THE BEST PLAYS OF 1986–1987

THE
BURNS MANTLE
YEARBOOK

THE
BEST PLAYS
OF 1986–1987

EDITED BY OTIS L. GUERNSEY JR.
AND JEFFREY SWEET

Illustrated with photographs and
with drawings by HIRSCHFELD

○○○○○○

DODD, MEAD & COMPANY, INC.

NEW YORK

Copyright © 1988 by Dodd, Mead & Company, Inc.
ISBN: 0-396-09077-X
Library of Congress Catalog Card Number: 20-21432
Printed in the United States of America

EDITOR'S NOTE

THE BROADWAY THEATER reversed the backsliding of recent seasons and moved forward in many respects in 1986–87. The number of productions was up by more than 10 percent, much of the increase being new American plays. The attenuating 12-month box office gross rallied and rose back up above the $200 million mark, with attendance also up and the average price of a Broadway ticket up only very slightly. (And while we're on this subject, please note that the price of our annual *Best Plays* volume has risen over the decades, but not more sharply than the price of an orchestra seat; from its 1919–20 beginning, *Best Plays* has been priced within the scale of one Broadway straight-play ticket.) These and other favorable Broadway developments, together with off Broadway's continuing importance as a catalyst of theater art and excitement, are set forth in detail in associate editor Jeffrey Sweet's report and analysis of the 1986–87 New York theater season, his second year of this assignment in this, the 68th *Best Plays* theater yearbook in continuous publication by Dodd, Mead & Company.

Like Broadway itself, the *Best Plays* series continuously strives to broaden its vision and grasp, while maintaining the highest standards of accuracy possible in the human condition. Jonathan Dodd of Dodd, Mead has provided his invaluable oversight of the publication process of *The Best Plays of 1986–87*. And the editors' wives give annually much more than moral support, Dorianne Guernsey correcting the text and Sheridan Sweet supplying the cast-and-credits listing of new scripts produced across the United States.

In a self-contained section devoted to activity in the New York tributary theater loosely known and inexactly defined as "off off Broadway," or OOB, Mel Gussow, distinguished member of the New York *Times* critical staff, reviews the high spots of the OOB season and selects its very best for special attention. In her comprehensive listing of 1986–87 OOB productions, Camille Croce makes no claim to following the exact boundaries of this busy production area—no one could, it stretches from 42d Street to backyard sheds in farthest Queens—but year after year Miss Croce collects the broadest (in scope) and most accurate (in detail) annual record of OOB published anywhere.

In our cast-replacement section, the eminent musical theater historian Stanley Green keeps track of those performers, many of them stars, who in the long course of New York runs and road tours take over important roles vacated by their original incumbents. And the American Theater Critics Association, through its playreading committee chaired this year by Dan Sullivan, distinguished critic of the Los Angeles *Times,* has made its annual selection for *Best Plays* of the best new scripts professionally produced from coast to coast, so that we join their applause, for the record, with excerpts from the ATCA-selected scripts (many of which in the years of our publication of the ATCA choices have later appeared on the New York stage and won Best Play citations). And the indispensible yearly contributions of Rue E. Canvin (necrology and publications),

William Schelble (Tony Awards facts), Richard Hummler (Critics Awards voting), Sally Dixon Wiener (two Best Plays synopses) and Thomas T. Foose (historical footnotes) have greatly enhanced our *Best Plays* coverage, as has the consultational help of Henry Hewes, Dorothy Swerdlove, Ralph Newman of the Drama Book Shop, Robert Nahas of the Theater Arts Book Shop, Glenn Young of Applause Theater Books and, most particularly, the dozens of helpful men and women in the producers' press departments, without whose advice and patient fact-gathering assistance this yearbook couldn't possible take its present wide-ranging form.

Among our graphics, Al Hirschfeld continues to hold a special place, as he does in the theater at large, showing it how it looks season after season. We are also most grateful to Loy Arcenas for permission to run a photo of his set-design model as an example of the year's best on New York stages. And we point with pride to the excellent theater photography illustrating this volume, the work of Martha Swope and her associates (including Carol Rosegg) and Richard Anderson, Adam Bartos, Marc Bryan-Brown, Terrance Carney, William B. Carter, Peter Cunningham, Chris Davies, John Dugdale, T. Charles Erickson, Deborah Feingold, Cynthia Friedman, Jennifer Girard, Goodness Gracious Photography, Gerry Goodstein, Chris Gulker, Bobbi Hazeltine, Martha Holmes, Peter Jacobs, Nathaniel Kramer, Brigitte Lacombe, Michael Le Poer Trench/Bob Barshak, Babette Mangolte, Joan Marcus, Adam Newman, Frederic Ohringer, Liselotte Riva, George Rose, Ron Scherl, Anita & Steve Shevett and John Peter Weiss.

We point with special admiration to the plays and musicals themselves—all of them, the Best Plays, the almost-bests, the not-near-bests. Manifesting the stubborn courage and dedicated effort of their authors, these scripts and scores succeeded in founding a vital and eclectic New York theater season in 1986–87. As has happened in each of the previous 67 years, a Best Plays theater yearbook now appears as a literary exclamation point to the entirety of their authorship.

OTIS L. GUERNSEY Jr.
Editor

July 1, 1987

CONTENTS

THE BEST PLAYS OF 1986–1987

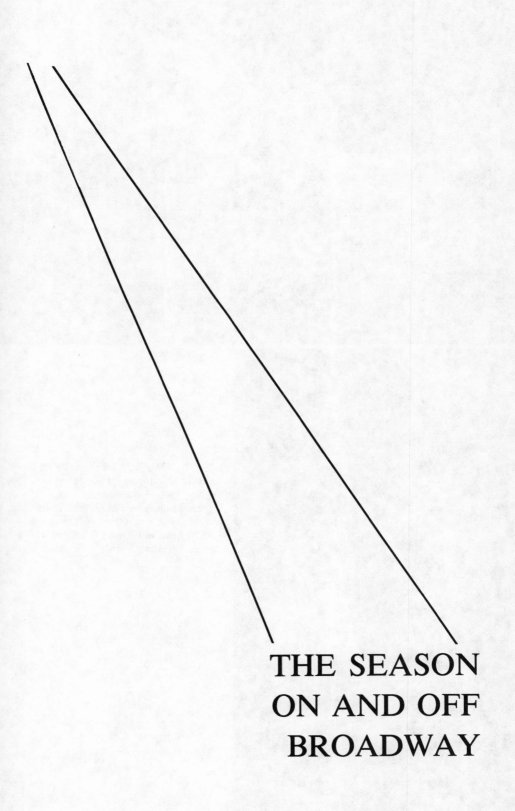

THE SEASON
ON AND OFF
BROADWAY

HIT MUSICALS FROM ABROAD—*Above,* Jane Summerhays as Lady Jaqueline Carstone and Robert Lindsay as Bill Snibson in *Me and My Girl; left,* Colm Wilkinson as Jean Valjean and Randy Graff as Fantine in *Les Misérables*

BROADWAY AND OFF BROADWAY

By Jeffrey Sweet

GEORGE ABBOTT celebrated his hundredth birthday on June 25, a few weeks after the close of this season. No attempt will be made here to count the number of productions in which he has been involved since 1913. Suffice it to say, in his more than seven decades as writer, director, producer and/or actor, he, more than any other individual, has been responsible for developing the brash, boisterous style which one associates with Broadway, particularly the Broadway musical. Collaborating with such artists as Richard Rodgers, Lorenz Hart, Oscar Hammerstein II, Jerome Robbins, Stephen Sondheim, Harold Prince, George Balanchine, Larry Gelbart, Burt Shevelove, Betty Comden, Adolph Green, Leonard Bernstein, Frank Loesser, John O'Hara, Jerry Bock, Sheldon Harnick, Jule Styne, Jerome Weidman and Bob Fosse, he helped establish American pre-eminence in musical comedy.

But the Broadway Mr. Abbott sustained and which sustained him for the bulk of his career is no longer with us. This season, for example, there wasn't a single successful Broadway musical by American authors. One after another they fell— *Honky Tonk Nights, Rags, Into the Light, Raggedy Ann* and *Smile.* In contrast, the British, from whom one rarely used to expect much by way of musical theater, dominated the field with *Me and My Girl, Starlight Express* and the sole Broadway musical to be named a Best Play, *Les Misérables,* all of which met with wide popular success. The American musicals off Broadway were generally a sad lot, too, including such ill-conceived works as *Staggerlee, Angry Housewives, The Rise of David Levinsky, Brownstone* and *Have I Got a Girl For You!* The British off-Broadway entry, *The Knife,* also failed. Not until May did this arena produce a musical of sustained distinction, a small gem called *Three Postcards,* a Best Play by a pair of Americans named Craig Lucas and Craig Carnelia.

British dramatists were responsible for a large proportion of the non-musical plays on and off Broadway as well. Three of these were Best Plays and, by coincidence, had non-British settings: *Les Liaisons Dangereuses* by Christopher Hampton took place in 18th century France, *Wild Honey* by Michael Frayn in 19th century Russia, and *Kvetch* by Steven Berkoff in contemporary America. Other British plays receiving their New York premieres included Simon Gray's *The Common Pursuit,* Willy Russell's *Educating Rita,* Bob Larbey's *A Month of Sundays* (revised with an American setting), Richard Harris's *Stepping Out* and David Pownall's *Master Class.*

The season was also uncommonly rich in works dealing with various aspects of black life, three of which were Best Plays—August Wilson's *Fences,* Alfred Uhry's *Driving Miss Daisy* and *Born in the R.S.A.,* written by director Barney

3

Simon in collaboration with his extraordinary multi-racial cast (in the Lincoln Center series entitled *Woza Afrika!*, which included three other evenings of South African plays). Lincoln Center also presented *Death and the King's Horseman* by the Nobel laureate Wole Soyinka. The Public Theater presented George C. Wolfe's widely acclaimed *The Colored Museum*, one scene of which parodied Lorraine Hansberry's *A Raisin in the Sun*—which, in the meantime, reaffirmed its place of honor in American theater in a strong revival a short walk north at the Roundabout. In addition to all this were the usual season of new plays by the Negro Ensemble Company, as well as *Lady Day at Emerson's Bar and Grill* and the musicals *Staggerlee* and *Honky Tonk Nights* mentioned above.

Fences was one of the two American Best Plays to play Broadway, the other being *Broadway Bound*, the third in a trilogy drawn by Neil Simon from his own and his family's experiences. Another veteran American dramatist, Horton Foote, has been taking inspiration from his family for a series of dramas, a nine-play cycle with the overall title *The Orphan's Home*; two of these, *Lily Dale* and the Best Play *The Widow Claire*, were produced off Broadway this season. (Filmed adaptations of three other plays in the cycle were presented on public television under the title *The Story of a Marriage*.) The other American Best Plays off Broadway were *Driving Miss Daisy* and *Three Postcards*.

Broadway Bound was a rarity, being one of the few plays to originate within the traditional commercial Broadway economy. Several of the productions which played under Broadway contracts this season were born in non-commercial houses in and outside of New York. *Fences* began at the O'Neill Center and played subsequent non-profit engagements at Yale, Rochester's GeVa Theater and Chicago's Goodman Theater. The Goodman was also the source of the Vivian Beaumont's presentations of *Death and the King's Horseman* and the "new vaudeville" version of *The Comedy of Errors*, not surprising given the fact they had been developed during Lincoln Center director Gregory Mosher's stewardship of the Goodman. Another Beaumont offering, Bill Irwin's *The Regard of Flight*, was first seen in New York at the American Place Theater. The Royal Shakespeare Company was responsible for three productions, *Les Misérables*, *Les Liaisons Dangereuses* and *Nicholas Nickleby*, and London's National Theater sent over *Wild Honey*. *Coastal Disturbances* started at the Second Stage, *The Musical Comedy Murders of 1940* at Circle Rep, *Stardust* at the Theater Off Park, *Asinamali!* in South Africa by a group called Committed Artists via Lincoln Center's Mitzi E. Newhouse, the revival of *Arsenic and Old Lace* at the Great Lakes Theater Festival, *The Mikado* at the Stratford Festival Canada, *All My Sons* at Long Wharf, *The Nerd* at the Milwaukee Rep, *Raggedy Ann* at the Empire State Institute for the Performing Arts in Albany and *Sweet Sue* at the Williamstown Theater Festival.

Off Broadway was a similar story. Among the companies which got earlier cracks at plays which played under off-Broadway contract here were Williamstown, Long Wharf, Chicago's Steppenwolf and Organic companies, Woodstock's River Arts Repertory, the Mark Taper, Odyssey, and Matrix of Los Angeles, Baltimore's Center Stage, the Oregon Shakespearean Festival, Seattle's Empty Space and Pioneer Square, Atlanta's Nexus Theater, Actors Theater of Louisville, Boston's Huntington Theater, Minneapolis's Guthrie Theater, Dallas's Stage

The 1986–1987 Season on Broadway

PLAYS (10)

Cuba and His Teddy Bear (transfer)
The Knee Plays
BROADWAY BOUND
Sweet Sue
Coastal Disturbances
The Nerd
FENCES
Safe Sex
The Musical Comedy Murders of 1940 (transfer)
Sleight of Hand

MUSICALS (7)

Honky Tonk Nights
Rags
Raggedy Ann
Into the Light
Smile
LES MISÉRABLES
Starlight Express

REVUES (3)

Flamenco Puro
L'Chaim to Life
Stardust

FOREIGN PLAYS IN ENGLISH (6)

WILD HONEY
Stepping Out
Death and the King's Horseman
A Month of Sundays
Asinamali! (transfer)
LES LIAISONS DANGEREUSES

HOLDOVERS WHICH BECAME HITS IN 1986–87

I'm Not Rappaport
Social Security

REVIVALS (11)

Arsenic and Old Lace
Me and My Girl
The Life and Adventures of Nicholas Nickleby
You Never Can Tell
Oh Coward!
The Front Page
The Mikado
Blithe Spirit
All My Sons
Pygmalion
The Comedy of Errors

SPECIALTIES (8)

Mummenschanz
Robert Klein on Broadway
Rowan Atkinson at the Atkinson
A Little Like Magic
The Magnificent Christmas Spectacular
Jackie Mason's "The World According to Me!"
The Regard of Flight & The Clown Bagatelles
Barbara Cook: A Concert for the Theater

Categorized above are all the new productions listed in the Plays Produced on Broadway section of this volume.
Plays listed in CAPITAL LETTERS have been designated Best Plays of 1986–87.
Plays listed in *italics* were still running June 1, 1987.
Plays listed in **bold face type** were classified as successes in *Variety's* annual estimate published June 3, 1987.

One, the Hartford Stage Company, San Diego's Old Globe Theater, Costa Mesa's South Coast Rep, the Crossroads Theater Company and George Street Playhouse of New Brunswick, the Lenox Arts Center, London's Royal Court, the National Theater of Norway, and New York's American Jewish and Vineyard Theaters.

Some of the reliable institutional theaters had bumpy seasons. Manhattan Theater Club's production of Janusz Glowacki's *Hunting Cockroaches* did well with the critics, but the other mainstage offerings there, featuring lesser plays by writers of proven abilities, were not warmly received. Playwrights Horizons's season began inauspiciously with productions of *The Maderati* and *Highest Standard of Living*, but ended strongly with two Best Plays, *Driving Miss Daisy* and *Three Postcards*. Circle Rep scored modest successes with *The Early Girl*, *The Musical Comedy Murders of 1940* and *Road Show* and stumbled with *In This Fallen City*. A good deal of excitement was generated by a limited run of *Burn This* by Circle's resident playwright Lanford Wilson, but he and his collaborator, director Marshall W. Mason, decided not to open the play to the press, preferring instead to invite critics when it moves to Broadway next season. The Public Theater, which did so well last year, presented only a handful of works, including Colleen Dewhurst in a disappointing solo show about Carlotta O'Neill by Barbara Gelb called *My Gene*, Eric Bogosian and Tad Savinar's *Talk Radio* and the aforementioned *The Knife* and *The Colored Museum*.

Circle in the Square had two popular successes, the transfer of Tina Howe's *Coastal Disturbances* and the star-laden revival of Shaw's *You Never Can Tell*. The Roundabout had little luck with its premieres but delivered solid revivals of *The Miracle Worker* and the aforementioned *A Raisin in the Sun*, *A Man for All Seasons* and *Rosencrantz and Guildenstern Are Dead*.

In addition to *Death and the King's Horseman*, *The Regard of Flight* and *The Comedy of Errors*, Lincoln Center's Vivian Beaumont re-teamed the Tony-winning combination of director Jerry Zaks and designer Tony Walton from last season's marvelous *The House of Blue Leaves* for an admirable *The Front Page*. Downstairs at the Mitzi Newhouse, new scripts by Arthur Miller and Roger Hedden fared less well than the series of plays by South African writers.

As always, there were performances to admire. Stars familiar from film and television included Matthew Broderick, Mary Tyler Moore, James Earl Jones, Molly Ringwald, Lynn Redgrave, Jason Robards, Sigourney Weaver, Jean Stapleton, Richard Chamberlain, Geraldine Page, Richard Thomas, Karen Allen, Mark Hamill, Amy Madigan, Andrew McCarthy, John Mills, Demi Moore and, making his Broadway debut, Peter O'Toole. Stars best known for their theatrical work were also in abundance, including Richard Kiley, Uta Hagen, Blythe Danner, Andrea McArdle, Barbara Cook, Judith Ivey, John Rubinstein, Stephen Lang, John Wood, Victor Garber, Phyllis Frelich, Dianne Wiest, Mandy Patinkin, Ron Silver, Colleen Dewhurst, Joe Morton, Len Cariou, Ernestine Jackson, Ben Harney, Robert Joy, Peter Riegert, Trish Hawkins, Lonette McKee, Anita Gillette, Morgan Freeman, Ian McKellen and John Lithgow. Some busy actors appeared in two or more productions this season, among them Philip Bosco, Austin Pendleton, Laurie Metcalf, Larry Kert, Jeffrey DeMunn, Mary Stuart Masterson, Jonathan Hadary, Ethyl Eichelberger, Kelly Connell, Lee Wilkof, Terrence Mann, Leo Burmester, Judy Kuhn, Meagan Fay and Amanda Plummer.

SWEET SUE—Lynn Redgrave and Mary Tyler Moore as different aspects of the same character in A.R. Gurney Jr.'s play, restoring "good, old-fashioned star power" to the Broadway stage

Several of this season's performers appeared in works they had helped create. Harvey Fierstein starred in his *Safe Sex*, Eric Bogosian in *Talk Radio*, Craig Carnelia in *Three Postcards*, the late Charles Ludlam in *The Artificial Jungle* (which he also directed), Ray Stricklyn in *Confessions of a Nightingale*, Rebecca Wackler, Larry Larson and Levi Lee in *Tent Meeting* and, as mentioned above, the company of *Born in the R.S.A.*, who collaborated on its text. In addition, company members' experiences were the source material for the new version of *The Concept*, and the cast of *Sills & Company*, with a little input from the audience, spontaneously created a new show every performance.

Writer-directors were also common. All of the African plays at Lincoln Center—*Asinamali!*, *Bopha!*, *Born in the R.S.A.*, *Children of Asazi*, *Gangsters* and

Death and the King's Horseman—were staged by their authors. Simon Gray co-staged *The Common Pursuit* with Michael McGuire, Arthur Marx staged *Groucho: A Life in Revue* which he wrote with Robert Fisher, David Hare directed and wrote the book for *The Knife*, Barry Harman directed and wrote the book and lyrics for *Olympus on My Mind*, Howard Ashman did likewise for *Smile*, Vernel Bagneris directed, wrote the book and co-authored the lyrics of *Staggerlee*, Steven Berkoff directed his *Kvetch*, and John Bishop his *The Musical Comedy Murders of 1940*.

Some directors came up to bat more than once. Trevor Nunn did the honors on *Starlight Express* and co-directed *Les Misérables* and the revival of *Nicholas Nickleby* with John Caird. Gene Saks staged *Broadway Bound*, *A Month of Sundays* and *Rags*. Andre Ernotte guided two biographical shows, *Lady Day at Emerson's Bar and Grill* and *My Gene*. Norman René directed *Tent Meeting* and *Three Postcards*. Brian Murray revived *Arsenic and Old Lace* and *Blithe Spirit*. John Tillinger shuttled from *Confessions of a Nightingale* to A.R. Gurney Jr.'s *Sweet Sue* before heading to a regional company to stage a pre–New York run of Gurney's *Another Antigone*. Among the other distinguished directors who had projects this season were Arthur Penn, Mike Nichols, Arvin Brown, Vivian Matalon, Stephen Porter, Gregory Mosher, Lloyd Richards, Mel Shapiro and Michael Lindsay-Hogg.

Among designers who had busy seasons were Marjorie Bradley Kellogg, Pat Collins, Beverly Emmons, Tharon Musser, Martin Aronstein, Ken Billington, Paul Gallo, David Hersey, Richard Nelson, Dennis Parichy and David Jenkins. British designer John Napier was responsible for the two most spectacular sets to be seen on Broadway in recent years—the multi-level racetrack featuring choreographed ramps and bridges in *Starlight Express* and the virtually non-stop parade of images of Victor Hugo's France for *Les Misérables*. Also spectacular was John Gunter's design of various locations in a Russian backwater (lighting by Martin Aronstein) for *Wild Honey*, climaxing with the sight of a locomotive bearing down on the play's ill-fated protagonist. Many designers were able to serve their projects equally well on a smaller scale. Bob Crowley provided the arresting unit set and costumes—designed primarily in various shades of off-white—which, in combination with Chris Parry and Beverly Emmons's lighting—gave visual unity to the peripatetic scenario of *Les Liaisons Dangereuses*. Dennis Parichy's lighting caught the many moods of summer on a New England beach for *Coastal Disturbances* and displayed both the romantic and tawdry sides of John Lee Beatty's roadhouse set for *The Lucky Spot*. Loy Arcenas's set and Debra J. Kletter's lighting for *Three Postcards* managed simultaneously to satirize a trendy New York restaurant and suggest the characters' inner worlds.

Of course, all of these worlds began in the imaginations of the dramatists, and it is those dramatists whose work the *Best Plays* annual is primarily dedicated to honoring. As noted in past editions, in making these choices we place our emphasis on the script rather than the production. Indeed, some of the scripts selected in this and past years deserved better productions than they received, and it is one of the happier aspects of this book to have the opportunity to draw attention to such works.

As noted by Otis L. Guernsey Jr. in past volumes, "The choice is made without any regard whatever to a play's type—musical, comedy or drama—or origin on or off Broadway, or popularity at the box office or lack of same.

"We don't take the scripts of bygone eras into consideration for the Best Play citation in this one, whatever their technical status as American or New York 'premieres' which didn't happen to have a previous production of record. We draw the line between adaptations and revivals, the former eligible for Best Play selection but the latter not, on a case-by-case basis . . . . . If a script influences the character of a season, or by some function of consensus wins the Critics, Pulitzer or Tony Awards, we take into account its future historical as well as present esthetic importance. This is the only special consideration we give, and we don't always tilt in its direction, as the record shows."

The Best Plays of 1986–87 are listed below for visual convenience in the order in which they opened in New York (a plus sign + with the performance numbers signifies that the play was still running after June 1, 1987).

Born in the R.S.A. (Off B'way, 8 perfs.)	*Les Misérables* (B'way, 88+ perfs.)
Broadway Bound (B'way, 205+ perfs.)	*Fences* (B'way, 77+ perfs.)
The Widow Claire (Off B'way, 150 perfs.)	*Driving Miss Daisy* (Off B'way, 55+ perfs.)
Wild Honey (B'way, 28 perfs.)	*Les Liaisons Dangereuses* (B'way, 37+ perfs.)
Kvetch (Off B'way, 31 perfs.)	*Three Postcards* (Off B'way, 22 perfs.)

New Plays

Lope de Vega described the requirements for theater as "four trestles, four boards, two actors, and a passion," and quite a few of this season's plays employed little more. Small-cast, single-set plays were common, and several were one-acts barely 90 minutes in length. Modesty of scale should not be confused with modesty of achievement, however. A number of these little packages brought major satisfactions.

Driving Miss Daisy epitomized the virtues of smallness. Alfred Uhry's Best Play concerned Daisy Werthan, an elderly Jewish lady of means in Atlanta, and Hoke Coleburn, the black man her son hires to drive her after she has one auto accident too many. The play begins in 1948 and depicts the relationship between the two through 1973. Those 25 years saw enormous changes in race relations in the South, and the script subtly reflects these changes through the impact on their lives of such public events as the bombing of her temple, a Klan lynching and the coming of Martin Luther King Jr. More subtly, despite the difference in economic status and race, the piece dramatizes what they have in common— being members of minorities in a frequently hostile society, both are constantly embroiled in the battle to maintain their dignity, a battle in which they often find themselves squared off against each other. Under Ron Lagomarsino's direction, Morgan Freeman and Dana Ivey beautifully realized this double portrait of an unconventional friendship.

Like *Driving Miss Daisy*, Horton Foote's *The Widow Claire* was an intermissionless play of small gestures hinting at larger truths. Horace Robedaux is a shy and profoundly decent young man trying to make a life for himself during hard times in a small Texas town in 1911. Part of the life he is hoping to build is with Claire, a widow a few years older than he. One night he calls on her. The attraction between Horace and Claire is great, and, in the moonlight, they dream of a future together. But with daylight comes Claire's recognition that her responsibility to her children requires that she accept a financially more advantageous proposal. Through the frustration of this courtship, Foote is depicting a world in which even modest dreams must bend before the reality of financial depression. Without a word of editorializing, Foote conveys the idea that poverty is not simply a matter of a lack of money but also the constraint of hope.

Another Foote play produced this season, *Lily Dale*, offered a view of Horace two years earlier and detailed the circumstances of his estrangement from his mother and sister, an estrangement which again could be traced to choosing security over the claims of the heart. Each production honored the richness of the playwright's subtext, Matthew Broderick and Don Bloomfield both creating complex Horaces out of the simplest of elements. I didn't have the pleasure of seeing Molly Ringwald as Lily Dale, but her successor Mary Stuart Masterson somehow managed to find a point of sympathy in Horace's selfish and spoiled sister. In the other play, the playwright's daughter, Hallie Foote, was a luminous Claire.

In the cases of the South African plays produced at Lincoln Center under the collective title *Woza Afrika!*, the modesty of the presentations was dictated by the circumstances under which the works were created. As there are no legitimate stages in the black townships, these works, focussing on the evils of a society built on legalized racism, were originally designed to be presented in such spaces as churches, community halls and classrooms. Unfortunately, most of the productions were admirable more for their commitment than their writing. Mbongeni Ngema's *Asinamali!* wove together the varied paths which led five blacks to be imprisoned together, but the stories were presented with such a constant and unmodulated intensity that the effect was ultimately numbing rather than stirring. *Bopha!* by Percy Mtwa began with a fascinating question: What leads a black to join a police force whose primary job is to oppress other blacks, and what rationales sustain him in this odious job? Unfortunately, the writing never investigated the moral complexity of the situation, getting sidetracked into a series of cartoon-like scenes before seizing on a sudden change of heart to bring about an unconvincing upbeat resolution. Maishe Maponya's *Gangsters* again presented a black South African policeman, this time locked in battle with an idealistic black poet. There was a great deal of promise in a play about the ways in which these two affect each other, but the author-director chose instead to keep them rigidly fixed in exactly the same positions as they were in when we first met them; so, though the play dramatized the poet's eventual murder at the policeman's hands,

The 1986–87 Season Off Broadway

PLAYS (32)

The Nice and the Nasty
Today I Am a Fountain Pen
Lady Day at Emerson's Bar and Grill (transfer)
Double Image:
The Return of Pinocchio
The Dreamer Examines His Pillow
Playwrights Horizons:
The Young Playwrights Festival
Highest Standard of Living
The Maderati
DRIVING MISS DAISY
Circle Repertory:
In This Fallen City
The Early Girl
The Musical Comedy Murders of 1940
Road Show
The Concept (new version)
Groucho: A Life in Revue
Neon Psalms
Tigers Wild
The War Party
Manhattan Theater Club:
The Hands of Its Enemy
Bloody Poetry

MTC (continued):
Hunting Cockroaches
Death of a Buick
The Lucky Spot
Lily Dale
THE WIDOW CLAIRE
Lincoln Center:
Bodies, Rest and Motion
Danger: Memory!
N.Y. Shakespeare
The Colored Museum
My Gene
Talk Radio
Cast Me Down
On the Verge
Tent Meeting

SPECIALTIES (8)

Swimming to Cambodia
Terrors of Pleasure
Vienna: Lusthaus
Confessions of a Nightingale
Black Sea Follies
Mona Rogers in Person
The Garden of Earthly Delights
Eno

MUSICALS (9)

Olympus on My Mind
Angry Housewives
Brownstone
Have I Got a Girl for You!
The Transposed Heads
The Rise of David Levinsky
The Knife
Staggerlee
THREE POSTCARDS

REVUES (4)

Sills & Company
Sex Tips for Modern Girls
Standup Shakespeare
Funny Feet

REVIVALS (18)

A Raisin in the Sun
Twelfth Night
LOOM:
The Drunkard
(6 operettas in running repertory)
Krapp's Last Tape
CSC:
The Maids
The Skin of Our Teeth
The Merchant of Venice
Roundabout:
A Man for All Seasons
The Miracle Worker
Rosencrantz and Guildenstern Are Dead
Much Ado About Nothing
As Is

FOREIGN PLAYS IN ENGLISH (11)

Master Class
Woza Afrika!
Asinamali!
Bophal
Children of Asazi & Gangsters
BORN IN THE R.S.A.
The Common Pursuit
Face to Face
The Double Bass
KVETCH
Women Beware Women
Educating Rita

FOREIGN-LANGUAGE PRODUCTION (1)

Medea

Categorized above are all the productions listed in the Plays Produced Off Broadway section of this volume.
Plays listed in CAPITAL LETTERS have been designated Best Plays of 1986–87.
Plays listed in *italics* were still running after June 1, 1987.

there was surprisingly little real dramatic development. Matsemela Manaka's *Children of Asazi*, a one-act which played on a bill with *Gangsters*, provided intriguing glimpses into the nature of living in a community under the constant threat of bulldozers, but the family story in front of this backdrop was hobbled with incredible coincidences undermining the play's effectiveness.

Apart from these plays' technical failings, some of them were disturbing for ethical reasons. *Asinamali!* purported to champion the cause of human rights and dignity, but how was one to reconcile this with the fact that the bulk of the characters' references to women were degrading? Program notes accompanying *Children of Asazi* claimed that "black people . . . never seem to . . . surrender to the forces of evil," but how is one to view the scene in which the young hero threatens to set fire to one of the other characters? The hero ultimately relents, but that he believes putting a flaming tire around the neck of an enemy to be a legitimate expression of his politics hardly supports the contention that there has been no surrender to the forces of evil.

The final offering of the series, however, more than justified the entire enterprise. *Born in the R.S.A.*, a Best Play researched, developed and written by the cast in collaboration with its director Barney Simon, presented in documentary fashion the interrelationship of a group of contemporary South African blacks and whites. Early on we are introduced to a young man named Glen, a white student with an easygoing charm and an appealing attitude of bemusement. Having given him our affection, we are initially inclined to follow Glen's fortunes with a sympathetic eye; but, without any particular political motive, Glen allows himself to be recruited by the security police to spy on a Marxist teacher. Then, with the same easygoing charm and very few apparent moral qualms, he betrays his wife by beginning an affair with Susan, an art teacher involved with an activist group. And then he betrays Susan and the activist group to the police, a move which leads to the imprisonment and torture of people who had called him friend.

Alone among the five plays presented in this series, *Born in the R.S.A.* seriously explored the psychology underlying the institutionalized moral corruption of the Republic of South Africa. The excellence of the cast's collective writing was complemented by the excellence of their performances, particularly those of Neil McCarthy as Glen, Timmy Zwebulana as a sweet-natured black musician pushed by injustice to the threshold of violence and Thoko Tshinga as the charismatic woman whose passion sustains the group Glen betrays.

Whereas *Born in the R.S.A.* charted the journey of a soul into corruption, another Best Play, *Les Liaisons Dangereuses*, Christopher Hampton's adaptation of Choderlos de Laclos's 18th century novel, introduced a character who is corrupt at the start and dramatized the beginnings of his rejuvenation, a process which, paradoxically, leads to his destruction. The Vicomte de Valmont is a thoroughgoing bastard whose sport is to garnish his notoriety through assaults on others' innocence and honor. His female counterpart is the Marquise de Merteuil, and, for a combination of amusement and revenge, she asks Valmont to do her the favor of seducing Cecile Volanges, a convent-schooled virgin. Valmont, however, already has a project—Madame de Tourvel, a young woman whose initial appeal lies in the challenge represented by her virtue. Gamely, Valmont decides to attempt both women and is successful in both ventures. But there is defeat in his victory over Madame de Tourvel; for the first time he finds himself genuinely in love. The Marquise will not and cannot let this situation stand, and she compels Valmont brutally to break off the relationship. Too late Valmont understands that the Marquise's vengeance has been aimed at him all along. Her final move is to manipulate him into a duel that he hasn't the heart to win.

In some respects *Les Liaisons Dangereuses* is analogous to Nathaniel Hawthorne's *Rappaccini's Daughter*. That story told of a young girl who, having been brought up in and become immune to the fumes of her father's poisonous garden, dies upon drinking a potion meant to wean her from them. "As poison had been life, so the powerful antidote was death," wrote Hawthorne. Similarly, Valmont's cynicism has been his life. In becoming a human being, he becomes vulnerable and cannot live where he once flourished. To move an audience over the destruction of a character who has richly deserved his fate is no small feat, but Hampton pulls it off brilliantly, making one realize that Valmont's cynicism is an inverted form of naivete. Alan Rickman as Valmont and Lindsay Duncan as the Marquise were justly acclaimed for their work. As memorable was Suzanne Burden's heartbreaking performance as the tragic Madame de Tourvel. Bob Crowley's unit set, a masterpiece of elegance and suggestion, housed this chronicle of intrigue. Howard Davies was the first-rate director.

Talk Radio, written by Eric Bogosian from an idea by artist Tad Savinar, featured another cynic as a central character, an abrasive radio personality who calls himself Barry Champlain (not his real name) who chastises, mocks or diddles everyone who talks with him during his broadcast. In one breath he tells a Jew-baiter a patently phony story about his visit to a concentration camp, soon after he tries to incite a black caller to bigotry by telling him that Jewish landlords victimize his race. What does Champlain really believe? He probably doesn't know. All he is certain of is that he must keep the show interesting at any cost. Having lost his moral compass long ago, he has stoked up the energy that fuels his pose as a man who is outrageous because he is outraged.

Bogosian, the author and star of last year's Best Play *Drinking in America*, was fiercely effective as Champlain and—Savinar's unnecessary rear-projected visuals aside—director Frederick Zollo's production was appropriately lean and relentless. Though moment by moment the vitality of the writing compels attention, however, the play does not develop so much as repeat itself, primarily constructed as it is as a series of dialogues in which Barry's behavior is predictably abrasive and perverse. Despite a frenzied breakdown during which Barry harangues his listeners at the play's climax, one finally knows little more about him than was apparent after the first 15 minutes.

Michael Frayn has twice previously been represented on Broadway—by *Noises Off* and *Benefactors*—both of which were named Best Plays. *Wild Honey*, his adaptation of an early and unstageable play by Anton Chekhov, strikes me as the most satisfying of his work to reach these parts. The action of the play revolves around Platonov, who has something in common with the leprechaun in *Finian's Rainbow* in that when he is not near the girl he loves, he loves the girl he is near. But Platonov is not merely a philanderer. A once-promising scholar whose lack of discipline resulted in his being consigned to a backwater province as a school-

COASTAL DISTURBANCES—Annette Bening and Timothy Daly in a scene from Tina Howe's play

teacher, his compulsive self-indulgence makes him a kind of anarchist, and his anarchy has the effect of disrupting the order of the whole community. (There is wonderful irony in his being a fallen scholar. Scholarship is concerned with trying to determine the order of things, whereas anarchy's objective, of course, is the disruption of order.) The results are by turns farcical, romantic and tragic. That these elements coexist in one script without clashing is a measure of Frayn's considerable achievement.

Unfortunately, some of this achievement was obscured by the production, and for this star Ian McKellen and his director Christopher Morahan must share the blame. When I saw the play in London, McKellen portrayed the character's self-indulgence without falling into the trap of self-indulgence as an actor. In the intervening year and a half, the part seemed to have gotten away from him with the result that, just as Platonov's sexual and intellectual anarchy undoes the town in which he lives, so did McKellen's theatrical anarchy, apparently endorsed by the director, undo the American production. The other characters revolve around Platonov like the spokes of a wheel around its center. With the histrionic center of the production out of balance, the actors playing the other roles seemed to be in the uncomfortable position of having to fend for themselves. This some did with greater success than others. Kathryn Walker did strong work as Anna Petrovna, a woman whose values would be more comfortably located in a later time. Kate Burton also fared well as Platonov's long-suffering wife, and Frank Maraden scored as Platonov's unfortunate friend, whose wife is among those pursuing and pursued by the schoolmaster. The world which embraced them, replete with woods and trains and twilight, was the inspired creation of set designer John Gunter in association with lighting designer Martin Aronstein. One hopes that the play's further fortunes will not be inhibited by its flawed American premiere. This is a script that should find a happy place on the stages of the world.

Our corresponding historian, Thomas T. Foose, comments that *"Wild Honey* is as acceptable as any title for this Chekhov play, since on the original manuscript the title was missing. I will list the earlier stagings of this play which I have at hand and the many different titles used: Williamstown, Mass. 1977–78, *Platonov*; 1975–76, New York City (CSC), *A Country Scandal*; London 1960–61, *Platonov* (with Rex Harrison); Bordeaux, France, 1955–56, *Ce Fou de Platonov*; 1953–54, New York City, *Fireworks on the James*; 1976, U.S.S.R. film version, *An Unfinished Piece for Mechanical Piano* (directed by Nikita Mikhalkov)."

August Wilson's *Fences* emerged as the best American play of the season. In it, Troy Maxson—a former ballplayer with the Negro League blocked from his rightful career in the majors because of racial prejudice—reigns over his world from the backyard of his battered house in a Northern ghetto. Society has frustrated his attempts to control the circumstances of his own life, so he compensates by exercising control over the lives of those within his sphere of influence, principally his son Cory. Cory has the opportunity to attend college on a football scholarship, but Troy, embittered by his frustrated career, will not allow his son to pursue a future in sports. By destroying Cory's opportunity, he drives his son away. In the meantime, an extramarital affair—an affair the primary attraction of which was the respite it offered from the pressures of work and family—makes him the object of yet more pressure when his lover becomes pregnant. The woman dies in childbirth, and Troy's wife Rose takes in her husband's daughter. But Rose, as proud and resolute in her way as her husband, makes it clear that Troy will no longer be welcome in her bed. Further complications involve Troy's dealings with a second son born of a pre-marital relationship, his simple-minded half brother and his unseen employers.

There was more than enough plot here for two plays, and there were times when the confluence of all these elements strained credibility. One could also argue that the exposition was frequently bald and that symbols were proclaimed heavy-handedly. But the magnitude of Wilson's achievement outweighs these objections. Wilson is writing about the nature of strength. Troy is powerful, but his inflexibility, paradoxically, makes his power a weakness. His intransigence isolates him. He has allowed his justifiable anger at a bigoted society to so harden him as to alienate the family that should have been his consolation. This is a grand role, grandly written, and in it that Promethean actor James Earl Jones gave perhaps the greatest performance of his career. As Cory, Courtney B. Vance seemed to mature in front of the audience's eyes, and Mary Alice was a volcano of eloquence as Troy's aggrieved wife. Lloyd Richards, whose association with the play began in 1983 when he directed a staged reading of the huge and unwieldy first draft at the Eugene O'Neill Theater Center (of which he is artistic director), was responsible for the admirable staging.

The most off-putting title of the season belonged to another Best Play, *Kvetch*, and, for much of the first act, the script it fronted was off-putting as well. The conceit of the play made the audience privy to the inner thought-monologues of a family of urban Jews and two men of their acquaintance. The monologues were filled with bitterness, vulgarity and other expressions of spiritual and emotional ugliness. At first the intensity of this incessant spewing was almost numbing in its purposeful offensiveness; and then, curiously, the play broke through to a new and arresting plane. Gradually, one became aware that underneath the loathing and vituperation there was a poignant yearning for a better, more forthright way of life. Author Steven Berkoff seemed to be saying that we eat our guts out largely as a result of enforced accommodations with society's constrictions and hypocrisies. I feel that many of the critics were too offended by the play's manner to appreciate its matter. Certainly it was not an easy play to embrace, but it was an electrifying experience. Berkoff, who also was his own admirable director, had the benefit of a remarkable company—Kurt Fuller as the chief kvetcher, Ruth Jaroslow as his aged mother-in-law, Mitch Kreindel as his unfortunate dinner guest and Hy Anzell as his contempt-ridden client. Most remarkable, however, was Laura Esterman as Fuller's longsuffering wife, giving a performance of elegant precision, even as she spoke lines the graphic nature of which might well have made Lenny Bruce blush.

George C. Wolfe's *The Colored Museum* consisted of a revue-like series of scenes regarding blacks' ambivalent feelings about their cultural identity. A sketch parodying Lorraine Hansberry's *A Raisin in the Sun* and Ntozake Shangé's *For Colored Girls* was pointed and entertaining, but Wolfe seemed better at mocking old conventions than creating new approaches to supplant them. The bulk of the other sketches, well performed by a cast of five under the direction of L. Kenneth Richardson, did not develop frequently promising premises so much as belabor them, strip-mining them for explicitly articulated Meaning. To be fair, several other critics embraced *The Colored Museum* and greeted Wolfe as a significant new talent.

Kathy Robbins in *The War Party* is a light-skinned young woman born of a white mother and a black father who, to her mother's dismay, choses to define herself as black. This in turn leads her to join a ghetto-based organization called Marching on Poverty and to become involved in the lives of her co-workers and superiors there. Playwright Leslie Lee had the makings of a fascinating look at bigotry within the black community, but the plot he constructed to support his theme was mechanical and prone to irrelevant detours. Kathy Robbins's death at the end seemed to occur more for the purpose of ending the play than the logical consequence of her choices. There is so much in the premise, however, that one hopes that Lee will make another attempt to realize it.

A two-character play is extremely difficult to sustain for a full evening. Generally the two leads have one key issue to resolve between them, and the playwright, knowing that when the issue is resolved the play must end, often artificially delays the resolution for the sake of cranking up enough material to qualify as a full-length piece. This was all-too-evidently the case with Bryan Williams's *In This Fallen City*, about a confrontation between an old man and the teacher of a student who was murdered on the old man's doorstep. From the start, it was obvious that the play was structured to deliver its payload of the old man's one big secret at the end. This stuck Williams with the problem of credibly forestalling the secret's revelation, necessitating the construction of reason after reason for the old man to delay telling the truth that is in his interest to reveal. Michael Higgins, a stalwart of Circle Rep, gave a rich and subtle performance as the old man, but Danton Stone was crippled by the jerry-built nature of the teacher's role.

Another two-hander, Willy Russell's *Educating Rita*, was already familiar to American audiences from a popular film version starring Julie Walters and Michael Caine, but its production by Chicago's Steppenwolf Theater Company represented the playscript's New York premiere. It concerns a working-class hairdresser who signs up with a hard-drinking, self-disgusted teacher for an "open university" tutorial in literature. During the course of the play, she becomes an enthusiastic scholar well on her way to academic success, while he goes into further decline. Clearly, Russell wants us to fall in love with Rita (one notes that Russell's biography describes him as a former hairdresser who found himself as a student in a night course in English literature), and this is partially the problem. Rita is so relentlessly self-congratulatory about her intentions and efforts that, instead of finding her endearing, I was put off. Laurie Metcalf and Austin Pendleton are both marvelous actors, and it is a measure of the script's limitations that both seemed to be frustrated by it. Metcalf was also seen in *Bodies, Rest and Motion*, a chronicle of lower-middle-class aimlessness by Roger Hedden. The play didn't have enough to say to sustain a full evening, but Hedden has a gift for quirky dialogue, and he gave Metcalf the material to score solidly as a woman trying to cope after being left in the lurch.

The action of Caroline Kava's *The Early Girl* begins with the arrival of a young woman named Lily at a house of prostitution in a mining town in the West. During the course of her initiation, we get to know the rules of the establishment and the other young women who work there under the supervision of Lana, the house's authoritarian owner. The first act of the play hits most of the dramatic bases familiar from countless other depictions of prostitution. Again we see it depicted as the logical, if distorted, extension of American business practices. Again we hear the women draw unconvincing distinctions between what they do and whoring. And again easy hay is made of the juxtaposition of the madam's delusions of sophistication and the reality of her vulgarity.

Having established business as usual in the first act, however, Kava moves on to more interesting developments in the second. Jean, the most intelligent and

AT THE PUBLIC THEA-TER—*Left,* Loretta Devine and Reggie Montgomery in George C. Wolfe's *The Colored Museum; below,* Eric Bogosian, Robyn Peterson, John C. McGinley and Mark Metcalf in *Talk Radio*

articulate of the women, in her efforts to keep Lily from sliding permanently into prostitution, manages to get the other women to band together in common cause against Lana. That these women, whose profession is based on exploitation, join together in a course of action recalling nothing so much as classic labor tactics makes for wonderful and thought-provoking irony. Film star Demi Moore made a strong stage debut as Lily, but the wise-cracking Jean was the plum part, and Robin Bartlett made the most of it.

A number of playwrights, real-life and fictional, peopled this season's stages. *Confessions of a Nightingale*, adapted by Charlotte Chandler and Ray Stricklyn from an interview Chandler had with Tennessee Williams, presented Stricklyn solo as the man many believe to have been America's greatest playwright. The construction of the evening was of uneven quality, too much of the piece being given over to familiar anecdotes about celebrities. But, in contrast to *Lillian,* William Luce's similarly conceived solo play about Lillian Hellman last season, this piece allowed the audience to arrive at conclusions about Williams distinct from Williams's self-evaluations. For example, his insistence that he refuses to give in to self-pity rings hollow coming as it does after an extended section in which he bitterly bemoans his fall from critical favor.

Perhaps the most impressive aspect of the script is the connection it makes between the playwright's work and his experience. Near the end of the piece, Williams talks of having spat out angry, hurtful words to his emotionally disturbed sister Rose. When he next saw her, his apology could mean nothing to her as, in the interim, Rose had been forced to undergo a lobotomy. This story instantly brings to mind the passage in *A Streetcar Named Desire* in which Blanche tells of the angry, hurtful words she said to her young husband minutes before he took his life. The link between the two stories is all the more potent because the writers have the wisdom not to draw explicit attention to it. Though Stricklyn did not bear an overwhelming physical resemblance to the late playwright, his performance under John Tillinger's direction was so expert that for long stretches one succumbed utterly to the illusion of being in Williams's presence.

The life of Eugene O'Neill was also dramatized this season, albeit indirectly through the eyes of his troubled widow Carlotta, in Barbara Gelb's play for solo actress, *My Gene*. The solo actress in question was the ever-compelling Colleen Dewhurst, but the bulk of the material, archly constructed as Carlotta's response to hallucinations of her late husband, was too much of a burden for her to support. The only times when Dewhurst had viable material to play were when Gelb segued to cuttings from several of O'Neill's works.

To move from works about mature playwrights to one about a playwright in germination, Neil Simon's Best Play *Broadway Bound* completes his autobiographical trilogy. It also represents an advance on his two previous plays. *Brighton Beach Memoirs* had a delightful first act, but in its second the author seemed to confuse development with repetition. *Biloxi Blues* gave full play to Simon's gift for individual scenes, but the plot that contained them was plagued by inconsistencies and relied on contrivance for its resolution. In happy contrast, *Broadway Bound*'s action develops according to the characters' logic rather than one imposed by the writer.

The success is not unqualified. As is true with most characters modeled on their authors, Eugene Jerome is passive and consequently dramatically recalcitrant. Simon seems to strain to come up with things for him to do, including an extended section concerning Eugene's collaboration with his brother Stanley. If there has ever been a persuasive scene depicting writers collaborating, it has escaped my notice. The attempt here is loaded with the bulk of the play's mechanical laughs, as if Simon were pressing jokes into service to distract our attention in the hope that we won't notice that he, too, cannot manage the illusion of creation in progress. (Archaeologists may recognize the sketch the brothers try to write as one that was performed by Alan Arkin and Valerie Harper on Simon's TV special, *The Trouble With People*.) In the second act, perhaps to give an alibi for Eugene's continued passivity, he hobbles his alter ego with an enervating case of the flu. It is not until late in the play, in a widely celebrated scene in which Eugene dances with his mother, that the writer as a young man achieves life onstage as something larger than an ironic narrator.

Simon does much better by his other characters. Stanley, played with fierce energy by Jason Alexander, is a sputtering firecracker of impatience. We laugh at his extreme reactions to petty irritations, but the same forces which lead him to throw himself to the floor in a comic explosion of frustration also fuel a later, grim confrontation with his wayward father. Eugene's grandfather Ben is the living embodiment of the sort of old Leftie who loves humanity in the plural but has little patience with it in the singular, and he was given full and contradictory life by the remarkable John Randolph. It has generally been agreed that the play's greatest cause for celebration, however, is Kate, the author's tribute to his mother. Simon has created a long gallery of memorable male characters, but never before has he written a female character as deeply felt and fully realized as Kate Jerome. Linda Lavin's seamless performance reached to the heart of a life proscribed by the assumption of soul-killing duty in the service of a family who are largely blind to her sacrifice. As was true of the two previous plays in the cycle, *Broadway Bound* was directed with gleaming precision by Gene Saks.

Mark Medoff attempted to pack so much meat into *The Hands of Its Enemy* that the play burst its sides. The central conflict was between Howard, an abusive, alcoholic director, and Marieta, the stubborn deaf dramatist whose play he is directing. It gradually becomes clear to Howard that Marieta's script is an autobiographic depiction of her childhood and that what is keeping it from being an important play is Marieta's resistance to revealing the whole painful story. As Howard works to get Marieta to confront the truth through her art, so Howard is hoping to heal himself through his art. Added to the brew—Marieta's daughter happens to be an actress playing the part based on her mother, and Howard's abused ex-lover happens to be playing the part based on Marieta's abused mother. The stage is so dense with coincidence and forced irony that *The Hands of Its Enemy* is, ultimately, unbelievable, though Medoff is too skillful to ever lose the audience's interest. The deaf playwright was played by Phyllis Frelich, whose previous collaboration with Medoff, *Children of a Lesser God*, was one of the major successes of the 1979–80 season.

Murray Schisgal's protagonist in *Road Show* was not a playwright but a screenwriter named Andy Broude. Travelling cross-country with his wife Bianca to a big future in Hollywood, he stops in a small town to discover that the wife of the local druggist is his first love, Evelyn. For a short time, the years drop away and the two, drawn to each other again, plan to run off together. But, overhearing a phone call, Evelyn discovers that Andy is no longer the man she remembers. She returns to her husband, Andy reunites with his wife, and the two couples go their separate ways.

In outline, the play sounds hackneyed, and indeed much of the press expressed impatience with the plot. But I believe there is more to *Road Show* than a replay of the "you can't go home again" theme. Since the days of *The Typists and the Tiger* and *Luv*, Schisgal has been fascinated by posturing. His characters put so much energy into trying to project (and protect) romanticized images of themselves that they begin to believe their own fictions. Andy keeps summoning up the myth of himself as an artist *manqué,* someone who made the Faustian bargain of succeeding in the movies at the cost of giving up his true work—writing essays. But what we learn of his essays gives no indication that Emerson had anything to fear from him, so clearly he had no great talent to betray. His has not been a tragic fall but a stumble of small consequence. But just because one is not special doesn't mean that one cannot experience pain. According to Schisgal, mediocrity provides no shield against suffering. Mel Shapiro directed the well-paced production, getting particularly moving performances out of Anita Gillette as Bianca and Jonathan Hadary as the eccentric druggist.

I thought that *Death and the King's Horseman* also deserved better than it received at the hands of the critics. Written and directed by Nobel Prize–winner Wole Soyinka, the play tells of a tribal chief who runs afoul of British colonials when they learn that, as custom dictates, he intends to follow his recently deceased leader to the other world by willing his own death. The chief sees this as the fulfillment of his life, the colonials as the sort of barbarism they are determined to stamp out.

In a program note, Soyinka warned against interpreting this as a "clash of cultures" play. Whatever his protestations, however, much of the script is devoted to showing what happens when one culture attempts to impose its will and values on another. Though the two leading figures are the old chief and the colonial district officer, embodying the two systems in contest, to me the most interesting figures are a pair of supporting characters who find themselves in a no-man's-land between the tribal and the colonial. As suggested by his name, Sergeant Amusa represents the comic side. A black policeman in the white man's employ, he is constantly in the awkward situation of being at cross-purposes with one aspect or another of his identity, and many of the jokes by the other characters are made at his expense.

Olunde, the chief's son, represents the tragic side. He has returned from medical school in London (in which he enrolled over his father's protests and with the assistance of the colonials) to find that the duties imposed by his place in the tribe are at war with the identity he has sought as a doctor. When, because of British interference, his father fails to achieve his responsibility to die, the son takes this responsibility onto himself. Yes, there was too much undramatic poetry, yes, the British were depicted as stick figures without a substantial argument to articulate, and yes, something is wrong with a play when the management feels it must print

THE COMMON PURSUIT—Peter Friedman, Nathan Lane, Dylan Baker and Michael Countryman in the drama written and directed by Simon Gray

a synopsis and an interpretation in the program. Still, this was one of the season's few attempts at tragedy and, imperfections and all, a frequently powerful and moving experience.

There were no great surprises in *Groucho: A Life in Revue*, which was directed and co-written with Robert Fisher by Groucho's son Arthur Marx and featured an expert impersonation of the comedian at various ages by Frank Ferrante. The familiar and welcome anecdotes and routines were revived with support from Les Marsden (who doubled as Chico and Harpo). The versatile Faith Prince was a particular delight as the various women in Groucho's life. This was not a necessary evening in the theater, but an amiable one.

In preparation for its improvisations, the cast at Second City solicits suggestions from the audience. As a rule, if a suggestion gets a laugh, the actors will not try to build a scene on it, understanding that the laugh indicates that the audience has already anticipated the humor which could be mined from the suggestion and that doing a scene based on it would be redundant. David Pownall's play *Master Class* faced a similar problem. As soon as one had learned that the play was about Stalin and his cultural commissar Zhdanov in a confrontation with Prokofiev and Shostakovich, one began to catalogue the immediately evident dramatic opportunities of the situation—Stalin's false courtesy to the composers, the accusations of cultural elitism, the point at which the pretense of civility falls away and Stalin's murderous nature stands nakedly revealed, and so forth.

Watching the play, one got a bit impatient waiting for Pownall to tag all of these anticipated bases. And tag them he indeed did with a kind of stolid intelligence which demanded appreciation without exciting much delight.

And then, in the second act, Pownall left the patch of the expected and gave us a scene in which the distinguished composers are compelled by Stalin to collaborate with him on a setting of one of the dictator's favorite Georgian poems. Suddenly, the grim irony of the composers' situation came to dramatic life as they tried to create music to the order of a barbarian. One sparkling 15-minute scene can't save a play, but even 15 minutes of intellectual comedy on this level is hard to come by. The problems in the writing were compounded by the casting. Philip Bosco, Werner Klemperer, Austin Pendleton and Len Cariou are fine actors all, but their accents and performing styles were so varied as to undermine belief that all four belonged in the same world.

While *Master Class* dealt with the tribulations of artists in a totalitarian society, *Hunting Cockroaches* concerned the tribulations a pair of Polish emigrés face in the freedom of New York. Stuck in a Lower East Side firetrap since their arrival three years ago, she is a classical actress whose accent is so thick she has no hope of working, and he is a writer suffering from a severe case of writer's block. In their battle with insomnia, they spend the night chewing over their situation and summoning up images of the various people and institutions that have contributed to the limbo in which they find themselves. An avowedly autobiographical work by Janusz Glowacki, the play was frequently witty, but one ached for it to move beyond exposition to some kind of event. Glowacki never answered the question of why we were watching this particular sleepless night as opposed to any other. Though it was less than satisfying as drama, under Arthur Penn's direction Dianne Wiest seized the opportunity it gave her to create a beautifully detailed performance as the actress.

Keith Reddin's *Highest Standard of Living* also juxtaposed American life with life behind the Iron Curtain. In the first act, an American graduate student in Moscow runs afoul of the institutionalized paranoia of Soviet society. In the second act, having been thrown out of the U.S.S.R., he returns to New York to confront a society which, in its own way, is as malign. Entirely apart from whether one agrees or disagrees with Reddin's conclusions, the play is a disappointment. The Moscow scenes are paraphrases of similar scenes from countless movies and TV shows.

I Can't Remember Anything, the first of two pieces by Arthur Miller under the collective title *Danger: Memory!*, was a wispy dialogue between a pair of elderly friends which provided the audience little but an hour or so of Geraldine Fitzgerald and Mason Adams's very agreeable company. The second play, *Clara*, concerning a father tortured by the possibility that his liberalism so influenced his daughter as to lead her to her violent death, did not successfully develop its provocative premise. The suspense of the piece was supposed to be derived from the investigating detective's drive to get the name of a likely suspect from the father in time for it to be of use, but this time pressure was all but lost in the rambling philosophizing in which the two men indulged.

The talented Beth Henley also stumbled this season with *The Lucky Spot*. Concerning an attempt to open a roadhouse in Pigeon, Louisiana on Christmas

Eve, 1934, the play was a jumble of whimsical conceits, as if, every few pages, Henley had asked herself the question, "What quirky thing can I toss in now?" Matters improved considerably, however, with the introduction of Sue Jack Tiller Hooker, a former cardsharp newly released from prison who arrives at the roadhouse in search of the husband she still loves. In contrast to the other characters—sketchy creatures thrown together with a handful of idiosyncrasies— Sue Jack's pain and wildness felt authentic, particularly in Amy Madigan's full-steam-ahead interpretation.

The effect of AIDS on the gay community was the unifying theme of Harvey Fierstein's triple bill, *Safe Sex*, which featured the author in the cast. *Manny and Jake*, about an encounter between two men whose desire for physical and emotional connection is frustrated by one of them having tested positive, reached for poetry but fell flat. In the title play, a pair of gay lovers engaged in a barbed dialogue on commitment and hygiene while perched on opposite sides of a teeter-totter archly intended to serve as a physical metaphor for their relationship. The third piece, *On Tidy Endings*, was the most affecting of Fierstein's three. The ex-wife of a recently deceased AIDS victim meets the man who provided her late husband companionship in his final days. The ensuing battle for mourning rights was conventionally developed, but Fierstein the writer composed several speeches filled with fury, pain and poignancy to which Fierstein as actor did full justice.

The Nerd, a comedy by the late Larry Shue, concerned a man who, for reasons too convoluted to summarize here, finds himself host to a fellow in whose character are combined tactlessness, physical ineptitude and gross stupidity. It was clumsily crafted, logically indefensible, and I was thoroughly ashamed of myself for laughing as much as I did. Mark Hamill played straight man to Robert Joy's exuberantly goofy visiting grotesque, and Peter Riegert, as Hamill's wry friend, batted out ironic wisecracks with aplomb. Most satisfying, however, was Pamela Blair's work in the secondary part of a model wife and mother constantly teetering on the brink of hysteria.

In *The Common Pursuit*, Simon Gray returned to subject matter he has mined so well in the past, the world of academia and literary in-fighting. The play's title is also the title of a magazine which, in the opening scene, is organized by a Cambridge student named Stuart Thorne in concert with fellow students. The play follows this circle of friends over the next 20 years during which Stuart, unable to maintain the magazine to his standards, closes it down. The standards of his circle of friends, too, cannot be maintained, and the ties between them disintegrate.

The dialogue bubbles with the wit one has come to expect from Gray, but *The Common Pursuit* is not in the same league as his *Butley*, *Quartermaine's Terms* and *Otherwise Engaged* (all of which were Best Plays). Gray's people, consumed with squabbling about esthetic issues and gaining petty advantage on the narrowest intellectual turf, seem oblivious to the larger world. (This obliviousness might have been the stuff of rich satiric comedy, but there was no suggestion that Gray himself was aware of it.) In order for the play to work, one must believe Stuart to be a compelling figure whose vision of excellence is the glue binding the others together. As written by Gray and performed by Kristoffer Tabori, however, Stuart may have been dogged and articulate, but he gave little evidence of the ability to inspire. Nor was Gray able to successfully give life to Stuart's relationship with Marigold, the woman he marries and subsequently loses to another member of his circle. Stuart and Marigold's thinness was especially noticeable in contrast to the richness of the play's four other characters, particularly Humphry Taylor, a homosexual poet-philosopher with such an intense devotion to his strict standards that he is condemned to be forever disappointed both in others and himself. Watching Peter Friedman's remarkable performance as the obsessed Taylor, one couldn't help speculating what the play might have been had Gray chosen this driven man as his central character rather than Stuart. The production was directed with becoming economy by Gray in association with Michael McGuire.

Israel Horovitz's *Today, I Am a Fountain Pen* dealt with a young Canadian Jewish boy in the 1940s and his confrontation with his parents when he discovers that they do not practice the same values they preach. The dramatic potential of this confrontation unfortunately was vitiated by its treatment which, with its wiseacre juvenile lead's non-stop spewing of one-liners and its overt sentimentality, resembled nothing so much as a situation comedy. Most successful in this enterprise were Marcia Jean Kurtz, who gave a nice edge to the stock character of a Jewish mother, and Sol Frieder as a font of wisdom.

Painters often do studies of other artists' works in order to develop their technique. In *Neon Psalms*, playwright Thomas Strelich seemed to be doing a study of Sam Shepard's technique. As a study it had merit. Strelich did well by his desert setting, highway imagery, and a grizzled father obsessed with turtles and old episodes of *Bonanza*. But, aside from isolated passages which showed actors Tom Aldredge, Scotty Bloch, Kelly Connell and Cara Duff-MacCormick to good advantage, the play didn't seem to be about much of anything.

A.R. Gurney Jr.'s *Sweet Sue* concerned the budding of a relationship between a woman in her 40s and her son's college roommate. The twist was that Gurney had each of the two characters played by two actors. Unlike Brian Friel's *Philadelphia, Here I Come!*, in which the protagonist was played by two actors (one representing the public face, one the inner voice), here no specific boundary was drawn between what the alter egos would say or do. Rather, the device was intended to dramatize the constant dialogue we all carry on with ourselves. Gurney furnished the two Susans with wonderful material. Torn by conflicting impulses, playing irony against doubt and foolishness against grit, she may be the most fully developed female character he has written. And what fun Mary Tyler Moore and Lynn Redgrave had with her!—Moore with a breathtaking precision that never seemed calculated, Redgrave with sheer exuberance. One had to be grateful to the writer for giving them the opportunity to generate the joys of good, old-fashioned star power.

Unfortunately, he did not give the two young actors playing Jake the same opportunity. Whereas the problems of Susan's maturity seemed to inspire Gurney, his response to Jake's youth was to create a generic young man, lacking in specificity. It was easy to see why Susan would spark Jake's adoration, but the reverse had to be taken on faith. John K. Linton and Barry Tubb gave it their best shots, but there was hardly enough for one actor to play, much less two.

A Girl's Guide to Chaos represented Cynthia Heimel's attempt to adapt her comic essays to the stage. Alternating uneasily between monologue and revue-like sketches, the piece's structural weaknesses kept it from being a persuasive play. But Heimel has a way with Dorothy Parker–style wisecracks and, in Debra Jo Rupp and Rita Jenrette, she had actresses who could put them over confidently.

Circle Rep was founded as part of the off-off-Broadway movement designed to provide an alternative to commercial fare. In this light, their production of John Bishop's *The Musical Comedy Murders of 1940* is particularly puzzling. Concerning a group of exaggerated theatrical types isolated in a mansion with an unknown killer and spies, it resembled nothing so much as an old Bob Hope vehicle without

THE NERD—Top to bottom, Peter Riegert, Mark Hamill and Robert Joy in the Broadway comedy by the late Larry Shue

Bob Hope. To his credit, Bishop (who also directed) was able to whip up a steady stream of gags, but one hopes for more than pastiche from the author of the underrated *The Trip Back Down*. And one wonders why Circle Rep produced a play more appropriate for summer stock.

Tina Howe's *Coastal Disturbances* focused on a young photographer coping with emotional disrepair over a summer on a New England beach. There are several monologues in this script that will surely become standards in acting classes. As enchanting as they are as writing *per se,* they are stylistically so similar—extrapolating from reality into finely spun fable and fantasy—that they undermine belief in the individuality of the characters. With almost every character speaking the same kind of poetry, one ceases to accept them as human beings with distinct and specific desires and perspectives. Instead, one often felt one was at a reading of excerpts from Howe's notebooks. These passages are surrounded by a play filled with delightful detail and telling incident, but the central story, concerning the photographer's summertime romance with a sensitive lifeguard, is so wispy that the effect is rather like coming across a random selection of unstrung pearls. Carole Rothman's production, however, was exemplary, carefully orchestrating the voices of the beach's regulars in counterpoint. Exemplary, too, were Dennis Parichy's lighting design, which subtly conveyed the many moods of the beach, and Annette Bening, who made a beguiling New York debut in the role of the photographer.

Eric Overmyer's *On the Verge* was a theatrical entry in the currently popular "fish-out-of-water" genre. In common with pictures like *Star Trek IV, Back to the Future* and *Peggy Sue Got Married,* the central characters, through some time travel gimmick, found themselves transported to another era, and much of the intended humor was mined from looking at the new milieu from the perspective of another age. Specifically, *On the Verge* moved three female American explorers from the turn of the century to 1955. Though Overmyer can turn a clever phrase, too much of the play depended on exploiting his travellers' befuddlement in the face of 1950s jargon and brand names. The portrait of the 1950s values, too, didn't cut very deeply, concentrating on easy jokes based on old TV shows and the obligatory cheap shots at Richard Nixon. (Mind you, I'm not objecting to shots at Richard Nixon, but genuine satire would have addressed his character and philosophy rather than making cracks about his physical appearance.) The set by John Arnone, the lighting by James F. Ingalls and the costumes by Ann Hould-Ward were full of happy surprises, and Lisa Banes, Laura Hicks and Patricia Hodges brought intelligence and energy to their roles.

Plays that don't work are not always without rewards. *The Maderati*, Richard Greenberg's farce about shallow pseudo-literary types, lacked narrative discipline, but was filled with good jokes. *Sleight of Hand*, John Pielmeier's thriller about a magician, sacrificed credibility for effect, but many of the effects (credited to magic consultant Charles Reynolds) were arresting. Rebecca Wackler, Larry Larson and Levi Lee's *Tent Meeting*, a black comedy about an itinerant preacher and his unbalanced children, also had problems with dramatic logic, but no play in which an organless infant types messages from God can lack interest. Bob Larbey's *A Month of Sundays*, a by-the-numbers construction featuring Jason Robards as a sprightly curmudgeon in a rest home, at least gave Felicity LaFortune and Lynne Thigpen opportunities to shine through the cliches. Richard Harris's *Stepping Out*, a chronicle of a group of Londoners in a tap class for amateurs, was peopled by stock characters and unsurprising epiphanies, but an admirable cast, including Carole Shelley and Meagan Fay, still held the attention, if not for their characters' sake then for the performers' skills. As for *Women Beware Women*, in which contemporary British playwright Howard Barker came up with a new resolution to Thomas Middleton's 1623 tragedy, though Barker's amendation lacked coherence, its baroque rhetorical flourishes were often exhilarating.

Here's where we list the Best Plays choices for the outstanding achievements of the season in New York, on and off Broadway. In the acting categories, clear distinction among "starring," "featured" or "supporting" players can't be made on the basis of official billing, which is as much a matter of contracts as of esthetics. Here in these volumes we divide acting into "primary" or "secondary" roles, a primary role being one which might some day cause a star to inspire a revival in order to appear in that character. All others, be they vivid as Mercutio, are classed a secondary. Furthermore, our list of individual standouts makes room for more than a single choice when appropriate. We believe that no useful purpose is served by forcing ourselves into an arbitrary selection of a single best when we come upon multiple examples of equal distinction.

Here, then, are the Best Plays bests of 1986–87:

PLAYS

BEST PLAY: *Fences* by August Wilson

BEST FOREIGN PLAY: *Les Liaisons Dangereuses* by Christopher Hampton; *Wild Honey* by Michael Frayn

BEST REVIVAL: *The Life and Adventures of Nicholas Nickleby* by David Edgar

BEST ACTOR IN A PRIMARY ROLE: Philip Bosco as Sir Thomas More in *A Man for All Seasons*; James Earl Jones as Troy Maxson in *Fences*; Alan Rickman as Vicomte de Valmont in *Les Liaisons Dangereuses*

BEST ACTRESS IN A PRIMARY ROLE: Laura Esterman as Donna in *Kvetch*; Amy Madigan as Sue Jack Tiller Hooker in *The Lucky Spot*; Mary Tyler Moore as Susan in *Sweet Sue*

SPECIAL CITATION: Barney Simon, Vanessa Cooke, Timmy Kwebulana, Neil McCarthy, Geina Mhlophe, Terry Norton, Thoko Tshinga and Fiona Ramsay for the collaborative creation of *Born in the R.S.A.*; Severn Darden in *Sills & Company*

BEST ACTOR IN A SECONDARY ROLE: Peter Friedman as Humphry Taylor in *The Common Pursuit*; John Randolph as Ben in *Broadway Bound*; Courtney B. Vance as Cory in *Fences*

BEST ACTRESS IN A SECONDARY ROLE: Mary Alice as Rose in *Fences*; Suzanne Burden as La Presidente de Tourvel in *Les Liaisons Dangereuses*; Jane Carr as Fanny Squeers and others in *The Life and Adventures of Nicholas Nickleby*

BEST DIRECTOR: Howard Davies for *Les Liaisons Dangereuses*; Lloyd Richards for *Fences*

BEST SCENERY: Bob Crowley for *Les Liaisons Dangereuses*; John Gunter for *Wild Honey*

BEST COSTUMES: Deirdre Clancy for *Wild Honey*; Bob Crowley for *Les Liaisons Dangereuses*

BEST LIGHTING: Martin Aronstein for *Wild Honey*; Dennis Parichy for *Coastal Disturbances* and *The Lucky Spot*; Chris Parry and Beverly Emmons for *Les Liaisons Dangereuses*

MUSICALS

BEST MUSICAL: *Three Postcards*

BEST BOOK: Craig Lucas for *Three Postcards*

BEST MUSIC: Craig Carnelia for *Three Postcards*; Charles Strouse for *Rags*

BEST LYRICS: Craig Carnelia for *Three Postcards*

BEST ACTOR IN A PRIMARY ROLE: Robert Lindsay as Bill Snibson in *Me and My Girl*; Colm Wilkinson as Jean Valjean in *Les Misérables*

BEST ACTRESS IN A PRIMARY ROLE: Teresa Burrell as Lily Meadows in *Honky Tonk Nights*; Lonette McKee as Billie Holiday in *Lady Day at Emerson's Bar and Grill*; Teresa Stratas as Rebecca Hershkowitz in *Rags*

BEST ACTOR IN A SECONDARY ROLE: Timothy Jerome as Herbert Parchester in *Me and My Girl*

BEST ACTRESS IN A SECONDARY ROLE: Judy Kuhn as Bella Cohen in *Rags*

BEST DIRECTOR: Trevor Nunn and John Caird for *Les Misérables*; Norman René for *Three Postcards*

BEST CHOREOGRAPHY: Gillian Gregory for *Me and My Girl*

BEST SCENERY: Loy Arcenas for *Three Postcards*; John Napier for *Les Misérables*

BEST LIGHTING: David Hersey for *Les Misérables*; Debra J. Kletter for *Three Postcards*

BEST COSTUMES: Mardi Philips for *Honky Tonk Nights*

SPECIAL CITATION: Michael Starobin for orchestrations for *Rags*

Musicals

Richard Rodgers once said that anything could be musicalized, even a heart operation. This season, several writers seemed inclined to test that statement by undertaking decidedly chancy subjects, including an operation on an organ somewhat south of the heart. Other writers tried to create shows well within the established traditions of the form. The results for adventurers and traditionalists alike were mostly undistinguished, though moments and performances provided consolations.

Rags told the story of immigrants Rebecca Hershkowitz and her young son David as they try to build new lives on the Lower East Side of New York in 1910. Certainly there was enough raw material here for a rousing evening of musical theater, and the first act, dealing with Rebecca's introduction to the ways of the Lower East Side, made good on much of that potential. But, after a promising start, Joseph Stein's book succumbed to formula, one which Stein himself helped to develop in his book for *Fiddler on the Roof*. At the end of the first act of that show, the wedding of one of Tevye's daughters is disrupted by a pogrom, and variations of that pogrom have rung down the first-act curtains of a number of musicals of serious intention since. In *Cabaret*, an engagement party is disrupted by Nazis. In *Grind*, a black boy's birthday present of a bicycle is destroyed by bigoted hooligans. And, again, in *Rags*, David, having refused to bow to extortionists, is beaten, and the stall he is tending is wrecked.

Alas, the second act continued to present thinly disguised revisions of scenes from older works rather than a freshly imagined account of an important chapter in American history. Stephen Schwartz's lyrics, too, were disappointing, generally constructed to explicate matters already understood by the audience. But *Rags* gave cause for celebration on a few counts. Opera star Teresa Stratas, making her Broadway debut, gave a commanding performance as Rebecca, the force of her own personality going a long way towards offsetting the passivity in which the character as written languished for the bulk of the second act. And Judy Kuhn stood out in the supporting cast as a young woman bridling against constraints laid down by her tradition-bound father. Perhaps challenged by Stratas and Kuhn's extraordinary voices, Charles Strouse composed one of his finest scores, which benefitted from the orchestrations of the remarkable Michael Starobin.

Larry Kert, featured in *Rags*, soon reappeared in another musical set on the Lower East Side, *The Rise of David Levinsky*. In contrast to *Rags*'s narrative confusion, *David Levinsky*, based on a novel by Abraham Cahan, had a strong story to tell about the evolution of an idealistic immigrant into an exploitative manufacturer, but Isaiah Sheffer's book and lyrics constantly had its characters clumsily verbalize the piece's themes and ironies rather than embody them in dramatic action. The result was a frustrating fizzle.

The action of *Honky Tonk Nights* began two years after *Rags* and also dealt with a minority's struggle for bread and dignity in New York. The subject was the black music halls of the time and the talented artists segregated there. Unfortunately, the creators didn't seem to have a clear idea of what they were after. Did they want the show to be a conventional musical about backstage love? Or an idealized recreation of a music hall? Or did they want to use the music hall as a device through which to comment satirically on black-white relations in the early years of this century? This confusion of purpose and style ultimately was the project's undoing, though there were bracing moments when toothless pastiche was put aside and the anger and frustration of the victims of discrimination were inverted into burlesque routines. Even when invention flagged, however, the cast, led by the engaging Joe Morton, buoyed the evening with their high spirits. The best reason to see the show was to watch the beautiful Teresa Burrell sing a wide variety of songs and more than hold her own with the company's broadest clowns. Hers was an unforgettable performance in an also-ran effort.

Above is a photo of the model for Loy Arcenas's acclaimed set for the off-Broadway musical *Three Postcards,* which its designer describes as follows: "It is a raked cobalt-blue floor; the table splits into three to allow isolation for the women in fantasy scenes; the mural is done in the style of Matisse."

Lanie Robertson's *Lady Day at Emerson's Bar and Grill* also focused on an aspect of black show business history. A musical play structured as a cabaret act, it featured Lonette McKee as Billie Holiday singing a program of songs on a night four months before Holiday's death. Shortly into the show, Holiday's patter between the songs shifts from the usual segues into an emotion-drenched autobiography. Though the form offered few dramatic surprises (one knows from the start that Holiday is going to fall to pieces in front of us), McKee more than justified the evening with a *tour de force* acting and singing performance.

A black folk hero gave his name to another off-Broadway musical, *Staggerlee,* but whatever qualities the character possessed to encourage the writers to build a show around him were lost somewhere along the way. The book by Vernel Bagneris ostensibly concerned Staggerlee's efforts to keep from being framed for murder; but whereas there were plenty of incidents, they didn't gather into a coherent story. What the show did have in abundance was the exuberant music composed and played by Allen Toussaint.

The creators of *Raggedy Ann,* a musical derived from the popular rag doll character, clearly hoped it would find a place as a *Wizard of Oz*–style family entertainment. But the genre requires a clarity that *Raggedy Ann* lacked. In *The Wizard of Oz,* which apparently served as a model, the motion of the story is based on Dorothy's desire to go home. In *Raggedy Ann,* the goal was to reinstill in a little girl named Marcella the desire to live. But the means by which this was to be accomplished were never clearly delineated. Instead, a lot of brightly costumed characters dashed to no particular purpose through cluttered fantasy sets, with the occasional intrusion of an explosion and a belch of smoke. Though some of Joe Raposo's music was tuneful, the lyrics were consistently flat. (Some of the songs, in fact, were plucked from an animated Raggedy Ann movie that featured a completely different story.) William Gibson, a considerable craftsman and the distinguished author of such plays as *The Miracle Worker* and *A Cry of Players*, wrote the surprisingly muddled book.

The big news in *Smile*, the musical by Howard Ashman and Marvin Hamlisch, was that the contestants in beauty pageants are not all selfless and idealistic American roses and that the pageants' promoters do not always hew to the standards of fair play and integrity their displays allegedly promote. It would have taken a lot of imagination to breathe new life into such timeworn insights, but such was not in evidence here. Howard Ashman, who did such a delightful job as writer-director of off Broadway's *Little Shop of Horrors*, did solid work as director, but his book generated little dramatic tension. As jaundiced a view as one might have of the musical's subject, a show about a pageant should at least stimulate some interest in who is going to win. The subplot held some promise, focusing on the fortyish former beauty contestant who runs the local pageant around which the story centered and how her obsession with making her pageant a success—an obsession which threatens her marriage—is the virulent extension of the American obsession with winning which lies at the heart of beauty contests. But this strain, too, was not developed to its full potential. The movie on which the musical was based was less than an ideal piece to begin with, but it didn't shrink from looking frankly at the ugly consequences of warped values. Here one got the feeling that Ashman and his colleagues were overly concerned with keeping the material palatable for a Broadway musical audience.

Marvin Hamlisch's score was thin, settling for easy spoofs of the musical wallpaper which usually accompanies such events, rather than going for the vigor and tunefulness that have been the hallmarks of his best work. Ultimately, the show suffered from what seemed to be mixed motives. On the one hand, it seemed to aspire to being a fearless exposé; on the other, it seemed to want to be good, light family entertainment. Despite a strong cast and sporadically witty musical staging by Mary Kyte, *Smile* was mild to a fault.

In a more frivolous vein, *Olympus on My Mind* attempted to create a musical adaptation of the Amphitryon legend in the cheerily anachronistic manner in which Rodgers and Hart and Abbott refashioned Shakespeare's *The Comedy of Errors* into *The Boys from Syracuse*, but only composer Grant Sturiale's sprightly music came close. Barry Harman's book and lyrics aspired to zippiness, but the essence of true zip is the appearance of effortlessness, and here one was constantly aware of the strain to be clever. Harman did rather better as director, getting engaging performances out of an energetic cast, particularly the production's two strongest singers, Ron Raines and Emily Zacharias.

Some show business cliches have been parodied so frequently that the parodies themselves have become cliches. Such was the case with *Have I Got a Girl For You!*, a camp musical travesty of the *Frankenstein* movies that offered nothing that hadn't been done before, better and more succinctly on *The Carol Burnett Show*. Another offering, *Stardust*, was the latest in a long series of salutes to well-known songwriters, this time focusing on the lyrics of Mitchell Parish, who wrote the lyrics to a number of familiar songs including "Moonlight Serenade," "Sophisticated Lady" and "The Syncopated Clock." But director Albert Harris couldn't lick the problem of making this amiable pop material hold the stage. Certainly, playing in a large Broadway house didn't help such a modest show, nor did Harris do any favor to Parish by placing next to each other two songs in which "together" was rhymed with "birds of a feather." The shame of it is that several of the cast—most notably Maureen Brennan and Kim Criswell—have previously proved themselves to be more than capable of fine work with genuinely theatrical material.

Angry Housewives was about four middle-class, middle-aged women who, despite the objections of the men in their lives, form a punk rock band to give expression to their frustrations. Their big song? "Eat Your Fucking Corn Flakes." What might have been the basis of an entertaining revue sketch was puffed by author A.M. Collins and songwriter Chad Henry into two repetitive acts. The characters were both caricatures and stereotypes, and the lyrics (littered with nonrhyming rhymes) did little but state and restate obvious points. What small pleasure the evening afforded was in watching a cast including such first-

STARLIGHT EXPRESS—Roller skaters portray an engine (Greg Mowry, *left*) pulling passenger cars (Reva Rice, Jane Krakowski, Lola Knox and Andrea McArdle) in Andrew Lloyd Webber-Richard Stilgoe musical fantasy about railroad trains

rate musical theater performers as Carolyn Casanave, Vicki Lewis and Lee Wilkof attack the intractable material with so much zest. (In the interest of fairness, it should be reported that *Angry Housewives* was a long-running hit in Seattle at the Pioneer Square Theater, of which Ms. Collins is artistic director.)

Composer Andrew Lloyd Webber and director Trevor Nunn, having dressed a squad of actors up as felines in *Cats*, turned his attention to trains with *Starlight Express*. Wearing roller skates and headdresses suggestive of the various engines and cars they represented, the actors zoomed up, down and around the ramps, banks and bridges of John Napier's gargantuan and colorful three-tiered set. The story concerned a plucky young steam engine who successfully challenges more modern locomotives in a race across America, but there was little pretense that this was meant to be anything but an occasion for songs, dances and spectacular effects. The effects, including clouds of smoke and thousands of flashing lights, were indeed spectacular, and the choreography Arlene Phillips invented for her skating dancers was vivid and athletic. But the songs displayed little of Webber's usual melodic flair, and Richard Stilgoe's lyrics were so thin as to barely register.

If *Starlight Express* represented the Broadway musical at its least consequential, the rock opera version of Victor Hugo's *Les Misérables* represented its most substantial effort. Here at last was a story with meat on it. The central figure is Jean Valjean, the convict who breaks parole and, after a crucible of conscience, emerges with a new identity and a passion to do good in the world. His nemesis is the dogged Inspector Javert, whose obsession with his severe brand of justice drives him to pursue Valjean down the years and across the breadth of 19th century France. The tale is a huge one, and the production, reteaming the ubiquitous Trevor Nunn with his *Nicholas Nickleby* co-director John Caird, was correspondingly huge and frequently exhilarating in its cinematic sweep. John Napier was again the resourceful designer; making use of a giant turntable, he shifted us with breathtaking swiftness from penal camp to village to tavern to slum to barricade to sewer to ballroom. For my taste, however, the score fell short of the scenario. Time and again, composer Claude-Michel Schönberg introduced a promising melodic idea only to fritter it away with banal development. The lyrics by Herbert Kretzmer and James Fenton, based on the French originals by Alain Boublil and Jean-Marc Natel, mostly consisted of rhymed cliches. Still, there was enough to the material for the cast to register solidly, particularly Colm Wilkinson as Valjean. His performance in the second act of the score's one truly distinguished song, a prayer that a young man facing death be spared called "Bring Him Home," was the high point of the Broadway musical theater season.

Downtown, the Public Theater premiered another rock opera, an exploration of the world of the transsexual called *The Knife*. Mandy Patinkin played a chef in a hotel who, when he encounters a naked female guest, suddenly realizes he wants to be a woman. The guest, seeing him as a soul-mate, obligingly helps him finance his operation, then disappears after quarreling with him on the eve of his transformation. There was a good deal more to David Hare's plot, all thumpingly earnest but thoroughly incredible. Composer Nick Bicat's lush score supplied Patinkin and co-star Mary Elizabeth Mastrantonio with some lovely music to display their fine voices, but Tim Rose Price's lyrics mostly consisted of awkward stabs at poetry. Hare, who has proved himself to be a gifted director in the past, was unable to do much on this occasion.

The most satisfying musical theater work on or off Broadway this season was a small-scale piece, about three women having dinner together, called *Three Postcards*. Initially, playwright Craig Lucas and composer-lyricist Craig Carnelia concentrate on having fun with their heroines' catch phrases and jargon-saturated conversation. But then the dramatists go inward, filling the stage with fantasy, memory and images from their private worlds. One of them indulges in an erotic daydream in which the indifferent pianist and the detached waiter suddenly and passionately sing to her of their desire; the second reflects on the various disasters which have turned her life into endless fodder for her companions' anecdotes; and the third tries to come to grips with the recent loss of her mother. This is a musical not of plot but of nuance, the theatrical equivalent of a *New Yorker* short story in which a detail may speak volumes. Though other shows this season featured music to be admired, this was the sole score in which the lyrics were of consistent distinction, encouraging the audience to search out their implications rather than bludgeoning with declamation. Norman René directed his excellent cast—including Carnelia and Brad O'Hare as the pianist and waiter and Jane Galloway, Maureen Silliman and Karen Trott as their customers—with grace and precision, proving again that one doesn't need a multimillion-dollar budget to produce a first-rate musical.

Specialties

Among the non-dramatic presentations to play Broadway this season were three showcases for stars. Barbara Cook, in an evening named *A Concert for the Theater*, brought an expanded version of her cabaret act to the Ambassador. The talk between the numbers was trivial, but the singing was magnificent, particularly in selections from musicals with which she has been associated—"Ice Cream" from *She Loves Me* and "When I Marry Mr. Snow" from *Carousel*. As pleasurable as the program was, it was the source of frustration, too. If American musical theater were healthy, she would be playing new roles rather than having to wax nostalgic about old.

Two comics held forth in evenings at the Atkinson Theater. Rowan Atkinson, a popular British comic, appeared in a series of sketches and monologues of variable quality, the best of these an exercise in black humor in which a grotesquely severe schoolmaster complained to a dazed parent of the inconvenience his son's death has caused. Too many of the other pieces, however, depended on easy vulgarity for their humor, and almost none of them had satisfactory resolutions.

He was followed by comedian Jackie Mason in a presentation entitled *The World According to Me!* Mason's targets are the standards for stand-up comics—cultural and racial differences, celebrities, sex. What is special is the delivery, in which the germ of an idea is given a nudge and, like a snowball sent down a steep hill in a cartoon, gathers mass and speed and the ability to flatten anything in its path.

Off-Broadway, *Eno* featured Israeli entertainer Eno Rosenn in a program of mime performed to an original score by Nir Brandt. Rosenn's technical control was awesome, particularly in an extended piece concerning a heart-attack victim floating in the ether of an out-of-body experience. The evening was flawed, however, by calculated cutenesses which stopped just short of winking at the audience.

Dance works appeared both on Broadway and off. Presented by the producers of last season's *Tango Argentino, Flamenco Puro* aimed to do for flamenco dancing what the other show had done for the tango. The dancing was indeed spectacular, but the evening appealed more to cognoscenti who could appreciate the subtleties and distinctions of the various performers' styles than to a general audience of sufficient size to fill the Mark Hellinger. Martha Clarke began and ended the season off Broadway with critically acclaimed pieces of dance theater: *Vienna: Lusthaus*, a depiction of the culture which went from the Strauss waltz to the Nazi goosestep, and *The Garden of Earthly Delights*, a vivid exploration of Hieronymus Bosch's famous painting.

Paul Sills's importance to the American stage can hardly be exaggerated. With the Compass Players and the Second City of Chicago, he helped create the American improvisational theater movement which has introduced and developed the skills of dozens of leading actors, directors and writers. He followed this by developing story theater, a widely emulated form in which a group of actors relates a tale by alternating between playing the story's characters and narrating these characters' actions in the third person. (As critic Julius Novick has pointed out, what is *Nicholas Nickleby* but a story theater piece on a grand scale?)

This season Sills assembled a group of old colleagues, some of whom have been working with him since the early 1950s, to improvise nightly as *Sills & Company*. The theater games developed by his mother, Viola Spolin, provided the structures of these voyages into spontaneous creation. The audience provided the specifics— where scenes should take place, what characters should people them, what issues they should wrestle with, etc. Being completely improvised, the success of the performances varied from night to night depending on the chemistry between the cast and the audience. At its best the shows were a remarkable blend of innocence and sophistication, the actors giving themselves over to the spirit of play but bringing to the games quick minds and seasoned technical skills. Severn Darden proved particularly popular. Assuming the identity of an expert on a topic suggested by a patron, in response to interviewer Garry Goodrow's questions he spun intricate webs of fantastic intellectual nonsense. As delightful as the shows frequently were, however, they represented something of a retrenchment for Sills. One looks forward to him undertaking new challenges in future projects.

Revivals

A large proportion of this season's revivals were of major plays by 20th-century British dramatists, ranging from Shaw and Coward to Stoppard, Bolt and Edgar (by way of Dickens).

The first of the two revivals of Shaw was Stephen Porter's production at Circle in the Square of *You Never Can Tell,* a play about a liberated woman, her three unconventional children, and their encounter with the husband she'd left some 20 years before. The play gives the impression of moving from scene to scene, not because of purposes organic to the people concerned, but because Shaw figured another combination of his mouthpieces could afford him the opportunity to write an amusing series of exchanges on another topic. To its credit, this production did have the benefit of some very agreeable mouthpieces, chief among them Philip Bosco as a waiter of unusual sagacity, Stephen McHattie (in a performance that recalled the young George C. Scott) as his brusque solicitor son, Victor Garber as a dentist whose conversation is livelier than his practice, Uta Hagen as the liberated mother and Amanda Plummer, Lise Hilboldt and John David Cullum as her children.

In contrast to *You Never Can Tell*, the characters in Shaw's *Pygmalion* are credible as human beings at war with conflicting emotions, which may explain why *Pygmalion* is among the most popular of his plays. Amanda Plummer again starred, playing Liza Doolittle to Peter O'Toole's Henry Higgins in an odd but ultimately valuable production. Perhaps because of *My Fair Lady* and the film version of *Pygmalion*, in which Higgins and Liza end up together, we are used to seeing this as a love story. There was little trace of that this time around. Instead, under Val May's direction, the play seemed to be an essay on adolescence. Higgins and Pickering take up Eliza with an almost teenage enthusiasm, as if (as Higgins's mother comments) they were playing with a doll. When, at the end, Higgins tries to persuade Eliza to return to Wimpole Street "for the fun of it," it's in the manner of one kid asking another to come back to the clubhouse to do some neat stuff. But, by play's end, Eliza has learned what she can from Higgins and Pickering. She's outgrown them, so it's time for her to move on. The play implies that people who seek to be liberated truly achieve their goal only when they can break their dependence on their benefactors.

Whether this approach to the script was arrived at intentionally or in reaction to Peter O'Toole's performance is a matter of conjecture. Some were offended by the shamelessness of O'Toole's star turn, but I thought O'Toole's shamelessness was consistent with Higgins's. O'Toole's reluctance to give his colleagues focus onstage was in line with Higgins's cheerful self-centeredness. His Higgins didn't much care about other people, only about the sounds they made, so he didn't bother to look at them much. This provided Amanda Plummer's Eliza with a powerful objective: to *make* O'Toole-Higgins look at her and actually see and consider her, an objective she ultimately achieved in the ferociously played final scene. If Plummer didn't entirely convince in her transformation from flower girl to lady, she did impress in her transformation from juvenile into an adult. In supporting parts, Dora Bryan was an admirable Mrs. Pearce and Lionel Jeffries a solid Pickering. That wonderful actor John Mills, on the other hand, didn't seem to possess enough of the anarchic spirit to do Doolittle full justice.

In the meantime, Plummer's *You Never Can Tell* co-star, Philip Bosco, had moved from waiter to martyr, playing Sir Thomas More in the Roundabout's 25th anniversary presentation of Robert Bolt's *A Man for All Seasons*. Happily, Bosco played not the saint but the man, depicting More as a canny politician who deployed every honorable device in his strategic arsenal in hope of avoiding martyrdom. As a result, More registered not as a sanctimonious, self-approbating bore, but as a human being trying to accommodate both his times and his conscience. Bolt's use of the Common Man as a kind of Greek chorus struck me as arch and self-conscious, but the rest of the play held up admirably.

The Roundabout also produced another British classic from the 1960s, Tom

THE LIFE AND ADVENTURES OF NICHOLAS NICKLEBY—DeNica Fairman (as Kate, *at top*), Michael Siberry (as Nicholas) and Frances Cuka (as Mrs. Nickleby) in the Royal Shakespeare Company revival

Stoppard's *Rosencrantz and Guildenstern are Dead*. John Wood, who had played Guildenstern in the original production, this time took on the Player King in an exuberant and royally hammy performance. The title characters were played by John Rubinstein and Stephen Lang, their open-faced Americanness, juxtaposed against Wood's convoluted old-style British theatricality, underscoring the characters' naïvete.

Having directed a near-flawless production of Noel Coward's *Hay Fever* last season, Brian Murray returned to Coward with a star-laden production of *Blithe Spirit* featuring Richard Chamberlain as Charles, a writer who, after a seance run by an eccentric medium, finds himself caught between his current wife, Ruth, and the materialized spirit of his late first wife, Elvira. The critical reaction to the opening performances of this revival was mixed, but when I saw it, several weeks into its run, it was in fine shape, Chamberlain doing trim and economical work, and Blythe Danner and Judith Ivey making their very different wives both charming and insufferable. Geraldine Page (in what turned out to be her final role) was a Ronald Searle drawing come to life as the eccentric Madame Arcati, and Nicola Cavendish was virtually flawless as the harried maid.

Less successful was the other Coward revival, a Broadway version of the musical revue, *Oh Coward!*, an assemblage of his songs devised and directed by and starring Roderick Cook which had a long run off Broadway several years back. In a season in which there were so few creditable new lyrics, it was a pleasure to be surprised again by Coward's extraordinary facility, but there was not enough variety in the material to sustain a full evening. One could not complain too much, however, about an entertainment which gave the beguiling Catherine Cox so much to do.

Me and My Girl received its Broadway premiere this season, but one hesitates to call a musical which originally opened in London in the 1930s a new work. Part of its intended charm was this lack of newness, the very fact of its having been conceived at a time when nothing was expected out of a musical except a few hours of light entertainment. But even for light entertainment, *Me and My Girl* was thin. The plot concerned a Cockney named Bill Snibson who, having been discovered to be the missing heir to a title and a fortune, tries to bridge the gaps between his two worlds. Having established this workable premise, however, the book, rather than developing it, relentlessly reiterated it. In scene after scene, Snibson tweaks the world of the upper class and threatens to leave it, yet it isn't until the end of the second act that he makes any significant gesture to make good his threat. The chief excuse for the production's existence—and it was excuse enough for most of the audience—was to provide a platform for its star, Robert Lindsay. Lindsay made the most of the opportunity, alternating between intricate setpieces of involved physical comedy (most notably a run-in with an ornamental cape which threatened to engulf him and most of the stage) and disarming song-and-dance routines. Choreographer Gillian Gregory and director Mike Ockrent moved the show along nimbly, and Maryann Plunkett, George S. Irving, Jane Summerhays and Timothy Jerome abetted.

Our corresponding historian, Thomas T. Foose, provides a footnote on the background and authorship of this immensely popular Broadway revival: "The original London production of *Me and My Girl* was at the Victoria Palace, opening on Dec. 16, 1937 for a run of 1,646 performances. There were revivals in 1945 and 1949. Lupino Lane created the role played by Robert Lindsay on Broadway.

"All three of the original British people who created this musical were highly prolific, but I do not believe that a book musical by anyone of the three has previously reached New York. Douglas Furber (1885–1961), the co-author of the book, was also a performer, and he appeared in New York in *Charlot's Revue* in 1926 He was also a lyricist and for the London *Charlot's Revue* in 1924 wrote the lyric for the famous song 'Limehouse Blues.' Furber's collaborator, L. Arthur

Rose (1887–1958), also wrote many musicals, but these titles are not familiar in America. Why the composer, Reginald Moxon Armitage (1898–1954) chose the pen name of 'Noel Gay' I have never found out. His musicals are also mostly unfamiliar here. What is familiar is one of his songs for a 1931 London musical, *Folly To Be Wise*, entitled 'All the King's Horses.' "

Another musical revival on Broadway was *The Mikado*, in a production directed and choreographed by Brian Macdonald. The cast mugged too much, but the singing was excellent, Susan Benson's sets and costumes were handsome and the staging was full of witty surprises. Karen Wood was a particular pleasure as Pitti-Sing.

That fine and beautiful actress Sigourney Weaver, under the direction of her husband James Simpson, met with mixed success playing Portia in the Classic Stage Company production of *The Merchant of Venice*. She had a clear line on Portia's mischeviousness, but seemed not to know how to play Portia in love. The production did, however, have the benefit of John Seitz's strong, sober Shylock.

The other Shakespearean productions were also of comedies. The Acting Company presented a well-received *Much Ado About Nothing*, and in Central Park Joseph Papp presented Wilford Leach's messy *Twelfth Night*, the primary assets of which were Peter MacNicol's Sir Andrew and Meagan Fay's Maria. The most unconventional Shakespeare was Robert Woodruff's production of *The Comedy of Errors* at the Vivian Beaumont, with The Flying Karamazov Brothers playing the two sets of twins and Shakespeare himself. There was a lot of juggling, tumbling and raw, rude physical comedy, much of it ingenious and hilarious, and some of it simply too much. In a production that was comprised of almost non-stop clamor, I was particularly grateful for the graceful and charming interludes featuring Avner Eisenberg, better known as Avner the Eccentric. Prior to this new vaudeville extravaganza, Lincoln Center played host to another evening of new vaudeville, a revival of Bill Irwin's dizzying combination of mime, slapstick and verbal wit, *The Regard of Flight*, which proved to be as much at home in the Vivian Beaumont as it had a few years back in the smaller American Place Theater.

The Beaumont was also the home of a revival of *The Front Page*, perhaps the earliest American play which can be revived without having to make apologies or special allowances. The dramas from the 1920s are seldom produced today, and in most cases it is all too easy to see why. They tend to advertise their serious intentions with explicitly articulated morals and speeches which, to contemporary ears, clank rather than ring. In contrast, *The Front Page* goes efficiently about its comic business. Under its surface guise as a light-hearted valentine to Chicago journalism, however, lurks a rather grim depiction of American values, institutions and practices. Yes, the reporters have an engaging vitality, but they are also blatantly bigoted, exploitative and mean-spirited. As much as they enjoy each other's company and proclaim their brotherhood, when the possibility of getting an exclusive story raises its head, they don't hesitate for a moment to betray each other.

If the boys in the pressroom are appalling, even worse are many of those they cover—graft-ridden, cynical cops and politicians, not above staging a gratuitous execution to win votes. As Lincoln Center's producing director Gregory Mosher has noted, *The Front Page* set the pattern for that other flamboyant Chicago play about men at work, David Mamet's *Glengarry Glen Ross*, as well as such other notable enterprises as *E/R* and *Bleacher Bums* (rough and tumble ensemble pieces by Chicago's Organic Theater about an inner-city emergency room and fans of the Chicago Cubs, respectively). All of these are invigorating combinations of farce and sociology, drawing energy from the arenas depicted without white-washing the morally questionable behavior of those who frequent them.

If Jerry Zaks's production of *The Front Page* was not quite on a par with his flawless *House of Blue Leaves* last season, its virtues were considerable, chief among them a sparkling supporting cast including Jerome Dempsey, Richard B. Shull, Ed Lauter, Jeffrey Weiss, Jack Wallace and Lee Wilkof. Richard Thomas achieved a hitherto unseen rakishness as Hildy Johnson opposite John Lithgow's jaunty Walter Burns. For my very personal taste, though Lithgow had the look and all the right moves, there was something a bit too sunny, too cheerful about his point of attack. I missed the meanness that the late Robert Ryan brought to the part in the Broadway revival of 1969, an interpretation which suggested that, while Hildy's affection for Walter had a personal base, Walter's for Hildy might end should Hildy ever stop being of use.

Bearing in mind that rats in an overcrowded cage become more aggressive, I also wished that Tony Walton's set were more claustrophobic. The reporters' territorial quibblings were undercut by what seemed like acres of unclaimed space. These quibbles aside, *The Front Page* was an impressive piece of work.

American corruption was also the theme of another major revival. With the revelations concerning the cause of last year's fatal space shuttle launching fresh in the audience's mind, Arthur Miller's *All My Sons* packed considerable contemporary relevance. One had to make allowances for a large number of coincidences and creaky devices employed to push the story forward, but the center of the play—Chris Keller's awful realization that the father he idealizes was in fact responsible for shipping defective parts which ultimately caused the deaths of many young American pilots during World War II—still compelled attention and stimulated thought. Under Arvin Brown's assured direction, Jamey Sheridan was able to give flesh and body to Chris. Richard Kiley made Joe Keller's journey from joviality to ruin tremendously affecting.

Broadway also saw a revival of *Arsenic and Old Lace*, Joseph Kesselring's comedy about two elderly Brooklyn sisters and their peculiar charity, relieving lonely old men of the cares of this world by giving them gentle pushes into the next with augmented elderberry wine. The script, doctored by the producers of the original production, Howard Lindsay and Russel Crouse, held up well after 40-odd years, but director Brian Murray had less success here than with Coward. Polly Holliday and William Hickey alone seemed to key into the script's peculiar blend of the quaint and the demented.

The original version of *The Concept* played to great success off Broadway 20 years ago. This season brought a new version, which, like its predecessor, followed a group of young addicts from street life to treatment at the Daytop Village. The actors were, in fact, recovering addicts from Daytop who, in collaboration with writer Casey Kurtti and director Lawrence Sacharow, drew on their own lives and experiences in building this piece. The material dealing with life at

ROSENCRANTZ AND GUILDENSTERN ARE DEAD—John Rubinstein, Stephen Lang and John Wood in the Roundabout Theater Company's revival of the Tom Stoppard play

Daytop inevitably got bogged down in preachiness, but the material which preceded it had a thrilling and brutal immediacy. Carl Cohen, one of the performers, could probably parlay his arresting combination of insolence and vulnerability into a continuing career.

Karen Allen, who played Helen Keller on Broadway in William Gibson's *Monday After the Miracle*, played Helen's teacher in the Roundabout revival of *The Miracle Worker*. One wished designer Neil Peter Jampolis had been able to come up with more elegant solutions to the set problems Gibson's script poses, but this story about Annie Sullivan's battle to bring intellectual light to the deaf and blind Helen still has the capacity to move an audience (and a critic) to tears. Vivian Matalon directed, with special assistance from B.H. Barry on the demanding fight scenes. Allen and Eevin Hartsough, as Helen, made a strong teacher-student team.

In 1959, *A Raisin in the Sun*, a drama about the black experience by a young black woman directed by a young black director (Lloyd Richards) must have been an easy play to embrace for political reasons. These days, plays about the black experience presented by black artists are, if not common, then not so infrequent that their very existence excites comment. Happily, the production of *Raisin*, also at the Roundabout, proved that no special allowances need be made for Lorraine

Hansberry's script. What is particularly striking about the play today is that, despite being a kitchen sink drama, it resounds with national and international concerns. An example: Beneatha Younger, a young black college student, plays a record of Nigerian music and, dressed in tribal clothes, begins to dance a dance with which Nigerian women welcome their men home from hunting expeditions. At this point, her brother Walter stumbles in, drunk and angry. Getting caught up in the music, he begins to pretend he is an African freedom fighter. The pretense slips away and, for a thrilling moment, this man, so frustrated by the daily humiliations at the hands of white society, gets an illusory taste of what it is to be brave, a warrior of the soul. The moment is rich with irony: the dance which would greet hunters in an African village is greeting a drunk in a Chicago slum. And yet, in that moment stirs also the promise of what Walter is to become. By the end of the play, he has found a way to be a warrior, a freedom fighter in his own world. Hal Scott's stirring production was alive to the many levels of the text and featured a remarkable set of performances by James Pickens Jr. as Walter, Kim Yancey as his sister, Olivia Cole as his mother and Starletta DuPois as his wife Ruth.

But for the most stirring revival of the season, we return again to the British and David Edgar's adaptation of Charles Dickens's *The Life and Adventures of Nicholas Nickleby*, which came back to Broadway in a stripped-down and substantially recast version of the production which took New York by storm in the 1981–82 season. My familiarity with the early production is based only on the television adaptation, so I am reluctant to make comparisons. Whatever cutbacks or compromises may have been made, however, the revival was still a magnificent achievement. Contemporary drama has tended toward plays that are the equivalent of hors d'oeuvres—tiny slices of little worlds—so it was thrilling to be reminded that the stage can also offer up a feast, in this case, the depiction of a huge cross-section of Victorian England. It was thrilling, too, in these days, in which so many plays are content to explore the ramifications of a single incident, to encounter such an abundance of high-calorie plot. Theater was born out of community, out of the need to share central values and myths and so to reaffirm the bonds of citizenship. At a time when much of our art romanticizes alienation from others, the company of *Nicholas Nickleby*, during the course of eight and one-half magical hours, forged with its enthusiastic audience a precious and rare sense of fellowship.

Offstage

Midway through the season, Wendy Wasserstein, the accomplished playwright of *Isn't It Romantic* and *Uncommon Women and Others*, published an article in the New York *Times* in which she reported that restaurants, discos and bowling alleys were losing their customers at 7:30 to the theaters. According to Wasserstein's scenario, British tourists were flocking to America to get the jump on the treats in store next season on the West End, 15 daily newspapers were staffed with critics who could hardly restrain their enthusiasm for the glorious new batch of American works adventurous producers were introducing in unprecedented numbers to unprecedented numbers, and the plays' authors were making handsome livings.

It was this last detail which positively revealed the piece to be a fraud. (Playwrights? Making *livings?*) Happy fiction though Wasserstein's article was, still there was genuinely good news about the economic health of the New York stage: More people paid more money to see more shows this season than last on Broadway. *Variety's* Richard Hummler spelled out the cheerful news in the following figures: Paid attendance this season was 6,968,277, as opposed to last season's 6,527,498, an increase of 6.7 percent. The box office total this season was $207,239,749, compared to last season's $190,619,862, an increase of 8.7 percent. The total of new productions listed in the Plays Produced on Broadway section of this 1986–87 *Best Plays* volume is 45 (see the one-page summary accompanying the first chapter of this report). Last season the number was 42, but that's not the only favorable comparison; this year the Broadway total includes one-third more new plays—10 American, 6 foreign—than last season. And there were 7 new musicals (5 American, 2 British), 3 revues, 8 specialty shows of one stripe or another and 11 revivals of plays and musicals, as described in the previous chapter.

Much of the financial good news was owing to the three new blockbuster British shows, *Les Misérables*, *Starlight Express* and *Me and My Girl*, as well as the continuing vitality of *Cats*. Reportedly, for several weeks these four shows accounted for more than 40 percent of Broadway's weekly receipts. *Les Misérables* had a strong start. *Variety* reported that well before it had even begun previews the show had already beaten *Cats's* record for the largest advance sale in Broadway history. (As of January 18, more than six weeks before it was scheduled to begin previews, *Les Misérables* had taken in a whopping $7,118,622. *Cats's* advance had been $6,200,000.) Of course, the capitalization was substantial as well—$4,500,000, equal to that of *Rags*. Even higher was *Starlight Express's* capitalization—$8,000,000, a Broadway record, and ten times what it cost to mount *Sweet Sue*, A.R. Gurney Jr.'s one-set play featuring four actors.

At the end of the season, only four shows that opened on Broadway had earned their money back: the Broadway transfer of last season's off-Broadway play *Cuba and His Teddy Bear* (presumably on the strength of superstar Robert DeNiro's presence) and three evenings of comedy—Jackie Mason's solo show *The World According to Me!*, Neil Simon's *Broadway Bound* and the revival of *Arsenic and Old Lace*. Several other shows are more or less likely to pay off, including the three new British musicals mentioned above plus the multi-award–winning *Fences*, and *Les Liaisons Dangereuses* and the revival of *Pygmalion*. Most of the above were generally well received by the press, with the exception of *Starlight Express*, for which the majority of the critics had little use or tolerance. This didn't prevent the huge, noisy and expensive show from posting record grosses several weeks in the spring.

The news was less cheery on the road, where touring productions' playing weeks declined from last season's 983 to 901, and income slipped from $235,616,902 to $224,287,315.

Off Broadway, the clear hit among commercial productions was *The Common Pursuit*, which was still running at season's end and recovered its $256,044 cost in about four months. Other 1986–87 long-running off-Broadway offerings were *Olympus on My Mind*, *The Colored Museum* and *Groucho: A Life in Revue*. As for production activity, there are 84 productions listed in the Plays Produced Off Broadway section of this 1986–87 *Best Plays* volume (see the one-page summary in the New Plays chapter of this report) as compared with 108 in 1985–86, a drop-off of 24 shows. The new-play and new-musical categories held up pretty well, however, with 44 plays this year (33 American and 11 foreign) and 9 musicals, as compared with 45 and 11 last year, whose volume was padded with 18 more revivals than in 1986–87.

Despite the improvement in Broadway's financial picture this year, the League of American Theaters and Producers was able to negotiate wage concessions from Actors' Equity Association (for bus-and-truck companies) and from the Association of Theatrical Press Agents and Managers (for members working in five Broadway theaters designated as "endangered"). The League also negotiated a new contract with the Society of Stage Directors and Choreographers under which Broadway artists in that organization would receive higher advance payments against future earnings, though only a modest advance in minimum fees.

The League also went head-to-head with the American Federation of Musicians over the issue of synthesizers. Some synthesizers are capable of simulating several instruments, and the musicians, fearing that producers would ultimately attempt to cut down expenses by substituting small combos of these electronic wonders for conventionally scaled orchestras, refused the League's request to be allowed their unlimited use for three years, despite League officials' pledge that current employment quotas would be frozen during that time. It seemed certain that both the synthesizers and the quota system (under which a predetermined number of musicians must be employed in designated houses, even if that means paying musicians for not playing) will make return appearances as issues when a new contract between the union and the producers is negotiated next season.

To turn to an intra-union issue, the British and U.S. chapters of Actors Equity agreed to renew an agreement under which non-star actors from one country are allowed to work in the other. The arrangement calls for a one-for-one exchange; that is to say, for every British actor welcomed to America, one American actor must be brought to Britain. Stars of major international reputation—such as John Gielgud or Lauren Bacall—are exempt from restriction, so no trade-off is required when they work across the sea.

For the first time since it was founded in 1930, the League held a convention. Over a weekend in Stamford, Connecticut, approximately 170 producers and managers discussed common concerns. Reportedly among the more controversial topics was the function of TKTS, the Theater Development Fund–sponsored booth which sells half-priced tickets on the day of performance and which is responsible for about 15 percent of Broadway's annual income. Some expressed the belief that the booth is doing more harm than good, discouraging rather than encouraging ticket sales. Henry Guettel, the executive director of T.D.F., proposed that instead of offering all listed shows at half price, producers might wish to determine for themselves how much to discount their tickets. Conceivably, a popular show could thus be sold at the TKTS booth for more than 50 percent of the ticket's face value, and a less popular show at less. Such a shift in policy,

GROUCHO: A LIFE IN REVUE—Faith Prince, Frank Ferrante and Les Marsden in the play by Arthur Marx

however, would require computerization of the box office. Other matters discussed at the convention included new strategies in Broadway financing in response to changing tax laws, the high cost of advertising in the New York *Times* and the need to develop better relations between New York producers and the local presenters of touring shows.

A substantial contingent of playwrights, literary managers and artistic directors held a conference of their own to discuss lessons learned during the four-year New Plays Program co-sponsored by the Foundation of the Dramatists Guild and CBS. Under the New Plays Program, 90 new scripts had been presented at a number of theaters around the country; 20 of these scripts had been given full productions, two of them, *The Colored Museum* and *Neon Psalms*, achieving off Broadway this season. Though generally the program was rated a success, participants at the conference had mixed feelings about the issue of play development and the problems playwrights face in trying to sustain themselves by their work. A number noted ironically that it seemed that more people supported themselves by handling (and rejecting) scripts than writing them. Simply speaking, even if one beats the odds and gets his or her play produced in a regional theater, the income from this production is seldom sufficient to support the writer during the composition of the next play. The clear consensus was that the theater is not doing enough to sustain the very people whose talents generate its projects.

Also, though much lip service is given to the support of playwrights, true support—in the form of companies sticking with dramatists through scripts that are unsuccessful as well as hits—is rare. More grumbling was heard about the nature of some so-called development programs, under which some writers felt that, rather than being given the opportunity to refine scripts to express what they wanted to say, they were being pressured to revise to suit management's ideas of marketability. Further, the proliferation of development programs has given rise to a breed of playwright whose career is limited to workshops and readings without ever receiving the satisfaction of full production, a condition likened to purgatory. The proposals discussed included putting playwrights on salary; assigning the English adaptation of foreign-language classics to resident writers rather than automatically using and paying royalties on already published adaptations; and the idea of theaters pooling resources to co-sponsor playwrights they couldn't support individually.

An organization called the Non-Traditional Casting Project held a two-day seminar at the Shubert Theater. Through discussions and demonstrations, it intended to open the theater community's minds to hiring actors without regard to race or, in some cases, gender. In unconventionally cast scenes from established works, the Project's organizers proved their contention that roles which are not race-specific could be played successfully by performers from backgrounds different than those who had originally played them (e.g., Joanne in *Company*, a role originally played by white Elaine Stritch, was played at the seminar by black Josephine Premice).

The issue gets more complicated when a character's ethnicity is a central part of his or her identity. For instance, would an audience accept a black Big Daddy playing opposite a white Brick in a production of *Cat on a Hot Tin Roof*? Evidently so, when Big Daddy is played by James Earl Jones and Brick by Stephen Collins, as was the case in another of the seminar's presentations. But here more issues arose. Watching Jones, one simply made an adjustment—this black actor is in a white role—and sat back to enjoy him and Collins play the hell out of one of the great scenes in American theater. But the reason one could make the adjustment is that one *knew* there was an adjustment to make. *Cat* is a well-known play, after all. It is questionable, however, if it would have been appropriate to have Jones play Big Daddy in the first production of *Cat*.

The new theater in the controversial Marriott Hotel made its debut as a legitimate house. There were complaints that patrons had to negotiate an inconvenient gauntlet of stairs and corridors to get to the Marquis Theater, and also that the lobby bar was placed so near a series of steps as to actively discourage patronage. The house itself, a 1,600-seat auditorium decorated in burgundy, seems well-suited for large musicals such as the one that was its premiere theatrical tenant, *Me and My Girl*. (The addition of a new musical house, however, does not make up for the loss of the three smaller houses that were demolished to make way for the Marriott, two of which, the Morosco and the old Helen Hayes, had been among the more attractive venues for straight plays.) In addition to this new building containing a new theater, plans were afoot to build a new building over an old theater. The Shubert Organization leased the air rights over the Belasco Theater to a real estate developer, who is planning to construct a new office tower.

There were some noticeable shifts in personnel. Marshall W. Mason was succeeded as president of the Society of Stage Directors and Choreographers by Gene Saks, who was elected to a three-year term. Mason, the artistic director of the Circle Repertory Theater since its founding, also resigned from that position and was replaced by co-founder and company member Tanya Berezin. The Ridiculous Theatrical Company also lost its artistic director, Charles Ludlam, not because of resignation but to an early death from AIDS. He was, unfortunately, but one of a growing number of valued artists stricken with it. There can be little doubt that the theater has been and will continue to be profoundly altered by AIDS. As the community joined the rest of society in prayers that a cure be found quickly, it continued to mount plays on AIDS-related subjects in a struggle to make some sense of a world in which this grim disease is a fact. Among the productions: *Safe Sex*, a revival of the acclaimed Best Play *As Is*, and, just after the close of the season, Alan Bowne's *Beirut*.

Business was not as usual with the Tony Awards. As reported last season, the administration committee was restructured. In the past, 13 of the 20 seats had been held by members of the League of American Theaters and Producers, with three of the remaining seven apportioned to designees of the American Theater Wing (owner of the Tony trademark) and the final four to representatives of the playwrights', actors', directors' and designers' professional organizations. Under pressure, the committee was reconstituted to give the League and the Wing equal weight.

Among the tasks faced by the committee was the formulation of new rules to prevent the repeat of a situation which embarrassed the Tonys last year—the nomination of old plays in the new-play catagory. *The House of Blue Leaves* and *The Blood Knot* had competed for the 1986 "Best Play" award rather than for "Best Revival" because, although they had been produced off Broadway in earlier decades, they technically received their Broadway premieres in the 1985–86 season. The committee decided that any play mounted on Broadway within three years of its non-Broadway New York premiere would be considered a new play. A Broadway production mounted after this would be considered a revival. The committee also once again declined to make off-Broadway productions eligible for the awards, despite growing pressure to acknowledge these smaller-scale offerings.

The Tony organization also was faced with the need to find a replacement for Alex Cohen, who, with his wife Hildy Parks, had run the awards show for 20 years. Although it was generally agreed that Cohen had done a fine job, members of the League did not smile on his agitation against their interests and were unwilling to keep working with him on the show. To replace him, Tony Awards Productions (the entity the League and the Wing co-established to serve as executive producer of the show) chose Don Mischer, a producer-director whose credits included the televising of such special events as the annual Kennedy Center honors and the Liberty Weekend spectacular. A four-year deal was signed with CBS for the broadcast rights, to commence as of the 1987 edition.

The show went off smoothly, with Mischer including in the program excerpts from the four nominated plays as well as the usual samplings from the scores of the nominated musicals. Some of the plays lent themselves to television excerpting better than others. A tense confrontation between father and son from *Fences* worked particularly well; the chunk of *Les Liaisons Dangereuses* made little sense out of context.

Two of the winners from *Les Misérables* devoted part of their acceptance speeches to statements of disgruntlement. Trevor Nunn, co-winner with John Caird as best director of a musical, made remarks which were interpreted as an attack on the critics who had had the temerity not to endorse the show. John Napier suggested that he would trade the Tony he'd just won for the design of *Les Misérables* to find out why the nominating committee did not nominate his work on *Starlight Express*. The implication was that members of the committee had somehow agreed amongst themselves not to honor that design. (Having been a member of the nominating committee, I can report that, except for comments on the quality of the coffee and the pastry, there was no discussion at all prior to the voting. *Starlight*'s design was not nominated because an insufficient number of the committee thought it one of the top four designs of the season. Mr. Napier is welcome to send his award to me.)

The New York Drama Critics echoed the Tony Awards by naming *Fences* best play and *Les Misérables* best musical. In addition, *Les Liaisons Dangereuses* was cited as the best foreign play of the 1986–87 season. (A fuller account of the voting will be found in the Facts and Figures section of this volume, courtesy of the organization's secretary, Richard Hummler.) *Fences* pulled off a triple crown by also winning the Pulitzer Prize.

All in all, a rather encouraging season. If it didn't match Wendy Wasserstein's fantasy, well, there's always next year . . .

A GRAPHIC GLANCE

(Clockwise left to right) Maryann Plunkett, Robert Lindsay, Nick Ullett, Jane Summerhays, George S. Irving and Jane Connell in *Me and My Girl*

Jane Summerhays in *Me and My Girl*

Jim Dale in *Me and My Girl*

Terrence Mann and Colm Wilkinson *(top center)* in *Les Misérables*

Colm Wilkinson in *Les Misérables*

Terrence Mann in *Les Misérables*

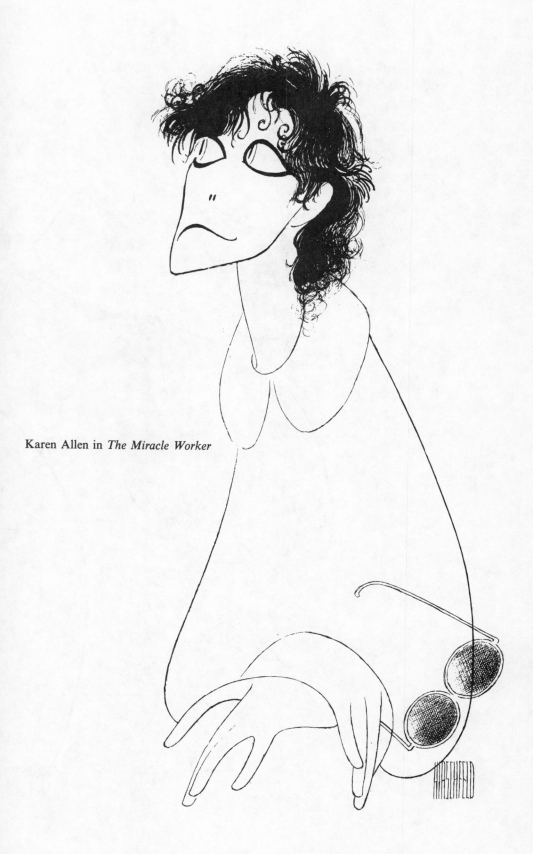

Karen Allen in *The Miracle Worker*

(Left to right) Frankie R. Faison, Charles Brown, Courtney B. Vance, James Earl Jones *(foreground)* and Mary Alice in *Fences*

James Earl Jones in *Fences*

Courtney B. Vance in *Fences*

Salem Ludwig and Jason Robards in *A Month of Sundays*

Tony Roberts, Jean Stapleton, Polly Holliday, William Hickey and Abe Vigoda in *Arsenic and Old Lace*

Polly Holliday in *Arsenic and Old Lace*

Jean Stapleton in *Arsenic and Old Lace*

John Wood in *Rosencrantz and Guildenstern Are Dead*

Kathryn Walker, George Hall, Kim Cattrall, Franklin Cover, Frank Maraden, Kate Burton, J. Smith-Cameron and Ian McKellen in *Wild Honey*

Kristoffer Tabori in *The Common Pursuit*

HIRSCHFELD

June Gable in *No Way to Treat a Lady*

Richard Thomas in *The Front Page*

Richard Thomas, John Lithgow and Julie Hagerty in *The Front Page*

Alan Rickman and Lindsay Duncan in *Les Liaisons Dangereuses*

Suzanne Burden in *Les Liaisons Dangereuses*

Timothy Daly in *Coastal Disturbances*

Annette Bening in *Coastal Disturbances*

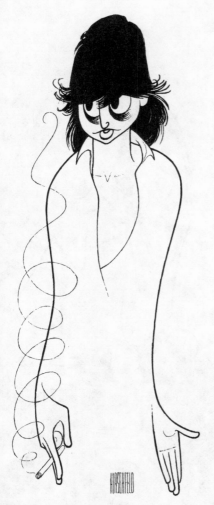

Ralph Macchio in *Cuba and His Teddy Bear*

Debra Jo Rupp in *A Girl's Guide to Chaos*

Judith Ivey, Richard Chamberlain, Blythe Danner and Geraldine Page in *Blithe Spirit*

HIRSCHFELD BALTIMORE, MD. 3

Jeff McCarthy and Marsha Waterbury in *Smile*

BALTIMORE HIRSCHFELD 3

Peggy Hewett in *Olympus on My Mind*

Elizabeth Austin in *Olympus on My Mind*

Michael Higgins in *In This Fallen City*

Frances Sternhagen in *Little Murders*

(Top left to right) Jane Carr, Michael Siberry, DeNica Fairman, Pat Keen

(bottom row left to right) John Lynch, David Delve, Rebecca Saire, John Carlisle and the boys at Dotheboys Hall in *The Life and Adventures of Nicholas Nickleby*

Tony Jay in *The Life and Adventures of Nicholas Nickleby*

Danitra Vance in *The Colored Museum*

Bobo Lewis in *The Musical Comedy Murders of 1940*

Gerrit Graham in *Sills & Company*

Larry Kert, Lonny Price, Josh Blake, Teresa Stratas *et al* in *Rags*

Philip Bosco, Uta Hagen and Amanda Plummer in *You Never Can Tell*

Victor Garber in *You Never Can Tell*

Lonette McKee in *Lady Day at Emerson's Bar and Grill*

John Pankow in *North Shore Fish*

Bob Bowyer in *Funny Feet*

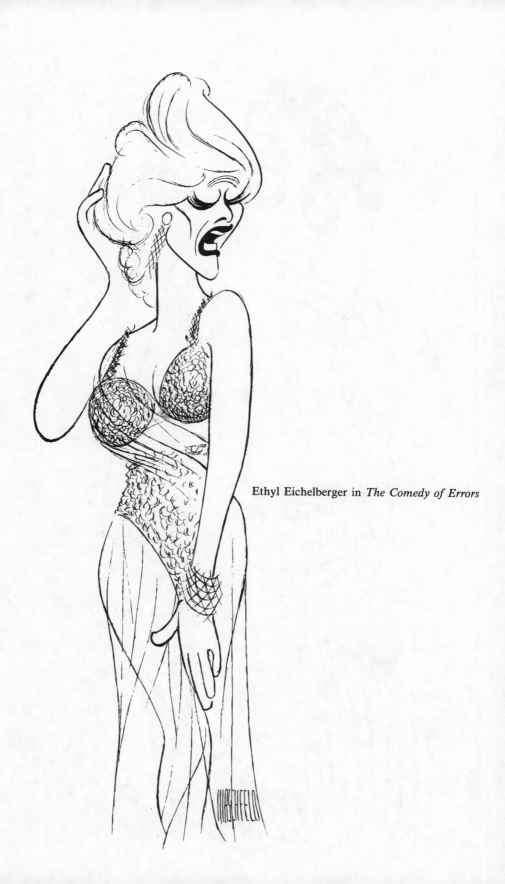

Ethyl Eichelberger in *The Comedy of Errors*

(Clockwise from top left) Timothy Daniel Furst, Paul Magid, Howard Jay Patterson, Avner Eisenberg, Randy Nelson and Sam Williams in *The Comedy of Errors*

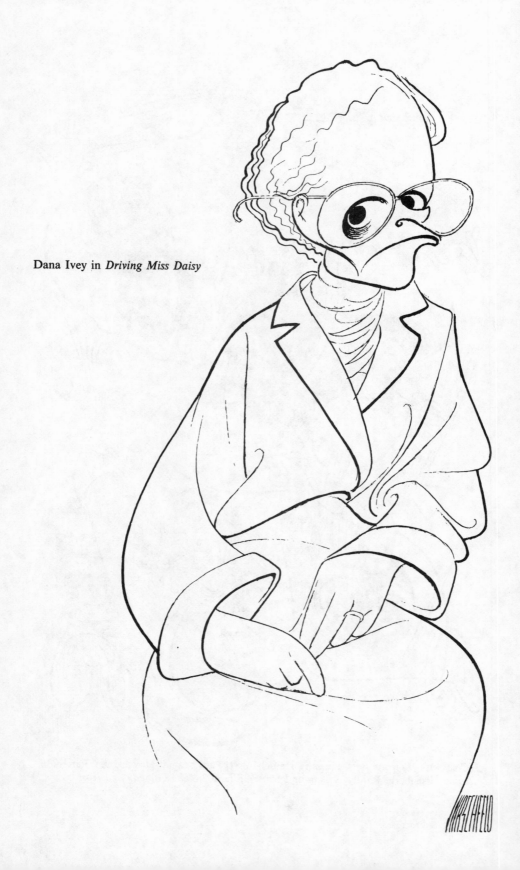

Dana Ivey in *Driving Miss Daisy*

Jackie Mason in *The World According to Me!*

Barry Tubb, John K. Linton, Lynn Redgrave and Mary Tyler Moore in *Sweet Sue*

Lynn Redgrave in *Sweet Sue*

Rosemary Prinz in *Steel Magnolias*

Blanche Baker in *Steel Magnolias*

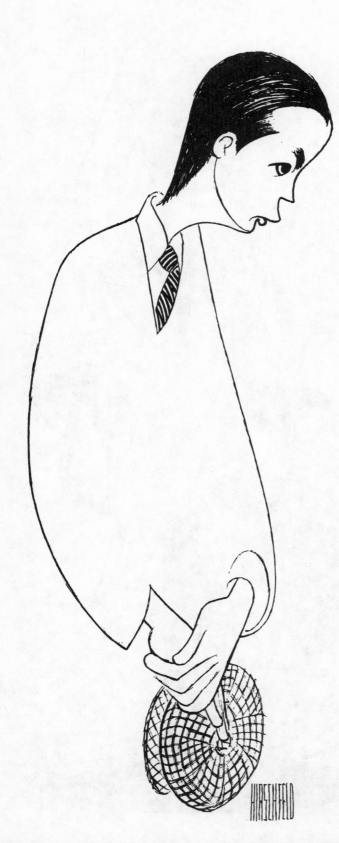

Don Bloomfield in *Lily Dale*

Donna McKechnie in *A Chorus Line*

Linda Lavin, Jonathan Silverman, Jason Alexander, Phyllis Newman, John Randolph and Philip Sterling in *Broadway Bound*

HIRSCHFELD WASHINGTON, D.C. 3

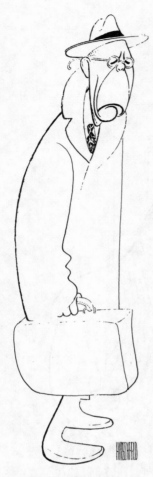

John Randolph in *Broadway Bound*

Jonathan Silverman in *Broadway Bound*

Hallie Foote in *The Widow Claire*

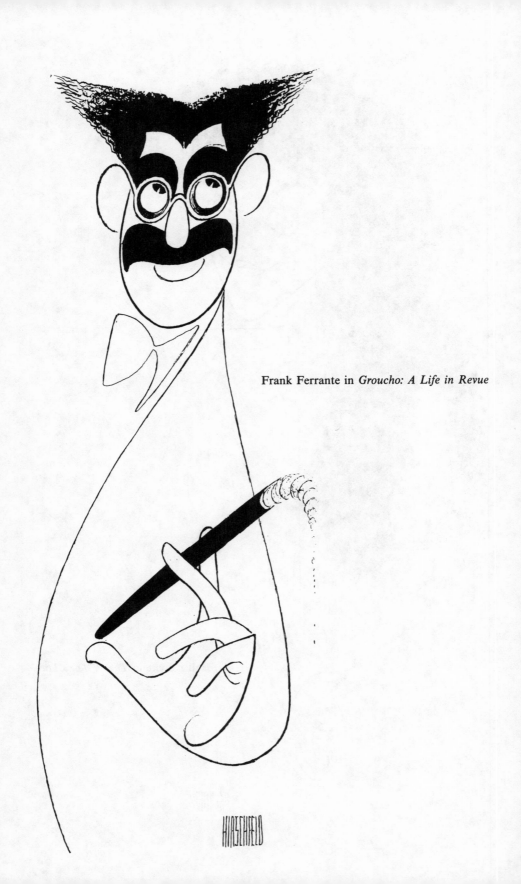

Frank Ferrante in *Groucho: A Life in Revue*

Arthur Miller

Michele Bautier in *Stardust*

Barbara Cook in *Barbara Cook: A Concert for the Theater*

Michael Wincott in *Talk Radio*

Starletta DuPois in *A Raisin in the Sun*

Dora Bryan in *Pygmalion*

Amanda Plummer and Peter O'Toole in *Pygmalion*

Alan Mintz, Danny Gerard, Dean Jones and Susan Bigelow in *Into the Light*

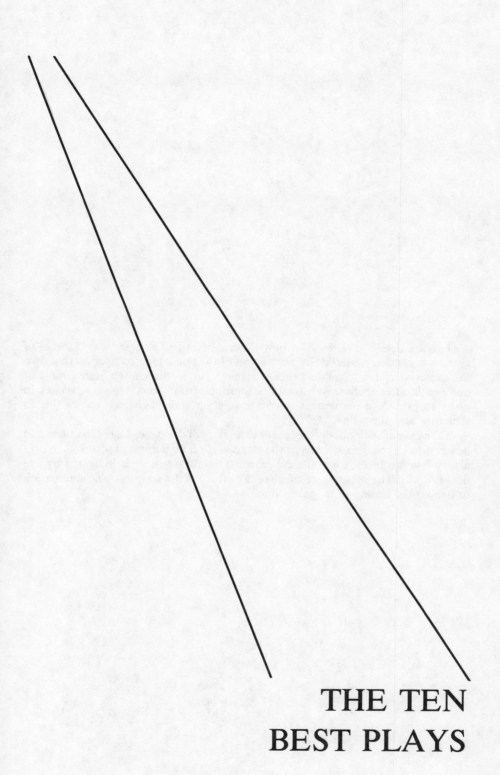

THE TEN
BEST PLAYS

Here are details of 1986–87's Best Plays—synopses, biographical sketches of authors and other material. By permission of the publishing companies that own the exclusive rights to publish these scripts in full in the United States, most of our continuities include substantial quotations from crucial/pivotal scenes in order to provide a permanent reference to style and quality as well as theme, structure and story line.

In the case of such quotations, scenes and lines of dialogue, stage directions and descriptions appear *exactly* as in the stage version or published script unless (in a very few instances, for technical reasons) an abridgement is indicated by five dots (. . . . .). The appearance of three dots (. . .) is the script's own punctuation to denote the timing of a spoken line.

BORN IN THE R.S.A.

A Full-Length Play in One Act

BY BARNEY SIMON IN COLLABORATION
WITH THE CAST: VANESSA COOKE,
TIMMY KWEBULANA, NEIL McCARTHY,
GEINA MHLOPHE, TERRY NORTON,
THOKO NTSHINGA, FIONA RAMSAY

Cast and credits appear on pages 331-332

BARNEY SIMON was born in Johannesburg, Republic of South Africa. He worked backstage for Joan Littlewood in the late 1950s, and in 1961 he joined Athol Fugard in the Dorkay House Rehearsal Room. During the next several years he conducted workshops and directed Fugard performances in Krapp's Last Tape *and* Hello and Goodbye. *He came to the United States in 1968 as a director in New York and Boston and was associate editor of* New American Review. *In 1970 he returned to his native land to form a theater group known as Mirror I—"a reflecting surface in which we might find an image of ourselves"—and in 1973 founded The Company and put on many classical and modern works including Fugard's* People Are Living There.

Simon, a three-time winner of the Breytenbach Epathlon, has collaborated with actors in creating a number of playscripts including Woza Albert! *(with Percy Mtwa and Mbongeni Ngema), which was produced off Broadway February 23, 1984 for 79 performances, and now* Born in the R.S.A., *a Best Play produced off Broadway this season October 1 for 8 performances by Lincoln Center as part of its four-program festival of South African plays entitled* Woza Afrika! *("woza" means "arise").*

Simon's other theater activities have included three scripts for Nadine Gordimer's Six Feet of Country *series, a production of of* Black Dog Inj'emnyama *at the 1984 Edinburgh Festival and London's Tricycle Theater, the direction of* Antigone *at the Haifa Municipal Theater in Israel and participation in a Massachusetts Arts Council playmaking project at Brandeis University.*

SYNOPSIS: Mia, a lawyer, recites a portion of the law protecting the Republic of South Africa government and its members from being held responsible for its actions in civil or criminal court proceedings. Speaking directly to the audience, she introduces herself (born in the R.S.A., both parents Afrikaans, a widow without children). She explains that she is the daughter of an active political lawyer and thus grew up listening to the conversation of such as Nelson Mandela at her family's dinner table. She herself is now devoted to the law: "Now my life is extraordinary—I wouldn't want it to be different. I'd like my world to be different, but not me . . . . . Aagh—times have changed, faces have changed, but I still feel privileged to be part of a community that is mine—some are clients, a lot are potential clients. We all have one basic thing in common—a desperate need to change the world we live in. Until the insanity of today's mass arrests, there were very few political people I did not know, or at least, did not know each other. Some call it an incestuous world—at times it really seems so. But not all my clients are political—not all of them are friends."

Among Mia's clients are Nicky Donahue and Susan Lang (an art teacher), both also born in the R.S.A. and both attracted to Glen (an R.S.A.–born graduate student), partly because of his impressive 6-foot-3-inch height. Nicky and Glen Donahue were teen-aged lovers, then both came to Witwatersrand University in Johannesburg, after Glen did his national service in the police force. Nicky couldn't cope with university life, became less and less involved in it and finally became pregnant, which gave her a good excuse to abandon it. Glen married Nicky, at the same time carrying on an affair with Susan.

When he first arrived at "Wits" college, Glen was "naive" and non-political: "There were things that I didn't like about the government if I thought about it, but I'd seen shit happening on both sides in the police force, and I like my life and didn't want that to change." But, as Nicky comments, "He got involved with this political crowd. I don't know—they just got so boring, and we'd usually end up at these multiracial parties, or curry suppers with Indians, and all they could do was talk politics." Glen especially disliked his tutor's, Feigle's, expounding on Marxism, Glen tells the audience.

GLEN: One day this guy Peter Moore phoned me up, and he says that he met me in the force. I don't remember him but I say, O.K., I'll meet him at the Devonshire for a drink, which I do . . . To cut a long story short, it turns out he's a lieutenant and he's handling the campus, he says he's heard some good things about me, we have a long chat about Marxist stuff-ups, and then he says that Feigle is causing lots of dangerous shit. Would I watch him—only during classes? And they're going to pay me. First I said no, then I said let me think about it. But it wouldn't be for money. I was very confused, and then I find myself in a Feigle tutorial, and this guy starts rapping way off the subject, on this heavy rap about Nicaragua. Again. And I start—just out of frustration—to take notes, and suddenly I think, hey, shit, it's happening. And I look at this guy, and I think no, what you're saying—that is trouble, man. Then I think no wait, wait, it's in my hands, in my handwriting. There was this double feeling you know, this feeling of my own power and of Feigle as . . . as innocent. There he was, he was rapping away with that same slick certainty I knew, but he didn't know what was happening to him, I knew, because I was happening to him. It was a new feeling, it was a good feeling, and then that night I took Nicky out to dinner. It felt like the first time in months.

Neil McCarthy as Glen and Vanessa Cooke as Susan in *Born in the R.S.A.*

NICKY: Ja, we never really went out much, as a couple I mean. We began to argue a lot about Glen's political friends. We'd fight and make up, fight and then make up, and then, well, I just stopped going.

GLEN: Anyway, two days later Moore phoned me up, so I played it cool, he says, howzit—I say fine. He says, "How's Feigle?" I said—plugging away as usual, red flags flying. And he says, "Ja, he's going to get a lot of nice people into very bad trouble. Did you take anything down?" I say ja, I've got some stuff, but I don't know how valuable it's going to be, but he drives over, comes and picks it up. And then, a week later, there was this check in the post. Now look, I had intended to send this thing back, but then it lay around in various pockets, and then the next month there's another one there. I mean, there was a baby coming and anyway . . . that was it, I was employed.

Zacharia, black, an unemployed double bass player, steps forward and raises his right hand to testify that he was born in the R.S.A. When he came to Johannesburg from Cape Town to play a couple of engagements, he had no place to stay. A friend loaned him his quarters in a garage behind the place belonging to his cousin, Thenjiwe Bona, "an amazing woman." Thenjiwe and her husband (jailed for the past two years) were active trade unionists, "Then she became a prime target for the special branch. She is famous for her courage. She'd been in and out of detention. In and out of house arrests."

Mia was so impressed by Thenjiwe Bona the first time she heard her speak, she believed that Thenjiwe might become the first woman president of South Africa. Zacharia thought her "much prettier than her pictures" as she showed him the room, apologizing for storing pamphlets there in a hidden drawer. One of Thenjiwe's two girls was in boarding school, and Zacharia found that her ten-year-old son, Dumisani, liked music.

The events and personalities so far described have been addressed to the audience as though the characters were giving sworn evidence in a court of law. Now, "Stage transforms to a party scene," but the characters continue addressing the audience directly, in monologue. Nicky tells how she accepted a joint from a black guest and smoked it with him. Glen tells how he helped a colleague of Feigle's arrange to get away from Johannesburg, where he was under restriction, but betrayed the would-be escapee to the police (he was promoted to Warrant Officer for this achievement). He was assigned to investigate the activists for black women workers' rights and became interested in Susan because she was the only white woman in the group.

Sindiswa introduces herself to the audience as Thenjiwe's sister, a school teacher, fond of her sister and her children, but perhaps a bit envious of Thenjiwe's efficiency and celebrity.

At Mia's birthday party, the group imitates the Andrews Sisters in an episode of singing and dancing. Then Nicky confesses that she is still attracted to Glen—who has other matters on his mind, however.

GLEN: I started going to functions where I knew Sue would be. Pretty soon things were cooking. One night after supper in her flat she just wouldn't let me out of the door.

SUSAN: You know what I was just wondering—who would have to move what for us to kiss?

GLEN: Actually, she's amazing, she never once said, "What are you thinking about?" in all that time I knew her. It became a very complicated situation. One day she confronted me, and I thought, "Oh fuck, this is it." But it turned out to be about Nicky.

SUSAN *(from behind, leaning over face to face):* Why didn't you tell me you were married?

GLEN: Because I'm not.

SUSAN: You are.

GLEN: Not in any way that matters.
        Kisses her lightly.

SUSAN: I didn't know how to take that, but I didn't want to let him go—not yet. I didn't know why—but not yet.

NICKY: Sometimes Glen didn't come home until five or six in the morning—I've got this job in a framing shop, so by the time I got up for work he was either sleeping or had gone out again, how's that for a marriage?

GLEN: One morning—Sue was making breakfast and I was getting dressed. I picked up this *Mad* magazine and this pamphlet fell out. I picked it up "UMK-HONTO WE SIZWE." The real thing.

SUSAN *(back turned to him):* Hey, what you doing?

GLEN: Nothing—just thinking about you.

SUSAN: Liar!

GLEN: It was a good breakfast—bacon, eggs, fresh orange juice. Gunning for Feigle had been easy—but this—this was the ultimate test—I really cared for Susan, but I felt this crazy kind of high, it was like standing on the edge of the top board waiting to jump. I decided to hand it in.

The police were pleased but told Glen that they were really after Thenjiwe Bona (and in the meantime Nicky realized she was losing Glen when she happened to see him with Susan on the street, and Glen soon moved out). From Susan, Glen learned that Thenjiwe was going to attend a meeting one Sunday. He tipped off the police, who raided the meeting and seized Thenjiwe. Susan escaped being arrested only because she had left to go get some takeout supper for the others. She immediately left messages for Zacharia, Sindiswa and especially the lawyer Mia.

THENJIWE: One minute I was dreaming of a fat Fontana Russian sausage and chips, and the next I was on my way to Jon Voster Square with a Boer on either side, well that's life in the R.S.A. They took us in three cars. That little cop, Klaasen, came to identify us. He looked me over and said, "Ja, dis die kaffermaid op wie ons wag (It is the kaffir maid that we have been waiting for)" and you know I was wearing my nice clothes and they said, "Ja, where did you steal those clothes from?"

When Zacharia found Susan's message he carried the pamphlets out of his room and dumped them a good distance away, on a football field. The police came to Susan's flat about 4:30 A.M., searched it for three hours, then took her off to Jon Voster Square. They also came and searched Zacharia's place about an hour after he'd disposed of the pamphlets, but they found nothing, not even the secret drawer. Mia sums up the situation: "You get a message Thenjiwe's been taken! You get a message Suzie's been taken! You're hearing about friends! You know what 'taken' means. You know who does the taking. You know what could be happening to them because of who they are and what they believe in. So what do you do? You apply here, you apply there, you apply here, you apply there, you apply, you apply, you apply—and then—YOU JUST WAIT!!"

Susan describes her jail quarters: "My cell was black cemented floors. There were three felt mats and a few blankets. There was a toilet, a cement bench, a bible, kotch green walls and that was it. No, there was a small box high in the corner—a TV camera." When Susan moved her mats out of the camera's range, policemen came in and shifted it.

Thenjiwe was alone for 28 days with no company except the whispered exchanges from other cells. When they finally came for her, they took her down to an office to be interrogated by "four cops, three rooinecks and one bantu." They gave her a 100-page notebook and ordered her to fill it with every detail about her life. When she could fill only 11 pages with a sketchy account of her birth, schooling, occupation, etc., one of the policemen told her, "You are being very stubborn. So now you are just going to stand until you tell the truth. The only time you will sit is when you go to the toilet, and that will be for one minute— that's all." Thenjiwe told herself, "O.K., I will stand until I die." At first she stood in 18-hour-a-day sessions, after which she could hardly bend her body, which began to swell. On the seventh day they began keeping her standing 24 hours a day and were beating her.

Back at Thenjiwe's house, her ten-year-old son Dumisani failed to show up after school. A neighbor had heard that his son and Dumisani were among those taken away by the police after the burning of a bus, so they went to the police station to try to find them. The black policeman at the desk hardly looked up from his comic book to tell them that no one had been brought here today, they should look elsewhere.

At the jail, they continued to punish Thenjiwe: "By now my body was so accustomed to standing that I began to dread the time when they would lead me back to my cell and I would have to struggle to lie down again." As for Susan, she was questioned from early morning to 6 P.M. daily.

SUSAN: They got heavier and heavier. They knew everything. Not only about the boycott we were organizing, but about my sex life, my contacts, my mother's bowling club. And then—they came to the point. They asked me what I'd done in Botswana.
COP: Do you like riding around in the backs of bakkies?
SUSAN: Depends on the company.
COP: Oh you mean, like black men?
SUSAN: Perhaps. Depends what black man.
COP: And on what he's wearing?
SUSAN: That's a point.
COP: Like an ANC T-short.

SUSAN: This is boring.
COP: Is food boring?
SUSAN: Sometimes.
COP: Grilled chicken?
SUSAN: No, I like grilled chicken.
COP: Do you like Molefe's grilled chicken?
SUSAN: Bit too salty. I had grilled chicken at Molefe's the night I left Gaberone. *(To the audience.)* Then they asked me about the ANC pamphlets that I had collected from Molefe and the people I had delivered them to in Johannesburg.

Thenjiwe's sister, Sindiswa, has taken up the search for missing ten-year-old Dumisani, who may have been arrested with a group who stoned and burned a bus. She consults Mia, and Mia advises her that it's no use querying official police sources, they'll have to "snoop around" to find where Dumisani is being held. Mia tries to borrow an English colleague's Telex machine to send out some queries. She is turned away and told, "In these times we really shouldn't deal with messages of that nature."

Susan is sent back to her cell "for a month, to stew," but after ten days they go after her again. Thenjiwe dreams that her friends gather around her, armed, and that they dance a pantomime with these guns and sing a song whose last lines go, "Hold tight you brave ones, we are almost there. The cowards are scared and confused and are contemplating retreat."

Mia tells of a recent discussion with a prosecutor in which "We were talking about black kids—the exploitation of children by the ANC—the brutality of the children. . . . . I said, 'Have you got eyes, your bloody government has been waging war against CHILDREN since '76. You know how I see them? As our liberators—yours—mine—their parents. They are fighting for the freedom of us all!' 'Freedom?' he said, from what?' 'From all the lies that have been . . . strangling us since . . . agh I don't know when!!' "

Zacharia and Sindiswa continue searching, asking questions, peering through the windows of police vans, but no Dumisani. Mia remembers a boy, charged with public violence, who was brought to her office by his mother but who wouldn't speak to Mia because she was white: "I just looked at him—he has no doubt. He's so powerful he STINKS OF VICTORY. Aagh it's finished, man—Let them take him—let them lock him up. He's got ten little brothers to take his place."

And Glen comments, "Listen, no one in the world has any right to judge anyone else. I mean—they want to talk to us about shooting children, talk to Americans about burning them, man, Nagasaki, hey napalm, and Philadelphia, did you hear about that bomb they dropped on those blacks in Philadelphia? Racism is a problem everywhere, it's primal, man. And that goes for the Feigles too. They need us to be like this, it's the new pornography, we're the stars of the world. They watch us like voyeurs in some sleazy leather bar."

In her cell, Thenjiwe manages to ward off the attentions first of a young white policeman and then a wardress assigned to take her to the toilet.

THENJIWE: They were angry with me because they still had no statement to present to their senior. One of them held my hand, forced a pen between my fingers and tried to make me write.

Thoko Ntshinga (Thenjiwe), Vanessa Cooke (Susan) and Goine Mhlophe (Sindiswa) in a scene from *Born in the R.S.A.*

COP: Ja, you and your fucken ANC. Did you hear about Mamelodi? They incite the children, but this time they learned their lesson, because not only did your children get shot, but your grandmothers too.

THENJIWE: What do you want me to do? Do you want me to cry? I won't cry for those grandmothers. I know them, and they are proud because every grandmother that gets shot gives birth to a thousand freedom fighters. I threw the pen at them. One of them hit me. They dragged me back to my cell. *(She lies down.)* The last thing I heard was:

COP *(to fellow Cop):* She's definitely Chinese-trained—if she was Russian-trained, she would have given up long ago.

The police show Susan a canvas bag and ask her to guess what it's for. She can't, but then the lights come up on Thenjiwe, canvas bag over her head, *"jerking with electric shocks."*

Policemen knock on Sindiswa's door in the night. They have Dumisani with them, charged with stoning buses and cars, and they want Sindiswa to come with them to the police station, where "They showed me a statement they said Dumisani had written. My God, it was all there—how he had stoned buses and a Mercedes Benz and then hidden in the shelter . . . it was all there, in his scribbly little child's handwriting. I prayed—I said, please God, let them warn him and send him home with me. But He wasn't listening. They led Dumisani away and told me to go home. He was crying and calling my name. I just stood at the desk."

Sindiswa pleads that Dumisani has always been a good boy, but they tell her his schoolmaster says the contrary. Later, Sindiswa hears from the schoolmaster that exactly the opposite is true—he praised Dumisani and was told, "How come his mother says otherwise?"

Zacharia manages to make himself heard by Thenjiwe, calling up to her from the street, telling her everything is all right with her family. Susan could hear that there were a lot of children in the other cells, shouting to each other, crying and even singing a song whose lyrics begin, "The Boer don't sleep / They lie with guns / When they wake up they shoot children." Mia is alarmed at the stores of weapons, the crowds of army recruits: "They tell you apartheid is dead and they send you to fight people who knew it long ago. They talk about releasing Mandela and yet arrest people like Suzie and Thenjiwe! Don't you see what liars they are? How insane they are?"

The authorities took Sindiswa and Dumisani to a Commissioner of Oaths, requesting that he sign his statement. But Dumisani, urged to tell the truth, says he merely took shelter from the rain—he had nothing to do with stoning buses. Nevertheless, Dumisani signed the paper, and Sindiswa is convinced they'll never let him go. There is a place in hell, she believes, reserved for those who force children to lie under oath.

Nicky is becoming more and more withdrawn, not wanting to face what's happening around her. Mia prepares to defend Susan at a trial, and meanwhile a brutalized, battered Dumisani is released in her custody.

GLEN: They subpoenaed me for Susan's trial. When I walked into the dock she smiled at me and blew a kiss—shit, that killed me. I thought she knew. Mia was there of course and a whole lot of other people that were my friends. I just watched the judge the whole time, which is what they advised me to do.

MIA: That day in court when Glen was called to the witness box and announced himself as:

GLEN: Warrant Officer Glen Donahue!

MIA: Her face—her face will be imprinted here, like a third eye, for the rest of my life. Afterwards he tried to talk to me. "Just stay away from me. All I can see is a nice Kentucky Necklace, a huge burning tire around your neck!" . . . . .

GLEN: So now they've offered me a full-time job in the police—a commission. I've taken it for the moment—but I'm still not sure what I want to do. I've often thought about becoming a game ranger or a forester or something. No, I'm being serious. You must go to Soweto, you must look at these kids, look into their eyes. It looks like we are all going to have our houses burned down pretty soon, so I think the best place to be is in a place with no houses, you know—like a forest. Well, come to think of it—things are pretty quiet around here—people avoid me in the streets—they don't wave back—oh ja—Mia did—but it wasn't really a wave—only cops love me now.

Mia gives him an "up yours" sign.

Zacharia went to visit Dumisani at Mia's house, bringing the boy his baseball bat and his recorder. He was shocked at Dumisani's condition: "Lying on his back in a big double bed. His face was swollen, his eyes closed." When Zacharia headed home he had forgotten to leave Dumisani the bat and recorder. He passed a playground where little uniformed white girls were playing. He thought to himself, "Ja, do you know who's watching you? Your mummy told you to be afraid of me. I thought ja, every one of you has a nanny. She feeds you, she comforts you, she washes that uniform, she polishes those shoes, and every time she leaves Soweto or Alexandra and says goodbye to her own children, she doesn't know whether she'll see them again, alive or dead. Ja, your nanny knows where your kitchen knives are, she even knows where your daddy hides the revolver. Your mommy's nanny knew too. But how many of you do they kill? Ask her about our children, and the soldiers who shoot them dead. Ask her what she's waiting for? For us to prove that we can kill children as well as they can?"

Zacharia imagined himself going into the playground and attacking the little girls with the baseball bat. Then the bell rang for the children to go inside and he turned and left, cursing them for making him feel murderous.

Glen was assigned to try to get a statement from Thenjiwe, but she spat in his face and informed him that he wouldn't be worth the match to light a gasoline-filled tire around his neck. One morning Thenjiwe was informed that she was being transferred to Diepkloof Prison to be charged. She felt sad when the van left John Vorster Square, because "for this swollen lady, it was like leaving home," and she didn't know what she might expect in the new place.

THENJIWE: When we reached Diepkloof they hustled us out of the van. There were more people in the lobby—people detained under Section 10. Hey, I was so excited—so many of them were my friends. Ndondi, Thembi, Topsie—I forgot my guard and ran to them. For a moment they didn't recognize me—just for a moment. But then we were hugging and kissing each other and laughing and crying. We all started to sing: THINA SIZWE ESIMNYAMA SIZOFELA IZWE LETH ELATHATHWA NGAMABHUMU! (We the black nation will die for our land taken from us by the Boers!) The guards moved in on us. We didn't care.

> In the spotlight the song builds and builds. Thenjiwe dances wildly, passionately, ululating, whistling, calling out the actors, singing and clapping in the darkness along with her. Behind her, movie images of defiant placards and police armored cars. Fade into blackout.
>
> The music on tape continues and the movie continues as the audience leaves.

BROADWAY BOUND

A Play in Two Acts

BY NEIL SIMON

Cast and credits appear on page 306

NEIL SIMON was born in the Bronx, N.Y. on July 4, 1927. After graduating from DeWitt Clinton High School he managed to find time for writing while serving in the Army. Writing soon became his profession without the formalities of college (except for a few courses at New York University and the University of Denver). His first theater work consisted of sketches for camp shows at Tamiment, Pa., in collaboration with his brother Danny. He became a TV writer, supplying a good deal of material for Sid Caesar ("Caesar's Hour") and Phil Silvers ("Sergeant Bilko").

On Broadway, Simon contributed sketches to Catch a Star *(1955) and* New Faces of 1956. *His first Broadway play was* Come Blow Your Horn *(1961), followed by the book of the musical* Little Me *(1962). His next play, the comedy* Barefoot in the Park *(1963) was named a Best Play of its season, as was* The Odd Couple *(1965). Neither of these had closed when the musical* Sweet Charity, *for which Simon wrote the book, came along early in 1966; and none of the three had closed when Simon's* The Star-Spangled Girl *opened the following season in December 1966—so that Simon had the phenomenal total of four shows running simultaneously on Broadway during the season of 1966–67. When the last of the four closed that summer, they had played a total of 3,367 performances over four theater seasons.*

Simon immediately began stacking another pile of blue-chip shows. His Plaza Suite *(1968) was named a Best Play of its year, His book of the musical* Promises, Promises *(1968) was another smash, and his* Last of the Red Hot Lovers *(1969)*

127

became his third Simon show in grand simultaneous display on Broadway (and fourth Best Play). Plaza Suite *closed before* The Gingerbread Lady *(1970, also a Best Play) opened, so that Simon's second stack was "only" three plays and 3,084 performances high.*

There followed The Prisoner of Second Avenue *(1971, a Best Play),* The Sunshine Boys *(1972, a Best Play),* The Good Doctor *(1973, a Best Play) and* God's Favorite *(1974). There was no new Neil Simon play on Broadway the following year because he was moving himself and his family from New York to California, partly for personal reasons and partly to base himself closer to his screen activities. Movies or not, by April 1976 he had* California Suite *ready for production at Center Theater Group in Los Angeles en route to the Eugene O'Neill Theater—which for a time he owned—in June 1976 as his 15th Broadway script and ninth Best Play.*

To continue: Simon's tenth Best Play was Chapter Two, *also produced at Center Theater Group before coming to New York in December 1977. He wrote the book for* They're Playing Our Song, *the long-run 1979 musical with a Marvin Hamlisch score and Carole Bayer Sager lyrics. His 11th Best Play,* I Ought To Be in Pictures, *went the California-to-New York route in 1980. His shortest-run New York play,* Fools *(1981) survived for only 40 performances, and an attempt to revise and revive* Little Me *in 1982 also fell short of expectations, with only 36 performances. But Simon came roaring back in 1983 with the first of three semi-autobiographical works,* Brighton Beach Memoirs, *with the character "Eugene Jerome" standing in for Simon as an adolescent growing up in Brooklyn. This popular hit was still running when its sequel, the Jerome-in-the-Army Best Play* Biloxi Blues *opened in March 1985, both taking the California-to-New York route. The third play in the series is this season's* Broadway Bound *about "Jerome's" efforts at gag writing for radio in collaboration with his brother, which came in from a Washington, D.C. tryout to New York on December 4, 1986 as—let's see—its author's 23d Broadway script and 13th Best Play. Prior to this third in the Jerome series was a revised version of* The Odd Couple—*sex-changed so that the two leading characters were women instead of men as in the original version—produced on Broadway in June 1985.*

Simon wrote the screenplays for his own Barefoot in the Park *(in its time the longest-runner at Radio City Music Hall),* The Odd Couple *(which broke that record the following year),* Plaza Suite, The Prisoner of Second Avenue, The Sunshine Boys, California Suite, Chapter Two, I Ought To Be in Pictures *and* Brighton Beach Memoirs, *plus* The Out-of-Towners, The Heartbreak Kid, Murder by Death, The Goodbye Girl, The Cheap Detective, Seems Like Old Times, Only When I Laugh, Max Dugan Returns *and* The Slugger's Wife.

Simon's many honors and accolades have included Tony Awards every ten years: the 1965 Tony as author of The Odd Couple, *a special 1975 Tony for his overall contribution to the theater and the 1985 best-play Tony for* Biloxi Blues. *He received the 1982–83 New York Drama Critics Circle best-play award for* Brighton Beach Memoirs, *the Sam S. Shubert Award in 1968, Writers Guild motion picture awards in 1968, 1970 and 1975 and numerous Tony, Emmy and Oscar nominations—and two years ago Broadway's Alvin Theater was renamed the Neil Simon in his honor. He divides his time between New York and Los Angeles and has been thrice married, with two daughters by his first wife.*

The following synopsis of Broadway Bound *was prepared by Jeffrey Sweet.*

Time: The late 1940s

Place: Brighton Beach, Brooklyn, N.Y.

Playing the members of the Jerome family in Neil Simon's *Broadway Bound* are *(top row)* Phyllis Newman as Blanche, Philip Sterling as Jack, Jason Alexander as Stanley and *(bottom row)* Linda Lavin as Kate, Jonathan Silverman as Eugene and John Randolph as Ben.

ACT I

February, 6 P.M.

SYNOPSIS: We are in the Jerome house in Brooklyn—a working-class neighborhood *"about two blocks from the ocean."* We see parts of the house's two stories. On the first are the living room and dining room. One door leads to the kitchen, another leads to the outside world, of which we see the front steps and a bit of the neighborhood. There is also a staircase leading to the second story where the bedrooms are. We can see into two of these—those of Eugene and his brother Stanley. We also see doors leading to other bedrooms.

At rise, Kate Jerome, *"about 50 and graying,"* is setting dinner for five. Her father, Ben Epstein, comes downstairs carrying a brown paper bag. He tells his daughter that he's going out. She argues that it is too cold and slippery outside and that she can get Eugene to do for him whatever he was going to do. But he seems determined to go, citing a series of pressing errands, among them getting a new book on Trotsky.

Kate is certain she's not getting the real story and that the key to the truth lies in the brown paper bag. She takes it from him and looks inside. It's his bed sheet. He's soiled it. He'd wanted to take it to the Chinese laundry, to deal with it without anybody knowing. Kate can't understand his embarrassment. "So you had an accident," she says. "It's all right, Poppa." "At night I've had accidents. This is the first time during the day," he replies. He tells her that he doesn't want the boys to know. She says the boys aren't around enough for that to be a worry. Ben, still in his hat and coat, sits down in the living room to read the newspaper.

Twenty-three-year-old Eugene Jerome appears on the street outside and runs to his front door and inside the house. He yells upstairs for his brother Stanley; but finding that Stanley isn't home, he turns to his grandfather.

EUGENE: Why are you sitting in your coat?

BEN: I was going out. Your mother changed my mind.

EUGENE *(going to the dining table for an apple):* You're better off. It's freezing. I saw a man kissing his wife on the corner and they got stuck to each other. Mr. Jacobs, the tailor, is blowing hot steam on them.

BEN *(looks at him, concerned):* Two people got stuck?

EUGENE: If they can't get them apart, they're going to have to sew all their clothes together.

BEN: They can't get them apart?

EUGENE *(straddling a dining chair and facing Ben):* It was a joke, Grandpa.

BEN: That was a joke? *(He rises and starts toward the closet.)* What kind of joke?

EUGENE: I made it up. It's not really a joke. It's just funny.

BEN: To who?

EUGENE: To me.

BEN: So if it's funny to you, what are you telling it to *me* for?

Ben goes to the closet and hangs up his coat but leaves his hat on.

EUGENE *(to audience):* The strange thing about my grandfather is, he has totally no sense of humor. None. But everything he says I think is funny. Maybe because he doesn't mean it to be. If he tried to be funny, he wouldn't be. *(To Ben.)* Where's Mom?

BEN: What kind of animal wears a zipper?

EUGENE: A zipper? I don't know. What kind?

BEN: A horse fly.

EUGENE *(to audience):* See what I mean?

BEN *(crossing back to the sofa): That's* a joke! Not two people got stuck together. You understand?

EUGENE: Yes, Grandpa. Thanks for the priceless information. *(To audience.)* My mother and father are the same way. I could say something so funny that the pictures on the wall would get cramps from laughing, but those three just stare at me like dead bodies. I'm trying to become a comedy writer some day, and this is the encouragement I get.

BEN: What kind of a fish sings an opera?

EUGENE: What kind of a fish sings an opera? . . . I give up. What kind?

BEN: A halibut.

EUGENE: A halibut?

BEN: I got it wrong. I thought it was a halibut, but it doesn't sound right.

EUGENE *(to audience):* Okay? I guarantee you that a halibut is funnier than the real answer . . . I mean, look at him. Sitting there with a hat on. If he put it on to be funny, it would be dumb. But he doesn't know he's got it on, so it's hysterical.

BEN: Does a mackerel sound right?

EUGENE: Don't work on it, Grandpa. It'll come to you. *(To audience.)* My brother Stanley is the only one who appreciates my humor. When I make Stanley laugh, I feel like Charles Lindbergh landing in Paris . . . And Stanley comes up with great ideas. That's why the two of us teamed up. We're going to be a comedy writing team . . . *(Like a radio announcer.)* "The Jack Benny Show was brought to you by Lucky Strike and was written by Sam Perrin, Nate Monnister, Milt Josephsberg and Stanley and Eugene M. Jerome."

Kate reappears, putting plates onto the table. Eugene tells her he has to talk to everybody, but Kate doesn't think his father will be home for dinner. Apparently her husband's non-appearance is getting to be a habit, and Kate is none too pleased about it.

She returns to the kitchen. Eugene asks Ben what's going on with Kate, why she has closed off from everyone. Ben has no idea. His daughter has stopped confiding in him. Eugene begins asking questions about what his mother was like when she was younger. Was she really as good a dancer as she says she was? Did she really once dance with George Raft at the Primrose Ballroom? Ben confirms the story. Only Raft wasn't a movie star then: "He was just a greasy looking kid. He used to go around to all the different ballrooms and pick out the best dancer." One night, he picked the teenaged Kate. Then an accident in a sweatshop left Kate's back badly burned, putting an end to her dreams of becoming a professional dancer.

Kate returns to the room and Eugene tells her and Ben his big news: He's going to marry a wonderful girl named Josie. Kate doesn't believe this. How can he marry? He's not even going with anyone. Eugene says he has had lunch with her, and what a lunch! He and Josie talked philosophy, literature, sports and ate from the same chopsticks. There's only one slight complication: She's engaged to be married to someone else. But Eugene thinks he can change her mind about that. Kate and Ben don't take this seriously. Eugene says he wants to bring Josie to dinner on Sunday to meet the family. "We'll see," says Kate as she exits into the kitchen. Eugene tries to turn to Ben again, but he's fallen asleep. Eugene heads upstairs to his room to write in his journal.

Now Eugene's brother, 28-year-old Stanley, comes barrelling down the street and into the house. As soon as he's inside he calls upstairs to Eugene. Kate returns, tells Stan he's late for dinner. Stan tells her he and Eugene won't be able to sit down for dinner, they have work to do. Maybe they'll catch a sandwich later.

Eugene appears, and Stan tells him they've got a job writing at CBS! Stan bubbles over about the day he's had, wandering around the sacred halls of CBS, looking at the stars' pictures, even meeting the legendary Abe Burrows. Stan says Burrows wished him luck. Kate and Ben might be more impressed if they knew who Abe Burrows is. Stan, eager to get to work, turns to go upstairs.

KATE: Can't you talk this over at dinner?
STAN: Is that all you care about? Your dinner? The most important thing that's ever happened in our lives, and you're worried about a lousy pot roast?
KATE (obviously hurt, she goes to the kitchen): Just like your father. You're getting to be just like your father every day. Next thing you'll turn Eugene against me, too.
STAN: I'm sorry! . . . Mom? Ah, shit! (To Eugene.) Come on.
    Eugene and Stan run upstairs, as Kate comes charging out of the kitchen.
KATE: What did you say?
BEN (ushering her back into the kitchen): He didn't mean anything.

Upstairs in Stan's room, Eugene asks about their new job. It becomes apparent that it's more of an audition than a job. And the fabled meeting with Abe Burrows? It seems that Stan ran into Burrows in an elevator and burbled something to the effect of how much he'd like to work on Burrows's staff, to which Burrows had replied, "Good luck, kid." In Eugene's book that doesn't score full points as a conversation with Burrows: "That's like the Pope waving to you in the Vatican."

Stan brushes this aside. They'd better get started. They're supposed to bring a finished sketch in at 10 o'clock the next morning. Eugene points out that they've never written a sketch in under three weeks. They've never even *finished* writing a sketch, for that matter. Eugene wonders if they're ready for CBS. Stan fears that if Eugene has confidence problems, then the two of them will never get out of their current low-level jobs. Eugene doesn't understand why his lack of confidence should impede Stan's future. "We're a team," Stan says forcefully. "I need you; you need me. You have a great comic mind. I'm the best editor and idea man in the business." From their subsequent conversation, we gather that their experience till now has been limited to writing monologues for "a guy who plays weddings and Bar Mitzvahs."

There's another complication aside from confidence: Eugene was planning on visiting Josie to persuade her to break off her engagement. Her fiancé, a Harvard student, is coming back tomorrow, so tonight's the only chance Eugene has. "If I don't convince her I'm the guy for her, he's liable to talk her into going through with it."

STAN: If he can talk her into it, what do you want her for?

EUGENE: Because she's perfect. And you only get one chance in your life of meeting a perfect girl.

STAN: You know how many perfect girls there are in Hollywood? They're *all* perfect. In two years you'll be *sick* of perfect girls. You'll be begging for a plain one.

> *Eugene goes to his own room and begins to dress for his date. Stan is in pursuit.*

EUGENE: An hour and a half, that's all I'll be gone. If I don't talk to her face to face, I'll lose her, Stan. I know it.

STAN: Eugene, as much confidence as I have in us, I don't have that much confidence that we can write the sketch by tonight. But we have to try. Remember the story Pop told us? How he had the opportunity to go into his own business with a friend . . . how he stayed up all night thinking about it . . . and he couldn't make up his mind. A week later it was too late. His friend lives on Park Avenue now, and Pop is still cutting raincoats . . . Maybe this is the only chance we'll ever get. Maybe not. But are you willing to risk everything for a girl you might not even be interested in by next week?

EUGENE: I'll be interested in her for the rest of my life.

STAN: Then go out with her. Take as much time as you want. I'll write the sketch myself. *(Storming back to his own room.)* I mean it. I'm not going to blow this opportunity.

EUGENE: Never mind. I won't see her.

STAN: I said, I'll do it myself.

EUGENE *(going downstairs):* Don't do me any favors.

Eugene goes into the kitchen with his mother to make some sandwiches for the night ahead. Ben moves to the table and begins eating the soup Kate has served.

Blanche Morton, Ben's other daughter, appears on the street dressed in fur. Getting no response when she rings the doorbell (Ben doesn't hear so well), she enters the house. Ben looks up from his soup and comments that he didn't hear her limousine pull up. "It's not a limousine, Poppa. It's just a plain Cadillac," says Blanche. "Like John D. Rockefeller is just a plain businessman," says Ben. Ben and Blanche don't get along all that well. Kate and Eugene emerge briefly to say hello, then return to the kitchen to negotiate over the art of cutting pot roast.

Blanche has come to talk to Ben about her mother, his wife. She's living with Blanche and her husband. Ben reminds Blanche they had an agreement not to talk about Momma, but Blanche persists. The doctors say that Momma is sick and that she should move to Florida or she might not last much longer. Moving her to Florida would be fine by Ben. "She'll outlive the palm trees," he predicts.

Blanche tells him that Momma cannot stop asking why Ben hates her so much. Ben has little patience with this. He still has strong feelings for Momma, but he can't leave his roots in Brighton Beach. He can't live in comfort on Park Avenue or in Miami Beach when so many others do without. He refers Blanche to Trotsky in support of his arguments. Blanche says this is not a political discussion, but to Ben everything is political: "The soup in my dish is political. The bread on my plate is political. And the four-thousand-dollar coat on your back is political."

Aside from the questions of love and the Socialist ethic there is a more pressing reason why Ben cannot leave Brighton Beach. Jack, Kate's husband, is going to walk out on her. Blanche is shocked: "Jack loves Kate. He's always loved her." "Absolutely," agrees Ben, "but at fifty-five, he can overlook it." Ben explains that Jack is looking at the fact that he only has a few years left, and he doesn't want to spend the rest of his life living this way. So, Ben continues, Jack will leave; and soon Eugene and Stan will leave. If Ben joins Momma in Miami, what will be left for Kate, "who doesn't know a thing in this world except how to serve someone?" Without someone in the house to care for, Kate's life will be over. Ben intends to be that someone as long as he's alive.

Blanche suggests that Kate could come down to Florida with Ben and Momma, but Ben, his own aversion to Florida entirely apart, doesn't think Kate would be willing to leave her house or to accept charity from her sister. Blanche doesn't see why Kate wouldn't allow her to repay Kate for when Kate took Blanche and her daughters in when Blanche's first husband Dave died. Ben insists Blanche doesn't understand her own sister. Blanche doubts if Ben approves of—much less likes—her, his own daughter. "I have three daughters, and I love them the same," Ben replies. "But the one who's in trouble is the one that I help." What about helping Momma? Blanche persists. Ben tells Blanche she's the only one who can afford to help Momma, so it's her job.

During this, Eugene has returned upstairs where an irritable Stan snaps about his having brought up sandwiches without cucumber in them and banishes him until he is needed. So Eugene sits alone in his room while on the other side of the wall Stan wrestles with his recalcitrant muse for an idea for a comedy sketch.

Downstairs, Kate emerges from the kitchen with dinner for Ben and a present for Blanche's new grandchild (born to Blanche's daughter Nora). Nora and the baby are going to be visiting Blanche and her husband Saul on Sunday. Blanche makes a bid to get Kate to bring Ben, but Kate doubts she'll be able to get Ben to do it. The train is too long and hard a ride for him, and he refuses to be driven there by a chauffeur. If he won't come visit, Blanche presses, would he at least call Momma? Ben insists his time will be taken up with various political meetings, but Kate assures Blanche that Ben will call.

Kate takes Blanche to the side. Will Blanche meet her for lunch in the city? There's something Kate needs to talk to her about. Blanche sees that Kate is on the verge of tears. Of course they'll meet for lunch as soon as Kate wants.

Just as this has been agreed, Ben, sitting at the table, has some kind of an attack—loses his sense of balance, begins to breathe hard. His daughters rush to help. The moment passes, and Ben waves it away, claiming the attack was brought on by how long he's had to wait to eat.

BLANCHE: It's this climate. Two blocks from the ocean in February, how can you keep the cold out of the house?

BEN: It's not the cold. It's not the climate. It's nerves, that's what it is.

KATE: How do you know it's not your heart? You haven't seen a doctor in over a year.

BEN: A heart attack God gives you. Nerves you get from people who worry about you too much.

BLANCHE: Is that meant for me, Poppa?

KATE: It's meant for both of us. You learn not to pay attention. He doesn't mean it.

BLANCHE: He can't stand the winters here any more than Momma. *(She sits at the table.)* I don't mean to upset you, Poppa. If you're happier here, then stay. Forget what we talked about. I'll get somebody to stay with Momma. I'll work it out myself.

KATE *(returning Ben's hat to the closet):* All right, Blanche. Leave it alone for now. We've got time yet.

BLANCHE *(to Ben):* Why is it so hard for us to talk to each other? Why is it so hard for you to take anything from me? I'm afraid to kiss you when I see you, I know how uncomfortable it makes you . . . Why is that, Poppa?

BEN *(banging his fist on the table): YOU ASK TOO MUCH OF ME!*
        Kate and Blanche are stunned by this outburst.
I am not an affectionate man. I don't trust affection . . . Sometimes people give it to you instead of the truth.

BLANCHE *(visibly hurt, going to sofa to collect her purse and package):* I see . . . And what's the truth about me, Poppa? Have I betrayed you because the man I married became wealthy? When I met him, he was on the verge of bankruptcy. Whatever he got, he earned. Whatever he has, he worked for.

KATE: Blanche, stop it. That's enough. Everybody has said enough.

BEN: Let her say what she wants. She's a good girl, my Blanche, but sometimes she forgets where she came from . . . Is it cold outside, Blanche? You bet your life it is . . . Is it hard on the people who live out there? Ask them, they'll tell you . . . Take them *all* to Florida, they'll put up a statue to you on the boardwalk . . . But not even Saul could afford that. They all can't escape, Blanche. They all don't get a ticket to Miami.

BLANCHE: And my sin is that I can afford to buy you one?

BEN: That's no sin, Blanche. You're a generous woman. Even *I* can see that. I thank God you're able to take care of your mother. But I can't enjoy the benefits of a society that made my daughter rich and starves half the people in the country.

BLANCHE: I can't take care of all the people in the country. I didn't ask for all this. I was happier when I had no money and Dave was alive. But I'm not going to curse God because He gave me a kind and loving husband and, yes, a mink coat and a Cadillac car. You want them, take them. I didn't ask for it. I found the coat in my closet on my birthday. Some good it does me. It keeps out the cold, but it also stops my father from reaching out and holding me . . . Is that the politics you believe in, Poppa?

BEN: I believe in what I was taught from the day I was born.

BLANCHE: I believe in what I was taught, too . . . I was taught that a family who loves each other takes care of each other . . . You're seventy-seven years old,

Poppa, you've done enough. You've worked hard all your life. It's time to play pinochle and walk on the beach. Maybe you'll meet a few retired Socialists. *(Going to Kate.)* I'll see you tomorrow, Kate?

KATE: Let me see what happens. I'll call you in the morning.

BLANCHE *(walks to the door, then turns to look at Ben):* I love you, Poppa . . . and I'll accept whatever affection you can give me. But you're not going to stop me and Momma from giving you ours. We're women, we don't know any better. *(Blanche exits.)*

EUGENE *(from his bedroom, to audience):* Can you see now why I want to write comedy? Even God has a terrific sense of humor. Why else would He make Grandpa a dedicated Socialist, fighting against the wealthy class, and then give him a daughter who marries the richest guy in the garment district? I wonder if we could sell it to CBS?

Downstairs, Ben tells Kate he knows she's having problems with Jack, that's what she's going to talk to Blanche about. He asks why she won't confide in him. "I don't know," she replies. "Maybe I'm afraid you'll think it's all my fault." Ben retreats to his room upstairs, and Kate returns to the kitchen.

The boys, in the meantime, are not faring well. Frustrated because he hasn't been able to come up with an idea for a sketch, Stan turns on Eugene, accusing him of not taking writing seriously. Eugene's quippy protestations ("I would rather write a comedy sketch than feed all the starving children in the world") fuel Stan's irritation. Stan thinks maybe he'll find a more mature partner. Eugene suggests Abe Burrows. After a fury of door-slamming on Stan's part, Eugene acknowledges to the audience that his lack of concentration might have something to do with his anxiety over losing his dream girl.

Stan returns. Perhaps they will do better if they simply remember the essential elements of a good comedy sketch. First: conflict. Second: wanting. "In every comedy, every drama, somebody has to want something and want it bad. He wants money, he wants a girl, he wants to get to Philadelphia. When somebody tries to stop him from getting money or a girl or getting to Philadelphia, that's conflict."

Something Stan said has triggered an idea in Eugene, and he begins to develop it. It's not easy. Ben, who can be maddeningly deaf at times, keeps yelling at them that their collaboration is disturbing his sleep. But the brothers persevere, putting together the elements of a sketch about a man and a woman who, because of ill health, disability and accident, on a freezing night cannot close the window of their bedroom. The process is more or less a Socratic dialogue, Eugene being stimulated to create by answering Stan's frequently tough questions. Stan is a stickler for credibility, asserting, "It's not funny if it's not believable."

Eugene tells the audience they then went to work on the idea and, more than four and a half hours later, had filled up lots of pages with unusable writing. At 11:30, exhausted, they decide to take a short break.

As the boys lie down in their respective rooms, Jack Jerome, Kate's 55-year-old husband, returns home. Jack wants to take a shower, but Kate prevails upon him to stay with her, drink a cup of tea, talk. She tells him about the boys' audition for CBS. Jack doesn't think much of their choice of career nor of Stan's plan to

quit his lower-level management job at a department store. Kate tells him that
writing is what the boys want to do, the boys want their chance; taking a chance
is a luxury they have that their father didn't have. Kate is mindful of what Jack
gave up to support his family. Jack insists he's not complaining; besides, he's
proud of his reputation as a cutter. But Kate will not be sidetracked by his
responses from stating what she knows must be true—that Jack is unhappy and
disappointed with his life. What she wants to know is, does his disappointment
extend to her?

JACK: Listen, Kate. I've had a long day. I'm tired. Whatever this is about, we'll
talk about it in the morning.
KATE: I want to know what you're planning to do.
JACK: Planning to do about what?
KATE (folding the tablecloth, carefully): Whatever's been going on, I want it
to stop. I don't want to know who she is or what she's like. And I don't want
to hear any lies. I just want tonight to be the end of it, and I'll never talk about
it again, as God is my judge.
JACK: You think I'm carrying on with some woman? Where do you get such
ideas from?
KATE: Two things a woman doesn't have to be told. When she's pregnant and
when her husband stops loving her. Maybe we've had enough years of loving each
other. But I will not live out the rest of my life being humiliated.
JACK: Who's been talking to you? What God damn liars tell you such things?
Nothing is going on. What's happened to us when we can't believe each other
anymore?
KATE: Maybe it's the way you look at me when you say you're telling me the
truth.
JACK (deliberately): There is no other woman.
KATE: Why not?
JACK: What?
KATE: Why not? You're a healthy man, you're affectionate, you're as normal
as anyone else. We haven't been together as man and wife since God knows when.
So, if it's not me and you're swearing it's no one else, I'm asking you, "Why not?"
JACK: Kate, let's not get into this. I beg of you.
KATE: Don't beg me!! . . . Don't tell me how trusting we were. We passed all
that when our children grew up. Now it's just you and me, Jack, and if I'm not
enough for you any more, then you tell me and get out. Get out, God damn it!
I will not be pointed at from windows as I walk down the street.
JACK: There is no other woman.
KATE: I don't care. Stop it anyway.

Jack acknowledges he's changed. When he was a boy he believed growing older
meant growing wiser, but now he is older himself, and he is painfully aware of
his lack of wisdom. He hasn't learned what he'd hoped. He hasn't even learned
to lie well, so he proceeds to tell Kate about another woman: "There was a
woman. About a year ago. I met her in a restaurant on Seventh Avenue. She
worked in a bank, a widow. Not all that attractive, but refined woman, spoke very

well, better educated than I was." It didn't go on for long, and it's long over. He apologizes if he has hurt her. Kate brushes the apology aside. She may have said before she didn't want to know what any other woman he's seen was like, but now she presses him for details. How old was she? What did they talk about together? Why did he pick *her*? Jack believes it is a great mistake for both of them to go on about this, nevertheless he answers her.

JACK: . . . . . Why this woman? Because she had an interest in life besides working in a bank or taking care of her house. To her, the world was bigger than that. She read books I never heard of, talked about places I never knew existed. When she talked, I just listened. And when *I* talked, I suddenly heard myself say things I never knew I felt. Because she asked questions that I had to answer . . . Learning about yourself can be a very dangerous thing, Kate. Some people, like me, should leave well enough alone . . . The things you were afraid to hear, I won't tell you, because they're true. It lasted less time than you think, but once was enough to hurt, I realize that . . . I never ate in that restaurant again, and I have never once seen her again . . . If either one of us feels better now that I've told you all that, then shame on both of us.

Jack sits at the table, opposite Kate. She turns away from him.
If I killed a man on the street, you would probably stand by me. Maybe even understand it. So why is this the greatest sin that can happen to a man and wife?
KATE: Because I'm not strong enough to forgive it.
JACK: I didn't expect you to.
KATE: What *do* you expect?
JACK: I'm not clever enough to answer that.
KATE: This woman—this refined, educated woman—if I left you, would you go to her?
JACK: She wouldn't have me. She's content with her life the way it is.
KATE: If she *would* have you, would you go to her?
JACK: No.
KATE: Why not?
JACK: Because I know where I belong.

Kate challenges this: does he really belong with her, given the fact *she* can't provoke him to new thoughts? Bitterly she continues: "I am so hurt by your selfishness. You break what was good between us and leave me to pick up the pieces . . . and *still* you continue to lie to me."
Kate now reveals that she knew about the affair when it happened. She got a phone call from a friend who had seen Jack eating lunch with this woman every day. Kate had hoped it would pass, and she thought her hope was realized. There had been no more reports of him meeting this woman in restaurants—until this morning, another phone call. Kate knows he's been eating lunch with her again. What else is he doing with her? Jack acknowledges he's seen her again, but not to resume the affair. The woman's son has died in an accident, and he had lunch with her to talk about anything but that death. Kate gives Jack an ultimatum: He must not see her again or else move out. Jack doesn't understand Kate's response. "I slept with her before, and you forgave me," he says. "Now I buy the

woman lunch and offer her compassion, and for this you want to end the marriage." Kate turns to him with a fierceness and says, "I didn't expect to get through a lifetime without you touching another woman. But having feelings for her is something I can never forgive." She marches upstairs to bed. Jack goes into the kitchen.

Stan suddenly awakens, checks the time and runs to Eugene's room to wake him. They've overslept by five minutes! When he asks Eugene to read what they have of the sketch, Eugene replies they have nothing. Stan has a severe confidence attack. Maybe he isn't a writer. Maybe he's an editor. Maybe he should stick to that. And maybe Eugene should find somebody else to work with. Somebody who won't hold him back. Eugene insists he doesn't want to write with anybody else, and this sinks in. Stan is comforted that Eugene wants to remain a team. Now all Stan needs to make him happy is a good idea. He looks up and makes a direct plea to God: "Give us an idea for a sketch you're not using. Tell me an idea that makes you laugh." Eugene and Stan wait for a response as the first act ends. *Curtain.*

ACT II

Saturday evening, a month later, 5:45 P.M.

From his room upstairs, Eugene fills us in on events. Apparently, Josie is still an open question, for Eugene tells of his ice skating with her at Rockefeller Center, from which he returned with a swell case of the flu. Turning from love to work, the sketch he and Stan ultimately wrote (and turned in a few days late) led CBS to hire them, not for big-time TV as they'd hoped, but for a radio show on Saturday nights at 6 o'clock, a show designed to develop new talent. He and Stan are two out of six writers on the show, and their first sketch is to be broadcast tonight. As concerned as they are about CBS's reaction, they're more concerned about getting their parents' approval.

Stan and Kate are readying the living room for the grand debut. Kate is calm, but Stan is working himself into a nervous state. Where are Pop and Grandpa? The show's going to start soon. Why is the radio taking so long to warm up? Is it broken? Doesn't Kate realize she shouldn't serve food? How will anybody be able to hear their writing over the chewing? In a frenzy of nerves, at one point Stan throws himself onto the floor. Kate warns him that if he goes on like this he'll grow an ulcer.

Stan goes upstairs to wake Grandpa, as Eugene explains to us that Kate and Jack have barely said a word to each other since the night of the big fight. Stan pounds on Eugene's door, telling him it's time for him to come down. "This is some audience we've got," fumes Stan. "A mother who doesn't talk to a father who hasn't come home yet, and a grandfather who hasn't laughed since the stock market crashed." Eventually, Eugene, Stan, Kate and Ben are gathered in the living room. There is a great deal of debate over who should sit where, which only continues to rattle Stan, who is peering through the window, looking for Jack.

Ben asks Eugene about their show. Eugene explains that it's a variety show, entertainment. Ben takes this to mean that it is devoid of social significance. "They didn't want any sketches on economic slavery, Grandpa," Stan interjects. "They're looking for laughs, not an uprising."

To hear Kate talk, half of the world is listening—Aunt Blanche, all of Brighton Beach and Grandma (who has apparently moved to an apartment in Miami since last we heard of her). And now, with an introduction by the announcer, "The Chubby Waters Show" is on the air.

Chubby Waters begins his monologue, most of it jokes about how small his home town is: "Decatur's sort of an agricultural town. We sell all the fruit and vegetables that drop offa trucks passing through." Kate doesn't get most of the jokes. Ben's opinion of Waters: "In Russia, he'd be shot by now." The monologue ends, and the band begins to play a tune.

Jack returns home now, apologizing for his lateness. Eugene tells him he timed his arrival perfectly: their part of the show will be on next. As Jack settles down to listen, we see evidence of the continuing chill between him and Kate.

Eugene and Stan's sketch begins. In it, the bumpkin Chubby Waters visits with a "typical" Jewish family in Coney Island. "I'm trying to familiarize myself with New Yorkers," says Chubby, "and I wondered if I could come in and say hello to your family." "Why?" replies Mrs. Pitkin. "My *family* doesn't say hello to my family." Chubby compliments her on the furniture, asking her what style it is. "Sacrifice! That's what you have to do to get it," says Mrs. Pitkin. Chubby asks what her husband does for a living. "He's in ladies' pajamas," replies Mrs. Pitkin. Chubby asks how she feels about that, and Mrs. Pitkin says, "That's the sacrifice I had to make to get the furniture."

All this is going over great with the studio audience at CBS, but (Eugene tells us) the reaction in the Jerome home was less than enthusiastic. The half-hour show seemed to stretch on forever. And reading the credits at the end, the announcer got Stan and Eugene's last name wrong.

Stanley switches the set off. Kate wants to compliment and congratulate her boys, but the strain shows. Eugene noticed that she didn't laugh. "There were too many funny lines," says Kate. "They came so fast, I couldn't find a place to laugh." She leaves the house to borrow some honey from next door.

The boys turn to Ben for his reaction. Ben didn't hate it. He tells them they should accept this as praise. "When I don't hate something, it's not bad." Ben doesn't care much about comedy for comedy's sake. He likes political satire. Maybe the boys could try to slip some in? Eugene remarks to Stan, "Can't you just see it? . . . *The Socialist Revue* starring Chubby Trotsky . . . We'd be writing it from jail." As he exits upstairs, Ben allows he did like the act that featured the dog who could talk Spanish (one word, "Si!"): "He didn't make any points, but he made me laugh."

Now it's time for Jack to have his say. Jack isn't pleased. "That was us you were writing about tonight, wasn't it? The family." Stan denies it, but Jack underscores the similarities—the husband and wife who don't talk to each other, the grandfather who falls asleep wherever he happens to be. "You don't poke fun of your own grandfather in front of the whole world." Eugene insists it wasn't poking fun. Now Jack gets to his big gripe, the jokes about Mr. Pitkin being in ladies' pajamas. What do they expect their neighbors will gather from this sketch?

"What do you think happens when the people in Brighton Beach hear a radio program with a woman on it who sounds familiar, tells us her husband's in ladies' pajamas—and they know what that means—they understand the innuendo . . . when they hear that on the radio, what are they thinking when they know that the two sons of the man in ladies' pajamas wrote the program?" Jack feels ridiculed in front of his neighbors, neighbors he had urged to listen to the show because he was so proud of his sons. "You may have been proud to *them*," says Stan tartly, "but you never encouraged *us*. If it were up to you, I'd still be selling boys' clothing." "After what I heard tonight, I wish to God you were," Jack snaps in reply.

EUGENE: . . . . . I'm sorry you feel this way, Pop. We both are. But I swear, we never thought of you and Mom when we wrote the sketch. We just thought of older couples who lived in this neighborhood, but when it got down on paper, I guess it sounded like the ones we knew best . . . It wasn't intentional, I swear.
> *Stan sits in the armchair. Jack sits between the two boys, but talks to Stan.*
JACK: You know what I thought when I heard it? . . . . . I thought it was their way of getting back at me for hurting their mother . . . Is that so impossible to imagine?
STAN: No. Not so impossible.
JACK: Ah, maybe we're getting closer to the truth now . . . What did she tell you about this woman? Did she tell you what she was like?
STAN: . . . . . She never talked to me about any of it.
JACK: But you seem to have feelings about it. Where did you get them from? Someone you know from New York? You have lots of friends there, right? Because, let me tell you something . . . No matter what you heard about this woman, you will never find a kinder or more decent human being on this earth. You understand me?
STAN: Go to hell.
JACK: What did you say to me?
STAN: I said, "Go to hell!"
EUGENE: Stan. Please. Don't do this.
STAN (*standing*): I don't care if she's Joan of Arc, that's still my mother we're talking about. Do whatever you God damn please, but don't blame Gene and me of humiliating you when you're the one who's been humiliating *us* . . . You're so damn guilty for what you've done, you're accusing everyone else of betraying *you* . . . I never wanted to hear what was happening between you and Mom. I prayed every night you would both work it out and it would pass out of our lives. You could have called each other "him" and "her" forever as long as it kept you together . . . All my life you taught me things about dignity and principles and I believed them. I still do, I guess . . . But what kind of principles does a man have when he tells his sons the woman he's seeing on the side is a wonderful, decent human being?
JACK (*stands, composes himself, then walks slowly to Stan*): Either you've grown up too fast . . . or I've outlived my place in this house.
> *Jack looks at both boys, then goes up the stairs to his bedroom and closes the door.*

Eugene is shaking in the aftermath of the confrontation. Stan is still furious. It's no surprise that fathers sometimes play around—Stan knows that the fathers of a lot of his friends have—but they don't have the gall to ask their sons to take the other woman into the family. Eugene suggests that perhaps there's more to Jack's side than they understand, but Stan doesn't want to hear any more of Jack's side. He doesn't want to be on the receiving end of his father's transferred guilt. Stan wants out of the house, and he wants Eugene to join him. They'll get an apartment in New York and begin to live like grownups.

EUGENE: Stan? . . . When we were writing the sketch, did you think we were writing about Mom and Pop?

STAN (coming back to sit next to Eugene): No. It was like you said. It's everybody out here. I thought the father was Mr. Greenblatt . . . Joe Pinotti's grandfather once fell asleep in his oatmeal. He almost suffocated.

EUGENE: I did. I thought it was Mom and Pop. And Grandpa. They were the ones I was writing about.

STAN: Okay. So? It was a little bit of them, too.

EUGENE: No. It was only them. The joke about him being in ladies' pajamas . . . I didn't mean it the way he said. To me it was just a joke. But maybe I did it subconsciously the way Pop said.

STAN: If it's subconscious, it's not a crime, Eugene.

EUGENE: I was the one who should have had the fight with him. Only I didn't know I was so angry. Like there's a part of my head that makes me this nice, likeable, funny kid . . . and there's the other part, the part that writes, that's an angry, hostile, real son of a bitch. . . . . .

STAN: Well, you'd better make friends with the son of a bitch, because he's the one who's going to make you a big living.

Joe Pinotti phones to tell Stan that his family thought it was about *them,* and they loved it. Stan lies about how well it went over in the Jerome house. Kate returns while Stan is on the phone. Eugene tells her Jack's gone upstairs. Kate asks what Jack thought of the show. "He thought it was very lifelike," says Eugene.

To the audience, Eugene compares where his parents are now and how they must have felt when they first met—maybe the way he and Josie feel about each other now. If he and Josie marry, what his folks are going through will never happen to them. But an element of doubt nibbles at his certainty.

Stan, off the phone now, is on his way out the door for a date with a girl he's been seeing for months. Tonight he thinks he's going to get lucky. After all, he's a celebrity now!

Kate gets a phone call from Grandma in Miami. She loved the program, of course, but she doesn't quite understand that the Pitkin family doesn't exist, that they're characters Eugene and Stan made up and are played by actors. From the Pitkins, the conversation moves to Grandpa. Grandma is obviously hurt that he not only has refused to go to Miami but hasn't picked up the phone to talk to her since she went there. In her upset, apparently Grandma accuses Kate of siding with Ben. This angers Kate. "I'm not yelling at you, but don't accuse me of what you make up in your own head," says Kate. A sort of peace is made between daughter and mother, and the phone call is over. Kate hangs up, obviously disturbed by the conversation.

Eugene tries to cheer up his mother, offering to make her a milkshake and promising some day to hire a maid to help her. She resists both. She only seems to spring to life when she catches him sitting on the corner of the dining room table. She orders him off. He mustn't show it such disrespect! This table was made by hand by his great-grandfather for his great-grandmother. A treat for Kate as a little girl was to be allowed to help her grandmother polish this table. Her grandmother bequeathed it to her. "The table you eat on means everything," she insists. "It's the one time in the day when the whole family is together . . . This is where you share things . . . People who eat out all the time don't get to be a family . . ." If Eugene and Josie marry, Kate will leave the table to them. If they have a daughter, Kate will invite her over to polish.

Eugene wants to know more about his great-grandmother. Kate tells him about when she and his great-grandfather immigrated and how, when they first saw the Statue of Liberty, they cried and prayed. Can Eugene guess why? "Because they were free," he guesses. Kate tells him, "Because they took one look at that statue and said, 'That's not a Jewish woman. We're going to have problems again.' "

Ben is not the first Socialist in the family. Apparently all the men have been. Kate's politics, however, have no theoretical base. She votes for those she feels she can trust, like Harry Truman. He used to own a store so he "knows what it's like to be a working man."

And now a request from Eugene. He wants to hear (again) about the fabled night she danced with George Raft. She resists. Whenever she tells it to him, he doesn't believe her. He promises to believe her. He picks up a skein of yarn, puts it around his hands and pushes the ball of yarn connected to it toward her. She picks up the ball and begins to wind and remember.

She committed a sin that night, a sin that God would punish. Her Aunt Sipra had died, and she was supposed to sit in mourning with the family at her grandmother's. But Kate had told her mother she wasn't feeling well and was given permission to go home—except she didn't go home. She joined her girl friend Adele Abrams and went to the Primrose Ballroom. George Raft, known then as the best ballroom dancer in New York, was a friend of the owner of the Primrose and had promised to come by to dance. Kate—a terrific dancer herself—*had* to see him in action. Not that she had a crush on him (Raft was Italian, after all), no, the person she had a crush on was Jack. For years, in fact, she'd had a crush on Jack. There was an integrity about Jack. "He didn't smile a lot, but when he did, you knew he meant it." Not being a smiler meant that Jack didn't get to be a boss or a salesman. "Your father paid the price for not being a phony . . . It was so hard to impress him. That's why I went to the Primrose that night. I thought if Jack heard that I danced with George Raft, maybe I'd get him to notice me." Eugene is thrilled by this story. Some day, he promises, he will write this as a movie.

Kate continues with her story. It was raining that night, and her hair got wet, ruining her curls, so she combed it straight and left it wet. "I looked like a Latin from Manhattan . . . The perfect partner for George Raft." When she walked onto the dance floor, she was deluged with offers to dance, but she held off. She wanted to save her energy until Raft showed up.

KATE: . . . . . And then I started to get scared. Because it was ten after eleven and he still didn't show up. If I wasn't home by twelve, my parents would walk in and find out I was lying to them. And with my mother, I didn't need God to punish me.

EUGENE: Twelve o'clock! Cinderella! This story has everything.

KATE: And then, at twenty after eleven, he walks in . . . Like the King of Spain. My heart was beating louder than the drummer in the band . . . He had two friends with him, one on each side, like bodyguards. And I swear, there was something in their inside pockets. I thought to myself, they're either guns or more jars of grease for his hair.

EUGENE (to audience): She actually had a sense of humor. This was a side of my mother I hardly ever saw. (To Kate.) So, he walks in with these two guys.

KATE (taking off her sweater and standing center): So, he walks in with these two friends, and I don't have much time. So I grabbed Bobby Zugetti, a shoe clerk, who was the best dancer at the Primose, and said, "Bobby, dance with me!" . . . I knew he had a crush on me, and I never gave him a tumble before. He didn't know what hit him. So out on the floor we go, and we foxtrotted from one side of the ballroom and back. In and out, bobbing and weaving through the crowd, gliding across the floor like a pair of ice skaters.

EUGENE: "Begin the Beguine" . . . Maybe "Night and Day." That's what I would use in the picture.

KATE: And I never once looked over to see if George Raft was looking at me . . . I wanted to get his attention, I didn't want to give him mine . . . The music finishes, and Bobby dips me down to the floor. It was a little lower than a nice girl should dip, but I figured one more sin wouldn't kill me . . . And I walk over to Adele, I'm dripping with perspiration, and I said, "Well? Did he watch me?" . . . And she said, "It's hard to tell. His eyes didn't move." . . . So I look over and he's sitting at a table with his two friends and Adele is right. His eyes don't move. And it's twenty-five to twelve, and he's never even noticed me. And I said to myself, "Well, if it's not meant to be, it's not meant to be." . . . and Adele and I started for the door.

EUGENE: The tension mounts. The audience is on the edge of their seats.

KATE: And as we pass their table, George Raft stands up and says, "Excuse me." And he's looking straight at Adele Abrams. He says, "Could I ask you a question, please?" . . . Adele is shaking like a leaf. And she walks over to him.

EUGENE: Adele? He's talking to Adele Abrams?

KATE: And he says, "I wonder if your friend would care to dance with me?" . . . And she says, "You want me to ask her?" . . . And he says, "Please. I'm a little shy."

EUGENE: I don't believe it. I don't believe George Raft said that.

KATE: I swear to God. May I never live to see another day.

EUGENE: Even if it's true, it's out of the picture. An audience would never believe it.

KATE: Fine. So Adele says, "I'll ask her" . . . So she comes back and asks me

. . . And I look at him and he smiles at me . . . And his eyes moved for the first time. Not fresh or anything, but he had the look of a man with a lot of confidence and I never saw that before. Scared the life out of me. So I walk over to him, and he takes my hand and leads me out to the floor . . . Everyone in the Primrose is watching. Even the band. Someone had to whisper, "Start playing," so they would begin . . . And they began. And we danced around that room. And I held my head high and my back straight as a board . . . And I looked down at the floor and up at the ceiling, but never in his eyes. I saw a professional do that once . . . His hands were so gentle. Hardly touching me at all, but I knew exactly when he wanted me to move and which way he wanted me to turn.

Jonathan Silverman and Linda Lavin in a scene from *Broadway Bound*

EUGENE *(dropping the knitting and rushing to the radio):* Wait a minute! Wait a minute!

KATE: What are you doing?

EUGENE: I want you to show me how you danced.

He has to coax her, but finally she agrees. Eugene pretends to slick his hair down like George Raft and takes his mother in his arms *"and they begin to dance—awkwardly at first, then more gracefully."* And for a few minutes, the years fall away. His mother is 16 and back in the Primrose Ballroom again.

The music ends. *"Eugene turns off the radio. Kate is embarrassed, but flushed with excitement. He smiles at her . . . . . She sits at the dining table."*

KATE: . . . . . My God, I'm drenched in perspiration. In the middle of the winter. I don't know how I let you get me to do such things.

EUGENE *(sitting on the sofa arm, opposite Kate):* Because you liked it. Why do you always stop doing the things that make you feel good?"

KATE: What's the matter? Raising you and Stanley wasn't something that made me feel good?

EUGENE: There's other things besides raising a family, Ma.

KATE: Yeah. So I've heard . . . . .

She tries to shoo him off to bed, but he wants to hear the end of the story. She was late getting home, but, lucky for her, her parents stayed elsewhere that night. But the dance was big news in the neighborhood so her mother found out anyway. "People were congratulating my mother. They treated her like her daughter was a movie star. She was angry with me, but she knew she couldn't say anything . . . But when I saw my grandmother, she winked at me, squeezed my hand and said, 'I know, darling. I know.' "

Kate is exhausted from telling the story. She says she won't tell it again. Telling it was harder than living it. As she heads upstairs to her bedroom Eugene points out that she didn't get caught by her folks or punished by God, so this movie has a happy ending. "The movie isn't over yet," she says, and goes into her room.

EUGENE *(Going into his bedroom and closing the door; to audience.):* I'll be honest about one thing. Dancing with my mother was very scary. I was doing what my father should have been doing with her but wasn't. And holding her like that and seeing her smile was too intimate for me to enjoy. Intimacy is a complex thing. You had to be careful who you shared it with . . . but without it, life was just breakfast, lunch, dinner and a good night's sleep. Most people would settle for that. Most people do . . . I was determined not to be most people.

Ben comes out of his room the next morning to see Jack about to tiptoe out of the house with a large suitcase. Jack is indeed walking out. He hasn't told Kate. He figures he'll call her in a few days when he has a better handle on what to say. Ben tries to persuade him to stay.

BEN: . . . . . This thing with the other woman won't last . . . I know, because I've had enough other women in my life . . . Kate will find a way to deal with it. She'll ignore it, she'll pretend it's not happening. She'll live with you and not talk to you to protect her dignity, but she won't leave you . . . I'm her own father and I'm saying to you, *have* your affair until it's over, but don't break up what'll last you the rest of your life.

JACK: You don't understand. It's not an affair. I don't sleep with this woman. I did once, not now . . . She's sick. She'll live another five, six more months. Maybe not even that.

BEN *(nods):* Maybe to you that's a noble gesture, but to me it stinks.

JACK: Don't be so God damn hypocritical. You've got a seventy-two-year-old wife living alone in Florida, and you stay here pretending you're martyring yourself for a political cause that you haven't been interested in for the last twenty years. I'm the last one to blame you . . . Where is it written that a man must love the same woman until the day he dies?

BEN: In the marriage vow he took.

JACK: If I took it, then you took it, too.

BEN: True. And maybe I don't love any more. Maybe I am a hypocrite. I don't have another woman, no . . . My mistress is my privacy. I am unfaithful with a room upstairs that lets me do what I want. I'm having an affair with peace and quiet . . . But you're right. I'm no better than you.

JACK *(at the front door with his suitcase):* I'm fifty-five years old, Ben. I'm not ready for a room yet. I need to run. I need to get away from myself and everything I was. I have no more children to raise. I have nothing waiting out there for me except one thing . . . Something else! *(Jack starts to go out the front door.)*

BEN: I still think you're making a big mistake, Jack. A big, big mistake.

JACK *(turning back):* Why?

BEN: . . . Because Kate is my daughter.

JACK: I'll call the boys tomorrow. *(Jack goes.)*

Ben is alone for a moment. Then Kate comes downstairs. She offers to make Ben breakfast. He doesn't really want anything. He tells her he overheard her talking to Eugene last night. He tells her she's raised good boys. She wonders where Jack is—in the kitchen? Out for a walk? Ben tells her no. She realizes what has happened. Ben confirms it. *"She stands there a moment, not saying a word. Then she goes out to the porch, lights a cigarette and looks out."*

Up in his room, Eugene addresses the audience: "When Mom heard the news about Pop, she didn't cry, she didn't reach for anyone to hug, she didn't make a sound . . . When I was in the Army, they told us, in battle, don't bother attending the wounded who were crying for help . . . Go to those who didn't make a sound. They were the ones in real trouble . . ." Eugene comes downstairs and brings us up to date on his and Stan's careers. They've done well. Their salaries have been doubled and they use the same john as Arthur Godfrey.

Stan comes running in and gathers Eugene and Kate to tell them the big news: He and Eugene are moving up from Chubby Waters. They're going to write for Phil Silvers at much increased salaries (negotiated by Stan). Now is the time for changes. For all of them. He and Eugene are moving to Manhattan, and he wants

Kate to move, too. He saw a terrific place two blocks from where they'll be that will be great for her and Grandpa. But Kate's plans aren't Stan's. Except for her sister, everyone she knows is in Brighton Beach. And she shudders to think what a chicken costs in Manhattan. No, this is where she intends to stay.

Kate goes into the kitchen, and Stan and Eugene go upstairs to pack. Stan has other news. He saw Pop. They went to a restaurant. Jack's lady friend is dying in the hospital, and he's taking it bad. Pop asked about Kate, held Stan's hand and started to cry. But Jack won't be coming back to Kate. He's certain she wouldn't take him. "Sure she would," says Eugene. "She still loves him." That may be so, but Kate can be as stubborn as Grandpa, says Stan.

The boys can't figure out why their parents are treating each other this way. Stan thinks perhaps Jack's perspective is explained in a pair of letters to his two sons. But Jack made Stan promise not to open the letters until after his death. The two speculate on what is in the letters. Maybe apologies? Or maybe saying he doesn't forgive Stan for telling him to go to hell. "He already forgave you. He held your hand in the restaurant," says Eugene. Stan says he's going to try to respect his father's request regarding the letter. Eugene wonders, if he dies before Jack, does he get his letter back? "You've got a wonderfully inventive mind," Stan tells him, "but sometimes it lacks respect."

Stan goes to his room and begins to pack, as Eugene addresses the audience again. The time is now the Monday they are to leave Brighton Beach. Eugene and Stan come downstairs. They remind Ben of his promise to come to the studio to watch their first show. To make sure he comes, they'll name a character after Trotsky. Ben lets them in on a secret: All the time they thought they were getting away with kidding him, he was kidding them back twice as much.

Kate comes out with freshly baked cookies. Stan and Eugene give Ben a hug, which, despite his protestations, he seems to appreciate. Stan gives Kate a hug. Now it's Eugene's turn. He has something to say. She asks him not to. "I don't deal with these things too good," she says. Eugene replies, "It's not that horrible. And it's quick . . . I love you. Okay? That wasn't so bad, was it?" And he embraces her.

Moving to the door, Stan tells Ben, ". . . . . just so you know, I always knew you were kidding me." Ben and Kate disappear into the kitchen as Stan and Eugene go outside. Stan goes off to get a cab. Eugene stays where he is, looking at the house for the last time as an occupant.

EUGENE *(to audience):* I knew then that no matter how many times I came back to see this house, it would never be my home again . . . Mom and Pop split up for good and never got back together . . . As a matter of fact, he remarried about two years later to a pretty nice woman. Mom would really be hurt if she heard me say that, but the truth is the truth . . . Grandpa found it rough going in his seventy-eighth year and finally surrendered to Capitalism and Miami Beach . . . He plays pinochle every day and donates half his winnings to the Socialist Party . . . Josie and I got married and we sleep each night with her hand lying gently across my chest. I won't even breathe for fear she'll move it away.

STAN *(running down the street to Eugene):* Gene! Come on! I got a cab!

EUGENE: I'm coming. I'm coming.

STAN: I never realized how cold it was out here before.

Stan exits up the street, taking Eugene's box of cookies with him.

EUGENE *(to audience):* I didn't keep my promise to Pop. I opened his letter and read it. He didn't apologize, and he wasn't mad at Stan and me for what we wrote. The only thing he wanted was for Stan and me to understand his side of the story . . . Only he never said what his side was . . . Contrary to popular belief, everything in life doesn't come to a clear-cut conclusion. Mom didn't do anything very exciting with the rest of her life except wax her grandmother's table and bask in the joy of her sons' success. But I never got the feeling that Mom felt she sacrificed herself for us. Whatever she gave, she found her own quiet pleasure in. I guess she was never comfortable with words like "I love you." A hard life can sometimes knock the sentiment out of you . . . But all in all, she considers herself to be a pretty lucky woman. After all, she did once dance with George Raft.

Eugene turns away from the house, grabs his suitcase and runs up the street to the cab. Curtain.

THE WIDOW CLAIRE

A Full-Length Play in One Act

BY HORTON FOOTE

Cast and credits appear on page 351

HORTON FOOTE was born in Wharton, Tex. March 14, 1916 into a family with deep, multigenerational roots in that Gulf Coast town. His father ran a local clothing store, and his mother was a gifted pianist. He left home at 16 for an acting apprenticeship at the Pasadena Playhouse and later studied with a Stanislavski protegée, Tamara Daykarhanova, in New York City. His acting career merged with a writing career at the turn of the decade, as he joined American Actors Theater and that group put on his one-act Wharton Dance *in the fall of 1940 and his full-length* Texas Town *the following spring.*

Foote's playscripts produced in New York at various levels have included Only the Heart *(1942),* Two Southern Idylls *(Miss Lou and The Girls, 1943),* The Lonely *and* Goodby to Richmond *(1944),* Daisy Lee *(1944),* Celebration *(1948),* The Chase *(1952),* The Trip to Bountiful *(1953) and* The Traveling Lady *(1954). His parallel career of distinguished authorship for the large and small screen (and the novel, for that matter) has taken in more than a dozen major works for Fred Coe, "Playhouse 90" and others in TV's golden age and numerous screenplays including the Academy Award–winning* To Kill a Mockingbird *and* Tender Mercies.

Foote withdrew from the fray to a farm in New Hampshire for most of the 1970s. There he began writing the nine-play cycle The Orphans' Home, *based on stories his father had told him about the family, beginning in 1902 with his father's leaving home at age 12 and ending with the death of Foote's maternal grandfather in 1928,* set against the background of the decline of the cotton plantations and the rise of the mercantile class in the Gulf Coast area. The nine, some already produced on the stage and screen and all to be published by Grove Press in sets of three, are Roots in a Parched Ground, Convicts, Lily Dale (produced off Broadway this season), The Widow Claire (also produced off Broadway December 17 for 150 performances and cited as a Best Play, Foote's first), Courtship, On Valentine's Day, 1918, Cousins and The Death of Papa.

Foote is married, with two sons and two daughters, and lives in New York City.

Time: 1911

Place: Harrison, Texas

SYNOPSIS: In a room furnished with double bed, dresser, etc., four young men in their 20s—Archie, Felix, Spence and Ed—are playing poker while a fifth— Horace Robedaux, 21, well-groomed—is tying his tie, preparing to go out on a date. Soon Ed is tapped out and tries to borrow some money from Horace, but the latter is leaving for business school the next day and needs every cent he has. As Horace adds the finishing touches to his dark three-piece suit for his date with the Widow Claire, both Felix and Ed warn him that her children get in the way on any date and would be a burden to a more meaningful future relationship.

ARCHIE: Do you think she's good-looking?
ED: Kind of.
FELIX: She used to be. I think she's losing her looks. She used to be a beauty.
  Horace looks at his watch.
Are we keeping you, boy? Don't let your old pals keep you from your date.
HORACE: No, it's still early. I want to give her time to put the kids to bed.
ED: How many dates have you had with her, Horace?
HORACE: Two.
SPENCE: Were those kids always there?
HORACE: In the house. Sometimes they are in bed.
FELIX: They weren't in bed the night I was there. They were crawling all over me the whole time, asking me every five minutes if I'd brought them a present. Finally I had to give them both a nickel to shut them up.
ED: I never went out with a widow.
ARCHIE: Hell, you never go out with anybody.

They warn Horace that widows can be dangerous, telling him that Claire sees other men (Horace knows this, she makes no secret of it). Horace exits whistling "Waltz Me Around Again, Willie," and the poker players disperse.

As the scene shifts to Claire's house, in the living room the gramophone is playing a record of that tune, and Claire is smoking a cigarette, which she puts out when Horace crosses the yard and knocks on the door. Horace has brought Claire a box of chocolates. Claire had to draw the curtains in order to prevent the neighbors from seeing her smoking, and she deplores the lack of privacy in this neighborhood. Privacy is in short supply indoors, too, because in the middle of a kiss they are interrupted by Claire's 9-year-old daughter, Molly, who is being prevented from going to sleep by her rambunctious brother. She demands to be told a bedtime story. Horace offers to supply one while Claire goes to quiet her son.

John Daman as Buddy, Sarah Michelle Gellar as Molly, Hallie Foote as Claire and Matthew Broderick as Horace Robedaux in Horton Foote's *The Widow Claire*

MOLLY: What stories did your mama and daddy tell you when you were a little boy?

HORACE: They didn't tell me any.

MOLLY: Didn't you have a mama and a daddy?

HORACE: Yes, but they didn't tell me any stories.

MOLLY: How did they get you to go to sleep?

HORACE: My daddy used to sing to me when I was real little. He would rock me and sing.

MOLLY: Do you know the story about Goldilocks?

HORACE: Yes, I do.

MOLLY: Tell me that one.

HORACE: All right. Once upon a time . . . there was a little girl with long golden curls. They called her Goldilocks . . .

MOLLY *(interrupting):* Don't tell me that one. Tell me about Red Riding Hood.

HORACE: All right. Red Riding Hood was going to see her grandmother one day and . . .

MOLLY *(interrupting again):* What was the song your daddy used to sing to you?

HORACE: He sang a lot.

MOLLY: Do you live with your mama and daddy?

HORACE: No, my daddy is dead.

MOLLY: Is your mama dead too?

HORACE: No, she lives in Houston.

Horace sings "Lily Dale" in response to Molly's request for a song. Molly decides she likes him better than the other men who come here to visit her mother. She mentions Val, who has been known to hit Claire and make her cry. Claire, having entered unnoticed and overheard this, orders Molly to bed (Horace agrees to go tell her a story there). They exit while Claire puts out the makings for drinks, and when Horace returns he tells her, "I don't want Val pushing you around. I'm going to speak to Val."

Claire pours drinks for them both and explains that she sees lots of fellows, Val included, without any emotional involvement, just to help pass the time. They embrace, but Buddy, Claire's 10-year-old son, enters to report that Molly is crying, so Claire goes to cope. Buddy extracts a nickel from Horace (and one for Molly too) and explains that Molly is crying because their daddy died of typhoid last year. Molly has told Buddy that Horace has no daddy either.

BUDDY: Were you sad when your daddy died?

HORACE: Yes, I was.

BUDDY: Did you cry?

HORACE: Yes, I did.

BUDDY: I cried too. Do you have a picture of your daddy?

HORACE: Yes, somewhere.

BUDDY: We don't have a picture of my daddy. He died before he even had his picture taken. I remember him, though. Do you remember him?

HORACE: Sure I do.

BUDDY: Tell me what he looked like?

HORACE: Well, he was good-looking and he had a real nice personality and he was certainly well liked by everybody.

BUDDY: Mama says he had good character. Do you think he did?

HORACE: Oh, yes, I do. And he was smart, Buddy. He was a very smart man and a good businessman. I expect in time he would have been rich.

BUDDY: Are you rich?

HORACE: No, I'm just starting out in life.

Buddy shows Horace a pocket knife given to him by "Uncle Ned"—a drummer and a frequent visitor. He also brought Molly a doll, in contrast to "Uncle Val," who never brings them anything. Asked by Buddy what he does, Horace explains that he's been working in a store but is going away to business school for about six weeks.

Claire comes back with Molly, who is carrying her doll. Horace opens the box of assorted chocolates and passes them around. The children quarrel routinely over their selections. Horace's largesse reminds them of the many presents "Uncle Ned" the drummer is always bringing them. Buddy allows as how he might like to come over to Horace's house and see him once in a while when Horace gets back from business school.

Horace compliments Claire on the new dress she is wearing. Molly informs him that her mother smokes cigarettes, and it develops that Horace doesn't but smokes cigars instead. The children ask to see their mother and Horace dance. They oblige, twirling and dipping around the room—it's obvious that both Horace and Claire are good dancers. Molly remarks that Val can't dance and repeats her dislike of Val, calling him "mean."

MOLLY: Can Uncle Ned dance, Mama?

CLAIRE: He sure can.

BUDDY: Uncle Ned is an old man. He's too old to dance.

CLAIRE: He is not old, Buddy.

BUDDY: He is too.

CLAIRE: Well, don't you ever tell him that. He would die. *(To Horace.)* He's a lonely fellow. He travels with the J.C. Taylor Tailoring Company. They have headquarters in Chicago. He has the Southern Territory.

HORACE: I know him. He sold tailoring to my uncle.

BUDDY: He asked Mama to marry him.

CLAIRE: Buddy!!

BUDDY: Didn't he?

CLAIRE: Yes, but you're not supposed to tell the whole world.

MOLLY: Are you going to marry him?

CLAIRE: I don't know. One day I think I will and the next day I decide nothing can ever get me to marry again.

Ned has gone so far as to give Claire an engagement ring, but she hasn't decided to keep it. Horace and Claire dance again, while talking of his forthcoming trip—they agree that they will miss each other during his six weeks' absence. She wishes he'd stay until after the dance at the Courthouse next week, but he can't, he has to be in Houston for the beginning of the term. Tactlessly, Buddy asks how old Horace is, then points out that he's six years younger than Claire, who is 27. "That don't make any difference, Buddy," Horace tells him, "My Aunt Virgie is six years older than my Uncle Doc."

Horace has a friend who has offered to help him get a job "in the traveling line" when he gets out of school. They discuss who's going to the dance with whom, and Horace notes that Felix and Ed don't have dates yet, though the latter is probably too shy to ask anyone.

CLAIRE: Sissy said she would watch the children for me if I wanted to go, but I don't think I will. Even if anybody asks me, which they haven't. Sissy said, "You've mourned a year. No one can criticize your going to the dance now." "I'm not worrying about that," I said, "but no one has asked me. I can't go by myself." No one wants to take an old married woman with two half-grown children to a dance. "You were a child when you married," Sissy said, "all of 16." "I can't help that," I said, "I'm not a child now."

HORACE: I wish I were going to be here. I would take you.

CLAIRE: You're just saying that to be nice.

HORACE: No. I would love to take you.

CLAIRE: You're not just saying that?

HORACE: No.

CLAIRE: I haven't been to a dance in so long I wouldn't know how to act.

HORACE: You know, I don't think I've ever seen you at a dance.

CLAIRE: I guess you haven't. When I went you were still in knee breeches.

HORACE: Didn't you ever go after you were married?

CLAIRE: No. We went to the first Christmas dance after we were married, and then we stopped going.

Horace remembers the day of Claire's wedding (though he didn't attend it), a big church wedding, Claire was a mother at 17 and then a widow whose beloved husband left her this house and two rental houses bringing in an income. Sometimes she thinks about selling out and moving to Houston with the children. Horace can't live with his mother in Houston—her house is too small—so he's going to stay at a boarding house. As they compliment each other on their dancing and put on another record, Horace promises to try to get home to see Claire one weekend during his Houston stay.

The children, exhausted, are asleep, so Claire lets Horace kiss her while they're dancing. Claire is somewhat disturbed because Horace's Aunt Inez, who was Claire's matron of honor, has stopped calling here or asking Claire to parties, probably because she disapproves of Claire's entertaining men. They pick up the sleeping children and carry them off to bed, as a voice outside calls Claire's name. It is Val and his friend Roger. Claire tells them at the door that she is having a date with Horace, enjoying his dancing ability. Roger can dance a little, but Val can't dance at all and declares that "Dancing is for sissies." Claire hints that she'd like to be asked to the dance next week, making it plain that Horace can't take her because he's going away.

Trying to improve an awkward situation, Claire asks the two callers in for a drink of Ned's whiskey (as Val makes a slighting remark about the traveling salesman's age). They swig directly from the bottle, and Val asserts that Ned dyes his hair. When Claire lights up a cigarette, Val bums one, as does Roger, but Horace refuses.

HORACE: No, I smoke cigars.

VAL: What are you trying to do? Act the big man and show off? When did you start smoking cigars?

HORACE: I always have.

The music has stopped Claire puts it on again.

CLAIRE: Anybody feel like dancing?

A pause. No one says anything.

Horace? . . .

HORACE: Sure.

They dance. Molly comes in.

MOLLY: Mama, I can't sleep with that music.

CLAIRE: All right, honey.

She turns it off.

Go on back to bed now.

MOLLY: I want Horace to take me to bed.

CLAIRE: Oh, Molly!

HORACE: I don't mind.

He takes her up and goes out with her.

VAL: Get rid of him.

CLAIRE: You go on and then I will.

VAL: Come on, Roger.

The two leave. Claire apologizes for the intrusion when Horace comes back. She pleads a headache, and Horace tells her he has to go, anyway. They declare that they'll miss each other while Horace is away, they kiss goodbye, and Horace promises to write. As he leaves, Horace hears Claire tell him, "You're very sweet . . ."

Back in the rooming house, Felix is drinking whiskey, and Archie goes off to look in on an all-night poker game. Horace comes in and immediately hints to dateless Felix that Claire might like to have someone offer to take her to the dance. "A date costs a lot of money. It's cheaper going stag," Felix informs Horace, who declares that he'd take her himself if he were going to be in town. Horace admits that he likes Claire and that "She likes me. I don't know how much." They have a drink, as the Courthouse clock strikes twelve. Felix heads for bed, but once again Horace asks him to take Claire to the dance, if only as a favor to him, and Horace will give Felix the money for the date. Grudgingly, Felix agrees and goes off but soon returns to tell Horace he's changed his mind— let Val take her and learn to dance if he has to.

Buddy is heard calling for Horace and comes in with the news that Val came back to the house and is beating up his mother. Felix warns Horace to stay out of this, but Horace goes off declaring, "I can take care of myself," followed by Buddy.

Ed comes in, so drunk he couldn't even find this house until it was pointed out to him by a friend across the street. Ed falls into bed.

At Claire's, the house is in darkness when Horace and Buddy arrive, the latter having extracted another nickel, after assuring Horace that his mother sent him for help. Claire comes outside.

CLAIRE: Horace, you're going to think we're crazy. Val came over here after you left, and Buddy and Molly heard him and asked me to tell him to go, and I did, and he began to get upset and started talking loud and arguing . . .
BUDDY: He hit you.
CLAIRE: He didn't hit me, Buddy.
BUDDY: He did too.
CLAIRE: He did not, now. He threatened to hit me. He's a bully, but I'm not afraid of him.
BUDDY: He hit you . . .
CLAIRE: Buddy, he didn't hit me.
BUDDY: He did, too, I saw him and Molly saw him.
CLAIRE: You thought you saw him hit me.
BUDDY: And he wouldn't leave when you asked him to go.
CLAIRE: Well, he's gone now, so let's all go to bed . . . . .

Buddy is sent off. Horace offers to stay the rest of the night on the couch, for protection, but Claire explains that Val won't be back tonight and only behaved in an unruly fashion because he'd been drinking heavily.

Claire makes a wish on the new moon. So does Horace, but they don't tell each other what they wished. Claire tells him that one of her new-moon wishes almost came true: she wished last summer she could go to Colorado to escape the heat and enjoy a change of scene after her husband's death—and at least she was able to get away to Galveston, where Ned has a house with his sister. Both of them would love to have Claire and the children come there again.

Claire asks Horace about the time after his father's death and his mother's remarriage.

CLAIRE: How long did she wait before she married again?
HORACE: Three or four years.
CLAIRE: Did your father leave her some money?
HORACE: No.
CLAIRE: How did she support you and your sister?
HORACE: Well, she kept a boarding house with her sister for awhile, but they couldn't make a go of it. They couldn't ever collect the money from the boarders. Then she went into Houston and got a job working as a seamstress in Munn's Department Store.
CLAIRE: Did you live with her in Houston?
HORACE: No. She left me back here with my grandparents. She took my sister with her. That's where she met Mr. Davenport.
CLAIRE: Who is that?
HORACE: The man she married.
CLAIRE: Why didn't you go and live with them then?

HORACE: Because Mr. Davenport didn't want me. He had to go to work when he was twelve, and he thought that was good for a boy, so they left me here, and I lived with my grandparents until they died, and then I lived with my Aunt Virgie. She has been like a mother to me. I'm crazy about my Aunt Virgie.

CLAIRE: She's a lovely lady.

In the still of the night, Horace admits to being "a pretty serious person." Claire assures him he's not too serious for her taste. He knows he is ambitious but isn't quite sure in which direction his ambition should take him. In any case, the first money he earns is going toward a tombstone on his father's grave. Claire put an expensive tombstone on her late husband's grave and wishes she had a picture of him, if only for her children's sake. She does have a picture of herself and agrees to give one to Horace to take to Houston.

Horace has the reputation of having a good singing voice, and at Claire's request renders "Sweet Alice Ben Bolt," a sad song with death in it. Again they declare that they'll miss each other while Horace is away.

Molly comes in, complaining that Buddy has eaten all the rest of the candy and won't go to sleep but is lying in bed, whistling.

MOLLY: . . . . . He says he's whistling to keep Val away. He says if Val comes back here and hears him whistling he'll think there is a man in the house and be scared and leave.

CLAIRE: Now you go tell Buddy not to worry. He's not coming back tonight.

MOLLY: Is he ever coming back?

CLAIRE: Yes, when he can behave like a gentleman.

MOLLY: Buddy says he heard Val say Uncle Ned dyes his hair. Is that true?

CLAIRE: No.

MOLLY: Why did he say it if it wasn't true?

CLAIRE: Because he's jealous of your Uncle Ned.

MOLLY: Why?

CLAIRE: Because Uncle Ned asked me to marry him and he thinks I might.

MOLLY: Please come to bed now, Mama.

CLAIRE: All right, darling.

She takes Horace's hand.

Good night, Horace.

HORACE: Good night.

CLAIRE: Write to us.

HORACE: I will. Good night, Molly.

Horace leaves. Claire hugs Molly, who asks her mother to sing "Goodnight Irene," as the scene changes to the boarding house. Felix and Archie enter and discuss their future. They've both had temporary jobs now and again, but neither knows what he is going to do, except that Felix hopes to get rich by marrying money. Archie suggests Claire, but Claire isn't rich enough for Felix.

Ed is still out cold on the bed. When Horace comes in Archie suggests a game of cards. Horace doesn't dare play: "I only have enough money to last me six weeks in Houston. I won't even be able to afford cigars or a newspaper. If I even lost a dollar I would be in trouble." He knows he was foolish to suggest paying for Felix to take Claire to the dance. The others insist—Archie will lend Horace a dollar, and if Horace loses it he can pay it back when he returns. Also, Horace would like to hire a guitar and fiddle player to serenade Claire some evening after he comes back.

Archie shuffles and deals while observing that Val may be courting Claire for her money—little as her three houses may represent, it's more than Val has. Archie reports that one of the locals, an insomniac given to walking around town when he can't sleep, saw Val coming out of Claire's house at 5 A.M. one morning: "He said he's seen him come out of there at all hours." Horace refuses to comment, and they play cards as Ed mutters "Roberta" in his sleep. They speculate that Ed never goes out with "nice" girls, so Roberta may be one of the other kind.

Buddy enters with the information that Val has come back to the house, and suggests that Horace come back and beat him up. Horace explains that it's no business of his whom Claire invites to her home, and Buddy argues that she's scared Val will hit her if she tells him to go. Horace doesn't believe this, but drunken Ed's cries and mutterings get Buddy so scared that Horace agrees to walk the boy back home. Horace escorts him as far as the porch, and before he can leave, Val comes outside.

BUDDY: Yonder comes Val. I told you he was in there. *(Calls.)* Val, Horace is going to beat you up.
VAL: Yeah? I'm scared to death.
He grabs Horace.
Look, I don't like being spied on.
HORACE: I'm not spying on you.
He throws Val's hands off. Val pushes him. He pushes Val back. They start to fight. It's a savage fight.
BUDDY *(yelling):* Mama . . . Molly . . . Come watch . . . They're having a fight! Horace is going to kill Val! Kill him, Horace! Kill him!
CLAIRE: Buddy, where are you? Buddy, is that you down there? Molly, why didn't you tell me he left his room?
MOLLY: He made me swear not to.
CLAIRE: What in the world is going on—do you know?
MOLLY: No, Ma'am.
CLAIRE: Buddy, Buddy, where are you?
Claire and Molly enter porch.
Stop it! Stop it! Val, have you gone crazy? Buddy, be careful!
The fight ends.
Go on home, Val.
VAL: That damn sneak was spying on us.
CLAIRE: Go on home, Val.
MOLLY: Is he dead, Mama?
CLAIRE: I don't think so.
Claire bends over Horace. Val exits.

Horace gets up, looking for more, but Val has gone. He assures Claire he wasn't spying and explains what happened. And Horace has decided to come back next weekend and take Claire to the dance himself—but it turns out that Val has already asked her and plans to let Claire teach him to dance. Val has also asked her to marry him (she tells Horace); but so has Ned, and she can't decide which one she ought to accept. She leans toward Val because he's nearer her age, but he has no job. The children make it clear they prefer Ned before they are sent off to bed. Claire continues on the subject of marriage, telling Horace that her sister thinks Val just wants her money.

CLAIRE: . . . . . She says he'll marry me and get me to sell my houses, spend the money and leave me flat. That's what Sissy says he'll do. Val says I'm the first girl he's ever asked to marry, because I'm the first girl he's ever loved. Ned says he's determined to be married before he's forty, and he'll be forty soon. I guess you're too young to be thinking about marrying yet, aren't you?
HORACE: I think about it.
CLAIRE: Did you ever meet a girl you'd like to marry?
HORACE: I like you.
CLAIRE: You don't think I'm too old for you?
HORACE: No. My Aunt Virgie is six years older than my Uncle Doc.
CLAIRE: You told me that . . . And are they happily married?
HORACE: Oh, yes. I think so.
CLAIRE: They certainly seem congenial.
HORACE: But I couldn't consider marriage to anyone at present . . .
CLAIRE: You couldn't?
HORACE: No. I couldn't. I have no job. I have no money. I would want to have a job and a little money saved before I married.

Claire was determined never to get married again until she heard from her sister that it was her husband's deathbed wish for Claire to provide another father for their growing children. Claire doesn't know whether or not to believe her sister, who simply wants Claire to marry again and favors Ned because he has money.

Molly comes in, having been looking for Ned's picture on Claire's dresser and, failing to find it, brought the ring and wrist watch Ned gave Claire to show to Horace. Buddy comes in—he has the picture and has brought it to show to Horace. Once more Claire sends them off to bed, this time commenting, "Sissy says they need a man's discipline and I guess they do."

As Claire and Horace embrace and kiss, Claire sees that he has blood on his face and wipes it off. He tells her that he is going to arrange to serenade her when he gets back. They are interrupted by the arrival of Val's friend Roger who was sent to fetch a bottle of whiskey. Told that Val has gone, he apologizes for being late and hands the bottle to Claire, supposing that it was to be a present for her. Roger asks Claire to the dance and is told she already has a date with Val. He takes a swig from his own bottle; then, when Claire goes inside to settle another minor problem of Molly's, Roger comments to Horace, "Val says he stays over here sometimes. You know, like a husband and wife. But Val is such a big liar

Hallie Foote and Matthew Broderick in a scene from *The Widow Claire*

I don't know if he's telling the truth or not . . . . . He says he tells her he's going to marry her, so she'll let him stay. But he says he don't have no intention of marrying nobody . . . . . I think she's right pretty. Don't you?"

Horace agrees but restrains himself from further comment, as Roger goes on about Claire's family of four sisters—Sissy married but the other three unmarried. Roger wonders whether Claire would marry him if he asked her, but Horace declines to offer an opinion (it is Val's opinion that Roger "is not refined enough" for Claire). Roger continues to make conversation to which Horace responds with laconic answers. How far did Horace get in school? "Sixth." Why did he quit? "I had to go to work." Where? "All over." Finally Roger notices that dawn is breaking and makes his departure, leaving goodbyes for Claire.

Claire joins Horace, having made up her mind that she's not going to marry anyone, she's going to sell her three houses and go live in Houston. She kisses Horace again and gives him the picture she promised. "I'm certainly glad you're not marrying right away. I'm certainly glad about that," says Horace before he leaves.

Back at Horace's boarding house, Ed is still in bed, and Archie, Felix and Spence are still up. When Horace comes in they inform him they've found out who Roberta is—a twin traveling with a medicine show. Spence has been watching the all-night poker game and tells Horace his Uncle Albert lost $15,000 to a pair of gamblers from Galveston. Felix reads the inscription on Claire's picture: "For Horace, lest he forget his friend Claire." The others notice that Horace has been in a fight, and Spence warns Horace to keep away from Val: "He cut a man once, you know, fighting over a woman."

Buddy comes in with a message that his mother has something to tell Horace, who agrees to stop by Claire's house on his way to the railroad station. Buddy goes off, and Spence offers a bet of $5 that Horace will never come back (Horace admits he doesn't know whether he will or not). Archie and Felix decide to go across the tracks to obtain the services of a woman for 50 cents apiece, taking Ed with them. Horace turns down their invitation to accompany them and continues his packing.

Claire has finally gotten her children off to school and has put on the record of "Waltz Me Around Again, Willie," when Horace arrives, carrying his suitcase. Claire goes outdoors to greet him. After Horace left, Claire got to thinking that she couldn't take the financial risk of selling out and trying to reestablish herself in Houston, because of the children, "So I woke them both up and we had a good long talk and I decided then and there to marry Ned for their sake." She has even sent Ned a telegram, and the children immediately went over to their Aunt Sissy's to tell her the news.

CLAIRE: . . . . . Anyway, right or wrong, we won't be here when you come home.
HORACE: You won't?
CLAIRE: No. Because Ned wants us to live in his house in Galveston. So we'll move there after we're married. I don't know what will happen to his sister.
HORACE: Maybe she'll live on with you.
CLAIRE: Maybe so. Ned says she's sweet and easy to get along with and likes children as much as he does. If you're ever in Galveston, come to see us and have a meal with us.
HORACE: Thank you.
CLAIRE *(hands him paper):* I wrote out the address for you.
HORACE: Thank you.
CLAIRE: Ned says they have a lot of oleander in the front and back yard. I love them. Don't you?
HORACE: Yes. My father's people all lived in Galveston.
CLAIRE: Did they?
HORACE: Yes, his father was sent there by the Confederate government. He was in charge of shipping cotton for the Confederacy.

CLAIRE: If you're going to be a traveling man, you and Ned will have a lot in common.

HORACE: Well, I'm not sure, of course, that I'll be a traveling man. It's just that when I finish my business course, I hope to get a job traveling.

CLAIRE: Well, if you do, I hope you will have great success at it. Ned says it pays very well if you're good at it.

HORACE: I've heard that, too.

CLAIRE: And I'm sure you'll be good at it. You have a very nice personality.

HORACE: Thank you.

The Courthouse clock strikes eight.

I guess I'll have to go now, Claire.

CLAIRE: I know. I'd ask you to kiss me goodbye, but it's daylight, and all the neighbors are watching.

HORACE: I understand.

CLAIRE: It's been very nice knowing you and the children, and I wish you a lot of luck.

HORACE: Good luck to you, too. *(A pause.)* Claire, if I come into the house could I kiss you goodbye?

CLAIRE: Sure.

She goes inside. He follows her. He kisses her. A train whistle blows.

CLAIRE: There's your train. Hurry, or you'll miss it.

HORACE: So long, Claire.

CLAIRE: So long.

HORACE *(takes his suitcase):* Good luck.

CLAIRE: Good luck to you.

The train whistle blows again, He goes hurrying out. She follows to the porch. As he gets to the edge of the yard, she calls.

Good luck.

HORACE: Thank you. Good luck to you.

The train whistle blows again as he runs out of sight. She waves a last farewell, and if he sees her or not, we never know. Curtain.

WILD HONEY

A Comedy in Two Acts

BY MICHAEL FRAYN

FROM AN UNTITLED PLAY BY ANTON CHEKHOV

Cast and credits appear on pages 306-307

MICHAEL FRAYN was born August 9, 1925 in northwest London, the son of a sales representative. He attended Kingston Grammar School but left in 1952 and went into the Army, which assigned him to train for the job of interpreter studying Russian at Cambridge and in Moscow. He received a commission as an intelligence officer before his discharge in 1954, when he returned to Cambridge to study philosophy and—in 1957—to co-author a college-produced musical comedy, Zounds!.

Frayn worked for the Manchester Guardian *as reporter and satirical columnist until 1962, and for the London* Observer *until 1968, the year in which his first dramatic work,* Jamie on a Flying Visit, *was televised on the BBC. His London stage debut took place in 1970 at the Garrick Theater with* The Two of Us, *a program of four short works:* Black and Silver, The New Quixote, Mr. Foot *and* Chinamen. *There followed* The Sandboy *(1971 at the Greenwich Theater);* Alphabetical Order *(1975 in London and later in the U.S.A. at the Long Wharf Theater);* Donkeys' Years *(1976);* Clouds *(1976);* Balmoral *(1979), revised as* Liberty Hall *(1980); and* Make and Break *(1980). Frayn's first Best Play* Noises Off *had its premiere at the Lyric Theater, Hammersmith, February 11, 1982 and soon trans-*

ferred to the Savoy Theater in the heart of London, where it continued as a long-run hit while its American production was being staged on Broadway December 11, 1983 for 553 performances. His second Best Play Benefactors *opened at the Vaude- ville Theater in London April 4, 1984 and was presented on Broadway December 22, 1985 for 217 performances after having received multiple London best-play awards (Frayn's* Alphabetical Order, Donkeys' Years, Make and Break *and* Noises Off *were also best-play award winners in London). His third New York Best Play citation was won this season by* Wild Honey, *an adaptation of Anton Chek- hov's first, untitled playscript, which premiered at the National Theater in London July 19, 1974 and opened on Broadway December 18, 1986. Like too many other plays of exceptional quality, it failed to find an audience in New York and closed after a run of only 28 performances, having made its mark, however, as a Best Play of this 1986–87 season.*

Frayn's stage credits also include an adaptation of Jean Anouilh's Le Nombril, *retitled* Number One, *and translations of Tolstoy's* The Fruits of Enlightenment *and Chekhov's* The Cherry Orchard, *the latter two produced by the National Theater. His published works include collections of his newspaper writings, a volume of philosophy (*Constructions*) and the novels* The Tin Men, The Russian Interpreter *(for which he won the Hawthornden Prize),* Towards the End of the Morning, A Very Private Life *and* Sweet Dreams. *Among his numerous TV productions have been documentaries on Berlin, Vienna, Australia, Jerusalem and the London suburbs. Frayn is married, with three daughters, and lives near Black- heath in southeast London.*

Place: *The Voynitzev family estate in one of the southern provinces of Russia*

ACT I

Scene 1

SYNOPSIS: On the verandah of the Voynitzev country house overlooking a sunny garden, the sound of a skyrocket is heard, followed by the rocket's stick falling into the garden. It has just been launched by Yakov (a Voynitzev servant) and Dr. Triletzky, a Voynitzev family connection by marriage. Yakov is holding a box of rockets for a fireworks display, and, excitedly, Dr. Triletzky lights some of the other fuses.

Anna Petrovna—widow of the late Gen. Voynitzev and therefore chateleine of this establishment—enters and orders Yakov to take the box of rockets away, quickly, before they burn down the house. Yakov obeys; there is the sound of rockets offstage, and when Yakov returns it is with a blackened, empty box which he then removes as he exits.

Dr. Triletzky tells Anna Petrovna how delighted and excited everyone is that she has returned from the city and is now in residence. Porfiry Semyonovich Glagolyev enters, making frequent halts and leaning heavily on his stick, in the company of Sergey Voynitzev, the late general's son and Anna Petrovna's stepson, a co-proprietor of the estate. Old Glagolyev is pontificating to young Sergey on the subject of women.

GLAGOLYEV: . . . . . We had real respect for them, you see.
SERGEY: Like the knights of old.
GLAGOLYEV: We looked up to them.
SERGEY: You put them on a pedestal.
GLAGOLYEV: We put them on a pedestal.
DR. TRILETZKY: I think they've got on to the subject of women.
GLAGOLYEV: We loved women, certainly. But we loved them in the way that the knights of old loved them.
SERGEY: You had respect for them.
GLAGOLYEV: We had respect for them.
DR. TRILETZKY (to Anna Petrovna): Your stepson has become the most agreeable of men.
ANNA PETROVNA: Poor Sergey!
DR. TRILETZKY: He goes away an artist and poet. He comes back with his beard shaved off—and underneath he's not an artist and poet at all! He's a very agreeable young man like everybody else.
ANNA PETROVNA: He doesn't need an artistic nature now. He has a wife instead.
GLAGOLYEV (to Sergey): So you see, we poor old setting stars have the advantage of you young rising stars!
SERGEY: You knew the world when the world was young.

Dr. Triletzky thinks this gathering needs the schoolmaster Platonov to provide extra amusement, and he exists to send for him. Glagolyev greets Anna Petrovna and sits to recover his strength, as another old gentleman, Col. Triletsky (father of the Doctor and his sister Sasha, married to Platonov), comes in from the garden leaning on his stick. He greets all including his son, and he looks forward to the fireworks, a "21-gun salute" to Anna Petrovna's return.

Sergey brings his new bride Sofya in from the garden—she is enchanted with the estate which is now her home. Anna Petrovna introduces Sonya to the others: the Colonel, who offers to take her snipe shooting; the Doctor, who will watch over her health. But Platonov, "our local Socrates," is still missing, though sent for.

Marko, a process server, arrives with envelopes for all present (Sergey fears he might be in danger of losing the estate because of some debts incurred by his late father the General). The envelopes turn out to contain invitations to the christening of the Justice of the Peace's son.

Meanwhile, Marya Yefimova Grekova appears and stands there shyly. When the others notice and greet her she "takes one horrified look at them and flees back into the garden." Col. Triletzky comments, "Poor girl! Comes seven miles on a hot afternoon, and what happens? Gets her head blown off! Same thing every time she comes here. Walks in—head blown off." Sergey adds that "It's usually Platonov who does it."

The two old gentlemen, Glagolyev and the Colonel, move off after Grekova, and the servants depart. Dr. Triletzky and Anna Petrovna agree that they both like Grekova, the Doctor commenting, "Platonov thinks she's a fool. That's what the trouble was last summer. He's got it into that unkempt head of his that he has some kind of mission to rebuke fools." Anna preceives that the Doctor is a bit in love with Grekova.

"Misha" Platonov and his wife Sasha (the Colonel's daughter, the Doctor's sister) enter and exchange cordial greetings with the others, congratulating Sergey on his marriage.

PLATONOV: . . . . . Have you found a job?

SERGEY: I've been offered a job in a high school of sorts, and I don't know what to do. It's not what I should have chosen.

Ian McKellen as Platonov in *Wild Honey*

PLATONOV: You'll take it, though?

SERGEY: I really don't know. Probably not.

PLATONOV: So you'll be letting more time slip by. Three years now, isn't it, since you left university? You need someone to give you a bit of a kick. I must have a word with your wife. Three good years wasted! Isn't that right?

DR. TRILETZKY: He hasn't been in the house five minutes, and already he's flaying us all!

GLAGOLYEV: Well, it's rare enough these days—someone with clear moral standards.

COL. TRILETZKY: My own son-in-law—the village Savonarola!

ANNA PETROVNA *(to Platonov):* Yes, go on! How have we got through the winter without your moral refreshment?

PLATONOV: It's too hot today to be serious. And it's far too pleasant sitting here again to be indignant at the evils of the world . . . I can see Sasha positively sniffing the air.

SASHA: Yes, I was.

PLATONOV *(laughs):* You know what it smells of here? Human flesh! And what a delightful smell it is! I feel as if we hadn't seen each other for a hundred years. The winter went on and on forever! And there's my old armchair! Recognize it, Sasha? Six months ago I was never out of it. Sat there day and night talking to Anna Petrovna about the nature of the world, and losing all the housekeeping at cards.

ANNA PETROVNA: I've been so longing to see you again! I was quite out of patience . . . And you're well?

PLATONOV: Very well . . . But I must tell you one piece of news: you have grown just a shade more beautiful than before.

ANNA PETROVNA: And you've put on weight! Such lucky people! So how have things been?

PLATONOV: Terrible, as usual. Never saw the sky for the whole six months. Ate, drank, slept. And read schoolboy adventure stories aloud to my wife. Terrible!

ANNA PETROVNA *(to Sasha):* Was it?

SASHA: I thought it was lovely.

PLATONOV: Sasha, it was appalling!

SASHA: It was a little bit dull, naturally.

PLATONOV: It wasn't a little bit dull, my love—it was extremely dull. *(To Anna Petrovna.)* I was pining for you!

Col. Triletzky expresses his regrets that he hasn't found the time to visit his daughter Sasha and his grandson. Anna Petrovna goes off to see about the food, as Sofya brings Grekova in from the garden. Seeing Grekova, Platonov exclaims, "Oh, it's the beetle-juice girl!" This stops Grekova in her tracks, but Platonov goes to her and kisses her hand.

GREKOVA *(pulls her hand back):* I don't want my hand kissed. Thank you.

PLATONOV: I'm not worthy to kiss your hand, even?

GREKOVA: I've no idea whether you're worthy or not. I just know you don't mean it.

PLATONOV: Don't mean it? What makes you think that?

GREKOVA: You know I don't like it. That's the only reason you do it. It's always the same—you only like doing things that I don't like you doing.

DR. TRILETZKY: Leave her alone, Misha.

PLATONOV: All in good time. *(To Grekova.)* How are you progressing with your beetle-juice?

GREKOVA: Beetle-juice? What is this about beetle-juice?

PLATONOV: Someone told me you were trying to make ether out of crushed beetles. Pushing forward the boundaries of science. Admirable!

GREKOVA: You must always make a joke of everything, mustn't you.

DR. TRILETZKY: Always! Of everything!

PLATONOV: I make the Doctor my model.

SERGEY: Platonov . . .

PLATONOV: But what a charming pink your cheeks are! You're feeling the heat, I can see.

GREKOVA: Why do you keep saying these things to me?

PLATONOV: I'm merely trying to hold a conversation with you. I haven't talked to you for six months or more. Why are you getting so cross about it?

GREKOVA: The sight of me seems to have some strange effect on you. I don't know how I've managed to upset you so. I stay out of your way as far as I possibly can . . . . .

Grekova exits in tears, followed by the Doctor who goes to comfort her. Platonov admits he treated Grekova somewhat stupidly. Sofya, a onetime friend of Platonov's back in their student days, sees that Platonov has failed to recognize her and reproaches him. In those days, much had been expected in the future from the promising Platonov.

SOFYA: And in fact you're the local schoolmaster?

PLATONOV: Yes.

SOFYA: The local schoolmaster. I find that difficult to believe. Why haven't you . . . done better?

PLATONOV: Why haven't I done better?

SERGEY *(to Platonov):* Now *you're* being called to account!

COL. TRILETZKY: This makes a change!

PLATONOV: Why haven't I done better? What can I say?

SOFYA: You finished university, at any rate?

SERGEY: No, he gave it up.

COL. TRILETZKY: He knew it all. Nothing more they could teach him.

PLATONOV: I got married.

SOFYA: I see. Still, that doesn't stop you leading a decent life, does it?

PLATONOV: A decent life?

COL. TRILETZKY: The boot's on the other foot now, and no mistake!

SOFYA: Perhaps I shouldn't have put it like that. But giving up university doesn't stop you doing something worthwhile, does it? It doesn't stop you fighting for political freedom or the emancipation of women? It doesn't stop you serving a cause?

PLATONOV: Oh, dear. What can I say to that?

GLAGOLYEV: I think our Savonarola has met his match!

COL. TRILETZKY: Come on, Misha! Return her fire!

PLATONOV: No, she's right. There's nothing to stop me. The question is whether there was ever anything there to be stopped. I wasn't put into this world to do things; I was put here to prevent others from doing them.

Petrin appears in the garden.

To lie here like some great flat stone and trip them up. To make them stub their toes against me.

SOFYA: And shall you lie in the same place for the rest of your life?

Petrin, a merchant who owns 63 taverns, joins the party, muttering about bills and promissory notes, reminding the Voynitzevs that the late General left them in precarious financial condition. Platonov, aside, sneers at Petrin and comments, "They all bend the knee before this jumped-up nobody. And why? Because they're all up to their ears in debt to him!"

Platonov sees Osip, a peasant thief and jailbird, approaching. Called to the party by Platonov, Osip enters uneasily, concealing something in his shirt. Members of the group are outraged when Platonov makes it clear he considers the wealthy Petrin a more arrant thief than Osip—who takes a baby owl from beneath his shirt and presents it to Anna Petrovna. Ordered off by Sergey, Osip departs. "If he goes. I go!" declares Platonov, exiting in sympathy with Osip. Petrin tries to engage Anna Petrovna's attention, but she goes off after Platonov.

Petrin and Glagolyev put their heads together, scheming that Glagolyev is to marry Anna Petrovna and should get the matter settled before the old Colonel can compete for her hand. Glagolyev is "not averse to the idea," but there is a hitch.

GLAGOLYEV: But will *she* want to marry *me?* That could be the difficulty, you see.

PETRIN: Of course she will!

GLAGOLYEV: Will she? Which of us knows the secrets of another's heart?

PETRIN: Lovely woman—handsome man. You're made for each other! Shall I ask her for you?

GLAGOLYEV: I can do my own courting, thank you! What's it to do with you?

PETRIN: A man needs a wife, Porfiry Semyonovich! An estate needs a man! And debts need someone to pay them! I don't want to take her to court and force her to sell up! I'm a reasonable man, Porfiry Semyonovich! All I want is my money!

Anna Petrovna appears in the garden, her arm in Platonov's.

Here she is, Porfiry Semyonovich! Ask her now!

GLAGOLYEV *(hesitates):* I can't do it on an empty stomach. Lunch first!

PETRIN: Your happiness—that's all I want! Your happiness and my money.

Glagolyev and Petrin exit in the direction of lunch. Anna Petrovna and Platonov enter from the garden.

ANNA PETROVNA: But I *can't* get rid of them, you see. Nor can you, for all your eloquence. I depend upon them! It's like a very complicated position on a chess board. If I didn't make Porphiry Semyonovich just a little bit jealous of the

Colonel . . . if I didn't make the Colonel just a little bit jealous of the Doctor
. . . if I wasn't protected from the Doctor by poor little Grekova . . . if Petrin
didn't believe he'd get his money from Glagolyev . . . if you weren't here to lighten
my heart . . . why, then the queen would fall. I should lose the estate, Platonov!
I should lose everything. Then what would you do? Any of you? The lion must
roar—of course he must—but a little more softly, Platonov, or he'll roar the
whole house down. Yes? Now you wait here. I'm going to send Marya Yefimovna
out to you. I found *her* in tears, Platonov! So you're going to give her your paw
and apologize.

While Anna goes to fetch Grekova, Sergey wonders whether Platonov and
Sasha are happy. "We're the perfect couple," Platonov replies, "she's a fool and
I'm a rogue," and he would be nothing without her. When Grekova comes in,
Platonov apologizes to her profusely and tries to kiss her hand, in his somewhat
mocking fashion. She exits, again in tears.

Scene 2

In the garden (without the verandah), Sasha is taking some food to Osip, while
looking forward to the fireworks display as soon as it gets dark. As a far-off train
whistle and sound of a locomotive are heard, Osip tells Sasha how he once kissed
Anna Petrovna. He came upon her drinking water from a forest stream, and "felt
as if I'd been thrown into a furnace" when she granted him permission to kiss
her. He did so, on cheek and neck, and then she sent him away. From then on,
before and after she was widowed, Osip adored Anna Petrovna from afar, bringing her gifts from the forest, willing to do anything for her.

Sasha in her turn remembers that when she first fell in love with Platonov "I
went through terrible torments. Wandered around the forest like a lost soul."
Osip resents Platonov's dancing attendance on Anna Petrovna when he has Sasha
and so many others admiring him. Osip disappears into the forest as Sergey comes
in looking for Sofya and the Doctor wanders in and out, obviously drunk.

Platonov enters with Sofya, who is telling him that their schoolgirl-student love
affair was an "old and trite" story, meaningless in the present. Platonov would
prefer to believe that the flame is still burning. He is still rankling over her
greeting him with a question about why he hasn't made more of himself.

SOFYA: I'm sorry.
PLATONOV: No, you're right. Why haven't I? Teeming evil all around me,
fouling the earth, swallowing up my brothers in Christ, while I sit here with
folded hands. I shall be the same when I'm forty, the same when I'm fifty. I shan't
change now. Not until I decline into shuffling old age, and stupefied indifference
to everything outside my own body. A wasted life! Then death. And when I think
of that death, I'm terrified.
     Pause.
Why haven't I done better? I might ask the same of you. What's happened to that
pure heart you used to have? Where's the old sincerity, the truthfulness, the
boldness? You ask me why I haven't done better; do you ever ask your husband?

You've let the years go by in idleness. You watch others callous their hands and hearts on your behalf. And still you manage to meet their eye. That is depravity.
    Sofya gets to her feet. Platonov makes her sit down again.
One last word, and then I'll let you go. You were so splendid once! No, let me finish . . . You were good. You had greatness in you.
    He takes her hand.
What in all the wide world made you marry that man?
    SOFYA: Sergey? He's a fine man!
    PLATONOV: He's a moral pygmy!
    SOFYA: He's my husband!
    PLATONOV: He's bogged down in debt—he's helpless with doing nothing!
    SOFYA: Lower your voice, will you! There are people about!
    PLATONOV: I don't care! Let them all hear! *(Quietly.)* I'm sorry if I spoke sharply. I loved you, though. Loved you more than all the world. This hair. These hands. This face . . . And what can you do here? You'll only go deeper and deeper into the mire. Why do we never lead the life we have it in us to lead? If I had the strength I should uproot us from this mudhole—uproot us both! We'd leave! Tonight! Take the night train and never return!
    SOFYA: What are you saying?
    PLATONOV: You know what I'm saying.

Sofya runs off, followed by Platonov, as they are interrupted by the entrance of Petrin and Glagolyev, both slightly drunk, planning to pursue Anna Petrovna. Others come in and out, and when Sergey happens upon Sofya she begs him to come away with her, now, even before the fireworks, on the night train. Sergey thinks she is merely bored and suggests that she talk to Platonov for amusement.

Anna Petrovna and Platonov find themselves alone in the garden, and she takes this opportunity to tell him, "I'm more in love with you than ever." She suggests that they are great friends and should "take that one short step" to becoming lovers.

    PLATONOV: It's not worth it, I promise you, Anna Petrovna—it's simply not worth it.
    ANNA PETROVNA: Isn't it? Now you listen to me. Sit down . . . Sit down!
    He sits beside her.
Look, if you were free, I shouldn't think twice—I'd make myself your wife. I'd bestow my rank and station on you. But as it is . . .
    Pause.
Am I to take your silence as a sign of agreement?
    Pause.
I think in the circumstances it is a little ungentlemanly of you not to say *something*.
    PLATONOV *(jumps to his feet):* Let's forget this conversation! Let's pretend it never took place!
    ANNA PETROVNA: You are a clown, Misha.
    PLATONOV: I respect you! And I respect myself in the respect I have for you! I'm not against harmless diversion . . .

ANNA PETROVNA: I know, Platonov.

PLATONOV: But not with a beautiful, intelligent, untrammeled woman like you! What—a month or two of foolishness, and then go our ways in shame? I couldn't do it!

ANNA PETROVNA: I wasn't talking about foolishness, I was talking about love.

PLATONOV: And do you think I don't love you? I love you for your goodness, for your generous heart. I love you desperately—I love you to distraction! I'll lay down my life for you, if that's what you want! Does every love have to be reduced to the same common denominator? I love you as a woman, yes, but I also love you as a person. On top of which, my dear, I am just a tiny bit married.

As Platonov goes off, Glagolyev takes his place and, hearing the Colonel approaching, quickly asks Anna Petrovna to become "the angel in my paradise." She manages to get away, pursued by Glagolyev, before the entrance of Petrin and the Colonel, the latter so obviously drunk that his daughter Sasha persuades him to let her take him home. Sergey and the Doctor come in and out looking for Platonov, who enters with Sofya. Again he tells her to go away, "Otherwise I can't answer for the consequences." Sofya runs off when Grekova enters.

PLATONOV: Beetle-juice! Come here, you lovely creature!

GREKOVA: What?

     She crosses to him nervously.

PLATONOV: You weird and wonderful woman!

     He kisses her.

GREKOVA: Why are you kissing me?

PLATONOV: I've got to kiss someone!

GREKOVA: Do you . . . do you love me, then?

PLATONOV: Why, do you love me, you foolish headstrong woman?

GREKOVA: I don't know. That depends on whether you . . .

     He kisses her.

You shouldn't do that if you don't.

     He kisses her.

Do you love me?

PLATONOV: Not at all, my precious! That's why I'm kissing you!

This puts Grekova in tears, but Sergey and the Doctor prevent her from running off, and the three exit to light the fireworks. Anna Petrovna comes to join Platonov, followed by Glagolyev, who continues to woo her, promising to "renounce the usual rights of a husband" if she will marry him. She ignores his suit, and they all go to watch the fireworks, as Sofya enters.

SOFYA *(to herself):* Is it ruin, or is it happiness? Is it the beginning of a new life, or is it the end of everything?

     Enter Col. Triletzky.

COL. TRILETSKY: It's the fireworks!

     Col. Triltzky and Sofya exit after the others. Osip enters from under the trees.

SERGEY: *(off)*: Look out, everyone! We're starting!
> *Osip whips out a long-bladed hunting knife; and at the same moment there is the whoosh of a rocket taking off. Osip stands gazing upwards, knife raised, as the colored stars burst in the sky. There is a collective sigh of satisfaction from the spectators, off. The stars fade. Osip brings the knife down into the back of one of the garden chairs. Curtain.*

ACT II

Scene 1

In a forest clearing with the schoolhouse at right and a railroad crossing downstage, the clanking sound of a train is heard. Platonov steps through the smoke left by the locomotive as the red tail light of the train can be seen disappearing. Sasha, in her nightgown, joins him on the steps of the schoolhouse. Platonov wants to be assured that she loves him—if only because he's her husband—but reacts to her assurances sardonically: "Where should we be if you understood me, if you realized how little there was to love in me?"

Platonov reports on the events of the evening after Sasha left—he fled from the fireworks party after having told Sofya she had married a moral pygmy; Glagolyev had a heart attack in the summer house and was treated by the Doctor. Platonov continues to address Sasha as though she were a "silly little noodle," and, irritated, she goes back into the house.

Anna Petrovna now emerges from the forest shadows in this brightly moonlit night. She has come to find out why Platonov left the party so abruptly, and to resolve whatever is between them, "to finish the thing one way or another."

PLATONOV: Finish it? We haven't started it!

ANNA PETROVNA: How can you say that? How can you lie to me, on such a night as this, beneath such a sky? Tell your lies in the autumn, if you must, in the gloom and the mud, but not now, not here. You're being watched! Look up, you absurd man! A thousand eyes, all shining with indignation! You must be good and true, just as all this is good and true. Don't break this silence with your little words!
> *She takes his hands, and they sit down on the timbers of the crossing, facing each other.*

There's no man in the world I could ever love as I love you. There's no woman in the world you could ever love as you love me. Let's take that love; and all the rest, that so torments you—we'll leave that to others to worry about.

PLATONOV *(kisses her hands)*: Odysseus was worth the sirens' song, but I'm no Odysseus, you lovely siren of the forest. If only I could give you happiness! But I can't, and I shan't. I shall do what I've done to every woman who has thrown herself at me; I shall make you unhappy!

ANNA PETROVNA: Are you really such a terrible Don Juan? You look so handsome in the moonlight!

PLATONOV: I know myself! The only stories that end happily are the ones that don't have me in them.

ANNA PETROVNA: Such a solemn face! It's a woman who's come to call, not a wild animal! All right—if you really hate it all so much I'll go away again. Is that what you want? I'll go away, and everything will be just as it was before. Yes . . . ? *(She laughs.)* Idiot! Take it! Snatch it! Seize it! What more do you want? Smoke it to the end, like a cigarette—pinch it out—tread it under your heel. Be human! . . . . .

They have both forgotten Sasha, who calls sleepily from inside the house. They will meet at the old summerhouse; meanwhile, Platonov goes in to get Sasha to go to sleep. Osip comes onto the scene, and Anna Petrovna, perceiving that he is still carrying the torch for her and is murderously jealous of Platonov, extracts Osip's promise never to hurt the schoolmaster.

Osip goes off. Dr. Triletzky enters, drunker than before, seeking to spend the night with his sister Sasha and Platonov. While Anna Petrovna remains hidden in the shadows, Platonov persuades the Doctor that his duty lies in treating the village storekeeper, who is ill. The Doctor finally leaves, "To save a human life," as Platonov puts it while castigating himself for having no such high purpose in *his* life.

A shot is heard. Thinking it's Osip come to revenge himself on Platonov, Anna Petrovna pulls the schoolteacher into hiding—but it's only Sergey and the Colonel, drunk, and come to fire a 21-gun salute outside Platonov's window. Platonov comes forth and begs them not to awaken Sasha. Sergey and the Colonel decide to go and fire their salute under Anna Petrovna's window instead, and, after placing their guns against each other's lips as a signal to maintain silence, they depart into the forest.

Sasha calls from the house. Platonov goes in to quiet her down again. Meanwhile, the Doctor enters supporting an equally drunken Petrin, muttering that Glagolyev meant to propose marriage to Anna Petrovna but had a heart attack instead. Dr. Triletzky points Petrin down the railroad track and instructs him to follow it home, which Petrin proceeds to do. Platonov joins the Doctor and manages to induce him once again to go off to attend to the sick storekeeper.

Now Sasha comes out, sees Anna Petrovna and assumes from her clothing that she is going for a drive, decides that she and Platonov should go too and exits into the house to get dressed. Exasperated at all the interruptions, Anna Petrovna leaves after telling Platonov, "I shall be in the old summerhouse. If you want to see me you must come to me there."

Sasha reappears, dressed, but by this time the Doctor has wandered back and Platonov tells Sasha to put him to bed in the house. As Platonov stumbles over Petrin (who hasn't gotten very far either and is mumbling his resolve, now that he's overheard all, to sue Anna Petrovna for his money), Sofya appears, begging to be "uprooted" and carried off as Platonov promised. Platonov sends her off, promising to meet her in the *new* summerhouse. He hasn't made up his mind which of the women to follow, when Sasha comes back outside. He starts off in the direction taken by Anna Petrovna, meets Osip coming from that way and turns and exits in the direction taken by Sofya.

SASHA: Osip! What's happening? I don't understand . . . Osip, what are you doing?

Osip lies down across the level crossing. The headlight of the approaching train grows slowly bigger.

You can't lie there! Osip, get up! The train's coming!

OSIP *(sobs):* He's gone to her! Gone to Anna Petrovna! And she loves him! She loves him!

SASHA: You're lying.

OSIP: God strike me down—I heard every word!

SASHA: He's left me, then! He's left me! Kill me, Lord! Mother of God, kill me! *The whistle of the approaching train. Sasha runs toward it with outstretched arms. Osip jumps up and runs after her.*

OSIP: No! No!

They stumble over Petrin, who sits up. They stop and turn round to gaze at him in astonishment.

PETRIN: Yes! Yes! You'll see! Tomorrow!

Sasha and Osip drag Petrin clear of the track as the headlight widens, and the roar of the approaching train and the scream of the whistle rise to a crescendo. The locomotive emerges from the darkness and comes toward us just as the curtain falls. The roar of the train and the scream of the whistle continue through the auditorium in the darkness until the lights come up.

Scene 2

In the combined schoolroom and living room of Platonov's house, with forest and railroad tracks outside, Sofya enters and wakes Platonov. He is sleeping on the sofa, though it's only 6:30 in the evening. She's angry because he is already half an hour late for a rendezvous. She demands that Platonov do some hard thinking about the possible consequences of this affair of theirs, which is now three weeks old.

PLATONOV: . . . . . I've ruined you, and that's all there is to say about it! And you're not the only one! Wait until your husband finds out!

SOFYA: You're afraid he's going to kill you?

PLATONOV: No. I'm afraid it's going to kill him.

SOFYA: He already knows!

PLATONOV: What?

SOFYA: Yes! I told him this afternoon.

PLATONOV: You're not serious!

SOFYA: Look at you. You're as white as a sheet. I don't know why I should love you. I must be mad!

PLATONOV: How did he take it?

SOFYA: Just like you. He was afraid. His skin went grey. He started to cry. Then he crumpled up. He went down and crawled on all fours . . . And he had just the same repellent look on his face as you have now.

PLATONOV: You've killed him! Do you realize that? How could you sit there and tell me it all so calmly? You've killed him! Did you . . . did you say it was me?

SOFYA: Of course. What else could I have done?

PLATONOV: How could you say the words?

SOFYA: Platonov! Have some shame! You mean I shouldn't have told him?

PLATONOV: Of course you shouldn't have told him! You shouldn't have told him anything! *(He sinks to his knees and puts his head down on the sofa.)* Cried! Crawled on all fours! Oh, that poor wretched man! If you hadn't told him he'd have gone to his grave without ever finding out!

SOFYA: I had to tell him! I do have a little self-respect!

PLATONOV: You know what you've done, don't you? You've parted forever.

SOFYA: Forever, yes. What alternative did I have?

PLATONOV: But what's going to happen to you when *we* part? Because part we very soon shall! You'll be the first to shake off the spell. You'll be the first to open your eyes. And then you'll leave me! *(He flaps his hand.)* Well, you do whatever you think best. You're a better person than I am. You've got a cleverer head on your shoulders. You take the whole mess over! Just tell me what to do! Get me up on my feet again, if you have the power. And do it now, for the love of God, before I go out of my mind!

SOFYA: We'll leave tonight.

PLATONOV: The sooner the better.

They must get ready to leave and meet at "the usual place" (Sofya tells Platonov) at 8:15, then catch the evening train. Platonov pledges his word of honor that he'll be there, and Sofya goes off. Platonov opens the cupboard looking for things he'll need on the journey but is distracted by bottles of liquor. He pours himself a drink, lies down on the sofa and shuffles a bunch of unopened letters from Anna Petrovna.

A knock on the door precedes the entry of Marko delivering an envelope—this time it's a real summons to appear before the Justice of the Peace to answer a charge of indecent assault, per a complaint by Grekova. Platonov asks Marko to pass the word to Grekova that he can't answer the summons, he's going away, but admittedly "I behaved like a swine, but then I've behaved like a swine with everybody." He offers Marko three rubles if he will report this to Grekova. Marko leaves on this errand.

Platonov is trying to hide the Anna Petrovna letters, when another sharp knock on the door heralds the arrival of Osip, who has come to say goodbye to Platonov and then send him to hell. Osip draws his knife menacingly, stating, "I've watched you these past weeks . . . . . Slipping off into the forest at all hours of the day and night . . . Well, that's no business of mine, who the General's widow meets on her rides through the forest. But I saw something else tonight. I saw the young mistress come running down here. And I waited. And I saw her go running back again. So then I went and fetched my knife. Because I reckon you're making a fool of the General's widow, and I'm not having that."

Sasha enters as Osip moves to stab Platonov. She tries to protect her husband, and Osip, unable to kill him in front of her, throws down his knife and exits. Sasha learns that Platonov is unharmed, apart from a twisted arm, then tells him that their little son Vova (who is staying with Sasha at her father the Colonel's) is quite sick. She is very worried. Platonov comforts her and promises to make a man of their boy.

PLATONOV: . . . . . I haven't been much of a man myself, I know, but as a father I shall be mighty! . . . . . Don't cry, love! *(He pulls her head down on to his chest.)* You're home again. Why did you ever leave? I love you, lass! I love you deeply! My sins are black, I know, but what can we do? You'll just have to forgive me, won't you?

SASHA: Is the affair over, then?

PLATONOV: The affair . . . What a word to choose!

SASHA: Or isn't it over?

PLATONOV: What can I say? There never was an affair. It's just some kind of absurd nonsense. You should never have let yourself be upset by it. And if it's not over yet then it soon will be!

SASHA: When?

PLATONOV: Sooner rather than later, I should imagine. Sofya isn't the one for me. The ferment hasn't quite died down in her yet, but, believe me, Sofya won't be your rival for long . . . Sasha, what's the matter?

SASHA: Sofya? It's *Sofya* that you're having an affair with?

PLATONOV: You didn't know?

SASHA: Sofya? But that's terrible!

PLATONOV: Sasha, don't torment me any more! I'm in agony with my arm as it is! Why did you leave me, then? You mean, it wasn't because of Sofya?

SASHA: I thought it was Anna Petrovna! That was bad enough! But another man's wife! That's vile, Misha, that's wicked! . . . . .

Platonov admits to being Sofya's actual and Anna Petrovna's potential lover but begs Sasha to stay and take care of him, as a nurse if not as a wife. Sasha, sobbing because she can't live either with him or without him, goes off, bound back to her father's.

Anna Petrovna appears and wonders why Platonov didn't respond to her letters (which Platonov is trying to stuff back into the cupboard). Anna Petrovna sees that Platonov has been drinking and decides to join him, commenting, "We'll have to get your wife back . . . . . It was no part of my plans to get you divorced." She pours, and they drink, while she tells him that Glagolyev is going to buy the estate and settle all debts, so that she can give Platonov enough money to go to Moscow or St. Petersburg and pull himself together, begin a new life—and she will join him after the estate is settled. They drink again and again, as he explains that he is going away, but not with her, and means to "disappear off the face of the earth."

ANNA PETROVNA *(pours):* Drink, my love. Drink and to hell with it!

PLATONOV *(drinks):* Be happy! Just go on quietly living here, and never mind about me.

ANNA PETROVNA: If we're going to drink, let's drink. *(She pours.)* You die if you drink. But then you die if you don't drink. *(She drinks.)* I'm one too, Platonov. I'm a drinker . . . Another glass? No, I mustn't, or the words will go. Then what shall I have left? Oh, Misha, it's terrible to be an educated woman. An educated woman with nothing to do. What am I here for? Why am I alive? *(She laughs.)* They should make me a professor somewhere, or a director of

J. Smith-Cameron (Grekova) and Ian McKellen (Platonov) in a scene from *Wild Honey*

something . . . If I were a diplomat I'd turn the whole world upside down
. . . An educated woman . . . And nothing to do.

PLATONOV: We're both in a sorry case.

ANNA PETROVNA: Won't you stay? You do . . . love me, don't you? You funny
man. Don't you?

PLATONOV: How could any mortal man not love you?

ANNA PETROVNA: You love me—I love you; what more do you want . . . ? Why
didn't you come to me that night . . . ? That wild night . . . Such a strange month
it's been. Their honeymoon month. A sort of honeymoon for all of us. A month
of wild honey.

PLATONOV: Please go now. If you stay I shall tell you everything, and if I tell you I shall kill myself . . . . .

Platonov bids her a mournful farewell, and she goes off in an attempt to catch Glagolyev at the station and get some money from him, still determined to carry out her plan to go to the city with Platonov. Alone, the latter muses that they might have enjoyed some weeks in Moscow—perhaps he could put Sofya off for a bit. His thoughts are interrupted by the arrival of Sergey, in despair because Platonov's affair with Sofya has robbed him of his only happiness. He is armed with a revolver but so upset he's unable to use it. Weeping, Sergey throws the weapon onto the table, as Glagolyev enters and begs Platonov to take pity on him and tell him whether or not he knows of any reason why Anna Petrovna should be unworthy to become his wife. Platonov simply picks up the revolver and walks out on the two of them. Glagolyev assumes that Sergey's tears are in response to his question about Anna Petrovna, so that when she suddenly appears he speaks to her harshly and goes off, bound for Paris, abandoning her and the estate to their fate.

"We're finished!" Anna Petrovna declares to Sergey, who replies that he doesn't care about losing the estate now that he has lost his precious wife Sofya to her lover. Anna Petrovna is at first skeptical but finally thunderstruck as it dawns on her that this imagined lover is her own would-be lover, the very real and apparently promiscuous Platonov. She keeps her head, though, and assures Sergey that Platonov doesn't love Sofya, he has merely seduced her. "Nonsense!" she cries when Sergey tells her that Platonov and Sofya are leaving together this very evening—and at this moment Sofya comes in, bags packed, ready to go.

SERGEY: I'm going to shoot myself.
SOFYA (quietly): Where is he?
SERGEY: Where's my revolver?
ANNA PETROVNA: What could he begin to see in a little ninny like you? I'm sorry, but that's what you are—an insipid little ninny!
SOFYA: Where is he?
ANNA PETROVNA: And now you've lost him again!
SERGEY: I've lost my revolver.
ANNA PETROVNA: Your revolver?
SERGEY: I put it on the table.
ANNA PETROVNA: Your estate—your wife—your revolver . . . ! Can't you keep your hands on anything?
SERGEY: He must have picked it up, and . . .
SOFYA (urgently): Where is he?
    A shot, off.
ANNA PETROVNA (to Sergey): You've killed him.

But they find that such is not the case, as Platinov enters, puts the revolver back on the table and explains that the peasants have shot and killed Osip, who made no effort to run away but was sitting staring at the schoolhouse. Platonov had considered shooting himself with the revolver but finally opted for life over death.

It is their forgiveness he wants and expects, not their reproaches. He lies down on the sofa but is soon roused by the arrival of the Colonel, anguished because his daughter Sasha has tried to poison herself by swallowing matches (she'll be all right, her brother the Doctor is taking care of her). The Colonel begs Platonov to go comfort Sasha, but Platonov pleads that he is too drunk and too ill. The women and Sergey go off to Sasha's bedside, soon followed by the Colonel when he finds he can do nothing with Platonov.

Grekova comes in and manages to get the revolver away from a now half-delerious Platonov, who is about to shoot it at some imagined flies he has been trying to brush away with his hand. Grekova offers to nurse Platonov. He kisses her, declaring that he loves her, that he loves everyone.

PLATONOV: . . . . . There are so many of you! And I'm in love with you all! I love everyone—and everyone loves me. I insult them, I treat them abominably—and they love me just the same!
He puts his arm round her.
Take that Beetle-juice girl, for example. I indecently assaulted her—I kissed her . . .
He kisses her.
. . . and she's still in love with me . . . Oh you are Beetle-juice, aren't you. Sorry.
GREKOVA: You're all muddled up inside that head of yours.
She embraces him. He flinches.
You're in pain, too. Tell me where it hurts.
PLATONOV: In Platonov—that's where it hurts . . . *Are* you in love with me, then? Are you really?
GREKOVA: Yes.
She kisses him.
I am in love with you.
PLATONOV: Yes, they're all in love with me. Once I used to moralize away to them all, and they loved me for it. Now I seduce them instead, and they still love me.
GREKOVA: You do what you like with me. I don't mind. *(She weeps.)* You're only human, after all. And that's enough for me.

Sasha enters, preceded by Dr. Triletzky who is supported by Anna Petrovna and Sofya, followed by Sergey and Col. Triletzky. They surprise Platonov hugging Grekova, his face buried in her neck so that he doesn't see them; thus their expected happy ending turns into a nightmare. Sofya points the revolver at Platonov, but Anna Petrovna tries to take it from her, offering to do the deed herself. When Grekova declares their love, Sasha sinks to her knees and asks to be shot instead of Platonov. In the midst of this pandemonium, Marko enters, his errand discharged, seeking his fee of three rubles. Platonov uses this distraction to make good his escape, jumping out of the window. The sound of a train approaching is heard as the others follow him outdoors.

. . . . . *The world falls apart. Amidst the gathering roar of the train the rear wall of the house moves aside and the lights go down. The forest and the railway line of the previous scene are revealed beyond, with everyone going away upstage, searching and calling Platonov's name. Platonov emerges from the shadows behind their backs. He steps onto the railway line and runs in the opposite direction—downstage—glancing back over his shoulder at them like a fugitive. Then he stops, blinded by the brilliant headlight of the train approaching from behind the heads of the audience, its whistle screaming. He staggers back a step or two, trying to wave the train away like the flies. Then sudden blackness and the great roar of the train, its note falling as it passes us. The red tail light of the train appears at the front of the stage and dwindles rapidly into the smoke left by the locomotive. There is a smell of sulphur in the air. Curtain.*

KVETCH

A Play in Two Acts

BY STEVEN BERKOFF

Cast and credits appear on page 353

STEVEN BERKOFF, a theatrical triple-threat actor, writer and director, was born in London August 3, 1937. After attending the Raines Foundation in Stepney and the Hackney Downs Grammar School, he trained for the stage in acting and mime at the Ecole Jacques Le Coq in Paris and the Webber-Douglas Academy in London. His first professional appearance onstage took place in 1959, beginning almost a decade of appearances in British repertory companies, after which he formed his own London Theater Group with a base at the Round House Theater. They produced his first playscript, an adaptation of Kafka's The Penal Colony *in 1968. There followed his adaptations of* Metamorphosis *(1969),* The Trial *(1971),* Knock at the Manor Gate *(1972),* Miss Julie, The Zoo Story *and* Agamemnon *(1973) and* Fall of the House of Usher *(1974).*

Berkoff's first original plays were the trilogy East *(first produced in 1975 at the Edinburgh Festival),* West *and* Greek. East *was also produced in the West End, as was his later play* Decadence, *which was one of his Los Angeles productions (others were* Metamorphosis *and* Greek, *winning a Los Angeles Critics Award for his direction). His New York writing debut took place in June 1983 with 6 performances of* Greek *off Broadway. His* Kvetch *was also short-lived in its off-Broadway premiere February 18, 1987 for 31 performances (after its world premiere at the Odyssey Theater, Los Angeles, March 15, 1986), but it will be long remembered as its versatile author's first Best Play.*

Berkoff's many other accomplishments have included a collection of short stories, Gross Intrusion; *playing the title role in his own production of* Hamlet *at the Edinburgh Festival and on tour; and numerous screen roles including those in* Rambo *and* Beverly Hills Cop. *He continues to make his home in London.*

ACT I

Scene 1

SYNOPSIS: The various locations in which the action takes place are symbolized with an all-purpose setting consisting of a backdrop with Los Angeles freeways, *"a surreal multi-laned jam of cars"* on about 20 lanes, converging in the distance, with blue sky above. Downstage are a table and four chairs. The dialogue consists of words spoken aloud and thoughts (expressed in *italics* in the quotes from the script below) that the audience can "hear."

In Frank's home, Frank's wife Donna is worrying that she won't have timed the dinner correctly—she'll either have overcooked it or be keeping her husband waiting when he gets home from work. Meanwhile, Frank is having a couple of beers in a bar with his friend Hal and, impulsively, asks Hal to come home with him for dinner. Hal is divorced, lives alone and—socially shy but reluctant to return to his lonely apartment—accepts with some trepidation the invitation which now, on second thought, Frank wishes he hadn't offered.

During the dinner—which is somewhat overcooked because the men were late in arriving and skimpy because the notice of a guest was so short—Frank's aged mother-in-law criticizes Donna's household management while Hal worries about how he is presenting himself to the others. Frank is disgusted by his mother-in-law's recurring digestive problems. Donna worries that she has presented a bad dinner. In their thoughts, secret from each other but not from the audience, Hal envies Frank and Donna's companionship, while Frank wants to relieve the somewhat awkward social situation by telling a joke but fears he will forget the tag line and make a fool of himself. The mother-in-law believes that she is coldly treated, filed away in a tiny apartment and relieved from the confinement of its four walls only once a week to come to dinner here.

The open conversation of all of them is awkward, inconsequential and halting, but fires burn within: Donna is sick and tired of Frank's continuous complaints and wishes she had the courage to leave him. She even thinks she might get along better with Hal. Hal embarrasses Frank by telling the others what Frank's nickname at work is: "The Kvetch," a Yiddish word meaning "anxiety." Desperately, Frank searches his memory for a joke he can tell to change the subject. Hal is beginning to become more confident in conversation. Donna now has acquired some confidence that the dinner is going well. Hal plans in his mind a return dinner party at his apartment. Frank bulls ahead with his joke.

FRANK: So there was an Englishman, an Irishman and a Jew . . . *Ah, they're smiling . . . like I hope we'll enjoy ourselves . . .* And they meet in a bar . . .
DONNA: You know Jews don't go to bars.
FRANK: I have never been to a bar? Eh! You have never seen me in a bar?
DONNA: Yeah, but you're not a real Jew . . .
FRANK: What?
DONNA: No, no, I mean, not like these Jews . . . er . . . real ones like . . . *Oh, shit, why does he embarrass me? . . . He knows what I mean . . . he knows I mean the Jews like his father who wear a hat in the house and dandruff over their coats*

and smell of onions, yellow flaccid ones with round backs and beards . . . You
know, like Orthodox . . .

FRANK: Listen to her, Hal . . . like a Jew can't be seen in a bar . . . What do
you think, they can't mix a bit? You think all Gentiles are uncircumcised anti-
Semitic yid-kicking bastards . . . where the kitchen stinks of grease and they never
wash their hands after going to the toilet? . . . What, you carry that old legend
that the goy just drink till they vomit, and at weddings you're lucky to get a
hamburger and a can of beer? . . . No . . . you're wrong . . . some of my best friends

Laura Esterman as Donna, Ruth Jaroslow as Mother-in-Law and Kurt Fuller
as Frank in *Kvetch*

are goyim . . . very decent people . . . 'cause they don't shtipp lox down their guts on Sunday until it comes out of their ears and have stomach ulcers it down't mean they're bad . . . so I'll carry on . . . *I've found my voice again . . . Hal is quiet with a new-found respect for my acid humor, and the party is not so bad . . . Wonderful, I've got the floor and no kvetch . . . I'll tell the joke . . . this is wonderful* . . . So they were in a bar and the Englishman says drunkenly . . . "I've been mistaken for some very important people in my time . . . You know, once I was taken for Winston Churchill" . . . and then the Irishman says . . . "Oh, that's not such a big deal, you know, once I was walking down Dublin High Street and a woman come up to me, 'Holy Father, if it's not the Pope himself' " . . . and the Jew says . . . "That's nothing . . . well, I was sitting in a movie house and the picture was so wonderful I thought why not see it again . . ."

DONNA: Hahahahahahahahahahaha!

FRANK: Wait a minute . . . I ain't finished yet . . .

MOTHER-IN-LAW: Here's the coffee . . .

DONNA: Shush, Ma . . . he's telling a joke . . . just a minute . . . he's nearly finished.

HAL: Come on, Frank . . . go on . . . "Vy not," he says . . . vy not indeed . . . haw haw haw haw haw haw haw haw!

FRANK: So he's sitting in the movie house and thinks, "So vy not see it again" . . . *Gosh, this is going really well . . . I'm excited . . . Hey, I can easily hold them there in the palm of my hand . . . I knew I could do it, so why do I hold back, why lack confidence when I'm such a marvellous story-teller? . . . I have the power . . . I know I do . . . but I always let the others do it . . . let them be funny . . . take the stage . . . impress the ladies and I go quiet and choke and then I open my mouth with a prepared speech and it sounds like death 'cause it didn't come out when it went in my head . . . I let it spoil and then when I let it out it stinks like a day-old herring you forgot to put back in the fridge . . . Oh, God, the joke's a prepared speech so what am I talking about? Yeah, but it's different, you got to use timing. Now timing's the gold of the comic . . . without timing, a shitty story will come across like a shitty story. But with timing a shitty story will sound like poetry . . . no, not poetry . . . but like amazing . . . like brilliant . . . A golden observation . . . but a brilliant observation will sound like drek in the mouth of a shmock! You know . . . don't laugh, but maybe I could do cabaret . . . Yeah, get up on volunteer night in the bar down the street . . . "Hey, ladies and gentlemen, what's a Jewish-American princess's favorite wine?" . . . Gentiles love Jewish jokes . . . I could get up and tell a lot of anti-Semitic jokes and I could get away with it . . . Oh, I know a beauty . . . I'll save it for after this . . .* Yeah, vy not indeed . . . so he sees the film again, he likes it so much that he stays for the last show . . . *Why are they yawning? . . . No, it's not going down too well . . . it's terrible . . . I promise God I won't tell anti-Semitic jokes . . . Just let me get to the end . . . please . . . I wish I never started . . . Why do I want to be funny and tell jokes? . . . I hate telling jokes . . . I hate it . . . I can't tell jokes . . . I'll never be able to tell them . . . I've never told them so why did I insist? . . . I loathe it . . . I'm going hot and cold . . . why on earth do I give myself this torture? . . .*

HAL: So vat happened? . . . *I wish I could tell jokes . . . He's so easy and relaxed in front of his wife . . . maybe I can think of one . . . now let me see . . .*

DONNA: *I wonder how much time he really spends in bars . . . Does he find shiksas in there . . . maybe, they're so easy. They drop their panties at any excuse, loose dirty sluts . . .*

FRANK: Yeah, so the Jew stays for the last show and the usherette says . . .

DONNA: *A real shiksa usherette with a short skirt and she probably made a date with him in the bar . . .*

FRANK: So the usherette says to the Jew after seeing him in there for the third showing . . . she says . . . "Jesus Christ! You here again." . . . hahahaha—

MOTHER-IN-LAW: Yours is with the milk . . .

FRANK: Ma! Later! You see, she thought he was Jesus Christ!

MOTHER-IN-LAW: You have half a sugar . . .

FRANK: Ma! Not now! No, not really, though for the sake of the joke he pretends to believe that she thought he was Jesus Christ.

MOTHER-IN-LAW: . . . and yours is black . . .

FRANK: Ma!!! Later!!! . . . Or that he thought that she thought that she thought he was . . . 'cause he was there three times for the three movies . . .

HAL: I think we have the wrong coffee.
        Exchanges his cup with Frank's.

FRANK: . . . so she said . . . hawhawhaw . . . "J.C., you here again!!" No! Of course she didn't think he was . . . it was an expression . . .
        Pause.

DONNA, HAL, MOTHER-IN-LAW: Ooooooohhh. Hahahahahahahahahahahaha.

HAL: *I don't get it . . . I wasn't paying attention . . . I was thinking of a joke to tell and I missed the tag line . . . And now he thinks I'm not too bright . . . Can he see the blank stare in my eyes? . . . I have to fake it . . .* Hawhawhawhawhawhaw! . . .

FRANK: *I fucked it up . . . My mind went in the middle . . . I was going well and my mind went . . . I didn't make it clear . . . and then she came in with her fucking coffee fucking milk her fucking sugar, fuck you!!! . . . Oh, God . . . my stomach aches . . . my voice is going . . . (Cough, cough.)*

HAL: Haw haw! that's good . . . *My laugh is unconvincing . . . He knows I didn't get it . . . He's looking at me like I'm a killjoy, one that spoils the party. I'm not free any more . . . I was having a good time . . . He's staring at me like he'll never have me round again . . .* Good, Frank!

FRANK: *He's looking at me like I'm crazy . . . He's thinking I'm crazy . . . I'm sweating . . . He's staring at my sweat and wondering about it . . . They're all staring at my sweat. I'll slowly take a handkerchief out and mop it casually . . .*

HAL: *He's staring at me waiting for me to do something . . . tell a joke or what I do with myself . . . I'm stuck . . . I'm stuck in life . . . I can't move or open my mouth . . . my jaw feels clamped . . .* Hahahahahahahahaha . . .

Donna throws Hal into stammering confusion by asking him what he does with his nights. *Blackout.*

Scene 2

DONNA: Hold me, Frank . . . don't just sleep . . . kiss me goodnight . . . don't just lie there like a lump . . . I might as well be alone . . .

FRANK: Hmmmf . . . hummmf . . . g'nigh' . . .

DONNA: Frank . . . kiss me goodnight . . . come on, turn over . . .

FRANK: Tirrrrreeed.

DONNA: Then just kiss me and say goodnight, darling . . .

FRANK: G'nigh', daarrrrling . . .

DONNA: Look at me and say it . . . turn your head . . .

FRANK: *Oh, for fuck's sake . . . I just want to bury myself in sleep . . . I just want to drag sleep over me like a sack and die in it until the morning . . . It was a terrible night but at least I did it . . . Now sleep . . . that's what I need, but she keeps asking to be kissed . . . "Kiss me . . . kiss me . . . kiss me" . . . It's like a goldfish coming at you every time you stand still . . . It's kiss kiss like I was giving resuscitation . . . What is it about the kisses? . . . It's enough already . . . The mouth keeps coming at me followed by the face . . . Sure I love her but tell you the truth I can't shtipp it in any more . . . Sometimes I roll over . . . you know, I've got to make a gesture and stick it in . . . I think of the shiksa in the bar . . . I see her with those tits ripe to plop out like melons . . . so I roll over but it's difficult . . . but I've got a card index to help out . . . the chick in the bus who kept crossing her legs . . . the one who eyed me walking down the street with the kids . . . the girl who smiled at me on the beach all those years ago . . . What might have happened if I made a move always fascinated me . . . so I go through it as I roll over . . . Her legs on the beach . . . long . . . long beautiful legs . . .*

   Frank kisses Donna perfunctorily and climbs aboard.

There . . . there . . . ouch . . . ow! what are you wearing? . . . ouch! . . .

DONNA: Ouch . . . ow! . . . here let me do it . . . there . . . *I want to be raped . . . Sometimes I want the garbagemen to throw me on the bed in the morning after the lump has gone to work and just use me . . . the three of them . . . and I know they've been eyeing me . . . They empty the garbage cans and I'm still in my nightdress . . . I know they're horny for me . . . They smile and talk after they've gone about the dirty things they'd like to do to me . . . . .*

Donna achieves satisfaction by dwelling on her fantasy of the garbage men while Frank is making love to her. Frank thinks he is causing her excitement, but his own is at first interrupted and then enhanced by an intruding fantasy of Hal.

ACT II

Scene 1

Frank, in the process of trying to sell gabardine to a potential buyer, George, lets his mind catalogue his fears: "*I'm afraid . . . I'm afraid of my rates going up . . . I'm afraid to go to the door and look at the bills . . . I'm afraid of brown envelopes . . . I'm afraid of not having enough money . . . . . I'm afraid to look at the tax demand . . . I'm afraid I'll never make enough.*"

George tells Frank how well his son is doing in college and advises Frank not to work so hard but to pick up a book and relax with it and enjoy himself once in a while. Frank claims that he's just finished a book. He can't remember the title, but "It was a great book . . . a very, very good book . . . deep, mind you."

Meanwhile George is thinking, "*Look at the pathetic schmock . . . He makes me grow old . . . He reminds me of what I might have become . . . So I shudder inside like I might have some of that contamination inside me . . . Tell you the truth, he makes me sick . . . an ass-kissing slug that creeps around . . . but I see him out of pity and to remind myself what not to become . . . I look at his wheedling pathetic face . . . his greasy skin and the kvetch lines ingrained into his forehead . . . his attempts to smarten up . . . his hopes whenever he comes into the building . . . To be a salesman is to be a wheedling ingratiating creep . . . because you need . . . all the time you need our good will so you can stay alive . . . I hate salesmen because they make you responsible for their livelihood . . . I hate the guilt trip they lay on you . . . Look at this fake trying to remember a book he never read . . . Who could even bear to live with him? . . . What his poor wife Donna must think staring at this shuffling wreck with hairs on his collar . . . his yellow face . . . Why do I hate him so much?*"

Frank has no less contempt for George than George for Frank, as Frank thinks, "*So I have to kiss his ass 'cause he spends a few bucks . . . I have to suffer this ignorant fat pig telling me I'm a shmock because his ability to be greedy is bigger than mine . . . Who is he to make me sweat? . . . Don't I do enough sweating? . . . Up yours, you fat greasy bastard . . .*" But on the surface all is routinely jovial in this salesman-client encounter, though George tends to be a bit patronizing as Frank tries to get in his sales pitch. George is thinking about what he's going to have for lunch, after which he might visit a woman, while Frank imagines Donna and his mother-in-law pushing him to swallow his pride, make a sale and bring home more money. But Frank resolves, "*I'll do what I want to do . . . I'll tell him for once in my life I'm gonna stand up for myself . . .*"

FRANK: You know what, George?

GEORGE: Yeah . . . tell me about it, old boy . . .

DONNA (*voice offstage*): *Frank, don't do it . . . The microwave . . . the second TV in Jennifer's bedroom . . . the VCR . . . the weekend at the Golden Nugget three nights for the price of two . . . the Cuisinart . . . the four-wheel drive . . . the computer for Josh . . .*

FRANK: I remember the book now . . .

GEORGE: Oh, yeah . . . *Shirley or Susan? . . .* What?

FRANK: "How to Increase Your Earning Power" . . .

GEORGE: Good for you . . . Frank . . .

      Blackout.

Scene 2

Frank dreams of buying and installing a brand new stereo with multiple speakers, while a chorus of Hal, Donna, George and Mother-in-Law ohs and ahs in unison as he dreams. Frank and the chorus finally decide a new stereo is not feasible and exit, leaving George with Donna, who accepts his invitation to take her out to dinner. At the restaurant, Donna thinks to herself, "*He's quite nice,*" while George informs her that he and his wife have decided to separate.

Ruth Jaroslow (Mother-in-Law), Mitch Kreindel (Hal), Kurt Fuller (Frank), Laura Esterman (Donna) and Hy Anzell (George) in a scene from *Kvetch*

DONNA: Yeah, my husband . . . well, we fight a lot . . . *Oh dear, maybe I shouldn't have said that . . . He'll think I'm difficult . . .*

GEORGE: Oh yeah . . . fight, fight . . . yeah . . . ha ha! . . . *That's all I need . . . a trouble maker.*

Chorus of the Fearful appear against the wall in identity parade.

HAL: *I'm afraid . . . I fear . . . I'm lonely . . . I want . . . I need . . . I must . . . I hunger . . . I feel . . . I desire . . . friends . . . yeah . . . I need friends . . . I won't tell you this because this is embarrassing but I am going out of my mind with loneliness . . .*

FRANK: *I'm afraid . . . I fear . . . I was on the seventeenth floor today and a window was open . . . and there was nothing but space between me and the deck and I kept seeing myself flying through . . . like in the movies . . .*

DONNA: *I'm afraid . . . what will happen? He doesn't love me . . . He leaves me alone . . . I'm getting old . . . I must be loved . . . I'm neglected and shriveled from it . . .*

GEORGE: *I'm afraid . . . I can't pay alimony . . . My taxes are awful . . .*

HAL: *I'm desperate . . . I can't breathe . . . I am not popular . . . I have few friends . . . few . . . but I am not liked . . . not popular . . . get nervous . . . not*

funny . . . not handsome . . . not suave . . . ugly . . . plain . . . ordinary . . .
simple . . .

GEORGE: *And I can't keep it up . . . I couldn't get it up there last night . . . So*
what? . . . So what? . . . I didn't feel right . . . I couldn't get it stiff!! I couldn't
say this to anyone . . . I couldn't speak these thoughts even to my shrink . . . I daren't
even think it to myself . . . but I'm afraid of not having a stiff prick . . .

FRANK: *I saw myself sail through space and hit the deck . . . like a hand was*
pulling me out or beckoning me . . . a soft invisible hand gathered me up and I
was flying . . . What a thrill . . . a five-second thrill . . . That's a good one . . .

DONNA: *I want to escape . . . I'll find a room but I'm afraid . . . I'll be lonely*
. . . I'll sit there . . . I'm not so attractive any more . . . I've only one tit . . . Who
will desire me now? . . . How can I be alone and undesired? . . . I'm bored
. . . so bored . . . I hate . . . The day starts and I hate the light threatening me
with another empty day . . .

HAL: *But I die in company . . . I have to think out lines before I say them*
. . . It doesn't gush out like a spring . . . like a torrent . . . but within I have a
waterfall . . . a giant explosion could come gushing out . . . but then an iron door
clamps shut on it . . .

GEORGE: *I can't say this to anyone . . . So I pulled this hooker . . . this shiksa*
. . . and I started but my will collapsed in my dick . . . My soul and my will is
in my dick and it collapsed and so my spirits collapsed if the dick is the barometer
of my will . . .

DONNA: *I'll have an operation . . . I hear they can make one now . . . It's simple*
. . . Yeah, but costs an arm and a leg just to get a pair of decent tits . . . Yeah,
but supposing it fails . . . or looks worse . . . oh, I don't know . . .

FRANK: *Stood there with an empty order book and the window beckoning*
. . . So this is the life . . . to shlapp my guts up and down and lick ass to keep the
shreik at home and for what? . . .

HAL: *So I escape to my room and sit and sit . . . I'm sorry for myself . . . See*
yourself growing fat in the mirror . . . stare . . . smoke a cigarette . . .

DONNA: *I'm afraid . . . I fear . . . I want . . . I need . . . I ache . . . I hunger*
. . . I cry . . . I sicken . . .

FRANK: *So the window was a ticket . . . like a check that I can cash . . . splattered*
out on the sidewalk and the crowd . . . circling and feasting on the mess . . . as
my skull lay cracked open like an egg . . . So I looked out at all the space I would
soon occupy but I was afraid . . .

GEORGE: *And so I'm afraid . . . each new woman inspires the greatest terror*
. . . that I'll shrink because I lack . . . or feel I lack . . . some kind of power
. . . Maybe I'm a fruit . . . no . . . God forbid . . .

   Blackout and return to restaurant.
You're sure he doesn't know? . . .

DONNA: No! . . . he doesn't even suspect . . .

George declares that he loves Donna—and respects her. Secretly, Donna fears
that her having only one breast will put George off if they sleep with each other.
The scene changes to Frank and Donna's kitchen, where the two are arguing

about whether there should be wine and beer in the house. Donna is curious about why Frank (who cannot get intrusive images of Hal out of his mind) has taken up drinking. Frank confesses to Donna that "I'm sick of hustling to that slimy dress manufacturer." Donna takes this opportunity to tell Frank she is sleeping with "that slimy dress manufacturer," but even though she describes the affair in graphic physical detail, Frank is so preoccupied with his dislike of George that Donna's words don't sink in until she finally demands his attention.

DONNA: Shut up! Shut up! Shut up! Shut up! . . . Shut up!

FRANK: Donna?

DONNA: He sticks it into me . . . the manufacturer . . . I had to tell you . . .

FRANK: Wad!!!? Wayasay!!? Wadya saying . . . Wad's coming out of your mouth??? Donna, am I hearing you??? Is that you??

DONNA: Yeah . . . listen . . . it's kvetching me and I have to let it out . . . that fat greasy manufacturer . . . the one who bosses you around . . . well, he really likes me and though he's screwing you, metaphorically of course, he's screwing me . . . so we're both being screwed so put that in your mouth and smoke it . . .

FRANK: Donna . . . I never heard you talk like that.

DONNA: I decided to kick kvetching . . . and suddenly like a dam . . . it all comes tumbling out.

FRANK: You kicked *kvetching!!!!!* How?????

DONNA: By deciding to do what I want and let the guilt go fuck itself . . . you know . . . at that Christmas party for the wholesalers . . . you introduced me and he's been after me ever since but I've been afraid 'cause of my one tit and he's been afraid in case he couldn't make it after his wife walked out . . . so we put our two minuses together and came up with a plus . . . It's O.K. . . . I told you . . . I let it out . . . I won't kvetch any more . . . I'm sorry, Frank . . . I'm sorry . . . My suitcases are packed . . . and your dirty laundry has been done . . . and there's three pints of milk in the fridge . . .

 Donna leaves.

Frank repeats to himself Donna's words *"Deciding what I want and let the guilt go fuck itself . . . hmmmnn . . ."* Hal comes in, and while telling him what has happened Frank feels attracted to Hal. Later, in bed together, Frank suggests that he and Hal take up housekeeping together.

HAL: Kvetches gone now, huh? . . .

FRANK: Oh, yeah . . .

HAL: Y'know, Frank . . . I'll give up my apartment if it's all right with you . . . It's an expensive dump . . . We can split expenses . . . Listen, it'll be so much cheaper . . .

FRANK: Listen, we'll save a fortune . . . *We get on fine . . . but suppose after a while we don't get on so good? . . . I mean it's possible . . . maybe I should move into his and rent mine out . . . but I like my house . . . Shit, I've just got my freedom!*

HAL: You will want to give it a whirl?

FRANK: Er . . . sure, Hal . . .

HAL: Are you sure? . . . I mean, level with me? . . .

FRANK: Yeah, of course I am . . . Let's give it a whirl . . . Hell, it's not the end of the world . . . *Oh, shiiiit!* . . . G'night, Hal . . . *I don't want him to give up his place and I don't want to move . . . What's going on? . . . I should tell him . . . but I don't want him to take it bad . . . but I suggested it . . .*

HAL: Frank . . . aren't you going to kiss me goodnight??

Slow fade to black—threatening music. Curtain.

LES MISÉRABLES

A Musical in Two Acts

BOOK BY ALAIN BOUBLIL AND
CLAUDE-MICHEL SCHÖNBERG

ORIGINAL FRENCH TEXT BY ALAIN
BOUBLIL AND JEAN-MARC NATEL

MUSIC BY CLAUDE-MICHEL SCHÖNBERG

LYRICS BY HERBERT KRETZMER

ADDITIONAL MATERIAL BY JAMES FENTON

BASED ON THE NOVEL BY VICTOR HUGO

Cast and credits appear on pages 311-313

ALAIN BOUBLIL (co-author of book and original French text) conceived the idea for the musical version of Les Misérables. *With Jean-Marc Natel and Claude-Michel Schönberg as collaborators, he initiated the project as a record album which had already sold more than 260,000 copies by the time the French stage version opened in Paris at the Palais des Sports in September 1980. He made his entrance onto the British musical stage in 1983 with* Abbacadabra *at London's Lyric Hammersmith Theater and then with* Les Misérables *in the English-language version which was produced by Cameron Mackintosh and the Royal Shakespeare Company under the direction of Trevor Nunn and John Caird at the Barbican on October 8, 1985, then moving to London's Palace Theater December 4, 1985. Its American production under the same direction opened in Washington, D.C. at the Kennedy Center Opera House on December 20, 1986 and on Broadway on March 12, 1987, where it won a Best Play citation and the Critics and Tony Awards as the best musical of the season, with Boublil also sharing the best-book Tony.*

Boublil's first collaboration with Schönberg took place in 1973 with France's first rock opera La Revolution Française *which was staged at the Palais des Sports. Their double-album of this show sold 350,000 copies, and the double-album of* Les Misérables *with the London cast has already "gone gold." The Messrs. Boublil and Schönberg are preparing a Japanese production of* Les Misérables *as well as collaborating on a new musical.*

CLAUDE-MICHEL SCHÖNBERG (music and co-author of book) is a performer as well as a record producer and songwriter and played King Louis XVI in the hit production of his and Alain Boublil's La Revolution Française, *their first collaboration, in 1973 on the Paris stage and in a recording. That same year Schönberg sang his own compositions and lyrics for another album, one of whose numbers, "Le Premier Pas," rose to the top of the popularity scale. In 1983 he produced an opera album in Paris with Julia Migenes-Johnson and the Monte Carlo Philharmonic Orchestra. Like his collaborator, he closely supervised all productions of* Les Misérables, *for which he shared the best-book and won the best-score Tonys, and now has turned his attention to a new work for the musical stage.*

HERBERT KRETZMER (lyrics) was born in Kronstad, South Africa on Oct. 5, 1925 and was educated at Rhodes University in Grahamstown. He embarked on a career in journalism in 1946, came to London in 1954 and worked at the Daily Sketch, *the* Sunday Dispatch, *the* Daily Express *(where he has been drama critic since 1960) and the* Daily Mail *(where he has won two national press awards as its TV critic since 1979). He wrote the lyrics for* Our Man Crichton *(1964),* The Four Musketeers *(1967), many works in other media including the film* Hieronymous Merkin *and the TV show* "That Was the Week That Was" *and now* Les Misérables. *The latter has added a best-lyrics Tony to his long list of other awards for such songs as "Goodness Gracious Me" (a Peter Sellers–Sophia Loren comedy number), "Yesterday When I Was Young" and "She" (the latter two written for Charles Aznavour). Kretzmer is married and lives in London.*

JEAN-MARC NATEL (co-author of original French text) was born in 1942 and studied art at the Beaux Arts in Toulon before coming to the conclusion that his destiny lay in the written word. He turned his hand to poetry and has since published two volumes of it. In 1968 he moved to Paris, met Alain Boublil and became interested in writing songs for a number of performers as well as collaborating on the original French text of Les Misérables. *Some of his poems have recently been set to music by Franck Pourcel.*

JAMES FENTON (additional material) was born in 1949 and educated at Repton School and Magdelen College, Oxford. He is a journalist who has served as theater critic for the Sunday Times *and chief book reviewer for the daily* Times, *both of London, and as an editor and correspondent of the* New Statesman *and* The Guardian *at various times between 1971 and 1979. Among his many published works is a translation of* Rigoletto.

Our method of synopsizing Les Misérables *in these pages differs from that of the other Best Plays. In order to illustrate the distinctive "look" of its characters and production numbers, its outstanding stagecraft (rather than outline its well-known sequence of events from the Victor Hugo novel), the musical is represented here mostly in photographs, with occasional short excerpts from its all-sung text to portray its verbal style and flavor. These photographs of* Les Misérables *depict scenes as produced March 12, 1987 at the Broadway Theater by Cameron Mackintosh, as directed and adapted by Trevor Nunn and John Caird, with scenery by John Napier, costumes by Andreane Neofitou and lighting by David Hersey.*

Our special thanks are tendered to the producer and his press representatives, the Fred Nathan Company, Inc. and Anne Abrams, for making available these selections from the excellent photographs of the show by Michael Le Poer Trench/Bob Marshak.

PROLOGUE

1815, DIGNE

1. After 19 years on a chain gang for stealing bread for a starving child, Jean Valjean is released with a warning from his warder Javert: "You are a thief . . . You will starve unless you learn the meaning of the law." But Valjean finds that the "ticket-of-leave" he must carry at all times brands him as an ex-convict and prevents him from making a fresh start. Caught stealing silver, he's saved from the police by a kindly bishop who pretends the silver was a gift and sends him off, declaring, "I have bought your soul for God!" Valjean (Colm Wilkinson, *above*), shaken by kindness, sings "Soliloquy":

. . . I had come to hate the world.
This world that had always hated me!
Take an eye for an eye.
Turn your heart into stone.
This is all I have lived for
This is all I have known.
One word from him and I'd be back
Beneath the lash, upon the rack.
Instead, he offers me my freedom.
I feel my shame inside me
                  like a knife.
He told me that I have a soul.

How does he know?
What spirit comes to move my life?
Is there another way to go?
I am reaching, but I fall,
And the night is closing in,
And I stare into the void—
To the whirlpool of my sin.
I'll escape now from the world
From the world of Jean Valjean.
Jean Valjean is nothing now
Another story must begin.
        Tears up yellow ticket-of-leave.

ACT I

1823, MONTREUIL-SUR-MER

2. Valjean, 8 years later under another name, is a Mayor and factory owner. One of his employees is Fantine (Randy Graff, *right*). She recalls better days in the song "I Dreamed a Dream":

I dreamed a dream in time gone by
When hope was high / And life worth living
I dreamed that love would never die
I dreamed that God would be forgiving . . . . .
But the tigers came at night
With their voices soft as thunder
As they tear your hope apart
As they turn your dreams to shame
He slept a summer by my side
He filled my days / With endless wonder
He took my childhood in his stride
But he was gone when autumn came . . .

Fellow workers learn of the child Fantine is secretly supporting in another town and have her fired. She turns to prostitution and is arrested by Javert (Terrence Mann, *below right*). But before he can take her to prison, Valjean *(below left)* intervenes and sends her to a hospital.

3. The Mayor's great strength enables him to lift a capsized cart off a victim. Javert comments, "I have only known one other man / Who can do as you have done," former prisoner Valjean, who broke parole but has been recaptured and is now in jail (Javert believes) awaiting resentencing. Valjean can't let that man suffer in his place. In court, he reveals his true identity.

At the hospital, Valjean swears to dying Fantine that he'll care for her daughter Cosette. But Javert arrives to arrest him. They quarrel, in duet:

VALJEAN:
..... I'm warning you, Javert
I'm a stronger man by far
There is power in me yet
My race is not yet run
I'm warning you, Javert
There is nothing I won't dare
If I have to kill you here
I'll do what must be done! .....

JAVERT:
..... Dare you talk to me of crime
And the price you had to pay
Every man is born in sin
Every man must choose his way
You know nothing of Javert
I was born inside a jail
I was born with scum like you
I am from the gutter too .....

Valjean and Javert fight. Valjean knocks Javert out and escapes.

1823, MONTFERMEIL

4. Fantine's daughter Cosette has been boarded and greatly abused at a tavern whose keeper Thenardier (Leo Burmester, *below left*) boasts that he is "Master of the House": "Master of the house / Keeper of the zoo / Ready to relieve 'em / Of a sou, or two / Watering the wine / Making up the weight / Pickin' up their knick-knacks when they can't see straight ....."

5. Keeping his deathbed promise to Fantine, Valjean buys the child Cosette (Donna Vivino, *above right*) from the greedy Thenardiers and tells her, "Come Cosette / Come my dear / From now on I will always be here." She asks, "Will there be children / And castles to see?" Valjean assures her there will.

1832, PARIS

6. Nine years later, the Thenardiers are in Paris, reduced to beggary, and their daughter Eponine (Frances Ruffelle, *left*) is now a grown woman. Her friends the students are waiting only for the death of their ally Gen. Lamarque to join the oppressed poor in rebellion against the government.

Valjean and Cosette, also now living in Paris, pay a charitable visit to the beggars' quarter and are threatened by Thenardier's gang. They escape, but Thenardier has recognized Valjean and informs on him to Police Inspector Javert.

Meanwhile, one of the students, Marius, has fallen in love with Cosette at sight and sends Eponine—who is herself in love with Marius (and has recognized Cosette as her childhood playmate)—to find where she lives.

7. Javert calls upon "Stars" to help him pursue and find Valjean:

There out in the darkness
A fugitive running
Fallen from grace / Fallen from grace
God be my witness
I shall never yield
Till we come face to face
Till we come face to face.

He knows his way in the dark
But mine is the way of the Lord
And those who follow the path
                        of the righteous
Shall have their reward
And if they fall / As Lucifer fell
The flame / The sword.

Stars in your multitudes
Scarce to be counted
Filling the darkness
With order and light.
You are the sentinels
Silent and sure
Keeping watch in the night
Keeping watch in the night . . . . .

Lord let me find him
That I may see him / Safe behind bars
I will never rest
Till then / This I swear
This I swear by the stars.

8. Marius (David Bryant, *left*) finds Cosette, thanks to Eponine. He sings to Cosette that he has "A heart full of love / A heart full of song." To Eponine's intense distress, Cosette replies in song that she also has "A heart full of love" for Marius and "No fear, no regret."

9. While Marius and Cosette declare their love, Eponine is keeping watch and screams a warning when her father Thenardier and his gang approach to rob the Valjean house. The gang escapes to the sewers, and Cosette pretends to Valjean it was she who cried the warning. Valjean, believing "Must be Javert / He's found my cover at last!" plans to take Cosette away from France the next day.

10. The death of popular Gen. Lamarque signals Enjolras (Michael Maguire, holding gun, *above center*) and the students to take to the streets in revolt. As all join in the song "One Day More," Enjolras declares "One day more before the storm! / At the barricades of freedom;" Valjean assures Cosette (Judy Kuhn, *extreme right above*) "Tomorrow we'll be far away;" Marius pledges to Enjolras "My place is here / I fight with you" but wonders with Cosette "How can I live when we are parted?"; Javert asserts "We will nip it in the bud / We'll be ready for these schoolboys;" and the scavenging Thenardiers chortle "Watch 'em run amuck / Catch 'em as they fall / Never know your luck / When there's a free-for-all."

ALL:
Tomorrow we'll discover
What our God in heaven has in store
One more dawn
One more day
One day more. *Curtain.*

ACT II

1832, PARIS (Continued)

11. As the students build their barricade, Javert joins them pretending to be on their side. He is soon exposed by an all-knowing, all-seeing gamin, Gavroche. An armed rebel, Courfeyrac (Jesse Corti, *above left*), wants to shoot the spy out of hand, but Enjolras orders Javert to be held prisoner.

Marius, committed with the others to almost certain death, sends Eponine to Cosette with a farewell love letter. Valjean intercepts and reads it: "Now that I know that you love me as well / It is harder to die." While returning to the barricade, Eponine is shot and dies in Marius's arms *(below)* declaring "I'm at rest / A breath away from where you are."

12: Having learned that Cosette loves Marius, Valjean makes his way to the barricade to try to protect the young man. The rebels give him a gun, and he helps repel the first attack by government soldiery *(above)*.

Thanked for his help, Valjean asks only that Javert's fate be put in his hands. Enjolras agrees, and Valjean draws his knife. Javert exclaims bitterly, "You've hungered for this all your life / Take your revenge!" Valjean replies, "Your life is safe in my hands" and cuts Javert's bonds.

Javert reacts, "Don't understand," then warns "If you let me go, beware / You'll still answer to Javert!" Valjean tells him, "There is nothing that I blame you for / You've done your duty, nothing more," fires a shot in the air and lets his prisoner escape.

13. In the night, Valjean *(above)* prays for Marius's safety in the song "Bring Him Home:"

God on high
Hear my prayer
In my need
You have always been there
He is young / He's afraid
Let him rest
Heaven blessed
Bring him home . . . . .
He's like the son
            I might have known
If God had granted me a son.
The summers die / One by one

How soon they fly

On and on / And I am old
And will be gone
Bring him peace
Bring him joy
He is young
He is only a boy.
You can take
You can give
Let him be / Let him live.
If I die, let me die
Let him live, bring him home
Bring him home / Bring him home.

        Dawn breaks.

14. Next morning it is obvious the students are doomed because the people haven't risen in support of their revolt. Enjolras rallies his friends *(opposite page)* to receive the final attack. They are wiped out—all but Marius, severely wounded, and Valjean, who is strong enough to raise a grating in the street and escape, carrying Marius, into the sewers of Paris.

15. Thenardier is robbing corpses *(above)* but flees at the approach of Valjean carrying Marius home.

    Javert *(left)* easily guesses how Valjean, with his great strength, has escaped. He catches Valjean emerging from the sewers with his burden. Valjean pledges to give himself up after carrying the wounded youth to safety. Javert, weakened by Valjean's previous act of mercy, lets him go. Alone on a bridge over the Seine, Javert is then tormented by the first misgivings of his obsessive life:

. . . . . And must I now begin to doubt,
Who never doubted all these years?
My heart is stone and still it trembles
The world I have known is lost in shadow.
Is he from heaven or from hell?
And does he know / That, granting me my life today
This man has killed me even so?

I am reaching but I fall
And the stars are black and cold
As I stare into the void / Of a world that cannot hold.
I'll escape now from the world
From the world of Jean Valjean.
There is nowhere I can go
There is no way to go on . . .

Javert jumps to his death.

16. Marius, recovering under Colette's loving care, expresses his and the people's discouraged sadness at the failure of the students' revolt in "Empty Chairs at Empty Tables": "Here they talked of revolution / Here it was they lit the flame / Here they sang about 'tomorrow' / And tomorrow never came."

Valjean blesses the young couple but reveals to Marius the guilty secret of his past. He has decided to go "A long way away" to avoid ever shaming them—and Cosette must never know. Marius objects strenuously, but Valjean insists. Marius and Cosette are married in Valjean's absence. At the wedding, Marius learns from the Thenardiers, for the first time, that Valjean was the one who rescued him from the fray and saved his life.

17. Marius and Cosette hasten to find Valjean, alone in a room praying for their happiness and for his own release: "Take me now / To Thy care . . . . . / Bring me home." When he perceives the young couple's devotion to him, particularly Cosette's ready forgiveness for his past, Valjean almost wishes to keep on living. But the spirit of Fantine is also there, gently urging "Come with me / Where chains will never bind you." Torn between Cosette and Fantine (as *above*), Valjean decides to follow Fantine at last.

Forgive all my trespasses
And take me to your glory.
Take my hand
And lead me to salvation
Take my love

For love is everlasting
And remember
The truth that once was spoken,
To love another person
Is to see the face of God.

18. The spirits of the brave young people who died on the barricade join Valjean and Fantine *(above)* in a finale of song:

For the wretched of the earth
There is a flame that never dies.
Even the darkest night will end
And the sun will rise.

They will live again in freedom
In the garden of the Lord.
They will walk
       behind the ploughshare
They will put away the sword
The chain will be broken
And all men will have
       their reward . . . . .

Will you join in our crusade?
Who will be strong
       and stand with me?
Somewhere beyond the barricade
Is there a world you long to see?
Do you hear the people sing
Say, do you hear the distant drums?
It is the future that they bring
When tomorrow comes . . .
Tomorrow comes!
   Curtain.

FENCES

A Play in Two Acts

BY AUGUST WILSON

Cast and credits appear on pages 315–316

AUGUST WILSON was born in 1945 in Pittsburgh, where his father worked as a baker and his mother determinedly introduced her son to the written word and had him reading at 4 years old. Despite his early acquaintance and continuing fascination with words, he didn't long pursue formal education, leaving Central Catholic High School before graduating. He can clearly remember when he began to approach writing as a profession: It was April 1, 1965; he had just earned $20 writing a term paper for his sister, and he bought a typewriter which, he says, "represented my total commitment" because it took every penny he had. Lacking bus fare, he carried it home.

Wilson started with poetry. By 1972 he was writing one-acts. His first production was Jitney, *staged in 1978 by Black Horizons Theater, a group which he himself founded in 1968.* Jitney *was repeated in 1982 by Allegheny Repertory Theater; meanwhile Wilson's* Black Bart and the Sacred Hills *was produced in 1981 by Penumbra Theater in St. Paul. After a staged reading at the O'Neill Theater Center in Waterford, Conn. in 1982 and production by Yale Repertory Theater April 3, 1984, Wilson's* Ma Rainey's Black Bottom *was brought to Broadway October 11, 1984 for 275 performances, becoming its author's first full New York production, a Best Play and the winner of the New York Drama Critics Circle Award for the best play of the season.*

Wilson's Fences *was also developed at the O'Neill Theater Center and premiered at Yale Rep on April 25, 1985, where it received the first annual American Theater Critics Association New Play Award, as recorded in* The Best Plays of 1985–86. *It was produced on Broadway March 26, 1987 and carried off its author's second*

Best Play citation, the 1986–87 Pulitzer Prize, the Critics Prize and the best-play Tony. His Joe Turner's Come and Gone *was presented by Yale Rep in May, 1986, and his new play* The Piano Lesson *is scheduled for production there during the 1987–88 season.*

Wilson is a member of New Dramatists in New York (which presented his The Mill Hand's Lunch Bucket *in staged readings in 1983 and 1984) and the Playwrights Center in Minneapolis. He has been a recipient of Bush, McKnight, Rockefeller and Guggenheim fellowships in playwriting and a Whiting Writer's Award. He is married, with one daughter, and lives in St. Paul.*

The following synopsis of Fences *was prepared by Sally Dixon Wiener.*

Time: 1957 to 1965

Place: A northern industrial city in the United States

ACT I

Scene 1: A Friday evening, fall 1957

SYNOPSIS: The small dirt backyard and the porch of the Maxsons' old two-story red brick house is part of a decaying urban neighborhood. The porch, with a chair or two, and its wooden railing sadly in need of paint, is up three wide steps from the yard and is the sole entryway to the house from the brick-paved alley at stage left. The yard, only partly fenced-in, has a sawhorse and a lumber pile. From the branch of a tree, at stage right, hangs a rag ball, and a much-taped baseball bat is propped against the tree. There is a kitchen window, and the screen door to the kitchen is flanked on the opposite side by an old icebox. Two oil drums alongside the alley are garbage containers. A portion of skyline, upstage of the alley, reflects the industrial area.

Troy Maxson, a larger-than-life character, fills and dominates this compact environment as he enters with Jim Bono, his friend of 30-odd years, conversing. Troy is 53. *"A large man with thick, heavy hands, it is this largeness that he strives to fill out and make an accommodation with. Together with his blackness, his largeness informs his sensibilities and the choices he has made in his life. Of the two men, Bono is obviously the follower."* Both wear faded green refuse worker uniforms with work gloves stuck under their belts and high black work shoes. They carry their lunch buckets and aprons of burlap. *"It is Friday night, payday, and the one night of the week the two men engage in a ritual of talk and drink."*

BONO: I don't believe that! Troy, you ought to stop that lying!

TROY: I ain't lying! The nigger had a watermelon this big. *(He indicates with his hands.)* Talking about . . . "What watermelon, Mr. Rand?" I liked to fell out! "What watermelon, Mr. Rand?" . . . And it sitting there big as life.

BONO: What did Mr. Rand say?

TROY: Ain't said nothing. Figure if the nigger too dumb to know he carrying a watermelon, he wasn't gonna get much sense out of him. Trying to hide the great big old watermelon under his coat. Afraid to let the white man see him carry it home.

BONO: I'm like you . . . I ain't got no time for them kind of people.

TROY: Now what he look like getting mad cause he see the man from the union talking to Mr. Rand?

BONO: He come to me talking about . . . "Maxson gonna get us fired." I told him to get away from me with that. He walked away from me calling you a troublemaker. What Mr. Rand say?

TROY: Ain't said nothing. He told me to go down the Commissioner's office next Friday. They called me down there to see them.

BONO: Well, as long as you got your complaint filed they can't fire you. That's what one of them white fellows tell me.

TROY: I ain't worried about them firing me. They gonna fire me cause I asked a question? That's all I did. I went to Mr. Rand and asked him, "Why?" Why you got the white mens driving and the colored lifting? Told him, what's the matter, don't I count? You think only white fellows got sense enough to drive a truck. That ain't no paper job! Hell, anybody can drive a truck. How come you got all whites driving and the colored lifting? He told me "take it to the union." Well, hell, that's what I done! Now they wanna come up with this pack of lies.

BONO: I told Brownie if the man come and ask me any questions . . . just tell the truth! It ain't nothing but something they done trumped up on you cause you done filed a complaint on them.

TROY: Brownie don't understand nothing. All I want them to do is change the job description. Give everybody a chance to drive the truck. Brownie can't see that. He ain't got that much sense.

Bono wonders if Brownie is making out with a woman named Alberta who spends a lot of time at Taylor's place. Troy guesses about as well as the two of them are, meaning not at all, but Bono thinks Troy could be making out better than he himself is. Troy kids him, saying if Bono had been getting anywhere with Alberta, he would have been bragging about it in 20 minutes. Troy admits to eyeing her, he eyes all women, and to buying her a drink. Bono points out that buying her one drink is polite—"But when you wanna be buying two or three . . . that's what you call eyeing her." Troy claims he hasn't been a woman-chaser since he and Rose got married.

Rose, an appealing, slight woman in a yellow cotton dress and a red print apron, her hair back in a bun, comes out of the house. She is ten years younger than her husband and devoted to him. *"She either ignores or forgives his faults, only some of which she recognizes."* She doesn't participate in the men's Friday night gin-drinking but banters cheerfully with them as she goes back and forth from the porch to the kitchen where supper is cooking. They're having man talk, but Troy tells Rose he'll have some talk for her later. With his arm around her, he recalls how, when he "got out of there," he went looking for a woman. He found Rose but told her he didn't want to marry her, just wanted to be her man, Rose told him to get out of the way so the marrying kind could find her. He thought it over—"two or three days," he tells Bono—but Rose claims he came back the same night.

Bono reminisces about the years when he and his wife lived in a place with an outhouse, not realizing he could do better. Rose believes it's something people have to learn, like the people who still shop at a neighborhood grocery that charges more than the A&P. Troy defends the neighborhood grocery for over-charging: the woman who runs it lets you have something on credit when you need it. The only good he'll say for the A&P is that their son Cory's got a job there. It helps to provide money for his school clothes since Troy's brother Gabe moved out and things got tighter—and it gives Cory a way to start looking out for himself.

ROSE: Cory done went and got recruited by a college football team.

TROY: I told that boy about that football stuff. The white man ain't gonna let him get nowhere with that football. I told him when he first come to me with it. Now you come telling me he done went and got more tied up in it. He ought to go and get recruited in how to fix cars or something where he can make a living.

ROSE: He ain't talking about making no living playing football. It's just something the boys in school do. They gonna send a recruiter by to talk to you. He'll tell you he ain't talking about making no living playing football. It's an honor to be recruited.

TROY: It ain't gonna get him nowhere. Bono'll tell you that.

BONO: If he be like you in the sports . . . he's gonna be all right. Ain't but two men ever played baseball as good as you. That's Babe Ruth and Josh Gibson. Them's the only two men ever hit more home runs than you.

TROY: What it ever get me? Ain't got a pot to piss in or a window to throw it out of.

ROSE: Times have changed since you was playing baseball, Troy. That was before the war. Times have changed a lot since then.

TROY: How in the hell they done changed?

ROSE: They got lots of colored boys playing ball now. Baseball and football.

BONO: You right about that, Rose. Times have changed, Troy. You just come along too early.

TROY: There ought not never have been no time called too early! Now you take that fellow . . . what's the fellow they had playing right field for the Yankees back then? You know who I'm talking about, Bono. Used to play right field for the Yankees.

ROSE: Selkirk?

TROY: Selkirk! That's it! Man batting .269, understand? .269. What kind of sense that make? I was hitting .432 with thirty-seven home runs! Man batting .269 and playing right field for the Yankees! I saw Josh Gibson's daughter yesterday. She walking around with raggedy shoes on her feet. Now I bet you Selkirk's daughter ain't walking around with raggedy shoes on her feet! I bet you that!

ROSE: They got a lot of colored baseball players now. Jackie Robinson was the first. Folks had to wait for Jackie Robinson.

TROY: I done seen a hundred niggers play baseball better than Jackie Robinson. Hell, I know some teams Jackie Robinson couldn't even make! What you talking about Jackie Robinson. Jackie Robinson wasn't nobody. I'm talking about if you could play ball then they ought to have let you play. Don't care what color you are. Come telling me I come along too early. If you could play . . . then they ought to have let you play.

Troy takes a big swig of gin, Rose warns him he's going to drink himself to death, but Troy claims death isn't anything. He has wrestled with death—"it's nothing but a fast ball on the outside corner." It's part of life, and everybody is going to die. He only drinks like this on Friday night, just "to where I can handle it," and then leaves it alone. Rose shouldn't worry about him, because he isn't worried about death. It was in July 1941; he had felt as cold as ice, and Death stood there grinning at him, but he was ready then—and now.

ROSE: Troy was right down there in Mercy Hospital. You remember he had pneumonia? Laying there with a fever talking plumb out of his head.
TROY: Death standing there staring at me . . . carrying that sickle in his hand. Finally he say . . . "You want to bound over for another year?" See, just like that . . . "You want to bound over for another year?" I told him . . . "Bound over, hell! Let's settle this now!" It seem like he kinda fell back when I said that, and all the cold went out of me. I reached down and grabbed that sickle and threw it just as far as I could throw it . . . and me and him commenced to wrassling.

Charles Brown as Lyons, James Earl Jones as Troy Maxson, Mary Alice as Rose and Ray Aranha as Jim Bono in *Fences*

We wrassled for three days and three nights. I can't say where I found the strength from. Every time it seemed like he was gonna get the best of me, I'd reach way down deep inside myself and find the strength to do him one better.

ROSE: Every time Troy tell that story he find different ways to tell it. Different things to make up about it.

TROY: I ain't making up nothing. I'm telling you the facts of what happened. I wrassled with Death for three days and three nights and I'm standing here to tell you about it.

Their conversation is interrupted by the arrival of Lyons, Troy's oldest son by a previous marriage. Lyons, 34, wears a brown suit with a white shirt and a flashy tie, a straw hat and polished shoes. He has a mustache. *"Though he fancies himself a musician, he is more caught up in the rituals and the 'idea' of being a musician than in the actual practice of the music."* Lyons is coming to borrow money. Troy knows why he's coming to see him, and Lyons knows that Troy knows, but they play out the game. And Troy knows he's here today and not yesterday because it's payday. Yes, Lyons would like ten dollars, but Troy says he'll "die and go to hell and play blackjack with the devil" before he gives him the money.

Lyons insists he'll return the money because his woman, Bonnie, has got a job. Troy wants to know why Lyons doesn't. Troy could help him get a job, but Lyons doesn't want the kind of job that Troy has, carrying rubbish and punching a time clock. Troy says he can't afford to give Lyons money now that Gabe, Troy's brother, has moved and is paying his rent elsewhere. If Lyons is living "the fast life" he's got to learn to take care of himself, life doesn't owe Lyons anything.

Rose urges Troy to give Lyons the money. He tells Rose to give it to Lyons if she wants him to have it. She says she will, as soon as Troy gives it to her. Troy hands over his pay to Rose, and she gives Lyons the ten dollars. He thanks Rose, tells his father that he knows it came from him, and he'll be giving it back. After he leaves, Bono tries to reassure Troy, saying Lyons is still young. As Bono is leaving to go home to his wife, Troy puts his arms around Rose, saying that he loves her and that Bono shouldn't come by for him Monday morning because he'll still be busy loving her.

Scene 2: The next morning

Rose is singing a gospel hymn in a soft voice and hanging up the wash when Troy comes out of the house. She matter-of-factly reports that for the second time in a month number 651 came up the day before. Troy complains about her playing the numbers, and Lyons too—it's throwing away money. Rose only plays a nickel or so, and when she does hit, he doesn't complain. He calls it foolishness, but Rose argues that people aren't going to stop doing it, pointing out that someone of their acquaintance won enough to buy a restaurant.

Troy wants to know where their son Cory is, convinced he's gone out to avoid his chores. Cory has gone to football practice, Rose tells him. She suggests that Troy go back to bed and "get up on the other side"—he's complaining about everything.

Offstage there is singing—it is Gabriel, seven years his brother Troy's junior.

"Injured in World War II, he has a metal plate in his head. He carries an old trumpet tied around his waist and believes with every fibre of his being that he is the Archangel Gabriel." He comes on with a basket of the discarded vegetables and fruits that he tries to sell. Rose asks him about his plums that he's been singing about, but it turns out he doesn't have any. He confides to Rose that Troy is mad at him for moving to Miss Pearl's "to keep out from in your way." Troy insists he's not mad at him. Gabriel proudly shows them his key to his two basement rooms—his key, his rooms.

Rose offers to give Gabriel some breakfast, and he allows as how he'd like some biscuits. Convinced that he died and went to heaven, he claims that he and St. Peter used to sit down to "big fat biscuits" until St. Peter would fall asleep, telling Gabriel to awaken him in time to open the judgment gates. He claims Troy's name is in the book, and he's sure Rose's is too.

Troy urges him to go on into the house and have something to eat, but Gabriel now wants to go off selling his fruit and vegetables. He's saving to buy a new horn. He "hears" the hellhounds and must go chase them. He goes off singing about getting ready for the judgment.

Rose is worried that his landlady, Miss Pearl, reports she can't get Gabriel to eat right. Troy's done everything he can for his brother, and there's no way he can be cured and no point in sending him to some hospital.

ROSE: Least he be eating right. They can help him take care of himself.

TROY: Don't nobody wanna be locked up, Rose. What you wanna lock him up for? Man go over there and fight the war . . . messin' around with them Japs, get half his head blown off . . . and they give him a lousy three thousand dollars. And I had to swoop down on that.

ROSE: Is you fixing to go into that again?

TROY: That's the only way I got a roof over my head . . . cause of that metal plate.

ROSE: Ain't no sense you blaming yourself for nothing. Gabe wasn't in no condition to manage that money. You done what was right by him. Can't nobody say you ain't done what was right by him. Look how long you took care of him . . . till he wanted to have his own place and moved over there with Miss Pearl.

TROY: That ain't what I'm saying, woman! I'm just stating the facts. If my brother hadn't had that metal plate in his head . . . I wouldn't have a pot to piss in or a window to throw it out of. And I'm fifty-three years old. Now see if you can understand that!

Troy gets up from the porch and starts to exit the yard.

ROSE: Where you going off to? You been running out of here every Saturday for weeks. I thought you was gonna work on this fence?

TROY: I'm gonna walk down to Taylor's. Listen to the ball game. I'll be back in a bit. I'll work on it when I get back.

Scene 3: A few hours later

As Rose is taking the wash off the line, Cory comes in, calling football signals and carrying a football. He is Rose and Troy's high-school-aged son, a little awkward, unprepossessing, and with his mother's slighter build rather than his father's massiveness. He's in jeans, high sneakers, and wears a sweater over his shirt.

Rose informs him his father was annoyed with him for leaving in the morning before completing his chores, and that he'd wanted Cory to help him with the fence. Cory wants to know if Rose told his father about the recruiter and what his reaction was. Rose reports that he didn't have too much to say about it. She wants Cory to get on with his chores before Troy returns, but Cory is hungry so she sends him into the kitchen to make a sandwich.

Rose is still taking down the wash when Troy comes in, sneaking up behind her and grabbing her. She asks him what the score of the game was, because she'd been on the telephone and missed it. Troy doesn't care about the game—he's more interested in her. He calls to Cory to come out and berates him for not having done his chores; right now he wants Cory to help him with the fence. Cory begins sawing boards and after a bit asks Troy why he doesn't buy a television set, everybody has one, and Troy could watch the ball games. Troy gets interested enough to wonder how much one would cost. Cory thinks maybe about $200. "That ain't that much, Pop" he argues, but Troy points out that the roof needs retarring and is going to cost $264. Cory would buy the television and when the roof starts to leak, he'd fix it then. Troy claims the money would be gone then, and his bank book now shows only $73.22. He could just make a down payment, but Troy doesn't want to owe anybody anything. He offers to make a deal with Cory, though: if Cory gets $100, Troy will put the other hundred in. Cory says he will show him and goes back to sawing and talking baseball.

CORY: The Pirates won today. That makes five in a row.

TROY: I ain't thinking about the Pirates. Got an all-white team. God that boy . . . that Puerto Rican boy . . . Clemente. Don't even half play him. That boy could be something if they give him a chance. Play him one day and sit him on the bench the next.

CORY: He gets a lot of chances to play.

TROY: I'm talking about playing regular. Playing every day so you can get your timing. That's what I'm talking about.

CORY: They got some white guys on the team that don't play every day. You can't play everybody at the same time.

TROY: If they got a white fellow sitting on the bench . . . you can bet your last dollar he can't play! The colored guy got to be twice as good before he get on the team. That's why I don't want you to get all tied up in them sports. Man on the team and what it get him? They got colored on the team and don't use them. Same as not having them. All them teams the same.

CORY: The Braves got Hank Aaron and Wes Covington. Hank Aaron hit two home runs today. That makes forty-three.

TROY: Hank Aaron ain't nobody. That's what you supposed to do. That's how you supposed to play the game. Ain't nothing to it. It's just a matter of timing . . . getting the right follow-through. Hell, I can hit forty-three home runs right now!

CORY: Not off no major league pitching, you couldn't.

TROY: We had better pitching in the Negro leagues! I hit seven home runs off of Satchel Paige. You can't get no better than that.

Troy gets around to the subject of the college football recruiter, and Cory tells him the man will be coming to speak to Troy and to get him to sign the papers. Cory also tells him that Mr. Stawicki at the A&P has agreed to hold his after-school job for him until football season ends. Next week he can start working there on the weekends. Troy is angry that Cory has left the after-school job and doesn't want anybody to come to get him to sign anything—the white man won't let Cory get anywhere with football. Troy wants Cory to get on with his studies so he can get ahead at the A&P or learn to be an auto mechanic or a builder, to get a trade—something nobody can take away from him, something "besides hauling people's garbage." Cory argues that he gets good grades—you have to, to be recruited—and this way he'll go to college and have a chance. Troy orders him to go and get his job back, but Mr. Stawicki has already hired a replacement. Anyway, Cory can't have an after-school job and play football at the same time.

CORY: . . . . . Can I ask you a question?

TROY: What the hell you wanna ask me? Mr. Stawicki the one you got the questions for.

CORY: How come you ain't never liked me?

TROY: Liked you. Who the hell say I got to like you? What law is there say I got to like you? Wanna stand up in my face and ask a damn fool-ass question like that. Talking about liking somebody. Come here, boy, when I talk to you.

> Cory comes over to where Troy is working. He stands slouched over, and Troy shoves him on his shoulder.

Straighten up, goddammit! I asked you a question . . . what law is there say I got to like you?

CORY: None.

TROY: Well, all right then! Don't you eat every day?

> Pause.

Answer me when I talk to you! Don't you eat every day?

CORY: Yeah.

TROY: Nigger, as long as you in my house, you put that sir on the end of it when you talk to me!

CORY: Yes . . . sir.

TROY: You eat every day.

CORY: Yessir!

TROY: Got a roof over your head.

CORY: Yessir!

TROY: Got clothes on your back.

CORY: Yessir!

TROY: Why you think that is?

CORY: Cause of you.

TROY: Aw, hell, I know it's cause of me . . . but why do you think that is?

CORY (hesitant): Cause you like me.

TROY: Like you? I go out of here every morning . . . bust my butt . . . putting up with them crackers every day . . . cause I like you? You about the biggest fool I ever saw.

    Pause.

It's my job. It's my responsibility! You understand that? A man got to take care of his family. You live in my house . . . sleep you behind on my bedclothes . . . fill you belly up with my food . . . cause you my son. You my flesh and blood. Not cause I like you! Cause it's my duty to take care of you. I owe a responsibility to you! Let's get this straight right here . . . before it go along any further . . . I ain't got to like you. Mr. Rand don't give me my money come payday cause he likes me. He gives me cause he owe me. I done give you everything I had to give you. I gave you your life! Me and your mama worked that out between us. And liking your black ass wasn't part of the bargain. Don't you try and go through life worrying about if somebody like you or not. You best be making sure they doing right by you. You understand what I'm saying, boy?

As Troy sends Cory off to the A&P to see Mr. Stawicki, Rose, who has overheard the conversation from behind the screen door comes on and urges Troy to let Cory play football. She tries to persuade him that the boy is emulating him in wanting to participate in sports.

TROY: I don't want him to be like me! I want him to move as far away from my life as he can get. You the only decent thing that ever happened to me. I wish him that. But I don't wish him a thing else from my life. I decided seventeen years ago that boy wasn't getting involved in no sports. Not after what they did to me in the sports.

ROSE: Troy, why don't you admit you was too old to play in the major leagues? For once . . . why don't you admit that?

TROY: What do you mean too old? Don't come telling me I was too old. I just wasn't the right color. Hell, I'm fifty-three years old and can do better than Selkirk's .269 right now!

ROSE: How's was you gonna play ball when you were over forty? Sometimes I can't get no sense out of you.

TROY: I got good sense, woman. I got sense enough not to let my boy get hurt over playing no sports. You been mothering that boy too much. Worried about if people like him.

ROSE: Everything that boy do . . . he do for you. He wants you to say, "Good job, son." That's all.

TROY: Rose, I ain't got time for that. He's alive. He's healthy. He's got to make his own way. I made mine. Ain't nobody gonna hold his hand when he get out there in that world.

ROSE: Times have changed from when you was young, Troy. People change. The world's changing around you and you can't even see it.

TROY (*slow, methodical*): Woman . . . I do the best I can do. I come in here every Friday. I carry a sack of potatoes and a bucket of lard. You all line up at the door with your hands out. I give you the lint from my pockets. I give you my sweat and my blood. I ain't got no tears. I done spent them. We go upstairs in that room at night . . . and I fall down on you and try to blast a hole into forever.

I get up Monday morning . . . find my lunch on the table. I go out. Make my way. Find my strength to carry me through to the next Friday.
        Pause.
That's all I got, Rose. That's all I got to give. I can't give nothing else.

Scene 4: *The following Friday*

Cory is ready to leave for the football game, and Rose is distressed because he's torn his room apart looking for some spikes that a friend wants to borrow. She's worried about what Troy will think about the mess. Cory leaves, saying he'll clean it up when he returns, and Rose goes into the house.

Troy and Bono come in. Troy is dressed other than in his work clothes because he's been to the Commissioner's office. Troy has gotten a driver's job after all, despite the fact that Mr. Rand thought Troy was going to be fired, as others also thought. Bono mentions that he saw Troy going to Taylor's to tell "that Alberta gal" the news, but Troy claims he was telling everybody, and that he went to Taylor's to cash his paycheck.

Troy hollers to Rose a couple of times to come out. When she does, he tells her she is supposed to come when he calls her. Rose tells him to hush, she isn't a dog who must come when called. Troy used to sing a song about an old dog named Blue (he sings it now), though she's impatient to learn what happened at work today. She figures the way Troy came in he hasn't been fired and is excited to hear that they are making him a driver, that Mr. Rand called him into the office to tell him so after he'd gotten back from the Commissioner's office.

Lyons arrives, and Troy expresses surprise at seeing him because the police have raided a gambling place where Lyons hangs out. Lyons assures his father he only sits in with the band there.

Bono tells Lyons about Troy's promotion. He'll be the first colored driver and won't have anything to do but sit reading the paper like the white fellows. Lyons is pleased, but kids Troy: "If you knew how to read you'd be all right." Actually, if he knew how to drive he would be all right; Troy has been fighting to become a driver and doesn't have a driver's license. That doesn't bother Troy, who claims all you have to do is "point the truck where you want it to go." By the time Mr. Rand finds out he didn't have a license he will have two or three.

Lyons digs in his pocket, and Troy assumes he's looking for a loan again; instead, Lyons has a ten to repay Troy. Troy won't take it. He tells Lyons to deposit it in the bank and then when he gets the urge to ask him for another loan he can get it out of the bank instead. Lyons is insistent that Troy take it, that it was a loan, and he doesn't want Troy to give him anything. Rose urges Troy to let Lyons repay him. Lyons finally gives it to Rose, who tells Troy he should hand over his money too.

Offstage singing signals Gabriel's arrival. He's pleased to see Lyons and pleased with his joke as he calls Lyons "The King of the Jungle." He has brought Rose a flower—a rose, like her name. He's been busy chasing hellhounds and waiting with his trumpet for the Judgment time. Rose and Troy start wrangling about Gabriel's having moved to Miss Pearl's, to the point where Rose doesn't want to hear any more about that, and she tells Troy that when the football recruiter comes next week, she wants him to sign the paper so that that will be the last she'll hear about that, too.

Rose goes inside. Lyons is interested to hear about Cory being recruited and asks Troy what school he will attend.

TROY: That boy walking around here smelling his piss . . . thinking he's grown. Thinking he's gonna do what he want, irrespective of what I say. Look here, Bono . . . I left the Commissioner's office and went down to the A&P . . . that boy ain't working down there. He lying to me. Telling me he got his job back . . . telling me he working weekends . . . telling me he working after school . . . Mr. Stawicki tell me he ain't working down there at all!

LYONS: Cory just growing up. He's just busting at the seams trying to fill out your shoes.

TROY: I don't care what he's doing. When he get to the point where he wanna disobey me . . . then it's time for him to move on. Bono'll tell you that. I bet he ain't never disobeyed his daddy without paying the consequences.

BONO: I ain't never had a chance. My daddy came on through . . . but I ain't never knew him to see him . . . or what he had on his mind or where he went. Just moving on through. Searching out the New Land. That's what the old folks used to call it. See a fellow moving around from place to place . . . woman to woman . . . called it searching out the New Land. I can't say if he ever found it. I come along, didn't want no kids. Didn't know if I was gonna be in one place long enough to fix on them right as their daddy. I figured I was going searching too. As it turned out I been hooked up with Lucille near about as long as your daddy been with Rose. Going on sixteen years.

TROY: Sometimes I wish I hadn't known my daddy. He ain't cared nothing about no kids. A kid to him wasn't nothing. All he wanted was for you to learn how to walk so he could start you working. When it come time for eating . . . he ate first. If there was anything left over, that's what you got. Man would sit down and eat two chickens and give you the wing.

Lyons is upset and tells his father he should stop, that everyone feeds their children, no matter how bad things are, that everyone cares about them. Troy declares that all his father was concerned about was getting the cotton bales to Mr. Lubin, and then he'd find out he'd owe him something. Lyons claims he ought to have left if he knew he couldn't get anywhere there.

Troy's father had eleven children, how could he have left, and where would he have gone? He only knew farming. He was in a trap, and Troy suspects he realized that. But even though he didn't treat them in a manner he should have, he did feel the responsibility of the children. If it hadn't been for that, he could have left. Many did in those times. They just walked out the door and kept walking. Taking off like that, it's called having "the walking blues".

TROY: My daddy ain't had them walking blues . . . . . But he was just as evil as he could be. My mama couldn't stand him. Couldn't stand that evilness. She run off when I was about eight. She sneaked off one night after he had gone to sleep. Told me she was coming back for me. I ain't never seen her no more. All his women run off and left him. He wasn't good for nobody. When my turn come

to head out, I was fourteen and got to sniffing around Joe Canewell's daughter. Had us an old mule we called Greyboy. My daddy sent me out to do some plowing and I tied up Greyboy and went to fooling around with Joe Canewell's daughter. We done found us a nice little spot . . . got real cozy with each other. She about thirteen and we done figured we was grown anyway . . . so we down there enjoying ourselves . . . ain't thinking about nothing. We didn't know Greyboy had got loose and wandered back to the house and my daddy was looking for me. We down there by the creek enjoying ourselves when my daddy come up on us. Surprised us. He had them leather straps off the mule and commenced to whupping me like there was no tomorrow. I jumped up, mad and embarrassed. I was scared of my daddy. When he commenced to whupping on me . . . quite naturally I run to get out of the way.
Pause.
Now I thought he was mad cause I ain't done my work. But I see where he was chasing me off so he could have the gal for himself. When I see what the matter of it was, I lost all fear of my daddy. Right there is where I become a man . . . at fourteen years of age.
Pause.
Now it was my turn to run him off. I picked up them same reins that he had used on me. I picked up them reins and commenced to whupping on him. The gal jumped up and run off . . . and when my daddy turned to face me, I could see why the devil had never come to get him . . . cause he was the devil himself.

Troy left home after that, "And right then the world suddenly got big. It was a long time before I could cut it down to where I could handle it. Part of that cutting down was when I got to the place where I could feel him kicking in my blood and knew that the only thing that separated us was the matter of a few years." He lost touch with everybody in the family except Gabriel, but he hopes his father has died and found peace. Lyons had had no idea Troy had gone out on his own at fourteen. Lyons doubts he could have handled being on his own at that age. He got up and walked 200 miles to Mobile, Troy tells him. Lyons can't believe that, but Troy points out that this was in 1918, and he continues with his story after Rose comes out to give Lyons a phone message.

TROY: I walked on down to Mobile and hitched up with some of them fellows that was heading this way. Got up here and found out . . . not only couldn't you get a job . . . you couldn't find no place to live. I thought I was in freedom. Shhhh. Colored folks living down there on the riverbanks in whatever kind of shelter they could find for themselves. Right down there under the Brady Street Bridge. Living in shacks made of sticks and tarpaper. Messed around there and went from bad to worse. Started stealing. First it was food. Then I figured, hell, if I steal money I can buy me some food. Buy me some shoes too! One thing led to another. Met your mama. I was young and anxious to be a man. Met your mama and had you. What I do that for? Now I got to worry about feeding you and her. Got to steal three times as much. Went out one day looking for somebody to rob . . . that's what I was, a robber. I'll tell you the truth. I'm ashamed of it today. But it's the truth. Went to rob this fellow . . . pulled out my knife . . . and he pulled out a gun. Shot me in the chest. It felt just like somebody had taken a hot branding iron and laid it on me. When he shot me I jumped at him with my knife. They told me I killed him and they put me in the penitentiary and locked me up for fifteen years. That's where I met Bono. That's where I learned how to play baseball. Got out that place and your mama had taken you and went on to make life without me. Fifteen years was a long time for her to wait. But that fifteen years cured me of that robbing stuff. Rose'll tell you. She asked me when I met her if I had gotten all that foolishness out of my system. And I told her, "Baby, it's you and baseball all what count with me." You hear me, Bono. I meant it too. She say, "Which one comes first?" I told her, "Baby, ain't no doubt it's baseball . . . but you stick and get old with me and we'll both outlive this baseball." Am I right, Rose? And it's true.

Rose claims Troy told her she was "number one" with him. Lyons tries to persuade Troy to come and hear him play at a club that night, but Troy says he's too old for that. He's going to have supper and get to bed.

Lyons leaves, and Bono is starting off when Cory, in his football uniform, comes on. *"He gives Troy a hard, uncompromising look,"* then throws down his helmet and accuses his father of having come to the school, told the coach Cory was not to play football and cancelled the appointment with the recruiter.

CORY: Why you wanna do that to me? That was the one chance I had.

ROSE: Ain't nothing wrong with Cory playing football, Troy.

TROY: The boy lied to me. I told the nigger if he wanna play football . . . to keep up with his chores and hold down that job at the A&P. That was the conditions. Stopped down there to see Mr. Stawicki . . .

CORY: I can't work after school during the football season, Pop! I tried to tell you that Mr. Stawicki's holding my job for me. You don't never want to listen to nobody. And then you wanna go and do this to me!

TROY: I ain't done nothing to you. You done it to yourself.

CORY: Just cause you didn't have a chance! You just scared I'm gonna be better than you, that's all!

TROY: Come here.

ROSE: Troy . . .

    Cory reluctantly crosses over to Troy.

TROY: All right! See. You done made a mistake.

CORY: I didn't even do nothing!

TROY: I'm gonna tell you what your mistake was. See . . . you swung at the ball and didn't hit it. That's strike one. See, you in the batter's box now. You swung and you missed. That's strike one. Don't you strike out! *Curtain.*

ACT II

Scene 1: Saturday, fall of 1957

Cory is in the yard with the ball and the bat. When Rose steps out to ask him to help her with something inside, he tells her he's not going to quit the team.

Rose says she'll speak to his father when he comes back from seeing about Gabriel, who's been arrested for disturbing the peace. Cory goes inside as Troy and Bono come on. For $50 they let Gabriel go, Troy reports (it's happened a half-dozen times or more before).

Troy and Bono are going to work on the fence. Bono begins sawing but complains that Troy doesn't need this hard wood—pine would be good enough. Bono is needling Troy about Alberta as Cory comes out and takes over the sawing at Troy's request. "Strong as a mule," Troy says when Bono is impressed with Cory's prowess. But Cory doesn't see why his mother wants the fence, and neither does Troy. Rose doesn't have anything anybody else would want.

BONO: Some people build fences to keep people out . . . and other people build fences to keep people in. Rose wants to hold on to you all. She loves you.

TROY: Hell, nigger, I don't need nobody to tell me my wife loves me. Cory . . . go on in the house and see if you can find that other saw.

CORY: Where's it at?

TROY: I said find it! Look for it till you find it!

Cory exits into the house.

What's that supposed to mean? Wanna keep us in?

BONO: Troy . . . I done known you seem like damn near my whole life. You and Rose both. I done know both of you all for a long time. I remember when you met Rose. When you was hitting them baseballs out of the park. A lot of them old gals was after you then. You had the pick of the litter. When you picked Rose, I was happy for you. That was the first time I knew you had any sense. I said . . . My man Troy knows what he's doing . . . I'm gonna follow this nigger . . . he might take me somewhere. I been following you too. I done learned a whole heap of things about life watching you. I done learned how to tell where the shit lies. How to tell it from the alfalfa. You done learned me a lot of things. You showed me how to not make the same mistakes . . . to take life as it comes along and keep putting one foot in front of the other.

Pause.

Rose a good woman, Troy.

TROY: Hell, nigger, I know she a good woman. I been married to her for eighteen years. What you got on your mind, Bono?

BONO: I just say she a good woman. Just like I say anything. I ain't got to have nothing on my mind.

TROY: You just gonna say she a good woman and leave it hanging out there like that? Why you telling me she's a good woman?

BONO: She loves you, Troy. Rose loves you.

TROY: You saying I don't measure up. That's what you trying to say. I don't measure up cause I'm seeing this other gal. I know what you trying to say.

BONO: I know what Rose means to you, Troy. I'm just trying to say I don't want to see you mess up.

Troy appreciates Bono's concern, but it's as if Alberta kind of stuck to him to the point where he can't get shed of her. He's tried, he insists, but "she's stuck on for good." Troy doesn't disclaim responsibility, but he's counting on his heart

James Earl Jones and Mary Alice in a scene from *Fences*

to tell him right from wrong. He doesn't want to do Rose any harm—he loves
and respects her. Bono doesn't like to get in the middle of Troy's and Rose's
business, but he warns Troy to "work it out right."

Troy reminds Bono he's been into Bono's and Lucille's business, too, and wants
to know when Bono is ever going to buy Lucille her refrigerator. Bono says he'll
buy Lucille's refrigerator when Troy finishes building Rose's fence, and he leaves.

Troy is back at work on the fence as Rose comes to ask the details about Gabe's
arrest. Kids were teasing him. He ran them off with a lot of hollering, and
someone called the police. The judge has set a hearing in three weeks, when
they're "to show cause why he shouldn't be re-committed." Troy told the judge
he would take care of Gabe. There's no sense in re-committing him, Troy believes.

Rose isn't sure. She thinks he might be better off in the hospital, but Troy claims he isn't bothering anybody and should be free.

Rose wants Troy to come in for lunch, but he wants to tell her something first. With a great deal of difficulty he finally gets it out that he is going to be a daddy. Rose is incredulous.

Gabriel comes wandering in, rose in hand for Rose, as they try to pursue the conversation. Rose is in a state of shock but finally manages to send the gabbling Gabe into the house to get a piece of watermelon.

ROSE: Why, Troy? Why? After all these years to come dragging this in to me now. It don't make no sense at your age. I could have expected this ten or fifteen years ago, but not now.

TROY: Age ain't got nothing to do with it, Rose.

ROSE: I done tried to be everything a wife should be. Everything a wife could be. Been married eighteen years and I got to live to see the day you tell me you been seeing another woman and done fathered a child by her. And you know I ain't never wanted no half nothing in my family. My whole family is half. Everybody got different fathers and mothers . . . my two sisters and my brother. Can't hardly tell who's who. Can't never sit down and talk about Papa and Mama. It your papa and your mama and my papa and my mama . . .

TROY: Rose . . . stop it now.

ROSE: I ain't never wanted that for none of my children. And now you wanna drag your behind in here and tell me something like this.

TROY: You ought to know. It's time for you to know.

ROSE: Well, I don't want to know, goddamn it!

TROY: I can't just make it go away. It's done now. I can't wish the circumstance of the thing away.

ROSE: And you don't want to either. Maybe you want to wish me and my boy away. Maybe that's what you want? Well, you can't wish us away. I've got eighteen years of my life invested in you. You ought to have stayed upstairs in my bed where you belong.

TROY: Rose . . . now listen to me . . . we can get a handle on this thing. We can talk this out . . . come to an understanding.

ROSE: All of a sudden it's "we." Where was "we" at when you was down there rolling around with some god-forsaken woman? "We" should have come to an understanding before you started making a damn fool of yourself. You're a day late and a dollar short when it comes to an understanding with me.

TROY: It's just . . . she gives me a different idea . . . a different understanding about myself. I can step out of this house and forget about the pressures and problems . . . be a different man. I ain't got to wonder how I'm gonna pay the bills or get the roof fixed. I can just be a part of myself that I ain't never seen.

ROSE: What I want to know . . . is do you plan to continue seeing her? That's all you can say to me.

TROY: I can sit up in her house and laugh. Do you understand what I'm saying? I can laugh out loud . . . and it feels good. It reaches all the way down to the bottom of my shoes.

Pause.
Rose, I can't give that up.

If the other woman is a better woman, Rose suggests he go and stay with her, but Troy says that's not what it's about. A man couldn't want a better wife than Rose, but living has become such a pattern of "trying to take care of you all" and trying to be a good husband that he's forgotten about his own life.

Using baseball analogies, he attempts to explain it to her. If you're born with two strikes against you before you come up to bat, you must watch for "the curve ball on the inside corner" and not risk a called strike. It's better to go down swinging. But he bunted and was safe—with Rose and Cory and a job. He wasn't going to strike out. He was on first base waiting for one of the boys to knock him safely home. Seeing "that gal," though, made him think that maybe, after standing on first base for 18 years, he could steal second. Rose cries out that she's been standing with him there on first base all this time, and she has frustrations of her own and might have wanted other men to cheer her up: "You not the only one who's got wants and needs. But I held on to you, Troy. I took all my feelings, my wants and needs, my dreams . . . and I buried them inside you. I planted a seed and watched and prayed over it. I planted myself inside you and waited to bloom. And it didn't take me no eighteen years to find out the soil was hard and rocky and it wasn't never gonna bloom. But I held on to you, Troy. I held you tighter. You was my husband. I owed you everything I had. Every part of me I could find to give you. And upstairs in that room . . . with the darkness falling in on me . . . I gave everything I had to try and erase the doubt that you wasn't the finest man in the world. And wherever you was going . . . I wanted to be there with you. Cause you was my husband. Cause that's the only way I was gonna survive as your wife. You always talking about what you give . . . and what you don't have to give. But you take too. You take . . . and don't even know nobody's giving!"

Troy grabs Rose's arm as she turns to go inside, hurting her, claiming that she's lying if she says he takes and doesn't give, that he gives everything he's got. Cory comes out of the house, as Rose again tells Troy that he's hurting her. Cory grabs Troy, catching him off guard. Troy loses his balance, and Cory's blow to Troy's chest fells him. Cory is as stunned as Troy. Troy gets up and goes for Cory. Rose tries to hold Troy back, pleading with him to stop, and he does. But before Troy goes off, he tells Cory that that was the second strike, and he'd better not strike out.

Scene 2: Friday, spring of 1958

Troy has come out of the house and is about to go off when Rose follows him out and says she wants to talk to him. He's indignant because she hasn't wanted to talk to him in months. He never comes home right after work, Rose claims, and she and wants to know if he's coming home tomorrow after work. Troy hadn't planned to, even though it's Friday tomorrow and he doesn't have any money except the money she gives back to him. He's living on borrowed time with her, Rose warns him and wants to know if the best he can do is to come home (as he has today) just to change clothes and leave. Troy says he won't be too long, but Alberta has gone to the hospital—the baby might be coming early—and he has to go see her.

Rose tells Troy that Gabe was taken away today and that Miss Pearl says Troy told them to do it. Troy says Pearl is lying, but Rose saw the papers he had signed. The papers say the government is to send part of Gabe's check to the hospital and the rest to Troy. Troy claims they've made a mistake, and as far as the money's concerned, he doesn't make the rules.

ROSE: You did Gabe just like you did Cory. You wouldn't sign the paper for Cory . . . but you signed for Gabe. You signed that paper.

TROY: I told you I ain't signed nothing, woman! The only thing I signed was the release form. Hell, I can't read, I don't know what they had on that paper! I ain't signed nothing about sending Gabe away.

ROSE: I said send him to the hospital . . . you said let him be free . . . now you done went down there and signed him to the hospital for half his money. You went back on yourself, Troy. You gonna have to answer for that.

TROY: See now . . . you been over there talking to Miss Pearl. She done got mad cause she ain't getting Gabe's rent money. That's all it is. She's liable to say anything.

ROSE: Troy, I seen where you signed the paper.

TROY: You ain't seen nothing I signed. What she doing to papers on my brother anyway. Miss Pearl telling a big fat lie. And I'm gonna tell her about it too! You ain't seen nothing I signed. Say . . . you ain't seen nothing I signed!

Rose goes into the house to answer the telephone and comes back to tell Troy that Alberta's had a baby, a healthy girl; but, despite doing all they could for her, Alberta died.

Troy takes umbrage when Rose wonders about Alberta's burial—he claims she'll be wondering next if Alberta had insurance. Rose reminds Troy that she's his wife and urges him not to push her away. He isn't, he says, he just wants her to give him breathing room. Rose goes back into the house, leaving Troy to walk in the yard.

TROY (with a quiet rage that threatens to consume him): All right . . . Mr. Death. See now . . . I'm gonna tell you what I'm gonna do. I'm gonna take and build me a fence around this yard. See? I'm gonna build me a fence around what belongs to me. And then I want you to stay on the other side. See? You stay over there until you're ready for me. Then you come on. Bring your army. Bring your sickle. Bring your wrestling clothes. I ain't gonna fall down on my vigilance this time. You ain't gonna sneak up on me no more. When you ready for me . . . when the top of your list say Troy Maxson . . . that's when you come around here. You come up and knock on the front door. Ain't nobody else got nothing to do with this. This is between you and me. Man to man. You stay on the other side of that fence until you ready for me. Then you come up and knock on the front door. Any time you want. I'll be ready for you.

Scene 3: Three days later

It's late, and Rose, who has been listening to the ball game on the radio, turns it off as the game ends. Troy comes on and into the yard with a blanket-wrapped baby. He calls out, and Rose steps out onto the porch.

> *There is a long, awkward silence, the weight of which grows heavier with each passing second.*

TROY: Rose . . . I'm standing here with my daughter in my arms. She ain't but a wee bittie little old thing. She don't know nothing about grownups business. She innocent . . . and she ain't got no mama.

ROSE: What you telling me for, Troy?

> *She turns and exits into the house.*

TROY: Well . . . I guess we'll just sit out here on the porch.

> *He sits down on the porch. There is an awkward indelicateness about the way he handles the baby. His largeness engulfs and seems to swallow it. He speaks loud enough for Rose to hear.*

A man's got to do what's right for him. I ain't sorry for nothing I done. It felt right in my heart. *(To the baby.)* What you smiling at? Your daddy's a big man. Got these great big old hands. But sometimes he's scared. And right now your daddy's scared cause we sitting out here and ain't got no home. Oh, I been homeless before. I ain't had no little baby with me. But I been homeless . . . . .

> *Rose enters from the house. Troy, hearing her step behind him, stands and faces her.*

She's my daughter, Rose. My own flesh and blood. I can't deny her no more than I can deny my boys.

> *Pause.*

You and them boys is my family. You and them and this child is all I got in the world. So I guess what I'm saying is . . . I'd appreciate it if you'd help me take care of her.

ROSE: Okay, Troy . . . you're right . . . I'll help you take care of your baby . . . cause like you say . . . she's innocent . . . and you can't visit the sins of the father upon the child. A motherless child has got a hard time.

> *She takes the baby from him.*

From right now . . . this child got a mother. But you a womanless man.

> *Rose turns and exits into the house with the baby.*

Scene 4: Two months later

Cory has graduated and is job-hunting. Lyons comes by briefly to repay $20 Troy has loaned him. Cory is swinging the bat when Troy comes on, and Cory goes off without either of them speaking. Rose is about to go off, too, with the baby, whose name is Raynell, to take a cake to the church bake sale. The tables seem to have turned, and now Troy is asking when she'll return. Rose barely gives him the time of day, however, other than to tell him his dinner is on the stove.

Troy is sitting on the porch steps having a drink from his payday pint singing "Old Dog Blue" as Bono comes on. It becomes evident that they haven't seen much of each other lately. Bono's thinking of retiring in two years, and Troy is thinking of it, too. He hasn't got anybody to talk with now that he's up in the driver's seat of the truck. Troy's heard from Rose that Lucille got her refrigerator, which Bono bought her when he'd heard Troy had finished the fence—so they're even (but their earlier bantering intimacy is gone).

Bono leaves, and Troy is singing again when Cory comes back. He wants to get by Troy to go into the house and tells Troy he's in the way. Troy wants Cory to say "excuse me" like his mother's taught him, but Cory says he doesn't have to because his father doesn't count there now.

TROY: Oh, I see . . . I don't count around here no more. You ain't got to say "excuse me" to your daddy. All of a sudden you done got so grown that your daddy don't count around here no more . . . Around here in his own house and yard that he done paid for with the sweat of his brow. You done got so grown to where you gonna take over. You gonna take over my house. Is that right? You gonna wear my pants. You gonna go in there and stretch out on my bed. You ain't got to say "excuse me" cause I don't count around here no more. Is that right?

CORY: That's right. You always talking this dumb stuff. Now why don't you just get out of my way.

TROY: I guess you got some place to sleep and something to put in your belly. You got that, huh? You got that? That's what you need. You got that, huh?

CORY: You don't know what I got. You ain't got to worry about what I got.

TROY: You right! You one hundred percent right! I done spent the last seventeen years worrying about what you got. Now it's your turn, see? I'll tell you what to do. You grown . . . we done established that. You a man. Now, let's see you act like one. Turn your behind around and walk out this yard. And when you get out there in the alley . . . you can forget about this house. See? Cause this is my house. You go on and be a man and get your own house. You can forget about this. Cause this is mine. You go on and get yours cause I'm through with doing for you.

CORY: You talking about what you did for me . . . what'd you ever give me?

TROY: Them feet and bones! That pumping heart, nigger! I give you more than anybody else is ever gonna give you.

CORY: You ain't never gave me nothing. You ain't never done nothing but hold me back. Afraid I was gonna be better than you. All you ever did was try and make me scared of you. I used to tremble every time you called my name. Every time I heard your footsteps in the house. Wondering all the time . . . what's Papa gonna say if I do this? . . . What's Papa gonna say if I do that? . . . What's he gonna say if I turn on the radio? And Mama too . . . she tries . . . but she's scared of you.

TROY: You leave your mama out of this. She ain't got nothing to do with this.

CORY: I don't know how she stand you . . . after what you did to her.

Troy goes toward Cory, who tells him he's too old to give him a whipping any more and that he's crazy. Troy orders Cory to get out of his yard, but Cory says it isn't his yard, he took Uncle Gabe's money from the army to buy the house and then put Uncle Gabe out. Troy again orders Cory to get out, but Cory picks up the baseball bat and dares him to put him out, saying he's not afraid. He goes on taunting his father and finally swings at him. Troy tells Cory that is strike three and he's struck out. He'll have to use the bat, he'll have to kill him. Cory swings at Troy again, and when Troy grabs at the bat the two of them struggle for it. Troy gets it and stands over Cory, ready to swing, but stops. For the last time he orders Cory to get away from his house. Cory says he'll come back for his things, and Troy tells him they will be outside the fence.

Troy, alone, talks to himself about not being able to taste anything any more. Once more he hollers out to Death, claiming Death hasn't been following him all this time "to be messing with my boy"—that it's between Death and himself now. He calls to Death to "Come on!" He'll be ready, but he won't be easy.

Scene 5: Summer of 1965

"It is the morning of Troy's funeral. A funeral plaque with a light hangs beside the door." Rose, Lyons and Bono are in the house when Raynell, now seven, comes out in a flannel nightgown to a little garden plot off to one side and pokes around in it with a stick. Rose, in a black dress, calls from the door to ask Raynell what she is doing. Raynell has come out to see if her garden has grown, but she must get ready for the funeral now.

Raynell keeps poking with her stick. Cory comes on in his Marine corporal's uniform and carrying a duffle bag. "His posture is that of a military man, and his speech has a clipped sternness." Raynell runs to call Rose, and Rose and Cory embrace tearfully. Lyons and Bono also come out of the house to greet Cory before Bono leaves to see about lining up the pallbearers. Rose is glad Lyons has been allowed to come to the funeral and hopes Gabriel will be let out of the hospital to come also.

Lyons wants to know if Cory's going to be a career Marine. Cory's not sure; he's put in six years and thinks that's enough. Lyons, who "thought he was being slick cashing other people's checks," as he puts it, has served all but nine months of three years in the workhouse and claims it isn't so bad. "You got to take the crookeds with the straights," he recalls their father saying when he would strike out. Lyons remembers him striking out three times in a row and then hitting a ball over the grandstand—and two hundred people would wait to shake his hand after the game. They have a silent moment together before Lyons goes into breakfast, which Cory has refused.

Raynell tells Cory that Papa called her room "Cory's room" and that his football is in the closet. Rose and Cory talk while Raynell goes in to change her shoes. Troy had been outside swinging the bat, and "just fell over," Rose tells him. They took him to the hospital, but she knew it was unnecessary. To Rose's dismay, Cory declares he's not going to the funeral.

CORY: I can't drag Papa with me everywhere I go. I've got to say no to him. One time in my life I've got to say no.
ROSE: Don't nobody have to listen to nothing like that. I know you and your daddy ain't seen eye to eye, but I ain't got to listen to that kind of talk this

morning. Whatever was between you and your daddy . . . the time has come to put it aside. Just take it and set it over there on the shelf and forget about it. Disrespecting your daddy ain't gonna make you a man, Cory. You got to find a way to come to that on your own. Not going to your daddy's funeral ain't gonna make you a man.

Cory tries to explain to his mother that when he was growing up his father was like a shadow following him, ". . . . . digging into your flesh. Trying to crawl in. Trying to live through you," and he has to find some way to be rid of the shadow. Rose claims Cory's like Troy, that he's Troy all over. But Cory doesn't want to be Troy, he wants to be himself.

ROSE: You can't be nobody but who you are, Cory. That shadow wasn't nothing but you growing into yourself. You either got to grow into it or cut it down to fit you. But that's all you got to make life with. That's all you got to measure yourself against that world out there. Your daddy wanted you to be everything he wasn't . . . and at the same time he tried to make you into everything he was. I don't know if he was right or wrong . . . but I do know he meant to do more good than he meant to do harm. He wasn't always right. Sometimes when he touched he bruised. And sometimes when he took me in his arms he cut. When I first met your daddy I thought . . . Here is a man I can lay down with and make a baby. That's the first thing I thought when I seen him. I was thirty years old and had done seen my share of men. But when he walked up to me and said "I can dance a waltz that'll make you dizzy," I thought, Rose Lee, here is a man you can open yourself up to and be filled to bursting. Here is a man that can fill all them empty spaces you been tipping around the edges of. One of them empty spaces was being somebody's mother. I married your daddy and settled down to cooking his supper and keeping clean sheets on the bed. When your daddy walked through the house he was so big he filled it up. That was my first mistake. Not to make him leave some room for me. For my part in the matter. But at that time I wanted that. I wanted a house I could sing in. And that's what your daddy gave me. I didn't know to keep up his strength I had to give up little pieces of mine. I did that. I took on his life as mine and mixed up the pieces so that you couldn't hardly tell which was which anymore. It was my choice. It was my life and I didn't have to live it like that. But that's what life offered me in the way of being a woman and I took it. I grabbed hold of it with both hands. By the time Raynell came into the house, me and your daddy had done lost touch with one another. I didn't want to make my blessing off of nobody's misfortune . . . but I took on to Raynell like she was all them babies I had wanted and never had. Like I had been blessed to relive a part of my life. And if the Lord see fit to keep up my strength . . . I'm gonna do her just like your daddy did you. I'm gonna give her the best of what's in me.

Rev. Tolliver is on the telephone, and Rose goes in to speak to him. Raynell wants to know if Cory knew Blue, "Papa's dog what he sings about all the time." Cory starts singing the song, with Raynell joining in. When Rose returns, saying they're going to be leaving shortly, Cory tells Raynell to go and change her shoes as her mother had told her before "so we can go to Papa's funeral."

From the alley, Gabriel comes on, calling to Rose that he is here.

GABRIEL: Hey, Rose. It's time. It's time to tell St. Peter to open the gates. Troy, you ready? You ready, Troy? I'm gonna tell St. Peter to open the gates. You get ready now.

> *Gabriel, with great fanfare, braces himself to blow. The trumpet is without a mouthpiece. He puts the end of it into his mouth and blows with great force, like a man who has been waiting some 20-odd years for this single moment. No sound comes out of the trumpet. He braces himself and blows again with the same result. A third time he blows. There is a weight of impossible description that falls away and leaves him bare and exposed to a frightful realization. It is a trauma that a sane and normal mind would be unable to withstand. He begins to dance. A slow, strange dance, eerie and life-giving. A dance of atavistic signature and ritual.*

LYONS: Come on, Uncle Gabe, it's all right. Come on:

> *Gabriel begins to howl in what is an attempt at song, or perhaps a song turning back into itself in an attempt at speech. He finishes his dance and the gates of heaven stand open as wide as God's closet.*

GABRIEL: That's the way that go! *Curtain.*

DRIVING MISS DAISY

A Full-Length Play in One Act

BY ALFRED UHRY

Cast and credits appear on pages 335-336

ALFRED UHRY was born in Atlanta in 1936. His father was a furniture dealer and by avocation an artist whose paintings are now hung in museums. Uhry can't remember when he didn't write—he didn't care much for the novel he wrote at age 9, so he immediately switched to writing for the theater, partly inspired by family visits to New York to see such shows as South Pacific *and* Kiss Me Kate. *At Brown University, from which he graduated in 1958, he won the competition to write the book and lyrics for the varsity shows (Robert Waldman wrote the music). His first New York production of record, a 1968 Broadway musical version of* East of Eden *entitled* Here's Where I Belong, *written with Waldman and Alex Gordon, closed after only 1 performance, but Uhry was taken under the broad wing of Frank Loesser, and soon his work was appearing on all three TV networks and on various stages. The latter has included* The Robber Bridegroom *(music by Waldman, 1974 OOB at St. Clement's, 1975 on Broadway by the Acting Company, winning Tony and Drama Desk nominations, and returning to Broadway the following season); lyrics for the musical* Swing *at Kennedy Center in 1980; a new adaptation of* Little Johnny Jones *on Broadway (but again for only 1 performance) in 1982;* America's Sweetheart *at the Hartford Stage Company in 1985, and five reconstructions of period musicals for the Goodspeed Opera House.*

Driving Miss Daisy, *which opened off Broadway April 15 at Playwrights Horizons, is Uhry's first straight play and first Best Play. He is married, with four daughters, and lives in New York City.*

The following synopsis of Driving Miss Daisy *was prepared by Sally Dixon Wiener.*

Time: 1948 to 1973

Place: Atlanta, Georgia

SYNOPSIS: A flowered upholstered armchair is situated downstage right. On a table next to it are an Oriental-style shaded lamp, photographs in silver frames and an old-fashioned black dial telephone. An upstage scrim has a curtain effect, and during scenes which occur in an office, a Venetian blind becomes visible. Two black pedestal stools, downstage left, are the front and back seats for scenes in a car. Other props appear as needed and disappear as the fluid action of the play continues, sometimes with blackouts, sometimes with just a lighting change.

As the play begins, we hear music, strings and a banjo. *"In the dark we hear a car ignition turn on and then a horrible crash. Bangs and booms and wood splintering. When the noise is very loud, it stops suddenly, and the lights come up on Daisy Werthan's living room, or a portion thereof. Daisy, age 72, is wearing a summer dress and high-heeled shoes. Her hair, her clothes, her walk, everything about her suggests bristle and feist and high energy. She appears to be in excellent health. Her son Boolie Werthan, 40, is a businessman, Junior Chamber of Commerce style. He has a strong, capable air. The Werthans are Jewish, but they have strong Atlanta accents."*

Daisy and Boolie are arguing. Boolie claims it's miraculous his mother isn't in the hospital or at the funeral home as the result of her car accident in which not even her glasses were broken—an accident which Daisy claims was the fault of the car. Boolie ought to have allowed her to keep her LaSalle, she insists, as it wouldn't have behaved that way. Boolie, sorely tried, points out that by putting the car in reverse she's demolished a Packard only three weeks old, a two-car garage and a tool shed.

The insurance company has to buy her a new car, but the gist of Boolie's argument with her is that she shouldn't be driving a car. Even if she did get a new insurance policy, he would worry. He is insisting that she have someone to drive her, as many of her friends do. Daisy is angry, insulted and adamant about not having a driver and furthermore claims her friends are rich. Boolie says his father left her enough money, and he'll even do the interviewing at his office. He'll find her a driver.

DAISY: No. Now stop running your mouth! I am seventy-two years old as you so gallantly reminded me, and I am a widow, but unless they rewrote the Constitution and didn't tell me, I still have rights. And one of my rights is the right to invite who I want—not who you want—into my house. You do accept the fact that this is my house? What I do not want—and absolutely will not have is some—*(She gropes for a bad enough word.)*—some chauffeur sitting in my kitchen, gobbling my food, running up my phone bill. Oh, I hate all that in my house!

BOOLIE: You have Idella.

DAISY: Idella is different. She's been coming to me three times a week since you were in the eighth grade, and we know how to stay out of each other's way. And even so, there are nicks and chips in most of my wedding china, and I've seen her throw silver forks in the garbage more than once.

BOOLIE: Do you think Idella has a vendetta against your silverware?

DAISY: Stop being sassy. You know what I mean. I was brought up to do for myself. On Forsyth Street we couldn't afford them, and we did for ourselves. That's still the best way, if you ask me.

Dana Ivey as Daisy and Morgan Freeman as Hoke in *Driving Miss Daisy*

BOOLIE: Them! You sound like Governor Talmadge.

DAISY: Why, Boolie! What a thing to say! I'm not prejudiced! Aren't you ashamed?

Boolie must leave because he and his wife Florine are invited to a dinner at the Ansleys. Daisy tartly comments that Florine must have bought a new dress for "socializing with Episcopalians." Boolie still insists, despite her protests, that he's going to start interviewing for a chauffeur. Daisy begins singing to put an end to the talk.

The scene changes to Boolie's office at the Werthan plant. Boolie is busy at his desk when Hoke Coleburn comes in to be interviewed, *"a black man of about 60, dressed in a somewhat shiny suit and carrying a fedora, a man clearly down on his luck but anxious to keep up appearances."* He has been out of work for quite a while.

Hoke asks Boolie if his family is Jewish and expresses his preference for working for Jews, especially after an experience he had working for a woman who was a holier-than-thou do-gooder connected with the Baptist Church. He quit that job in a hurry and went to work for a Jewish judge until the judge died. His widow wanted Hoke to go to Savannah with her when she moved, but he stayed in Atlanta because he was a widower then and wanted to be close to his grandchildren. The judge, it turns out, had been a friend of Boolie's father.

Hoke assumes Boolie wants a driver for his family, to take the children to school and his wife to the beauty parlor and such, and Boolie admits to not having children. Hoke feels badly about that, his daughter is the "bes' thing ever happen to me," but advises Boolie not to worry because he's still young. Boolie gets Hoke back on the subject at hand and finds out that Hoke also was a milk truck driver for a dairy all during the war.

Boolie reveals that what he needs is someone to drive for his mother. Hoke is curious as to why she isn't doing the hiring herself. Boolie assures him that it isn't that she's around the bend, but that it isn't safe for her to drive now, although she won't admit it. He tells Hoke frankly that he's desperate. His mother doesn't want anybody to drive her, and she's high-strung. He puts it to Hoke that he'd be working for him, not for her, and although she can say whatever she likes, she can't fire him. Hoke understands, he tells Boolie: "I hold on no matter what way she runs me." The two strike a bargain—Hoke will get $20 a week.

> *Lights fade on them and come up on Daisy who enters her living room with the morning paper. She reads with interest. Hoke enters the living room. He carries a chauffeur's cap instead of his hat. Daisy's concentration on the paper becomes fierce when she senses Hoke's presence.*

HOKE: Mornin', Miz Daisy.

DAISY: Good morning.

HOKE: Right cool in the night, wadn't it?

DAISY: I wouldn't know. I was asleep.

HOKE: Yassum. What yo plans today?

DAISY: That's my business.

HOKE: You right about dat. Idella say we runnin' outa coffee and Dutch cleanser.

DAISY: We?

HOKE: She say we low on silver polish too.

DAISY: Thank you. I will go to the Piggly Wiggly on the trolley this afternoon.

HOKE: Now, Miz Daisy, how come you doan' let me carry you?

DAISY: No thank you.

HOKE: Aint that what Mist' Werthan hire me for?

DAISY: That's his problem.

HOKE: All right den. I find something to do. I tend yo zinnias.

DAISY: Leave my flowerbed alone.

HOKE: Yassum. You got a nice place back beyond the garage ain' doin' nothin' but sittin' there. I could put you in some butterbeans and some tomatoes and even some Irish potatoes could we get some ones with good eyes.

DAISY: If I want a vegetable garden, I'll plant it for myself.

HOKE: Well, I go out and set in the kitchen, then, like I been doin' all week.

Hoke, the soul of patience, keeps working on her and tries a new tack. It's a shame, he despairs, that Daisy's new Oldsmobile has been sitting there since her son drove it home from the dealers'. It's only been driven 19 miles. In his opinion, it's as if the insurance company gave her the car for nothing. And it's also his opinion that "a fine rich Jewish lady" shouldn't be getting on and off a trolley with grocery bags.

Daisy doesn't like him to say she's rich and wonders if that's what he and Idella talk about in the kitchen. She doesn't need or want Hoke, she reiterates, and doesn't want to be talked about behind her own back in her own house. She lectures Hoke on the subject of her early upbringing on Forsyth Street. They didn't have anything, she tells him, not even enough to feed a cat her brother brought home once. Her sisters saved their money in order that she could become a teacher.

Even so, Hoke says, it seems as if she's doing well now, and he feels badly taking her son's money for doing nothing. Daisy picks up on that quickly enough. She wants to know how much Hoke is getting, but he says it's between him and Mr. Werthan. It shouldn't be more than seven dollars a week, she remarks. Hoke, as if to agree with her, points out it's especially so when he just sits on a kitchen stool all day. When he suggests that he hose down the front steps while she goes to the Piggly Wiggly on the trolley, she finally concedes and puts on her hat. She will go with him to the Piggly Wiggly, but that's all, then home.

Hoke, in his chauffeur's cap, assists her into the car, and they set off. "*Daisy, in the rear, is in full bristle.*" She's not a fool, she cautions, and can read the speedometer from where's she's sitting. She claims he's speeding. They're only going 19 miles an hour, and the speed limit is 35 miles an hour, but Daisy likes to stay below the speed limit. At this rate they are hardly moving and might just as well walk, Hoke grumbles, but Daisy is insistent, because her husband had told her that the slower they go, the more they'll save on gas.

Despite the fact that her son believes she is losing her abilities, she's bound and determined she is going to stay in control of her car and demands to know why

Hoke isn't turning where she thinks he should to get to the store—meaning the way she used to drive there. She is still ordering him to turn back and go the other way when they arrive at the Piggly Wiggly. When she gets out of the car to go into the store she takes the car keys with her.

Hoke goes to a pay telephone while she is marketing and calls Boolie's office triumphantly to report that he has driven his mother to the store. He is pleased that it took only six days to get her to allow him to drive her there. "Same time it take the Lawd to make the worl'," he adds.

There is the sound of a choir singing as the scene changes. Hoke is by the car, looking at the newspaper, as Daisy comes on with a different hat and wearing a fur piece. He inquires as to how her temple service had gone, but Daisy is in a huff and tells him to hurry and get her away from there. Hoke wonders what's happened to put her in such a bad mood. The fact is, she's embarrassed because Hoke has parked the car directly in front of the temple entrance, so that everyone can notice that she has a driver and will think she is putting on airs, pretending to be rich. Rich or not, if Hoke had her means he would flaunt it, he tells her.

The lights go up briefly on Boolie, at home, talking to his mother on the telephone. It's early morning, and she's called him because she wants him to come over right away. Daisy is in her bathrobe when Boolie arrives to determine what the crisis is. Daisy is convinced Hoke is stealing from her and wants Boolie to be there when Hoke arrives. Her evidence, which she produces from her bathrobe pocket, is an empty salmon can she found in the garbage under the coffee grounds. "They all take things," she declares, so she has been counting her possessions and found only eight cans of salmon where there should have been nine.

BOOLIE: Very clever, Mama. You made me miss my breakfast and be late for a meeting at the bank for a thirty-three cent can of salmon.
    He jams his hands in his pocket and pulls out some bills.
Here! You want thirty-three cents? Here's a dollar! Here's ten dollars! Buy a pantry full of salmon!

DAISY: Why, Boolie! The idea! Waving money at me like I don't know what! I don't want the money. I want my things!

BOOLIE: One can of salmon?

DAISY: It was mine. I bought it and I put it there and he went into my pantry and took it, and he never said a word. I leave him plenty of food every day, and I always tell him exactly what it is. They are like having little children in the house. They want something so they just take it. Not a smidgin of manners. No conscience. He'll never admit this. "Nome," he'll say. "I doan know nothin' bout that." And I don't like it! I don't like living this way! I have no privacy.

BOOLIE: Mama!

DAISY: Go ahead. Defend him. You always do.

BOOLIE: All right. I give up. You want to drive yourself again, you just go ahead and arrange it with the insurance company. Take your blessed trolley. Buy yourself a taxicab. Anything you want. Just leave me out of it.

Daisy's high dudgeon turns to embarrassment when Hoke arrives with a can of salmon in a paper bag in his overcoat pocket, explaining to Daisy that the pork chops she'd left for him to eat yesterday when she was away with her sister were "stiff," and so he'd eaten a can of salmon, which he's now replacing. Hoke goes off to put it in the cupboard. Daisy, looking at the empty can she's holding, dismisses Boolie with what dignity she can muster.

Birds are singing as Daisy, in the sunshine, is busy with a trowel by a gravestone at the cemetery. Hoke comments that her husband's grave is certainly well-tended. Daisy isn't a believer in the perpetual care program, and Hoke agrees with her it's more proper for the family to tend a grave. She sends Hoke to the car to get the potted azalea she's promised Mrs. Bauer to place on Mr. Bauer's grave. She tells Hoke to put it on the grave which is a little way off beyond a cherry tree, that he'll see the headstone. Hoke seems confused about where to take it. The truth is, he painfully admits, that he can't read; that when Daisy has been watching him with the newspaper, he's just trying to figure out things from looking at the pictures.

DAISY: You know your letters, don't you?
HOKE: My ABC's? Yassum, pretty good. I jes' cain' read.
DAISY: Stop saying that. It's making me mad. If you know your letters then you can read. You just don't know you can read. I taught some of the stupidest children God ever put on the face of this earth, and all of them could read enough to find a name on a tombstone. The name is Bauer. Buh buh buh buh Bauer. What does that buh letter sound like?
HOKE: Sound like a B.
DAISY: Of course. Buh Bauer. Er er er er er. BauER. That's the last part. What letter sounds like er?
HOKE: R?
DAISY: So the first letter is a—
HOKE: B.
DAISY: And the last letter is an—
HOKE: R.
DAISY: B-R. B-R. B-R. Brr. Brr. It even sounds like Bauer, doesn't it?
HOKE: Sho' do Miz Daisy. Thass it?
DAISY: That's it. Now go over there like I told you in the first place and look for a headstone with a B at the beginning and an R at the end and that will be Bauer.
HOKE: We ain' gon' worry 'bout what come in the middle?
DAISY: Not right now. This will be enough for you to find it. Go on now.
HOKE: Yassum.
DAISY: And don't come back here telling me you can't do it. You can.

The scene changes, as Daisy and Hoke are on the way to Christmas dinner at Boolie and Florine's house. Daisy is definitely not in a "ho, ho, ho" mood, but Hoke is enjoying the lighted decorations as they drive along. Florine goes over-board with Christmas lighting and decoration every year, with a wreath in every window, a Santa Claus on the front door—and this year, as they now can see, a Rudolph the Red-Nosed Reindeer in the dogwood. Hoke allows as how he enjoys Christmas at this house, and Daisy replies, "I don't wonder. You're the only Christian in the place!"

Hoke helps Daisy out of the car, and she hands him a package wrapped in plain paper tied with grocery twine—it's not a Christmas present because she doesn't give Christmas presents, it's just something she happened to find that morning. It's a book, and Hoke, deeply touched as nobody has ever given him a book before, slowly and carefully reads the title. "Hand Writing Copy Book—Grade Five." It's the book Daisy used as a teacher. She assures Hoke that if he practices, and he has to, he will write "nicely." She taught the mayor with the same textbook. She doesn't want Hoke to go "yapping" about it to Boolie and Florine, though.

The lights come up on Boolie in slacks and sport shirt by the car, calling to Hoke to hurry so he can get to his golf game at the club on time. In answer to Boolie's question as to where his mother is, Hoke tells him she's in her room, upset over the fact that Boolie is trading in her car for a new one. She's watched over her car "like a chicken hawk," Hoke points out, and she even went so far as to get out one day when a man put his satchel on the hood of her car while he was opening the trunk of his car and "run that man every which way. She wicked 'bout her paint job." Boolie acknowledges his mother fought with him about the trade-in and concedes that probably she and Hoke will miss this car. Not him, Hoke tells him.

HOKE: It ain' goin' nowhere. I done bought it.
BOOLIE: You didn't!
HOKE: I already made the deal with Mist' Red Mitchell at the car place.
BOOLIE: For how much?
HOKE: Dat for him and me to know.
BOOLIE: For God's sake! Why didn't you just buy it right from Mama? You'd have saved money.
HOKE: Yo' Mama in my business enough as it is. I ain' studyin' makin' no monthly car payments to her. Dis mine the regular way.
BOOLIE: It's a good car, all right. I guess nobody knows that better than you.
HOKE: Best ever come off the line. And dis new one, Miz Daisy doan' take to it, I let her ride in disheah now an' again.
BOOLIE: Mighty nice of you.
HOKE: Well, we all doin' what we can. Keep them ashes off my 'polstry.

Daisy, dressed for traveling, comes on with a large suitcase, obviously in a determined dither, looks at her watch and goes off to return with a dress bag and a shoe box lunch. Her agitation increasing by the moment, she goes off again and comes back with a big beribboned package. Hoke appears with his small suitcase, and Daisy opens fire, telling him it's three minutes past seven. Hoke reminds her they were not to leave until a quarter to eight and is upset because she's carried out all her things by herself. Well, there wasn't anyone to help her, she snaps, and she hates to do things at the last minute. Hoke claims she's been ready to go for a week and a half.

Boolie comes on to see them off, bearing a gift package. It's from Florine for Uncle Walter's 90th birthday, which is the reason for Daisy's forthcoming trip to Mobile. Boolie thinks the gift is notepaper, which Daisy remarks ironically as being appropriate, insofar as Uncle Walter can't see.

She is livid because Boolie is not going to the birthday party. She knows it's not just because he has to go to New York for a convention, it's because he and Florine have tickets, written away for eight months previously, for *My Fair Lady*.

Daisy is impatient to leave, but Boolie wants to talk to Hoke. He commiserates with him and gives him $50 in the event they should run into trouble. He asks Hoke about the map, which Hoke says Daisy has with her in the back seat and has studied "every inch of the way."

They are on their way, and at lunch time they are eating Idella's stuffed eggs, as Hoke continues driving. Daisy is remembering her first trip to Mobile, for Walter's wedding in 1888.

DAISY: I was twelve. We went on the train. And I was so excited. I'd never been on a train, I'd never been in a wedding party and I'd never seen the ocean. Papa said it was the Gulf of Mexico and not the ocean, but it was all the same to me. I remember we were at a picnic somewhere—somebody must have taken us all bathing—and I asked Papa if it was all right to dip my hand in the water. He laughed because I was so timid. And then I tasted the salt water on my fingers. Isn't it silly to remember that?

HOKE: No sillier than most of what folks remember. You talkin' about first time. I tell you 'bout the first time I ever leave the state of Georgia?

DAISY: When was that?

HOKE: 'Bout twenty-five minutes back.

DAISY: Go on!

HOKE: Thass right. First time. My daughter, she married to Pullman porter on the N C & St. L, you know, and she all time goin'—Detroit, New York, St. Louis—talkin 'bout snow up aroun' her waist and ridin' in de subway car, and I say, "Well, that very nice Tommie Lee, but I jes' doan' feel the need." So dis it, Miz Daisy, and I got to tell you, Alabama ain' lookin' like much so far.

Suddenly Daisy realizes they're going the wrong way. Studying her map, she accuses Hoke of taking a wrong turn. Hoke says she took it, too, then, and she was the one with the map. Daisy's all wound up and furious with herself for letting Boolie make her take the car trip with Hoke. She should have taken the train and been safe. Hoke agrees.

The lights dim again briefly to indicate the passage of time. It's night, both show their weariness, and Daisy is distressed that the crab dish her hosts always go to such trouble to fix for her will be ruined by now. Hoke tells her they have to stop. It isn't car trouble, he's got to be excused.

DAISY: You should have thought of that back at the Standard Oil Station.

HOKE: Colored cain' use the toilet at no Standard Oil . . . You know dat.

DAISY: Well there's no time to stop. We'll be in Mobile soon. You can wait.

HOKE: Yassum.

He drives a minute, then stops the car.

Nome.

DAISY: I told you to wait!

HOKE: Yassum. I hear you. How you think I feel havin' to ax you when can I make my water like I some damn dog?

DAISY: Why, Hoke! I'd be ashamed!

HOKE: I ain' no dog and I ain' no chile and I ain' jes' a back of the neck you look at while you goin' wherever you want to go. I am man nearly seventy-two years old and I know when my bladder full and I gettin' out dis car and goin' off down de road like I got to do. And I'm takin' de car key dis time. And that's de end of it.

Hoke slams the car door as he goes off, leaving Daisy in the dark of a country night with only the sounds of crickets chirping and a dog barking, and her anger changes to fright as she calls out his name.

On his day off, Hoke comes to Boolie's office to talk to him. It seems that Boolie's cousin's wife—"the one talk funny" (because she's from Canton, Ohio)—has been trying to hire him. She telephoned when she knew Daisy wouldn't be there and asked him how he was being treated. He told her fine, but she said that if he was thinking about a change he'd know who to call. Hoke thought Boolie would want to know and Boolie is dumfounded. Hoke also tells Boolie that she said he should name his salary. Boolie asks Hoke if he did.

HOKE: Now what you think I am? I ain' studyin' workin' for no trashy some-thing' like her.

BOOLIE: But she got you to thinking, didn't she?

HOKE: You might could say dat.

BOOLIE: Name your salary?

HOKE: Dat what she say.

BOOLIE: Well, how does sixty-five dollars a week sound?

HOKE: Sounds pretty good. Seventy-five sounds better.

BOOLIE: So it does. Beginning this week.

HOKE: Das mighty nice of you Mist' Werthan. I 'preciate it. Mist' Werthan, you ever had people fightin over you?

BOOLIE: No.

HOKE: Well, I tell you. It feel good.

The phone is ringing at Daisy's house. She enters with a coat on over her bathrobe, carrying a lighted candle in a candlestick. Now into her 80s, she's still spry but moves a bit more carefully. It's Boolie, at home, calling her, and we see him, too. He was worried that Daisy's phone might be out. There's been an ice storm, and all the power's out. Boolie can't get over to Daisy's because his driveway is covered with ice. She assures him she's fine and sends her love to Florine before she hangs up, then tells herself she gueses "that's the biggest lie I'll tell today."

She's attempting to read by candlelight when Hoke arrives with a paper bag and wearing galoshes. He'd learned to drive on ice when he was delivering for the dairy, and he's stopped on his way to Daisy's to pick up hot coffee at a service store because he assumed her stove would be out. Daisy is touched at his thoughtfulness. As Hoke sips his coffee, he mentions that they haven't had good coffee since Idella died. Daisy agrees. She can make biscuits the way Idella did and Hoke can fry chicken like she did, but they don't know how to make her coffee. Hoke confesses that every time he hears the Hit Parade it makes him think of Idella, who, according to Idella's daughter, during the Lucky Strike Extra "all of a sudden, she belch and she gone." Daisy says Idella was lucky, and Hoke figures she probably was.

When Boolie calls again he says the ice will be melted by afternoon and he'll be there as soon as he can to get Daisy. She tells him to stay home, that Hoke is with her. Boolie wonders how he managed that, and Daisy says that he is very handy. Boolie asks if he has the right phone number—he never heard her say "loving things" about Hoke. She didn't say she loved him, Daisy retorts. She'd said he was handy.

There are horns blowing, the sounds of a bad traffic jam, as the lights go up on Daisy. She is wearing a hat and anxiously looking out of the window of the car. Hoke comes to report "a big mess up yonder"—she wont be going to temple today because it's been bombed. A policeman told him it happened half an hour or so ago. He doesn't know if anyone was injured.

When Daisy asks who would do it, Hoke tells her she knows as well as he does that it's always "the same ones." Daisy's convinced that it's a mistake because her temple is Reform, not Conservative or Orthodox. Hoke says that doesn't matter—"A Jew is a Jew to them folks. Jes like light or dark we all the same nigger."

DAISY: I can't believe it!
HOKE: I know jes' how you feel, Miz Daisy. Back down there above Macon on the farm—I 'bout ten or 'leven years old and one day my frien' Porter, his daddy hangin' from a tree. And the day befo', he laughin' and pitchin' horseshoes wid us. Talkin' bout Porter and me gon' have strong good right arms like him and den he hangin' up yonder wid his hands tie behind his back an' the flies all over him. And I seed it with my own eyes and I throw up right where I standin'. You go on and cry.
DAISY: I'm not crying.
HOKE: Yassum.
DAISY: The idea! Why did you tell me that?
HOKE: I doan' know. Seem like disheah mess put me in mind of it.
DAISY: Ridiculous! The temple has nothing to do with that!
HOKE: So you say.
DAISY: We don't even know what happened. How do you know that policeman was telling the truth?
HOKE: Now why would that policeman go and lie 'bout a thing like that?
DAISY: You never get things right anyway.
HOKE: Miz Daisy, somebody done bomb that place and you know it too.
DAISY: Go on. Just go on now. I don't want to hear any more about it.
HOKE: I see if I can get us outta here and take you home. You feel better at home.
DAISY: I don't feel bad.

Ray Gill (Boolie), Dana Ivey (Daisy) and Morgan Freeman (Hoke) in a scene from *Driving Miss Daisy*

HOKE: You de boss.
DAISY: Stop talking to me!

There is the sound of applause at the lights come up on Boolie, now in his late 50s, with a big silver bowl, making his acceptance speech as Atlanta Business Council's man of the year. The Werthan Company was started with one printing press 72 years ago and "believes we want what Atlanta wants." He adds, to more applause, that he'd be completely happy "if the jackets whup the dawgs up in Athens Saturday afternoon."
In Daisy's living room she is dialing the phone with difficulty and leaves a message with Boolie's secretary that she has bought tickets for the UJA banquet in honor of Martin Luther King. The lights dim briefly, and Boolie comes into the living room. He asks Daisy how she is, a question she regards as not a good one for somebody almost 90.
He's gotten her message about the banquet. Daisy tells him Florine is also invited. She suggests Hoke drive them. Boolie is hedging. Daisy asks him point-blank why he doesn't just say so if he doesn't want to go. He does, Boolie says. It's Florine, then, Daisy assumes, but that isn't it; it's that he still has to do business in Atlanta.

DAISY: I see. The Werthan Company will go out of business if you attend the King dinner?
BOOLIE: Not exactly. But a lot of the men I do business with wouldn't like it. They wouldn't come right out and say so. They'd just snicker and call me Martin

Luther Werthan behind my back—something like that. And I'd begin to notice that my banking business wasn't being handled by the top dogs. Maybe I'd start to miss out on a few special favors, a few tips. I wouldn't hear about certain lunch meetings at the Commerce Club. Little things you can't quite put your finger on. And Jack Raphael over at Ideal Press, he's a New York Jew instead of a Georgia Jew, and as long as you got to deal with Jews, the really smart ones come from New York, don't they? So some of the boys might start throwing business to Jack instead of old Martin Luther Werthan. I don't know. Maybe it wouldn't happen, but that's the way it works. If we don't use those seats, somebody else will, and the good Doctor King will never know the difference, will he?

DAISY: If we don't use the seats? I'm not supposed to go either?

BOOLIE: Mama, you can do whatever you want.

DAISY: Thanks for your permission.

BOOLIE: Can I ask you something? When did you get so fired up about Martin Luther King? Time was, I'd have heard a different story.

DAISY: Why, Boolie! I've never been prejudiced and you know it!

BOOLIE: Okay. Why don't you ask Hoke to go to the dinner with you?

DAISY: Hoke? Don't be ridiculous. He wouldn't go.

BOOLIE: Ask him and see.

Daisy is putting on her evening wrap and a chiffon scarf over her hair, moving very slowly. Hoke comes on and assists her in getting into the car. After a bit, Daisy starts complaining that Hoke shouldn't be driving, that he can't see. The car has scratches, she insists, and Hoke insists it doesn't. Daisy asks how he would know since he can't see. She continues her carping, saying he's forgotten to turn, that she knows the way to the Biltmore, she's lived here all her life. And not driven a car in 20 years, Hoke comments.

Daisy asks Hoke if he knows Martin Luther King. Hoke says he doesn't, he's heard him preach the same way she has, on the television. She pussyfoots around some more, suggesting that Hoke could see him any time if he went over to the Ebenezer Baptist Church. Finally Hoke asks her straight out what she's getting at. It's silly, she says, but Boolie told her that Hoke wanted to attend the dinner with her. Hoke denies it. Daisy hadn't thought so—after all, Hoke can hear him whenever he wants. Daisy remarks how wonderful it is the way things are changing.

HOKE: What do you think I am, Miz Daisy?

DAISY: What do you mean?

HOKE: You think I some somethin' sittin' up here doan' know nothin' 'bout how to do?

DAISY: I don't know what you're talking about.

HOKE: Invitation to disheah dinner come in the mail a mont' ago. Did be you want me to go wid you, how come you wait till we in the car on the way to ask me?

DAISY: What? All I said was that Boolie said you wanted to go.

HOKE (sulking): Mmm hmmm.

DAISY: You know you're welcome to come, Hoke.

HOKE: Mmmm hmmm.
DAISY: Oh my stars. Well, aren't you a great big baby!
HOKE: Never mind baby, next time you ask me someplace, ask me regular.
DAISY: You don't have to carry on so much!
HOKE: Das' all. Less drop it.
DAISY: Honestly!
HOKE: Things changin', but they ain't change all dat much.

Hoke offers to help her up to the door, but Daisy refuses. Hoke stays in his seat while she slowly gets out, then looks at him. Whatever she was going to say to him, she thinks better of it and walks to the door.

Boolie, at home, is on the phone. It's Hoke, calling from Daisy's, to tell him his mother is "worked up," but not in the usual way—she thinks she is still teaching school and not making any sense. Hoke's worried. Boolie says he'll come right over.

Daisy comes on, her hair uncombed, her slip showing under her open housecoat, asking Hoke where he's put her papers, the papers she corrected last night and put in the front of the house ready to take to school. Hoke tries to persuade her there aren't any papers, but she's fretting because the children are upset if she doesn't hand their papers back to them promptly. She always does, and they like her for that.

She can't understand why Hoke won't help her find them. She's not angry if he moved them, she tells him, but she must find them and go to school or she will be late, and her class will be left by themselves. "I do everything wrong," she says, as Hoke tries to calm her before she can fall and hurt herself. She carries on, mostly quite out of it, as Hoke continues to try to persuade her that she isn't teaching any more, and that those children are "ole men and women by now." Her mind has just taken a turn, and, if she will let herself, she will snap back. Hoke reminds her she's a lucky old woman, rich, healthy for her age, and with people who care about her. Daisy grasps that she is being troublesome and insists she doesn't want to be. If she wants something to cry about, Hoke tells her, he will show her the state home and the people lying there in the hallways.

Daisy says she's sorry but slips back into worrying about the children. Hoke, trying to jolt her into reality again, warns her that if she keeps on this way her son will call the doctor to put her in the insane asylum. Does she want that? he asks her.

Daisy looks at him. She speaks in her normal voice.
DAISY: Hoke, do you still have that Oldsmobile?
HOKE: From when I firs' come here? Go on, Miz Daisy, that thing been in the junkyard fifteen years or more. I drivin' yo' next to las' car now. '63 Cadillac, runnin' fine as wine.
DAISY: You ought not to be driving anything, the way you see.
HOKE: How you know the way I see, less you lookin' outta my eyes?
DAISY: Hoke?
HOKE: Yassum?
DAISY: You're my best friend.

HOKE: Come on, Miz Daisy. You jes—
DAISY: No. Really. You are. You are.
She takes his hand. The light fades on them.

Boolie, 65, comes on and is walking around Daisy's living room. He picks up a book, looks at an ashtray and flips through his mother's small phone book, which he pockets. Hoke, 85, arrives, shuffling a little and wearing very thick glasses. Boolie is worried that Hoke has driven himself to Daisy's house, but Hoke doesn't drive any more. His granddaughter Michelle drove him there. Boolie is surprised that she's old enough and even more surprised to hear that Michelle is 37 and a college biology teacher.

Daisy's house is being sold, although Boolie feels odd about selling it while she's still living. But Daisy hasn't been in the house for two years, and Boolie feels confident he's made the right decision. He seems to be looking to Hoke for affirmation, but Hoke just comments, "Don' get me into it."

Boolie has already removed whatever he wanted from the house and wants to know if there's anything Hoke wants before the Goodwill arrives. Hoke claims he has more than enough at his place. Boolie also tells Hoke he can rest assured that a check from him will still keep coming to Hoke every week.

It's hard for Hoke to get out to see Daisy very often, now that he's not driving, and the place isn't on a bus line, but he goes in a taxi sometimes, he tells Boolie.

It's Thanksgiving Day and Boolie and Hoke are going together, from Daisy's house, to pay a call on her.

The lights come up on Daisy, 97, moving slowly with her walker. "*She seems fragile and diminished, but still vital.*" Near her are a hospital chair and table. Boolie and Hoke arrive and greet her, and Boolie helps her into the chair. Hoke asks Daisy if she's been keeping busy. When she doesn't respond, Boolie reports that Daisy goes to jewelry-making classes. "She's a regular Tiffany's." To cover her inattentiveness, he mentions to Hoke that he'd thought of him recently when he saw a milk truck from the dairy Hoke once drove for, describing it as having 16 wheels. Suddenly Daisy interrupts him to point out that Hoke came to see her, not him. It's one of her good days, Hoke comments.

Florine has sent Thanksgiving greetings to Daisy. She is in Washington, a Republican National Committeewoman, Boolie reminds her. Daisy's retort is brief: "Good God!" She tells Boolie to go away and "charm the nurses." He leaves, fondly calling her a "doodle."

Daisy dozes for a minute in her chair. Then she looks at Hoke.
DAISY: Boolie payin' you still?
HOKE: Every week.
DAISY: How much?
HOKE: That between me an' him, Miz Daisy.
DAISY: Highway robbery.
She closes her eyes again. Then opens them.
How are you?
HOKE: Doin the bes' I can.
DAISY: Me too.

HOKE: Well, thass all there is to it, then.
She nods, smiles. Silence. He sees the piece of pie on the table.
Looka here. You ain eat yo' Thanksgiving pie.
She tries to pick up her fork. Hoke takes the plate and fork from her.
Lemme hep you wid this.
He cuts a small piece of pie with the fork and gently feeds it to her. Then another as the lights fade slowly out. Curtain.

LES LIAISONS DANGEREUSES

A Play in Two Acts

BY CHRISTOPHER HAMPTON

FROM THE NOVEL BY CHODERLOS DE LACLOS

Cast and credits appear on page 319

CHRISTOPHER HAMPTON was born in the Azores at Fayal on Jan. 26, 1944 and finished his education at New College, Oxford. His first play, When Did You Last See My Mother?, *was put on by the Royal Court Theater (where he later served as resident dramatist, 1968–1970) in London in June 1966 and transferred to the West End and then to New York at the Sheridan Square Playhouse in January 1967. His New York productions have included new versions of Henrik Ibsen's* A Doll's House *and* Hedda Gabler *(Broadway, January 1971),* The Philanthropist *(Broadway, March 15, 1971, for 72 performances and citations as a Best Play and in* Variety's *poll as most promising playwright),* Total Eclipse *(off Broadway, February 1974, at Chelsea Theater of Brooklyn),* Savages *and* Treats *(OOB at the Hudson Guild Theater, 1977) and a translation of Odon Von Horvath's* Don Juan Comes Back From the Wars *(off Broadway at Manhattan Theater Club, April 1979), not to mention the many New York and cross-country reproductions of these works.*

Hampton's second Best Play, Les Liaisons Dangereuses, *adapted from the 18th-century novel of pre-Revolution French manners and mores by Choderlos de Laclos, was produced by Royal Shakespeare Company January 8, 1986 in London, where it won the Laurence Olivier Award for the season's best. That RSC production was transferred to Broadway April 30, 1987 for what promises to be a long run.*

The list of Hampton playscripts includes The Portage to San Cristobal of A.H. *and* Tales From Hollywood *and new translations of* Don Juan, Tales From the Vienna Woods, Ghosts, The Wild Duck *and* Tartuffe, *and his list of TV and film scripts is a long one.*

PIERRE AMBROSE-FRANCOIS CHODERLOS DE LACLOS (original novel) was born in 1741 and pursued a military career. It was while he was assigned to boring duty on a Bay of Biscay island at age 40 that he determined, as he wrote to a friend, to use the time to create something "out of the ordinary, eyecatching, something that would resound around the world" and live on after de Laclos's death. The result was Les Liaisons Dangereuses, *his first and only and immediately successful novel (his two other writings were a treatise on women's education and an attack on Maréchal de Vauban). During the French Revolution he was a Jacobin, a friend of Danton, secretary to "Philippe-Égalité" and was twice jailed but managed to avoid the guillotine. At the turn of the century, Napoleon made de Laclos a general and assigned him to southern Italy, where he died in 1803.*

Time: One autumn and winter in the 1780s

Place: Various salons and bedrooms in a number of hotels and chateaux in and around Paris, and in the Bois de Vincennes

ACT I

Scene 1: Mme. la Marquise de Merteuil's salon, an August evening

SYNOPSIS: In her opulent salon, the Marquise de Merteuil is playing cards with Mme. de Volanges, a widow whose daughter Cecile—*"a slim and attractive blonde girl of 15"*—is just out of the convent. A major-domo comes in to announce that the Vicomte de Valmont has come to call, then exits to show him in.

VOLANGES: You receive him, do you?
MERTEUIL: Yes. So do you.
VOLANGES: I thought perhaps that under the circumstances . . .
MERTEUIL: Under what circumstances? I don't believe I have any grounds for self-reproach . . .
VOLANGES: On the contrary. As far as I know, you're virtually unique in that respect.
MERTEUIL: . . . and, of course, if I had, he would no longer be calling on me.
Cecile has been following this exchange closely, frowning in the attempt to make sense of it. Now Mme. de Volanges turns to her.

VOLANGES: Monseur le Vicomte de Valmont, my child, whom you very probably don't remember, except that he is conspicuously charming, never opens his mouth without first calculating what damage he can do.

CECILE: Then why do you receive him, Mama?

VOLANGES: Everyone receives him. He has a distinguished name, a large fortune and a very pleasant manner. You'll soon find that society is riddled with such inconsistencies; we're all aware of them, we all deplore them and in the end we all accommodate to them. Besides which, people are quite rightly afraid to provoke his malice. No one has the slightest respect for him; but everyone is very nice to him.

Mme. de Volanges breaks off as the major-domo escorts Valmont *("a strikingly elegant figure")* into the room and then exits. Valmont greets the ladies formally, particularly noticing Cecile. But while Valmont is explaining that he is soon going to the country to visit his aunt, Mme. de Rosemonde, Cecile falls asleep (being accustomed to a 9 P.M. bedtime at the convent). It is clearly time for Mme. de Volanges and daughter to depart, which they do.

Alone with Valmont, the Marquise de Merteuil tells him why she has summoned him: her lover, M. de Gercourt, who left her and ran off with Valmont's current mistress, is to marry Cecile Volanges. The Marquise suggests that she and Valmont can both be revenged if Valmont will seduce Cecile while her intended is off with his regiment in Corsica. Valmont considers, then shakes his head: "You

The company of *Les Liaisons Dangereuses* posed in Bob Crowley's scenery and costumes

know how difficult I find it to disobey your orders," but he feels it would be too easy to seduce this 15-year-old. Besides, he has other plans.

VALMONT: . . . My trip to the country to visit my more or less immortal aunt. The fact of the matter is that it's the first step towards the most ambitious plan I've ever undertaken.

MERTEUIL: Well, go on.

VALMONT: You see, my aunt is not on her own just at the moment. She has a young friend staying with her. Madame de Tourvel.

MERTEUIL: Yes.

VALMONT: She is my plan.

MERTEUIL: You can't mean it.

VALMONT: Why not? To seduce a woman famous for strict morals, religious fervor and the happiness of her marriage: what could possibly be more prestigious?

MERTEUIL: I think there's something very degrading about having a husband for a rival. It's humiliating if you fail and commonplace if you succeed. Where is he, anyway?

VALMONT: He's presiding over some labyrinthine case in Burgundy, which I'm reliably informed will drag on for months.

MERTEUIL: I can't believe this. Apart from anything else, she's such a frump. Bodice up to her ears in case you might catch a glimpse of a square inch of flesh . . .

VALMONT: You're right, clothes don't suit her.

MERTEUIL: How old is she?

VALMONT: Twenty-two.

MERTEUIL: And she's been married . . . ?

VALMONT: Two years.

MERTEUIL: Even if you succeed, you know what?

VALMONT: What?

MERTEUIL: All you'll get from her is what she gives her husband. I don't think you can hope for any actual pleasure. They never let themselves go, those people. If you ever make her heart beat faster, it won't be love, it'll be fear. I sometimes wonder about you, Vicomte. How could you make such a fool of yourself over a complete nonentity?

VALMONT: Take care, now, you're speaking of the woman . . .

MERTEUIL: Yes?

VALMONT: I've set my heart on.

   Silence. Valmont smiles at her.

I haven't felt so strongly about anything since you and I were together.

Valmont doesn't want to change the ways of his prey, he wants to seduce her in *spite* of her convictions: "I want the excitement of watching her betray everything that's most important to her." He indicates that he and the Marquise have been collaborators in a deliberate program of such dissipation, telling her, "Since we started this little mission, you've made many more converts than I have."

The Marquise reminds Valmont to avoid any taint of love, which is "like medicine, you use it as a lubricant to nature." Her present lover, Belleroche, is in fact in love with her, and Valmont suggests that perhaps it's time, then, for the Marquise to practice a little infidelity—with him. She refuses to indulge him, however, but promises to reward him if he can bring her written proof of victory in his proposed campaign. As for Cecile, Mme. de Merteuil comments, "She's so lovely. If my morals were less austere, I'd take it on myself." "You are an astonishing woman," Valmont comments, kissing her hand and taking his leave.

Scene 2: The principal salon in Mme. de Rosemonde's chateau in the country,
early evening three weeks later

Valmont's valet, Azolan, has taken Mme. de Tourvel's maid, Julie, to bed, per instructions from his master, but the lass has proved uncooperative and won't steal her mistress's letters so that Valmont can discover who has warned Madame against him. They arrange for Valmont to break into his valet's room at 2 A.M. that morning to find Julie in bed with him, hoping that blackmail will succeed where cajoling has failed.

As Azolan departs, Mme. de Rosemonde (*"84, arthritic but lively, intelligent and sympathetic"*) comes in with Mme. de Tourvel (*"a handsome woman of 22, dressed . . . . . in an elegantly plain linen gown. She is clearly in a state of considerable excitement"*). The latter *"cannot help reacting"* to Valmont's presence and can hardly wait to reveal a secret about Valmont she's learned from her footman Georges, who saw the Vicomte in this village this morning. Valmont (she blurts out) came upon a poor family in distress and rescued them by paying their debt and giving them a contribution to put them back on their feet. (With Azolan's help, Valmont staged this particular event this morning so that it would be witnessed and repeated to his credit back at the chateau, but the two ladies don't know that—they think it was an act of extraordinary kindness.) Valmont's aged aunt hugs him for his generosity as well as his modesty for not wanting to reveal it. *"Then Valmont turns and advances toward Mme. de Tourvel, smiling radiantly, his arms outstretched. A spasm of panic crosses her face, but she has no choice but to submit to the embrace: Valmont squeezes her powerfully. Then he releases her, and, as she looks at him, ashen and mesmerized, he turns aside, wiping away a surreptitious tear."* Valmont's aunt rushes off to tell the curé of her nephew's good deed. Left alone with Mme. de Tourvel, Valmont waits her out until she's forced to break the silence.

TOURVEL: I can't understand how someone whose instincts are so generous could lead such a dissolute life.

VALMONT: I'm afraid you have an exaggerated idea both of my generosity and of my depravity. If I knew who'd given you such a dire account of me, I might be able to defend myself; since I don't, let me make a confession: I'm afraid the key to the paradox lies in a certain weakness of character.

TOURVEL: I don't see how so thoughtful an act of charity could be described as weak.

VALMONT: This appalling reputation of mine, you see, there is some justification for it. I've spent my life surrounded by immoral people; I've allowed myself to be influenced by them and sometimes even taken pride in outshining them. Whereas, in this case, I've simply fallen under a quite opposite influence: yours.

TOURVEL: You mean you wouldn't have done it . . .

VALMONT: Not without your example, no. It was by way of an innocent tribute to your goodness.

Valmont kneels before her, takes her hands and begs for her encouragement, which throws her into tearful confusion. She pulls herself together and declares herself offended by Valmont's behavior, suspecting he may have planned this whole episode. Valmont protests, "As I got to know you, I began to realize that beauty is the least of your qualities. I became fascinated by your goodness . . . . . It finally dawned on me: I was in love, for the first time in my life. I knew it was hopeless, of course, but that didn't matter to me, because it wasn't like it always has been, it wasn't that I wanted to have you, no. All I wanted was to deserve you."

Mme. de Tourvel wishes to hear no more of this kind of talk and asks Valmont, as a favor, to leave this house. He agrees (with the proviso that he can give his aunt 24 hours notice), and he asks her to return the favor by telling him which of his friends has been blackening his name. She refuses. He withdraws this request and asks only that after he leaves he be permitted to write to her—and have her answer his letters. She makes no commitment, but Valmont drops to one knee again and kisses her hand in farewell, then *"hurries away into the darkness, just failing to muffle a discreet sob. Mme. de Tourvel is left alone, rooted to the chaise-longue. She looks terrified."*

Scene 3: Emilie's bedroom in her house on the outskirts of Paris, a couple of days later, the middle of the night.

Emilie is a courtesan, and Valmont is in bed with her. Emilie's protector owns this house, but Valmont has gotten him drunk and sent him off with the coachman so they won't be disturbed. Valmont gets out of bed to fetch pen and paper, then uses Emilie's back to write a love letter to Mme. de Tourvel.

Scene 4: The grand salon of the Marquise de Merteuil, a September afternoon ten days later

Valmont and the Marquise are having tea, the Marquise advising him that he should have taken Mme. de Tourvel right there on his aunt's chaise-longue. But Valmont wants to prolong the pursuit. He is sure now that Mme. de Tourvel loves him, because he has left his valet Azolan behind to keep watch, and the valet reported that "when my first letter arrived, she took it to her room and sat turning it over for hours, sighing and weeping." And Valmont has found out from the chambermaid (who is much more cooperative now after Valmont "caught" her in bed) that it is Mme. de Volanges who has been writing to Mme. de Tourvel warning her against Valmont and thus setting his "campaign" back a month or more.

Valmont is so angry with Mme. de Volanges that he is now ready to help the

Marquise with her scheme for seducing Cecile. The Marquise has seen a lot of Cecile recently and has decided that "She has no character and no morals, she's altogether delicious." The Marquise has poisoned Cecile's mind against the "geriatric" of 36 her mother intends her to marry and has encouraged Cecile's emotional involvement with the young intellectual Danceny. They are in love, the Marquise is certain, and discouraged only by the advice of Cecile's confessor. Mme. de Merteuil hopes that Valmont will strengthen Danceny's resolve and help her plan to succeed. He observes, "I often wonder how you managed to invent yourself," and she replies, "Women are obliged to be far more skilful than men." She goes on to detail her philosophy for Valmont.

MERTEUIL: . . . . . You hold every ace in the pack. You can ruin us whenever the fancy takes you. All we can achieve by denouncing you is to enhance your prestige. We can't even get rid of you when we want to: we're compelled to unstitch, painstakingly, what you would just cut through. We either have to devise some way of making you want to leave us, so you'll feel too guilty to harm us; or find a reliable means of blackmail: otherwise you can destroy our reputation and our life with a few well-chosen words. So of course I had to invent: not only myself, but ways of escape no one else has ever thought of, not even I, because I had to be fast enough on my feet to know how to improvise. And I've succeeded, because I always knew I was born to dominate your sex and avenge my own.

VALMONT: Yes; but what I asked you was how.

MERTREUIL: When I came out into society, I'd already realized that the role I was condemned to, namely to keep quiet and do what I was told, gave me the perfect opportunity to listen and pay attention: not to what people told me, which was naturally of no interest, but to whatever it was they were trying to hide. I practiced detachment, I learned how to smile pleasantly while, under the table, I stuck a fork into the back of my hand. I became not merely impenetrable, but a virtuoso of deceit. Needless to say, at that stage nobody told me anything: and it wasn't pleasure I was after, it was knowledge. But when, in the interests of furthering that knowledge, I told my confessor I'd done "everything," his reaction was so appalled, I began to get a sense of how extreme pleasure might be. No sooner had I made this discovery than my mother announced my marriage: so I was able to contain my curiosity and arrived in Monsieur de Merteuil's arms a virgin. All in all, Merteuil gave me little cause for complaint: and the minute I began to find him something of a nuisance, he very tactfully died. I used my year of mourning to complete my studies: I consulted the strictest moralists to learn how to appear; philosophers to find out what to think; and novelists to see what I could get away with. And finally I was well placed to perfect my techniques.

VALMONT: Describe them.

MERTEUIL: Only flirt with those you intend to refuse; then you acquire a reputation for invincibility, whilst slipping safely away with the lover of your choice. A poor choice is less dangerous than an obvious choice. Never write letters. Get them to write letters. Always be sure they think they're the only one. Win or die.

Valmont smiles. He looks at Merteuil for a moment.

VALMONT: These principles are infallible, are they?

MERTEUIL: When I want a man, I have him; when he wants to tell, he finds he can't. That's the whole story.

VALMONT: And was that our story?

Merteuil pauses before answering.

MERTEUIL: I wanted you before we'd even met. My self-esteem demanded it. Then, when you began to pursue me . . . I wanted you so badly. It's the only one of my notions has ever got the better of me. Single combat.

VALMONT: Thank you . . .

They are interrupted when the major-domo brings in the Chevalier Danceny *("a Knight of Malta, an eager and handsome young man of about 20")*. The Marquise suggest that Danceny might profit from Valmont's advice in his pursuit of Cecile, but Danceny reminds Valmont that this is not a common affair but a worshipful courtship which must proceed with utmost delicacy.

The major-domo reappears and announces the arrival of Mme. de Volanges, so that Danceny must leave. Before he goes, Valmont makes an appointment with him for the next day. Valmont remains, but he goes behind a screen to conceal his presence, as Mme. de Volanges comes in.

The Marquise reminds her visitor that she has become extremely friendly with her daughter Cecile, and she now has the unpleasant duty to tell her that Cecile is having a "dangerous liaison" with Danceny. Mme. de Volanges cannot believe it: Cecile is an innocent, Danceny is an honorable man, and they have always been chaperoned by the Marquise. But the Marquise has seen Cecile concealing letters, she insists, and she advises Mme. de Volanges to send Cecile to the country for a visit with Mme. de Rosemonde, now that Valmont has returned from there to Paris. Mme. de Volanges departs, grateful for the Marquise's information and for her advice.

Valmont comes out of his hiding place making faces at the lady's back as she exits. The Marquise points out to Valmont that she has now set it up so that Valmont can return to his aunt's and kill two birds with one stone. Valmont suggests she now take his success for granted, but Mme. de Merteuil reminds him that there will be no favors, no reward, until she has the required proof of his conquest of Mme. de Tourvel in writing.

Scene 5: The salon in Mme. de Rosemonde's chateau, a week later, after lunch.

Mme. de Tourvel, *"ashen,"* rests on the chaise-longue; Cecile is working on her tapestry, and Valmont observes them while Mmes. de Rosemonde and de Volanges play cards. After dallying with Mme. de Tourvel through eye contact, Valmont suddenly observes that she looks ill; and while the older women's attention is distracted, he throws a letter into Cecile's lap. Cecile is amazed but conceals the letter and joins the others bending over Mme. de Tourvel on the chaise-longue. They suggest some air would do Mme. de Tourvel good and proceed to take her out for a walk.

Valmont signals for Cecile to leave her scarf behind, and, after the ladies have all gone out, she returns to get it. Valmont seizes the opportunity to tell her the letter is from Danceny. Cecile can't answer the letter, because they've taken away her writing materials—but Valmont has a plan: writing materials have been concealed in her anteroom cupboard. Valmont will act as messenger back and forth if she will exchange the key to her bedroom on her mother's mantelpiece for one which resembles it, oil the hinges of her bedroom door and bring Valmont the key to have a copy made. Cecile goes out to join the others, prepared to follow instructions.

The lights change to denote the passage of time to early evening. Valmont is reading, when Mme. de Tourvel enters and reproaches him for returning to this place, when he had promised to go away.

> *Valmont contrives, imperceptibly, to maneuver himself between her and the door.*

VALMONT: Why are you so angry with me?

TOURVEL: I'm not angry. Although, since you gave me a solemn undertaking not to offend me when you wrote and then in your very first letter spoke of nothing but the disorders of love, I'm certainly entitled to be.

VALMONT: I was away almost three weeks and wrote to you only three times. Since I was quite unable to think about anything but you, some might say I showed heroic restraint.

TOURVEL: Not insofar as you persisted in writing about your love, despite my pleas for you not to do so.

VALMONT: It's true: I couldn't find the strength to obey you.

TOURVEL: You claim to think there's some connection between what you call love and happiness: I can't believe that there is.

VALMONT: In these circumstances, I agree. When the love is unrequited . . .

TOURVEL: As it must be. You know it's impossible for me to reciprocate your feelings; and even if I did, it could only cause me suffering, without making you any the happier.

VALMONT: But what else could I have written to you about, other than my love? What else is there? I believe I've done everything you've asked of me.

TOURVEL: You've done nothing of the sort.

VALMONT: I left here when you wanted me to.

TOURVEL: And you came back.

> *Silence, as Valmont searches for a way forward, momentarily at a loss.*

Mme. de Tourvel has offered Valmont friendship, which is not enough for him, and now she regrets her rashness in permitting him to write to her. He assures her he's a better person now—"More celibate than a monk"—and asks only that they don't try to avoid each other while they're here at the chateau. Valmont takes his leave of her, politely, and she *"stands for a long time, not moving, locked in some personal struggle."*

Scene 6: Cecile's bedroom in the chateau, a fortnight later, the middle of the night

Availing himself of the key he acquired by deceit, Valmont, wearing a dressing gown and carrying a dark-lantern, comes into the bedroom where Cecile is fast asleep. She awakens and thinks that Valmont has come to bring her a letter from Danceny. He caresses her, gently at first and then more forcefully as she resists. She struggles to reach the bell pull. Valmont reminds her that she would be embarrassed if she had to explain how he came by the key to her bedroom.

Valmont assures Cecile that if she will give him a kiss he will go.

CECILE: You really promise?
VALMONT: Let's just get ourselves more comfortable, shall we?
CECILE: Do you?
> *Valmont disposes the cover over them, then leans back to look down on her. He replaces his hand, and Cecile reacts with a start.*

Please don't do that.
VALMONT: I'll take it away. After the kiss.
CECILE: Promise?
VALMONT: Yes, yes.
CECILE: Swear?
VALMONT: I swear. Now put your arms around me.
> *Cecile gives a long, surprisingly intense kiss, her eyes tightly closed. Suddenly, she pulls away from him as much as she can, her eyes now wide with amazement. Valmont's hand comes slowly up from under the cover. Cecile continues to look appalled.*

See. I told you I'd take my hand away.

Scene 7: The salon in Mme. de Rosemonde's chateau, the following day, Oct. 1, afternoon

Cecile enters with Mme. de Merteuil whom Cecile, in tears, accepts as a confidante and comforter. Cecil is upset because her mother found her letters from Danceny (someone informed her, and she went straight to the cupboard where they were hidden); and even more because Valmont used the key to her bedroom last night.

CECILE: . . . . . And by the time I realized what he had come for, it was, well, it was too late to stop him . . .
> *Cecile bursts into tears again; but this time Mme. de Merteuil doesn't take her into her arms. Instead, she considers her coolly for a moment before speaking.*

MERTEUIL: You mean to tell me you're upset because Monsieur de Valmont has taught you something you've undoubtedly been dying to learn?
> *Cecile's tears are cut off, and she looks up in shock.*

CECILE: What?
MERTEUIL: And am I to understand that what generally brings a girl to her senses has deprived you of yours?
CECILE: I thought you'd be horrified.
MERTEUIL: Tell me: you resisted him, did you?
CECILE: Of course I did, as much as I could.

MERTEUIL: But he forced you?

CECILE: It wasn't that exactly, but I found it almost impossible to defend myself.

MERTEUIL: Why was that? Did he tie you up?

CECILE: No, no, but he has a way of putting things, you just can't think of an answer.

MERTEUIL: Not even no?

CECILE: I kept saying no, all the time; but somehow that wasn't what I was doing. And in the end . . .

MERTEUIL: Yes?

CECILE: I told him he could come back tonight.

Cecile is ashamed and this morning burst into tears at the very sight of her mother. The Marquise advises Cecile 1) let Valmont continue his "instruction," 2) make no objection to marrying M. de Gercourt and 3) take up with Danceny again after marriage, while convincing everyone she's dropped him. "Provided you take a few elementary precautions," the Marquise advises her, "you can do it, or not, with as many men as you like, as often as you like, in as many different ways as you like. Our sex has few enough advantages, you may as well make the most of those you have."

Mme. de Volanges enters, sees that Cecile looks strained and sends her off to her room to rest. Cecile seems to be pining for "that young man"—Mme. de Volanges believes—and it is affecting her health, so that the mother is now almost ready to give up the idea of the daughter's marriage to de Gercourt and allow her to marry Danceny, whom Cecile so obviously loves and who isn't all that bad a match, even without money, of which Cecile will have enough for both of them.

This development doesn't suit the Marquise's plan for revenge on de Gercourt, so she advises Mme. de Volanges against it. When Valmont enters, Mme. de Volanges leaves the room, still undecided about her daughter's future.

Alone with Valmont, the Marquise congratulates him on his success with Cecile, and Valmont tells her, "I was malicious enough to use no more strength than could easily be resisted." The Marquise has come to visit at "this lugubrious address" because she hoped that Valmont would have also succeeded with Mme. de Tourvel. He isn't in any hurry in that enterprise, however, because he is enjoying the love-versus-virtue conflict which it has generated. Mme. de Tourvel is coming around slowly, going for longer and longer walks with Valmont every day. Mesdames de Tourvel and de Rosemonde enter.

Mme. de Rosemonde bustles over to Mme. de Merteuil to embrace her; Mme. de Merteuil responds convincingly, but it's clear she has immediately registered the look which passes between Valmont and Mme. de Tourvel, a look that indicates that there has indeed been some progress in their relationship.

ROSEMONDE: I'm so delighted you could manage to visit us, my dear, even if only for such a short time.

MERTEUIL: I wish I could stay longer, Madame, but my husband's estate . . .

ROSEMONDE: Do you know, I was thinking yesterday, it's more than five years since you were last here, with your dear husband. Such a kind and such a vigorous man, who could have imagined . . . ah well . . .

Mme. de Merteuil, who is centrally placed, has been watching Mme. de Tourvel and, particularly, Valmont, who really is lost in contemplation of Mme. de Tourvel. She doesn't like what she sees: it clearly troubles her, even though, after only the briefest pause, she manages a civil reply to Mme. de Rosemonde.

MERTEUIL: Yes, Madame, there's no denying that life is frighteningly unpredictable.

Scene 8: Valmont's bedroom in the chateau, two nights later

Valmont escorts Cecile into his room, where they can make more noise without being overheard than in Cecile's quarters. Cecile jumps into bed and eagerly summons Valmont, who instructs her that haste isn't desirable in these circumstances. He means to take the time to show her subtleties of lovemaking that will gratify her husband on her wedding night and and probably cause him to believe that Cecile's mother, who once was "one of the most notorious young women in Paris," coached her well.

"Education is never a waste," Valmont finally declares, drawing Cecile to him. "Now I think we might begin with one or two Latin terms."

Scene 9: The salon in the chateau, late the following evening

Mme. de Tourvel is alone, putting away the playing cards, when Valmont enters. Helping her, Valmont contrives to touch her hand, which throws her into confusion. She relies on his integrity (she tells him) and wishes he would leave the chateau, but when he takes her hand she doesn't withdraw it. Valmont begs her to let him know if she loves him, and when he looks into her eyes he sees that she does. When he tries to embrace her, however, she cries out, "For God's sake, you must leave me, if you don't want to kill me, you must help, it's killing me!"

Mme. de Tourvel then collapses into shock and convulsions. Valmont carries her to the chaise-longue, alarmed at the intensity of her reaction. As she lies there helpless, he loosens her bodice, and when her convulsions cease, he *"pauses for a moment, looking down at her, as her features return to normal. They look at each other. Something passes between them; and this time it's Valmont who looks away, something almost like shame darkening his expression. Mme. de Tourvel begins to go into shock again; and Valmont breaks away and races over to the door,"* calling for help. She reaches out her hand to him; he takes it, holds it and releases it only when Mme. de Rosemonde and her maid enter and go to Mme de Tourvel's assistance. As Valmont leaves the room, they offer to fetch the doctor, but Mme. de Tourvel wishes only to have a word alone with Mme. de Rosemonde, who sends the maid away.

TOURVEL: I have to leave this house first thing in the morning. I'm most desperately in love.

Mme. de Rosemonde, unsurprised, bows her head.

To leave here is the last thing in the world I want to do: but I'd rather die than have to live with the guilt. I don't mind if I die: to live without him is going to be no life at all. But that's what I have to do. Can you understand what I'm saying?

ROSEMONDE: Of course. My dear girl. None of this is any surprise to me. The only thing which might surprise one is how little the world changes. Of course you must leave if you feel it's the right thing to do.

TOURVEL: And what should I do then? What's your advice?

ROSEMONDE: If I remember rightly, in such matters all advice is useless. You can't speak to the patient in the grip of a fever. We must talk again when you're closer to recovery.

TOURVEL: I've never been so unhappy.

ROSEMONDE: I'm sorry to say this: but those who are most worthy of love are never made happy by it. You're too young to have understood that.

TOURVEL: But why, why should that be?

ROSEMONDE: Do you still think men love the way we do? No. Men enjoy the happiness they feel; we can only enjoy the happiness we give. They're not capable of devoting themselves exclusively to one person. So to hope to be made happy by love is a certain cause of grief. I'm devoted to my nephew, but what is true of most men is doubly so of him.

TOURVEL: And yet . . . he could have . . . just now. He took pity on me, I saw it happen, I saw his decision not to take advantage of me.

ROSEMONDE: If he has released you, my dear child, it's because your example over these last few weeks has genuinely affected and improved him. If he's let you go, you must go.

TOURVEL: I will. I will.

> *Mme. de Tourvel starts crying again and twists round, letting her head drop into Mme. de Rosemonde's lap. Mme. de Rosemonde sits, looking down, stroking Mme. de Tourvel's hair.*

ROSEMONDE: There. And even if you had given way, my dear girl, God knows how hard you've struggled against it. There now.

> *She strokes Mme. de Tourvel's hair. The lights fade to blackout. Curtain.*

ACT II

Scene 1: The principal salon in Valmont's Paris house, late October

Mme. de Tourvel has returned home, but Azolan's relationship with her maid Julie permits him to keep an eye on Madame and even intercept her mail. He hands two letters to his master—one addressed to Mme. de Rosemonde and one to Mme. de Tourvel's confessor. Valmont peruses them and rewards his manservant handsomely.

A footman escorts Danceny and Mme. de Merteuil into the salon. Valmont dismisses his servants and hears that Danceny believes the Vicomte has been advancing Danceny's romantic cause with Cecile so successfully that even Cecile's mother may come around to countenancing their marriage. Mme. de Merteuil requests a few moments alone with Valmont. When Danceny exits to wait in the carriage, the two conspirators *"fall into each other's arms"* with laughter. Valmont then informs her that Cecile is now pregnant, so that the Marquise's revenge on Gercourt should be considered complete: "I've provided him with a wife trained by me to perform quite naturally services you would hesitate to request from a professional. And very likely pregnant as well. What more do you want?" Mme. de Merteuil fears that Valmont may have gone too far with Cecile but agrees that he's done his duty in this case.

"Shame you let the other one slip through your fingers," she comments, and Valmont agrees. He doesn't know what came over him to allow Mme. de Tourvel to escape: "I was . . . moved." It won't happen again, though, he assures her: "I have an appointment to visit her house on Thursday. And this time, I shall be merciless. I'm going to punish her . . . . . I shan't have a moment's peace until it's over, you know. I love her, I hate her, I'm furious with her, my life's a misery; I've got to have her so that I can pass all these feelings on to her and be rid of them."

On her part, the Marquise is ready to drop her present lover and take another one, but she won't tell Valmont who the next one is to be. She directs Valmont not to call on her until he has succeeded with Mme. de Tourvel: "I'm not sure I could face another catalogue of incompetence."

Scene 2: The salon in Mme. de Tourvel's house, two days later, 6 P.M.

Mme. de Tourvel is seated when Valmont is shown in by a footman. She tries to rise but, weakly, she is trembling and cannot. Valmont hands her a packet of letters and explains that he has come to be reconciled with her before beginning to take instruction from a priest. He pretends that reconciliation is necessary because she has maltreated him by leaving him abruptly in the lurch at Mme. de Rosemonde's and then refusing to accept or answer his letters to her. He begs her forgiveness for whatever wrong she believes he has done her.

Desperately, Mme. de Tourvel tries to explain that duty forbids her responding to him, so that she must avoid him forever more. Valmont *"falls to his knees and buries his face in her lap"* as he voices his despair.

VALMONT: I must have you or die.
> *Mme. de Tourvel scrambles to her feet and retreats across the room. Valmont watches her and then mutters a bitter aside, loud enough, however, to be heard by her.*
Death it is.
> *Silence. Mme. de Tourvel is plainly distraught. Valmont appears to make a great effort to calm himself. He rises to his feet.*
I'm sorry. I wanted to live for your happiness and I destroyed it. Now I want to give you back your peace of mind and I destroy that too. I'm not used to passion, I can't deal with it. At least, this is the last time. So be calm.
TOURVEL: It's difficult when you are in this state, Monsieur.
VALMONT: Yes; well, don't worry, it won't last very long.

> *Valmont picks up the packet of letters which Mme. de Tourvel has let drop by her chair.*

These are the very things which might weaken my courage: these deceitful pledges of your friendship. They were all that reconciled me to life.

> *Valmont puts them down on the chair. Mme. de Tourvel moves toward him, concerned.*

TOURVEL: I understood you wanted to return them to me. And that you now approved of the choice my duty has compelled me to make.

VALMONT: Yes. And your choice has determined mine.

TOURVEL: Which is what?

VALMONT: The only choice capable of putting an end to my suffering.

TOURVEL: What do you mean?

> *Mme. de Tourvel's voice is full of fear. Valmont is beside her now, and she doesn't resist as he takes her in his arms.*

VALMONT: Listen. I love you. You've no idea how much. Remember, I've made far more difficult sacrifices than the one I'm about to make. Now goodbye.

> *Valmont pulls away from Mme. de Tourvel, but she clutches at his wrist.*

TOURVEL: No.

VALMONT: Let me go.

TOURVEL: You must listen to me!

VALMONT: I have to go.

TOURVEL: No!

> *Mme. de Tourvel collapses into Valmont's arms. He begins to kiss her, and she responds: for a moment they kiss each other greedily. Then he sweeps her up in his arms, carries her across the room, sets her down gently on the ottoman and kneels alongside her. She bursts into tears and clutches onto him as if she's drowning. He looks down at her as she sobs helplessly and speaks with unusual tenderness.*

VALMONT: Why should you be so upset by the idea of making me happy?

> *Gradually, Mme. de Tourvel stops crying and looks up at him.*

TOURVEL: Yes. You're right. I can't live either unless I make you happy. So I promise. No more refusals and no more regrets.

> *Mme. de Tourvel kisses Valmont. He begins, slowly, to undress her.*

Scene 3: Mme. de Merteuil's salon, the following evening

Exuberantly, Valmont enters and tells Mme. de Merteuil of his successful conquest of Mme. de Tourvel. When he learned that his aunt had become Mme. de Tourvel's confidante (he explains), he hinted to her that he was "losing the will to live, knowing that this would be passed on"; and he induced Mme. de Tourvel's confessor to set up the appointment with her. As for the seduction itself, "It had a kind of charm I don't think I've ever experienced before. Once she'd surrendered, she behaved with perfect candor. Total mutual delirium: which for the first time ever with me outlasted the pleasure itself. She was astonishing. So much so that I ended by falling on my knees and pledging her eternal love. And do you know, at the time, and for several hours afterwards, I actually meant it!"

Mme. de Merteuil receives this information coolly. Valmont claims his reward, but the Marquise refuses him in the absence of the agreed-upon written evidence of his conquest; moreover, she feels that Valmont is taking her favors too much for granted. Valmont pleads that this is "really only eagerness," and that no other compares with her in his estimation. But she continues to refuse him at this time. She is going away for a couple of weeks, during which time Valmont can procure the essential letter; and then, she agrees, "You and I will spend a single night together. I'm sure we shall find it quite sufficient. We shall enjoy it enough to regret that it's to be our last; but then we shall remember that regret is an essential component of happiness. And part the best of friends."

The Marquise believes that Valmont is in love with Mme. de Tourvel, but Valmont calls it an infatuation which won't last, in contrast to their relationship, which was love suspended by "failure of the imagination" and now ready to be rekindled. She lets him kiss her, briefly, then dismisses him.

> *Merteuil stands a moment, collecting herself, then she crosses the room and opens a door.*
> MERTEUIL: He's gone.
> *Presently, Danceny steps into the room. He embraces Merteuil impulsively and, once again, she submits only briefly.*
> DANCENY: I thought he'd be here all night. Time has no logic when I'm not with you: an hour is like a century.
> MERTEUIL: We shall get on a good deal better if you make a concerted effort not to sound like the latest novel.
> DANCENY *(blushes):* I'm sorry, I . . .
> *Merteuil softens and reaches a hand to Danceny's cheek.*
> MERTEUIL: Never mind. Take me upstairs.
> *Arm in arm, Merteuil and Danceny begin to move towards the door.*

Scene 4: The salon in Valmont's house, a fortnight later, afternoon

Valmont is drinking champagne with Emilie when a visitor is announced. He lets Emilie linger in the room long enough so that as Mme. de Tourvel enters Emilie is just leaving. She passes Mme. de Tourvel, staring, without a word, but breaks into laughter as she exits.

Mme. de Tourvel is confused and upset; she recognizes Emilie as someone who has been pointed out to her at the opera as a courtesan. She turns and tries to walk out, but Valmont holds her back, insisting on her hearing his explanation: Emilie, a relic of Valmont's past life, does much charity work and came to collect a donation. Mme. de Tourvel wants to believe him, so she does, telling him "I love you so much." In spite of himself, the Vicomte is moved by her jealousy and sincerity; he is *"no longer in command of his emotions, his expression pained and uncharacteristically tender."*

Scene 5: Mme. de Merteuil's salon, ten days later, evening

Valmont enters unannounced and observes Danceny lying on the sofa with his head in the Marquise's lap. She had instructed her porter to tell visitors she is out of town, but Valmont refused to be put off and has come looking for Danceny on Cecile's behalf. She has been so ill that it was necessary to call the doctor in the middle of the night, possibly because (Valmont suggests) she was anxious about the whereabouts of Danceny, who now reproaches himself bitterly for not having been at Cecile's side in her time of need.

Valmont also announces that he's brought a letter which might be of interest to the Marquise. She sends Danceny upstairs with his worries about Cecile and glances at the letter. It is satisfactory proof of his conquest of Mme. de Tourvel, but the situation, in Valmont's opinion, is not—the Marquise has allowed a "mawkish schoolboy" to preempt her attentions. "Mawkish or not, he's completely devoted to me," the Marquise replies, "and, I suspect, better equipped to provide me with happiness and pleasure than you in your present mood."

Valmont is put out by this remark but nevertheless answers the Marquise's questions about Cecile, informing her that Cecile has suffered a miscarriage. The moment has now come to pass Cecile along to Danceny, the Vicomte declares, and of course Mme. de Merteuil cannot have that. Flirtatiously, she suggests, "If I thought you would be your old charming self, I might invite you to visit me one evening next week . . . . . I still love you, you see, in spite of all your faults and my complaints." She tells him of a friend who extracted himself from any and all awkward situations by announcing, "It's beyond my control." Valmont exits, pondering her meaning and his own situation.

Scene 6: The salon in Mme. de Tourvel's house, the following afternoon

The footman shows Valmont in, and Mme. de Tourvel is delighted to see him. But he is standoffish, pushing away from her embrace and shocking her with brutal confessions that after four months he is bored with her, he has been unfaithful to her with Emilie, he now wishes to take another woman, whom he adores, for a mistress—all of which is "beyond my control." Goaded to fury, Mme. de Tourvel suddenly beats at him with her fists.

TOURVEL *(screams):* Liar!
VALMONT: You're right, I am a liar. It's like your fidelity, a fact of life, no more or less irritating. Certainly it's beyond my control.
TOURVEL: Stop it, don't keep saying that!
VALMONT: Sorry, it's beyond my control.
      Mme. de Tourvel screams.
Why don't you take another lover?
      Mme. de Tourvel bursts into tears, shaking her head and moaning incoherently.
Just as you like, of course, it's beyond my control.
TOURVEL: Do you want to kill me?
      Valmont strides over to Mme. de Tourvel, takes her by the hair and jerks her head up, shocking her into a moment's silence.
VALMONT: Listen. Listen to me. You've given me great pleasure. But I just can't bring myself to regret leaving you. It's the way of the world. Quite beyond my control.

Alan Rickman as the Vicomte de Valmont and Lindsay Duncan as the Marquise de Merteuil in a scene from *Les Liaisons Dangereuses*

> *When Valmont lets go of her hair, Mme. de Tourvel collapses full-length, moaning and sobbing helplessly. Valmont crosses to the doorway and turns to look back at her. His triumphant expression has lasted only a moment; and now gives way to a queasy, haunted, tormented look. His eyes are full of fear and regret. For a moment, it's almost as if he's going to run back to help her. Abruptly, Valmont turns and guiltily scuttles away.*

Scene 7: Mme. de Merteuil's salon, a December evening about a week later

Again Valmont enters unannounced, startling the Marquise, who is seated at her escritoire, writing. To the Marquise's satisfaction, she learns that Valmont broke with Mme. de Tourvel using the "beyond my control" gambit, and that the lady has retired to a convent. Valmont calls this his "most famous exploit" which could only be topped by winning Mme. de Tourvel back. That would be impossible, Mme. de Merteuil counters; she sees this as one of her greatest triumphs, too, and "When one woman strikes at the heart of another, she seldom misses; and the wound is invariably fatal." And the Marquise goes on to explain that her victory was over the Vicomte, not Mme. de Tourvel, and this brings the fear once again into Valmont's eyes, as the Marquise continues: "You loved that woman, Vicomte. What's more, you still do. Quite desperately. If you hadn't been so ashamed of it, how could you possibly have treated her so viciously? You couldn't bear even the vague possibility of being laughed at. And this has proved something I've always suspected. That vanity and happiness are incompatible."

The Vicomte reminds the Marquise that now she must get rid of Danceny, but she refuses to be ordered around like a married woman. She is waiting for an assignation with Danceny here this very night, but Valmont takes pleasure in informing her that her lover isn't coming. Instead, Valmont has persuaded Danceny that he must choose between Cecile and the Marquise, and Danceny has chosen Cecile, He will call on Mme. de Merteuil the next day to announce this and pledge his continuing friendship; in the meantime, Valmont has arranged a reconciliation between Danceny and Cecile.

The time has come, Valmont states firmly, for the Marquise to redeem her pledge.

VALMONT: . . . . . Shall we go up?
MERTEUIL: Shall we what?
VALMONT: Go up. Unless you prefer this, if memory serves, rather purgatorial sofa.
MERTEUIL: I believe it's time you were going.
    Silence.
VALMONT: No, I don't think so. We made an arrangement. I really don't think I can allow myself to be taken advantage of a moment longer.
MERTEUIL: Remember I'm better at this than you are.
VALMONT: Perhaps. But it's always the best swimmers who drown. Now. Yes or no? Up to you, of course. I wouldn't dream of trying to influence you. I therefore confine myself to remarking that a "no" will be regarded as a declaration of war. So. One single word is all that's required.
MERTEUIL: All right. *(She looks at Valmont evenly for a moment, almost long enough for him to conclude that she has made her answer. But she hasn't. It follows now, calm and authoritative.)* War.
    Blackout.

Scene 8: The Bois de Vincennes, a misty December dawn

Valmont and Danceny, accompanied by manservants, are preparing to fight a duel with epées. Apparently Danceny has learned that the Vicomte made a fool of him and has challenged his older and obviously confident rival.

The two are evenly matched. Danceny, the aggressor, wounds the Vicomte in the arm, not his sword arm. After a pause, the fight resumes but *"Valmont seems to have lost heart"* and fails to take an advantage of an obvious opportunity, with his great skill, to strike a decisive blow. Valmont seems to become almost careless, *"which allows Danceny through his guard with a thrust which enters Valmont's body somewhere just below his heart."* Danceny withdraws his sword from the wound, and Valmont falls to the ground. He rejects the offer to call a surgeon and draws Danceny over to hear his painfully murmured advice: Beware the Marquise de Merteuil, she has manipulated both of them to this duel. Valmont also asks Danceny to take a last message to the now very ill Mme. de Tourvel: "Tell her it's lucky for her that I've gone and I'm glad not to have to live without her. Tell her her love was the only real happiness I've ever known." . . . . . *"He raises a hand towards Danceny: but the effort of doing so is too great, and he slumps back before Danceny can take his hand. He's dead."*

Scene 9: Mme. de Merteuil's salon, New Year's Eve

The three ladies—Mesdames de Merteuil, de Volanges and de Rosemonde—are playing cards, but Mme. de Rosemonde, dressed in mourning, is distracted by reverie. She has much to occupy her thoughts, with the death of her nephew in the duel and the death in the convent of Mme. de Tourvel. Mme. de Volanges, who was at Mme. de Tourvel's side, describes how she gradually wasted away. The Marquise cannot hide *"the glitter of satisfaction in her eyes,"* but her satisfaction is soon soured by traces of bitter jealousy as Mme. de Volanges declares that Mme. de Tourvel still might have managed to pull through, except that Danceny visited her, informed her of Valmont's death and delivered the Vicomte's message that Mme. de Tourvel was "the only woman he'd ever loved."

Mme. de Merteuil manages to regain her composure and diverts Mme. de Volanges into changing the subject to her daughter Cecile's future prospects.

VOLANGES: . . . . . I did want to ask your advice about this, both of you. Monsieur de Gercourt is expected back anyday now. Is there nothing to be done? Must I really break off such an advantageous match?

MERTEUIL: Oh, surely not.

ROSEMONDE: I'm afraid you must.

VOLANGES: But why?

MERTEUIL: I think you must provide a reason, Madame, if you ask our friend to sacrifice so glorious a future.

> *Her fighting spirit has returned now, and her voice is as crisp and decisive as ever.*

VOLANGES: To be honest with you, Madame, and in spite of his crime, I'd rather marry Cecile to Danceny than see my only child become a nun.

ROSEMONDE: As a matter of fact, I've heard from Danceny. He sent me a very strange letter. From Malta.

VOLANGES: Oh, that's where he's run away to?

> *A silence falls. Merteuil is busy digesting what Mme. de Rosemonde has said. When she's done so, she turns to Mme. de Volanges.*

MERTEUIL: On second thoughts, my dear, I suppose it might be best to defer to Madame's wisdom and experience. Perhaps you should leave Cecile in the convent.

VOLANGES: But there must be a reason?

> *Silence. No one seems disposed to add anything, and Mme. de Volange's question hangs in the air. Eventually, Merteuil speaks, with all her customary authority.*

MERTEUIL: This has been a terrible few weeks. But time passes so quickly. A new year tomorrow and more than halfway through the eighties already. I used to be afraid of growing old, but now I trust in God and accept. I dare say we would not be wrong to look forward to whatever the nineties may bring. Meanwhile, I suggest our best course is to continue with the game.

Merteuil's words seem to exert a calming effect on her companions: and indeed, they resume playing. The atmosphere is serene. Very slowly, the lights fade: but just before they vanish, there appears on the back wall, fleeting but sharp, the unmistakeable silhouette of the guillotine. Curtain.

THREE POSTCARDS

A Full-Length Musical in One Act

BOOK BY CRAIG LUCAS

MUSIC AND LYRICS BY CRAIG CARNELIA

Cast and credits appear on pages 335 & 337

CRAIG LUCAS (book), a graduate of Boston University where he studied with the poets Anne Sexton and George Starbuck, first came to the attention of New York audiences as a musical theater performer in the role of "Confederate Sniper" in Shenandoah *in January 1975. Like his collaborator, Craig Carnelia, he branched out from acting into authorship. After his appearance in* Sweeney Todd, the Demon Barber of Fleet Street *in 1979, he joined with Norman René in the conception and development of* Marry Me a Little, *the collection of Stephen Sondheim songs which opened OOB at The Production Company in November 1980 and moved off Broadway March 12, 1981 for 96 performances. His* Blue Window *also began at The Production Company, opening June 12, 1984 and then rising to full off-Broadway status December 9th of that year, also playing 96 performances.* Blue Window *won Lucas the George and Elisabeth Marton Award for Playwriting, "to recognize and encourage a new American playwright" and the 1985–86 Los Angeles Drama Critics Award for outstanding writing. His* Three Postcards *opened late this season—May 14—at Playwrights Horizons and was taken off after only 22 performances, but it won its author a Best Play citation and has a brightly promising future.*

Lucas is also the author of the playscripts Missing Persons *and* Reckless *presented at The Production Company and* Prelude to a Kiss *commissioned by South*

Coast Repertory in Costa Mesa, Calif.; the librettos for two operas, Cousin Lillie *and* Orpheus in Love; *and the film version of his own* Blue Window. *He is the recipient of a 1987 Guggenheim Fellowship.*

CRAIG CARNELIA (music, lyrics) was born on Long Island in Floral Park in 1949, the son of an accountant. He attended Memorial High School there and went on to Hofstra but dropped out to become an actor. In January 1969 he was cast as Matt in The Fantasticks *and played the role for about six months, during which time he discovered in himself "a more distinctive talent" than acting and began to try his hand at writing music and lyrics. His first produced work of record was* Notes: Songs *OOB at Manhattan Theater Club's Upstage in January 1977. He contributed song numbers to the Goodman Theater production of* Working *in Chicago at the end of that year and was included in its best-score Tony nomination after it played Broadway for 25 performances beginning May 14, 1978. He did the score for* Is There Life After High School? *at the Hartford, Conn. Stage Company in April 1981 and on Broadway May 7, 1982 for 12 performances, and he contributed a song to the 122-performance off-Broadway musical* Diamonds *which opened December 16, 1984.*

Three Postcards was produced off Broadway by Playwrights Horizons May 14, 1987 for only 22 performances, but it won both its authors their first Best Play citation. Carnelia is married to the actress Maureen Silliman (who played one of the three major roles in Three Postcards*), and they live in New York City.*

Not being organized around a formal plot in the usual sense of the word, Three Postcards *doesn't lend itself to representation by detailed synopsis, as in the case of most of the other Best Plays. Instead, to suggest its flavor, we emphasize substantial excerpts from the book and lyrics of this unusual work, with brief suggestions of the connecting activity.*

Place: A restaurant

Three women—K.C., Big Jane and Little Jane—meet for dinner in a trendy restaurant. Having been friends since childhood, they speak in shorthand about their shared pasts. But the show is as much about their private worlds as the one they share.

In "What the Song Should Say," the three women, each singing from a private perspective, simultaneously articulate their feelings about the restaurant and their meeting, all of which is informed by a yearning that this evening will be in some way special and fulfilling.

> *They smile at one another. K.C. looks around the restaurant.*
K.C.: This is nice.
LITTLE JANE: Isn't it?

BIG JANE: Isn't it nice?
LITTLE JANE: . . . . . It's great to see you.
K.C.: Thanks.
THREE WOMEN *(sing):*

> The song should say . . . a restaurant.
> The song should say . . . evening.
> And in the words, a chance of rain,
> A table and three chairs.
>
> The song should have city sounds,
> Far away and fast.
> And as it flows the song should have
> The waiter brushing past.
> And it should say a piano plays
> All the evening long,
> And we should be . . . in the song.
>
> Father, mother, brother, naked.
> How's the puppy? Did you drive?
> Tuesday, thank you, my umbrella.
> Just to be alive.

Night will fall, the restaurant will fill with people (the lyrics continue), and the three friends will lose themselves in their song.

Karen Trott as K.C., Jane Galloway as Big Jane and Maureen Silliman as Little Jane in *Three Postcards*

K.C. *(sings):*
Finding . . .
Father, mother
In the fall.
Father, mother
In the chill.
Father, mother
In the hall,
Standing perfectly,
Perfectly still.

LITTLE JANE *(sings):*
Finding . . .
I'm very young.
I'm very small
And I'm standing,
Standing still.
And I understand
Everything
Standing perfectly,
Perfectly still.

BIG JANE *(sings):*
Finding . . .
Husbands,
Lovers

In the song.
Young
Girls
Dancing, dancing,
Dancing
In each other's arms
In the song . . . . .

ALL THREE *(sing):*
But there should be more.
Somehow . . .
Somehow the music should soar,
And so should we.
So should we.
We should soar in the song.
Somehow . . . perfectly . . .
We should be, should be carried along
Carried along
By the song.
On and on and on and on and
On and on and on and on . . .
Restaurant music resumes. Waiter returns with drinks and menus.

Big Jane is a would-be poet who is about to begin part-time work doing phone sales of magazine subscriptions. She also has a history of fairly disastrous and humiliating relationships with men. In the following section, what starts out as a realistic discussion among the friends of Big Jane's situation takes a leap into fantasy when the waiter, Walter, assumes the role of a therapist. Then what started as a private session between the two of them is broken open when K.C. and Little Jane insist on adding their perspectives on Big Jane's dilemma.

K.C. *(to Big Jane):* How's the poetry?
BIG JANE: Good.
K.C.: Have you submitted anything?
BIG JANE: No. But . . .
K.C.: When do you start the job?
BIG JANE: Oh, any time.
K.C.: Oh.
BIG JANE: But, you know, I have to decide.
K.C.: Uh-huh.
BIG JANE: But I can make my own hours, I can work out of the apartment.
K.C.: Great.
LITTLE JANE: Yeah.

BIG JANE: We'll see.

LITTLE JANE: Do you ever hear from the airline steward?

BIG JANE: No, but I heard from Tommy!

LITTLE JANE: Oh.

K.C.: Oh, you did.

BIG JANE: Oh, he's terrific.

K.C.: Uh-huh.

BIG JANE: And he's still with Mark. And they want me to clean their apartment. You know.

K.C.: What do you mean?

BIG JANE: You know, I said I needed money. Who knows, I don't know.

K.C.: Is that wise?

BIG JANE: No. But I mean, why shouldn't I?

LITTLE JANE: I'm out of it.

BIG JANE: Really. You know.

K.C.: You're going to clean your ex-boy friend's apartment and his boy friend's?

BIG JANE: Only if I want to. I mean . . .

LITTLE JANE: I have no opinion.

BIG JANE *(to K.C.):* Why not?

K.C.: Well, here in America we sometimes consider it a small indignity to—

BIG JANE: I know—

K.C.:—clean other people's apartments.

BIG JANE: I know.

K.C.: Our *own* apartments, for that matter, but of course we do it, or we hire someone we don't know to do it and feel guilty about it. But there are those who would say—

BIG JANE: You're right.

K.C.:—that to clean the apartment of the man we were in love with who left us for another man—

BIG JANE: Well, I knew he was bisexual.

K.C.: Still, there are those who would say that to accept the offer at all is in some small way to make a putz out of one's own nose.

> *Walter presents the wine to Little Jane, who nods her approval.*

Don't do it. I will pay you not to do it.

BIG JANE: Well, I'm not going to, so—

K.C.: Good . . .

WALTER *(to Big Jane, as all others freeze):* Why lie?

BIG JANE: Excuse me?

WALTER: Why did you lie?

BIG JANE: I didn't. No, you know, I don't know, I mean, you're the doctor, but I think she's just saying don't let people run over you, that's all.

WALTER: Oh. Is that what you think you're doing?

BIG JANE: No, but I can understand why she might think that's what I would be doing. If I were to clean his apartment.

WALTER: Why didn't you say that?

BIG JANE: Because. Then I'd have to say that I already did.

WALTER: Ohhh.

BIG JANE: No, I mean, I just sort of straightened up a little, I don't know, that's not really the problem . . .

WALTER: What's the problem?

BIG JANE: I don't know. I guess I just don't feel like I really need to be seeing you right now.

LITTLE JANE *(unfreezing):* Oh, please.

BIG JANE: You know?

LITTLE JANE: Are you kidding?

BIG JANE: And I can't really afford it either.

BIG JANE *(continued):* I mean—You   LITTLE JANE: You can't *not* afford it.
know. I don't know . . . I just . . . I guess
I feel . . . You know . . .

LITTLE JANE: You see, you can't even say what you mean, because you don't know what you mean, because your feelings are like tofu. *(To Walter.)* I'm sorry, I know this is her session.

WALTER: Please.

> *He pours himself a glass of wine and sips it.*

LITTLE JANE: All right. O.K., I'm sorry, you know I love you dearly, but somebody has to tell you the truth. Your poetry stinks. It stinks.

BIG JANE: My . . . ?

LITTLE JANE *(to K.C.):* Yes?

K.C. *(unfreezing):* It stinks.

LITTLE JANE *(to Big Jane):* You have the vocabulary of a fruit fly. You're thirty-five years old, you have no skills, you've been through seventeen boy friends in three years, you don't know when to pay your income tax, how to drive a car or keep an apartment, you can't even keep a job as a waitress because you don't know what half the foodstuffs are. "Oh, is *that* a scallop?"

BIG JANE: We never had them.

LITTLE JANE: When are you going to face up to the fact that you need help? Jane, look at me. You are a train wreck. A big one. The governor is on his way over here.

K.C.: Tell him about—

LITTLE JANE: Oh, O.K. *(Getting up.)* All right, here is the supreme example of what we're talking about.

> *She motions for Walter to take her seat, which he does.*

BIG JANE: Please—

LITTLE JANE: Bear with me.

WALTER: Hey, take your time.

> *Walter butters Little Jane's roll and eats it. Bill, the piano player, unfreezes and begins playing and whistling.*

LITTLE JANE: Seven years ago we decided it was time that Big Jane had a vacation. She doesn't have a job at the time and she's just broken up with, I can't even remember.

BIG JANE: Marco.

LITTLE JANE: Marco. Is he the one who gave you herpes?

BIG JANE AND K.C. *(in unison):* No.

LITTLE JANE: Oh, that's right, he's the one who is now in prison.

BIG JANE: He's not in—

LITTLE JANE: So we agree to put up the money for Big Jane to take ten carefree days in Martinique. Have you ever been to Martinique?

WALTER: No.

LITTLE JANE: Neither have we.

BIG JANE: It's very nice.

LITTLE JANE: And I agree to water the plants, pick up the mail, the usual announcements that the phone is being shut off—

WALTER: Un-huh.

LITTLE JANE: Because what's ten days? Ten days. *(To Big Jane.)* Would you care to tell the rest of the story . . . Somehow in the amazing, mind-numbing way of our best friend in all the world, ten days becomes . . . five years.

WALTER: *Seriously?*

BIG JANE: Wellll, it was really only four. And a half.

LITTLE JANE: O.K., it was really only four and a half. Years. And during those four and a half years—*(To K.C.)* Back me up on this.

K.C.: All true.

LITTLE JANE: We find, slowly but strangely, that we're not really even welcome to come to Martinique because, as it turns out, our best friend's boy friend—and please, I don't care to hear his name right now—has a small jealous streak—

K.C.: Maniac.

LITTLE JANE: But quote, "He's really very nice," which I'm sure he was—

K.C.: Surrrrrrre.

> *Walter nods.*

LITTLE JANE:—other than his beating you to a pulp, getting you pregnant and disappearing forever, and—that's right, you were living illegally in Martinique, weren't you?

WALTER: No, no.

LITTLE JANE: That's right, but listen, hey, it   K.C.: Wait.
was no trouble, Jane, just contacting the
American consulate, our Congressman, you
had no passport oddly enough—

WALTER: No. Why *should* she?

LITTLE JANE:—and paying for your flight back, your abortion, your new apartment, and oh yes, your landlord was suing me, too—

K.C.: Suing her. *Suing* her!

LITTLE JANE:—wasn't he? Because I had to cosign on the sublease, and the new tenant turned out to be . . .

WALTER: What? Don't tell me! Don't tell me!

LITTLE JANE AND K.C. *(in unison):* A heroin addict!

> *Bill finishes playing as the laughter plays itself out and everyone returns to their earlier positions.*

In the following excerpt, while the three chat about K.C.'s new dog, Little Jane (whose marriage is in a bumpy patch) dreams that first Bill, the cocktail pianist, and then Walter, the waiter, harbor lascivious thoughts about her, expressed in the lyrics of the song "I've Been Watching You."

*The table conversation fades as Bill continues singing to Little Jane.
Walter arrives with the appetizers, serving K.C. first and pouring everyone more wine.*

BILL *(sings):*
   Ho, it's not every night
   Not every night
   That someone like you walks in the cafe.
   Other women come in,
   They don't begin
   To stir me like you do.
   By the way,

   I've been thinking about your panties.
   I've been guessing they might be pink.
WALTER *(sings):*
   No no. Black.
BILL *(sings):*
   And it's giving me shakes.
   I've been making mistakes.
WALTER *(sings):*
   Oh, the way you fit in that chair.
WALTER AND BILL *(sing):*
   Oh, hoo, la la la, la la la, la la la.
WALTER *(sings):*
   I've been thinking of *you*, Jane, 'til it hurts.
WALTER AND BILL *(sing):*
   Mmmm, oo, hoo, la la la, la la love
WALTER *(sings):*
   The way you sit,
BILL *(sings):*
   The way you smile,
WALTER *(sings):*
   The way you talk,
WALTER AND BILL *(sing):*
   The way you . . .
   The way you move me.

   Oh, it's not every night,
   Not every night
   That someone like you
   Walks in the cafe . . . . .

   Not every night,
   Not every night
   There's someone like . . .
   Quite so hot every night,
   Not every night.
   Not every night
   There's someone like . . .

Maureen Silliman (as Little Jane) with Craig Carnelia, composer and lyricist of *Three Postcards* (as Bill), in a scene from the musical

WALTER *(sings):*
The way you sit,
The way you smile,
The way you talk,
The way you . . .
The way you smell,
The way you laugh,
The way you . . .
The way you walk in a room
The way you . . .

BILL *(sings):*
The way you move,

The way you walk in a room,

The way you touch,
The way you butter your bread,

The way you move in that blouse,   The way you tease,
The way . . .   The way . . . the way . . .
The way you dressed for me   The way you dressed for me
Tonight . . . . .   Tonight . . . . .

The song "Three Postcards" is a contrapuntal setting of postcard messages Big Jane sent to Little Jane (who then passed them on to K.C.) during the Martinique adventure.

BIG JANE *(sings):*
  Jane,
  You would love this hotel.
  My flight was O.K.
  Boy, that water's blue.
  I go snorkling today.
  The suit fits me fine.
  See you Wednesday night.
  Pass this on to K.C.
  Jane.

BIG JANE *(sings):*   LITTLE JANE *(sings):*
Jane,   Jane,
Thank you, thank you, thank you.   You would love this hotel.
This vacation was the greatest idea.   My flight was O.K.
I met this guy   Boy, that water's blue.
He teaches snorkling   I go snorkling today
I won't be home 'til Thursday,   The suit fits me fine
Or at the latest Friday.   See you Wednesday night.
I found that perfume you asked for.   Pass this on to K.C.,
Give you a call the minute I get in.   Jane
Pass this on to K.C.,
Jane.

BIG JANE *(sings):*   LITTLE JANE *(sings):*   K.C. *(sings):*
Jane,   Jane,   Jane,
Have left my hotel,   Thank you, thank you,   You would love this
And moved in with   thank you.   hotel.
            Philippe.   This vacation was the   My flight was O.K.
I'm gonna stay down   greatest idea. Boy that water's
            here awhile.   I met this guy,   blue.
You know me.   He teaches snorkling.   I go snorkling
Please call my mother   I won't be home 'til   today.
And tell her I'm fine.   Thursday.   The suit fits me
Philippe says hello.   Or at the latest Friday.   fine.
Pass this on to K.C.   I found that perfume   See you Wednesday
Yo ho ho, and a   you asked for.   night.
            bottle of rum. Give you a call the   Pass this on
Your island girl.   minute I get in.   to K.C.
                            Pass it on to K.C.,   Jane
                            Jane

LITTLE JANE *(sings):*
Jane,
Have left my hotel
And moved in with Philippe,
I'm gonna stay down here
                                    awhile.
You know me.
Please call my mother
And tell her I'm fine.
Philippe says hello.

Yo ho ho,
And a bottle of rum.
Your island girl.

K.C. *(sings):*
Jane,
Thank you, thank you, thank you.
This vacation was the greatest
                                    idea.
I met this guy.
He teaches snorkling.
I won't be home 'til Thursday,
Or at the latest Friday.
I found that perfume you asked
                                    for.
Give you a call the minute I get
                                    in.
Pass it on to K.C.,
Jane.

K.C. *(sings):*
Jane,
Have left my hotel,
And moved in with Philippe,
I'm gonna stay down here awhile.
You know me.
Please call my mother
And tell her I'm fine.
Philippe says hello.
Pass this on to K.C.
Yo ho ho, and a bottle of rum.
Your island girl.
Jane.
       The chairs and table join together on the last note of the song. Lights
       and restaurant music restore.

K.C. is trying to adjust to the death of her mother. In a private moment, she
thinks of a photograph taken on her mother's wedding day, examining it for clues
to who her mother was, in the lyrics of "The Picture in the Hall."

K.C. *(sings):*
       In her hand she holds a small bouquet.
       In the distance there's a Chevrolet.
       In the corner there's a tree
       Only half of which we see
       In the churchyard with the bride
       And the soldier at her side.

       And she's got wavy hair
       And she wears her shoulders all but bare.
       And the soldier looks her way
       On a breezy Brooklyn day

In the forties
In the fall
In the picture
In the hall.

And a cloud is passing by
In the moment, in the sky.
And it's captured like the faces
And the flowers,
And the car
And the gown
In a hundred shades of brown
In the churchyard
In the fall
In the picture
In the hall . . . . .

The women aren't the only ones with interior lives. Having just served the dessert, the waiter shares with us scenes from his life in which it becomes apparent that for him these women are part of a "Cast of Thousands" supporting his own personal drama. The women freeze as he sings his song.

WALTER (sings):
There's a house near Chicago
Where I slept with a light on,
Where I showed my report cards,
And I had a lot of dreams
You don't need to know.
There's a town near Chicago
With my name in the sidewalk . . .
There you go.

And oh, there's a cast of thousands
Making a scene.
Oh, there's a cast of thousands
Filling the screen.

There's a school up in Boston
Where I majored in Science.
Don't ask.
Where I crashed in a car.
Here's the scar.
And I once was up all night
Walking in the snow.
There's a courthouse in Boston
Where I think I got married . . .
Hard to know . . . . .

When we pick up our story next
We find we're in New York.
There's a bar in the Village
Where I used to go
I bought a couch this year,
So I guess I plan to stay.
There's nothing big I can tell you about.
I don't yet know how it all turns out,

But oh, there's a cast of thousands
Making a scene,
Putting on such a show.
There's a cast of thousands
Filling the screen.

The three women prepare to leave the restaurant. Little Jane remarks that it's been raining.

K.C.: It's still coming down.
BIG JANE: There goes a cab, too.
LITTLE JANE: That's right, Jane, the last cab that will ever go by.
K.C.: There's another one.
BIG JANE: That's the last one.
LITTLE JANE: That's the last one.
> *They laugh and are gone. Lights fade and music concludes as Walter puts out the candle and begins to clear the table. Freeze. Curtain.*

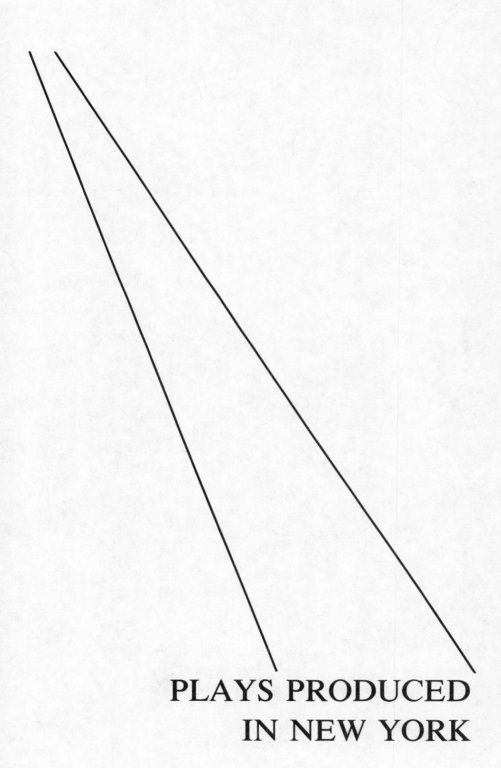

PLAYS PRODUCED
IN NEW YORK

PLAYS PRODUCED ON BROADWAY

Figures in parentheses following a play's title give number of performances. These figures are acquired directly from the production offices and do not include previews or extra non-profit performances. In the case of a transfer, the off-Broadway run is noted but not added to the figure in parentheses.

Plays marked with an asterisk (*) were still running on June 1, 1987. Their number of performances is figured through May 31, 1987.

In a listing of a show's numbers—dances, sketches, musical scenes, etc.—the titles of songs are identified wherever possible by their appearance in quotation marks (").

HOLDOVERS FROM PREVIOUS SEASONS

Plays which were running on June 2, 1986 are listed below. More detailed information about them appears in previous *Best Plays* volumes of appropriate years. Important cast changes since opening night are recorded in the Cast Replacements section of this volume.

*A Chorus Line (4,920; longest run in Broadway history). Musical conceived by Michael Bennett; book by James Kirkwood and Nicholas Dante; music by Marvin Hamlisch; lyrics by Edward Kleban. Opened April 15, 1975 off Broadway where it played 101 performances through July 13, 1975; transferred to Broadway July 25, 1975.

*Oh! Calcutta! (4,786). Revival of the musical devised by Kenneth Tynan; with contributions (in this version) by Jules Feiffer, Dan Greenberg, Lenore Kandel, John Lennon, Jacques Levy, Leonard Melfi, David Newman & Robert Benton, Sam Shepard, Clovis Trouille, Kenneth Tynan and Sherman Yellen; music and lyrics (in this version) by Robert Dennis, Peter Schickele and Stanley Walden, additional music by Stanley Walden and Jacques Levy. Opened September 24, 1976 in alternating performances with *Me and Bessie* through December 7, 1976, continuing alone thereafter.

*42nd Street (2,816). Musical based on the novel by Bradford Ropes, book by Michael Stewart and Mark Bramble, music and lyrics by Harry Warren and Al Dubin; other lyrics by Johnny Mercer and Mort Dixon. Opened August 25, 1980.

*Cats (1,940). Musical based on *Old Possum's Book of Practical Cats* by T.S. Eliot; music by Andrew Lloyd Webber; additional lyrics by Trevor Nunn and Richard Stilgoe. Opened October 7, 1982.

*La Cage aux Folles (1,577). Musical based on the play *La Cage aux Folles* by Jean Poiret; book by Harvey Fierstein; music and lyrics by Jerry Herman. Opened August 21, 1983.

Biloxi Blues (524). By Neil Simon. Opened March 28, 1985. (Closed June 28, 1986).

*Big River: The Adventures of Huckleberry Finn (889). Musical based on the novel by Mark Twain; book by William Hauptman; music and lyrics by Roger Miller. Opened April 25, 1985.

Song & Dance (474). Musical with music by Andrew Lloyd Webber; lyrics by Don Black; American adaptation and additional lyrics by Richard Maltby Jr. Opened September 18, 1985. (Closed November 8, 1986)

The Search for Signs of Intelligent Life in the Universe (398). One-woman performance by Lily Tomlin; written by Jane Wagner. Opened September 26, 1985. (Closed October 4, 1986)

*I'm Not Rappaport (639). Transfer from off Broadway of the play by Herb Gardner. Opened off Broadway June 6, 1985 where it played 181 performances through November 10, 1985; transferred to Broadway November 18, 1985.

The Mystery of Edwin Drood (608). Transfer from off Broadway of the musical by Rupert Holmes; suggested by the unfinished novel by Charles Dickens. Opened off Broadway August 4, 1985 where it played 25 performances through September 1, 1985; transferred to Broadway December 2, 1985, where the title was later changed to *Drood*. (Closed May 16, 1987)

Benefactors (217). By Michael Frayn. Opened December 22, 1985. (Closed June 29, 1985)

Loot (96). Transfer from off Broadway of the revival of the play by Joe Orton. Opened February 18, 1986 off Broadway where it played 32 performances through March 15, 1986; transferred to Broadway April 7, 1986. (Closed June 28, 1986)

Big Deal (70). Musical by Bob Fosse based on the film *Big Deal on Madonna Street*; music and lyrics by various authors. Opened April 10, 1986. (Closed June 8, 1986)

Social Security (385). By Andrew Bergman. Opened April 17, 1986. (Closed March 22, 1987)

The Petition (77). By Brian Clark. Opened April 24, 1986. (Closed June 29, 1986)

Sweet Charity (368). Revival of the musical originally conceived, directed and choreographed by Bob Fosse; based on an original screenplay by Federico Fellini, Tullio Pinelli and Ennia Faiano; book by Neil Simon; music by Cy Coleman; lyrics by Dorothy Fields. Opened April 27, 1986. (Closed March 15, 1987)

Long Day's Journey Into Night (54). Revival of the play by Eugene O'Neill. Opened April 28, 1986. (Closed June 29, 1986)

The House of Blue Leaves (398). Transfer from off Broadway of the revival of the play by John Guare. Opened off Broadway (Lincoln Center's Mitzi E. Newhouse Theater) March 19, 1986 where it played 38 performances through April 20, 1986; transferred to Broadway (Lincoln Center's Vivian Beaumont Theater) April 29, 1986 where it played 184 performances through October 5, 1986; reopened October 14, 1986. (Closed March 15, 1987)

The Boys in Autumn (70). By Bernard Sabath. Opened April 30, 1986. (Closed June 29, 1986)

PLAYS PRODUCED JUNE 1, 1986—MAY 31, 1987

Mummenschanz (152). New version of the program of Swiss pantomime by and with Andres Bossard, Floriana Frassetto and Bernie Schurch. Produced by ICM Artists, Ltd. in association with Mummenschanz, Ltd. at the Helen Hayes Theater, Opened June 24, 1986. (Closed October 26, 1986)

Lee Dassler and Walter Flohr, stage assistants; lighting, Beverly Emmons; production stage manager, Dino De Maio; press, Marilynn LeVine/PR Partners, Meg Gordean, Patricia Robert.

An entertainment of mime and masks, suggested by Swiss folk traditions and presented in two parts. An earlier version was presented on a national U.S. tour beginning in 1973, including a Broadway presentation 3/30/77 for 1,326 performances. This new version, a transfer from off Broadway, was presented there 4/24/86–5/25/86 for 39 performances; see its entry in the Plays Produced Off Broadway section of *The Best Plays of 1985–86.*

Robert Klein on Broadway (2). One-man performance by and with Robert Klein. Produced by Home Box Office at the Nederlander Theater. Opened and closed June 25, 1986.

Directed by Thomas Schlamme; musical direction, Bob Atein; art direction, Frank Lopez.

Two sessions of standup comedy presented on the same evening in a limited engagement taped and edited for TV showing.

Arsenic and Old Lace (221). Revival of the play by Joseph Kesselring. Produced by Elliot Martin, Act III Productions, James M. Nederlander and Burton Kaiser at the 46th Street Theater. Opened June 26, 1986. (Closed January 3, 1987)

Abby Brewster	Jean Stapleton	Mortimer	Tony Roberts
Rev. Dr. Harper	Gwyllum Evans	Mr. Gibbs	William Preston
Teddy Brewster	Michaeljohn McGann	Jonathan Brewster	Abe Vigoda
Officer Brophy	Andrew Gorman	Dr. Einstein	William Hickey
Officer Klein	J.J. Johnston	Officer O'Hara	Kevin McClarnon
Martha Brewster	Polly Holliday	Lt. Rooney	Barry Snider
Elaine Harper	Mary Layne	Mr. Witherspoon	Phillip Pruneau

Standby: Messrs. Roberts, McGann—Timothy Landfield. Understudies: Misses Stapleton, Holliday—Virginia Downing; Mr. Vigoda—J.J. Johnston; Mr. Hickey—Phillip Pruneau; Miss Layne—Karen Trott; Messrs. Evans, Preston, Snider, Pruneau—John Leighton; Mr. McClarnon—Andrew Gorman.

Directed by Brian Murray; scenery, Marjorie Bradley Kellogg; costumes, Jeanne Button; lighting, Pat Collins; associate producer, Marjorie Martin; production stage manager, Elliott Woodruff; stage manager, Wally Peterson; press, Jeffrey Richards Associates, C. George Willard.

Place: The living room of the Brewster home in Brooklyn. Act I: An afternoon in September 1941. Act II: That same night. Act III, Scene 1: Later that night. Scene 2: Early the next morning.

Arsenic and Old Lace was first produced on Broadway 1/10/41 for 1,444 performances and was named a Best Play of its season. This is its first major New York revival.

Marion Rose replaced Polly Holliday, Gary Sandy replaced Tony Roberts, Larry Storch replaced William Hickey and Jonathan Frid replaced Abe Vigoda 12/23/86.

Honky Tonk Nights (4). Musical with book and lyrics by Ralph Allen and David Campbell; music by Michael Valenti. Produced by Edward H. Davis and Allen M. Shore in association with Marty Feinberg and Schellie Archbold at the Biltmore Theater. Opened August 7, 1986. (Closed August 9, 1986)

Barney Walker	Joe Morton	Countess Aida	Susan Beaubian
Billy Sampson	Ira Hawkins	Kitty Stark	Robin Kersey
Armistead Sampson	Danny Strayhorn	Montgomery Boyd	Michael-Demby Cain
Lily Meadows	Teresa Burrell	Winston Grey	Keith Rozie
George Gooseberry	Reginald Veljohnson	Sparks Roberts	Lloyd Culbreath
Ruby Bush	Yolanda Graves	Patron	Charles Bernard Murray
Ivy Vine	Kyme		

The Sampson Philharmonia: George Broderick, Kaman Adilifu, Robert Keller, Gregory Maker, Andrew Stein, John Gale, David Krane, James Sedlar, Quinten White.

Understudies: Mr. Morton—Danny Strayhorn; Messrs. Hawkins, Veljohnson—Keith Rozie; Mr.

Strayhorn—Lloyd Culbreath; Miss Burrell—Susan Beaubian; Misses Graves, Beaubian, Kersey—Julia Lema-Jackson; Miss Kyme—Yolanda Graves; Messrs. Cain, Rozie, Culbreath—Charles Bernard Murray.

Directed and choreographed by Ernest O. Flatt; musical direction and vocal arrangements, George Broderick; scenery, Robert Cothran; costumes, Mardi Philips; lighting, Natasha Katz; sound, Jack Mann; orchestrations, Jim Tyler; dance arrangements, David Krane; associate choreographer, Toni Kaye; production stage manager, Larry Forde; stage manager, Mark Rubinsky; press, Mark Goldstaub Public Relations, Kevin P. McAnarney.

Time and Place: Act I: Sampson's Music Hall on a winter evening, New York City's Hell's Kitchen, 1912. Act II: The Promised Land Saloon, summer, 1922, Harlem.

Musical about black vaudeville, subtitled "How Billy Sampson and company left Hell's Kitchen for the Promised Land and what they found there."

ACT I

Overture, or "The Honky Tonk Nights Rag,"
    or "Professor Walker and His Solo Symphony" . . . . The Sampson Philharmonia
"Honky Tonk Nights" . . . . Sampson, His Company
"Hot and Bothered" . . . . Lily
"Roll With the Punches" . . . . Barney, Armistead, Countess Aida, Ivy Vine, Kitty, Ruby Bush
"Lily of the Alley" . . . . Sampson, Winston, Montgomery, Sparks, Barney, Lily
"Choosing a Husband's a Delicate Thing" . . . . Armistead, Barney, Gooseberry
"Little Dark Bird" . . . . Lily
"Withered Irish Rose" . . . . Barney, Armistead, Gooseberry, Montgomery, Lily
"Tapaholics" . . . . Sparks, Ivy, Montgomery
"Eggs" . . . . Barney, Lily
"A Ticket to the Promised Land" . . . . The Sampson Company

ACT II

Overture: "The Promised Land" . . . . The Pyromaniacs
"Stomp the Blues Away" . . . . The Sampson Company
"I've Had It" . . . . Barney, Lily
"The Sampson Beauties" . . . . Ivy Vine, Kitty, Ruby Bush
"The Reform Song" . . . . Barney, Gooseberry, Armistead
"I Took My Time" . . . . Lily
"The Brothers Vendetto" . . . . Barney, Gooseberry, Armistead
"A Man of Many Parts" . . . . Barney
Finale . . . . The Sampson Company

Cuba and His Teddy Bear (53). By Reinaldo Povod. Produced by New York Shakespeare Festival, Joseph Papp producer, at the Longacre Theater. Opened July 16, 1986. (Closed September 21, 1986)

Cuba	Robert DeNiro	Lourdes	Wanda DeJesus
Teddy	Ralph Macchio	Che	Michael Carmine
Jackie	Burt Young	Dealer	Paul Calderon
Redlights	Nestor Sorrano		

Directed by Bill Hart; scenery, Donald Eastman; costumes, Gabriel Berry; lighting, Anne E. Militello; production stage manager, Ruth Kreshka; stage manager, Joel Elins; press, Merle Debuskey, Richard Kornberg, Barbara Carroll, Kevin Patterson, Patricia Krawitz, Don Summa.

Macho drug pusher is alarmed when his teen-aged son falls into bad company and experiments with drugs. The play was presented in two parts. Transfer from off Broadway presented there 5/18/86–6/14/86 for 24 performances; see its entry in the Plays Produced Off Broadway section of *The Best Plays of 1985–86.*

*Me and My Girl (337). Revival of the musical with book and lyrics by L. Arthur Rose and Douglas Furber; music by Noel Gay; book revised by Stephen Fry; contributions to revisions by Mike Ockrent. Produced by Richard Armitage, Terry Allen Kramer, James

M. Nederlander and Stage Promotions Limited & Co. at the Marquis Theater. Opened August 10, 1986.

Lady Jacqueline Carstone... Jane Summerhays	Sally Smith............. Maryann Plunkett
Hon. Gerald Bolingbroke....... Nick Ullett	Pub Pianist................... John Spalla
Lord Battersby............... Eric Hutson	Mrs. Worthington-
Lady Battersby .... Justine Johnston	Worthington .... Gloria Hodes
Herbert Parchester .... Timothy Jerome	Lady Diss; Mrs. Brown .... Elizabeth Larner
Sir Jasper Tring................ Leo Leyden	Lady Brighten .... Susan Cella
Duchess of Dene.............. Jane Connell	Bob Barking............ Kenneth H. Waller
Sir John Tremayne .... George S. Irving	Telegraph Boy................. Bill Brassea
Charles Hethersett.......... Thomas Toner	Constable .... Eric Johnson
Bill Snibson .... Robert Lindsay	

Ensemble: Cleve Asbury, Bill Brassea, Jonathan Brody, Frankie Cassady, Susan Cella, Sheri Cowart, Bob Freschi, Anne-Marie Gerard, Larry Hansen, Isa Henry, Randy Hills, Gloria Hodes, K. Craig Innes, Eric Johnson, Michael Hayward-Jones, Barry McNabb, Donna Monroe, Barbara Moroz, William Ryall, John Spalla, Cynthia Thole, Michael Turner, Dana Walker, Kenneth H. Waller. Swings: Corinne Melancon, Tony Parise.

Understudies: Messrs. Lindsay, Ullett—James Brennan; Mr. Ullett—Larry Hansen; Miss Plunkett—Sheri Cowart; Miss Connell—Justine Johnston; Mr. Irving—Eric Hutson; Miss Summerhays—Susan Cella; Mr. Jerome—John Spalla; Messrs. Toner, Leyden, Hutson—Kenneth H. Waller; Miss Johnston—Elizabeth Larner; Miss Larner—Donna Monroe, Barbara Moroz; Miss Cella—Barbara Moroz; Mr. Johnson—Michael Hayward-Jones; Mr. Waller—Jonathan Brody.

Directed by Mike Ockrent; choreography, Gillian Gregory; musical direction, Stanley Lebowsky; scenery, Martin Johns; costumes, Ann Curtis; lighting, Chris Ellis, Roger Morgan; conductor, Thomas Helm; sound, Tom Morse; orchestrations and dance arrangements, Chris Walker; production stage manager, Steven Zweigbaum; stage manager, Arturo E. Porazzi; press, Jeffrey Richards Associates, C. George Willard, Ben Morse.

Time: The late 1930s. Place: In and around Hareford Hall, Hampshire, Mayfair and Lambeth.

Me and My Girl, the romance of a Lambeth Cockney who becomes an earl, was originally produced in London 12/16/37 for 1,646 performances. This Olivier Award–winning revival opened 2/12/85 in London and is still running (Robert Lindsay, star of the London cast, repeats his role in the New York version), while still another production is touring Australia.

Jim Dale replaced Robert Lindsay 12/16/86 for one week.

ACT I

Prologue: Mayfair
Scene 1: Hareford Hall, Hampshire
"A Weekend at Hareford"... Ensemble
"Thinking of No-One But Me".................................... Lady Jaquie, Gerald
"The Family Solicitor" .... Parchester, Family
"Me and My Girl"... Bill, Sally
Scene 2: The kitchen
"An English Gentleman"... Heathersett, Staff
Scene 3: The drawing room
"You Would if You Could" .... Lady Jaquie, Bill
"Hold My Hand"... Bill, Sally, Dancers
Scene 4: The Hareford Arms
"Once You Lose Your Heart" .... Sally
Scene 5: The terrace
"Preparation Fugue" .... Company
"The Lambeth Walk" .... Bill, Sally, Company

ACT II

Scene 1: The garden at Hareford Hall, the next afternoon
"The Sun Has Got Its Hat On"....................... Gerald, Lady Jaquie, Ensemble
"Take It on the Chin"... Sally

Scene 2: The library
"Once You Lose Your Heart" (Reprise) .... Sally
"Song of Hareford" .... Duchess, Bill, Ensemble
"Love Makes the World Go Round" .... Bill, Sir John
Scene 3: Lambeth
"Leaning on a Lamppost" .... Bill, Ensemble
Scene 4: Hareford Hall
Finale .... Company

Rags (4). Musical with book by Joseph Stein; music by Charles Strouse; lyrics by Stephen Schwartz. Produced by Lee Guber, Martin Heinfling and Marvin A. Krauss at the Mark Hellinger Theater. Opened August 21, 1986. (Closed August 23, 1986)

ACT I

Scene 1: Ellis Island, April
Homesick Immigrant .... Andy Gale
Rebecca Hershkowitz .... Teresa Stratas
David Hershkowitz .... Josh Blake
Guards .... John Aller, Peter Samuel
Scene 2: Battery Park, immediately following
Americans .... Michael Cone, Michael Davis
Bella Cohen .... Judy Kuhn
Avram Cohen .... Dick Latessa
Ben .... Lonny Price
Recruiters .... Andy Gale, Stan Rubin
Scene 3: East Side streets and Cohen tenement apartment, that afternoon
Anna Cohen .... Evalyn Baron
Jack Cohen .... Mordecai Lawner
Scene 4: East Broadway and offices on the Lower East Side, the next few days
Nathan's Landlady .... Irma Rogers
Millie .... Bonnie Schon

Editor of Newspaper .... Stan Rubin
Social Worker .... Joanna Glushak
Scene 9: The Cohen apartment, evening, July 3
Irish Tenor on Recording .... Michael Cone
Scene 10: Suffolk Street and above 14th Street
Ragman .... Gabriel Barre
Wealthy New Yorkers: Bill Hastings, John Aller, Michael Davis, Joan Finkelstein, Joanna Glushak, Wendy Kimball, Robert Radford, Peter Samuel, Catherine Ulissey
Scene 11: Pat's Tavern
Frankie .... Michael Cone
Mike .... Michael Davis
"Big Tim" Sullivan .... Rex Everhart
Nathan Hershkowitz .... Larry Kert
Scene 12: The street market, July 4
Man on Stilts .... Gabriel Barre
Thugs .... Andy Gale, Peter Samuel
Scene 13: Suffolk Street, immediately following

ACT II

Scene 1: The rooftop, evening, July 4
Scene 2: The rooftop, later that night
Scene 3: The street market, the next day
Scene 4: A few days later
Passerby .... Stan Rubin
Morris .... Devon Michaels
His Mother .... Bonnie Schon
Scene 5: A street and sweatshops, a few days later
Klezmorim:
Tuba .... Teddy Bragin
Trombone .... Sean Mahony
Trumpet .... Bruce Engel
Clarinet .... Harold Seletsky
Violin .... Marshall Coid
Rachel Halpern .... Marcia Lewis
Mr. Bronstein .... Stan Rubin
Scene 6: Outside Bronstein's sweatshop, later that day and weeks following
Scene 7: A Yiddish theater, a few weeks later
Hamlet .... Peter Samuel
Ophelia .... Joanna Glushak
Gertrude .... Irma Rogers

Violinist .... Marshall Coid
His Mother .... Irma Rogers
Irish Girl .... Wendy Kimball

Sweatshop Workers:
Rosa .... Audrey Lavine
Esther .... Joan Finkelstein
Sam .... Gabriel Barre
Saul .... Terrence Mann
Cigar Boss .... Peter Samuel
Avid Shopper .... Joanna Glushak
Mr. Rosen .... John Aller

Rosencrantz .... Michael Cone
Laertes .... Gabriel Barre

Scene 8: Suffolk Street and under the Brooklyn Bridge, later that night

Her Mother...............	Audrey Lavine	His Mother..............	Joanna Glushak
Italian Tenor.................	Andy Gale		

Scene 5: The Lower East Side Democratic Club, a week later

Mrs. Sullivan .... Bonnie Schon

Scene 6: "Prayer"

Scene 7: The Cohen apartment, some time later

Scene 8: Bronstein's Sweatshop

Scene 9: Union Square, a protest demonstration, later that day

Scene 10: Suffolk Street and Battery Park, a few weeks later

Herschel Cohen .... John Aller

Finale

Swings: Patti Mariano, Ciccy Rebich, Mark Fotopoulos.

Understudies: Miss Stratas—Audrey Lavine; Mr. Mann—Peter Samuel; Mr. Blake—Devon Michaels; Miss Kuhn—Joanna Glushak; Messrs. Latessa, Lawner—Stan Rubin; Mr. Price—John Aller; Miss Baron—Irma Rogers.

Directed by Gene Saks; musical staging, Ron Field; musical direction and additional arrangements, Eric Stern; scenery, Beni Montresor; costumes, Florence Klotz; lighting, Jules Fisher; sound, Peter Fitzgerald; orchestrations, Michael Starobin; associate producer, Madeline Lee Gilford; stage managers, Joel Tropper, John Actman; press, Solters/Roskin/Friedman, Joshua Ellis, Cindy Valk, James Sapp.

Jewish immigrant makes a life for herself on New York's Lower East Side in the ragtime era.

MUSICAL NUMBERS, ACT I, Scene 1: "I Remember"—Homesick Immigrant. Scene 2: "Greenhorns"—Americans, New Immigrants. Scene 3: "Brand New World"—Rebecca, David. Scene 4: "Children of the Wind"—Rebecca, Avram, David. Scene 5: "Penny a Time"—Rachel, Klezmorim, Peddlers, Workers. Scene 6: "Easy for You"—Saul, Rebecca, David. Scene 7: "Hard To Be a Prince"—Hamlet, Company. Scene 8: "Blame It on the Summer Night"—Rebecca, Clarinetist. Scene 9: "For My Mary"—Irish Tenor, Ben. Scene 10: "Rags"—Bella, Avram. Scene 11: "What's Wrong With That?"—Frankie, Mike, "Big Tim"—Nathan. Scene 12: "On the Fourth Day of July"— Picknickers, Band. Scene 13: "In America"—Rebecca, Nathan.

ACT II, Scene 1: "Yankee Boy"—Nathan, Neighbors; Scene 2: "Uptown"—Nathan, Rebecca; "Wanting"—Rebecca, Saul. Scene 3: "Three Sunny Rooms"—Rachel, Avram. Scene 4: "The Sound of Love"—Ben, David, Shoppers; "For My Mary" (Reprise)—Bella, Ben. Scene 5: "Democratic Club Dance"—Rebecca, "Big Tim," Nathan, Mike, Mrs. Sullivan, Democrats, Band. Scene 6: "Prayer"— Avram, Rebecca, Men. Scene 8: "Bread and Freedom"—Rosa, Rebecca, Nathan, Strikers. "Scene 9: "Dancing With the Fools"—Rebecca, Nathan, Strikers. Scene 10: Finale—Rebecca, David, Americans, New Immigrants.

The Life and Adventures of Nicholas Nickleby (29 each of parts I and II; 58 programs). Revival of David Edgar's adaptation of Charles Dickens's novel. Produced by The Shubert Organization, Three Knights, Ltd. and Robert Fox, Ltd. in the Royal Shakespeare Company production at the Broadhurst Theater Opened August 24, 1986. (Closed October 12, 1986)

The Nickleby Family		Newman Noggs	David Collings
Nicholas Nickleby	Michael Siberry	Hannah	Jane Whittenshaw
Kate Nickleby..........	DeNica Fairman	Miss La Creevy	Eve Pearce
Mrs. Nickleby..............	Frances Cuka	William	Jimmy Yuill
Ralph Nickleby.............	John Carlisle	Waitresses	Karen Lancaster,
London			Rebecca Saire
Sir Matthew Pupker..........	Hubert Rees	Belling.................	Allan Hendrick
Mr. Bonney...................	Alan Gill	Mr. Snawley	Richard Simpson
Irate Gentleman	George Raistrick	Snawley Major	Jane Whittenshaw
Furious Man...............	David Delve	Snawley Minor	Raymond Platt
Flunkey	Timothy Kightley	Coachman	George Raistrick

A LITTLE LIKE MAGIC—Black light effects *(above left)* and celebrity puppets (Elvis Presley, *above right*) were major elements of this Famous People Players production

Guard .... Ian East
Flunkey .... Jimmy Gardner
Mr. Mantalini................ Alan David
Mme. Mantalini .... Karen Archer
Miss Knag................. Frances Cuka
Rich Ladies.... Shirley King, Rebecca Saire
Milliners: Jane Carr, Ian East, Allan Hendrick, Karen Lancaster, Eve Pearce, Raymond Platt, Alison Rose, Richard Simpson, Jane Whittenshaw.
Yorkshire
Mr. Squeers................. David Delve
Mrs. Squeers.................. Pat Keen
Smike......................John Lynch
Phib .... Rebecca Saire
Fanny Squeers .... Jane Carr
Young Wackford Squeers ..... Jimmy Yuill
John Browdie .... Clive Wood
Tilda Price .... Alison Rose
Boys:
Tomkins .... Timothy Kightley
Coates................. Jimmy Gardner
Graymarsh.................... Alan Gill
Jennings .... George Raistrick
Mobbs.................... Alan David

Bolder................... Bryan Torfeh
Pitcher .... Karen Lancaster
Jackson.............. Simon Templeman
Cobbey .... DeNica Fairman
Peters .... Frances Cuka
Sprouter .... Karen Archer
Roberts..................... Ian East
London Again
Mr. Crowl.................... Ian East
Mr. Kenwigs............ George Raistrick
Mrs. Kenwigs.............. Shirley King
Morleena Kenwigs ...... Jane Whittenshaw
Baby Kenwigses .... Jane Carr, Alison Rose
Mr. Lillyvick.......... Timothy Kightley
Miss Henrietta Petowker ... Karen Lancaster
George...................... Alan Gill
Mr. Cutler.............. Richard Simpson
Mrs. Cutler............... Karen Archer
Mrs. Kenwigs's Sister .... Rebecca Saire
Lady From Downstairs .... Eve Pearce
Miss Green .... Frances Cuka
Babysitter .... Allan Hendrick
Pugstyles .... Roderick Horn
Old Lord................ Jimmy Gardner
Young Fiancee .... Jane Whittenshaw

Landlord . . . . Richard Simpson
Stable Boy . . . . Alan Gill
Portsmouth
Mr. Vincent Crummles . . . . Tony Jay
Mrs. Crummles . . . . Pat Keen
Master Crummles . . . . Bryan Torfeh
Master Percy Crummles . . . . Raymond Platt
Infant Phenomenon . . . . Alison Rose
Mr. Folair . . . . Alan David
Mr. Lenville . . . . Roderick Horn
Miss Snevellicci . . . . Jane Carr
Mr. Bane . . . . Allan Hendrick
Mr. Wagstaff . . . . David Delve
Mr. Fluggers . . . . Jimmy Gardner
Mr. Bightey . . . . Richard Simpson
Mr. Hetherington . . . . Simon Templeman
Mr. Pailey . . . . Jimmy Yuill
Miss Ledrock . . . . Rebecca Saire
Miss Belvawney . . . . Jane Whittenshaw
Mrs. Lenville . . . . Shirley King
Miss Bravassa . . . . Karen Archer
Mrs. Grudden . . . . Eve Pearce
Mr. Curdle . . . . Hubert Rees
Mrs. Curdle . . . . DeNica Fairman
Mr. Snevellicci . . . . : John Carlisle
Mrs. Snevellicci . . . . Shirley King
London Again
Scaley . . . . Jimmy Yuill
Tix . . . . Raymond Platt
Lord Frederick
    Verisopht . . . . Simon Templeman
Sir Mulberry Hawk . . . . Clive Wood
Mr. Pyke . . . . Bryan Torfeh
Mr. Pluck . . . . Raymond Platt
Mr. Snobb . . . . Richard Simpson
Col. Chowser . . . . Timothy Kightley
Brooker . . . . George Raistrick

Mrs. Wititterly . . . . Karen Archer
Alphonse . . . . Allan Hendrick
Mr. Wititterly . . . . Hubert Rees
Opera Singers . . . . Roderick Horn,
                Karen Lancaster, Bryan Torfeh
Box-Keeper . . . . Jimmy Gardner
Head Waiter . . . . George Raistrick
Waiters . . . . . . Alan Gill, Jane Whittenshaw
Charles Cheeryble . . . . Timothy Kightley
Ned Cheeryble . . . . Hubert Rees
Tim Linkinwater . . . . Jimmy Gardner
Man Next Door . . . . Raymond Platt
Keeper . . . . Alan Gill
Angry Fellow . . . . Simon Templeman
Frank Cheeryble . . . . Allan Hendrick
Nurse . . . . Karen Archer
Dr. Lumbey . . . . Roderick Horn
Stout Lady . . . . Pat Keen
Married Women . . . . Ian East,
             Raymond Platt, Richard Simpson
Arthur Gride . . . . Alan David
Walter Bray . . . . Tony Jay
Madeline Bray . . . . Rebecca Saire
Peg Sliderskew . . . . Jane Carr
Minister . . . . Roderick Horn
Croupier . . . . Timothy Kightley
Casino Proprietor . . . . George Raistrick
Hawk's Rival . . . . David Collings
Westwood . . . . Alan Gill
Capt. Adams . . . . Jimmy Yuill
Umpire . . . . Roderick Horn
Surgeon . . . . Timothy Kightley
Policemen . . . . Simon Templeman,
                                 Bryan Torfeh
Mrs. Snawley . . . . Karen Archer
Young Woman . . . . Jane Whittenshaw

Understudies: All members of the acting company, plus Colin Campbell, Stephen Finlay, Caroline Ryder and Ruth Trouncer.

Directed by Trevor Nunn and John Caird. Scenery, John Napier, from an original design by John Napier and Dermot Hayes; costumes, Andreane Neofitou, from an original concept by John Napier; lighting, David Hersey; music and lyrics, Stephen Oliver; sound, T. Richard Fitzgerald; musical direction, Donald Johnston; executive producer, Nelle Nugent; stage manager, Michael Townsend; press, The Fred Nathan Company, Marc P. Thibodeau.

The 8½-hour play was presented in two parts, the first with one intermission and the second with two intermissions.

The Life and Adventures (Life & Adventures in previous billing) *of Nicholas Nickleby* was produced on Broadway in the Royal Shakespeare production 10/4/81 for 49 performances each of Parts I and II and was named a Best Play of its season and won the Critics Award for best play regardless of category.

*Circle in the Square. Schedule of two programs. **You Never Can Tell** (125). Revival of the play by George Bernard Shaw. Opened October 9, 1986. (Closed January 25, 1987) ***Coastal Disturbances** (102). By Tina Howe; presented in the Second Stage production. Opened March 4, 1987. Produced by Circle in the Square, Theodore Mann artistic director, Paul Libin producing director, at Circle in the Square Theater

YOU NEVER CAN TELL

Dolly Clandon .... Amanda Plummer
Valentine .... Victor Garber
Parlormaid.. Tracy Sallows
Philip Clandon .... John David Cullum
Mrs. Clandon .... Uta Hagen
Gloria Clandon... Lise Hilboldt
Mr. Crampton... Stefan Gierasch
Mr. M'Comas .... Gordon Sterne
Waiter .... Philip Bosco
2d Waiter .... Eric Swanson
Mr. Bohun... Stephen McHattie

Understudies: Messrs. Gierasch, Sterne, Bosco—Tom Brennan; Misses Plummer, Hilboldt—Tracy Sallows; Mr. Cullum—Eric Swanson; Misses Hagen, Sallows—Glynis Bell; Messrs. Garber, McHattie, Swanson—John Hutton.

Directed by Stephen Porter; scenery, Thomas Lynch; costumes, Martin Pakledinaz; lighting, Richard Nelson; wigs, Paul Huntley; production stage manager, Michael F. Ritchie; stage manager, Carol Klein; press, Merle Debuskey, William Schelble.

Act I, Scene 1: A dentist's office. Scene 2: The terrace of the Marine Hotel. Act II, Scene 1: The sitting room of a suite in the Marine Hotel. Scene 2: The same.

The last major New York production of *You Never Can Tell* was by Roundabout Theater Company off Broadway 10/4/77 for 31 performances.

John Cullum replaced Philip Bosco 12/9/86. Richard Backus replaced Stephen McHattie 12/16/86. Susan Diol replaced Amanda Plummer 12/23/86.

COASTAL DISTURBANCES

Leo Hart .... Timothy Daly
Holly Dancer .... Annette Bening
Winston Took... Jonas Abry
Miranda Bigelow .... Angela Goethals
Ariel Took... Jean De Baer
Faith Bigelow .... Heather Mac Rae
M.J. Adams... Rosemary Murphy
Dr. Hamilton Adams... Addison Powell
Andre Sor .... Ronald Guttman

Understudies: Misses Bening, Mac Rae, De Baer—Susan Wands; Mr. Daly—Don Fischer; Messrs. Powell, Guttman—David Cryer; Mr. Abry—Christopher Cunningham Jr.; Miss Goethals—Monique Lawrence.

Directed by Carole Rothman; scenery, Bob Shaw; lighting, Dennis Parichy; costumes, Susan Hilferty; sound, Gary Harris; production manager, Michael F. Richie; production stage manager, Pamela Edington.

Time: The last two weeks of August. Place: A private beach on Massachusetts's North Shore. Act I, Scene 1: Tuesday morning, around 10. Scene 2: Friday, noon. Scene 3: Monday afternoon, around 1. Scene 4: Wednesday, 2 p.m. Scene 5: Friday, end of the day. Act II, Scene 1: Dawn, the next morning. Scene 2: Several hours later. Scene 3: The next day, Sunday, around noon. Scene 4: Monday, mid-afternoon. Scene 5: Tuesday, near dusk.

The joys and heartbreaks of love in a late summer environment, previously produced off off Broadway at Second Stage.

Rowan Atkinson at the Atkinson (6). By Richard Curtis, Rowan Atkinson and Ben Elton; music by Howard Goodall. Produced by Arthur Cantor in association with Caroline Hirsch, Peter Wilson and Tony Aljoe at the Brooks Atkinson Theater. Opened October 14, 1986. (Closed October 18, 1986)

CAST: Rowan Atkinson, Angus Deayton.

Musicians: Steven Margoshes musical director, Miles Chase keyboards, Roger Rosenberg saxophone.

Directed by Mike Ockrent; design, Will Bowen; lighting, Mark Henderson; sound, Tony Meola; production supervisor, Mitchell Erickson; technical supervisor, Peter Fulbright; press, Arthur Cantor Associates, Stephen Cole.

Comedy sketches (*Schoolmaster* monologue by Richard Sparks) performed by the celebrated British comedian Rowan Atkinson. The play was presented in two parts.

Raggedy Ann (5). Musical with book by William Gibson; music and lyrics by Joe Raposo. Produced by Jon Silverman Associates, Ltd., Kennedy Center, Empire State Institute for the Performing Arts and Donald K. Donald in association with CBS at the Nederlander Theater. Opened October 16, 1986. (Closed October 19, 1986)

Poppa . . . . Bob Morrisey	General D . . . . Leo Burmester
Marcella . . . . Lisa Rieffel	Bat . . . . Gail Benedict
Raggedy Ann . . . . Ivy Austin	Wolf . . . . Gordon Weiss
Raggedy Andy . . . . Scott Schafer	Camel With Wrinkled Knees . . . . Joel Aroeste
Baby Doll . . . . Carolyn Marble	Mommy . . . . Elizabeth Austin
Panda . . . . Michelan Sisti	

Doctors: Dick Decareau, Joe Barrett, Richard Ryder.

Company: Melinda Buckley, Gregory Butler, Anny De Gange, Susann Fletcher, Michaela Hughes, Steve Owsley, Andrea Wright.

Understudies: Mr. Weiss—Joe Barrett; Messrs. Schafer, Sisti and Swing—Kenneth Boys; Miss Benedict—Melinda Buckley; Miss Rieffel—Sara Carbone; Mr. Morrisey—Dick Decareau; Miss Austin—Anny De Gange; Miss Austin—Susann Fletcher; Messrs. Decareau, Barrett, Ryder—Steve Owsley; Mr. Aroeste—Richard Ryder; Mr. Burmester—Gordon Weiss; Miss Marble—Andrea Wright; Swing—Helena Andreyko.

Directed and choreographed by Patricia Birch; musical direction, Ross Allen, Roy Rogosin; scenery, Gerry Hariton, Vicki Baral; costumes, Carrie Robbins; lighting, Marc B. Weiss; sound, Abe Jacob; flying, Foy; musical supervision and dance arrangements, Louis St. Louis; orchestrations, Stan Applebaum; conductor, Ross Allen; assistant choreographer, Helena Andreyko; production stage manager, Peggy Peterson; stage managers, Franklin Keysar, Amy Pell; press, Shirley Herz Associates, Glenna Freedman, Peter Cromarty.

Time: Sometime earlier this century. Place: A New York riverfront.

Good (personified by a Raggedy Ann Doll) and Evil contend for the spirit of a young girl. Previously produced in regional theater at ESIPA, Albany and abroad in Moscow (under the title of *Rag Dolly*) in the fall of 1985 as the first item in a cultural exchange program with the Soviet Union.

ACT I

Overture . . . . Orchestra
"Gingham and Yarn" . . . . Company
"Carry On" . . . . Poppa
"Diagnosis" . . . . Doctors
"The Light" . . . . Dolls, Marcella
"Make Believe" . . . . Raggedy Ann, General D
"Blue" . . . . Camel, Raggedy Ann
"Make Believe" (Reprise) . . . . Raggedy Ann, Marcell Dolls, Company
"Make Believe" (Reprise) . . . . Raggedy Ann, Marcella
"Something in the Air" . . . . Company
"Delighted" . . . . Clouds
"So Beautiful" . . . . Raggedy Ann, Marcella, Clouds
"A Heavenly Chorus" . . . . Yellow Yum Yum
"The Shooting Star" . . . . Mommy, Poppa, Rat in Rolls Royce
"The Wedding" . . . . Company
"Rag Dolly" . . . . Raggedy Ann

ACT II

"Gingham and Yarn" (reprise)... Company
"You'll Love It".. Bat, Raggedy Ann, Battettes
"A Little Music" .... Marcella, Camel, Raggedy Ann, Dolls
"Gone" .... Dolls, Company
"Why Not" .... Mommy
"What Did I Lose" .... Mommy
"Somewhere" .... Raggedy Ann
"Welcome to L.A." .... Nurses
"Diagnosis" (Reprise) .... Doctors
"I Come Riding" .... General D
"Gingham and Yarn" (Reprise) .... Company
"Rag Dolly (Reprise; finale) .... Company

Flamenco Puro (40). Flamenco revue conceived by Claudio Segovia and Hector Orezzoli. Produced by Mel Howard and Donald K. Donald at the Mark Hellinger Theater. Opened October 19, 1986. (Closed November 30, 1986)

Dancers:
  Mañuela Carrasco
  Jose Cortes
  Antonio Montoya
  Pilar Montoya
  Rosario Montoya
  Eduardo Serrano
  Angelita Vargas
Singers:
  Juan Jose Amador
  Diego Camacho
  Adela Chaqueta

Enrique
Fernanda de Utrera
Juan Fernandez
Antonio Nunez
Guitarists:
  Joaquin Amador
  Ramon Amador
  Agustin Carbonell
  Jose Carmona Carmona
  Juan Carmona Carmona
  Jose Miguel Carmona Nino

Directed and designed by Claudio Segovia and Hector Orezzoli; production stage manager, Demetrio; press. P.R. Partners, Meg Gordean, Susan Arons.

Flamenco songs, dances and instrumentals, previously produced in Seville (1980), Paris (1984) and at Gusman Center, Miami.

MUSICAL NUMBERS, PART I: Bulerias—Company; Martinete—Antonio Nunez; Toque—Pilar Montoya, Jose Carmona Carmona; Cana—Manuela Carrasco, Pilar Montoya, Rosario Montoya, Angelita Vargas, Enrique, Diego Camacho, Juan Fernandez, Agustin Carbonell, Juan Carmona Carmona, Joaquin Amador.

Also Cafe Cantante: Alegrias—Adela Chaqueta; Romeras—Jose Cortes; Garrotin—Vargas; Romance—Carrasco; Farruca—Eduardo Serrano; Allegrias—Rosario Montoya, Camacho, Enrique, Juan Jose Amador, Fernandez, Joaquin Amador, Ramon Amador, Carbonell, Jose Miguel Carmona Nino; Fandangos—Fernanda de Utrera, Nunez, Juan and Jose Carmona; Tarantos—Company.

PART II: Tangos—Chaqueta, Rosario Montoya, Pilar Montoya, Enrique, Fernandez, Juan Jose Amador, Carbonell, Carmona Nino; Tientos—Vargas, Jose and Juan Carmona Carmona, Camacho; Soleares—Fernanda de Utrera, Jose and Juan Carmona Carmona, Serrano, Carbonell, Enrique, Juan Jose Amador, Carrasco, Joaquin and Ramon Amador; Seguiriya—Antonio Montoya, Nunez, Jose Carmona Carmona, Ramon Amador, Fernandez; Bulerias—Company.

Into the Light (6). Musical with book by Jeff Tambornino; music by Lee Holdridge; lyrics by John Forster. Produced by Joseph Z. Nederlander, Richard Kughn and Jerrold Perenchio at the Neil Simon Theater. Opened October 22, 1986. (Closed October 26, 1986)

Friend...................... Alan Mintz
Mathew Prescott............ Danny Gerard
Kate Prescott............... Susan Bigelow
James Prescott................ Dean Jones

Colonel...................... Ted Forlow
Major...................... David Young
Father Frank Girella......... William Parry
Peter Vonn................. Lenny Wolpe

Nathan Gelb .... Peter Walker	Don Cesare .... Casper Roos
Vijay Bannerjee .... Mitchell Greenberg	Archbishop Parisi .... Thomas Batten
Phyllis Terwilliger .... Kathryn McAteer	Signor Bocciarelli .... Gordon Stanley
Paul Cooper .... Alan Brasington	

Ensemble: Michael Duran, David Young, Deborah Carlson, Terri Homberg, Valerie DePena. Swings: Cheri Butcher, Ron Chisholm.

Understudies: Mr. Jones—Alan Brasington; Mr. Mintz—Ron Chisholm; Mr. Gerard—Michael Marona; Miss Bigelow—Kathryn McAteer; Mr. Wolpe—David Young; Messrs. Parry, Batten—Gordon Stanley; Mr. Greenberg—Michael Duran; Miss McAteer—Deborah Carlson; Mr. Brasington—David Young; Messrs. Walker, Stanley—Ted Forlow; Mr. Roos—Peter Walker.

Directed by Michael Maurer; choreography, Mary Jane Houdina; musical direction, Peter Howard; scenery and projections, Neil Peter Jampolis, Hervig Libowitsky; costumes, Karen Roston; lighting, Neil Peter Jampolis; sound, Jack Mann; orchestrations, Ira Hearshen; laser design, Marilyn Lowey; special laser effects, Laser Media, Inc.; synthesizer programming, Jeff Waxman; music supervisor, Stan Sheldone; production stage manager, William Dodds; stage manager, Steven Shaw; press, the Jacksina Company, Judy Jacksina, Marcy Granata, Julianne Waldheim.

Time: Late summer. Place: Los Alamos, N.M.

Scientists run tests on the Shroud of Turin. Previously produced in tryout at Detroit.

ACT I

Scene 1: James Prescott's office and the Prescott home
"Neat/Not Neat" .... James, Girella, Kate
"It Can All Be Explained" .... James, Girella
Scene 2: The lab at Los Alamos
"The Data" .... James, Team
Scene 3: The Prescott home, late that night
"A Talk About Time" .... James, Kate
Scene 4: The next morning
"Trading Solos" .... Girella, Mathew, Friend
Scene 5: Turin, Italy—the council chambers of Il Centro di Sindonologia
"Let There Be Light" .... James, Don Cesare, Girella, Bocciarelli, Parisi
Scene 6: The Prescott home
"Wishes" .... Mathew
Scene 7: The airport and lab at Los Alamos
"The Three of Us" .... Kate, James
"Rainbow Logic" .... James

ACT II

Scene 1: Turin, Italy
"Fede, Fede" .... Don Cesare, Parisi, Team
Scene 2: Turin, Italy
"To Measure the Darkness" .... James, Kate
Scene 3: The Prescott home
Scene 4: The testing room, St. John's Cathedral
"The Testing" .... James, Team
Scene 5: Albergo Excelsiore
"The Rose and I" .... Kate
Scene 6: The testing room
"The Testing" (continued) .... James, Team
"To Measure the Darkness" (Reprise) .... James
"Be There" .... James, Mathew
Scene 7: Epilogue
"Into the Light" .... Company

A Little Like Magic (49). Puppet show conceived by Diane Lynn Dupuy; musical numbers by various authors (see credits below). Produced by Famous People Players at the Lyceum Theater. Opened October 26, 1986. (Closed December 7, 1986)

CAST: Darlene Arsenault, Michelle Busby, Sandra Ciccone, Charlene Clarke, Annastasia Danyliw, Benny D'Onofrio, Any Fitzpatrick, Kim Hansen, Greg Kozak, Debbie Lim, Renato Marulli, Debbie Rossen, Mary Thompson, Neil Thompson, Lenny Turner.

Directed by Diane Lynn Dupuy; visual art effects, Mary C. Thornton; lighting, Ken Billington; sound, Lewis Mead; production supervisor, Sam Ellis; press, Mark Goldstaub Public Relations, Kevin P. McAnarney.

Puppets presented with "black light" effects (performers invisible in black costumes) in a revue of singing, dancing and pantomime. A foreign (Canadian) play performed by Famous People Players on a worldwide tour.

MUSICAL NUMBERS, ACT I: "A Little Like Magic" (by Victor Davies, sung by Gord Masten), "Aruba Liberace" (by Liberace), "Aquarium" (by Camille Saint-Saëns), "The Sorcerer's Apprentice" (by Paul Dukas), "The Bear and Bee" (by Victor Davies, sound effects by James Macdonald, Walt Disney Studios), "Concertino for Carignan" (by Andre Gagnon), "Viva Las Vegas" (by Elvis Presley), "The Gambler" (by Kenny Rogers), "Theme from *Superman*" (by John Williams, voices by Cal Dodd & Philip Williams), "Music of 007" (by John Barry), "The Battle Hymn of the Republic" (by Edrich Siebert, voices by Philip Williams).

ACT II: "Divertissement" (by Jacques Ibert), "Night on Bald Mountain" (by Modeste Mussorgsky), "Fossils" and "The Swan" (by Camille Saint-Saëns), "Billie Jean" (by Michael Jackson), "Part-Time Lover" (by Stevie Wonder).

Also Entertainment/Broadway Medley: "That's Entertainment" (by Arthur Schwartz and Howard Dietz), "New York, New York" (by John Kander and Fred Ebb, sung by Liza Minnelli), "42nd Street (by Harry Warren), "Ease on Down the Road" (by Charlie Smalls-Fox), "Don't Rain on My Parade" (by Jule Styne and Bob Merrill, sung by Barbra Streisand), "Send in the Clowns" (by Stephen

THE MAGNIFICENT CHRISTMAS SPECTACULAR—The Rockettes in a scene from Radio City Music Hall's annual holiday show

Sondheim), "The Night They Invented Champagne" (by Alan Jay Lerner and Frederick Loewe, sung by Cal Dodd), "Get Me to the Church on Time" (by Alan Jay Lerner and Frederick Loewe, sung by Neil Thompson), "Oklahoma!" (by Richard Rodgers and Oscar Hammerstein II, sung by Kim Hansen), "Can-Can" (by Cole Porter), "Lullaby of Broadway" (by Harry Warren and Al Dubin), "A Little Like Magic" (Reprise) (by Victor Davies), "Give My Regards to Broadway" (by George M. Cohan, sung by Cal Dodd).

L'Chaim to Life (42). Musical revue in the Yiddish and English languages; by various authors (see list of credits). Produced by International Artistic Productions, Inc. and Ralph Mercado at Town Hall. Opened November 5, 1986. (Closed December 21, 1986)

ACT I

Overture
Opening
  "Shalom Aleichem" .... Company
    (music and lyrics by Leybele Schwartz)
  "Yiddish" and "Alleh Villn" .... Jackie Jacob
    (music and lyrics by Ben Zion Witler)
Yiddishe Gesheftn (by Martin Hamar)
  Mrs. Rivkeh .... Mina Bern
  Mr. Leybl .... Leon Liebgold
  "Naches Fin Kinder" .... Mina Bern
The Rebbe and His Chassidim (based on a work by Martin Buber; adapted by Neil Steinberg)
  Chassidic Folk Dance... Dance Ensemble
  "Dus Yiddishe Leid" .... Jackie Jacob, Gerri-Ann Frank, Ari Roussimoff, Company
    (music and lyrics by Sholom Secunda)
Roumanian Memories—Dreams (music by Eber Lobato)
  Grandson.. Eric Kaufman
  Zeyde (Moishe)... Jackie Jacob
  Moishe, Age 9... Michael Fritzke
  Moishe, Age 19.. Jesse Webb
  Chanele .... Mary Ann Marek
  Nurse.. Gerri-Ann Frank
  "Kinder Yurn" .... Jackie Jacob, Mary Ann Marek
    (music and lyrics by Mordechai Gebirtig)
  Roumanian Folk Dance... Dance Ensemble
  "Roumania, Roumania"............... Jackie Jacob, Mina Bern, Leon Liebgold, Company
    (music and lyrics by Aaron Lebedeff)

ACT II

Entr'acte
My Yiddishn Buenos Aires
  "This Is The Show"... Dance Ensemble
    (music by Eber Lobato)
  "Du Iz Mein Hartz" .... Jackie Jacob
    (music by Eber Lobato, lyrics by Neil Steinberg)
  "Papirossn".. Jackie Jacob
    (by Herman Yablokoff)
  "Tanguera" .... Dance Ensemble
    (music by Mariano Mores)
  "A Yiddish Tango" .... Mina Bern, Leon Liebgold
  "Dance, Milonga, Dance!"... Dance Ensemble
    (music by Eber Lobato)
The Painter (by Yitzhok Perlov)
  Actress.. Mina Bern
  Painter .... Leon Liebgold

Those Good Old Days

"La Vie en Rose" . . . . Gerri-Ann Frank
    (music by Louiguy, lyrics by Edith Piaf)
"C'est Si Bon" . . . . Gerri-Ann Frank
    (music by Henri Betti, lyrics by Andre Hornez)
"Valentine" . . . . Gerri-Ann Frank
    (music by H. Christine, lyrics by Albert Willemote)
"Far Mir Alayn" . . . . Jackie Jacob, Trish Kane, Mary Ann Marek
    (music and lyrics by Max Perlman)
"Ich Vel Dir Kayn Mol Nisht Farbeytn" . . . . . . Jackie Jacob, Trish Kane, Mary Ann Marek
    (music and lyrics by Ben Zion Witler)
"Mayn Ruchele". Jackie Jacob, Helen Frank, Trish Kane, Mary MacLeod, Mary Ann Marek
    (music and lyrics by Ben Zion Witler)
"Rivkele" and "Lomir Trachtn Nor Fin Haynt" . . . . Dance Ensemble
    (music and lyrics by Ben Zion Witler)
"Bei Mir Bistu Shayn" . . . . Jackie Jacob, Ensemble
    (music by Sholom Secunda, lyrics by Jackie Jacob)
"Shayn Vi Di Levune" . . . . Jackie Jacob, Ensemble
    (music by Joseph Rumshinsky, lyrics by Chaim Tauber)
"Chiribin" . . . . Jackie Jacob, Ensemble
"Shabbos" . . . . Jackie Jacob, Ensemble
    (music and lyrics by Ben Bonus)
"My Way" . . . . Jackie Jacob, Company
    (music and lyrics by Paul Anka)

Directed by Neil Steinberg; choreography, Eber Lobato; musical direction, Renee Solomon; scenery, Ari Roussimoff; costumes, Eber Lobato; lighting, Neil Steinberg; production stage manager, Sandy Levitt; press, Max Eisen, Madelon Rosen, Maria Somma.

Yiddish-English sketches and musical numbers, some in Latin style.

The Magnificent Christmas Spectacular (140). Return engagement of the spectacle conceived by Robert F. Jani. Produced by Radio City Music Hall Productions at Radio City Music Hall. Opened November 14, 1986. (Closed January 8, 1987)

Scrooge; Santa; Narrator	Douglas Broyles	Belinda	Amy Gear
Mr. Cratchit	Edward Prostak	Martha	Gillian Hemstead
Mrs. Cratchit	Ann-Marie Blake	Coachman	Marty McDonough
Sarah Cratchit; Princess	Stacy Latham	Poultry Man	Tony Cobb
Tiny Tim Cratchit	Bradley Latham	Mrs. Claus	Alison England
Peter Cratchit	Demetri Callas	Skaters	Laurie Welch, Greg Welch

The Rockettes: Carol Beatty, Catherine Beatty, Dottie Belle, Susan Boron, Katy Braff, Linda Deacon Burrington, Elizabeth Chanin, Stephanie Chase, Barbara Ann Cittadino, Eileen M. Collins, Prudy Gray Demmler, Susanne Doris, Joyce Dwyer, Deniene Fenn, Alexis Ficks, Carol Harbich, Gynny Hounsell, Connie House, Stephanie James, Joan Peer Kelleher, Dee Dee Knapp, Kim Leslie, Judy Little, Sonya Livingston, Setsuko Maruhashi, Mary McNamara, Laraine Memola, Cynthia Miller, Kerri Pearsall, Gerri Presky, Linda Riley D'Allessio, Mary Six Rupert, Maryellen Scilla, Jereme Sheehan, Terry Spano, Maureen Stevens, Lynn Sullivan, Susan Theobald, Pauline Achilles Tzikas, Darlene Wendy.

The New Yorkers: Ann-Marie Blake, Tony Cobb, Alison England, Tom Garrett, David Michael Johnson, Connie Kunkle, Mark McBride, Nancy Meyer, Steven Edward Moore, Patrice Pickering, Edward Prostak, Laurie Stephenson, Alberto Stevans, Amy Stoddart, Susan Streater.

Dancers: Brian Arsenault, Joseph Bowerman, Leigh Catlett, Amy Gear, Michael Graham, Edward Henkel, Gillian Hemstead, David Loring, Marty McDonough, Sharon Moore, Laura Streets, Greg Welch, Laurie Welch, Kevin Weldon, Travis Wright.

Elves: Wiggle—John Edward Allen; Squiggle—Melinda C. Keel; Giggle—Timothy Loomis; Jiggle—Scott Seidman; Bruce—David Steinberg.

Orchestra: Bo Ayars musical director, conductor; Don Smith assistant conductor; Louann Montesi concertmaster; Gilbert Bauer, Carmine Deleo, Howard Kaye, Joseph Kowalewski, Julius H. Kunstler, Nannette Levi, Samuel Marder, Holly Ovenden violin; Marris J. Sutow, Barbara Harrison viola; Frank Levy, Pamela Frame cello; Dean Crandall bass; Kenneth Emery flute; Gerard J. Niewood, Richard Oatts, Joseph Camilleri, Joshua Siegel, Kenneth Arzberger reeds; George Bartlett, Nancy Freimanis—French horn; Richard Raffio, Zachary Shnek, Norman Beatty trumpet; John Schnupp, David Jett, Mark Johansen trombone; John Bartlett tuba; Thomas J. Oldakowski drums; Mari DeCiutiis, Randall Max percussion; Anthony Cesarano guitar; Susanna Nason, Don Smith piano; Jeanne Maier harp; Robert MacDonald, George Wesner organ.

Directed and produced by Robert F. Jani; scenery, Charles Lisanby; costumes, Frank Spencer; lighting, Ken Billington; staging and choreography, Violet Holmes, Linda Lemac, Marilyn Magness; orchestrations, Elman Anderson, Robert M. Freedman, Michael Gibson, Don Harper, Arthur Harris, Bob Krogstad, Philip J. Lang; production stage manager, Howard Kolins; stage managers, Peter Muste, Tony Berk, Mimi Apfel, Chris Kelly; press, Helene Greece, Shara R. Sokol.

The Music Hall's annual Christmas show with its famous Nativity pageant.

MUSICAL NUMBERS AND SCENES: Overture, "We Wish You a Merry Christmas"—Orchestra; Scene 1, *The Nutcracker; A Teddy Bear's Dream;* Scene 2, *A Christmas Carol;* Scene 3, "Sleigh Ride"—Orchestra; Scene 4, *Christmas in New York*—Company; Scene 5, "The Twelve Days of Christmas"; Scene 6, *They Can't Start Christmas Without Us;* Scene 7, "The Parade of the Wooden Soldiers"—Rockettes; Scene 8, *Beginning of Santa's Journey;* Scene 9, *The Night Before Christmas;* Scene 10, "The Christmas Song"—The New Yorkers; Scene 11, *The Rockette Christmas Carousel*—Rockettes; Scene 12, *The Living Nativity;* Jubilant, "Joy to the World"—Orchestra.

Oh Coward! (56). Revival of the musical revue devised by Roderick Cook; words and music by Noel Coward. Produced by Raymond J. Greenwald at the Helen Hayes Theater. Opened November 17, 1986. (Closed January 3, 1987)

Roderick Cook   Patrick Quinn
Catherine Cox

Musicians: Dennis Buck, David Evans piano; Ray Kilday bass; David Cox drums/percussion.

Standbys: Miss Cox—Marianne Tatum; Messrs Cook, Quinn—Dalton Cathey.

Directed by Roderick Cook; musical direction, Dennis Buck; scenery, Helen Pond and Herbert Senn; costumes, David Toser; lighting, F. Mitchell Dana; arrangements, Rene Wiegert; executive producer, Richard Seader; production stage manager, Andrew Burgreen; stage manager, Jim Woolley; press, Jeffrey Richards Associates, C. George Willard, Ken Mandelbaum.

Oh Coward! was first produced off Broadway 10/4/72 for 294 performances. This production, its first major New York revival and its Broadway premiere, was previously presented at Westport, Conn. Country Playhouse.

ACT I

Introduction: The Boy Actor—Company

Oh Coward!: "Something to Do With Spring," "Bright Young People," "Poor Little Rich Girl," "Zigeuner," "Let's Say Goodbye," "This Is a Changing World," "We Were Dancing," "Dance Little Lady," "Room With a View," "Sail Away"—Company.

England: London Is a Little Bit of All Right—Patrick Quinn; "The End of the News"—Catherine Cox, Roderick Cook; "The Stately Homes of England"—Quinn, Cook; London Pride—Cox.

Family Album: Aunt Jessie—Cook; "Uncle Harry"— Cox, Quinn.

Music Hall: Introduction—Cook; "Chase Me Charlie"—Cox; "Saturday Night at the Rose and Crown"—Company; "Island of Bolamazoo"—Quinn; "What Ho, Mrs. Brisket!"—Cook; "Has Anybody Seen Our Ship?"—Company; "Men About Town"—Quinn, Cook.

"If Love Were All"—Cox.

Travel: Too Early or Too Late—Cook; "Why Do the Wrong People Travel?"—Cox, Quinn; "The Passenger's Always Right"—Company.

Mrs. Worthington: "Don't Put Your Daughter on the Stage, Mrs. Worthington"—Company.

ACT II

"Mad Dogs and Englishmen"—Company.
A Marvelous Party: "The Party's Over Now"—Cook.
Design for Dancing: "Dance Little Lady" (Reprise)—Company.
"You Were There"—Quinn.
Theater: "Three White Feathers"—Cox, Cook; The Star—Quinn; The Critic—Cook; The Elderly Actress—Cox.
Love: Gertie—Cook. Loving—Quinn; I Am No Good at Love—Cook; Sex Talk—Quinn; A Question of Lighting—Quinn, Cook; "Mad About the Boy"—Cox.
Women: Introduction—Cook; "Nina"—Quinn; "Mrs. Wentworth-Brewster"—Cook.
"World Weary"—Company.
"Let's Do It" (music by Cole Porter)—Company.
Finale: "Where Are the Songs We Sung"—Quinn; "Someday I'll Find You"—Cook; "I'll Follow My Secret Heart"—Cox; "If Love Were All"—Company; "Play Orchestra Play"—Company; "I'll See You Again"—Company.

*Lincoln Center Theater. Schedule of four programs. **The Front Page** (57). Revival of the play by Ben Hecht and Charles MacArthur. Opened November 23, 1986. (Closed January 11, 1987) **Death and the King's Horseman** (33). By Wole Soyinka. Opened March 1, 1987. (Closed March 29, 1987) **The Regard of Flight** and **The Clown Bagatelles** (16). Return engagement of the comedy entertainment written by Bill Irwin in collaboration with the company and Nancy Harrington; original music by Doug Skinner. Opened April 12, 1987. (Closed April 26, 1987) ***The Comedy of Errors** (1) Revival of the play by William Shakespeare; adapted by The Flying Karamazov Brothers and Robert Woodruff; prologue by Avner the Eccentric. Opened May 31, 1987. Produced by Lincoln Center Theater, Gregory Mosher director, Bernard Gersten executive producer, at the Vivian Beaumont Theater.

THE FRONT PAGE

McCue	Trey Wilson
Endicott	Bernie McInerney
Schwartz	Lee Wilkof
Murphy	Ed Lauter
Wilson	Charles Stransky
Kruger	Ronn Carroll
Woman	Amanda Carlin
Frank	Philip LeStrange
Bensinger	Jeff Weiss
Woodenshoes Eichorn	Jack Wallace
Diamond Louis	Raymond Serra
Hildy Johnson	Richard Thomas
Jennie	Mary Catherine Wright
Mollie Malloy	Deirdre O'Connell
Sheriff Hartman	Richard B. Shull
Peggy Grant	Julie Hagerty
Mrs. Grant	Beverly May
Mayor	Jerome Dempsey
Mr. Pincus	Bill McCutcheon
Earl Williams	Paul Stolarsky
Walter Burns	John Lithgow
Tony; Policeman	Patrick Garner
Carl	Michael Rothhaar
Policeman	Richard Peterson

Understudies: Misses Hagerty, O'Connell—Amanda Carlin; Misses May, Wright—Anita Dangler; Messrs. McCutcheon, Stolarsky, Rothhaar, LeStrange—Patrick Garner; Messrs. Lauter, Wilson,

McInerney—Philip LeStrange; Messrs. Carroll, Weiss, Wilkof, Garner—Richard Peterson; Messrs. Thomas, Serra, Wallace—Michael Rothhaar.

Directed by Jerry Zaks; scenery, Tony Walton; costumes, Willa Kim; lighting, Paul Gallo; sound, Otts Munderloh; production manager, Jeff Hamlin; production stage manager, George Darveris; press, Merle Debuskey, Robert Larkin, Tracy Gore.

Place: The press room of the Criminal Courts Building, Chicago. The play was presented in two parts.

The last major New York revival of *The Front Page* took place on Broadway 5/10/60 for 64 performances, with a return engagement 10/18/69 of 158 performances.

DEATH AND THE KING'S HORSEMAN

Olohun-iyo (Praise Singer)	Ben Halley Jr.
Elesin (Horseman)	Earle Hyman
Iyaloja	Trazana Beverley
Bride	Sylvia Best
Simon Pilkings	Alan Coates
Jane Pilkings	Jill Larson
Sgt. Amusa	Ernest Perry Jr.
Joseph	Abdoulaye N'gom
Resident	Dillon Evans
Aide de Camp	Graeme Malcolm
Prince	Roderick McLachlan
Consort	Erika Petersen
Conductor	Robert Cenedella
Olunde	Eriq La Salle
Constables	Kenneth Arch Johnson, Munir Salaam

Men, Women, Young Girls, Dancers at the Ball: Niamani Asante-Rich, Sylvia Best, John K. Blandford, Marilyn Buchanan, Gregory Ince, Kenneth Arch Johnson, Marcya A. Joseph, Nanama Amankwaa Moore, Abdoulaye N'gom, Munir Salaam, Phyllis Yvonne Stickney, Wilhelmena T. Taylor, Karen Thornton, Byron Utley, Vanessa Williams.

Drummers: Kimati Dinizulu, Yomi Obileye, Tunji Oyelana, Edwina Lee Tyler.

Standbys: Mr. Hyman—Arthur French; Messrs. Halley, La Salle—Byron Utley; Misses Beverley, Heard—Phyllis Yvonne Stickney; Mr. Coates—Roderick McLachlan; Miss Larson—Erika Petersen.

Directed by Wole Soyinka; scenery, David Gropman; costumes, Judy Dearing; lighting, Pat Collins; sound, John Kilgore; production stage manager, Clinton Turner Davis; stage manager, Bonnie Panson.

Time: 1944. Place: Nigeria. Scene 1: The market. Scene 2: The verandah of the District Officer's bungalow. Scene 3: The market. Scene 4: The Residency. Scene 5: The stockade behind the Residency. The play was presented in two parts with the intermission following Scene 3.

A chief's intended suicide brings on a clash of British colonial and African tribal morals, based on a true incident. A foreign (Nigerian) play produced in London, Chicago and elsewhere.

THE REGARD OF FLIGHT and THE CLOWN BAGATELLES

CAST: Bill Irwin, M.C. O'Connor, Doug Skinner.

Scenery, Douglas O. Stein; lighting, Robert W. Rosentel; production stage manager, Nancy Harrington.

The Regard of Flight and *The Clown Bagatelles* were produced off Broadway at American Place Theater 5/23/82 for 83 performances. They were presented without intermission in this production.

THE COMEDY OF ERRORS

Janitor; Dr. Pinch	Avner Eisenberg
Duke of Ephesus; Luce	Karla Burns
Egeon	Daniel Mankin
Antipholus of Ephesus	Howard Jay Patterson
Antipholus of Syracuse	Paul Magid

DEATH AND THE KING'S HORSEMAN—Trazana Beverley and Jill Larson
in the play by Wole Soyinka

Dromio of Ephesus..Randy Nelson
Dromio of Syracuse..Sam Williams
Balthasar..Mark Sackett
Angelo; 2d Merchant..Alec Willows
1st Merchant..Raz
Emilia; Courtesan..Ethyl Eichelberger
Adriana..Sophie Hayden
Luciana..Gina Leishman
William Shakespeare..Timothy Daniel Furst

    Citizens of Ephesus: Steven Bernstein, Karla Burns, Bud Chase, Ethyl Eichelberger, Danny Frankel, Timothy Daniel Furst, Sophie Hayden, Gina Leishman, Paul Magid, Daniel Mankin, Derique

McGee, Randy Nelson, Wendy Parkman, Howard Jay Patterson, Raz, Rosalinda Rojas, Mark Sackett, Douglas Wieselman, Sam Williams, Alec Willows.

Directed by Robert Woodruff; scenery, David Gropman; costumes, Susan Hilferty; lighting, Paul Gallo; music, Douglas Wieselman with Thaddeus Spae; sound, John Kilgore; musical direction and arrangements, Douglas Wieselman; production stage manager, George Darveris; stage manager, Chet Leaming.

Shakespeare's comedy freely interpreted by The Flying Karamazov Brothers, presented in two parts, previously presented in a similar version in regional theater at the Goodman Theater, Chicago.

Smile (48). Musical based on the screenplay by Jerry Belson; book and lyrics by Howard Ashman; music by Marvin Hamlisch. Produced by Lawrence Gordon, Richard M. Kagan and Sidney L. Shlenker at the Lunt-Fontanne Theater. Opened November 24, 1986. (Closed January 3, 1987)

Contestants:
Robin Gibson .... Anne Marie Bobby
Doria Hudson .... Jodi Benson
Sandra-Kay Macaffee........ Veanne Cox
Maria Gonzales .... Cheryl-Ann Rossi
Shawn Christianson .... Tia Riebling
Valerie Sherman............ Lauren Goler
Heidi Anderson .... Deanna D. Wells
Patti-Lynn Bird .... Mana Allen
Debralee Davis....... Andrea Leigh-Smith
Kate Gardner; Joanne Marshall . . Mia Malm
Linda Lee .... Valerie Lau-Kee
Kimberly Lyons .... Julia Tussey
Gina Minelli .... Donna Marie Elio
Dana Simpson............ Renee Veneziale
Connie-Sue Whipple......... Cindy Oakes
Cookie Wilson .... Nikki Rene

Adults:
Brenda DiCarlo
Freelander .... Marsha Waterbury
Big Bob Freelander .... Jeff McCarthy
Tommy French....... Michael O'Gorman
Dale Wilson-Shears .... Richard Woods
Ted Farley............... Dick Patterson
Carol .... Ruth Williamson
Tony .... Jeffrey Wilkins
Robin's Mom; Judge;
Volunteer .... Laura Gardner
Photographer; Judge;
Volunteer .... K.C. Wilson
Kids:
Little Bob Freelander...... Tommy Daggett
Freddy................. Andrew Cassese

Orchestra: John Beal, Michael Berkowitz, Francis Bonny, Anthony Cecere, Nick Cerrato, Andy Drelles, Dennis Elliot, Eileen M. Folson, Jack Gale, Clarissa Howell, Al Hunt, Stephen Marzullo, Ronald Melrose, John J. Moses, Brian O'Flaherty, Caryl Paisner, Dean Plank, Marilyn Reynolds, Gene Scholtens, Les Scott, Ron Sell, Steve Uscher, Lorraine Wolf, Ann Yarbrough.

Understudies: Miss Waterbury—Joyce Nolen; Mr. McCarthy—Jeffrey Wilkins; Miss Bobby—Mana Allen, Susan Dow; Miss Benson—Donna Marie Elio, Deanna D. Wells; Messrs. Patterson, Woods—K.C. Wilson; Miss Rossi—Donna Marie Elio, Nikki Rene; Miss Riebling—Lauren Goler, Deanna D. Wells; Miss Cox—Susan Dow, Cindy Oakes; Miss Goler—Andrea Leigh-Smith, Mia Malm; Mr. O'Gorman—Michael Bologna.

Swings: Michael Bologna, Susan Dow, Linda Hess, Woody Howard, Joyce Nolen.

Directed by Howard Ashman; musical staging, Mary Kyte; musical director, Paul Gemignani; scenery, Douglas W. Schmidt; costumes, William Ivey Long; lighting, Paul Gallo; sound, Otts Munderloh; orchestrations, Sid Ramin, Bill Byers, Dick Hazard, Torrie Zito; vocal arrangements, Buster Davis; associate producers, Barbara Livitz, Ronald and Barbara Balser; production stage manager, Alan Hall; stage manager, Ruth E. Rinklin; press, the Fred Nathan Company, Bert Fink.

Act I: Santa Rosa Junior College, three days last summer. Act II: Santa Rosa Junior College, Saturday night.

Satire of teenage beauty contests, based on a 1975 movie.

ACT I

Prologue .... Contestants
"Orientation/Postcard #1" .... Brenda, Robin, Contestants
"Disneyland" .... Doria
"Shine" .... Contestants, Tommy French, Brenda
"Postcard #2".. Robin

"Nerves" .... Contestants
"Young and American" (Preliminary Night) .... Contestants
"Until Tomorrow Night" .... Contestants, Brenda, Big Bob

ACT II

"Postcard #3/Dressing Room Scene"................. Robin, Doria, Ted Farley, Contestants
"Smile" .... Ted Farley, Contestants
"In Our Hands"... Contestants
"Pretty as a Picture" .... Ted Farley, Big Bob, Robin, Contestants

The Knee Plays (4). Scenario by Robert Wilson; words and music by David Byrne. Produced by Great Performers at Lincoln Center, sponsored by the American Telephone and Telegraph Company in association with IPA Presents, Inc. (Robert LoBianco and Jedediah Wheeler) at Alice Tully Hall. Opened December 2, 1986. (Closed December 3, 1986)

CAST: Narrator—Matthew Buckingham. Dancers: Frank Conversano—Admiral Perry, Basket; Denise Gustafson, Suzushi Hanayagi—(Lion, Snow Carrier); Jeannie Hill—Knee Dancer; Carl House—Reader; Cho Kyoo Hyun—Cannon, Basket Seller; Fabrizia Pinto—Passenger, Man in Library; Satoru Shimazaki—Knee Dancer; Sanghi Wagner—Fisherman; Gail Donnerfield—Dance Captain, Lion, Woman With Umbrella, Basket (parentheses indicate roles in which the performers alternated).

Les Miserables Brass Band: Charles Berg drums, Pablo Calogero baritone saxophone, Matt Darriau tenor saxophone, David Harris trombone, Frank London trumpet, Marcus Rojas tuba, Jeanne Snodgrass trumpet.

Directed by Robert Wilson; choreography, Suzushi Hanayagi; musical direction, Frank London; lighting, Heinrich Brunke; stage manager, Michele Stechler; press, Susan Bloch & Company, Ellen Zeisler, Peter Carzasty, Alison Sherman.

Thirteen entr'acte playlets excerpted from the Wilson-Byrne operatic extravaganza *the CIVIL warS: a tree is best measured when it is down* and presented without intermission as "The American Section" of that work. *the CIVIL warS* has been presented in part and in whole on several occasions including an OOB presentation of the Prologue and Act V for 10 performances 12/14/86 at the Brookyn Academy of Music. It was recommended for—but not given—the Pulitzer Prize last season.

*Broadway Bound (205). By Neil Simon. Produced by Emanuel Azenberg at the Broadhurst Theater. Opened December 4, 1986.

Kate	Linda Lavin	Jack......................	Philip Sterling
Ben	John Randolph	Radio Voices:	
Eugene	Jonathan Silverman	Mrs. Pitkin	Marilyn Cooper
Stanley	Jason Alexander	Chubby Waters..........	MacIntyre Dixon
Blanche..................	Phyllis Newman	Announcer..................	Ed Herlihy

Standbys: Misses Lavin, Newman—Carol Locatell; Messrs. Randolph, Sterling—Alan Manson; Messrs. Silverman, Alexander—Peter Birkenhead.

Directed by Gene Saks; scenery, David Mitchell; costumes, Joseph G. Aulisi; lighting, Tharon Musser; sound, Tom Morse; production stage manager, Peter Lawrence; stage manager, Henry Velez; press, Bill Evans & Associates, Sandra Manley, Jim Baldassare.

Act I: Brighton Beach, Brooklyn, N.Y., February, late 1940s, 6 P.M. Act II: Saturday evening, a month later, 5:45 P.M.

Third in the series of the author's semi-autobiographical comedies (first two were *Brighton Beach Memoirs* and *Biloxi Blues*), dealing with the writer and his brother's efforts at gag writing for radio. A Best Play; see page 127.

Wild Honey (28). By Michael Frayn; from an untitled play by Anton Chekhov. Produced by Duncan C. Weldon, Jerome Minskoff, Robert Fryer, Karl Allison, Douglas Urbanski,

Jujamcyn Theaters/Richard G. Wolff and Albert and Anita Waxman in association with the National Theater of Great Britain at the Virginia Theater. Opened December 18, 1986. (Closed January 11, 1987)

Dr. Triletsky .... Sullivan Brown	Marko...................... George Hall
Yakov.................. Timothy Landfield	Marya Yerfimovna
Maids ..... Vivienne Avramoff, Kitty Crooks	Grekova.............. J. Smith-Cameron
Anna Petrovna............ Kathryn Walker	Platonov.................... Ian McKellen
Porfiry Semyonovich	Sasha...................... Kate Burton
Glagolyev .... Jonathan Moore	Gerasim Kuzmich
Sergey Voynitzev........... Frank Maraden	Petrin.............. William Duff-Griffin
Col. Triletzky.............. Franklin Cover	Osip .... Stephen Mendillo
Sofya....................... Kim Cattrall	Peasant..................... William Cain
Vasily .... Ron Johnston	

Standby: Mr. McKellen—Guy Paul. Understudies: Misses Walker, Cattrall—Vivienne Avramoff; Misses Burton, Smith-Cameron—Kitty Crooks; Messrs. Cover, Moore, Johnston, Landfield—William Cain; Messrs. Brown, Mendillo—Timothy Landfield; Mr. Duff-Griffin—Ron Johnston; Mr. Maraden—Guy Paul.

Conceived and directed by Christopher Morahan; scenery, John Gunter; costumes, Deirdre Clancy; lighting, Martin Aronstein; incidental music, Dominic Muldowney; production stage manager, Bob Borod; stage manager, Joseph Cappelli; press, the Fred Nathan Company, Merle Frimark, Marc P. Thibodeau.

Place: The Voynitzev family estate in one of the southern provinces of Russia. The play was presented in two parts.

This version of Chekhov's comedy about a womanizing schoolmaster (Platonov) in 19th century Russia, his first known playscript, untitled but often known as *Platonov*, is a foreign play first produced by the National Theater in London 7/19/84. This production was previously mounted at the Ahmanson Theater, Los Angeles, 10/10/86.

A Best Play; see page 164.

*Jackie Mason's "The World According to Me!" (160). One-man show created, written and performed by Jackie Mason. Produced by Nick Vanoff at the Brooks Atkinson Theater. Opened December 22, 1986.

Scenery and lighting, Neil Peter Jampolis; sound, Bruce D. Cameron; associate producer, Jyll Rosenfeld; original production supervised by Ron Clark; production stage manager, Don Myers; press, Patt Dale Associates.

Stand-up comedy treatment of politics, Hollywood, sex, the army, the weather, etc., previously produced in Los Angeles. The show was presented in two parts.

Sweet Sue (164). By A.R. Gurney Jr. Produced by Arthur Whitelaw, Dick Button and Byron Goldman at the Music Box. Opened January 8, 1987. (Closed May 31, 1987)

Susan .... Mary Tyler Moore	Jake...................... John K. Linton
Susan Too .... Lynn Redgrave	Jake Too..................... Barry Tubb

Standby: Misses Moore, Redgrave—Karen Grassle. Understudy: Messrs. Linton, Tubb—Steven Flynn.

Directed by John Tillinger; scenery, Santo Loquasto; costumes, Jess Goldstein; lighting, Ken Billington; creative photography, FPG International; background display, Kodak Duratrans; associate producer, Norma Langworthy, David Langworthy; production stage manager, Ed Aldridge; stage manager, Noel Stern; press, David Powers.

Time: During the course of a recent summer. Place: Various rooms of Susan's house in a suburb outside New York. The play was presented in two parts.

Love affair between a woman and her son's roommate, a two-character play with each character played by two performers. Previously produced at Williamstown, Mass.

Stepping Out (72). By Richard Harris. Produced by James M. Nederlander, The Shubert Organization, Jerome Minskoff, Elizabeth I. McCann and Bill Kenwright at the John Golden Theater. Opened January 11, 1987. (Closed March 15, 1987)

Mavis	Pamela Sousa	Andy	Janet Eilber
Mrs. Fraser	Victoria Boothby	Geoffrey	Don Amendolia
Lynne	Cherry Jones	Vera	Meagen Fay
Dorothy	Marcell Rosenblatt	Sylvia	Sheryl Sciro
Maxine	Carole Shelley	Rose	Carol Woods

Standbys: Misses Sousa, Eilber—Candace Tovar; Miss Boothby—Roo Brown; Misses Shelley, Fay, Sciro—Nancy Callman; Misses Rosenblatt, Jones—Susanna Fraser. Miss Woods—Gwen Shepherd; Mr. Amendolia—David Doty.

Directed by Tommy Tune; scenery, David Jenkins; costumes, Neil Spisak; lighting, Beverly Emmons; sound, Otts Munderloh; musical supervision and arrangements, Peter Howard; choreographic assistant, Marge Champion; directorial associate, Bruce Lumpkin; production stage manager, Bruce Lumpkin; stage manager, David Wolfe; press, the Jacksina Company, Judy Jacksina, Marcy Granata, Julianne Waldhelm.

Time: The present. Place: A North London church hall. The play was presented in two parts.

Activities in a woman's tap dancing class culminate in a chorus-line demonstration. A foreign play previously produced in London.

The Mikado (46). Revival of the operetta with book and lyrics by W.S. Gilbert; music by Arthur Sullivan. Produced by Ed Mirvish, David Mirvish and Brian Macdonald in the Stratford Festival Canada production at the City Center. Opened January 13, 1987. (Closed January 18, 1937 after 8 performances) Reopened in a return engagement April 2, 1987 at the Virginia Theater. (Closed May 3, 1987)

Mikado	Avo Kittask	Yum-Yum	Marie Baron
Nanki-Poo	John Keane	Pitti-Sing	Karen Wood
Ko-Ko	Eric Donkin	Peep-Bo	Karen Skidmore
Pooh-Bah	Richard McMillan	Katisha	Arlene Meadows
Pish-Tush	Paul Massel	Tumblers	David Gonzales, Walter Quigley

Chorus of School Girls, Nobles, Guards: Stephen Beamish, Timothy Cruikshank, Aggie Gekuta Elliot, Glori Gage, Paul Gatchell, Larry Herbert, Deborah Joy, David Keeley, Calla Krause, Richard March, Janet Martin, Dale Mieske, Lyndsay Richardson, Bradley C. Rudy, Joy Thompson-Allen, Marcia Tratt, Jim White.

Understudies: Miss Baron—Janet Martin; Mr. Massel—Dale Mieske; Miss Wood—Karen Skidmore; Mr. Kittask—Timothy Cruikshank; Mr. McMillan—Stephen Beamish; Mr. Donkin—Jim White; Miss Meadows—Calla Krause; Miss Skidmore—Marcia Tratt; Mr. Keane—Richard March.

Orchestra: Berthold Carriere conductor; Laura Burton assistant conductor, synthesizers; Marilyn Dallman keyboards.

Directed and choreographed by Brian Macdonald; musical direction, Berthold Carriere; scenery, Susan Benson, Douglas McLean; costumes, Susan Benson; lighting, Michael J. Whitfield; press, Max Eisen, Madelon Rosen.

Visiting Canadian production of the Gilbert & Sullivan operetta, which has been in running revival in New York City for many seasons in Light Opera of Manhattan repertory off Broadway.

ACT I

"If You Want to Know Who We Are"	Chorus of Men
"A Wand'ring Minstrel I"	Nanki-Poo, Chorus
"Our Great Mikado, Virtuous Man"	Pish-Tush, Chorus
"Young Man, Despair, Likewise Go To"	Pooh-Bah, Nanki-Poo, Pish-Tush
"And Have I Journey'd for a Month"	Nanki-Poo, Pooh-Bah
"Behold the Lord High Executioner"	Ko-Ko
"As Some Day It May Happen"	Ko-Ko, Chorus

"Comes a Train of Little Ladies".................................... Chorus of Girls
"Three Little Maids From School" .... Yum-Yum, Peep-Bo, Pitti-Sing, Chorus
"So Please You, Sir, We Much Regret" ..... Yum-Yum, Peep-Bo, Pitti-Sing, Pooh-Bah, Chorus
"Were You Not to Ko-Ko Plighted"............................. Yum-Yum, Naki-Poo
"I Am So Proud".. Ko-Ko, Pooh-Bah, Pish-Tush
"With Aspect Stern and Gloomy Stride" .... Company

ACT II

"Braid the Raven Hair"... Pitti-Sing, Chorus of Girls
"The Sun, Whose Rays Are All Ablaze"...................................... Yum-Yum
"Brightly Dawns Our Wedding Day" .... Yum-Yum, Pitti-Sing, Nanki-Poo, Pish-Tush
"Here's a How-de-do! If I Marry You".................... Yum-Yum, Nanki-Poo, Ko-Ko
"Mi-ya-sa-ma-mi-ya-sa-ma".. Chorus
"A More Humane Mikado
  Never Did in Japan Exist" .... Mikado, Chorus
"The Criminal Cried as He Dropped
  Him Down" .... Pitti Sing, Ko-Ko, Pooh-Bah, Chorus
"The Flowers That Bloom in the Spring".. Nanki-Poo, Ko-Ko, Yum-Yum, Pitti-Sing, Pooh-Bah
"Alone, and Yet Alive"... Katisha
"On a Tree by a River, a Little Tom-tit
  Sang Willow, Tit-willow"... Ko-Ko
"There Is a Beauty in the Bellow
  of the Blast"... Katisha, Ko-Ko
"For He's Gone and Married Yum-Yum" .... Company

Stardust (102). Musical revue conceived by Albert Harris; lyrics by Mitchell Parish; music by various authors (see credits below). Produced by William H. Kessler Jr., Burton L. Litwin, Martin Rein, Howard Rose and Louise Westergaard in association with Paula Hutter Gilliam in the Theater Off Park (Arthur Harris artistic director, Bertha Lewis producing director) production at the Biltmore Theater. Opened February 19, 1987. (Closed May 17, 1987)

Michele Bautier   Andre De Shields
Maureen Brennan   Jason Graae
Kim Criswell   Jim Walton

Understudies: Misses Bautier, Brennan, Criswell—Leata Galloway, Deborah Graham. Messrs. De Shields, Graae, Walton—Joel Blum, Vondie Curtis-Hall.
Musicians: James Raitt piano; Clint DeGannon percussion; Bill Cadieux guitar, banjo; Greg Maker, bass/tuba; Bill Meade Reed I; Al Hunt Reed II; Ed Kalney trumpet; Wayne Andre trombone; Katherine Easter harp.
Directed by Albert Harris; musical staging, Patrice Soriero; musical supervision and direction, vocal arrangements and orchestrations, James Raitt; tap dance created and staged by Henry Le Tang; scenery, David Jenkins; costumes, Mardi Philips; lighting, Ken Billington; sound, Gary Harris; associate producer, Richard Jay Smith; production stage manager, William Hare; stage manager, Rachel S. Levine; press, Henry Luhrman Associates, Terry M. Lilly, Susan Chicoine, Andrew P. Shearer, Anne Holmes.
Cavalcade of songs by various composers, with Mitchell Parish lyrics, chosen from the latter's 700 numbers, transferred from OOB.

ACT I

"Carolina Rolling Stone"....................................... Jason Graae, Company
  (1921, music by Eleanor Young and Harry D. Squires)
"Riverboat Shuffle" .... Andre De Shields, Company
  (1924, music by Hoagy Carmichael, Dick Voynow and Irving Mills)
"Sweet Lorraine" .... Jim Walton
  (1928, music by Cliff Burwell)

STARDUST—Andre De Shields and Maureen Brennan in the show featuring Mitchell Parish lyrics

"Sentimental Gentleman From Georgia".. Women
    (1932, music by Frank Perkins)
"Sophisticated Lady".. Michele Bautier
    (1933, music by Duke Ellington and Irving Mills)
"Dixie After Dark" .... De Shields, Walton
    (1934, music by Ben Oakland and Irving Mills)
"Stairway to the Stars" .... Kim Criswell
    (1935, music by Matt Malnick and Frank Signorelli)
"Wealthy, Shmelthy, as Long as You're Healthy".................................. Graae
    (1935, music by Sammy Fain)
The 1930s Unrequited Love Montage:
    "Hands Across the Table"... Bautier
        (1934, music by Jean Delettre)
    "You're so Indiff'rent"... Graae
        (1935, music by Sammy Fain)
    "It Happens to the Best of Friends" .... Criswell
        (1934, music by Rube Bloom)
    "I Would if I Could but I Can't"............................. Graae, Maureen Brennan
        (1933, music by Bing Crosby and Alan Grey)
    "The Scat Song"... De Shields, Brennan
        (1932, music by Frank Perkins and Cab Calloway)
    "Sidewalks of Cuba" .... Criswell, Graae
        (1934, music by Ben Oakland and Irving Mills)
    "Evenin' " .... Bautier
        (1934, music by Harry White)
    "Deep Purple" .... De Shields, Company
        (1934, music by Peter DeRose)

ACT II

Entr'acte .... Orchestra
"Sophisticated Swing" .... Criswell, Brennan, Walton
  (1936, music by Will Hudson)
"Midnight at the Onyx" .... De Shields, Brennan, Walton
  (1937, music by Will Hudson)
"Tell Me Why"
  (1945, music by Michael Edwards and Sigmund Spaeth)
"Does Your Heart Beat for Me?" .... Graae
  (1936, music by Russ Morgan and Arnold Johnson)
"Stars Fell on Alabama" .... Walton, Brennan
  (1934, music by Frank Perkins)
"Don't Be That Way" .... De Shields, Bautier
  (1935, music by Benny Goodman and Edgar Sampson)
"Organ Grinder's Swing" .... Men
  (1936, music by Irving Mills and Will Hudson)
"Moonlight Serenade" .... Company
  (1939, music by Glenn Miller)
"Star Dust" .... Bautier
  (1929, music by Hoagy Carmichael)
Your Cavalcade of Hits:
  Host .... Andre De Shields
  "Belle of the Ball" .... Graae, Brennan
    (1951, music by Leroy Anderson)
  "The Syncopated Clock" .... Brennan, Graae, Criswell, Walton
    (1946, music by Leroy Anderson)
  "Take Me in Your Arms" .... Brennan
    (1932, music by Fred Markush)
  "Ciao, Ciao, Bambino" .... Criswell
    (1959, music by Domenico Modugno)
  "Sleigh Ride" .... Brennan, Graae, Criswell, Walton
    (1949, music by Leroy Anderson)
  "Volare" .... Walton, Company
    (1958, music by Domenico Modugno)
  "Your Cavalcade of Hits" Theme
    (music by James Raitt, lyrics by Jay Jeffries)
  "Happy Cigarettes" Theme
    (music by James Raitt, lyrics by Peter Jablonski)
"Ruby" .... De Shields
  (1953, music by Heinz Roemheld)
"Forgotten Dreams" .... Company
  (1954, music by Leroy Anderson)
"Star Dust" (Reprise) .... Company

*Les Misérables (88). Musical based on the novel by Victor Hugo; book by Alain Boublil and Claude-Michel Schönberg; music by Claude-Michel Schönberg; lyrics by Herbert Kretzmer; original French text by Alain Boublil and Jean-Marc Natel; additional material by James Fenton. Produced by Cameron Mackintosh at the Broadway Theater. Opened March 12, 1987.

Prologue: 1815, Digne
Jean Valjean .... Colm Wilkinson
Javert................... Terrence Mann
Farmer..................... Jesse Corti
Laborer .... Alex Santoriello
Innkeeper's Wife......... Susan Goodman
Innkeeper .... John Norman

Bishop of Digne .... Norman Large
Constables... Marcus Lovett, Steve Shocket
Chain Gang: Kevin Marcum, Paul Harman, Anthony Crivello, John Dewar, Joseph Kolinski, Leo Burmester, David Bryant, Alex Santoriello, Michael Maguire.
1823, Montreuil-sur-Mer

Fantine .... Randy Graff
Foreman .... Paul Harman
Workers.......... Jesse Corti, John Dewar
Factory Girl .... Ann Crumb
Old Woman .... Cindy Benson
Crone..................... Marcie Shaw
Pimp; Fauchelevent .... Steve Shocket
Bamatabois .... Anthony Crivello
Women Workers: Cindy Benson, Marcie Shaw, Jane Bodle, Joanna Glushak.
Sailors: Joseph Kolinski, Kevin Marcum, John Dewar.
Whores: Susan Goodman, Joanna Glushak, Jane Bodle, Kelli James, Ann Crumb, Frances Ruffelle, Judy Kuhn, Gretchen Kingsley-Weihe.
1823, Montfermeil
Young Cosette .... Donna Vivino
Mme. Thenardier .... Jennifer Butt
Thenardier................ Leo Burmester
Young Eponine........ Chrissie McDonald
Drinker .... Jesse Corti
Young Couple........... Alex Santoriello, Gretchen Kingsley-Weihe
Drunk .... John Norman
Diners .... Norman Large, Joanna Glushak
Young Man.............. Joseph Kolinski
Young Girls ...... Jane Bodle, Kelli James
Old Couple ..... Marcie Shaw, John Dewar

Travelers ..... Paul Harman, Marcus Lovett
Other Drinkers: Steve Shocket, Anthony Crivello, Kevin Marcum, Ann Crumb, Susan Goodman, Cindy Benson.
1832, Paris
Gavroche................. Braden Danner
Old Beggar Woman .... Susan Goodman
Young Prostitute .... Ann Crumb
Pimp .... John Norman
Eponine................ Frances Ruffelle
Thenardier's Gang:
  Montparnasse.......... Alex Santoriello
  Babet.................. Marcus Lovett
  Brujon.................. Kevin Marcum
  Claquesous .... Steve Shocket
Enjolras................ Michael Maguire
Marius.................... David Bryant
Cosette..................... Judy Kuhn
Combeferre .... Paul Harman
Feuilly .... Joseph Kolinski
Courfeyrac................. Jesse Corti
Joly .... John Dewar
Grantaire............... Anthony Crivello
Lesgles.................. Norman Large
Jean Prouvaire .... John Norman
(The play was presented in two parts with the intermission coming during this 1832, Paris sequence of events.)

Understudies: Mr. Wilkinson—Kevin Marcum, Paul Harman; Mr. Mann—Anthony Crivello, Norman Large; Mr. Large—Steve Shocket, John Dewar; Miss Graff—Ann Crumb, Joanna Glushak; Miss Vivino—Brandy Brown, Chrissie McDonald; Miss Butt—Cindy Benson, Susan Goodman; Mr. Burmester—John Norman, Norman Large; Miss McDonald—Brandy Brown; Mr. Danner—R.D. Robb, Kelli James; Miss Ruffelle—Kelli James, Gretchen Kingsley-Weihe; Mr. Bryant—Marcus Lovett, Joseph Kolinski; Miss Kuhn—Gretchen Kingsley-Weihe, Jane Bodle; Mr. Maguire—Joseph Kolinski, Paul Harman; Swings—Patrick A'Hearn, Diane Della Piazza, Jordan Leeds.

Directed and adapted by Trevor Nunn and John Caird; musical supervision and direction, Robert Billig; orchestral score, John Cameron; scenery, John Napier; costumes, Andreane Neofitou; lighting, David Hersey; sound, Andrew Bruce/Autograph; executive producers, Martin McCallum, Richard Jay-Alexander; produced in association with the John F. Kennedy Center for the Performing Arts, Roger L. Stevens chairman; original London production by Cameron Mackintosh and the Royal Shakespeare Company; production stage manager, Sam Stickler; stage managers, Mitchell Lemsky, Fredric Hanson; press, the Fred Nathan Company, Anne Abrams.

Victor Hugo's tale of a reformed ex-convict (Jean Valjean) relentlessly pursued by a nemesis of a policeman (Javert), climaxing in scenes from the 1832 student uprising in Paris. A foreign play previously produced in Paris, London and Washington, D.C.

A Best Play; see page 194.

ACT I

Prologue .... Company
"Soliloquy" .... Jean Valjean
"At the End of the Day" .... Unemployed, Factory Workers
"I Dreamed a Dream".. Fantine
"Lovely Ladies" .... Ladies, Clients
"Who Am I?"... Valjean
"Come to Me" .... Fantine, Valjean

"Castle on a Cloud".. Young Cosette
"Master of the House".......................... Thenardier, Mme. Thenardier, Customers
"Thenardier Waltz" .... M. & Mme. Thenardier, Valjean
"Look Down"... Gavroche, Beggars
"Stars"...Javert
"Red and Black" .... Enjolras, Marius, Students
"Do You Hear the People Sing?"............................ Enjolras, Students, Citizens
"In My Life" .... Cosette, Valjean, Marius, Eponine
"A Heart Full of Love".. Cosette, Marius, Eponine
"One Day More" .... Company

ACT II

"On My Own" .... Eponine
"A Little Fall of Rain" .... Eponine, Marius
"Drink With Me to Days Gone By" .... Grantaire, Students, Women
"Bring Him Home"... Valjean
"Dog Eats Dog".. Thenardier
"Soliloquy" ....Javert
"Turning" .... Women
"Empty Chairs at Empty Tables"... Marius
"Wedding Chorale" .... Guests
"Beggars at the Feast"... M. & Mme. Thenardier
Finale.. Company

*Starlight Express (89). Musical with music by Andrew Lloyd Webber; lyrics by Richard Stilgoe. Produced by Martin Starger and Lord Grade at the Gershwin Theater. Opened March 15, 1987.

Bobo........................	A.C. Ciulla	Rocky IV...................	Angel Vargas
Espresso...................	Philip Clayton	Dustin..............	Michael Scott Gregory
Weltschaft	Michael Berglund	Flat-Top....................	Todd Lester
Turnov	William Frey	Red Caboose	Barry K. Bernal
Hashamoto..............	D. Michael Heath	Krupp...................	Joey McKneely
Prince of Wales..........	Sean McDermott	Wrench...............	Christina Youngman
Greaseball	Robert Torti	Joule.....................	Nicole Picard
Rusty	Greg Mowry	Volta....................	Mary Ann Lamb
Pearl........................	Reva Rice	Purse......................	Gordon Owens
Dinah	Jane Krakowski	Electra	Ken Ard
Ashley	Andrea McArdle	Poppa......................	Steve Fowler
Buffy.................	Jamie Beth Chandler	Belle	Janet Williams Adderley
Rocky I	Frank Mastrocola	Voice of The Boy	Braden Danner
Rocky II....................	Sean Grant	Voice of The Mother	Melanie Vaughan
Rocky III..................	Ronald Garza		

Greaseball Gang: Todd Lester, Sean Grant, Ronald Garza, Angel Vargas, Joey McKneely, Gordon Owens. Starlight Chorus: Paul Binotto, Lon Hoyt, Melanie Vaughan, Mary Windholtz.

Orchestra: Paul Bogaev conductor; David Caddick associate conductor; Joe Mosello, Brian O'Flaherty, James Hynes, Greg Ruvolo trumpets; Ed Neumeister, Keith O'Quinn trombones; Joe Randazzo, George Moran bass trombones; Kaitlin Mahoney, French horn; Mort Silver, Bob Mintzer, Ralph Olsen, Robert Eldridge reeds; Nicholas Cerrato percussion; Lee Musiker, Brett Sommer, Gary Dienstadt, Jan Rosenberg keyboards; Steve Bargonetti, Robbie Kirshoff guitars; Jeff Ganz bass; Ray Marchica drums.

Understudies: Miss McArdle—Jamie Beth Chandler, Amelia Prentice, Christina Youngman; Miss Adderley—Lola Knox, Amelia Prentice; Mr. Ciulla—Mark Frawley, Anthony Galde, Ron Morgan, Dwight Toppin; Miss Chandler—Lola Knox, Mary Ann Lamb, Christine Langner; Miss Krakowski—Christine Langner, Nicole Picard; Mr. Gregory—Anthony Galde, D. Michael Heath, Sean McDermott; Mr. Ard—Michael-Demby Cain, Philip Clayton, Gordon Owens, Broderick Wilson;

Mr. Clayton—Mark Frawley, Ron Morgan, Broderick Wilson; Mr. Lester—Mark Frawley, Anthony Galde, Joey McKneely; Mr. Torti—Mark Frawley, William Frey, Frank Mastrocola; Mr. Heath—Mark Frawley, Ron Morgan, Dwight Toppin; Miss Picard—Lola Knox, Christine Langner, Amelia Prentice; Mr. McKneely—Mark Frawley, Anthony Galde, Ron Morgan, Dwight Toppin, Broderick Wilson.

Also Miss Rice—Lola Knox, Christine Langner; Mr. Fowler—Danny Strayhorn, Broderick Wilson; Mr. McDermott—Mark Frawley, Ron Morgan, Broderick Wilson; Mr. Owens—Michael-Demby Cain, Dwight Toppin, Broderick Wilson; Mr. Bernal—Mark Frawley, Anthony Galde, Todd Lester; Mr. Mastrocola—Michael-Demby Cain, William Frey, Broderick Wilson; Mr. Grant: Michael-Demby Cain, Dwight Toppin, Broderick Wilson; Mr. Garza—Michael-Demby Cain, A.C. Ciulla, Dwight Toppin; Mr. Vargas—Michael-Demby Cain, Dwight Toppin, Broderick Wilson; Mr. Mowry—Michael-Demby Cain, Sean Grant, Sean McDermott; Mr. Frey—Mark Frawley, Ron Morgan, Dwight Toppin; Miss Lamb—Lola Knox, Christine Langner, Christina Youngman; Mr. Berglund—Mark Frawley, Anthony Galde, Ron Morgan; Miss Youngman—Lola Knox, Christine Langner, Amelia Prentice.

Directed by Trevor Nunn; choreography, Arlene Phillips; musical director, Paul Bogaev; design, John Napier; lighting, David Hersey; sound, Martin Levan; musical direction and supervision, David Caddick; orchestrations, David Cullen, Andrew Lloyd Webber; original London production, The Really Useful Theater Company; executive producer, Gatchell & Neufeld, Ltd.; production advisor, Arthur Cantor; production stage manager, Frank Hartenstein; stage manager, Perry Cline; press, Bill Evans & Associates, Sandra Manley, Jim Baldassare.

Personification and glorification of railroad trains. A foreign play previously produced in London.

ACT I

Overture
"Rolling Stock" .... Greaseball, Gang
"Engine of Love" .... Rusty, Pearl, Dinah, Ashley, Buffy
  (derived from an original lyric by Peter Reeves)
"Lotta Locomotion".. Dinah, Ashley, Buffy, Rusty
"Freight".. Company
"AC/DC" .... Electra, Krupp, Wrench, Joule, Volta, Purse, Company
"Pumping Iron" .... Greaseball, Pearl, Ashley, Dinah, Buffy
"Freight" (Reprise) .... Company
"Make Up My Heart"... Pearl
"Race One".. Greaseball & Dinah, Weltschaft & Joule, Turnov & Red Caboose, Electra & Pearl
"There's Me" .... Red Caboose, Dinah
"Poppa's Blues" .... Poppa, Rocky I, II, III & IV, Rusty
"Belle" .... Belle, Poppa, Rocky I, II, III, & IV, Rusty, Dustin, Flat-Top
Race Two" .... Bobo & Buffy, Hashamoto & Volta, Espresso & Ashley, Poppa & Dustin
"Laughing Stock".. Company
"Starlight Express"... Rusty

ACT II

"Silver Dollar" .... Company
"U.N.C.O.U.P.L.E.D." .... Dinah, Ashley, Buffy
"Rolling Stock" (Reprise) .... Dinah, Ashley, Buffy
"Wide Smile, High Style, That's Me" .... Red Caboose, Electra, Krupp, Wrench,
                                                            Joule, Volta, Purse
"First Final".................... Greaseball & Pearl, Electra & Dinah, Hashamoto & Volta,
                                                      Rusty & Red Caboose
"Right Place, Right Time" .... Rocky I, II, III, & IV
"I Am the Starlight" .... Rusty, Poppa
"Final Selection" .... Rusty, Dusty, Dinah, Electra, Pearl, Greaseball, Red Caboose
"Only You".. Pearl, Rusty
"Chase"... Company
"One Rock & Roll Too Many" .... Greaseball, Electra, Red Caboose
"Light at the End of the Tunnell".. Company

SAFE SEX—John Wesley Shipp and Harvey Fierstein in the title one-acter of this program of three plays

*The Nerd (81). By Larry Shue. Produced by Kevin Dowling, Joan Stein, Melvyn J. Estrin, Susan Rose, Gail Berman and Lynn Dowling in association with F. Harlan Batrus, Gina Rogak and George A. Schapiro at the Helen Hayes Theater. Opened March 22, 1987.

Willum Cubbert	Mark Hamill	Clelia Waldgrave	Pamela Blair
Tansy McGinnis	Patricia Kalember	Thor Waldgrave	Timmy Geissler
Axel Hammond	Peter Riegert	Rick Steadman	Robert Joy
Warnock Waldgrave	Wayne Tippit		

Standby: Messrs. Hammill, Joy, Riegert, Tippit—Edward Edwards. Understudy: Mr. Geissler—Jeremy Cummins.

Directed by Charles Nelson Reilly; scenery, John Lee Beatty; costumes, Deborah Shaw; lighting, Dennis Parichy; sound, Timothy Helgeson; associate producers, Gintare Seleika Everett, Allan Matthews, Yentl Productions; production stage manager, Robert T. Bennett; stage manager, Daniel R. Bauer; press, Adrian Bryan-Brown, Joshua Ellis, Reva Cooper.

Place: Terra Haute, Ind. Act I: Nov. 4, 1981. Act II, Scene 1: Six days later. Scene 2: The following day.

A visiting nerd upsets the household of a Vietnam War veteran. Previously produced in Milwaukee and in England in London and Manchester.

*Fences (77). By August Wilson. Produced by Carole Shorenstein Hays in association with the Yale Repertory Theater, Lloyd Richards artistic director, Benjamin Mordecai managing director, at the 46th Street Theater Opened March 26, 1987.

Troy Maxson	James Earl Jones	Gabriel	Frankie R. Faison
Jim Bono	Ray Aranha	Cory	Courtney B. Vance
Rose	Mary Alice	Raynell	Karima Miller
Lyons	Charles Brown		

Understudies: Mr. Jones—Gilbert Lewis; Miss Alice—Ethel Ayler; Mr. Vance—Byron Keith Minns; Messrs. Aranha, Faison—Mike Hodge; Mr. Brown—Vince Williams; Miss Miller—Tatyana Ali.

Directed by Lloyd Richards; scenery, James D. Sandefur; costumes, Candice Donnelly; lighting, Danianne Mizzy; production stage manager, Martin Gold; stage manager, Terrence J. Witter; press, Joshua Ellis, Reva Cooper, Adrian Bryan-Brown.

Place: The backyard of the Maxson house, itself in an urban neighborhood of a Northern American industrial city. Act I, Scene 1: A Friday evening, fall of 1957. Scene 2: The next morning. Scene 3: A few hours later. Scene 4: The following Friday. Act II, Scene 1: Saturday, fall of 1957. Scene 2: Friday, Spring of 1958. Scene 3: Three days later. Scene 4: Two months later. Scene 5: Summer of 1965.

Black father and his family painfully approach the threshold of the Great Society. Previously produced in regional theater in San Francisco, New Haven, Chicago, Seattle and Rochester.

A Best Play; see page 209.

*Blithe Spirit (71). Revival of the play by Noel Coward. Produced by Karl Allison, Douglas Urbanski and Sandra Moss in association with Jerome Minskoff and Duncan C. Weldon at the Neil Simon Theater. Opened March 31, 1987.

Edith....................	Nicola Cavendish	Mrs. Bradman.............	Patricia Conolly
Ruth.......................	Judith Ivey	Mme. Arcati	Geraldine Page
Charles..............	Richard Chamberlain	Elvira	Blythe Danner
Dr. Bradman...........	William LeMassena		

Understudies: Messrs. Chamberlain, LeMassena—Lewis Arlt; Misses Ivey, Danner—Jennifer Harmon; Misses Cavendish, Conolly—le Clanché duRand.

Directed by Brian Murray; scenery, Finlay James; costumes, Theoni V. Aldredge; lighting, Richard Nelson; music arrangements, Marvin Hamlisch; sound, Jan Nebozenko; production stage managers, Murray Gitlin, T.L. Boston; press, Joshua Ellis, Adrian Bryan-Brown, Reva Cooper.

Time: The late 1930s. Place: Charles Condomine's house in Kent. Act I, Scene 1: Before dinner on a summer evening. Scene 2: After dinner. Act II, Scene 1: The next morning. Scene 2: Late the following afternoon. Scene 3: Early evening, a few days later. Act III, Scene 1: After dinner, a few days later. Scene 2: Several hours later.

The last major New York revivals of *Blithe Spirit* took place off Broadway in the season of 1951–52 and in a musical adaptation entitled *High Spirits* on Broadway for 63 performances 4/7/64.

Safe Sex (9). Program of three one-act plays by Harvey Fierstein: *Manny and Jake, Safe Sex* and *On Tidy Endings.* Produced by The Shubert Organization and MTM Entertainment, Ltd. at the Lyceum Theater. Opened April 5, 1987. (Closed April 12, 1987)

Manny and Jake
Manny.. John Mulkeen
Jake.. John Wesley Shipp

Safe Sex
Mead... John Wesley Shipp
Ghee... Harvey Fierstein

On Tidy Endings
Marion... Anne De Salvo
Jimmy .... Ricky Addison Reed
June .... Billie McBride
Arthur .... Harvey Fierstein

Standbys: Messrs. Fierstein, Shipp, Mulkeen—Stephen Bogardus; Misses McBride, De Salvo—Megan McTavish; Mr. Reed—Christopher Unger.

Directed by Eric Concklin; scenery, John Falabella; costumes, Nanzi Adzima; lighting, Craig Miller; sound, Tom Morse; music, Ada Janik; associate producer, Scott Robbe; production stage manager, Bob Borod; stage manager, Glen Gardali; press, Jim Baldassare.

Variations on the AIDS theme: *Manny and Jake* portrays the plight of a virus carrier; *Safe Sex* is an argument between male lovers; *On Tidy Endings* is a clash between the male lover and the widow of an AIDS victim. The play was presented in two parts with the intermission following *Safe Sex*. Previously produced OOB at La Mama E.T.C.

*The Musical Comedy Murders of 1940 (64). By John Bishop. Produced by Bill Wildin in the Circle Repertory Company production, Marshall W. Mason artistic director, at the Longacre Theater. Opened April 6, 1987.

Helsa Wenzel	Lily Knight	Nikki Crandall	Dorothy Cantwell
Elsa von Grossenknueten	Ruby Holbrook	Eddie McCuen	Kelly Connell
Michael Kelly	Willie C. Carpenter	Marjorie Baverstock	Pamela Dunlap
Patrick O'Reilly	Nicholas Wyman	Roger Hopewell	Richard Seff
Ken de la Maize	Michael Ayr	Bernice Roth	Bobo Lewis

Understudies: Messrs. Ayr, Seff, Wyman—Matthew Gottlieb; Messrs. Carpenter, Connell—Mark Enis; Misses Cantwell, Knight—Susan Bruce; Misses Holbrook, Dunlap, Lewis—Elizabeth Perry.

Directed by John Bishop; scenery, David Potts; costumes, Jennifer Von Mayrhauser; lighting, Jeff Davis; original music, Ted Simons; sound, Chuck London Media/Stewart Werner; production stage manager, Fred Reinglas; stage manager, Leslie Loeb; press, Jeffrey Richards Associates, C. George Willard, Ken Mandelbaum.

Time: December 1940, midnight. Place: An estate in Chappaqua, N.Y. The play was presented in two parts.

Comedy melodrama with people trapped by a snowstorm in a mansion with a maniac. Transfer from off Broadway where it played 88 performances 1/7/87–3/22/87; see its entry in the Plays Produced Off Broadway section of this volume.

Barbara Cook: A Concert for the Theater (13). One-woman program with Barbara Cook; original music by Wally Harper; lyrics by David Zippel; other music and lyrics by various authors (see credits below). Produced by Jerry Kravat, The Shubert Organization and Emanuel Azenberg at the Ambassador Theater. Opened April 15, 1987. (Closed April 26, 1987)

Musicians: Wally Harper piano, John Beal bass, Charles Loeb Guitar, John Redsecker drums, David Carey percussion, Mack Schlefer keyboard, John Clifton keyboard, Lawrence Feldman reeds.

Music arranged and conducted by Wally Harper; scenery, John Falabella; costumes, Joseph G. Aulisi; lighting, Richard Winkler; sound, Fred Miller; keyboard coordinator, John Clifton; associate producer, Perry B. Granoff; production stage manager, Martin Herzer; stage manager, Jane E. Cooper; press, Bill Evans & Associates, Becky Flora.

Barbara Cook in a concert of Broadway and other songs including works by these composers and lyricists: Harold Arlen, Irving Berlin, Ben Bernie, Leonard Bernstein, Jerry Bock, Ken Casey, Betty Comden, Noel Coward, Howard Dietz, Walter Donaldson, Adolph Green, Oscar Hammerstein II, Sheldon Harnick, Lorenz Hart, Rupert Holmes, Janis Ian, Gus Kahn, Michael Leonard, Melissa Manchester, Herbert Martin, Johnny Mercer, Harry Nilsson, Maceo Pinkard, Richard Rodgers, Carole Bayer Sager, Arthur Schwartz, Stephen Sondheim, Doris Tauber, William Tracy, Paul Zakrzewski.

A Month of Sundays (4). By Bob Larbey. Produced by Emanuel Azenberg, Jerome Minskoff and Jujamcyn Theaters/Richard G. Wolff at the Ritz Theater. Opened April 16, 1987. (Closed April 18, 1987)

Cooper	Jason Robards	Aylott	Salem Ludwig
Nurse Wilson	Felicity LaFortune	Julia	Patricia Elliott
Mrs. Baker	Lynne Thigpen	Peter	Richard Portnow

Standbys: Messrs. Robards, Ludwig—James Cahill; Miss Thigpen—L. Scott Caldwell; Misses Elliott, LaFortune—Alma Cuervo; Mr. Portnow—Curt Karibalis.

Directed by Gene Saks; scenery, Marjorie Bradley Kellogg; costumes, Joseph G. Aulisi; lighting, Tharon Musser; sound, Brian Lynch; production stage manager, William Buxton; stage manager, Steven Shaw; press, Bill Evans & Associates, Becky Flora.

Time: The first Sunday in April and the first Sunday in May. Place: Cooper's room in a rest and retirement home in Westchester County, N.Y. The play was presented in two parts.

Comedy, widower takes pleasure in harassing the staff of a retirement home. A foreign play previously produced in London, with locale changed to the U.S. for this production.

All My Sons (29). Revival of the play by Arthur Miller. Produced by Jay H. Fuchs and Steven Warnick in association with Charles Patsos in the Long Wharf Theater production at the John Golden Theater. Opened April 22, 1987. (Closed May 17, 1987)

Dr. Jim Bayliss	Dan Desmond	Chris Keller	Jamey Sheridan
Joe Keller	Richard Kiley	Bert	Michael Maronna
Frank Lubey	Stephen Root	Kate Keller	Joyce Ebert
Sue Bayliss	Kit Flanagan	Ann Deever	Jayne Atkinson
Lydia Lubey	Dawn Didawick	George Deever	Christopher Curry

Standbys: Mr. Kiley—Rex Robbins; Miss Ebert—Rose Arrick; Messrs. Sheridan, Curry, Desmond, Root—Tracy Griswold; Misses Atkinson, Didawick, Flanagan—Wendy Barrie-Wilson.

Directed by Arvin Brown; scenery, Hugh Landwehr; costumes, Bill Walker; lighting, Ronald Wallace; production stage manager, Zoya Wyeth; press, Shirley Herz Associates, Peter Cromarty.

Time: End of summer, 1946. Act I: The backyard of the Keller home on the outskirts of an American town. Act II: The same evening, as twilight falls. Act 3: 2 o'clock the following morning. The play was presented in two parts.

All My Sons was first produced on Broadway 1/29/47 for 328 performances and was named a Best Play of its season and won the Critics Award for best American play. It was revived off Broadway in the 1949–50 season and 9/27/74 for 60 performances.

Asinamali! (We Have No Money) (29). By Mbongeni Ngema. Produced by Kenneth Waissman, Robert A. Buckley, Jane Harmon, Nina Keneally and Edward L. Schuman at the Jack Lawrence Theater. Opened April 23, 1987. (Closed May 17, 1987)

CAST: Solomzi Bisholo, Thami Cele, Bongani Hlophe, Bheki Mqadi, Bhoyi Ngema.

Understudies: Fanya Kekana, Michael Xulu.

Directed by Mbongeni Ngema; lighting, Wesley France; production supervisor, Makalo Mofokeng; production stage manager, Bruce Hoover; stage manager, Judith Binus; press, Jeffrey Richards Associates, Ben Morse, Ken Mandelbaum.

Place: A prison cell at Leeuwkop Prison, outside Johannesburg. The play was presented without intermission.

Five men jailed during a 1983 rent strike describe in song, dance and dialogue how each came to be incarcerated. The play was presented without intermission. Transfer from off Broadway (Lincoln Center Theater) where it played 8 performances 9/10/86–9/14/86; see its entry in the Plays Produced Off Broadway section of this volume.

*Pygmalion (41). Revival of the play by George Bernard Shaw. Produced by The Shubert Organization, Jerome Minskoff and Duncan C. Wilson at the Plymouth Theater. Opened April 26, 1987.

Mrs. Eynsford Hill	Mary Peach	Prof. Higgins	Peter O'Toole
Clara Eynsford Hill	Kirstie Pooley	Mrs. Pearce	Dora Bryan
Sarcastic Bystander	Ivar Brogger	Alfred Doolittle	John Mills
Freddy Eynsford Hill	Osmund Bullock	Mrs. Higgins	Joyce Redman
Eliza Doolittle	Amanda Plummer	Parlormaid	Selena Carey-Jones
Col. Pickering	Lionel Jeffries	Teamaid	Wendy Makkena

Other Bystanders: Lucy Martin, Robertson Dean, Angela Thornton, Richard Neilson, Edward Conery.

Understudies: Mr. O'Toole—Ivar Brogger; Miss Plummer—Kirstie Pooley; Messrs. Mills, Brogger—Edward Conery; Mr. Jeffries—Richard Nelson; Misses Bryan, Peach—Lucy Martin; Miss Redman—Angela Thornton; Mr. Bullock—Robertson Dean; Miss Carey-Jones—Wendy Makkena; Miss Pooley—Selena Carey-Jones.

Directed by Val May; scenery, Douglas Heap; costumes, Terence Emery; lighting, Martin Aronstein; production stage manager, Martin Gold; stage manager, John Vivian; press, the Fred Nathan Company, Merle Frimark.

Time: 1912. Place: London. Act I, Scene 1: The portico of St. James's Church, Covent Garden, 11:15 P.M. Scene 2: Professor Higgins's phonetics laboratory in Wimpole Street, 11 A.M. the next day. Act II, Scene 1: Mrs. Higgins's drawing room in Chelsea, afternoon, several months later. Scene 2: Higgins's laboratory, midnight, several months later. Act III: Mrs. Higgins's drawing room, the next day.

The last major New York revival of *Pygmalion* was its musical adaptation *My Fair Lady* on Broadway 8/18/81 for 119 performances. There have been no major New York revivals of the original play since the opening of the musical 3/15/56. Before that, its most recent revivals were Raymond Massey's Prof. Higgins on Broadway 12/26/45 for 179 performances and an off-Broadway revival in the season of 1951–52.

*Les Liaisons Dangereuses (37). By Christopher Hampton; from the novel by Choderlos de Laclos. Produced by James M. Nederlander, The Shubert Organization, Jerome Minskoff, Elizabeth I. McCann and Stephen Graham in association with Jonathan Farkas in the Royal Shakespeare Company production, Terry Hands artistic director, at the Music Box. Opened April 30, 1987.

Major-Domo	Barry Heins	Azolan	Hugh Simon
Marquise de Merteuil	Lindsay Duncan	La Presidente de Tourvel	Suzanne Burden
Mme. de Volanges	Kristin Milward	Mme. de Rosemonde	Jean Anderson
Cecile Volanges	Beatie Edney	Emilie	Lucy Aston
Vicomte de Valmont	Alan Rickman	Chevalier Danceny	Hilton McRae

Harpsichord: Michael Dansicker.

Understudies: Misses Burden, Edney—Lucy Aston; Misses Anderson, Milward, Aston—Cissy Collins. Messrs. McRae, Simon—Barry Heins; Miss Duncan—Kristin Milward; Mr. Rickman—Hugh Simon.

Directed by Howard Davies; design, Bob Crowley; lighting, Chris Parry in association with Beverly Emmons; sound, Otts Munderloh in association with John A. Leonard; music, Ilona Sekacz; fight direction, Malcolm Ranson; production stage manager, Susie Cordon; company stage manager, Jane Tamlyn; stage manager, Paul Mills Holmes; press, Joshua Ellis, Adrian Bryan-Brown, Jim Sapp, Reva Cooper, Jackie Green.

Time: One autumn and winter in the 1780s. Place: Various salons and bedrooms in a number of hotels and chateaux in and around Paris and in the Bois de Vincennes. The play was presented in two parts.

Pre-revolution manners and mores of French aristocrats, with destructive consequences through a series of amours. A foreign play previously produced in London.

A Best Play; see page 249.

Sleight of Hand (9). By John Pielmeier. Produced by Suzanne J. Schwartz in association with Jennifer Manocherian. Opened May 3, 1987. (Closed May 10, 1987)

Paul	Harry Groener	Dancer	Jeffrey DeMunn
Sharon	Priscilla Shanks		

Understudy: Messrs. Groener, DeMunn—Stephen Rowe.

Directed by Walton Jones; scenery, Loren Sherman; costumes, William Ivey Long; lighting, Richard Nelson; magic consultant, Charles Reynolds; sound, Jan Nebozenko; special effects, Jauchem & Meeh; fight staging, B.H. Barry; title song recorded by Carly Simon; associate producers, Alison Clarkson, Douglas B. Leeds; production stage manager, Franklin Keysar; stage manager, R. Nelson Barbee; press, Patt Dale Associates.

PYGMALION—Amanda Plummer and Peter O'Toole in a scene from the George Bernard Shaw revival

Time: Christmas Eve. Act I: A loft apartment in New York City, 8 P.M. Act II: The stage of an empty Broadway theater, 10 P.M.

Suspense thriller, amateur magician performs a dangerous new trick.

PLAYS WHICH CLOSED PRIOR TO BROADWAY OPENING

Productions which were organized by New York producers for Broadway presentation but which closed during their production and tryout period are listed below.

Legends! By James Kirkwood. Produced by Ahmet E. Ertegun, Kevin Eggers, Robert Regester for EEE Ventures, Cheryl Crawford and Pace Theatrical Group, in association with the Tom Hughes Foundation and Center Theater Group/Ahmanson Theater in a pre-Broadway tryout. Opened at the Majestic Theater, Dallas, January 8, 1986. (Closed at the Royal Poinciana Theater, Palm Beach, January 18, 1987)

Sylvia Glenn	Carol Channing	Martin Klemmer	Gary Beach
Leatrice Monsee	Mary Martin	Policeman	Don Howard
Aretha Thomas	Annie-Joe	Young Man	Eric Riley

Directed by Clifford Williams; scenery, Douglas W. Schmidt; costumes, Freddy Wittop; lighting, Thomas Skelton; press, Gifford/Wallace, Marie Moschetta.

Comedy, two former movie greats in conflict. The play was presented in two parts.

Roxie Roker replaced Annie-Joe.

Sweet Bird of Youth. Revival of the play by Tennessee Williams. Produced by Duncan C. Weldon, Jerome Minskoff, Douglas Urbanski and Karl Allison in a pre-Broadway tryout. Opened November 19, 1986 at Denver Center. (Closed January 25, 1987 at the Ahmanson Theater, Los Angeles)

Chance Wayne	Mark Soper	Miss Lucy	Carol Goodheart
Princess Kosmonopolis	Lauren Bacall	Heckler	James Cahill
Fly	Mansoor Najee-Ullah	Page	Charles Douglass
George Scudder	Joseph McCaren	Violet	Sharon Ullrick
State Trooper	Ed Trotta	Edna	Alexandra Nelson
Boss Finley	Henderson Forsythe	Scotty	Lee Chew
Tom Junior	Howard Sherman	Bud	Robertson Carricart
Charles	Hugh L. Hurd	Hatcher	Saylor Creswell
Aunt Nonnie	Georgia Southcotte	Man #1	Hugh A. Rose
Heavenly Finley	Donna Bullock	Man #2	David Lee Taylor
Jackie	Jimmy Justice	Doctor	Alex Paul
Stuff	Peter Strong	Drum Majorette	Laurane Sheehan

Directed by Michael Blakemore; scenery, Michael Annals; costumes, Carrie Robbins; lighting, Martin Aronstein; consultant set designer, Michael Vale; music, Barrington Pheloung; sound, Jan Nebozenko; production stage manager, George Rondo; press, Joshua Ellis, Adrian Bryan-Brown.

Act I, Scene 1: A bedroom in the Royal Palms Hotel somewhere on the Gulf Coast. Scene 2: The same, later. Scene 3: The terrace of Boss Finley's house in St. Cloud. Act II, Scene 1: The cocktail lounge and Palm Garden of the Royal Palms Hotel. Scene 2: the Bedroom again.

The last major New York revival of *Sweet Bird of Youth* was the American Bicentennial Theater production 12/3/75 for 15 performances off Broadway and 12/29/75 for 48 performances on Broadway.

Light Up the Sky. Revival of the play by Moss Hart. Produced by Robert Fryer, Christopher Hart and Center Theater Group/Ahmanson Theater in a pre-Broadway tryout. Opened at the Ahmanson Theater, Los Angeles, March 6, 1987. (Closed April 25, 1987)

Miss Lowell	Patricia Kilgarriff	Sidney Black	Peter Falk
Carleton Fitzgerald	Fritz Weaver	Sven	Tim Loughlin
Frances Black	Deborah Rush	Irene Livingston	Carrie Nye
Owen Turner	Barry Nelson	Tyler Rayburn	Burt Edwards
Stella Livingston	Nancy Marchand	William H. Gallegher	Bill McCutcheon
Peter Sloan	Steven Culp	Plain Clothes Man	Richard Fancy

Shriners: David Bailey, Richard Fancy, Tim Loughlin.

Directed by Ellis Rabb; scenery, Douglas W. Schmidt; costumes, Ann Roth; lighting, James Tilton; press, Josh Ellis.

Light Up the Sky was produced on Broadway 11/18/48 for 216 performances and was named a Best Play of its season. This revival was presented in three parts.

PLAYS PRODUCED OFF BROADWAY

Some distinctions between off-Broadway and Broadway productions at one end of the scale and off-off-Broadway productions at the other were blurred in the New York theater of the 1970s and 1980s. For the purposes of this *Best Plays* listing the term "off Broadway" is used to distinguish a professional from a showcase (off-off-Broadway) production and signifies a show which opened for general audiences in a mid-Manhattan theater seating 499 or fewer and 1) employed an Equity cast, 2) planned a regular schedule of 8 performances a week in an open-ended run and 3) offered itself to public comment by critics at a designated opening performance.

Occasional exceptions of inclusion (never of exclusion) are made to take in visiting troupes, borderline cases and nonqualifying productions which readers might expect to find in this list because they appear under an off-Broadway heading in other major sources of record.

Figures in parentheses following a play's title give number of performances. These figures do not include previews or extra non-profit performances.

Plays marked with an asterisk (*) were still running on June 1, 1987. Their number of performances is figured from opening night through May 31, 1987.

Certain programs of off-Broadway companies are exceptions to our rule of counting the number of performances from the date of the press coverage. When the official opening takes place late in the run of a play's regularly-priced public or subscription performances (after previews) we count the first performance of record, not the press date, as opening night—and in each such case in the listing we note the variance and give the press date.

In a listing of a show's numbers—dances, sketches, musical scenes, etc.—the titles of songs are identified wherever possible by their appearance in quotation marks (").

Most entries of off-Broadway productions which ran fewer than 20 performances are somewhat abbreviated, as are entries on running repertory programs repeated from previous years.

HOLDOVERS FROM PREVIOUS SEASONS

Plays which were running on June 2, 1986 are listed below. More detailed information about them appears in previous *Best Plays* volumes of appropriate date. Important cast changes since opening night are recorded in a section of this volume.

*The Fantasticks (11,272; longest continuous run of record in the American theater). Musical suggested by the play *Les Romanesques* by Edmond Rostand; book and lyrics by Tom Jones; music by Harvey Schmidt. Opened May 3, 1960.

*Forbidden Broadway (2,229). Cabaret revue with concept and lyrics by Gerard Alessandrini. Opened May 4, 1982. Revised versions opened October 27, 1983, January 29, 1985, June 11, 1986.

*Little Shop of Horrors (2,033). Musical based on the film by Roger Corman; book and lyrics by Howard Ashman; music by Alan Menken. Opened July 27, 1982.

The Foreigner (686). By Larry Shue. Opened November 1, 1984. (Closed June 8, 1986)

Penn & Teller (666). Magic show by Penn Jillette and Teller. Opened April 18, 1985. (Closed January 4, 1987)

*Vampire Lesbians of Sodom and Sleeping Beauty or Coma (779). Program of two plays by Charles Busch. Opened June 19, 1985.

New York Shakespeare Festival. Aunt Dan and Lemon (191). By Wallace Shawn. Opened October 1, 1985. (Closed January 26, 1986 after 82 performances). Reopened after recasting March 23, 1986. (Closed June 29, 1986) Cuba and His Teddy Bear (24). By Reinaldo Povod. Opened May 18, 1986. (Closed June 14, 1986 and transferred to Broadway; see its entry in the Plays Produced on Broadway section of this volume)

The Golden Land (277). Musical revue in the Yiddish and English languages, created by Zalman Mlotek and Moishe Rosenfeld. Opened November 11, 1985. (Closed July 13, 1986)

Personals (265). Musical revue with words and lyrics by David Crane, Seth Friedman and Marta Kauffman; music by William Dreskin, Joel Phillip Friedman, Seth Friedman, Alan Menken, Stephen Schwartz and Michael Skloff. Opened November 24, 1985. (Closed July 13, 1986)

*Nunsense (591). Musical with book, music and lyrics by Dan Goggin. Opened December 12, 1985.

*Beehive (506). Musical revue conceived and written by Larry Gallagher. Opened March 30, 1986.

The Perfect Party (238). By A.R. Gurney Jr. Opened April 2, 1986. (Closed October 26, 1986)

Goblin Market (89). Musical adapted by Peggy Harmon and Polly Pen from the poem by Christina Rossetti, music by Polly Pen. Opened April 13, 1986. (Closed June 29, 1986)

Sweethearts (56). Revival of the operetta with book by Harry B. Smith and Fred De-Gresac; music by Victor Herbert; lyrics by Robert B. Smith. Opened May 7, 1986. (Closed June 29, 1986)

Louis and Ophelia (85). By Gus Edwards. Opened May 15, 1986. (Closed July 27, 1986)

Ten by Tennessee (53). Two programs of short plays by Tennessee Williams. Opened May 18, 1986. (Closed June 29, 1986)

National Lampoon's Class of '86 (53). Revue by Andrew Simmons (head writer) and various authors. Opened May 22, 1986. (Closed July 6, 1986)

Professionally Speaking (37). Musical revue with music and lyrics by Peter Winkler, Ernst Muller and Frederic Block. Opened May 22, 1986. (Closed June 15, 1986)

Women of Manhattan (25). By John Patrick Shanley. Opened May 25, 1986. (Closed June 15, 1986)

PLAYS PRODUCED JUNE 1, 1986—MAY 31, 1987

Lincoln Center Theater. 1985–86 schedule included **Spalding Gray** (51). Three monologue programs written and performed by Spalding Gray. **Swimming to Cambodia** (23). Opened June 4, 1986. (Closed June 22, 1986) Return engagement alternating **Swimming to Cambodia** (16) and **Terrors of Pleasure** (12). Opened July 8, 1986. (Closed August 3, 1986) Produced by Lincoln Center Theater, Gregory Mosher director, Bernard Gersten executive producer, at the Mitzi E. Newhouse Theater.

Press: Merle Debuskey, Robert W. Larkin.
One-man show with a minimum of theatrical trappings such as lighting and props, performed as a first-person, conversational autobiography. *Swimming to Cambodia* recounts experiences as a member of the cast of the movie *The Killing Ground*. *Terrors of Pleasure* is about a city dweller's problems in buying a house in the country and trying to acclimatize himself to country living, plus an actor's problems in a Hollywood career.

Playwrights Horizons. 1985–86 schedule included **The Nice and the Nasty** (14). By Mark O'Donnell. Produced by Playwrights Horizons, Andre Bishop artistic director, Paul S. Daniels executive director, James F. Priebe managing director, at Playwrights Horizons. Opened June 5, 1986. (Closed June 15, 1986)

Tippy Blite...................	Jane Adams	Smurgison	Kurt Beattie
Blade Crevvis..............	David O'Brien	Gad Allwyn.............	James McDonnell
Cathexa Heitz	Marianne Owen	Fanatic; Security Man;	
Junius Upsey	W.H. Macy	Simmons	Bill Fagerbakke
Lesser Lawyer;		Boyd Barnes...............	Charles Bradley
Deus ex Machina	Jerry Mayer	Needa Heitz...................	Jodi Thelen
Least Lawyer..............	Lawrence Eaton	Hobart Heitz	Thomas Barbour

Directed by Douglas Hughes; scenery, Loren Sherman; costumes, Andrew B. Marlay; lighting, Stephen Strawbridge; sound, Scott Lehrer; original music, Paul Sullivan; production stage manager, Robin Rumpf; press, Bob Ullman.
Time: Right now, exactly. Place: An absolutely enormous American city. The play was presented in two parts.
Comedy of contemporary manners, a huge food corporation threatens the environment.

Roundabout Theater Company. 1985–86 schedule included **Master Class** (45). By David Pownall. Opened June 5, 1986. (Closed July 13, 1986) **A Raisin in the Sun** (70) By Lorraine Hansberry. Opened July 23, 1986; see note. (Closed September 21, 1986) Produced by Roundabout Theater Company, Gene Feist artistic director, Todd Haimes executive director, at the Roundabout Theater.

MASTER CLASS

Zhdanov....................	Philip Bosco	Shostakovich	Austin Pendleton
Prokofiev	Werner Klemperer	Stalin	Len Cariou

Directed by Frank Corsaro; scenery and costumes, Franco Colavecchia; lighting, Robert Wierzel; original compositions and arrangements, John White; musical direction, Jack Lee; sound, Philip Campanella; production stage manager, Kathy J. Faul; dance staged by John Montgomery; press, Solters/Roskin/Friedman, Joshua Ellis, Adrian Bryan-Brown.
Time: 1948, January, evening. Place: A room in the Kremlin. The play was presented in two parts.
Black comedy, Stalin bullies two of Russia's great composers. A foreign play previously produced in London and elsewhere.

A RAISIN IN THE SUN

Ruth Younger . . . . Starletta DuPois
(Travis Younger) . . . . Richard Habersham,
Kimble Joyner
Walter Lee Younger . . . . James Pickens Jr.
Beneatha Younger . . . . Kim Yancey
Lena Younger . . . . Olivia Cole
Joseph Asagai . . . . Vondie Curtis-Hall

George Murchison . . . . Joseph C. Phillips
Bobo . . . . Stephen Henderson
Karl Lindner . . . . John Fiedler
Moving Men . . . . Jacob Moultrie,
Ron O.J. Parson
(Parentheses indicate role in which the performers alternated)

Directed by Harold Scott; scenery, Thomas Cariello; costumes, Judy Dearing; lighting, Shirley Prendergast; sound, Rich Menke, Philip Campanella; presented in collaboration with Robert Nemiroff; African dance staged by Loretta Abbott; production stage manager, Matthew T. Mundinger.

Time: The early 1950s. over a period of three weeks. Place: The Youngers' apartment on Chicago's Southside. The play was presented in three parts.

A Raisin in the Sun was first produced on Broadway 3/11/59 for 530 performances and was named a Best Play and received the Drama Critics Award as best American play. This is its first major New York revival other than its adaptation as a musical 11/18/73 for 847 performances.

Note: Press date for *A Raisin in the Sun* was 8/14/86.

Sills & Company (118). Improvisational revue created by the performers. Produced by Thomas Viertel, Steven Baruch, Richard Frankel and Jeffrey Joseph at the Lamb's Theater. Opened June 9, 1986. (Closed September 28, 1986)

Severn Darden
MacIntyre Dixon
Paul Dooley
Garry Goodrow
Gerrit Graham

Bruce Jarchow
Mina Kolb
Maggie Roswell
Rachel Sills

Directed by Paul Sills; theater games created by Viola Spolin; musical direction, David Hollister; scenery, Carol Sills; costume consultant, Deborah Shaw; lighting, Malcolm Sturchio; sound supervision, Chuck London Media/Stewart Werner; artistic consultant, Art Wolff; production stage manager, Karen Armstrong; press, Solters/Roskin/Friedman, Joshua Ellis, Adrian Bryan-Brown, Bill Shuttleworth, Jackie Green.

Comic material, improvised and changing somewhat with each performance, in the manner of Second City and Story Theater, presented without intermission.

Nancy McCabe-Kelly joined the company in the course of the run, and MacIntyre Dixon, Gerrit Graham, Maggie Roswell and Rachel Sills left it.

New York Shakespeare Festival. 1985–86 schedule included **Vienna: Lusthaus** (49). Performance piece conceived by Martha Clarke; created with the company; text by Charles Mee Jr.; music by Richard Peaslee. Produced by New York Shakespeare Festival, Joseph Papp producer, and Music-Theater Group-Lenox Arts Center, Lyn Austin producing director, with Robert De Rothschild at the Estelle R. Newman Theater. Opened June 15, 1986. (Closed July 27, 1986)

Rob Besserer
Brenda Currin
Timothy Doyle
Marie Fourcaut
Lotte Goslar
Robert Langdon-Lloyd

Rick Merrill
Gianfranco Paoluzi
Amy Spencer
Paola Styron
Lila York

Musicians: Carol Emanuel, Jill Jaffe, Matthias Naegele, Peter Reit, Steven Silverstein.
Directed by Martha Clarke; scenery and costumes, Robert Israel; lighting, Paul Gallo; costume execution, Sandra Woodall; produced in association with Crowsnest, Inc.; associate producers, Jason

Steven Cohen, Diane Wondisford, Mark Jones; production stage manager, Steven Ehrenberg; stage manager, Elizabeth Sherman; press, Merle Debuskey, Richard Kornberg, Bruce Campbell.

Erotic representation of turn-of-the-century Vienna in music (billed as "with the aid of Johann Sebastian Bach, Eugene Friesen and Johann Strauss") and dance, previously presented off off Broadway in this production by Music-Theater Group/Lenox Arts Center at St. Clement's Church. The play was presented without intermission.

New York Shakespeare Festival. Summer schedule of two outdoor revivals. **Twelfth Night, or What You Will** (26). By William Shakespeare. Opened June 20, 1986; see note. (Closed July 20, 1986) **Medea** (6). By Euripides; performed in the Japanese language. Opened September 3, 1986. (Closed September 8, 1986). Produced by New York Shakespeare Festival, Joseph Papp producer, with the cooperation of the City of New York, Edward I. Koch mayor, Bess Myerson commissioner of cultural affairs, Henry J. Stern commissioner of parks and recreation (*Twelfth Night* in association with New York Telephone, *Medea* in association with the Agency for Cultural Affairs of Japan, in the Toho Company, Ltd. production) at the Delacorte Theater in Central Park.

BOTH PLAYS: Associate producer, Jason Steven Cohen; plays and musicals development, Gail Merrifield; press, Merle Debuskey, Richard Kornberg, Barbara Carroll, Reva Cooper, Bruce Campbell, Kevin Patterson, Glenn Poppleton, Don Anthony Summa, Michelle Macau.

TWELFTH NIGHT

Entertainers of the Theater:
Singer, Clown . . . . Tony Azito
Musicians, Utility Players . . . . Ashley Crow,
    Michael Gerald, James Lancaster,
                  Kathleen McNenny
Shipwrecked in Illyria:
Viola . . . . Kim Greist
Sea Captain . . . . Jordan Lund
Sailor . . . . Renardo Johnson
Lodge of the Duke of Illyria:
Orsino . . . . Thomas Gibson
Curio . . . . Michael David Morrison
Valentine . . . . Tim Guinee
Officer . . . . Kevin Black
Attendant . . . . Jeff Bender

Also Shipwrecked:
Antonio . . . . Marco St. John
Sebastian . . . . Perry Lang
Olivia's Household:
Sir Toby Belch . . . . William Duff-Griffin
Maria . . . . Meagen Fay
Sir Andrew Aguecheek . . . . Peter MacNicol
Feste . . . . Tony Azito
Olivia . . . . Kathleen Layman
Malvolio . . . . F. Murray Abraham
Fabian . . . . James Lancaster
Olivia's Servant . . . . Michael Gerald
Ladies . . . Ashley Crow, Kathleen McNenny
Priest . . . . Michael Gerald

Understudies: Messrs. Lang, Lancaster, Guinee, Black—Jeff Bender; Messrs. MacNicol, Johnson—Kevin Black; Misses Layman, Fay—Ashley Crow; Messrs. Azito, Gerald—Renardo Johnson; Miss Greist—Kathleen McNenny; Mr. Abraham—Marco St. John; Mr. Duff-Griffin—Jordan Lund; Messrs. St. John, Lund, Morrison—Michael Gerald; Mr. Gibson—Michael David Morrison.

Directed by Wilford Leach; music, Rupert Holmes; entr'acte lyrics, Thomas Campion; scenery, Bob Shaw; costumes, Lindsay W. Davis; lighting, Stephen Strawbridge; fight direction, B.H. Barry; speech consultant, Elizabeth Himmelstein; production stage manager, Ginny Martino; stage manager, Alan Traynor.

Twelfth Night, opening Joseph Papp's 31st season of free productions in Central Park, was last seen in a major New York production for 5 performances off Broadway by the Acting Company.

Note: Press date for *Twelfth Night* was 7/1/86.

MEDEA

Medea . . . . Mikijiro Hira
Jason . . . . Masane Tsukayama
Creon . . . . Ryunosuke Kaneda
Nurse . . . . Hatsuo Yamaya
Tutor . . . . Kazuhisa Seshimo

Aegeus . . . . Ryuzaburo Otomo
Messenger . . . . Takayuki Sugo
Soldiers . . . . . . Fujiro Higashi, Takuzo Kaneda
Sons of Medea . . . Ken Osawa, Tatsuya Miura

Chorus: Kazunaga Tsuji, Goro Daimon, Tatsumi Aoyama, Susumu Kakuma, Hirofumi, Yamabi, Eiichi Seike, Chihiro Ito, Masahiko Nakata, Tsukasa Nakagoshi, Keita Oishi, Hiroki Okawa, Kazuhiro Kikuchi, Toru Takagi, Kunihiro Iida, Sho Shinohara, Hirokazu Aoyama.

Directed by Yukio Ninagawa; scenario, Mutsuo Takahashi; scenery, Setsu Asakura; art direction and costumes, Jusaburo Tsujimura; lighting, Sumio Yoshii; sound effects, Akira Honma; choreography, Kinnosuke Hanayagi; producer, Tadao Nakane; stage managers, Takayuki Yamada, Hideyasu Murai.

Originally produced in Japan in 1978, this *Medea* has a Japanese temple setting and is performed by an all-male cast.

Today, I Am a Fountain Pen (117). By Israel Horovitz; based on the book *A Good Place to Come From* by Morley Torgov. Produced by Lou Kramer, Ken Waissman and Robert A. Buckley in association with Louis W. Scheeder, Michael Lonergan and Roadworks Productions at Theater 890. Opened July 10, 1986. (Closed October 12, 1986)

Irving Yanover	Danny Gerard	Esther Yanover	Marcia Jean Kurtz
Emil Ilchak	Stan Lachow	Annie Ilchak	Barbara Garrick
Ardenshensky; Ukranian Priest	Sol Frieder	Moses Yanover	Sam Schacht
Mrs. Ilchak	Dana Keeler	Pete Lisanti	Grant Shaud

Understudies: Messrs. Lachow, Shaud—Joseph Giardina; Miss Garrick—Diane Gaidry; Misses Keeler, Kurtz—Ann Mantel.

Directed by Stephen Zuckerman; scenery, James Fenhagen; costumes, Mimi Maxmen; lighting, Curt Ostermann; sound, Aural Fixation; production stage manager, Michael S. Mantel; press, Jeffrey Richards Associates, Ben Morse.

Time: Early 1940s, during the early stages of the war in Europe. Place: The home of the Yanover family in Sault Ste. Marie, Ontario, Canada. The play was presented without intermission.

First play in a trilogy about growing up in a Jewish family in Canada, previously produced off off Broadway at American Jewish Theater.

Josh Blake replaced Danny Gerard 9/17/86, alternating in the role with Robert Dekelbaum.

Olympus on My Mind (207). Musical suggested by *Amphitryon* by Heinrich Von Kleist; book and lyrics by Barry Harman; music by Grant Sturiale. Produced by Harve Brosten and Mainstage Productions, Ltd. in association with "Murray the Furrier" at the Lamb's Theater. Opened July 15, 1986. (Closed January 10, 1987)

The Chorus:		Mercury	Jason Graae
Tom	Peter Kapetan	Charis	Peggy Hewett
Dick	Andy Spangler	Alcmene	Emily Zacharias
Horace	Keith Bennett	Sosia	Lewis J. Stadlen
Delores	Elizabeth Austin	Amphitryon	George Spelvin
Jupiter	Martin Vidnovic		

Understudies: Messrs. Graae, Stadlen—Paul Kassel; Misses Zacharias, Hewett, Austin—Nancy Johnston.

Directed by Barry Harman; choreography, Pamela Sousa; scenery, Christopher Stapleton; costumes, Steven Jones; lighting, Fabian Yeager; production stage manager, Joseph A. Onorato; press, Henry Luhrman Associates, David Mayhew, Susan Chicoine.

Place: The ancient Greek city of Thebes, during the course of a 41-hour day.

Musicalization of an 1807 German version of the Amphitryon legend, transferred from off-off-Broadway production.

Tom Wopat replaced Martin Vidnovic, Rusty Riegelman replaced Elizabeth Austin, Susan Powell replaced Emily Zacharias, Charles Repole replaced Lewis J. Stadlen, Naz Edwards replaced Peggy Hewett, John Scherer replaced Jason Graae 11/13/86.

ACT I

"Welcome to Greece" .... Chorus
"Heaven on Earth" .... Jupiter, Alcmene, Chorus

OLYMPUS ON MY MIND—Keith Bennett, Andy Spangler, Elizabeth Austin and Peter Kapetan in the Barry Harman–Grant Sturiale musical

"The Gods on Tap".................................... Delores, Jupiter, Mercury, Chorus
"Surprise!".. Sosia
"Wait 'Til It Dawns".. Mercury
"I Know My Wife"... Amphitryon
"It Was Me".. Sosia
"Back So Soon?".. Amphitryon, Sosia, Chorus
"Wonderful".. Alcmene
"At Liberty in Thebes"... Charis, Chorus
"Jupiter Slept Here"... Company

ACT II

"Back to the Play"... Chorus
"Don't Bring Her Flowers".. Mercury
"Generals' Pandemonium"........................... Amphitryon, Jupiter, Sosia, Chorus
"Heaven on Earth" (Reprise)..................................... Sosia, Charis
"Olympus Is a Lonely Town"... Jupiter
"A Star Is Born"... Delores, Company
"Final Sequence" .... Amphitryon, Alcmene, Mercury, Jupiter, Charis, Sosia, Chorus
"Heaven on Earth" (finale)................................. Jupiter, Alcmene, Company

Light Opera of Manhattan (LOOM). Repertory of one new operetta revival and six running operetta revivals. **The Drunkard** (21). By William H. Smith; music by various authors (see list of musical numbers). Produced by Light Opera of Manhattan. William Mount-Burke founder, Raymond Allen and Jerry Gotham artistic directors, Todd Ellison music director, at the Cherry Lane Theater. Opened August 6, 1986. (Closed August 24, 1986)

Mrs. Wilson	Rhanda Spotton	Landlord	Bill Partlow
Mary Wilson	Susan Davis Holmes	Mr. Stevens;	
Squire Cribbs	Tom Boyd	Messenger	Michael Dean Smith
Edward Middleton	Michael Scott	Julia Middleton	Claudia Egli
Sophia Spindle	Ann J. Kirschner	Arden Rencelaw	David Green
William Dowton	Jon Brothers	Boy	Donavon Armsbruster
Agnes Dowton	Andrea Calarco	Mr. Gates	Will Elliot

Quartet: Susan Irene Marshall, Will Elliot, Bill Partlow, Teri Bibb. Piano: Todd Ellison. Violinists: Maria Zimmermann, Paula Flatow.

Directed by Raymond Allen; choreography, Jerry Gotham; musical direction, Todd Ellison; scenery, Ellen Kurrelmeyer; lighting, Franklin Meisner Jr.; vocal and musical arrangements, Todd Ellison; musical consultant, Alfred Simon; press, Jean Dalrymple, Gregory Tarmin.

The Drunkard, a 19th century melodrama subtitled *The Fallen Saved* was first produced by P.T. Barnum in 1843. Its first major modern New York production of record was on Broadway 3/10/34 for 277 performances. It was revived off Broadway in the season of 1937–38 and in a musical version off Broadway 4/13/70 for 48 performances, adapted by Bro Herrod, with original musical numbers by Barry Manilow.

MUSICAL NUMBERS: "The Band Played On" (by Charles Ward and John F. Palmer), "By the Light of the Silvery Moon" (by Gus Edwards and Edward Madden), "Come Home Father" (by Henry C. Work), "Cuddle Up a Little Closer" (by Karl Joschna and Otto Harbach), "Elite Syncopations" and "Gladiolus Rag" (by Scott Joplin), "I Don't Care" (by Harry O. Sutton and Jean Lennox), "I Don't Want to Play in Your Yard" (by H.W. Petrie and Philip Wingate), "In My Merry Oldsmobile" (by Gus Edwards and Vincent Bryan), "In the Shade of the Old Apple Tree" (by Egbert Van Alstyne and Harry Williams), "Love's Old Sweet Song" (by J.L. Molloy), "Meet Me in St. Louis, Louis" (by George Evans and Ren Shields), "Oh Happy the Lily" (by W.S. Gilbert and Arthur Sullivan, from *Ruddigore*), "Sometimes Think of Me" (by Waldemar Malmene and George Birdseye), "Sweet Adeline" (by Harry Armstrong and Richard Gerard), "There's a Tavern in the Town" (Cornish folk song), "When You Were Sweet Sixteen" (by James Thornton), "Whispering Hope" (by Alice Hawthorne).

LOOM's 1986–87 repertory included six running productions mounted in previous seasons and presented on the following schedule (operettas have book and lyrics by W.S. Gilbert and music by Arthur Sullivan unless otherwise noted: *The Red Mill* (21), opened July 2, 1986, book and lyrics by Henry Blossom, music by Victor Herbert; *Patience* (14), opened July 23, 1986; *The Mikado* (14), opened August 27, 1986; *The Fortune Teller* (21), opened September 10, 1986, original book and lyrics by Harry B. Smith, music by Victor Herbert; *The Vagabond King* (14), opened October 1, 1986, music by Rudolf Friml, lyrics by Brian Hooker, Russell Janney and W.H. Post. (LOOM's repertory was discontinued and closed at the Cherry Lane Theater October 12, 1986) *Babes in Toyland* (39). Book by William Mount-Burke and Alice Hammerstein Mathias, music by Victor Herbert, lyrics by Alice Hammerstein Mathias. Opened November 28, 1986 at the Eastside Playhouse. (Closed January 4, 1987)

Performers in LOOM repertory during the 1986–87 season included Raymond Allen, Donavon Armbruster, Ruth Alison, Jon Brothers, Jensen Buchanan, Robert Conkling, Paul Chisolm, William Christofells, Andrea Calarco, Mary Jo Dugaw, Lindsay Dyett, Shawn Davis, Anthony Emeric, Claudia Egli, Stephen Fleming, Antonia Garza, David Green, Mary Gibboney, Theresa Hudson, David Thomas Hampson, John Jud Healey, Susan Davis Holmes, Mark Henderson, Robin Heagan, Teresa Haislip, Stuart Hult, Anne Jacobsen, Ann J. Kirschner, Stephan Kirchgraber, Martin J. Kugler, Robert Leary, Bruce McKillip, Eileen Merle, Grace Millo, Michael Muziko, Siobhan Marshall, Katherine Newlon, Marilyn E. Olsen, Susanna Organek, Bill Partlow, Sally Jo Reis, Michael Dean Smith, Helene Sanders, Linda Suda, Helmut Steibl, Kristopher Shaw, Rhanda Spotton, Ann Tulin, Stephen Todar, Richard Wyr.

Krapp's Last Tape (104). Revival of the play by Samuel Beckett. Produced by the Harold Clurman Theater, Jack Garfein artistic director, at the Samuel Beckett Theater. Opened August 27, 1986. (Closed November 30, 1986)

Krapp	Rick Cluchey
Sound Operator	Bud Thorpe

Directed by Samuel Beckett; scenery and lighting, Bud Thorpe; costumes, Teresita Garcia Suro; production stage manager, Bud Thorpe; press, Joe Wolhandler Associates.

This often-revived Beckett one-act was last done off Broadway on an Acting Company program 4/29/83 for 4 performances. The present production, directed by the author himself, was offered on a program with the American premieres of two 1984 films written and directed by Samuel Beckett: *Quad* and *Nacht und Traume*.

Lady Day at Emerson's Bar and Grill (281). By Lanie Robertson. Produced by Lady Day at Emerson's Company in the Vineyard Theater production at the Westside Arts Theater. Opened September 3, 1986. (Closed May 17, 1987)

Billie Holiday.............. Lonette McKee   Frankie Lee Jones (bass) ..... David Jackson
Jimmy Powers (piano) .... Danny Holgate   Pepe .... Bambi Herrera
Buck Wilson
(guitar, harmonica)........ Rudy Stevenson

Directed by Andre Ernotte; musical direction and arrangements, Danny Holgate; scenery, William Barclay; costumes, Muriel Stockdale; lighting, Phil Monat; sound, Phil Lee; associate producer, Kenneth Polokoff; production stage manager, Crystal Huntington; press, Bruce Cohen, Kathleen von Schmid.

Time: Midnight on a Friday night in March 1959, four months before Billie Holiday's death. Place: A bar in South Philly. The play was presented without intermission.

Presenting Billie Holiday at the end of her life, and some of her most popular song numbers, in a production which moved up to off-Broadway status after previous presentation off off Broadway 6/4/86 by the Vineyard Theater.

S. Epatha Merkerson replaced Lonette McKee 3/3/87.

Angry Housewives (137). Musical with book by A.M. Collins; music and lyrics by Chad Henry. Produced by M Square Entertainment, Inc., Mitchell Maxwell, Alan J. Schuster, Marvin R. Meit and Alice Field at the Minetta Lane Theater. Opened September 7, 1986. (Closed January 3, 1987)

Tim.................... Michael Manasseri   Carol...................... Camille Saviola
Bev .... Carolyn Casanave   Larry .... Nicholas Wyman
Wendy .... Lorna Patterson   Wallace................. Michael Lemback
Jetta .... Vicki Lewis   Lewd........................ Lee Wilkof

Understudy: Mary Munger.

Directed by Mitchell Maxwell; musical staging and choreography, Wayne Cilento; musical direction, Jonny Bowden; scenery, David Jenkins; costumes, Martha Hally; lighting, Allen Lee Hughes; sound, Otts Munderloh; musical supervision and orchestrations, Dave Brown; additional musical arrangements, Mark Hummel; assistant choreographer, Lisa Mordente; associate producers, Robert and Trinity Lind; production stage manager, Clayton Phillips; press, Shirley Herz, Peter Cromarty, Glenna Freedman.

Discontented wives scheme to form a hard-rock combo. Previously produced at Pioneer Square, Seattle and Organic Theater, Chicago.

ACT I

Scene 1: Bev's
   "Think Positive"... Bev
Scene 2: The bridge
   "It's Gonna Be Fun" .... Wendy, Bev, Carol, Jetta
Scene 3: Bev's
   "Generic Woman" .... Carol, Bev, Wendy, Jetta
Scene 4: Bev's and Jetta's
   "Not at Home"... Jetta

Scene 5: Lewd Fingers Club
  "Betsy Moberly"... Lewd, Wallace
  "Cold Cruel Dark".. Company

ACT II

Scene 1: Bev's
  "First Kid on the Block"............................... Tim, Bev, Carol, Jetta, Wendy
Scene 2: Lewd's/Bev's/Jetta's/An overlook
  "Love-O-Meter" .... Wallace, Wendy
Scene 3: Bon Poisson Restaurant
Scene 4: A park
  "Trouble With Me" .... Wendy, Larry
Scene 5: Lewd Fingers Club
  "Stalling for Time".. Lewd, Larry, Wallace, Tom
  "Eat Your @*!#@*!@#! Cornflakes"............................. Angry Housewives
Finale... Company

Lincoln Center Theater. Schedule of seven programs (see note). **Woza Afrika!** (32). Festival of four programs of South African plays, co-produced with the Woza Afrika Foundation, Duma Ndlovu Festival director. **Asinamali!** (We Have No Money) (8). By Mbongeni Ngema. Opened September 10, 1986. (Closed September 14, 1986 and transferred to Broadway; see its entry in the Plays Produced on Broadway section of this volume) **Bopha!** (Arrest) (8). By Percy Mtwa. Opened September 17, 1986. (Closed September 21, 1986) **Children of Asazi** by Matsemela Manaka, in the Soyikwa Institute of African Theater production, and **Gangsters** by Maishe Maponya, in the Bahumutsi Drama Group production (8). Program of two one-act plays. Opened September 25, 1986. (Closed September 28, 1986) **Born in the R.S.A.** (8). By Barney Simon in collaboration with the cast, in the Market Theater Company production. Opened October 1, 1986. (Closed October 5, 1986)

Also **The Transposed Heads** (4). Musical adapted by Julie Taymor and Sidney Goldfarb from Thomas Mann's novella: music by Elliot Goldenthal; lyrics by Sidney Goldfarb. Opened October 31, 1986. (Closed November 2, 1986) **Bodies, Rest and Motion** (22). By Roger Hedden. Opened December 21, 1986. (Closed January 4, 1987) **Danger: Memory!** (33). Program of two one-act plays by Arthur Miller: *I Can't Remember Anything* and *Clara*. Opened February 8, 1987. (Closed March 8, 1987) Produced by Lincoln Center Theater, Gregory Mosher director, Bernard Gersten executive producer, at the Mitzi E. Newhouse Theater.

ASINAMALI!

CAST: Solomzi Bisholo, Thami Cele, Bongani Hlophe, Bheki Mqadi, Bhoyi Ngema.

Directed by Mbongeni Ngema; lighting, Mannie Manim, supervised by Wesley France; stage manager, Makalo Mofokeng; press, Merle Debuskey, Robert W. Larkin.

Five men jailed during a 1983 rent strike describe in song, dance and dialogue how each came to be incarcerated. The play was presented without intermission.

BOPHA!

CAST: Sydney Khumalo, Aubrey Molefe Moalosi, Aubrey Radebe.

Directed by Percy Mtwa; lighting, Mannie Manim, supervised by Wesley France; stage manager, Small Ndaba.

Place: A prison cell at Leeuwkop Prison, outside Johannesburg. the play was presented without intermission.

Black policeman enforcing white laws in South Africa is confronted by his rebellious son.

CHILDREN OF ASAZI and GANGSTERS

Children of Asazi
Diliza Mabunu.............. Ali Hlongwane
Charmaine Legadima;
   Blind Woman............ Soentjie Thapeli
Nduna Mabunu.............. Peter Boroko
Gogo...................... Thelma Pooe
Majika .... Job Kubatsi

Mabu .... Khaya Mahlangu
Officer..................... Peter Boroko

Gangsters
Masechaba .... Nomathembe Mdini
Maj. Whitebeard .... Anthony Wilson
Jonathan.................. George Lamola

CHILDREN OF ASAZI: Directed by Matsemela Manaka; movement, Nomsa Manaka; lighting, Ali Hlongwane, Paul Abrams; music consultants, Sibongile Khumalo, Motsumi Makhene; stage manager, Simon Mosikidi.

Families made homeless by the bulldozing of their township.

GANGSTERS: Directed by Maishe Maponya; lighting, Simon Mosikidi; stage manager, Simon Mosikidi.

A poetess is punished for her writings by interrogation and death in prison.

BORN IN THE R.S.A.

Susan .... Vanessa Cooke
Zack .... Timmy Kwebulana
Glen .... Neil McCarthy
Sindiswa .... Geina Mhlophe

Nikki .... Terry Norton
Thenjiwe.................. Thoko Ntshinga
Mia...................... Fiona Ramsay

Directed by Barney Simon; scenery, Sarah Roberts; lighting, Mannie Manim, supervised by Wesley France; stage manager, Melanie Dobbs.

A collaborative piece, with the performers reflecting individual traits, emotions and experiences of persecutors and persecuted in the South African social and political emergency beginning in 1985.

A Best Play; see page 117.

THE TRANSPOSED HEADS

Sita .... Yamil Borges
Shridaman .... Scott Burkholder

Narrator..................... Rajika Puri
Nanda...................... Byron Utley

Puppeteers: Richard Hester, Stephen Kaplin, Barbara Pollitt. Puppeteer and assistant to Julie Taymor: Erin Cressida Wilson.

Musicians: Richard Martinez keyboards; Steve Gorn flute; Jamey Haddad percussion; William Moersch hammered dulcimer, percussion; Marilyn Gibson violin.

Directed by Julie Taymor; choreography, Margo Sappington, Julie Taymor and the Company; Indian choreography, Swati Gupte Bhise, Rajika Puri; musical direction, Richard Martinez; conductor, Joshua Rosenblum; scenery based on a concept by Alexander Okun; costumes, Carol Oditz; lighting, Marcia Madeira; sound, Tom Gould; lightscapes, Caterina Bertolotto; puppets and masks, Julie Taymor; production stage manager, Renee Lutz.

Thomas Mann's tale of mind vs. body, based on an East Indian legend, set to music in a drama of severed heads restored to the wrong bodies. Previously produced in another version at American Music Theater Festival, Philadelphia. The play was presented in two parts.

BODIES, REST AND MOTION

Nick .... W.H. Macy
Carol.................... Christina Moore
Beth .... Laurie Metcalf
Sid.................... Andrew McCarthy
Man Shopping for TV;
   Mr. August.............. Larry Bryggman

Elizabeth .... Carol Schneider
Mrs. Dotson.................. Lois Smith
Newlywed Couple........ Larry Bryggman,
                                Lois Smith

Directed by Billy Hopkins; scenery, Thomas Lynch; costumes, Isis Mussenden; lighting, James F. Ingalls; sound, Bruce Ellman; production manager, Jeff Hamlin: production stage manager, Susan Selig.

Set of characters coming to grips with life and love in a Connecticut living room. The play was presented in two parts.

Understudies: Messrs. Macy, McCarthy—Marcus Olson; Misses Moore, Metcalf, Schneider—Dani Klein.

DANGER: MEMORY!

I Can't Remember Anything	Tierney . . . . Victor Argo
Leonora . . . . Geraldine Fitzgerald	Albert Kroll . . . . Kenneth McMillan
Leo . . . . Mason Adams	Clara . . . . Karron Graves

Clara
Detective Lieutenant Fine . . . . . James Tolkan

Understudies: Messrs. Adams, McMillan—Vince O'Brien; Mr. Tolkan—Victor Argo.

Directed by Gregory Mosher; scenery, Michael Merritt; costumes, Nan Cibula; lighting, Kevin Rigdon; production manager, Jeff Hamlin; production stage manager, George Darveris.

In *I Can't Remember Anything*, a widow and her late husband's friend review the human condition. In *Clara*, a detective grills the victim's father in a murder investigation.

Note: In addition to its regular off-Broadway schedule, Lincoln Center Theater staged 4 performances before an invited audience 8/28/86–8/31/86 of *Goose and Tom-Tom*, by David Rabe, directed by David Rabe, with Sean Penn, Harvey Keitel, Barry Miller, Eric Bogosian, Lorraine Bracco and Madonna.

Double Image Theater. Schedule of three programs. **The Return of Pinocchio** (21), by Richard Nelson, opened September 21, 1986, (closed October 26, 1986); and **The Dreamer Examines His Pillow** (40), by John Patrick Shanley, opened October 5, 1986 (Closed November 23, 1986) Repertory of two programs. **The Double Bass** (26). By Patrick

DANGER: MEMORY!—Geraldine Fitzgerald and Mason Adams in *I Can't Remember Anything*, on a program of two one-act plays by Artuur Miller

Suskind; translated by Harry Newman and David Overmyer. Opened December 4, 1986. (Closed December 28, 1986) Produced by Double Image Theater, Helen Waren Mayer founder and executive director, Max Mayer artistic director, Leslie Urdang managing director, at the 47th Street Theater.

THE RETURN OF PINOCCHIO

Lucio . . . . Dan Moran	Silia. . . . . Jean Bacharach
Pinocchio . . . . Joe Urla	Rosina . . . . Marcell Rosenblatt
Lucio's Wife. . . . . Mary-Louise Gemmil	Carlo. . . . . Rob Morrow
Leone . . . . Daniel De Raey	Soldier . . . . Carles Cleveland
Mama . . . . Marylouise Burke	

Understudy: Messrs. Urla, Cleveland—Phil Kaufmann.

THE DREAMER EXAMINES HIS PILLOW

Tommy. . . . . Scott Renderer	Dad. . . . . Graham Beckel
Donna. . . . . Anne O'Sullivan	

BOTH PLAYS: Directed by Max Mayer; sound, Janet Kalas; production stage manager, William H. Lang; press, the Fred Nathan Company, Dennis Crowley.

THE RETURN OF PINOCCHIO: Scenery, Kate Edmunds; costumes, Candice Donnelly; lighting, Jennifer Tipton.

Pinocchio comes back home to Italy in 1946 after spending World War II as a U.S.O. entertainer. The play was presented without intermission. Previously produced at The Empty Space, Seattle and Vassar College, Poughkeepsie, N.Y.

THE DREAMER EXAMINES HIS PILLOW: Scenery, Adrianne Lobel; costumes, Dunya Ramicova; lighting, James F. Ingalls.

A would-be artist contemplates esthetics and his own identity. The play was presented without intermission. Previously produced at Vassar College, Poughkeepsie, N.Y.

THE DOUBLE BASS

The Double Bassist. . . . . Boyd Gaines

Directed by Kent Paul; scenery, William Barclay; costumes, Jared Aswegan; lighting, Phil Monat; sound, Tom Gould; production stage manager, Louis D. Pietig.

Time: The present. Place: Germany.

About "the existence of man in his small room" (author's note), in this case a lovesick musician. A foreign (German) play presented in two parts and previously produced in this version at the New Theater, Brooklyn.

Confessions of a Nightingale (48). By Charlotte Chandler and Ray Stricklyn; adapted from Charlotte Chandler's *The Ultimate Seduction*. Produced by Jack and Richard Lawrence at the Audrey Wood Playhouse. Opened September 23, 1986. (Closed November 2, 1986)

Tennessee Williams. . . . . Ray Stricklyn

Directed by John Tillinger; scenery and costumes, Richard Lawrence; lighting, Natasha Katz; production stage manager, Doug Laidlaw; press, Shirley Herz Associates, David Roggensack.

Ray Stricklyn in a one-man portrayal of the late, celebrated playwright.

*Playwrights Horizons. Schedule of six programs. **The Young Playwrights Festival** (23). Program of three one-act plays: *Coup D'Etat* by Carolyn Jones (age 18), *A Delicate Situation* by Eve Goldfarb (age 17), *Remedial English* by Evan Smith (age 18); in the Foundation of the Dramatists Guild production, Peggy C. Hansen producing director. Opened September 24, 1986. (Closed October 12, 1986) **Highest Standard of Living** (19).

By Keith Reddin. Opened November 13, 1986. (Closed November 30, 1986) **Black Sea Follies** (31). Music-theater piece conceived by Stanley Silverman; written by Paul Schmidt; music by Dmitri Shostakovich and other Russians; music adapted by Stanley Silverman; Russian lyrics translated by Paul Schmidt; additional material by Stanley Silverman. Co-produced by Music-Theater Group, Lyn Austin producing director. Opened December 16, 1986. (Closed January 11, 1987) **The Maderati** (12). By Richard Greenberg. Opened February 19, 1987. (Closed March 1, 1987.) *****Driving Miss Daisy** (55). By Alfred Uhry. Opened April 15, 1987. **Three Postcards** (22). Musical with book by Craig Lucas; music and lyrics by Craig Carnelia. Opened May 14, 1987. (Closed May 31, 1987) Produced by Playwrights Horizons, Andre Bishop artistic director, Paul S. Daniels executive director, at Playwrights Horizons.

THE YOUNG PLAYWRIGHTS FESTIVAL

Coup D'Etat
Mama; Stephanie........... Susan Greenhill
Juan .... Evan Handler
Papa; Enrico .... Shawn Elliott
King .... Tom Mardirosian
Abdul.......................... Ted Sod
Yuri Brushnik .... Larry Block
Troy LeFlame .... Jim Fyfe
Julio Fernandez........... Greg Germann
   Understudy: Mr. Mardirosian—Adam Redfield.
   Directed by Art Wolff. Time: The present. Place: The island of St. Passis. Satire on volatile Caribbean politics.

A Delicate Situation
Amelia .... Kelly Wolf
Derek .... Evan Handler
Susan .... Susan Greenhill

Lydia .... Fran Brill
Chuck................... Nicholas Kallsen
   Directed by Mary B. Robinson. Time: The present. Place: Two Manhattan apartments. Teen-aged daughter of a broken marriage in the process of self-destructing.

Remedial English
Vincent.................... Greg Germann
Sister Beatrice .... Anne Pitoniak
Rob.................... Nicholas Kallsen
Coach .... Shawn Elliott
Chris........................ Jim Fyfe
David .... Adam Redfield
   Directed by Ron Lagomarsino. Time: The present. Place: Cabrini Catholic Academy, a private high school for boys, and Vincent's living room. Comedy, sexual and other confusions of growing up.

ALL PLAYS: Scenery, Rick Dennis; costumes, Michael Krass; lighting, Ann G. Wrightson; sound, James M. Bay; production stage manager, Melissa Davis; stage managers, Anne Marie Kuehling, Johnna Murray; press, Bob Ullman.

These three plays by young authors (ages given at the time of submission of scripts) were selected from hundreds of entries in the Foundation of the Dramatists Guild's fifth annual playwriting contest for young people. In addition to the above full productions, staged readings were held of *Dinner at Eight* by Isa-Jill Gordon (age 15), *Once Upon a Time There Was a Family* by Kenn Adams (age 18) and *Waning Crescent Moon* by Stephen Serpas (age 18).

HIGHEST STANDARD OF LIVING

Bob........................ Steven Culp
Vlad; Jack .... Timothy Carhart
Man on Ferry; Gary; Yuri.... Kevin Skousen
Ludmilla..................... Leslie Lyles
Tom; Larry .... James Murtaugh
Tatiana; Lonnie; Jean;
   Adele................. Lola Pashalinski

Mother; Helen.............. Sloane Shelton
Sergei; Don .... Clement Fowler
Dmitri; Doug............... Peter Crombie
Rodger; Waiter; Man at Bus Stop;
   Eskimo Pie Man.......... Robert Stanton

Ensemble: Timothy Carhart, Peter Crombie, Clement Fowler, James Murtaugh, Lola Pashalinski, Sloane Shelton, Kevin Skousen, Robert Stanton.
Children: Phillip Daniels, David Jon, Robert Meltzer, Meredith Muller, Caryn Osofsky, Shiah Schwartz, Christopher Spellman.

Directed by Don Scardino; scenery, John Arnone; costumes, David C. Woolard; lighting, Joshua Dachs; sound, Scott Lehrer; production stage manager, Fredric H. Orner; stage manager, Amanda Mengden.

Parallels between Russia and the United States demonstrated in a play whose first act takes place in Moscow and second act in New York.

BLACK SEA FOLLIES

Shostakovich	David Chandler	Stepanych....	Robert Osborne (bass-baritone)
Stalin	Alan Scarfe	Violin	Martha Caplin, Carol Zeavin
Misha	Henry Stram	Viola	Sarah Clarke
Katerina Lvovna ...	Carmen Pelton (soprano)	Cello	Matthias Naegele
Seryozha	David Dusing (tenor)	Piano	Elena Ivanina

Directed by Stanley Silverman; scenery, James Noone; costumes, Jim Buff; lighting, Ken Tabachnick; music coordinated by Mark Bennett; dances, Liz Lerman; production stage manager, Roy Harris; stage manager, Anne Marie Kuehling.

Time: The early 1970s. Place: Moscow.

As per a program note, "A young ensemble of Soviet musicians has asked Dmitri Shostakovich to coach them in his late chamber music. It is the music of these pieces that reawakens Shostakovich's memories of the Stalin years," including a visit to Stalin's dacha on the Black Sea.

ACT I: 1. Rehearsal; 2. Leningrad—What War Was It? (from Quartet #8, Opus 110), "United Nations on the March" (lyrics by Harold Rome); 3. By the Beautiful Black Sea; 4. The State Film Industry at Work, "I'm Single" (Opus 121, No. 2); 5. A Night at the Movies, "The King Goes to War" (Opus 62, No. 6); 6. War and Peace (Dialectic in Action!), "Comin' Through the Rye" (Opus 62, No. 4, text by Robert Burns); 7. Rehearsal Break, Skipping Dance; 8. The Composing of "Tahiti Trot."

ACT II: 9. March vs. Waltz (Dialectic in Action! From Quartet #3, Opus 73), prison camp scene and Katerina's aria from *Lady Macbeth of Mtsensk* (Opus 29); 10. The Mad Tea Party (from Quartet #13, Opus 138), "Tchaikowsky" from *Lady in the Dark* (music by Kurt Weill, lyrics by Ira Gershwin), Duet from "Moscow Cheryomushki" (Opus 105, from Quartet #1, Opus 49); 11. Truth and Lies (Dialectic in Action! From Quartet #7, Opus 108); Dancing to the Tick of Terror (Coda, 1st Movement, 5th Symphony); 13. Rehearsal: Cantabile (from Piano Quintet, Opus 57); 14. Ant and Grasshopper (More Dialectic in Action!), "We Were Together" (Opus 127, No.3).

THE MADERATI

Rena deButts	Mary Joy	Kenne Esterhazy	David Pierce
Chuck deButts	Boyd Gaines	Cuddles Molotov	Anna Levine
Dewy Overlander	Patricia Clarkson	Charlotte Ebbinger	Amanda Carlin
Ritt Overlander	Lenny Von Dohlen	Danton Young	Philip Coccioletti
Martin Royale	Paul Collins		

Directed by Michael Engler; scenery, Philipp Jung; costumes, Candice Donnelly; lighting, Michael Orris Watson; sound, Lia Vollack; production stage manager, Melissa Davis.

Comedy of contemporary New York trend-setters in the world of the arts. The play was presented in two parts.

DRIVING MISS DAISY

Daisy Werthan	Dana Ivey	Hoke Coleburn	Morgan Freeman
Boolie Werthan	Ray Gill		

Directed by Ron Lagomarsino; scenery, Thomas Lynch; costumes, Michael Krass; lighting, Ken Tabachnick; incidental music, Robert Waldman; production manager, Carl Mulert; production stage manager, Anne Marie Kuehling.

Time: 1948 to 1973. Place: Atlanta, Ga. The play was presented without intermission.

Difficult Southern lady grows closer and closer to her black chauffeur over a 25-year period.

A Best Play; see page 233.

THREE POSTCARDS

Bill	Craig Carnelia	Little Jane	Maureen Silliman
Walter	Brad O'Hare	K.C.	Karen Trott
Big Jane	Jane Galloway		

Directed by Norman René; choreography, Linda Kostalik-Boussom; scenery, Loy Arcenas; costumes, Walter Hicklin; lighting, Debra J. Kletter; sound, Bruce D. Cameron; musical theater program director, Ira Weitzman; production stage manager, M.A. Howard.

Three women meet in a Manhattan restaurant to renew their old friendship and review their lives. Previously produced in regional theater at Costa Mesa, Calif. The play was presented without intermission.

A Best Play; see page 270.

MUSICAL NUMBERS: Opening, "She Was K.C.," "What the Song Should Say," Piano Effects, "See How the Sun Shines," "I've Been Watching You," Collage, "Three Postcards," "The Picture in the Hall," "Cast of Thousands," Rain, "I'm Standing in This Room."

*Circle Repertory Company. Schedule of five programs (see note). **In This Fallen City** (40) by Bryan Williams, opened September 25, 1986 (Closed November 14, 1986); and **The Early Girl** (47) by Caroline Kava, opened October 30, 1986 (Closed November 30, 1986). Repertory of two programs. **The Musical Comedy Murders of 1940** (88). By John Bishop. Opened January 7, 1987. (Closed March 22, 1987 and transferred to Broadway; see its entry in the Plays Produced on Broadway section of this volume) ***As Is** (28). Revival of the play by William M. Hoffman. Opened April 26, 1987. ***Road Show** (19). By Murray Schisgal. Opened May 21, 1987. Produced by Circle Repertory Company, Marshall W. Mason artistic director, Suzanne M. Sato managing director, B. Rodney Marriott associate artistic director, at Circle Repertory Company.

IN THIS FALLEN CITY

Paul Forrest	Danton Stone
Abner Abelson	Michael Higgins

Directed by Marshall W. Mason; scenery, David Potts; costumes, Jennifer Von Mayrhauser; lighting, Dennis Parichy; sound, Chuck London Media/Stewart Werner; production stage manager, Fred Reinglas; press, Burnham-Callaghan Associates, Jacqueline Burnham, Edward Callaghan, Gary Murphy.

Time: The present, Saturday and Sunday afternoon. Place: A small house in a run-down neighborhood in an American city. The play was presented in two parts.

Teacher investigates the mysterious death of a boy. Previously produced at White Barn Theater, Westport, Conn.

THE EARLY GIRL

Pat	Lily Knight	Lana	Pamela Dunlap
Jean	Robin Bartlett	Laurel	Sharon Schlarth
Lily	Demi Moore	Sally	Tisha Roth
George	Roxann Cabalero		

Directed by Munson Hicks; scenery, John Lee Beatty; costumes, Jennifer Von Mayrhauser; lighting, Dennis Parichy; sound, Chuck London Media/Stewart Werner; production stage manager, Denise Yaney.

Time: A few years ago. Place: A house of prostitution in a mining town out West. Act I: Late August. Act II: September to October.

Humanizing dramatization of the love-for-sale business. Previously produced by Central Casting, Ithaca, N.Y.

THE MUSICAL COMEDY MURDERS OF 1940

Helsa Wenzel.................	Lily Knight	Nikki Crandall..........	Dorothy Cantwell
Elsa von Grossenknueten....	Ruby Holbrook	Eddie McCuen...............	Kelly Connell
Michael Kelly..........	Willie C. Carpenter	Marjorie Baverstock.........	Pamela Dunlap
Patrick O'Reilly..........	Nicholas Wyman	Roger Hopewell...............	Richard Seff
Ken de la Maize..............	Michael Ayr	Bernice Roth..................	Bobo Lewis

Directed by John Bishop; scenery, David Potts; costumes, Jennifer Von Mayrhauser; lighting, Mal Sturchio, Dennis Parichy; sound, Chuck London Media/Stewart Werner; original music, Ted Simons; production stage manager, Fred Reinglas.

Time: Midnight, December 1940. Place: An estate in Chappaqua, N.Y. The play was presented in two parts.

Comedy melodrama with people trapped by a snowstorm in a mansion with a maniac.

AS IS

Hospice Worker; Business Partner;		Lily..........................	June Stein
Nurse....................	Claris Erickson	Brother; Barney............	Francis Guinan
Rich.......................	Steve Bassett	Clone	Mark Robert Myers,
Saul......................	Alan Feinstein	Pat; Orderly; Clone............	Rob Gomes
Chet	Steven Gregan		

Directed by Michael Warren Powell; scenery, David Potts; costumes, Susan Lyall, Michael Warren Powell; lighting, Dennis Parichy; sound, Chuck London Media/Stewart Werner; production stage manager, Denise Yaney.

As Is was first produced off Broadway by Circle Repertory Company 3/10/85 for 49 performances and transferred to Broadway 5/1/85 for 285 performances and was named a Best Play of its season.

ROAD SHOW

Bianca Broude...............	Anita Gillette	Robert Lester.............	Jonathan Hadary
Andy Broude.................	David Groh	Evelyn Lester...............	Trish Hawkins

Directed by Mel Shapiro; scenery, David Potts; costumes, Laura Crow; lighting, Dennis Parichy; sound, Chuck London Media/Stewart Werner; choreography, Candace Tovar; production stage manager, Kate Stewart.

Chance meeting of two couples on a cross-country trip brings together former childhood sweethearts.

Note: In addition to its regular off-Broadway schedule, Circle Repertory staged 21 subscription performances 2/18/87–3/8/87 of *Burn This* by Lanford Wilson, directed by Marshall W. Mason, with Joan Allen, John Malkovich, Jonathan Hogan and Lou Liberatore. It is planned to produce public performances of this play next season.

Sex Tips for Modern Girls (198). Musical revue collectively created by Edward Astley, Susan Astley, Kim Seary, John Sereda, Hilary Strang, Christine Willes and Peter Eliot Weiss. Produced by Ray Waves Productions/Raymond L. Gaspard in the Touchstone Theater production at the Susan Bloch Theater. Opened October 5, 1986. (Closed November 9, after 41 performances) Reopened at the Actors' Playhouse after recasting December 19, 1986. (Closed May 3, 1987)

Dot..........................	Kim Seary	Alyss......................	Hilary Strang
Helen	Christine Willes	Men	Edward Astley

Directed by Susan Astley; musical direction, John Sereda; scenery and costumes, Pearl Bellesen; set adaptation and lighting, Llewellyn Harrison; associate producers, Alan Harrison, Sharon and Bruce Miller; production stage manager, Llewellyn Harrison; press, Robert Ganshaw.

The woman's point of view put forth in revue form. A foreign play originally produced in Vancouver. The Canadian cast played 41 performances; the American cast (see below) played 157 performances.

MUSICAL NUMBERS (all songs by John Sereda except as noted), ACT I: "Ordinary Women," "Motherload," "Go for It," "Who Will Be There," "Easy for Them to Say," "Baby, Baby," "Penis Envoy" (additional lyrics by Gary Fisher).

ACT II: "Up to My Tits in Water" (by Kim Seary and Adrian Smith), "Victim of Normality," "Oh! K-Y Chorale (or, Beyond the Labia Majora)," "More and More."

Second cast as of 12/19/86:

		Alyss.....................	Briana Burke
Dot........................	Julie Ridge	Men	Alan Harrison
Helen	Laura Turnbull		

Understudy: Misses Ridge, Turnbull, Burke—C.J. Critt.
Musical direction, Kevin Wallace.

The Concept (48). New version of the play conceived by Lawrence Sacharow; text by Casey Kurtti in collaboration with the company. Produced by Arthur Cantor in the Daytop Village production at Circle in the Square Downtown. Opened October 7, 1986. (Closed November 16, 1986)

CAST: Melechi Bellamy, Ursula Carambo, Carl Cohen, Deborah Davis, Anthony Fischetti, Jennifer McNeill, Richard Murphy, Michele Zampello.
Understudy: Karen Billups.
Directed by Lawrence Sacharow; scenery, Derek McLane; costumes, Marianne Powell-Parker; lighting, Frances Aronson; press, Arthur Cantor Associates, Stephen Cole.
The experiences of recovering drug addicts dramatized and performed by members of Daytop Village, a drug rehabilitation center, without intermission. An earlier version by Lawrence Sacharow with different stories was produced in 1968. The present version was developed by River Arts Repertory at Byrdcliffe Theater, Woodstock, N.Y.

Groucho: A Life in Revue (254). By Arthur Marx and Robert Fisher. Produced by Louis C. Blau with Dennis D. Hennessy, Stockton Briggle and Richard Carrothers, Jon Wilner executive producer, at the Lucille Lortel Theater. Opened October 8, 1986. (Closed May 3, 1987)

Groucho...................	Frank Ferrante	Girls	Faith Prince
Chico; Harpo.................	Les Marsden	Deckhand...................	Rusty Magee

Understudy: Mr. Marsden—Rusty Magee.
Directed by Arthur Marx; scenery, Michael Hotopp; costumes, Baker Smith; lighting, Richard Winkler; sound, Tony Meola; musical direction, Brian Hurley; assistant director, David Storey; co-producers, Nancy and Ronnie Horowitz; associate producers, Helen Henderson, Howard Pechet; production stage manager, Robert T. Bennett; stage manager, Daniel R. Bauer; press, Shirley Herz Associates, Peter Cromarty.
Act I: Groucho's memories, the early years. Act II: Groucho's memories, the later years.
Play with music, biographical reminiscences of Groucho Marx in jokes, episodes and musical numbers from past hits.

*Roundabout Theater Company. Schedule of four programs. **Brownstone** (69). Musical with book by Josh Rubins and Andrew Cadiff; music and lyrics by Peter Larson and Josh Rubins. Opened October 8, 1986; see note. (Closed December 6, 1986) **A Man for All Seasons** (69). Revival of the play by Robert Bolt. Opened December 11, 1986; see note. (Closed February 8, 1987) **The Miracle Worker** (62). Revival of the play by William Gibson. Opened February 18, 1987; see note. (Closed April 12, 1987) ***Rosencrantz and Guildenstern Are Dead** (40). Revival of the play by Tom Stoppard. Opened April 29, 1987; see note. Produced by Roundabout Theater Company, Gene Feist artistic director, Todd Haimes executive director, at the Christian C. Yegen Theater.

THE MIRACLE WORKER—Karen Allen and Eevin Hartsough in the Round-about revival of William Gibson's play

BROWNSTONE

Claudia.................... Liz Callaway   Mary.................... Ernestine Jackson
Stuart........................ Rex Smith   Joan .... Kimberly Farr
Howard .... Ben Harney

Directed by Andrew Cadiff; musical direction, Don Jones; scenery, Loren Sherman; costumes, Ann Emonts; lighting, Richard Nelson; orchestrations, Harold Wheeler; additional musical staging, Don Bondi; sound, Peter Fitzgerald; production stage manager, Kathy J. Faul; press, Solters/Roskin/Friedman, Joshua Ellis, Adrian Bryan-Brown.

Time: During the course of one year from autumn to autumn. Place: In and around a brownstone apartment building in New York City. Act I, Scene 1: A day in autumn from very early one morning to early the next morning. Scene 2: A night in winter—from early evening until after midnight. Act II, scene 1: A Saturday in spring—from late morning to very late that night. Scene 2: A Sunday morning in summer. Epilogue: A day in autumn—very early one morning.

A year in the lives of one couple and three singles, all brownstone-dwellers. Previously produced in an earlier version OOB at Hudson Guild Theater.

ACT I

Scene 1
"Someone's Moving In".. Company
"Fiction Writer".. Howard
"I Just Want to Know".. Claudia
"There She Goes"... Joan, Claudia
"We Should Talk" .... Mary, Howard
"Camouflage".. Company
"Thanks a Lot" .... Joan, Stuart, Claudia
"Neighbors Above, Neighbors Below"....................................... Company
Scene 2
"I Wasn't Home for Christmas"... Stuart
"What Do People Do?".. Claudia
"Not Today"... Joan, Company
"The Water Through the Trees" .... Joan, Stuart
"You Still Don't Know" .... Mary
"Babies on the Brain" .... Howard, Company
"Almost There" .... Company

ACT II

Scene 1
"Don't Tell Me Everything"........................... Mary, Howard, Claudia, Stuart
"One of Them"... Joan, Stuart
"Spring Cleaning".. Claudia, Stuart
"Fiction Writer Duet"... Howard, Mary
"He Didn't Leave It Here"... Joan, Claudia
"It Isn't the End of the World" .... Mary, Howard
"See That Lady There"... Stuart, Joan
"Since You Stayed Here" .... Claudia
"We Came Along Too Late" .... Joan, Stuart, Claudia
Scene 2
"Hi There, Joan" .... Company
"It's a Funny Thing"... Joan, Stuart
"It Isn't the End of the World" (Reprise)................................... Howard
"There She Goes" (Reprise) .... Joan, Claudia
"Nevertheless".. Mary, Howard
"Almost There" (Reprise)... Stuart, Claudia
Epilogue: "Someone's Moving Out"... Company

A MAN FOR ALL SEASONS

Common Man .... Charles Keating
Sir Thomas More .... Philip Bosco
Master Richard Rich .... Campbell Scott
Duke of Norfolk .... George Guidall
Lady Alice More.............. Maria Tucci
Lady Margaret More .... Diane Venora
Cardinal Wolsey;
   Thomas Cranmer .... Ron Randell
Thomas Cromwell........... Robert Stattel
Signor Chapuys........ Ted van Griethuysen
Chapuys's Attendant........... Chip Davis
William Roper.......... Patrick O'Connell
King Henry VIII....... J. Kenneth Campbell
Woman.................... Evelyn Senter
Attendant...................... Jo Jones

Directed by Paul Giovanni; scenery, Daniel Ettinger; costumes, Abigail Murray; lighting, Dawn Chiang; sound, Philip Campanella; production stage manager, Franklin Keysar; speech consultant, Elizabeth Himmelstein.

Time: The 16th Century. Act I, Scene 1: Sir Thomas More's house at Chelsea. Scene 2: Wolsey's apartment at Richmond. Scene 3: The riverside at Richmond. Scene 4: Sir Thomas More's house. Scene 5: Hampton Court Palace. Scene 6: The garden of Sir Thomas More's house. Scene 7: An inn.

Act II, Scene 1: Sir Thomas More's house. Scene 2: Cromwell's apartment at Hampton Court. Scene 3: Sir Thomas More's house. Scene 4: Cromwell's apartment at Hampton Court. Scene 5: The riverside at Hampton Court. Scene 6: The Tower of London. Scene 7: The same. Scene 8: The Hall of Westminster. Scene 9. Tower Hill.

The last major New York revival of *A Man for All Seasons* was by ANTA with New York City Center 1/27/64 for 17 performances.

THE MIRACLE WORKER

Doctor; Voice of Doctor........ Tom Klunis	Anagnos.................... John Niespolo
Kate...................... Laurie Kennedy	Annie Sullivan................ Karen Allen
Keller...................... Jack Ryland	Viney..................... Kim Hamilton
Helen .... Eevin Hartsough	Voice of Jimmie......... Anthony Alexander
Martha.................... Tracy Yanger	Voices of Crones........... Kim Hamilton,
Percy................. Anthony Alexander	Elizabeth Owens
Aunt Ev................. Elizabeth Owens	Belle............................ Moose
James .... Victor Slezak	

Understudy: Miss Hartsough—Rachel West.

Directed by Vivian Matalon; scenery and lighting, Neil Peter Jampolis; costumes, Sigrid Insull; sound, Philip Campanella; fight coordinator, B.H. Barry; production stage manager, Kathy J. Faul.

Time: 1887. Place: The Keller homestead in Tuscumbia, Ala.; also briefly the Perkins Institution for the Blind in Boston, and a train station. The play was presented in two parts. This is its first major New York revival.

ROSENCRANTZ AND GUILDENSTERN ARE DEAD

Rosencrantz................. Stephen Lang	Claudius................ Stephen Newman
Guildenstern .... John Rubinstein	Gertrude............... Delphi Harrington
Player....................... John Wood	Polonius..................... Ron Randell
Alfred.................... William Russo	Horatio.................. Daniel Southern
Hamlet.................. David Purdham	Courtier .... James Sheerin
Ophelia.................. Barbara Garrick	

Tragedians: David Barbee, John Aaron Beall, Frandu, Robert Prichard. Musicians: Ken Forman, Joshua Worby.

Directed by Robert Carsen; scenery, Peter David Gould; costumes, Andrew B. Marlay; lighting, Robert Jared; original music, Peter Golub; movement director, fights, Carryer & Bailey; sound, Philip Campanella; production stage manager, Matthew T. Mundinger.

Rosencrantz and Guildenstern Are Dead was produced on Broadway 10/16/67 for 420 performances and was named a Best Play of its season and received the Critics and Tony Awards. This is its first major New York revival, which was presented in three parts.

Note: Press date for *Brownstone* was 11/6/86, for *A Man for All Seasons* was 1/4/87, for *The Miracle Worker* was 3/12/87, for *Rosencrantz and Guildenstern Are Dead* was 5/17/87.

The Classic Stage Company (CSC Repertory, Ltd.). Schedule of three revivals. **The Maids** (29). By Jean Genet; translated by Bernard Frechtman. Opened October 8, 1986; see note. (Closed November 1, 1986) **The Skin of Our Teeth** (28). By Thornton Wilder. Opened November 9, 1986; see note. (Closed December 7, 1986) **The Merchant of Venice** (36). By William Shakespeare. Opened December 14, 1986. (Closed January 18, 1987) Produced by The Classic Stage Company (see note), Carol Ostrow producing director, Jennifer Ober general manager, at CSC.

THE MAIDS

Claire . . . . Marceline Hugot   Madame . . . . Deborah Offner
Solange . . . . Etain O'Malley

Directed by David Kaplan; scenery, Rick Butler; costumes, Marcy Grace Froehlich; lighting, Ken Tabachnick; sound, Gary Harris; production stage manager, William H. Lang; stage manager, Liz Small; press, Dara Hershman.

Time: Midnight. Place: Paris, between the wars. The play was performed without intermission. The last major New York revival of *The Maids* was by CSC 1/3/78 for 21 performances.

THE SKIN OF OUR TEETH

Announcer . . . . Ron Orbach
Sabina . . . . Park Overall
Mrs. Antrobus . . . . Novella Nelson
Dinosaur; Conveneer . . . . Renaud Knapp
Mammoth . . . . Melissa Salack
Telegraph Boy . . . . John Aaron Beall
Gladys . . . . Lisa Goodman
Henry . . . . Peter Francis-James
Mr. Antrobus . . . . Steve Coats
Doctor; Conveneer . . . . Sanford Stokes

Moses; Broadcast Official;
  Mr. Tremayne . . . . George McGrath
Homer . . . . Joanne Bowling
Miss E. Muse . . . . Alexandra Rhodie
Miss T. Muse . . . . Kathy Karl
Miss M. Muse; Conveneer;
  Ivy . . . . Shawn Powers
Fortune Teller . . . . Elaine Hausman
Conveneers . . . . Aaron Kjennas,
                                      Anthony Ejarque

Directed by Carey Perloff; scenery, Loy Arcenas; costumes, Candice Donnelly; lighting, Anne Militello; sound, Tom Gould; composer, Wayne Horvitz; production stage manager, William H. Lang; stage manager, Liz Small.

Time: The present. Place: Various locations in New Jersey. The play was presented in two parts. The last major New York revival of *The Skin of Our Teeth* was by the Acting Company off Broadway 5/24/85 for 3 performances.

THE MERCHANT OF VENICE

Antonio . . . . George McGrath
Salerio; Old Gobbo;
  Morocco . . . . Reg E. Cathey
Sonalio; Lancelot Gobbo;
  Aragon . . . . Dan Moran
Bassanio . . . . Michael Hammond
Lorenzo . . . . John Wojda
Gratiano . . . . Sam Tsoutsouvas
Portia . . . . Sigourney Weaver

Nerissa . . . . Kristine Neilsen
Balthazar; Tubal;
  Duke of Venice . . . . Rocco Sisto
Shylock . . . . John Seitz
Leonardo;
  Man From Antonio . . . . . . John Aaron Beall
Jessica . . . . Elaine Hausman
Jailer . . . . Sanford Stokes

Koken: Renaud Knapp, Kathy Karl. Boat Boys: Aaron Kjenaas, Sandford Stokes, Anthony Ejarque.
Musicians: Tom Ericson, Michael Jung, Richard Porterfield.
Directed by James Simpson; scenery, Loy Arcenas; costumes, Claudia Brown; lighting, Anne Militello; music, Richard Porterfield.
The last major New York revival of *The Merchant of Venice* was 3/4/80 in CSC repertory.
Note: Christopher Martin's Classic Stage Company changed its name to City Stage Company in the season of 1983–84. In 1986–87, under new management it changed its name back to The Classic Stage Company, still known for short as CSC.
Note: Press date for *The Maids* was 10/17/86, for *The Skin of Our Teeth* was 11/16/86, for *The Merchant of Venice* was 12/21/86.

*The Common Pursuit (255). By Simon Gray. Produced by John A. McQuiggan in association with the Hart Entertainment Group and Douglas M. Lawson at the Promenade Theater. Opened October 19, 1986.

Stuart Thorne	Kristoffer Tabori	Humphry Taylor...........	Peter Friedman
Marigold Watson..............	Judy Geeson	Nick Finchling...............	Nathan Lane
Martin Musgrove.......	Michael Countryman	Peter Whetworth..............	Dylan Baker

Standbys: Messrs. Lane, Friedman—Robertson Dean; Miss Geeson—Sharon Scruggs.

Directed by Simon Gray and Michael McGuire; scenery, David Jenkins; costumes, David Murin; lighting, Frances Aronson; associate producers, Lois Deutchman, James Peck, Harold Reed, Sharon Scruggs; production stage manager, Lois Griffing; press, Henry Luhrman Associates, Terry M. Lilly, Andrew P. Shearer, Susan Chicoine.

Act I, Scene 1: Stuart's room in Cambridge, 20 years ago, mid-morning. Scene 2: Stuart's office in Holborn, nine years later, early summer, late morning. Act II, Scene 1: Stuart and Martin's office, three years later, later afternoon. Scene 2: Martin's office, a few years later, late autumn, early afternoon.

Cambridge University chums set out to publish a magazine after they graduate. A foreign play previously produced in London (1982), in regional theater at the Long Wharf, New Haven, Conn. (1985) and in this revised version at the Matrix Theater, Los Angeles (1986).

Lisa Eichhorn replaced Judy Geeson 1/13/87. Judy Geeson replaced Lisa Eichhorn 3/10/87. Charles Shaw Robinson replaced Kristoffer Tabori 2/10/87. Rex Smith replaced Charles Shaw Robinson 5/11/87. Daniel Gerroll replaced Rex Smith 5/26/87. Mark Nelson replaced Peter Friedman 3/3/87; Reed Birney replaced Michael Countryman; Bill Buell replaced Nathan Lane and Jack Coleman replaced Dylan Baker 5/12/87.

Neon Psalms (14). By Thomas Strelich. Produced by American Place Theater, Wynn Handman director, Julia Miles associate director, at the American Place Theater. Opened October 22, 1986. (Closed November 1, 1986)

Luton Mears	Tom Aldredge	Barbara Mears.......	Cara Duff-MacCormick
Patina Mears.................	Scotty Bloch	Ray.......................	Kelly Connell

Directed by Richard Hamburger; scenery, Christopher Barecca; costumes, Connie Singer; lighting, Stephen Strawbridge; sound design, Aural Fixation; production stage manager, Rebecca Green; stage manager, Mary Fran Loftus; press, the Fred Nathan Company, Merle Frimark, Marc P. Thibodeau.

Place: An isolated trailer near Boron, Calif., site of the world's largest open pit borax mine. Act I, Scene 1: 11 p.m., early summer. Scene 2: Late summer, dusk, about 8:30 p.m. Act II, Scene 1: Next day, late afternoon. Scene 2: Later that night, about 3 p.m.

Family life in a trailer in the Mojave Desert, a symbol of anti-technology. Previously produced at the Magic Theater, San Francisco.

Tigers Wild (8). By John Rechy. Produced by Artists Ensemble Productions, Inc. and Russell Barnard at Playhouse 91. Opened October 21, 1986. (Closed October 26, 1986)

Shell	Cordelia Richards	Stuart	Gary Matansky
Cob......................	Frank Whaley	Violet Fever...............	Lynn Chausow
Manny	Leonard P. Salazar	Pipe........................	Peter Zapp
Jerry..............	Michael David Morrison		

Directed by Michael Ewing; scenery, Nancy Thun; costumes, Kathleen Blake; lighting, Jan Kroeze; sound, Brian Ronan; production stage manager, Giles F. Colahan; press, Jeffrey Richards Associates, Irene Gandy.

Four troubled teenagers act out their emotional stresses in a West Texas setting.

Have I Got a Girl For You! (78). Musical with book by Joel Greenhouse and Penny Rockwell; music and lyrics by Dick Gallagher. Produced by Heide Mintzer, George Grec, Frank Laraia and David Singer in association with Gary H. Herman at the Second Avenue Theater. Opened October 29, 1986. (Closed January 4, 1987)

HUNTING COCKROACHES—Dianne Wiest and Ron Silver in the play by Janusz Glowacki, translated by Jadwiga Kosicka

The Monster .... Gregory Jbara
Baron John
  Von Frankenstein......... Walter Hudson
Nurse Mary Phillips .... Semina De Laurentis
Elke .... Angelina Fiordellisi

Dr. Pretorius .... J.P. Dougherty
Little Peasant Girl;
  Blind Peasant Girl .... Ritamarie Kelly
Igor...................... Dennis Parlato

Peasants, Movie Stars, Failed Experiments, Various Pieces of Furniture: Barry Finkel, Alain Freulon, Daniel Guzman, Heidi Joyce, Ritamarie Kelly, Erica Paulson.

Chorus Understudy: Russell Halley.

Directed by Bruce Hopkins; choreography, Felton Smith; musical director and conductor, Michael Rise; scenery, Harry Darrow; costumes, Kenneth M. Yount; lighting, Jeffrey Schissler; sound, James K. Morris; illusions, Ben Robinson; associate producer, Robert De Rothschild; production stage manager, Gary M. Zabinski; press, Shirley Herz Associates, Pete Sanders, Glenna Freedman.

Time: A long time ago. Place: A Bavarian forest just east of Hollywood.

Subtitled *The Frankenstein Musical*, a send-up of the movie *The Bride of Frankenstein* and others in the horror genre.

ACT I

Scene 1: A Bavarian forest
  "The Peasants' Song"... Ensemble
Scene 2: Baron Frankenstein's castle
  "Don't Open the Door"... Mary's Protectors
  "Always for Science".. Mary
Scene 3: A Bavarian forest
Scene 4: Dr. Pretorius's laboratory
  "Hollywood".. Dr. Pretorius, Ensemble
Scene 5: A peasant hut
Scene 6: Mary's bedroom
  "Girlfriends for Life".. Elke, Mary

Scene 7: A Bavarian forest
"The Monster's Song" .... Monster
Scene 8: Mary's bedroom
"I Love Me" .... John, Mary
Scene 9: Dr. Pretorius's laboratory
"Have I Got a Girl for You" .... Dr. Pretorius, Igor, Monster

ACT II

Dr. Pretorius's laboratory
"Mary's Lament" .... Mary
"The Opera" .... Company
"Something" .... Bride
Finale .... Company

*New York Shakespeare Festival. Schedule of four programs. *The Colored Museum (232). By George C. Wolfe. Opened November 2, 1986. My Gene (62). By Barbara Gelb. Opened January 29, 1987. (Closed March 22, 1987) The Knife (32). Musical with book by David Hare; music by Nick Bicat; lyrics by Tim Rose Price. Opened March 10, 1987. (Closed April 5, 1987) *Talk Radio (6). By Eric Bogosian; based on an original idea by Tad Savinar. Opened May 28, 1987. Produced by New York Shakespeare Festival, Joseph Papp producer, at the Public Theater (see note).

ALL PLAYS: Associate producer, Jason Steven Cohen; plays and musicals development, Gail Merrifield; press, Richard Kornberg, Kevin Patterson, Barbara Carroll, L. Glenn Poppleton III.

THE COLORED MUSEUM

CAST: Loretta Devine, Tommy Hollis, Reggie Montgomery, Vickilyn Reynolds, Jonea Thomas and Colette Baptiste (alternating), Danitra Vance.
Musicians: Musical direction and vocal arrangements, Daryl Waters; Ron McBee percussionist; Kysia Bostic synthesizer, vocals; Ken Brescia guitar; Bernard Fowler vocals; Luicco Hopper Bass; Dale Kleps saxophone; Anthony Lewis drums; Kit McClure saxophone; Keith O'Quinn trombone; Jon Paris harmonica; Emedin Rivera percussion; Alan Rubin trumpet; Daryl Waters piano.
Directed by L. Kenneth Richardson; composer/arranger, Kysia Bostic; choreographer, Hope Clarke; scenery, Brian Martin; costumes, Nancy L. Konrardy; lighting, Victor En Yu Tan, William H. Grant III; sound, Ron Gorton; slide projections, Anton Nelessen; production stage manager, Kenneth Johnson.
Satire on "the myths and madness" of being black in America in 11 playlets presented without intermission. Previously produced by Crossroads Theater Company, New Brunswick, N.J.

THE EXHIBITS IN THE COLORED MUSEUM: Git on Board (Miss Pat—Danitra Vance); Cooking With Aunt Ethel (Aunt Ethel—Vickilyn Reynolds); The Photo Session (Models—Loretta Devine, Reggie Montgomery); Soldier With a Secret (Soldier—Tommy Hollis); The Gospel According to Miss Roj (Waiter—Hollis, Miss Roj—Montgomery); The Hairpiece (Woman—Vance, Jeanine—Reynolds, LaWanda—Devine).
Also The Last Mama-on-the-Couch Play (Narrator—Hollis, Mama—Reynolds, Walter/Lee/Beau/Willy—Montgomery, Lady in Plaid—Devine, Medea Jones—Vance); Symbiosis (Man—Hollis, Kid—Montgomery); LaLa's Opening (LaLa—Devine; Admonia—Reynolds; Flo-rance—Hollis; Girl—Jonea Jones/Colette Baptiste); Permutations (Normal Jean—Vance); The Party (Topsy Washington—Reynolds).

MY GENE

Carlotta Monterey O'Neill. .... Colleen Dewhurst

Directed by Andre Ernotte; scenery, William Barclay; costumes, Muriel Stockdale; lighting, Phil Monat; production stage manager, Buzz Cohen.

Time: November 1968. Place: St. Luke's Hospital, New York City. The play was presented in two parts.

Eugene O'Neill's widow, a mental patient, relives episodes of her life with the playwright, in a one-woman performance which includes excerpts from the roles of Mildred Douglas in *The Hairy Ape*, Nina Leeds in *Strange Interlude*, Edmund Tyrone and Mary Tyrone in *Long Day's Journey Into Night*, Josie Hogan in *A Moon for the Misbegotten* and Deborah Hartford in *More Stately Mansions*.

THE KNIFE

Peter	Mandy Patinkin
Angela	Cass Morgan
Lifeboat Collector	Michael Willson
Johnny	Wade Raley
Ralph	William Parry
Jeremy	Tim Shew
Jenny	Mary Elizabeth Mastrantonio
Roxanne; Nurse	Mary Gordon Murray
Sally	Mary Testa
1st Waiter	Louis Padilla
Kitchen Boy	Reuben Gaumes
Chloe	Shelly Paul
Richard	Devon Michaels
Citizens Advice Bureau	Liz Vroman, Louisa Flaningham
G.P.; Michael	Ronn Carroll
Therapist	Olivia Virgil Harper
English Surgeon	Kevin Gray
Mariachi Singer	Mary Gutzi
Dr. Bauer	Dennis Parlato
Michael's Wife	Louisa Flaningham
Andrew	Hansford Rowe

Choir Boys: Jeremy Cummins, Reuben Gaumes, Roshi Handwerger.

Directed by David Hare; musical direction, Michael Starobin; choreography, Graciela Daniele; scenery, Hayden Griffin; costumes, Joan Greenwood; lighting, Tharon Musser; sound, Otts Munderloh; orchestrations, Chris Walker; production stage manager, Karen Armstrong; stage manager, Alan R. Traynor.

Time: Now. Place: Winchester, England. The play was presented in two parts.

All-singing musical about a man seeking a sex-change operation. A foreign (British) play having its world premiere in this production.

ACT I

"To Be at Sea" .... Peter, Angela, Chorus
"Hello Jeremy," "Agnus Dei," "Miserere" .... Peter, Ralph, Jeremy, Choir
"Between the Sheets" .... Angela
"Blow Slow Kisses" .... Jenny, Roxanne, Sally
"The Gay Rap" .... Waiters
"Men's Eyes" .... Jenny, Peter
"The Shape I'm In" .... Peter
"You're Not Unique" .... Peter, Doctor, Officials
"Macumba" .... Mariachi Singer
"Someone Who Touches Me" .... Jenny

ACT II

"Africa" .... Liz, Jenny
"Shadows Dance Behind You" .... Jenny
"The Knife," "To Be at Sea" (Reprise) .... Dr. Bauer, Hospital Staff
"Hello Peter We're Going Out" .... Angela, Liz, Ralph
"What Would You Do in My Place?" .... Johnny
"When I Was a Man" .... Liz
"At Least There Are Parties" .... Guests, Liz, Michael
"The Open Sea" .... Jenny, Liz
"Ache in Acorn" .... Schoolchildren
"What You Mean to Me" .... Liz, Johnny

TALK RADIO

Sid Greenberg	Zach Grenier
Bernie	Peter Onorati
Stu Noonan	John C. McGinley
Linda MacArthur	Robyn Peterson

Barry Champlain..............	Eric Bogosian	Dr. Susan Fleming	Linda Atkinson
Dan Woodruf................	Mark Metcalf	Robert	William DeAcutis
Kent....................	Michael Wincott		

Callers' Voices: Linda Atkinson, Susan Gabriel, Michele M. Mariana, William DeAcutis, Zach Grenier, Peter Onorati, Michael Wincott.

Directed by Frederick Zollo; visuals, Tad Savinar; scenery, David Jenkins; costumes, Pilar Limosner; lighting, Jan Kroeze; production stage manager, Alan R. Traynor; stage manager, Pat Sosnow.

Time: 7:45 p.m. Place: Studio B of radio station WTLK in Cleveland, Ohio. The play was presented without intermission.

Glib, hard-nosed radio talk show performer goes through an identity crisis in the verbal rough-and-tumble of one night's phone-in broadcasting. Previously produced at the Portland Center for the Visual Arts.

Note: In Joseph Papp's Public Theater there are many auditoriums. *The Colored Museum* played the Susan Stein Shiva Theater, *My Gene* and *Talk Radio* played Martinson Hall, *The Knife* played the Estelle Newman Theater.

Note: New York Shakespeare Festival also produced The Belasco Project, performances of *Macbeth*, *As You Like It* and *Romeo and Juliet* by a multicultural cast for New York City high school students, at the Belasco Theater beginning 11/12/86.

The War Party (31). By Leslie Lee. Produced by The Negro Ensemble Company, Douglas Turner Ward artistic director, Leon B. Denmark managing director, at Theater Four. Opened November 5, 1986. (Closed November 30, 1986)

Kathy Robbins	Carla Brothers	Joey Robbins	Kirk Taylor
Roosevelt Gwynne........	Vondie Curtis-Hall	Maddog	Brian Wesley Thomas
Sookie Jenkins.............	Kathryn Hunter	Outlaw	Tico Wells
David Hansen	Larry Sharp	Stan Younger................	Adam Wade
Cora Henry	Carmen Mathis	Diamond Streeter #1..........	Rome Neal
Dorothy Robbins............	Roberta Pikser	Diamond Streeter #2.........	Kevin Rock

Directed by Douglas Turner Ward; scenery, Charles H. McClennahan; costumes, Judy Dearing; lighting, Shirley Prendergast; sound, Harrison Williams; production stage manager, Ed De Shea; press, Howard Atlee.

Time: 1978. Place: Philadelphia, a ghetto office of the organization Marching on Poverty; a home in suburbia; the hospital. The play was presented in two parts.

Young woman of mixed parentage in search of identity within the black civil rights movement.

Manhattan Theater Club. Schedule of five programs. **The Hands of Its Enemy** (21). By Mark Medoff. Opened November 18, 1986. (Closed December 7, 1986) **Bloody Poetry** (24). By Howard Brenton. Opened January 6, 1987. (Closed January 25, 1987) **Hunting Cockroaches** (24). By Janusz Glowacki; translated by Jadwiga Kosicka. Opened March 3, 1987. (Closed March 22, 1987) **Death of a Buick** (16). By John Bunzel. Opened April 21, 1987. (Closed May 3, 1987) **The Lucky Spot** (24). By Beth Henley. Opened April 28, 1987 (Closed May 17, 1987). Produced by Manhattan Theater Club, Lynne Meadow artistic director, Barry Grove managing director, at City Center Theater.

THE HANDS OF ITS ENEMY

T.O. Finn.................	Ralph Williams	Elma Pafko	Joyce Reehling
Asst. Stage Manager.........	Tammy Taylor	Skip Donner.................	Dann Florek
Mel Katzman..............	Robert Steinberg	Howard Bellman	Jeffrey De Munn
Marieta Yerby	Phyllis Frelich	Diane Newburry	Jane Kaczmarek
Amanda Yerby	Lucy Deakins		

Directed by Kenneth Frankel; scenery, John Lee Beatty; costumes, Jennifer Von Mayrhauser; lighting, Pat Collins; sound, Aural Fixation; production stage manager, John Vivian; stage manager, Tammy Taylor; press, Helene Davis, Leisha DeHart.

Place: A university resident theater in the Southwest. The play was presented in two parts.

Deaf playwright, with a melodrama in rehearsal for a college production, in conflict with her director and just about everyone else.

BLOODY POETRY

Percy Bysshe Shelley	Thomas Gibson	Dr. William Polidori	Keith Reddin
Mary Shelley	Laila Robins	Harriet Westbrook;	
Claire Clairmont	Jayne Atkinson	Her Ghost	Denise Stephenson
Lord Byron	Daniel Gerroll		

Directed by Lynne Meadow; scenery, John Lee Beatty; costumes, Dunya Ramicova; lighting, Dennis Parichy; sound, Scott Lehrer; production stage manager, Peggy Peterson.

Time: Between the summers of 1816 and 1822. Place: Switzerland.

Shelley and Byron, free from the restraints of England, in full youthful cry on the Continent.

HUNTING COCKROACHES

She	Dianne Wiest	Bum	Paul Greco
He	Ron Silver	Mr. Thompson	Paul Sparer
Immigration Officer	Reathel Bean	Mrs. Thompson	Joan Copeland
Rysio	David Berman	Censor	Larry Block
Czesio	Martin Shakar		

Standbys: Mr. Berman—Paul Greco; Mr. Silver—David Berman.

Directed by Arthur Penn; scenery, Heidi Landesman; costumes, Rita Ryack; lighting, Richard Nelson; sound, Stan Metelits; production stage manager, Susie Cordon; stage manager, Laura deBuys.

Place: A Lower East Side Manhattan apartment. The play was presented in two parts.

Polish immigrants adjust to today's America. Previously produced at River Arts Repertory, Woodstock, N.Y.

DEATH OF A BUICK

Dad	Brian Evers	Mom	Christina Pickles
Benji	Tim Guinee	Arnie; Voice of Newscaster	Brian Cousins
Jack	Scott Plank		

Directed by Jonathan Alper; scenery, Philipp Jung; costumes, C.L. Hundley; lighting, Arden Fingerhut; sound, James M. Bay; production stage manager, Daniel S. Lewin; stage manager, Anita Ross.

Time: Christmas 1979. Place: In and around the Master's house in Pacific Palisades, Calif. Act I, Scene 1: 4 o'clock Christmas Eve morning. Scene 2: The same morning, about 8:30. Scene 3: The same morning, about 11. Scene 4: Later, about 1 p.m. Act II, Scene 1: Half an hour later. Scene 2: Later, about 2. Scene 3: Later that day, about 6. Scene 4: Christmas Day, about 10 a.m.

Comedy about the California lifestyle of a family living astride the San Andreas fault.

THE LUCKY SPOT

Cassidy Smith	Mary Stuart Masterson	Lacey Rollins	Belita Moreno
Turnip Moss	Alan Ruck	Sue Jack Tiller Hooker	Amy Madigan
Reed Hooker	Ray Baker	Sam	John Wylie
Whitt Carmichael	Lanny Flaherty		

Directed by Stephen Tobolowsky; scenery, John Lee Beatty; costumes, Jennifer Von Mayrhauser; lighting, Dennis Parichy; sound, Scott Lehrer; fight staging, B.H. Barry; production stage manager, Peggy Peterson; stage manager, Jim Fontaine.

Time: Christmas Eve, 1934. Place: The Lucky Spot Dance Hall in Pigeon, La. The play was presented in two parts.

Offbeat Southern characters try to beat the Depression by opening a taxi dance hall. Previously produced in Williamstown, Mass.

Face to Face (15). By Alexander Gelman; translated by Zora Essman. Produced by Judith Rubin in the Quaigh Theater production, Will Lieberson artistic director. Opened November 19, 1986. (Closed November 30, 1986)

Andrei . . . . David Groh
Natasha . . . . Ina Balin

FACE TO FACE—David Groh and Ina Balin in a scene from the play by Alexander Gelman, translated by Zora Essman

Directed by Will Lieberson; design, Donald L. Brooks; stage manager, Nancy Rutter; press, David Rothenberg, Marjorie Waxman.

Time: The present. Place: A major city in the Soviet Union. The play was presented in two parts. A foreign (Russian) play about marriage, with 56 productions in the Soviet Union.

Lily Dale (112). By Horton Foote. Produced by J.R. Productions at the Samuel Beckett Theater. Opened November 20, 1986. (Closed February 15, 1987)

Horace Robedaux	Don Bloomfield	Pete Davenport	Greg Zittel
Mrs. Coons	Jane Welch	Will Kidder	Johnny Kline
Lily Dale Robedaux	Molly Ringwald	Albert	Cullen Johnson
Corella Davenport	Julie Heberlein		

Standbys: Miss Ringwald—Kathleen Gibbons; Messrs. Bloomfield, Kline—Matthew Penn; Misses Heberlein, Welch—Sara Croft; Mr. Zittel—Cullen Johnson.

Directed by William Alderson; scenery, Daniel Conway; costumes, Deborah Shaw; lighting, John Hastings; production stage manager, Laura Kravets; stage manager, Laura Young; press, Burnham-Callaghan Associates.

Time: 1909. Place: On a train from Harrison, Tex. and in the home of Pete Davenport in Houston. Act I, Scene 1: Morning. Scene 2: Later that afternoon. Scene 3: Two hours later. Act II: Two weeks later.

Texan tries to go home again but is rejected by his remarried mother and teen-aged sister; third in nine-play cycle of autobiographical plays 1902–1928 under the portmanteau title *The Orphans' Home* (the first two were *Roots in a Parched Land* and *Convicts*; also see the *The Widow Claire* listing below).

The Widow Claire (150). By Horton Foote. Produced by Circle in the Square Theater, Theodore Mann artistic director, Paul Libin producing director, at Circle in the Square Downtown. Opened December 17, 1986. (Closed April 26, 1987)

Horace Robedaux	Matthew Broderick	Widow Claire	Hallie Foote
Archie	Anthony Weaver	Buddy	John Daman
Felix	Victor Slezak	Molly	Sarah Michelle Gellar
Spence	Spartan McClure	Val	Patrick James Clarke
Ed Cordray	William Youmans	Roger	Dan Butler

Understudies: Messrs. Broderick, Weaver, McClure, Youmans—Ned Bridges; Messrs. Butler, Clarke, Slezak—Kevin O'Meara; Miss Foote—Julie Swenson.

Directed by Michael Lindsay-Hogg; scenery, Eugene Lee; costumes, Van Broughton Ramsey; lighting, Natasha Katz; dance sequences, Margie Castleman; fight sequences, B.H. Barry; production stage manager, Carol Klein; stage manager, Julie Swenson; press, Merle Debuskey, Leo Stern.

Time: 1911. Place: Harrison, Texas. The play was performed without intermission.

The courting of a young widow with two children, part of the author's autobiographical nine-play cycle 1902–1928 with the portmanteau title "The Orphans' Home" (see the *Lily Dale* listing above).

Eric Stoltz replaced Matthew Broderick 3/3/87.

A Best Play; see page 150.

The Rise of David Levinsky (31). Musical based on the novel by Abraham Cahan; book and lyrics by Isaiah Sheffer; music by Bobby Paul. Produced by Eric Krebs at the John Houseman Theater. Opened January 12, 1987. (Closed February 8, 1987)

Maximum Max; Reb Shmerel;		Chaiken; Naphtali; Little Getzel	Jack Kenny
Diamond	Larry Raiken	Dora	Eleanor Reissa
Huntington; Manheimer	W.M. Hunt	Mrs. Noodleman;	
Blitt; Barber; Big Muttel;		Mrs. Deinstog	Judith Cohen
Moscowitz	David Vosburgh	Levinsky	Larry Kert

Shlanki; Bender . . . . Arthur Howard
David . . . . Avi Hoffman
Model; Matilda;
  Guddie; Rosie . . . . Jean Kauffman
Gitelson . . . . Bruce Adler

Model; Argentine Ruchel;
  Becky . . . . Rendé Rae Norman
Model; Shopgirl; Sadie . . . . Lynne Winterseller
Peddler; Strike Worker . . . . David Kenner
Shopgirl; Strike Worker . . . . Wendy Bala

Understudies: Mr. Hoffman—Jack Kenny; Mr. Raiken—Arthur Howard; Mr. Hunt—David Vosburgh; Miss Cohen—Rendé Rae Norman; Messrs. Vosburgh, Kenny, Howard—David Kenner; Miss Reissa—Jean Kauffman; Miss Kauffman—Wendy Baila.

Musicians: Lanny Meyers piano; Susan Shumway violin.

Directed by Sue Lawless; musical direction, Lanny Meyers; scenery, Kenneth Foy; costumes, Mimi Maxmen; lighting, Phil Monat; production stage manager, Donald Christy; stage manager, Anita Ross; press, Max Eisen, Maria Somma.

In a turn-of-the-century setting, the loss of belief in the American Dream.

ACT I

1910: A testimonial banquet
  "Who Is This Man?" . . . . Levinsky
1883: Antomir, Poland: The Yeshiva
  "Five Hundred Pages" . . . . David
  "Grand Street" . . . . Matilda, Naphtali, Reb Shmerel, David
The train station
Aboard ship
  "In America" . . . . Gitelson, Immigrants
The street in front of Castle Garden
A grocery store on Essex Street
  "The Boarder" . . . . Mrs. Dienstog
All around the East Side
  "The Transformation" . . . . David, Barber Shop People
Stanton Street
  Quartet: "Sharp" . . . . Maximum Max, Shlanki, Big Muttel, Little Getzel
  "Two of a Kind" . . . . Dora
  "Little Did I Know" . . . . Levinsky
In night school
Winter: The city streets
  "Hard Times" . . . . David, Levinsky
Manheimer's Sweat Shop
Maximum Max's Home
  "Two of a Kind" (Reprise)
A rented loft
  "Credit Face" . . . . Levinsky, David
  "Five Hundred Garments" . . . . David, Levinsky

ACT II

Some years later: The shop and office of Levinsky Suits and Cloaks
  "The Garment Trade" . . . . Ensemble, Levinsky
  "Some Incredible Guy" . . . . Gitelson, Ensemble
Maximum Max's home
  Trio: "Just . . . Like . . . Me" . . . . Max, Dora, Levinsky
Levinsky's hotel room
The office
A French restaurant
  "Be Flexible" . . . . David
The shop
Mrs. Noodleman's uptown salon
  "A Married Man" . . . . Mrs. Noodleman, Max, Moscowitz,
                                                              Becky, Rosie, Sadie, Levinsky

Maximum Max's home
  Duet: "Little Did We Know" . . . . Levinsky, Dora
  "Bittersweet" . . . . Dora, Levinsky
The Levinsky and Company showrooms
  "Survival of the Fittest" . . . . Levinsky
Seventh Avenue, in front of Levinsky and Company
1910: The testimonial banquet
  "A View From the Top" . . . . Levinsky, David
  "In America" (Reprise) . . . . Levinsky, David, Ensemble

Cast Me Down (26). By J. Howard Holland. Produced by CMD Productions, Inc., Lucy
Holland and Susan Watson Turner producers, at Theater Four. Opened February 15,
1987. (Recessed February 22, 1987) Reopened March 1, 1987. (Closed March 15, 1987)

T. Thomas Fortune	Marcus Naylor	Samuel Chapman Armstrong . .	Shannon Baker
Booker T. Washington	Eldon Bullock	Thomas Ferris	Leo V. Finnie III
Emmet Scott	Howard J. Garner		

Directed by Susan Watson Turner; scenery, Lisa L. Watson; costumes, Ali Turns; lighting, Kathy
Perkins; sound, Richard V. Turner; original direction, Meachie Jones; production stage manager, P.J.
Wilson; press, Howard Atlee.

Act I, Scene 1: Booker T. Washington's office, Tuskegee Institute, 1901. Scene 2: Flashback,
Brooklyn, N.Y., 1891. Scene 3: Brooklyn, later that afternoon. Act II, Scene 1: Tuskegee Institute,
spring 1892. Scene 2: A few months later. Scene 3: A few minutes later. Scene 4: The same. Scene
5: Same day, later that afternoon. Scene 6: The same. Scene 7: Next morning. Act III, Scene 1: Spring
1893 in Fortune's office, New York City. Scene 2: Several days later at Tuskegee. Scene 3: The next
morning, backlawn of The Oaks. Scene 4: Fall 1895 in New York City. Scene 5: Fall 1901, same as
in Act I, Scene 1. The play was presented in two parts with the intermission following Act II.

Subtitled "The tragedy of Booker T. Washington," the story of his struggle "to uplift his people."
Previously produced at Hunter College and Hampton University.

Kvetch (31). By Steven Berkoff. Produced by Gerry Roberts, Bunni Roberts and Larry
Spellman at the Westside Arts Theater. Opened February 18, 1987. (Closed March 15,
1987)

Donna	Laura Esterman	Hal	Mitch Kreindel
Frank	Kurt Fuller	George	Hy Anzell
Mother-in-Law	Ruth Jaroslow		

Understudies: Suzanne Toren, Ron Siebert.

Directed by Steven Berkoff; scenery, Don Llewellyn; costumes, Ruth A. Brown; lighting, Jason
Kantrowitz; production coordinator, Bernard Block; production stage manager, Jason Fogelson;
press, Max Eisen, Madelon Rosen.

Act I: Frank's home. Act II: Various locations.

Self-styled "An Uncommon Comedy," the orchestrated plaints of a group of five members of a
Jewish family. A foreign (British) play previously produced in Los Angeles.

A Best Play; see page 183.

Mona Rogers in Person (36). One-woman performance by Helen Shumaker; written by
Philip-Dimitri Galas. Produced by the Hart Entertainment Group, Inc. and Pamela
Koslow at the Cherry Lane Theater. Opened March 1, 1987. (Closed April 4, 1987)

Directed by Lynne Taylor-Corbett; based on the original direction by Philip-Dimitri Galas; lighting, Mimi Jordan Sherin; associate producers, Jane Holzer, Jon Kane; production stage manager,
Lynn Moffat; press, Shirley Herz Associates, Glenna Freedman, Peter Cromarty.

Portrayal of the invented character of a brainy former star of burlesque, presented without intermission. Previously produced at La Jolla and San Francisco.

Women Beware Women (65). Adapted by Howard Barker from the play by Thomas Middleton. Produced by Robert Klein and Overture Productions at Playhouse 91. Opened March 1, 1987. (Closed April 26, 1987)

Mother . . . . Florence Winston	Isabella . . . . Katell Pleven
Leantio . . . . Graves Kiely	Ward . . . . Barry Jon Lynch
Bianca . . . . Caroline Beck	Sordido . . . . Judson Camp
Guardiano . . . . John Heffernan	Duke of Florence . . . . Chet London
Fabritio . . . . Marcus Powell	Cardinal . . . . William Newman
Livia . . . . Sally Kirkland	Messenger . . . . William Castleman
Hippolito . . . . Roy Steinberg	Citizen; Servant . . . . Lynn Elliott, Dede Lowe

Standby: Messrs. Powell, Heffernan, London, Newman—Moutrie Patten. Understudy: Misses Beck, Pleven, Kirkland, Winston—Dede Lowe.

Directed by Sharon Gans; scenery, Wolfgang Roth; costumes, Ruth Morley; lighting, Jeff Davis; choreography, William Burdick; production stage manager, John Handy; stage manager, William Castleman; press, Jeffrey Richards Associates, C. George Willard, Ken Mandelbaum.

Time: 17th century to today. Place: Florence. Act I, Scene 1: Widow's house, early morning. Scene 2: Courtyard, afternoon of the same day. Scene 3: Widow's house, two days later. Scene 4: Courtyard, later the same day. Scene 5: Livia's house, the same day. Scene 6: Widow's house, five days later. Scene 7: Guardiano's home, two days later. Act II, Scene 1: Livia's room, one week later, late morning. Scene 2: Courtyard, immediately following. Scene 3: The Ward's garden, the next day. Scene 4: The Palace, the following day. Scene 5: The Street, the same day. Scene 6: Fort at Rouen, two days later. Scene 7: The Palace, two days later.

Adaptation of the 1623 Jacobean tragedy about a woman's sexual adventures, with a new final act in which she achieves a measure of redemption. A foreign play previously produced in London.

The Acting Company. Schedule of two programs. **On the Verge, or The Geography of Yearning** (72). By Eric Overmyer. Opened March 2, 1987. (Closed May 3, 1987) **Much Ado About Nothing** (8). Revival of the play by William Shakespeare. Opened May 11, 1987. (Closed May 17, 1987) Produced by the Acting Company, John Houseman producing artistic director, Michael Kahn artistic director, Margot Harley executive producer, at the John Houseman Theater.

ON THE VERGE,
or THE GEOGRAPHY OF YEARNING

Mary . . . . Lisa Banes	Alexandra . . . . Laura Hicks
Fanny . . . . Patricia Hodges	

Grover; Alphonse; George Troll; Yeti; Gus; Mme. Nhu; Mr. Coffee; Nicky Paradise—Tom Robbins.

Understudies: Misses Banes, Hodges, Hicks—Becky Borczon; Mr. Robbins—Jack Kenny.

Directed by Garland Wright; scenery, John Arnone; costumes, Ann Hould-Ward; lighting, James Ingalls; music, John McKinney; sound, Bruce D. Cameron; produced in association with Everett L. King in the New York Ensemble production; production stage manager, Robin Rumpf; press, The Fred Nathan Company, Marc P. Thibodeau.

Time 1888; Place: Terra Incognita. The play was presented in two parts.

Three Victorian time-travellers arrive in the world of the mid-1950s. Previously produced in regional theater at Baltimore, Hartford, San Diego and elsewhere.

MUCH ADO ABOUT NOTHING

Don Pedro . . . . Terrence Caza	Leonato . . . . Kevin McGuire
Don John; 2d Watchman . . . Joseph Houghton	Antonio; Verges . . . . Ralph Zito
Claudio . . . . Michael McKenzie	Balthazar; Friar; 1st Watchman;
Benedick . . . . Philip Goodwin	Sexton . . . . Douglas Krizner

Conrade . . . . Craig Bryant
Borachio. . . . . Matt Bradford Sullivan
Dogberry . . . . Joel Miller
Hero . . . . Melissa Gallagher
Beatrice . . . . Alison Stair Neet

Margaret. . . . . Constance Crawford
Ursula. . . . . Wendy Brennan
Celebrities at the Party. . . . . Craig Bryant,
Joel Miller

Directed by Gerald Gutierrez; choreography, Theodore Pappas; scenery, Douglas Stein; costumes, Ann Hould-Ward; lighting, Pat Collins; musical direction and original music, Bruce Pomahac; staff repertory director, Rob Bundy; production stage manager, Mark Baltazar; stage manager, Lisa Rollins.

Shakespeare's play performed as though it were set in Cuba in the 1930s. The last major New York revival of *Much Ado About Nothing* was by Royal Shakespeare Company on Broadway 10/14/84 for 53 performances.

*Staggerlee (86). Musical with book by Vernel Bagneris; music and lyrics by Allen Toussaint; additional lyrics by Vernel Bagneris. Produced by John H. Williams, Ruth Mieszkuc, The Program Development Company and The Encore A Partnership at the Second Avenue Theater. Opened March 18, 1987.

Staggerlee. . . . . Adam Wade
Zelita . . . . Juanita Brooks
Elenora. Ruth Brown
June . . . . Marva Hicks
Tiny . . . . Reginald Veljohnson
Bertha Ann . . . . Carol Sutton
Dolores. . . . . Angeles Echols

Andrea . . . . Christie Gaudet
Peat. . . . . Alfred Bruce Bradley
Piano Player; Policeman. . . . . . Kevin Ramsey
Bone; Billy Bottom . . . . Bernard J. Marsh
Silk . . . . Leon Williams
Pepper; Policeman. . . . . Ron Woodall

Understudies: Miss Brown—Yvonne Talton Kersey; Miss Hicks—Claire Bathé; Miss Brooks—Angeles Echols; Miss Sutton—Christie Gaudet; Messrs. Wade, Williams, Marsh, Woodall, Ramsey—Ronald Wyche; Mr. Bradley—Kenneth Hanson.

Musicians: Allen Toussaint piano, conductor; Walter Payton bass; Bernard "Bunchy" Johnson drums; Amadee Castanell saxophone; Trazi Williams percussion; Billy Butler guitar.

Directed by Vernel Bagneris; choreography, Pepsi Bethel; musical coordinator and conductor, Allen Toussaint; scenery, Akira Yoshimura; costumes, JoAnn Clevenger; lighting, Allen Lee Hughes; sound, Paul Garrity; associate producer, Kirk D'Amico; production stage manager, Diane F. Mazey; stage manager, Kenneth Hanson; press, Milly Schoenbaum.

Time: The late 1950s. Place: A local corner bar in the South.

Rhythm-and-blues musical based on a New Orleans folk tale about a bold young man's romance with a young girl against the wishes of her scheming mother.

ACT I

"Iko Iko" . . . . Tiny, Company
"Night People". . . . . Vocalist, Staggerlee, Company
"Staggerlee". . . . . Zelita, Company
"Discontented Blues". . . . . Elenora
"With You in Mind". . . . . Vocalist, Staggerlee, June
"Big Chief" . . . . Tiny, Company
"Mardi Gras Time". . . . . Staggerlee, Boys
"A Pimp Like That" . . . . Elenora, Tiny, Zelita
"You Knew I Was No Good" . . . . Bertha Ann, Girls
"Lover of Love". . . . . Staggerlee
"You Knew I Was No Good" (Reprise) . . . . Company
"Saved by Grace". . . . . Zelita, Company

ACT II

"Happy Time" (Entr'acte). . . . . The Band
"Victims of the Darkness" . . . . Vocalist, Staggerlee, Boys
"Devil's Disguise" . . . . June, Tiny, Staggerlee, Peat, Bertha Ann, Andrea

"One Monkey Don't Stop No Show"............................... Bertha Ann, Staggerlee
"Ruler of My Heart".. June
"Going Down Slowly".. Staggerlee, Boys
"Lighting a Candle".. Elenora
"Knocking Myself Out" .... Zelita
"We're Gonna Do It Good".. June
"Let's Live It Up" .... Elenora

Standup Shakespeare (2). Musical revue conceived by Ray Leslee and Kenneth Welsh; words by William Shakespeare; music by Ray Leslee. Produced by The Shubert Organization at Theater 890. Opened April 4, 1987. (Closed April 5, 1987)

Directed by Mike Nichols; scenery, John Arnone; costumes, Cynthia O'Neal; lighting, Mitchell Bogard; sound, Barbara J. Schwartz; musical direction and orchestral arrangements, Ray Leslee; vocal arrangements, Thomas Young; press, Milly Schoenbaum, Brian Drutman. With Taborah Johnson, Kenneth Welsh, Thomas Young. Musicians: Jack Bashkow, Marshall Coid, Dean Johnson, Ray Leslee.

Shakespearean dialogue and lyrics applied to jazzy love songs and other modern subjects.

Tent Meeting (15). By Rebecca Wackler, Larry Larson and Levi Lee. Produced by ERB Productions, Joan Stein, the Seco Production Company and John Roach at the Astor Place Theater. Opened April 7, 1987. (Closed April 19, 1987)

STAGGERLEE—Carol Sutton *(center)* with (clockwise from lamp post, *left*) Kevin Ramsey, Leon Williams, Alfred Bruce Bradley and Bernard J. Marsh and *(right)* Christie Gaudet and Angeles Echols in a scene from the Vernel Bagneris–Allen Toussaint musical

Directed by Norman René; scenery, Andrew Jackness; costumes, Walter Hicklin, lighting, Paul Gallo; sound, James M. Bay; associate producers, Judie Amsterdam, Elysa Lazar; production stage manager, Jerry Bihm; press, Henry Lurhman, Andrew P. Shearer. With Levi Lee, Larry Larson, Rebecca Wackler.

Cracks in the facade of religious revivalism. Previously produced by Southern Theater Conspiracy, Atlanta and other cross-country theaters. The play was presented in two parts.

*Funny Feet (48). Revue conceived by Bob Bowyer; musical numbers by various authors (see credits below). Produced by Nancy E. Diamond in association with Hieronymus Foundation, Inc. and Universal Arts Management, Inc., at the Lamb's Theater. Opened April 21, 1987.

CAST: Philippe, A Molotov Brother, X, Ray, Welcoming Committee, A Helping Hand—Wilton Anderson; A Molotov Brother, Beam, Host—Matthew Baker; A New Yorker, Baby Bobby, Older Man, Mr. Green, Mourner, Security—Bob Bowyer; Jeannine, Mother, Simone, Bobbi Jo, A Molotov Brother, A Paracomic, Welcoming Committee, Hostess—Veronica Castonguay; Natasha Roach, Playmate, Younger Woman, Z, The Dearly Departed—Sandra Chinn; Organism II, Betti Li—Irene Cho; Rhoda Fernandez, Brenda Sue, Older Woman, Danseuse, Hostess—Martha Connerton; Madelaine, Goldie, Danseuse, Hostess—Amy Flood; Rudolph Roach, Seymour Fernandez, Organism I, Younger Man, Sting, A Paracomic, Premier Danseur, A Party Giver—Zane Rankin; Jacques, Father, Eduardo, A Molotov Brother, Y, Haze, Man, Welcoming Committee, Host—D. Kevin Rhind.

Alternates: Organism I—Matthew Baker; Organism II—Veronica Castonguay; Natasha Roach, Playmate, Younger Woman, Z, The Dearly Departed—Irene Cho; Male Roles—Ramon Galindo.

Understudies: Rudolph Roach, Eduardo, X, Y—Matthew Baker; Rhoda Fernandez, Older Woman—Veronica Castonguay; Simone, Martine—Irene Cho; Mother, A Molotov Brother—Martha Connerton; Jeannine, Organism II, A Paracomic, A Molotov Brother—Amy Flood; A New Yorker, Mr. Green, Older Man, Security—D. Kevin Rhind.

Directed and choreographed by Bob Bowyer; creative supervision, Art Wolff; scenery and costumes, Lindsay W. Davis; lighting, Arden Fingerhut; sound, Bruce Ellman; associate producers, Andrea Pullman, Pearl Tisman Minsky; production stage manager, Vincent Paul; stage manager, Elizabeth Heeden; press, Shirley Herz Associates, Glenna Freedman.

Spoof of professional dancing, in revue format. The play was presented without intermission.

MUSICAL NUMBERS

"Black Cockroach Pas de Deux" . . . . A New Yorker, Rudolph Roach, Natasha Roach
("Grand Tarantella for Piano and Orchestra" by Louis Moreau Gottschalk, reconstructed and orchestrated by Hershey Kaye)
"Jacques and Jeannine". . . . . Jeannine, Jacques
("What I Did for Love" by Marvin Hamlisch and Edward Kleban)
"Baby Bobby's Backyard". . . . . Baby Bobby, Father, Playmate, Mother
("Meditation from Thais" by Jules Massenet)
"La Stampa de Feeta". . . . . Seymour Fernandez, Rhoda Fernandez
("Malaguena" by Ernesto Lecuona)
"Les Jazz Chics" . . . . Eduardo, Philippe, Simone, Madelaine
("I Hear a Symphony" by Eddie Holland, Lamont Dozier and Brian Holland)
"Duet for Mating Organisms" . . . . Organisms I & II
("Adagio for Strings, Op. 11" by Samuel Barber)
"Molotov Brothers". . . . . The Molotov Brothers
("Hungarian Dance No. 5" by Johannes Brahms)
"Remembrance Waltz" . . . . Older Couple, Younger Couple
("Nocturne" by Frederic Chopin)
"Pas de Trois Pour la Psychologie Contemporaine" . . . . X, Y, Z
("Piano Concerto #2 in C Minor" by Sergei Rachmaninoff)
"The Buttercups". . Betti Li, Brenda Sue, Bobbi Jo, Ray, Mr. Green, Haze, Goldie, Sting, Beam
("You Are My Friend" by Patti LaBelle, Budd Ellison and Armstead Edwards)

"Smile" .... Man, Paracomics
  ("Send in the Clowns" by Stephen Sondheim)
"Faux Pas de Trois" .... Premier Danseur, Danseuse
  ("Waltz" from *Faust* by Charles Francois Gounod)
"The Big Ballet in the Sky" .... The Dearly Departed, Mourner, Welcoming Committee,
                                   Security, Party Giver, Host, Hostesses
  ("Adagio in G Minor for Strings" by Romasso Albinoni)

*Educating Rita (30). By Willy Russell. Produced by Raymond L. Gaspard in the Steppenwolf Theater Company production at the Westside Arts Theater. Opened May 7, 1987.

Frank... Austin Pendleton
Rita .... Laurie Metcalf

Directed by Jeff Perry; scenery and lighting, Kevin Rigdon; costumes, Erin Quigley; sound, Jeffrey Webb; associate producer, Marc Sferrazza; production supervisor, Sam Ellis; original music, Ray Leslee; production stage managers, Jane Grey, Jeffrey Webb; press, Robert Ganshaw.

Time: The present. Place: A first-floor room in a university in the north of England. The play was presented in two parts.

Bibulous teacher takes on the job of educating a vulgar but ambitious hairdresser. Transfer of a Chicago production (2/8/87) of a foreign play first produced in London by the Royal Shakespeare Company, then in the West End, then made into a movie in 1983.

*The Garden of Earthly Delights (21). Performance piece conceived by Martha Clarke; created in collaboration with Robert Barnett, Felix Blaska, Robert Faust, Marie Fourcaut, Margie Gillis and Paola Styron; music composed by Richard Peaslee, created in collaboration with Eugene Friesen, Bill Ruyle and Steven Silverstein. Produced by M Square Entertainment, Inc., Mitchell Maxwell, Alan J. Schuster, Marvin L. Melt and Margo Lion in the Music-Theater Group (Lyn Austin, Diane Wondisford and Mark Jones) production at the Minetta Lane Theater. Opened May 15, 1987.

Rob Besserer	Raymond Kurshal
Felix Blaska	Matthias Naegele
Martha Clarke	Bill Ruyle
Marie Fourcaut	Steven Silverstein
Margie Gillis	Paola Styron

Directed by Martha Clarke; costumes, Jane Greenwood; lighting, Paul Gallo; flying, Foy; consultant, Peter Beagle; production associate, Warren Trepp; production stage manager, Steven Ehrenberg; stage manager, David Carriere; press, Shirley Herz Associates, Peter Cromarty.

Scenes: Eden; The Garden; The Seven Sins; Hell.

Dramatization of the painting by Hieronymus Bosch, previously produced off off Broadway by Music-Theater Group/Lenox Arts Center, Lyn Austin producing director, at St. Clement's.

*Eno (7). One-man performance by Eno Rosenn; written by Daniel Lappin and Eno Rosenn. Produced by Turner/Ross Productions in association with Gene S. Jones at the Cherry Lane Theater. Opened May 27, 1987.

Scenery and costumes, Yael Pardes; lighting, Zeev Navon; original score, Nir Brandt; sound, Stan Mark; press, Burnham/Callaghan.

Series of skits by an Israeli mime who has performed them previously in his own country and Europe.

CAST REPLACEMENTS AND TOURING COMPANIES

Compiled by Stanley Green

The following is a list of the more important cast replacements in productions which opened in previous years, but were still playing in New York during a substantial part of the 1986–87 season; or were still on a first-class tour in 1986–87, or opened in New York in 1986–87 and went on tour during the season (casts of first-class touring companies of previous seasons which were no longer playing in 1986–87 appear in previous *Best Plays* volumes of appropriate years).

The name of each major role is listed in *italics* beneath the title of the play in the first column. In the second column directly opposite appears the name of the actor who created the role in the original New York production (whose opening date appears in *italics* at the top of the column). Indented immediately beneath the original actor's name are the names of subsequent New York replacements, together with the date of replacement when available.

The third column gives information about first-class touring companies, including London companies (produced under the auspices of their original New York managements). When there is more than one roadshow company, #1, #2, etc., appear before the name of the performer who created the role in each company (and the city and date of each company's first performance appears in *italics* at the top of the column). Their subsequent replacements are also listed beneath their names, with dates when available.

ARSENIC AND OLD LACE

	New York 6/26/86	*Louisville 1/6/87*
Abby Brewster	Jean Stapleton	Jean Stapleton
Martha Brewster	Polly Holliday Marion Ross 12/23/86	Marion Ross
Mortimer Brewster	Tony Roberts Gary Sandy 12/23/86	Gary Sandy
Dr. Einstein	William Hickey Larry Storch 12/23/86	Larry Storch
Jonathan Brewster	Abe Vigoda Jonathan Frid 12/23/86	Jonathan Frid

BENEFACTORS

	New York
Jane	Glenn Close Maureen Anderman 6/17/86
David	Sam Waterston David Birney 6/17/86

359

BIG RIVER

New York 4/25/85

Huckleberry Finn	Daniel Jenkins
	Martin Moran 4/7/86
	Brian L. Green 10/21/86
	Jon Ehrlich 4/21/87
Jim	Ron Richardson
	Larry Riley 2/21/86
	George Merritt 6/1/86
The Duke	Rene Auberjonois
	Russell Leib 9/2/85
	Brent Spiner 10/8/85
	Ken Jenkins 1/7/86
	Stephen Mellor 9/2/86
The King	Bob Gunton
	Michael McCarty 7/8/86
Tom Sawyer	John Short
	Clint Allen 8/22/85
	Roger Bart 4/7/87
Mary Jane Wilkes	Patti Cohenour
	Karla DeVito 7/9/85
	Patti Cohenour 9/3/85
	Marin Mazzie 10/15/85
Pap Finn	John Goodman
	Leo Burmester 9/3/85
	Roger Miller 11/11/86
	Graham Pollock 12/9/86

CATS

New York 10/7/82

Bustopher Jones	Stephen Hanan
	Bill Carmichael
Cassandra	René Ceballos
	Roberta Stiehm
Demeter	Wendy Edmead
	Patricia Ruck
Mistoffelees	Timothy Scott
	Don Johanson
Old Deuteronomy	Ken Page
	Clent Bowers
Plato/Macavity/	Kenneth Ard
Rumpus Cat	Jamie Patterson
Rum Tum Tugger	Terrence V. Mann
	Steve Yudson
Skimbleshanks	Reed Jones
	Robert Burnett

Note: Only replacements during the 1986–1987 season are listed above under the names of the original cast members. For previous replacements (and the touring cast), see page 415 of *The Best Plays of 1983–1984* and page 414 of *The Best Plays of 1984–1985*.

A CHORUS LINE

N.Y.Off Bway 4/15/75
N.Y. Bway 7/25/75

Val
Pamela Blair
Delyse Lively-Mekka

Mike
Wayne Cilento
Mark Bove

Diana
Priscilla Lopez
Mercedes Perez 10/86

Zack
Robert LuPone
Eivind Harum

Cassie
Donna McKechnie
Angelique Ilo 7/86
Donna McKechnie 9/1/86
Laurie Gamache 5/18/87

Sheila
Carole Bishop
Cynthia Fleming 11/86

Mark
Cameron Mason
Andrew Grose 11/86

Richie
Ronald Dennis
Bruce Anthony Davis 12/86

Judy
Patricia Garland
Trish Ramish 2/87

Note: Only replacements during the 1986–87 season are listed above under the names of the original cast members. For previous replacements, see page 437 of *The Best Plays of 1982–83*, page 416 of *The Best Plays of 1983–84*, page 414 of *The Best Plays of 1984–85* and page 372 of *The Best Plays of 1985–86.*

THE FANTASTICKS

New York 5/3/60

Luisa
Rita Gardner
Lorrie Harrison 11/4/86

Note: As of May 31, 1987, 31 actors had played the role of El Gallo, 29 actresses had played Luisa and 23 actors had played Matt. Only the major cast replacement during the 1986–1987 season is listed above under the name of the original cast member. For previous replacements, see page 442 of *The Best Plays of 1982–1983*, page 418 of *The Best Plays of 1983–1984*, page 415 of *The Best Plays of 1984–1985*, and page 373 of *The Best Plays of 1985–1986.*

42nd STREET

New York 8/25/80

Julian Marsh
Jerry Orbach
Barry Nelson 7/22/86
Jamie Ross 9/2/86

Dorothy Brock
Tammy Grimes
Louise Troy
Dolores Gray 6/17/86
Elizabeth Allen 1/20/87

Peggy Sawyer	Wanda Richert
	Cathy Wydner 7/22/86
	Clare Leach 9/16/86
Maggie Jones	Carole Cook
	Denise Lor
Tommy Lawlor	Lee Roy Reams
	Jim Walton 7/22/86
	Lee Roy Reams 9/23/86

Note: Only replacements during the 1986–1987 season are listed above under the names of the original cast members. For previous replacements, see page 418 of *The Best Plays of 1983–1984* (also touring casts), page 417 of *The Best Plays of 1984–1985* (also London cast), and page 374 of *The Best Plays of 1985–1986.*

THE HOUSE OF BLUE LEAVES

New York 4/29/86

Artie Shaugnessy	John Mahoney
	Jack Wallace 7/29/86
	John Mahoney 10/10/86
Bananas Shaugnessy	Swoosie Kurtz
Bunny Flingus	Stockard Channing
	Christine Baranski 6/24/86
Billy Einhorn	Christopher Walken
	Danny Aiello 4/29/86
	Richard Portnow 1/27/87
	Danny Aiello
Corinna Stroller	Julie Hagerty
	Patricia Clarkson 6/3/86
	Julie Hagerty 1/27/87

I'M NOT RAPPAPORT

	N.Y. Off B'way 6/6/85		*#1 London 7/3/86*
	N.Y. B'way 11/19/85		*#2 Boston 11/28/86*
Nat	Judd Hirsch		#1 Paul Scofield
	Hal Linden 9/2/86		#2 Judd Hirsch
Midge	Cleavon Little		#1 Howard Rollins Jr.
	Ossie Davis 9/2/86		#2 Cleavon Little
Clara	Cheryl Giannini		
	Mercedes Ruehl 11/19/85		
	Marcia Rodd 9/30/86		
	Christine Estabrook 2/2/87		

LA CAGE AUX FOLLES

New York 8/21/83

Alban	George Hearn
	Jack Davison 7/15/86
	Walter Charles 7/22/86
	Keene Curtis 2/17/87

Georges	Gene Barry
	Tom Urich 7/22/86
	Steeve Arlen 7/29/86
	Peter Marshall 2/17/87

Note: Only replacements during the 1986–1987 season are listed above under the names of the original cast members. For previous replacements see page 418 of *The Best Plays of 1984–1985* (also touring casts) and page 374 of *The Best Plays of 1985–1986.*

THE MYSTERY OF EDWIN DROOD

	New York 12/1/85	*London 5/7/87*
William Cartwright	George Rose	Ernie Wise
Princess Puffer	Cleo Laine	Lulu
	Loretta Swit 6/9/86	
	Karen Morrow 12/8/86	
Edwin Drood	Betty Buckley	Julia Hills
	Donna Murphy 6/16/86	
	Paige O'Hara 12/15/86	
	Donna Murphy 12/22/86	
John Jasper	Howard McGillin	David Burt
Rosa Bud	Patti Cohenour	Patti Cohenour
	Karen Culliver 8/16/86	
Helena Landless	Jana Schneider	Marilyn Cutts
	Alison Fraser 8/13/86	
Neville Landless	John Herrera	Mark Ryan

Note: In New York only, title officially changed to *Drood* on November 13, 1986.

ON YOUR TOES

	New York 3/6/83	*Los Angeles 7/25/86*
Vera Baronova	Natalia Makarova	Natalia Makarova
Junior Dolan	Lara Teeter	Lara Teeter
Sergei Alexandrovitch	George S. Irving	Michael Kermoyan
Peggy Porterfield	Dina Merrill	Dina Merrill
Frankie Frayne	Christine Andreas	Kathleen Rowe McAllen
Konstantine Morrosine	George de la Pena	George de la Pena

Note: For New York cast changes and touring cast, see page 420 of *The Best Plays of 1983–1984;* for London cast see page 419 of *The Best Plays of 1984–1985.*

A RAISIN IN THE SUN

	New York 8/14/86	*Washington 11/16/86*
Ruth Younger	Starletta DuPois	Starletta DuPois
Travis Younger	Richard Habersham	Kimble Joyner
	Kimble Joyner	
	(alternating)	
Lena Younger	Olivia Cole	Esther Rolle

SOCIAL SECURITY

	New York	*Palm Beach 3/3/87*
Barbara Kahn	Marlo Thomas Maureen Anderman 11/25/86 Marilu Henner 2/10/87	Lucie Arnaz
David Kahn	Ron Silver Cliff Gorman 11/25/86	Laurence Luckinbill

SONG & DANCE

	New York 9/18/85
Emma	Bernadette Peters Betty Buckley 10/6/86
Joe	Christopher d'Amboise Victor Barbee 1/6/86 Christopher d'Amboise 3/31/86 Victor Barbee 6/23/86

SWEET CHARITY

	New York 4/27/86
Charity	Debbie Allen Ann Reinking 10/28/86

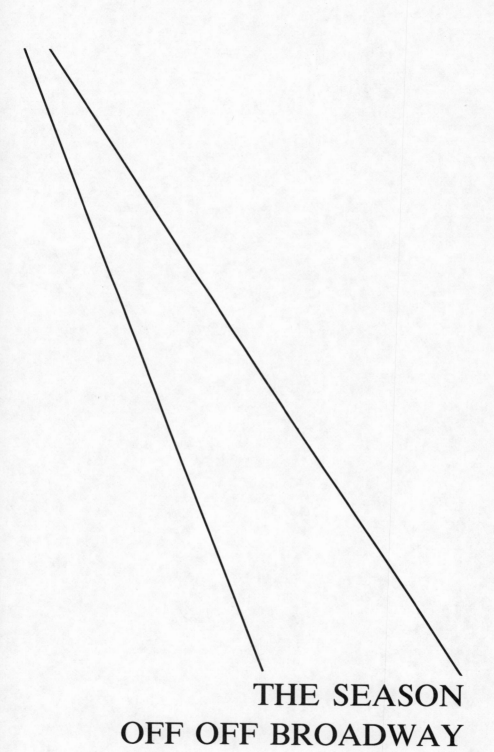

THE SEASON
OFF OFF BROADWAY

OFF OFF BROADWAY

By Mel Gussow

THE DEATH of Charles Ludlam ended one of off off Broadway's most illustrious careers. For 20 years—from his early work, such as *Bluebeard*, through his final play, *The Artificial Jungle*—Ludlam was the creative force behind the Ridiculous Theatrical Company. As director, playwright, actor and designer, he discovered new comic life in the detritus of popular culture. He was a revitalizer and also an interpretative artist. As much as anyone, he helped make off off Broadway a vital part of the American theater. Ludlam's death reminded us of his considerable achievement and of the ephemeral quality of much that is most important in this arena. None of his plays was recorded, although several have been published. One hopes that, increasingly, other artists will do the works of Charles Ludlam. After a brief initial run, off off Broadway plays disappear, perhaps to resurface on tour or in revival in New York.

This OOB season was, in fact, notable for its revivals. Celebrating the 25th anniversary of her LaMama theater, Ellen Stewart reprised several past successes, including *Fragments of a Greek Trilogy*, the Andrei Serban–Elizabeth Swados exploration of Greek tragedy, and Fernando Arrabal's desert island duet, *The Architect and the Emperor of Assyria*, in Tom O'Horgan's bold production (a new play by Arrabal, *The Red Madonna*, opened at INTAR, but with less success).

Mabou Mines, one of our most durable experimental theater companies, returned with a season of revivals, including Lee Breuer's *Prelude to Death in Venice*, the film version of JoAnne Akalaitis's *Dead End Kids*, and, the chef d'oeuvre, *Cold Harbor*. This Bill Raymond–Dale Worsley play was a fascinating study of Ulysses S. Grant, approaching him as a figure on exhibition in a museum. In the course of the show, Grant (played by Bill Raymond) came teeteringly to life and led us through his wars, both on and off the battlefield. Mabou Mines also offered the premieres of Frederick Neumann's stark visualization of Samuel Beckett's prose piece *Worstward Ho* and Greg Mehrten's soap operatic *It's a Man's World*.

Another important event was Richard Foreman's new play *Film Is Evil, Radio Is Good* (cited as an outstanding production). This was, in part, a return to Foreman's Ontological-Hysteric Theater past, a chamber epic presented in collaboration with the New York University Tisch School of the Arts. *Film Is Evil* was a multimedia battle between the visual and the aural for conceptual supremacy. John Jesurun, who has made an artistic livelihood out of combining theater, film and video techniques, was represented by *White Water* (theater and video) and *Black Maria* (theater and film). In the latter instance, he entirely eliminated live actors. This was a film on stage, surrounding an audience with cinematic

Cited by Mel Gussow as Outstanding OOB Productions

Right, John Kelly in *Pass the Blutwurst, Bitte* which he also wrote and directed—"An impressionistic canvas about the life and work of the painter Egon Schiele"

Below, the puppet figures of Madame Curie and Charles Darwin in Theodora Skipitares's *Defenders of the Code,* with music by Virgil Moorefield and lyrics by Andrea Balis—"Theodora Skipitares is one of a number of puppeteers investigating the outer limits of this performance art."

Above, David Patrick Kelly (*left,* with side of beef) Lola Pashalinski (*center,* in V-necked black gown), Kate Manheim (*foreground,* in white lab coat) and others in Richard Foreman's *Film Is Evil: Radio Is Good*—"A chamber epic. A multimedia battle between the visual and the aural for conceptual supremacy"

images, with characters conversing with one another across the heads of theatergoers.

Theodora Skipitares is one of a number of puppeteers, investigating the outer limits of this performance art, moving it very far from its position as an entertainment for children. Miss Skipitares has always been intrigued by history and science, and in her puppet musical *Defenders of the Code* (cited as an outstanding production) she set Darwin dancing, along with Mendel, Madame Curie and others in an animated educational journey. Her close collaborators included Andrea Balis (as lyricist), Virgil Moorefield (as composer) and a team of finely trained puppeteers. Janie Geiser, a talented Atlanta-based puppeteer-experimentalist, also visited New York this year with *Blue Night*.

In *Pass the Blutwurst, Bitte* (cited as an outstanding production), the performance artist John Kelly created an impressionistic canvas about the life and work of the painter Egon Schiele. Using himself as a stand-in for this demonic artist, he simulated and interpreted his paintings while also placing him within the cultural context of Vienna. *Pass the Blutwurst, Bitte* could be regarded as an enlightening footnote to Martha Clarke's *Vienna: Lusthaus* of last season.

Miss Clarke, herself, returned with *The Hunger Artist*, an evocation of Franz

Kafka in words and images, drawing upon the writer's letters as well as his stories, filtered through the conceptualist's imagination. The actor Anthony Holland portrayed a semblance of Kafka, in a company that also included Paola Styron and Rob Besserer. As in her previous work, Miss Clarke was greatly abetted by Robert Israel's set design, Paul Gallo's lighting and Richard Peaslee's music. Robert Wilson had two works on in New York this season, the Rome section of *The Civil Wars* (more of an opera than a play) and *The Knee Plays*, the entr'actes uniting the various divisions of this epic—and the more interesting of the two dramatic works. *The Knee Plays*, which played 4 performances at Alice Tully Hall, was a fanciful exercise in the art of transformation, featuring, among other things, choreographed lighting effects. *The Civil Wars* section was presented in the Brooklyn Academy of Music's Next Wave Festival, a worthy annual series having something of an off season (with *Social Amnesia* and Ping Chong's *The Angels of Swedenborg*, the play that covered the stage with a carpet of white turkey feathers).

Clowning continued to be an important element of New York theater, as represented by *Le Cirque Imaginaire*, a vest-pocket circus devised and performed by Victoria Chaplin and Jean Baptiste Thierrée. Miss Chaplin is a superb mime, in the tradition of her father, Charles Chaplin. Huck Snyder's *Circus* was an even smaller, confetti-size circus, in which actors pretended to be wild animals. An Australian troupe, *Los Trios Ringbarkus*, carried clowning in the opposite direction—with a broad, boisterous slapstick. A Home for Contemporary Art joined Dance Theater Workshop, P.S. 122 and the Kitchen as a space for avant-garde theater, presenting, among other shows, an evening of one-act vignettes by Stuart Sherman and Georg Osterman's *No Damn Good*, a lampoon of Broadway's *The Bad Seed*, done in Ridiculous style.

Though the most adventurous work off off Broadway continues be in performance art, there were, as usual, a number of interesting new plays, including the co-winners of this year's Susan Smith Blackburn Prize—Mary Gallagher's *How to Say Goodbye* (a sensitive study of a mother trying to cope with a disabled child) and Ellen McLaughlin's *A Narrow Bed* (a mood-filled reflection on the idealism of the 1960s). Another Blackburn finalist, Milcha Sanchez-Scott's *Roosters* was a provocative study of a family in crisis.

Mama Drama (at the Ensemble Studio Theater) was a spirited collage of sketches about women's problems, while Conrad Bromberg's revised version of *Dream of a Blacklisted Actor* was an unsubtle account of the effects of McCarthyism. The Ensemble once again honored the art of the one-act with its spring Marathon of new short plays, which presented, notably, Romulus Linney's *April Snow*, Richard Greenberg's *The Author's Voice*, Keith Reddin's *The Big Squirrel* and Frank D. Gilroy's *Real to Reel*. The WPA showcased a series of small naturalistic works, including Israel Horovitz's *North Shore Fish* (a close look at women working in a Massachusetts fish processing plant) and Robert Harling's *Steel Magnolias* (life in a Southern beauty parlor), which moved into an off-Broadway engagement in June. Brooklyn's BACA theater introduced New Yorkers to the work of a talented newcomer, Allan Havis, with his surrealistic *Mink Sonata*. Paul Selig's *Terminal Bar* was a "site-specific" end-of-the-world play performed in an abandoned Soho showroom. Alan Bowne's *Beirut* approached an AIDS-caused apocalypse as a science fiction yarn (*Beirut*, running 59 minutes, moved off Broadway in June). The Soho Rep imported two politically based English plays, David Lan's *Sergeant Ola and His Followers* (about a native cult that worships cargo) and Stephen Lowe's *The Ragged Trousered Philanthropists* (an environmentally staged study of the English labor movement).

On other stages, the English were represented by Arnold Wesker's *Annie Wobbler*, a one-actress jaunt through feminism, and Terry Johnson's *Insignificance*, which imagined a romantic meeting between Marilyn Monroe and Albert Einstein. *Insignificance* opened Geoffrey Sherman's first season as artistic director of the Hudson Guild, the theater that later offered *Moms*, Alice Childress's amusing play about the comedienne Moms Mabley, and a musical version of the serial-killer movie, *No Way to Treat a Lady*.

Tisa Chang's Pan Asian Repertory Theater presented its customary diversity of Asian-American plays, including *The Imposter* from China, *Wha . . . i, Whai, a Long Long Time Ago* from Korea and *Shogun Macbeth*, a Japanese reinterpretation of Shakespeare, with Ernest Abuba giving a visceral performance in the title role.

Musically the season was a disappointment, with *Bar Mitzvah Boy,* an Americanization of a British show with a score by Jule Styne, and *Shipwrecked Sofa*, a whimsical musicalization of nonsense rhymes by Mervyn Peake, conceived by many of the people who created the admirable *Goblin Market*.

A late-season high point was Joseph Chaikin's production of Eugene Ionesco's *The Bald Soprano*, with *The Leader* as a curtain-raiser. As co-directed by Nancy Gabor, this production represented both a return of Mr. Chaikin as an active force in New York experimental theater and a rare, expert revival by this influential absurdist.

PLAYS PRODUCED
OFF OFF BROADWAY

AND ADDITIONAL PRODUCTIONS

Here is a comprehensive sampling of off-off-Broadway and other experimental or peripheral 1986–87 productions in New York, compiled by Camille Croce. There is no definitive "off-off-Broadway" area or qualification. To try to define or regiment it would be untrue to its fluid, exploratory purpose. The listing below of hundreds of works produced by more than 110 OOB groups and others is as inclusive as reliable sources will allow, however, and takes in all leading Manhattan-based, new-play-producing, English-language organizations.

The more active and established producing groups are identified in **bold face type,** in alphabetical order, with artistic policies and the name of the managing director(s) given whenever these are a matter of record. Each group's 1986–87 schedule is listed with play titles in CAPITAL LETTERS. Often these are works-in-progress with changing scripts, casts and directors, sometimes without an engagement of record (but an opening or early performance date is included when available).

Many of these off-off-Broadway groups have long since outgrown a merely experimental status and are offering programs which are the equal in professionalism and quality (and in some cases the superior) of anything in the New York theater, with special contractual arrangements like the showcase code, letters of agreement (allowing for longer runs and higher admission prices than usual) and, closer to the edge of the commercial theater, a so-called "mini-contract." In the list below, all available data on opening dates, performance numbers and major production and acting credits (almost all of them Equity members) is included in the entries of these special-arrangement offerings.

A large selection of lesser-known groups and other shows that made appearances off off Broadway during the season appears under the "Miscellaneous" heading at the end of this listing.

Amas Repertory Theater. Dedicated to bringing all people, regardless of race, creed, color or economic background, together through the creative arts. Rosetta LeNoire, founder and artistic director.

16 performances each

HOT SAKE . . . WITH A PINCH OF SALT (musical) book and lyrics by Carol Baker and Lana Stein, based on Leonard Spigelgass's *A Majority of One*; music, Jerome I. Goldstein. October 23, 1986. Director, William Martin; choreographer, Audrey Tischler; scenery, Frank J. Boros; lighting, Ken Lapham; costumes, Howard Behar; musical director, Neal Tate. With Laurie Katzmann, Alvin K.U. Lum, Anne Allgood, Jim Donahoe, Gordon Kupperstein, Mary Rocco, Steven Steiner, Marzetta Tate, Kirby Wahl, Ann Yen.

DAZY (musical) book by Allan Knee; music by Lowell E. Mark; lyrics and concept by Norman Simon. February 12, 1987. Director, Philip Rose; choreographer, Clarence Teeters; scenery, Clarke Dunham; lighting, Ken Billington; costumes, Gail Cooper-Hecht; musical director, Jeffrey Roy. With Leah Hocking, Jack Landron, Tom Flagg, Peter Gunther, Joie Gallo, Philip Carrubba,

Norman Golden, Peter Lind Harris, Denise LeDonne, Ken McMullen, Sel Vitella, LaTonya Welch, Teresa Wolf, Wendy Worth.

PRIME TIME (musical) book by R.A. Shiomi; music and lyrics by Johnny Brandon. April 9, 1987. Director, Marvin Gordon; scenery and costumes, Vicki Davis; lighting, David Segal; musical director, Joyce Brown. With Kevin John Gee, Elly Barbour, George Constant, Marcia Dadds, Rommel Hyacinth, Valerie Lau-Kee, Eric Riley, Eddie Simon, Patricia Ward, Helena-Joyce Wright, Peter Yoshida.

American Place Theater. In addition to the regular off-Broadway season, cabaret and other special projects are presented. Wynn Handman, director, Julia Miles, associate director.

The Women's Project

CONSEQUENCE (14). By Kat Smith. March 29, 1987. Director, Alma Becker; scenery, Robert Perdziola; lighting, Anne Militello; costumes, Judy Dearing. With Didi Conn, Tino Juarez, Geraldine Librandi, Joan MacIntosh.

American Humorists Series

A GIRL'S GUIDE TO CHAOS (193). By Cynthia Heimel. November 5, 1986. Director, Wynn Handman; scenery, Brian Martin; lighting, Brian MacDevitt; costumes, Deborah Shaw. With Debra Jo Rupp, Mary Portser, Rita Jenrette, Eric Booth, Celeste Mancinelli, F.D. Herrick.

JAMES THURBER KINTYPES (one-man show) (12+). Works by James Thurber. May 19, 1987. Director, Wynn Handman. With John Valentine. (Part of the "Laugh at Lunch" series)

American Theater of Actors. Dedicated to providing a creative atmosphere for new American playwrights, actors, and directors. James Jennings, artistic director.

AMERICAN PLACE THEATER—Geraldine Librandi, Didi Conn and Joan MacIntosh in *Consequence* by Kat Smith, a production of The Women's Project

16 performances each

HENRY V by William Shakespeare. June 4, 1986. Directed by James Jennings; with Robert Blue, Tom Major, Joy Saylor, Jane Culley.

COMEBACK. By Claris Nelson. June 18, 1986. Director, Roy Steinberg; scenery and lighting, Shep Pamplin. With Keith Burns, David Hayes Andrews, Jolene Carroll.

SOME THINGS YOU REMEMBER. By Joseph MacDonald. July 23, 1986. Director, Barbara Nicoll. With Erin McLaughlin, J.J. Clark, Alison Byrne.

FIRST COUSINS. By Donald Kvares. August 6, 1986. Director, James Jennings; scenery and lighting, Shep Pamplin. With Myra Robbins, James Lorinz.

THE TEMPEST. By William Shakespeare. September 10, 1986. Directed by James Jennings; with Robert Blue, Tom Major, Pamela Welsh, Harold Simpson.

NORMAL DOESN'T MEAN PERFECT. By Don Gordon. September 17, 1986. Director, Bob Hoffmann. With Joy Saylor, Tom Ryan, Teresa Willis.

AFTERNOONS AT WARATAH. Written and directed by Jean Sterrett. September 24, 1986. Choreographer, Monica Kelly; scenery, Jane Sablow; lighting, Beau Kennedy; costumes, Shep Pamplin. With Nadine Browning, Reb Buxtom, Steve Daley, Ruth Hartung.

ABORTION? By Dick Zylstra. October 22, 1986. Director, Diane Van Beuren. With Perry Bernard, Susan Chandler, Elizabeth Karr, Lori Gittelson.

THE HOLY JUNKIE. By John Quinn. November 6, 1986. Director, James Jennings; scenery and lighting, Shep Pamplin. With Keith Burns, Jane Culley, Leverne Summers.

THE LAST WEEKEND. By E. Sharland-Jones. November 12, 1986. Director, James Jennings; scenery, Shep Pamplin; lighting, Beau Kennedy. With Will Buchanan, Barbara Ambrose, Shelley Conger.

WINDMILLS. Written and directed by Daniel Kalmann. December 26, 1986. Costumes, Irene Feldsher. With Tom Christy, Florence Galperin, Garth Miano, Stan Winston.

BEYOND ILLUSION. Written and directed by Mary Brendle. January 7, 1987. Scenery, Cynthia McLean; lighting, Margaret Fox. With Janet Aspinwall, Robert Blue, Will Buchanan.

ICE EATERS. By Nicholas Wenckheim. January 21, 1987. Director, Shep Pamplin. With Stephen John, Barbara Ambrose.

COSMIC CRAZINESS. By Michael Racanelli. January 28, 1987. Director, Shep Pamplin. With Barbara Ambrose, Stephen John, Curtis LeFevre, James Lorinz.

FLOWERS FOR MISS EPSTEIN. By Irving Leitner. February 11, 1987. Director, Judy Ramakers. With Claire Curtin, Richard Leitner, Eleanor Burke, Susanne Hayes.

DAUGHTERS OF JERUSALEM WEEPING. By James Crafford. March 4, 1987. Director, Alanna Fearing. With Michelle Cain, Bob Crafford, Roger Kabler, James Crafford.

ACCEPTANCE. Written and directed by David Lessoff. March 25, 1987. With Shannon Sorin, Richard Stockton, Robert Michaels, Shep Pamplin.

DESIGNER GENES. By Richmond Shepard and John Sinclair. April 1, 1987. Director, Douglas Sprigg. With Lee Beltzer, Sarah Watchman, Mitchell Calder.

INCONCEIVABLE. By Joseph Krawczyk. April 22, 1987. Director, James Jennings; scenery and lighting, Tom Major. With James Judy, Karen Flannery, Joy Saylor, Nick Giangiulio.

MOVING TARGETS. By Peter Chelnik. May 13, 1987. Director, James Jennings. With Jack Rodgerson, Carolyn Tenney, Mark Kiely, Mary Huner.

Circle Repertory Projects-in-Progress. Developmental programs for new plays. Marshall W. Mason, artistic director.

4 performances each

LIKE A LION by Rustam Imbrahimbekov. September 22, 1986. Directed by B. Rodney Marriott; with Michael Ayr, Lisa Emery, James Rice, Richard Seff, Ben Siegler, Elise Thoron, Angela Workman.

CAVE LIFE by David Steven Rappoport. October 13, 1986. Directed by Margaret Denithorne; with Susan Greenhill, James Goodwin Rice, Bruce McCarty, Bobo Lewis, Lisa Emery, Jack Fris, Natalya Sokeil.

NASTY LITTLE SECRETS by Lanie Robertson. January 19, 1987. Directed by B. Rodney Marriott; with Rob Gomes, Ken Kliban, Richard Seff, Michael Warren Powell.

EL SALVADOR by Rafael Lima. March 9, 1987. Directed by Mark Ramont; with Peter Guttmacher, John Bishop, Bruce McCarty, Michael Ayr, Stephen Singer, Cotter Smith, Erica McFarquhar.

RIGHT BEHIND THE FLAG by Kevin Heela. May 18, 1987. Directed by Robert Fuhrmann; with Danton Stone, Bruce McCarty, Kelly Connell, Tom Celli, Suzy Morris, Michael Warren Powell, Eddie Jones.

Ensemble Studio Theater. Membership organization of playwrights, actors, directors and designers dedicated to supporting individual theater artists and developing new works for the stage. Over 200 projects each season, initiated by E.S.T. members. Curt Dempster, artistic director.

DREAM OF A BLACKLISTED ACTOR (33). By Conrad Bromberg. December 1, 1986. Director, Jack Gelber; scenery, Steve Saklad; lighting, Karl Haas; costumes, Deborah Shaw. With Ryan Cutrona, Ned Eisenberg, Rose Gregorio, Michael Kaufman, Joseph McKenna, Frederica Meister, Barry Primus, Victor Raider-Wexler, Sam Schacht, Jodi Thelen.

CLEVELAND AND HALF-WAY BACK (18). By Leslie Lyles. February 10, 1987. Director, James Hammerstein; scenery, Richard Harmon; lighting, Tina Ann Byers; costumes, David Woolard. With Julie Garfield, Bruce MacVittie, Rebecca Nelson, Cynthia Nixon, Lola Pashalinski, Keith Reddin.

MAMA DRAMA (34). By Leslie Ayvazian, Donna Daley, Christine Farrell, Marianna Houston, Rita Nachtmann, Anne O'Sullivan and Ann Sachs. April 2, 1987. Director, Pamela Berlin; scenery, Philipp Jung; lighting, Jackie Manassee; costumes, Lindsay W. Davis. With Leslie Ayvazian, Christine Farrell, Rita Nachtmann, Anne O'Sullivan, Anne Sachs.

MARATHON '87 (festival of one-act plays) (48). THE ONE ABOUT THE GUY IN THE BAR by Ernest Thompson, directed by Curt Dempster; THE AUTHOR'S VOICE by Richard Greenberg, directed by Evan Yionoulis; THE LAST OUTPOST AT THE EDGE OF THE WORLD by Stuart Spencer, directed by Shirley Kaplan; A MILLION DOLLAR GLASS OF WATER by Anthony McKay, directed by Joel Bernstein; LADY OF FATIMA by Edward Allan Baker, directed by Risa Bramon; DINAH WASHINGTON IS DEAD by Kermit Frazier, directed by Fred Tyson; A RIPE BANANA by Jennifer Lombard, directed by W.H. Macy; AFTER SCHOOL SPECIAL by Keith Reddin, directed by Billy Hopkins; ALL FOR CHARITY by John Patrick Shanley, directed by Willie Reale; APRIL SNOW by Romulus Linney, directed by David Margulies; WAKING WOMEN by Cassandra Medley, directed by Irving Vincent; BAD BLOOD written and directed by Peter Maloney; REAL TO REEL by Frank D. Gilroy, directed by Curt Dempster. May 6–June 15, 1987.

Equity Library Theater. Actors' Equity sponsors a series of revivals each season as showcases for the work of its actor-members. George Wojtasik, managing director.

RELATIVE VALUES by Noël Coward. September 25, 1986. Directed by William Hopkins; with Ann Ducati, Ronald Wendschuh, Rica Martens, Mitchell Sugarman, Marla Johnson, Dennis Pfister.

THE PAJAMA GAME (musical) book by George Abbott and Richard Bissell, music and lyrics by Richard Adler and Jerry Ross. October 30, 1986. Directed by Bill Herndon; with Rick Porter, Connie Baker, Michael Piontek, Ann Fleuchaus, Daniel Marcus, Norma Crawford.

NIGHT WATCH by Lucille Fletcher. December 4, 1986. Directed by Licia Colombi; with Marlena Lustik, Walter Hook, Estelle Kemler, Edward Joseph, Herbert DuVal, Alison Edwards, Kevin Hagan, Mary McTigue, Richard Dahlia.

TAKE ME ALONG (musical) book by Joseph Stein and Robert Russell, based on Eugene O'Neill's *Ah, Wilderness!*; music and lyrics by Bob Merrill. January 8, 1987. Directed by Richard Casper; with Jase Draper, Tom Souhrada, Alisa Carroll, Richard Voigts, Mary Gant, Kathryn McAteer, Tony Carlin.

THE LITTLE FOXES by Lillian Hellman. February 12, 1987. Directed by Thomas Edward West; with Juanita Walsh, Mary Ed Porter, Gordon G. Jones, James Davies, Ed Easton, Frederick Walters, Gillian Ruth Hemstead, Ward Asquith.

TOO MANY GIRLS (musical) book by George Marion Jr., music by Richard Rodgers, lyrics by Lorenz Hart. March 12, 1987. Directed by Stephen G. Hults; with Carol Dilley, Teri Gibson, Lynne Kolber, Pamela Khoury, Richard Waterhouse, Chan Harris, Robert A. Woronoff, William Reynolds.

MISALLIANCE by George Bernard Shaw. April 16, 1987. Directed by Geoffrey Hitch; with Max Gulack, Lori Bezahler, Mark Diekmann, Aaron Lustig, John C. Talbot, Patricia Mertens, Don Sobolik, Craig Dudley, Elizabeth C. Loftus.

WISH YOU WERE HERE (musical) book by Arthur Kober and Joshua Logan, based on Arthur Kober's *Having Wonderful Time*; music and lyrics by Harold Rome. May 14, 1987. Directed by Don Price; with Larry Francer, Charles Mandracchia, Kari Nicolaisen, Sean Hopkins, Doug Tompos, Tia Riebling.

Hudson Guild Theater. Presents plays in their New York, American or world premieres. Geoffrey Sherman, producing director, James Abar, associate director.

28 performances each

INSIGNIFICANCE. By Terry Johnson. October 15, 1986. Director, Geoffrey Sherman; scenery and lighting, Paul Wonsek; costumes, Pamela Scofield. With Yusef Bulos, Lou Bedford, Polly Draper, Keith Langsdale.

PANTOMIME. By Derek Walcott. December 11, 1986. Director, Kay Matschullat; scenery, Rosario Provenza; lighting, Robert Wierzel; costumes, Pamela Peterson; musical director, Deborah R. Lapidus; musical staging, Edward Love. With Charles S. Dutton, Edmond Genest.

MOMS. By Alice Childress. February 4, 1987. Music and lyrics, Nathan Woodard and Alice Childress; director, Walter Dallas; choreographer, Andy Torres; scenery, Rosario Provenza; lighting, Robert Wierzel; costumes, Judy E. Dearing; musical director, Grenoldo Frazier. With Clarice Taylor, Grenoldo Frazier, S. Epatha Merkerson.

FESTIVAL '87 (readings and workshops to celebrate Black History Month): THE ROAD by Zakes Mda, directed by James Abar; HOT SAUCE by Karmyn Lott, directed by Seret Scott; THE CHOSEN by Clement J. Sumner, directed by Randy Frazier; TELEBRAIN by Billy Graham, directed by Sutton Bacote; HANG IN THERE! by the Chameleons, directed by Roni Dengel; FRIED CHICKEN AND INVISIBILITY by OyamO, directed by Peter Wallace; THE LAST PASSION PLAY by Kenshaka Ali, directed by Michael Rogers; TO DIE FOR GRENADA written and directed by Derek Walcott; SEPIA TONE: THE LIFE AND TIMES OF OSCAR MICHEAUX by John E. Byrd, directed by Carl Arnold; WILD MILK by Darrah Cloud, directed by Steven Ramay. February 10–26, 1987.

CRACKWALKER. By Judith Thompson. April 1, 1987. Directors, James Abar and Judith Thompson; scenery and lighting, Paul Wonsek; costumes, Karen Hummel. With Elizabeth Berridge, Matt Craven, Frances Fisher, Graham Greene, Joe Mantello.

NO WAY TO TREAT A LADY (musical) book, music and lyrics by Douglas J. Cohen, based on William Goldman's novel. May 27, 1987. Director, Jack Hofsiss; scenery, David Jenkins; lighting, Beverly Emmons; costumes, Michael Kaplan; musical director, Uel Wade. With Stephen Bogardus, Liz Callaway, June Gable, Peter Slutsker.

INTAR. Innovative cultural center for the Hispanic American community of New York focusing on the art of theater. Max Ferra, artistic director, Dennis Ferguson-Acosta, managing director.

THE RED MADONNA OR A DAMSEL FOR A GORILLA (27). Written and directed by Fernando Arrabal, translated by Lynne Alvarez. November 19, 1986. Scenery, David Peterson; lighting, John Gisondi; costumes, Donna Zakowska. With Anna Larreta, Ralph Marrero, Roger Rignack, Francisco Rivela, Elizabeth Ruiz, Bina Sharif, Frank Torren.

ROOSTERS (28). By Milcha Sanchez-Scott. March 11, 1987. Director, Jackson Phippin; scenery, Loy Arcenas; lighting, John Gisondi; costumes, C.L. Hundley. With Suzanne Costallos, Joaquim De Almeida, Jonathan Del Arco, Sara Erde, Albert Farrar, Ilka Tanya Payan. (Co-produced by the New York Shakespeare Festival.)

Interart Theater. Committed to producing innovative work by women theater artists and to introducing New York audiences to a bold range of theater that is non-traditional in form or theme. Margot Lewitin, artistic director.

WOMANTALK (15). By Sandra Fae Dietrick. September 2, 1986. Director, Olivia Negrón; scenery, Todd Lewey; lighting, video and sound, Larry G. Decle. With Jamie Cass, Carole Garcia, Kiya Ann Joyce, Essene R, Socorro Santiago, Julie DeLaurier, Ernestine M. Johnston, Bina Sharif, June Squibb. (Produced in association with C & L Collective.)

INTERART—Rob Erbert and Shirley Knight in *The Depot* by Eve Ensler

THE DEPOT (21). By Eve Ensler. March 3, 1987. Director, Joanne Woodward; scenery, Nina Jordan; lighting, Larry G. Decle. With Shirley Knight, Rob Erbert, Peter Gregory. (Produced in association with Center for Defense Information.)

PATIENCE AND SARAH (25+). By Isabel Miller, adapted from her novel. April 1, 1987. Director, Lois Weaver; scenery and lighting, Joni Wong; costumes, Susan Young; music, Shaz Nassauer. With Lois Weaver, Chris Brandt, Dan Crozier, Deborah Margolin, Peggy Shaw, Debra Miller, Sabrina Artel. (Co-produced by Split Britches.)

PATIENCE AND SARAH extended its run in rotating repertory with DRESS SUITS FOR HIRE by Holly Hughes. June 10, 1987 (17).

LaMama Experimental Theater Club (ETC). A busy workshop for experimental theater of all kinds. Ellen Stewart, founder and artistic director.

Schedule included:

RETURN. By Roger Babb. June 5, 1986. Music, Blue Gene Tyranny. With the Otrabanda Company.

AZAX/ATTRA II (performance art). By Sussan Deihim and Richard Horowitz. June 29, 1986. Director, Sussan Deihim.

CARMILLA: A VAMPIRE TALE. Adapted and directed from J.S. LeFanu's novella by Wilford Leach; music, Ben Johnston. October 1, 1986. With Nancy Heikin, Margaret Benczak, Ken Jennings, Don Harrington, Camille Tibaldeo, Audrey Levine.

SOLE SISTERS. Directed by Constance Valis-Hill. October 16, 1986.

THE DARK AND MR. STONE III: MURDER IN THE MUMMY'S TOMB. By Paul Foster. November 5, 1986. Director, Stephen Ahern; scenery, Susan Haskins; lighting, Howard Thies; costumes, Sharon Lynch; music and musical direction, Alkiviades Steriopoulos. With Jack Di Monte, James Lally, Steven Andresen, Lea Floden, Ken Gold, Peter Matthey, Robert Michael Tomlinson, Robin Westphal.

THE ARCHITECT AND THE EMPEROR OF ASSYRIA by Fernando Arrabal. November 12, 1986. Directed and music by Tom O'Horgan; with Alexi Mylonas, Ray Contreras, M.A. Whiteside.

ETIQUETTE (musical revue) book and lyrics by William M. Hoffman; music by John Braden. November 13, 1986. Director, John Vaccaro.

BETTY AND THE BLENDERS written and composed by Ellen Maddow, directed by Paul Zimet; LIFE SIMULATOR by Paul Zimet, music by Harry Mann, directed by Roger Babb. December 3, 1986. With The Talking Band.

FRAGMENTS OF A GREEK TRILOGY: MEDEA, ELECTRA AND THE TROJAN WOMEN conceived and directed by Andrei Serban; music by Elizabeth Swados. December 29, 1986. With Jane Lind, Priscilla Smith, Karen Evans-Kandel, William Duff-Griffin, Aneza Papadopoulos.

LUST AND THE UNICORN. Adapted by Osvaldo Rodriguez and Mark Waren from S. and S. Charnas's play *Body Work*. January 5, 1987. Director, Osvaldo Rodriguez; scenery, Paul Ginel, Brian Glover and Marcus Cerda; lighting, Joanna Schielke; costumes, Margo La Zaro. With Christiane McKenna, David Phillips, Brian Glover.

SAFE SEX. By Harvey Fierstein. January 8, 1987. Director, Eric Concklin.

CIRCUS. Conceived, directed and designed by Huck Snyder and realized in collaboration with John Kelly, Beatricia Sagar and Wendy Copp. February 5, 1987. With Kyle De Camp, Michael Gregor, Marleen Menard, Joseph Pupello, Kennon B. Raines, Stephen Tashjian. (Produced in association with Creative Time.)

MARY STUART. Based on Dacia Maraini's text; created, directed and performed by Denise Stoklos; translated by Maurice McClelland and Isla Jay. February 19, 1987.

TRES CEPAS (work-in-progress) by Edgar White. March 16, 1987. Directed by Basil Wallace.

THE SLEEPLESS CITY. By Jean Tardieu. April 4, 1987. Director, Francoise Kourilsky; environment, Jun Maeda; lighting, Watoku Ueno; costumes, Carol Ann Pelletier; music, Genji Ito. With James L. King, Philippe Ambrosini, Miguel Braganza, Alexi Mylonas, Laurence Gleason, Jennifer Rohn. (Co-produced by Ubu Repertory Theater.)

AN EVENING WITH FRANK MAYA (performance art). April 6, 1987.

DIAL 'M' FOR MODEL (cabaret musical) by John Epperson. April 7, 1987. Director, Michael Nee; scenery, Max Di Corsia; costumes, Pamela Goldman. With John Epperson, Stephen Pell, Edgar Oliver, Mark Oates.

BLACK MARIA. Written and directed by John Jesurun. April 8, 1987.

YAP THAW and DEAD RECKONING (one-act plays). Written and performed by Steve Buscemi and Mark Boone Jr. April 30, 1987. Director, T. Weir Wright.

PROPAGANDA. Written and directed by Matthew Maguire. May 1, 1987. Music, Fred Frith.

PUNCH. Written and directed by Leonardo Shapiro, adapted from a transcript of the *Punch and Judy* puppet shows. May 2, 1987.

HEIMLICH VARIATIONS and ORANGE GROVE. By Roger Babb and Sidney Goldfarb. May 20, 1987. Director, Roger Babb; music, Blue Gene Tyranny. With the Otrabanda Company.

A LEAP IN THE DARK. Written and directed by Timothy Buckley. May 27, 1987.

WE'RE MOVING ON (musical). By Ed Heath. May 29, 1987. Director, John McGee; choreography, Melvin Cooper. With Martha Baker, Ed Heath, Verna Day, Douglass Howell, John Carrington.

Lamb's Theater Company. Committed to developing and presenting new works in their most creative and delicate beginnings. Carolyn Rossi Copeland, executive director.

THE CHINA FISH (43). By David McFadzean. October 6, 1986. Director, Susan Gregg; scenery and lighting, Dale F. Jordan; costumes, Ellen Ryba. With Mary Armstrong, Leesa Bryte, Paul Collins, Clarke Gordon, Sally Prager, Leon Russom.

THE GIFT OF THE MAGI (musical) book and lyrics by Mark St. Germain, based on the O. Henry story, music and lyrics by Randy Courts. December 8, 1986. Directed by Carolyn Rossi Copeland; with Jeff Etjen, Sarah Knapp, Cissy Rebich, Clint Vriezelaar, John David Westfall, Ken Jennings.

THE WONDERFUL ICE CREAM SUIT (43). By Ray Bradbury. May 4, 1987. Director, Sonya Baehr; scenery, Bob Phillips; lighting, Jean Redmann; costumes, Susan Branch. With Cliff Batuello, Neal Bishop, Philip Carrubba, Emilio del Pozo, Jon Lerner, Yvonne Martin, Denise Nations, Luis Perez, Andres Rieloff, Anthony Ruiz, Ian Shupeck.

Mabou Mines. Theater collaborative whose work is a synthesis of motivational acting, narrative acting and mixed-media performance. Collective artistic leadership.

WORSTWARD HO! (20). By Samuel Beckett. September 10, 1986. Director, Frederick Neumann; scenery, John Arnone; lighting, Jennifer Tipton; costumes, Gabriel Berry; movement director, Terry O'Reilly. With Frederick Neumann, Terry O'Reilly, Honora Fergusson, Lute Ramblin'.

COLD HARBOR conceived, directed and performed by Bill Raymond; written by Dale Worsley. March 18, 1987.

A PRELUDE TO DEATH IN VENICE written and directed by Lee Breuer. March 25, 1987.

DEAD END KIDS: A STORY OF NUCLEAR POWER written and directed by JoAnne Akalaitis. April 20, 1987.

IT'S A MAN'S WORLD (34). By Greg Mehrten. May 27, 1987. Director, David Schweizer; scenery, Philipp Jung; lighting, Pat Dignan; costumes, Michael Kaplan. With Roger Guenveur Smith, Greg Mehrten, Paul Schmidt, Ruth Maleczech, Rhonda Aldrich, Dan Froot, Tom Cayler.

Manhattan Punch Line. New York's only theater company devoted to comedy. Steve Kaplan, artistic director, Craig Bowley, executive director.

EPIC PROPORTIONS (24). By Larry Coen and David Crane. November 24, 1986. Director, Paul Lazarus; scenery, William Barclay; lighting, Curt Ostermann; costumes, Mary L. Hayes. With Humbert Allen Astredo, Robert Blumenfeld, Michael Heintzman, Michael Murphy, Patricia Norcia, Paul O'Brien, Louise Roberts, Mark Kenneth Smaltz.

FESTIVAL OF ONE-ACT COMEDIES: WORDS, WORDS, WORDS by David Ives, directed by Fred Sanders; THE MOANER by Susan Sandler, directed by Pamela Berlin; THE DEEP END by Neil Cuthbert, directed by Charles Karchmer; CHILD'S PLAY by Peter Manos, directed by Lee Costello; ALMOST ROMANCE by Howard Morris, directed by Robin Saex; IN THE PARK by M.B. Valle, directed by Jason Buzas; THE GREENHOUSE KEEPER DIED OVER THE WEEKEND by Terri Wagener, directed by Gavin Cameron-Webb; THE TABLE-CLOTH OF TURIN by Ron Carlson, directed by Jason Buzas; IF WALLS COULD TALK by Lawrence Klavan, directed by Steve Kaplan. January 9–February 22, 1987. Scenery, Jane Clark, Christopher Stapleton and Kurt Rauchenberger; lighting, Mark Di Quinzio; costumes, Michael S. Schler and Lillian Pan. With Jo Anderson, Shirl Bernheim, Irving Burton, Bill Cohen, Ronnie Farer, Christopher Fields, Susan Greenhill, Terri Hawkes, Sally-Jane Heit, Ronald Hunter, Lee Kheel, Warren Keith, Michael Patterson, Oliver Platt, Leo Postrel, Victor Raider-Wexler, J. David Rozsa, Ron Lee Savin, Helen Slater, Fisher Stevens, Mary Testa, Robert Trebor, Robert Tyler, Roberta Wallach, Thomas Mills Wood.

SECOND AVENUE (24). By Allan Knee. April 25, 1987. Director, Steve Kaplan; scenery, Richard Harmon; lighting, Mark Di Quinzio; costumes, David Loveless; music, Barry Kleinbort. With Ned Eisenberg, David Lipman, Ralph Pochoda, Roberta Wallach, Max Jacobs, Nelson Avidon, Gerry Vichi, Natalie Priest, Julie Garfield, Buzz Bovshow.

BIGFOOT STOLE MY WIFE (24). By Ron Carlson. May 30, 1987. Director, Jason Buzas; scenery, Bobby Berg; lighting, Brian MacDevitt; costumes, Mimi Maxmen. With David Jaffe, Eddie Jones, Darren McGavin, Thomas Nahrwold, Hansford Rowe.

Music-Theater Group/Lenox Arts Center. Working with a core of artists in the development of ideas flowing in all directions from the participants, based in Lenox, Mass. and showcasing productions in New York City, Lyn Austin producer-director, Diane Wondisford, Mark Jones associate producing directors.

THE HUNGER ARTIST (68). Conceived and directed by Martha Clarke, based on Franz Kafka's writings; created with the company; adapted by Richard Greenberg. February 26, 1987. Scenery and costumes, Robert Israel; lighting, Paul Gallo; music, Richard Peaslee. With Rob Besserer, Brenda Currin, Anthony Holland, Jill Jaffe, David Jon, Bill Ruyle, Paola Styron.

New Dramatists. An organization devoted to playwrights; member writers may use the facilities for anything from private cold readings of their material to public script-in-hand readings. Thomas G. Dunn, executive director, David Milligan, program director, Susan Gregg, literary director.

Public readings

LOVE IN THE THIRD DEGREE by O-Lan Jones and Kathleen Cramer. October 6, 1986. Directed by Chris Silva; with Abra Bigham, Felicity LaFortune, Michelle Mais, O-Lan Jones, Kathleen Cramer, Ed Trotta, John Farrell, Willie Carpenter.
SWEETNESS by Glenn Lumsden. November 24, 1986. Directed by Alma Becker; with Deborah Stenard, Bruce Gooch, Susan Pellegrino, Wendy Barrie, Pirie MacDonald, Charlotte Colavin, Joel Rooks, James Goodwin Rice, Rick Casorla.

LAMB'S THEATER COMPANY—Sally Prager and Leon Russom in *The China Fish* by David McFadzean

GETTING THE MESSAGE ACROSS by Pedro Juan Pietri. December 4, 1986. Directed by Livia Perez; with John La Gioia, Laurie Klatscher, Lucien Douglas, John P. Connolly.

NIGHTMARE #9 by Mark Handley. December 15, 1986. Directed by Nick Flynn; with Steve Coats, William Verderber, Lachlan Macleay, James Mathers.

THE PERFECT LIGHT by Geraldine Sherman and Eduardo Machado. December 17, 1986. Directed by Joel Bishoff; with Jossie de Guzman, Joseph Adams, Evangelia Costantakos, Mark Nelson, Deborah Bremer, Judith Borne, Kate Flatland, Robert Jason, David Stamford, Spencer Beckwith, Berry Cooper, Brad Oscar, Mark Metcalf, Stan Tucker.

INSIDE OUT by Willy Holtzman. February 2, 1987. Directed by John Pynchon Holms; with Ellen Tobie, Adina Porter, Thomas Schall, Eriq Ki LaSalle. (Produced in cooperation with Theater for a New Audience.)

FINDING YOUR WAY by Eduardo Machado. February 9, 1987. Directed by Mark Lutwak; with Jossie de Guzman, Nickie Feliciano, Olga Merediz, Stanley W. Mathis, Carol Denise Clarke, Callan White, Jonathan Kline. (Produced in cooperation with Theater for a New Audience.)

NO PASSENGERS by Pedro Juan Pietri. March 18, 1987. Directed by Paul Ellis; with John Henry Redwood, Kathryn Markey, Susan Gosdick, Edward Henzel, Deborah Phelan, Dennis Pfister, Willy Corpus, Sean FitzSimons, Marcella Lowery.

ANNUAL FESTIVAL OF LUNCHTIME ONE-ACTS: THE MAN AT THE DOOR by Laura Cunningham. April 1, 1987. HEARTS by Willy Holtzman; directed by Robert Hall. April 15, 1987. SURE THING and SEVEN MENUES by David Ives; directed by Fred Sanders. April 22, 1987. THE ROAD TO RUIN by Richard Dresser; directed by John Pynchon Holms. April 29, 1987. VISITING HOURS ARE OVER by Pedro Juan Pietri; directed by Paul Ellis. May 6, 1987. THE WORLD AT ABSOLUTE ZERO by Sherry Kramer. May 13, 1987.

DOBBS IS DEAD by Sebastian Barry. April 13, 1987. Directed by Rhea Gaisner; with Ian O'Connell, David Strathairn, Alex Paul, John Seitz, Steven Coats, Maren Swenson.
BARGAINS by Jack Heifner. April 22, 1987. Directed by Diane Kamp; with Greg Grove, Brian Hinson, Margo Martindale, Lorraine Morgan, Sally Sockwell, Steven Weber.
PARADISE RE-LOST (musical) book by Charles F. (OyamO) Gordon; concept and music by Carman Moore; lyrics by Charles F. (OyamO) Gordon and Carman Moore. April 29, 1987. Directed by Thomas Gruenewald; with Nick Smith, Reg E. Cathey, Abra Bigham, William Campbell, Phillip Brown, Alice Cannon, Sheila Dabney, Philip Shultz, Lucile Ford, Mia Korf, Michael Oberlander, Robert Jason, Eleni Kelakos, Rhobye Wyatt, Lauri J. Taradash.
THREE VIEWS OF MT. FUJI by Ntozake Shangé. May 4, 1987. Directed by Laurie Carlos; with Ruben Hudson, Sue Parks, Karen Abercrombie, Nikos Valance, John Peck, Terria Joseph, Mia Katigbak, Verna Hampton, Nicky Paraiso, Bimbo Rivas, Luis Guzman, Alexander Bernstein, Samuel L. Jackson.
ALBANIAN SOFTSHOE by Mac Wellman. May 13, 1987. Directed by Gordon Edelstein; with Beth Browde, Jan Leslie Harding, John Seitz, Olek Krupa, Reg E. Cathey, Paul Zimet, William Duff-Griffin, Ryan Cutrona, Elzbieta Czyzewska, Michele Rigan.
VISIT FROM THE WILD by Anne Legault, translated by Jill MacDougall. May 28, 1987. Directed by Alma Becker; with Phyllis Somerville, Bradley Whitford, Kathy Danzer, Paul Vernet, Ben Siegler, Lisa Barnes, Steve Coats.

New Federal Theater. The Henry Street Settlement's training and showcase unit for playwrights, mostly black and Puerto Rican. Woodie King Jr., producer.

THE SOVEREIGN STATE OF BOOGEDY BOOGEDY (24). By Lonnie Carter. July 10, 1986. Director, Dennis Zacek; scenery, Bob Edmonds; lighting, William H. Grant III; costumes, Judy Dearing. With Reggie Montgomery, Helmar Augustus Cooper, Robert Jason, Angela Sargeant, Andre De Shields, Brian Thomas.

LILLIAN WALD: AT HOME ON HENRY STREET (one-woman show) (24). By Clare Coss. October 9, 1986. Director, Bryna Wortman; scenery, Richard Harmon; lighting, Jackie Manassee; costumes, Gail Cooper-Hecht. With Patricia Elliott.

TIME OUT OF TIME (24). By Clifford Mason. November 13, 1986. Director, Al Freeman Jr.; scenery, Charles McClennahan; lighting, James Worley; costumes, Judy Dearing. With Clifford Mason, Hazelle Goodman, Hazel Medina, Donald Lee Taylor, Helmar Augustus Cooper, Monica Williams, Vaughn Dwight Morrison, Thomas Anderson, Petronia Paley, Thomas Pinnock.

BOOGIE WOOGIE AND BOOKER T (30). By Wesley Brown. February 12, 1987. Director, A. Dean Irby; scenery, Charles H. McClennahan; lighting, Victor En Yu Tan; costumes, Judy Dearing. With Charles Dumas, Ruben S. Hudson, John McCallum, Cortez Nance Jr., La Tanya Richardson, Marie Thomas, Nick Smith.

HATS, A TRIBUTE TO HARRIET TUBMAN (one-woman show) (24). By and with Saundra Dunson Franks. February 12, 1987. Music, Joseph W. Jennings; vocal artist, Bernadine Mitchell. (Presented by the National Black Touring Circuit, Inc.)

THE MEETING (24). By Jeff Stetson. April 9, 1987. Director, Judyann Elder. With Dick Anthony Williams, Taurean Blacque, Felton Perry. (Presented by The Crossroads Theater of Los Angeles.)

New York Shakespeare Festival Public Theater. Schedule of workshop productions, in addition to its regular productions. Joseph Papp, producer.

ROOSTERS. (Co-produced by INTAR. For full entry, see INTAR listing.)

MEDEA by Euripides. September 3, 1986. Directed by Yukio Ninagawa; with Mikijiro Hira, Masane Tsukayama, Ryunosuke Kaneda, Hatsuo Yamaya, Kazuhisa Seshimo, Ryuzaburo Otomo, Takayuki Sugo.

FESTIVAL LATINO IN NEW YORK: Schedule included LA VERDADERA HISTORIA DE PEDRO NAVAJA written and directed by Pablo Cabrera, with Teatro del 60; LA TRAS-ESCENA written and directed by Fernando Penuela, translated by Martha Avellaneda and Rodney Reding, with Hernan Forero, Santiago Garcia, Marta Osorio; PRANZO DI FAMIGLIA by Roberto Lerici, translated by Nina Miller, directed by Tinto Brass, with Cooperative Teatrale Belli; SOBRE EL AMOR Y OTROS CUENTOS SOBRE EL AMOR created and directed by Norma Aleandro, based on texts by Lope de Vega, Garcia Lorca, Baltazar de Alcazar, Munos de Seca, J. Prevert, Garcia Marquez, Vargas Llosa, Norma Aleandro et al, translated by Julio Marzan; INTRODUCTION TO CHICANO HISTORY 101 written and directed by Anthony J. Garcia, with Micaela Garcia, Debora Martinez, Angelo Mendez-Soto, Alfredo Sandoval; GUADALUPE AÑOS SIN CUENTA by Teatro La Candelaria, translated by Fernando Torres, directed by Santiago Garcia; THE PLACE WHERE THE MAMMALS DIE by Jorge Dias, translated by Naomi Nelson, directed by Carlos Carrasco, with Gilbert Cruz, Anthony Ruiz, Alicia Kaplan, Blanca Camacho, Felix Pitre, Mary Lou Simo, Anthony Carrion; LOS MUSICOS AMBULANTES collective creation based on texts of Luis Henriquez and Sergio Baraotti, adapted and directed by Miguel Rubio Japata, with Grupo Yuyachkani; TODA NUDEZ SERA CASTIGADA by Nelson Rodrigues, translated by Leslie Damasceno, adapted and directed by Jose Antonio Teodoro, with Delta de Teatro; LA ZAPATERA PRODIGIOSA by Federico Garcia Lorca, directed by Margarita Galban, with Herberto Guillen, Maria Rubell, Pete Leal, Angela Estrada, Hecmar Lugo; FIGHT! (musical-in-progress) book, lyrics and directed by Manuel Martin Jr., music by Felix Mendez, with Manny Matos, Nancy Mayans, Carlos Collazo, Jorge Luis Ramos, Juan Manuel Aguero, Marcella White, Ricci Adan, Daniel Rivas, Arcadio Ruiz Castellano; LO QUE ESTA EN EL AIRE by ICTUS and Carlos Cerda, with ICTUS; BOX PLAYS (8 one-act plays): FIRST VOWS by Manuel Pereiras, directed by Donald Squires, DOG written and directed by Leo Garcia, NOT TIME'S FOOL written and directed by Migdalia Cruz, WHAT DO YOU SEE? written and directed by Ana Maria Simo, LOOKING FOR ANGELS written and directed by Lisa Loomer, SNAKES IN THE BREAD BOX written and directed by Lourdes Blanco, CADILLAC RANCH written and directed by Jose Pelaez, ART by Maria Irene Fornes, directed by Donald Squires; THE MANY DEATHS OF DANNY ROSALES by Carlos Morton, directed by Marvin Felix Camillo; SOMBRAS DE AGUA conceived by Eva Gasteazoro and Tony Gillotte, directed by Tony Gillotte; QUINTUPLES written and directed by Luis Rafael Sanchez, translated by Julio Marzan, with Idalia Perez Garay, Francisco Prado; MEMORY written and directed by Carlos Gimenez, translated by Julio Marzan, based on texts by Federico Garcia Lorca and Walt Whitman, with Gonzalo Velutini, Mildred Chirinos, Jorge Luis Morales, Javier Zapata, Luis Garban, Benigno Acuna; BOLIVAR by Jose Antonio Ral, translated by Julio Marzan, directed by Carlos Gimenez, with Daniel Lopez, Jose Tejera, Luis Garban, Roberto Moll, Pilar Romero; CULTURE CLASH (collaborative piece) written and performed by Richard Montoya, Jose Antonio Burciaga, Herbert Singueza, Ric Slic; ALGUNA COSITA QUE ALIVIE EL SUFRIR by Rene R. Aloma, translated by Alberto Sarrain, with Teatro Avante; LOS TIEMPOS DE RUIDO (collective work) written and performed by the LaMama group, translated by Rodney Reding and Martha Avellaneda, directed by Eddy Armando; RETRATO DE MUJER SOLA CON ESPEJO by Pedro Corradi, directed by Dumas Lerena, with Estela Castro; THE BIRDS FLY OUT WITH DEATH by Edilio Pena, directed by Vicente Castro, with Lillian Hurst, Bertila Damas; TIEMPO MUERTO by Manuel Mendez Ballester, adapted by Rosalba Colon, with Pregones. August 6-31, 1986.

THOMAS COLE, A WAKING DREAM (5). Written and directed by Donald Sanders; musical score, Henry Threadgill. September 9, 1986. Scenery, lighting and costumes, Vanessa James. With Guy Custis, Margot Gordon, Elliot Crown, Kate Farrell, Arthur McGuire, Peter Lane, Dan Farrell, Amy Rugland, John White, Karen Crumley, Roland Jones.

The Open Eye: New Stagings. Committed to innovative collaboration and excellence in performance of both classic and new material. Jean Erdman, founding director, Amie Brockway, artistic director.

Schedule included:

A TASTE OF HONEY by Shelagh Delaney. March 7, 1987. Directed by Betsy Shevey; with Michael Burg, Sam Currie, Deborah Laufer, Janet Mitchko, John Edmond Morgan, Kevin O'Neill.

THE DREAM OF KITAMURA by Philip Kan Gotanda. May 11, 1987. Directed by Jean Erdman and Philip Kan Gotanda; with June Angela, Stanford Egi, William Ha'o, Glenn Kubota, Jodi Long, Chris Odo, Maureen Fleming.

Pan Asian Repertory Theater. Strives to provide opportunities for Asian American artists to perform under the highest professional standards and to create and promote plays by and about Asians and Asian Americans. Tisa Chang, artistic director.

PAN ASIAN REPERTORY THEATER—Toshi Toda, Ako and Allan Tung in a scene from *Shogun Macbeth*

THE IMPOSTOR (IF I WERE REAL) (24). By Sha Yexin, Li Shoucheng and Yao Mingde. October 7, 1986. Director, Ron Nakahara; special consultant, William Sun; lighting, Victor En Yu Tan; costumes, Linda Taoka. With Kati Kuroda, Mary Lum, Norris M. Shimabuku, Keenan Shimizu, Hamilton Fong, Dalton Leong, Mary Lee-Aranas, Tom Matsusaka, Donald Li, Bea Soong, Ben Lin.

SHOGUN MACBETH (30). By William Shakespeare, adapted and directed by John R. Briggs. November 18, 1986. Scenery, Atsushi Moriyashu; lighting, Tina Charney; costumes, Eiko Yamaguchi. With Ernest Abuba, Freda Foh Shen, Donald Li, Raul Aranas, Mel Duane Gionson, Norris M. Shimabuku, Natsuko Ohama, Michael G. Chin, Toshi Toda, Ako, Allan Tung, Ron Nakahara, Lori Tanaka.

WHA . . . i, WHAI, A LONG LONG TIME AGO (30). By Che Inhoon, translated by Huijin Pak, with additional phrases by Oh-kon Cho. April 28, 1987. Director, Tisa Chang; scenery, Alex Polner; lighting, Victor En Yu Tan; costumes, Eiko Yamaguchi; puppet creations, Rebecca Kravetz. With Ginny Yang, Du-Yee Chang, Mary Lum, Hae Ryen Kim, Jung Nam Lee, Steve Park.

THE LIFE OF THE LAND (18). By Edward Sakamoto. June 2, 1987. Director, Kati Kuroda; scenery, Bob Phillips; lighting, Richard Dorfman; costumes, Eiko Yamaguchi. With Jeff Akaka, Kenny Baldwin, Mel Duane Gionson, Carol A. Honda, Eric Miji, Ron Nakahara, Barbara Pohlman, Lily Sakata, Norris M. Shimabuku, Lori Tanaka.

ROSIE'S CAFE (1). By R.A. Shiomi. June 13, 1987. Director, Raul Aranas. With Donald Li, Carol A. Honda, Mike Arkin, Mariye Inouye, Mary Lee-Aranas, Dalton Leong, Tom Matsusaka, Steve Park, Keenan Shimizu, Ron Yamamoto.

The Puerto Rican Traveling Theater. Professional company presenting bilingual productions primarily of Puerto Rican and Hispanic playwrights, emphasizing subjects of relevance today. Miriam Colon, founder and producer.

LADY WITH A VIEW. By Eduardo Ivan Lopez, music and lyrics, Fernando Rivas. August 8, 1986. Director, Max Ferra. With Linda Reyes, Anthony LaGuerre, James Callun, Edward Rodriguez, Milton Demel, Nina Laboy. (Summer touring production.)

A LITTLE SOMETHING TO EASE THE PAIN (42). By Rene R. Aloma; Spanish translation, Alberto Sarrain. January 14, 1987. Director, Mario Ernesto Sanchez; scenery, Rolando Moreno; lighting, Rachel Budin; costumes, Kay Panthaky. With Rita Ben-Or, Laura E. Delano, Cari Gorostiza, Graciela Lecube, Graciela Mas, Jeannette Mirabal, Ruben Pla, Jorge Luis Ramos, Jorge Rios, Carmen Rosario, Arcadio Ruiz Castellano.

A ROSE OF TWO AROMAS (42). By Emilio Carballido; translated by Margaret Peden. March 11, 1987. Director, Vicente Castro; scenery, Janice Davis; lighting, Rachel Budin; costumes, Gail Brassard. With Sully Diaz, Irene De Bari.

BODEGA by Federico Fraguada, Spanish translation by Freddy Valle. May 6, 1987. Directed by Alba Oms; with Antonio Aponte, Regina Baro, Rudy Fort, Olga Molina-Tobin, Jaime Rodriguez, John Rivera, Donald Silva, Jaime Tirelli, Puli Toro.

Playwrights Workshop Staged Readings
LAUGHTER ANONYMOUS by Allen Davis III. May 11, 1987. Directed by Nancy Rhodes.
FAST SHUFFLE by Fred Crecca. May 12, 1987.
THE CONSCIENCE OF THE KING by Maria Elena Torres. May 18, 1987. Directed by Robert Carver.
BARBEQUE by Harriet Levin. May 19, 1987. Directed by Peter Gordon.

Quaigh Theater. Primarily a playwrights' theater, devoted to the new playwright, the established contemporary playwright and the modern (post-1920) playwright. Will Lieberson, artistic director.

FACE TO FACE. By Alexander Gelman, translated by Zora Essman. November 17, 1986. Director, Will Lieberson; designer, Donald L. Brooks. With Ina Balin, David Groh.

DOWN AN ALLEY FILLED WITH CATS (125). By Warwick Moss. December 4, 1986. Director, Peter Askin; scenery, Roy Hine; lighting, Nancy Collings. With Theo Barnes, Stewart Finlay-McLennan.

Lunchtime Series

TRIFLES by Susan Glaspell. October 13, 1986. Directed by Solange Marsin; with Gail Gerber, Michael Patrick Hughes, Kricker James, Paul Henry Rosson.

A DAY FOR SURPRISES by John Guare, directed by Peter Askin; A BOY IN NEW YORK CALLS HIS MOM IN L.A. by John Ford Noonan, directed by Pat McNamara. October 27, 1986. With Cam Kornman, Jack Van Natter, Jim Rosin.

CANADIAN GOTHIC by Joanna M. Glass. November 10, 1986. Directed by Dennis Lieberson; with Patrick McCullough, Gretchen Trapp, Angelynn Bruno, Billy Wirth.

THE GIRL IN PINK by Peter Hedges. November 24, 1986. Directed by Frank Faranda; with Thomas Keith, Tisha Roth, Mary-Louise Parker, Joe Mantello, Martin Barter, Merri Biechler.

FLAT TIRE and AN EXCHANGE by Marcia Haufrecht. December 5, 1986. Directed by Solange Marsin; with Denise Lute, Brad Warner, Marcia Haufrecht, Scott Plank.

OUT TO LUNCH (musical revue) by Wally White. January 19, 1987. Directed by Kevin Walsh; with John Dollinger, Robyne Langsdorf, Dan Rubenstein, Joanna Hoty, Rachel Luxemburg, Kim Stengel.

The Ridiculous Theatrical Company. The late Charles Ludlam's camp-oriented group devoted to productions of his original scripts and broad adaptations of the classics. Charles Ludlam, artistic director.

THE ARTIFICIAL JUNGLE (162). Written and directed by Charles Ludlam. September 21, 1986. Scenery, Jack Kelly; lighting, Richard Currie; costumes, Everett Quinton; music, Peter Golub. With Philip Campanaro, Charles Ludlam, Black-Eyed Susan, Ethyl Eichelberger, Everett Quinton.

The Second Stage. Committed to producing plays of the last ten years believed to deserve another look, as well as new works. Robyn Goodman, Carole Rothman, artistic directors.

COASTAL DISTURBANCES (45). By Tina Howe. November 19, 1986. Director, Carole Rothman; scenery, Tony Straiges; lighting, Dennis Parichy; costumes, Susan Hilferty. With Annette Bening, Timothy Daly, Heather MacRae, Rachel Mathieu, Joanne Camp, Jonas Abry, Rosemary Murphy, Addison Powell, Ronald Guttman.

DIVISION STREET by Steve Tesich. February 3, 1987. Directed by Risa Bramon; with Saul Rubinek, Novella Nelson, Olek Krupa, Kathleen Wilhoite, John Spencer, Cecilia Hart.

LITTLE MURDERS by Jules Feiffer. May 6, 1987. Directed by John Tillinger; with Frances Sternhagen, Fisher Stevens, MacIntyre Dixon, Christine Lahti, Graham Beckel, Mike Nussbaum.

Shelter West. Aims to offer an atmosphere of trust and a place for unhurried and constructive work. Judith Joseph, artistic director.

TOPOKANA MARTYRS' DAY (24). By Jonathan Falla. February 18, 1987. Director, Judith Joseph; lighting, David Tasso; costumes, Rachel Kusnetz; sound, Kenn Dovel. With Dee Dee Friedman, Ray Iannicelli, Robert Jetter, William Lucas, Victor Castelli, Jane Sharp, Howard Wesson.

Staged readings

DANCIN' TO CALLIOPE by Jack Gilhooley. February 22, 1987.
BUT WHAT WILL WE DO ABOUT BETTY? by Roma Greth. February 23, 1987.
PHONE FUN by Bernard MacLaverty and HOW THE VOTE WAS WON (original words by Suffragettes). March 1, 1987.

HIDE THE BRIDE by Sari Bodi. March 2, 1987.
BARRY by Frederic Mohr. March 8, 1987.
LEGACY by Mark DeGasperi. March 9, 1987.

Soho Rep. Infrequently or never-before-performed plays by the world's greatest authors, with emphasis on language and theatricality. Marlene Swartz, Jerry Engelbach, artistic directors.

16 performances each

THE RAGGED TROUSERED PHILANTHROPISTS. By Stephen Lowe, based on Robert Tressell's book. November 15, 1986. Director, Julian Webber; scenery, David Nelson; lighting, Nancy Collings; costumes, Patricia Adshead. With Steve Hofvendahl, Michael Wetmore, John Gould Rubin, Ellen Mareneck, Time Winters, Ray Collins, George Taylor.

SERGEANT OLA AND HIS FOLLOWERS. By David Lan. January 30, 1987. Director, Tazewell Thompson; scenery, Dale F. Jordan; lighting, David Noling; costumes, Eiko Yamaguchi. With Jonathan Peck, Helmar Augustus Cooper, LaDonna Mabry, Karen Jackson, Mark Kenneth Smaltz, Leon Addison Brown.

EURYDICE and THE MOCK DOCTOR (one-act plays). By Henry Fielding. March 27, 1987. Director and music, Anthony Bowles; scenery, Joseph A. Varga; lighting, David Noling; costumes, Michael S. Schler. With Tory Alexander, Jim Bracchitta, Denise Dillard, Anna Lank, Dane Knell, DeAnn McDavid, Martin Moran, Nicholas Saunders, Mark Kenneth Smaltz, Steve Sterner.

YORK THEATER COMPANY—Rudolph Willrich, Fran Brill, Sam Robards and Michael Zaslow in a scene from *Taking Steps* by Alan Ayckbourn

Theater for the New City. Developmental theater and new American experimental works. George Bartenieff, Crystal Field, artistic directors.

Schedule included:

HOMECOMING (musical street play) (16). By Crystal Field, George Bartenieff and the company; music, Mark Hardwick. August 1, 1986. Director, Crystal Field; scenery, Anthony Angel; costumes, Animal X; masks and puppets, Stephen Kaplin, Pamela Mayo, Sarah Germain; musical director, Christopher Cherney. With Crystal Field, Michael David Gordon, Mark Marcante, George Bartenieff, Ben Silver, Marie McKinney.

ONE-ACT MARATHON (14 hours of new plays). Schedule included WHAT DO YOU CALL IT? by Rosalyn Drexler, LUST and LA BALANCE by Robert Patrick. December 6, 1986.

CARRYING SCHOOL CHILDREN (16). By Thomas Babe. February 26, 1987. Director, David Briggs; scenery, James Tilton; lighting, Peter A. West; costumes, Daphne Stevens-Pascucci; music and sound, Michael Brennan. With Fisher Stevens, Jodie Markell, Nealla Spano, Scott Hitchcock, Rush Pearson.

SECOND SPECIES (opera/music theater) (8). Conceived and directed by Keith King; music, Skip LaPlante. March 5, 1987. Scenery, James Finguerra; lighting, Ronald M. Katz; costumes, Mary Brecht. With Daniel Bridston, Iris Brooks, Michael Brown, Elizabeth Evans, Martha King, Peter Kisiluk, George McGrath, Claire Picher, David Simons, Richard Steen.

THE HEART THAT EATS ITSELF (16). By Rosalyn Drexler. April 2, 1987. Director, John Vaccaro; scenery, Abe Lubelski; lighting, Jeffrey Nash; costumes, Gabriel Berry; music, John Braden. With George Bartenieff, Tom Cayler, Crystal Field, Richard Ellis, Don Harrington.

FAMILY PRIDE IN THE 50'S (16). By Joan Schenkar. May 7, 1987. Director, Liz Diamond; scenery, Reagan Cook; lighting, Nicole Werner; costumes, Tracy Oleinick. With Adrien Brody, Jim Demarse, Deanna Duclos, Beverly Jacob, David Shuman, Christopher Spellman, Diana Puccerella, Shelley Wyant.

THREE UP, THREE DOWN (13). By Spiderwoman Theater. May 9, 1987. With Lisa Mayo, Muriel Miguel, Gloria Miguel.

Theater Off Park. Concentrates on producing new plays or musicals and revivals of obscure works by well-known writers, with an emphasis on social consciousness. Albert Harris, artistic director, Bertha Lewis, producing director.

STARDUST (59). Conceived and directed by Albert Harris; music, Hoagy Carmichael, Glenn Miller, Benny Goodman, Duke Ellington, Leroy Anderson and others; lyrics, Mitchell Parish. November 11, 1986. Choreography, Patrice Soriero; scenery, David Jenkins; lighting, Ken Billington; costumes, Mardi Philips; musical direction, James Raitt. With Michele Bautier, Maureen Brennan, Kim Criswell, Andre De Shields, Jason Graae, Jim Walton.

WPA Theater. Produces neglected American classics and new American plays in the realistic idiom. Kyle Renick artistic director, Edward T. Gianfrancesco resident designer, Wendy Bustard managing director.

ALTERATIONS (34). By Leigh Curran. October 15, 1986. Director, Austin Pendleton; scenery, Edward T. Gianfrancesco; lighting, Craig Evans; costumes, Don Newcomb. With Gretchen Cryer, Jane Hoffman, Mary Kane, Cynthia Nixon, Wayne Tippit.

NORTH SHORE FISH (49). By Israel Horovitz. December 31, 1986. Director, Stephen Zuckerman; scenery, Edward T. Gianfrancesco; lighting, Craig Evans; costumes, Mimi Maxmen. With John Pankow, Christine Estabrook, Mary Klug, Cordelia Richards, Thomas G. Waites, Michelle M. Faith, Elizabeth Kemp, Laura San Giacomo, Wendie Malick.

STEEL MAGNOLIAS (42). By Robert Harling. March 11, 1987. Director, Pamela Berlin; scenery, Edward T. Gianfrancesco; lighting, Craig Evans; costumes, Don Newcomb. With Margo Martindale, Constance Shulman, Kate Wilkinson, Blanche Baker, Rosemary Prinz, Mary Fogarty.

COPPERHEAD (28). By Erik Brogger. June 3, 1987. Director, Mary B. Robinson; scenery, Edward T. Gianfrancesco; lighting, Craig Evans; costumes, Mimi Maxmen. With Dave Florek, Kathleen Nolan, Campbell Scott, William Cain, William Wise.

York Theater Company. Each season, productions of classic and contemporary plays are mounted with professional casts, providing neighborhood residents with professional theater. Janet Hayes Walker, producing director.

TAKING STEPS (16). By Alan Ayckbourn. October 24, 1986. Director, Alex Dmitriev; scenery, James Morgan; lighting, Brian MacDevitt; costumes, Muriel Stockdale. With Fran Brill, Michael Zaslow, Sam Robards, Rudolph Willrich, Skip Hinnant, Marguerite Kelly.

MARRY ME A LITTLE (musical revue) conceived and developed by Craig Lucas and Norman René; songs by Stephen Sondheim. January 16, 1987. Directed by Stephen Lloyd Helper; with Liz Callaway, John Jellison.

BILLY BISHOP GOES TO WAR by John Gray and Eric Peterson. February 19, 1987. Directed by William S. Morris; with Robin Haynes.

THE APPLE TREE (musical) book, music and lyrics by Sheldon Harnick and Jerry Bock; additional material by Jerome Coopersmith; based on stories by Mark Twain, Frank R. Stockton and Jules Feiffer. March 20, 1987. Directed by Robert Nigro; with John Sloman, Kathy Morath, Rufus Bonds Jr., Lyle Garrett, Kimberly Harris, Ron LaRosa, Kevin Wallace.

SHYLOCK (12). Music and lyrics by Ed Dixon, based on William Shakespeare's *The Merchant of Venice*. April 23, 1987. Director, Lloyd Battista; scenery, Daniel Ettinger; lighting, Marcia Madeira; costumes, Robert W. Swasey. With Brooks Almay, Ann Brown, Ed Dixon, Joel Fredrickson, Dennis Parlato, Charles Pistone, Lisa Vroman.

Miscellaneous

In the additional listing of 1986–87 off-off-Broadway productions below, the names of the producing groups or theaters appear in CAPITAL LETTERS and the titles of the works in *italics*. This list consists largely of new or reconstituted works and excludes most revivals, especially of classics. It includes a few productions staged by groups which rented space from the more established organizations listed previously.

ACL COMPANY. *Atlantic City Lost* written and directed by Sidney Eden. October 1, 1986. With Sam Baum, Dennis Wit, James Earl Stewart.

ACTORS COLLECTIVE. *The Cork* by Samm-Art Williams. December 4, 1986. Directed by Warren Manzi; with Bernard Lunon, Geoffrey Ewing, Elain Graham, Paul Hart, Nan-Lynn Nelson, Regina Davis, Lois Raebeck, Bill King, Melissa Davis. *Between Time and Timbuktu* by Kurt Vonnegut Jr. January 24, 1987. Directed by Warren Manzi; with Perry Pirkkanen. *Perfect Crime* by Warren Manzi. April 18, 1987. With Cathy Russell, Perry Pirkkanen, Mark Lutsky, G. Gordon Cronce, W. MacGregor King.

ACTOR'S OUTLET. *The Dangerous Christmas of Red Riding Hood* (musical) book by Robert Emmett, music by Jule Styne, lyrics by Bob Merrill. December 19, 1986. Directed by Lee Costello. *Traveling* conceived and directed by Bob Berky. February, 1987. With Deborah Kaufmann, Peter Bruno, Julia Pearlstein, Christopher Agostino, Barbara Svoboda, Wellington Santos, Jeffrey Hess, Marilyn Galfin, Aaron Watkins. *The Delusion of Angels* by Don Rifkin. February, 1987. Directed by Neile Weissman; with Michael Ornstein, James Selby, Kathryn Layng, Richard M. Hughes. *Black Medea: A Tangle of Serpents* by Ernest Ferlita. Directed by Ken Lowstetter; with Daniel Barton, Lee Beltzer, Stephanie Berry, David Jeffryes, Monica Parks, Essene R, Cheryl Ann Scott, Brenda Thomas.

ACTOR'S PLAYHOUSE. *Electric Man* by Mark Eisenstein. June 9, 1986. Directed by James Karr; with Philip Bruns, Jerry Terheyden, Steve Potfora.

AMERICAN FOLK THEATER. *Autobahn* written and directed by Tony Brown and Kari Margolis. December 11, 1986. With the Adaptors. *Whores of Heaven* (musical) book by David Wells and Luisa Inez Newton, based on Machiavelli's; *The Mandrake*; music and lyrics by Michael Wright. March 2, 1987. Directed by Kim Johnson; with Suzanne Parke, Cindy Foster Jones, Ron Golding, Christopher Le Blanc. *Birth Rites* by Elaine Jackson. April 24, 1987. Directed by June Pyskacek; with John Bakos, Shelly Delaney, Jennifer Joseph, Eva Lopez, Lola Loui, Arlene Roman, Mercedes Tang, Alta Withers. *Territorial Rights* by Kerry Kennedy. April 30, 1987. Directed by Daniel Wilson; with James Harper, Sheila Russell, Terres Unsoeld.

AMERICAN JEWISH THEATER. *Kiddush* written and directed by Shmuel Has'fari. September, 1986. With Edna Fleidel, Yossi Graber, Don Navon. *Passover* by Lloyd Gold. November, 1986. Directed by Stanley Brechner. *Panache!* by Ron Mark. January 15, 1987. Directed by Stanley Brechner; with Sam Gray, Sol Frieder, Richard Parnell Habersham. *I Love You, I Love You Not* by Wendy Kesselman. March 26, 1987. Directed by Ben Levit; with Rita Karin, Daria Maazel.

APPLE CORPS. *Kill* by Hugh Leonard. December 11, 1986. Directed by Jerry Heymann; with Larry Pine, Paddy Croft, Maia Danziger. *Defenders of the Code* (musical with puppets) by Theodora Skipitares. February 12, 1987.

ARTISTS ENSEMBLE PRODUCTIONS. *Tigers Wild* by John Rechy. October, 1986. Directed by Michael Ewing; with Cordelia Richards, Frank Whaley, Leonard P. Salazar, Michael David Morrison.

BACA DOWNTOWN THEATER. *Mink Sonata* written and directed by Allan Havis; with Victoria Boothby, Randy Phillips, Gordana Rashovich.

BACK EAST PRODUCTIONS. *Scooncat* by Eve Ensler. April 4, 1987. Directed by Lamis Khalaf; with Dylan McDermott, Marylouise Burke, Ron Faber, Alexandra Gersten, Edwin Owens, Clayton Prince.

BALDWIN THEATER. *Day Six* by Martin Halpern. April 2, 1987. Directed by Louis D. Pietig; with Len Cariou, Heather Summerhayes. *Another Slice of Pizza* (musical) book and lyrics by Anita Sorel and David Young; music by Robert Curto, May 13, 1987. Directed by Anita Sorel and David Young.

THE BALLROOM. *Say It With Music* (cabaret revue) written and directed by Will Holt. September 9, 1986. With Rita Gardner.

BANDWAGON. *Miss Liberty* (musical) book by Robert E. Sherwood, music and lyrics by Irving Berlin. June 30, 1986. With Meg Bussert, Ann Corio, Anita Gillette, Tammy Grimes, Kurt Peterson, Ann Reinking.

BILLIE HOLIDAY THEATER. *A Star Ain't Nothin' But a Hole in Heaven* by Ann Mason. March 26, 1987. Directed by Mikell Pinkney; with Alexria Siglinda Davis, Cynthia Henderson, Gwendolyn Roberts-Frost, Sharon Hope, Clarenze Jarmon, Mike Jefferson, Rome Neal.

BREAD AND PUPPET THEATER. *The Hunger of the Hungry and the Hunger of the Overfed Cantata*. September 6, 1986. *Josephine* based on a parable by Franz Kafka. December 10, 1986.

BROOKLYN ACADEMY OF MUSIC. *Next Wave Festival*: works included *Social Amnesia: a Live Movie* conceived, written, designed and directed by Impossible Theater and John Schneider, inspired by Russell Jacoby's *Social Amnesia* and Howard Zinn's *People's History of the United States*. *The Angels of Swedenborg* conceived and directed by Ping Chong; with Roger Babb. *The Soldier's Tale* by Igor Stravinsky; text by Len Jenkin and Paul Magid. Directed by Robert Woodruff; with The Flying Karamazov Brothers. *the CIVIL warS: a tree is best measured when it is down* (Act V—the Rome Section) by Philip Glass and Robert Wilson, text by Maita di Nascemi and Robert Wilson; music by Philip Glass. With Claudia Cummings, Ruby Hinds, Paul Spencer Adkins, Harlan Foss, Paul Collins, Bruce Kramer. October 7–December 30, 1986.

CHRIST AND ST. STEPHEN'S CHURCH. *Narnia (musical)* adapted by Jules Tasca, Thomas Tierney and Ted Drachman from C.S. Lewis's *The Lion, the Witch and the Wardrobe*. October 3, 1986. Directed by Christopher Biggins; with Paddie O'Neil, Gareth Marks.

CREATIVE TIME. *The Memory Theater of Giulio Camillo* written and directed by Matthew Maguire. September 9, 1986. (See also entry for *Circus* under LaMama ETC.)

CORNER LOFT STUDIO. *Blue Is for Boys* written and directed by Robert Patrick. November 27, 1986.

COURTYARD PLAYHOUSE. *Duck Hunting* by Aleksandr Vampilov, translated by Alma H. Law. February 20, 1987.

CUBICULO. *The Horse's Mouth* by Mark J. Dunas. April 10, 1987. Directed by John Fleming.

DANCE THEATER WORKSHOP. *Blue Night*, *Hangman*, *Little Eddie* and *The Third Bank of the River* (short plays with puppets). September 1986. Directed by Janie Geiser; with Jottay Theater. *Los Trios Ringbarkus*, devised and directed by Neill Gladwin and Stephen Kearney. September 1986. *Keeping Up with the 80's* conceived by Michael Smith, written by Howard Mandel and Michael Smith. April 23, 1987. Directed by Howard Mandel; with Michael Smith, Andrew Black, Rachael Graham, Seth Granger.

AMERICAN FOLK THEATER—Eva Lopez, Arlene Roman and Alta Withers in *Birth Rites* by Elaine Jackson

THE DUPLEX. *Bittersuite* (musical cabaret) music by Eliot Weiss, lyrics and directed by Michael Champagne. April 12, 1987. With Claudine Cassan-Jellison, Joy Franz, John Jellison, Joseph Neal.

ECONOMY TIRES THEATER. *Pass the Blutwurst, Bitte* by and with John Kelly. November 18, 1986.

EN GARDE ARTS. *Terminal Bar* by Paul Selig. November 13, 1986. Directed by Michael Engler; with Jayne Haynes, Roxanne Rogers, Fisher Stevens, Kevin O'Rourke.

ERNIE MARTIN STUDIO THEATER. *Mama* by Paulene Myers. November 1, 1986. Directed by Terrence Shank and Paulene Myers; with Paulene Myers.

THE FAMILY. *Pardon/Permission* written and directed by Seret Scott. February 5, 1987. With O.L. Duke, Robyn Hatcher, Anthony Thomas Paige.

FREE THEATER PRODUCTIONS. Great Artist series, featuring a reading by William Hickey. September 30, 1986.

HAROLD CLURMAN THEATER. *An Acute Obsession* by Barbara Feldman. October 22, 1986. Directed by Gardner Compton; with Ben Frank, Eric Rosse, Kate Merrick, Christian Andrews, Michael Carey, Dianne Pagliai. *Henhouse* by Bo Brinkman. April 9, 1987. Directed by Linda Nerine; with Jayne Chamberlain, Jen Jones, Betty Pelzer, Vincent Procida, Stan Tracy, Eric Uhler, Frank Vohs.

HARTLEY HOUSE THEATER. *Chili Queen* by Jim Lehrer. November 15, 1986. Directed by Frances Hill; with Fred Burrell, Jayne Chamberlain, Paul Doherty, Rick J. Porter.

HOME FOR CONTEMPORARY THEATER AND ART. *An Evening of One-Act Plays* written and directed by Stuart Sherman. February 1987. With Mark Boone Jr., Perry Greaves, John Hagan, Yolanda Hawkins, Anne Iobst, Georg Osterman, Stuart Sherman, Scotty Snyder. *No Damn Good* by Georg Osterman. April 15, 1987. Directed by Linda Chapman; with Coco McPherson, John D. Brockmeyer, Bill Vehr, Susan Varon.

INTAR STAGE 2. *The Dixie Dewdrop* by R. Santinelli and Patrick Sky. August 22, 1986. Directed by Thomas J. Carroll; with Ralph P. Martin, Gilles Malkine. *Working One-Acts 1987:* schedule included *The Great Labor Day Classic* by Israel Horovitz, directed by Robert Owens Scott; *Montana* by David Kranes, directed by Richard Bly; *MacTerrance Moldoon's Dress Rehearsal* by John Heller, directed by Stephen Rosenfield; *Walking Papers* by Michael Stephens, directed by William Alderson; *San Antonio Sunset* by Willy Holtzman, directed by John Pynchon Holms. May, 1987.

IRISH ARTS CENTER. *The Tunnel* by Gregory Teer. January 6, 1987. Directed by Jim Sheridan; with Frank McCourt, Liam Clarke, Nye Heron, Jim Sheridan, Noel Comac, Ciaran Reilly.

JEAN COCTEAU REPERTORY. *Socrates: Theater of Life* by Edward Radzinsky. September 1986. Directed by Eve Adamson; with Craig Smith, John Schmerling, Coral S. Potter, Vincent Roppolo, William Dante, Craig Cook, Joseph Menino. *The Shoemakers* by Stanislaw Ignacy Witkiewicz, adapted by Wlodzimierz Herman and Daniel C. Gerould, translated by Daniel C. Gerould and C.S. Durer. March 1987. Directed by Wlodzimierz Herman; with John Schmerling, Craig Smith, Elise Stone, Harris Berlinsky, William Dante.

JEWISH REPERTORY THEATER. *Roots* by Arnold Wesker. November 12, 1986. Directed by Edward M. Cohen; with Bonnie Gallup, Fred Sanders, Nealla Spano, Roger DeKoven, Gloria Barret, Dermot McNamara, Christopher Merrill, Elaine Rinehart, Brian Drillinger. *Our Own Family* (one-act plays): *Zimmer* by Donald Margulies, directed by Michael Arabian; *The Renovation* by Susan Sandler, directed by Susan Einhorn; *The Converts* by Michael Taav, directed by William Partlan; *Scrabble* by David Rush, directed by Lynn Polan. March 6, 1987. With Joe Urla, Beth McDonald, Jennifer Blanc, Michael Albert Mantel, Bill Cohen, Alice Spivak, Victor Raider-Wexler, Maury Cooper. *Waving Goodbye* by Bob Morris. May 10, 1987. Directed by Robin Saex; with Michael Ornstein, Robert Dorfman.

JUDITH ANDERSON THEATER. *Out!* by Lawrence Kelly. July 11, 1986. Directed by Max Charruyer; with Arnie Mazer, Michael Countryman, Paul Christie, Steven Stahl. *Shots at Fate* by Steven Braunstein. August 11, 1986. With David Staller, Donna Snow. *A Scent of Almonds* by

Marjorie Osterman. October 3, 1986. Directed by Langdon Brown; with Heather Osterman, Carlotta Schoch, Mel Cobb, Robin Howard, Matt Conley, Peg Daloia. *Triangles* by June Bingham. October, 1986. Directed by Aaron Frankel; with Kathleen Butler, Redman Maxfield, Maggi-Meg Reed.

KINDRED PRODUCTIONS. *Loveplay* by Lawrence Leibowitz; translated from Arthur Schnitzler's *Liebelei*. May 18, 1987. Directed by Susan Einhorn; with Lawrence Prescott, Victor Raider-Wexler, Cynthia Crumlish, John Hickok, Katherine Hiler, Sarah Hornby.

THE KITCHEN. *White Water* written and directed by John Jesurun. October 22, 1986. With Valerie Charles, Larry Tighe, Michael Tighe.

LINCOLN CENTER OUT-OF-DOORS FESTIVAL. Events included Mime Day with performances by Daniel Stein, Branch Worsham, Yass Hakoshima Mime Theater. August 30, 1986. Clown Theater Day with performances by Paul Zaloom, Serious Foolishness, Jan Greenfield, The Wright Brothers. September 1, 1986.

LOAVES AND FISH THEATER COMPANY. *Return to the River* by C. Dumas. March 21, 1987. Directed by Douglas Farren; with Michael Haney, W. Allen Taylor, Joe Viviani, Gail O'Blenis Dukes, Nikki Barthen, Dan Kelley, Jonathan Peck.

MASS TRANSIT STREET THEATER. *House on Mayhem Street* (musical) book by Lynn Pyle, Skeeter Greene and Jerry Cofta; music by Greg Langdon; lyrics by Skeeter Greene, John-Martin Green, Sharita Hunt, Greg Langdon, Lynn Pyle and Jerry Cofta. November 20, 1986. With the ensemble.

MAZUR THEATER. *Swan Song* by John Greenwood and Jonathan Levi, based on Edmund Crispin's novel. November 9, 1986. Directed by Tony Tanner; with Jack Eddleman, Chip Cornelius, Ann Marie Lee, Michael Tartel, Adam Redfield, Tony Tanner.

MUMBO JUMBO THEATER COMPANY. *City on the Make* (musical) adapted from the works of Nelson Algren by Jeff Berkson, Denise DeClur and John Karraker. December 17, 1986. Directed by Tim Raphael.

MUSICAL THEATER WORKS. *Abyssinia* (gospel musical) book, music and lyrics by James Racheff and Ted Kociolek; based on Joyce Carol Thomas's short story. April 5, 1987. Directed by Tazewell Thompson; with Jennifer Lee Warren, Tina Fabrique, Cheryl Freeman, Zelda Pulliam, Karen Jackson, LaDonna Mabry. *Starmites* (musical) book by Stuart Ross and Barry Keating, music and lyrics by Barry Keating. April 26, 1987. Directed by Mark Herko; with Liz Larsen, Steven Watkins, Sharon McKnight, Gabriel Barre, Bennett Cole, Victor Cook. *212* (musical) book and lyrics by Victor Joseph; music by Donald Siegal. May 15, 1987. Directed by Maggie Harrer.

NAT HORNE THEATER. *The Magician* conceived and performed by Peter Samelson. December 5, 1986. *Class1acts: Language as Communication* by John Angell Grant, directed by Brian Mertes; *Tuba Solo* by Michael Lynch, directed by Pam Pepper; *Beirut* by Alan Bowne, directed by Jimmy Bohr; *Where Have All the Virgins Gone* by Anna Theresa Cascio, directed by Kevin Kelley; *A Capella Hardcore* by Erik Ehn, directed by Janet Herzenberg; *Sister Gloria's Pentecoastal Baby* by Michael Lynch, directed by Will Cantler. March 29, 1987. *Plain Brown Wrapper* (five skits) by Keith Reddin. April 16, 1987. Directed by Victor D'Altorio; with Richard Schiff, Robyn Lord, Cornelia Mills, Cyrus Newitt, Sally Brookbank. *The Great Truman Capote* by Murphy Martell and Fredrick Davies; based on the life and works of Truman Capote. May 31, 1987. Directed by Murphy Martell; with Fredrick Davies.

NATIONAL BLACK THEATER. *A Matter of Conscience* by Venona Thomas. January 24, 1987. Directed by Seret Scott; with Donna Smith, Wendi Franklin, Angeles Echols, Richard Lemerise, Stanley Earl Harrison, Bertilla Baker. *The Legacy* by Gordon Nelson. May 29, 1987. Directed by Elmo Terry Morgan; with JoHanna Daughtrey, Richard Malavet, Cheryl Hillard-Hewitt, Lottie E. Porch, Esther Pulliam, Billie Scott.

NEIGHBORHOOD GROUP THEATER. *Wild Oats* by James McClure. October 10, 1986. Directed by Kathryn Ballou.

NEW HERITAGE REPERTORY THEATER. *Brother Malcolm X* by Frank G. Greenwood. June 1986. Directed by Ron Milner; with Duane Shepard.

NEW MUSEUM OF CONTEMPORARY ART. *One Night Only* (performance art). March 22, 1987. With Ethyl Eichelberger, Pat Oleszko, Danny Mydlack, Danitra Vance, Flotilda Williams, Lucy Sexton, Anne Iobst.

NEW THEATER OF BROOKLYN. *Space Walk* by Alan Mokler; music by Brad Garton. October 23, 1986. Directed by Peter Wallace; with Paul Zimet, Nancy Mayans, Todd Oleson. *Donkeys' Years* by Michael Frayn. February 22, 1987. Directed by Steve Stettler; with Regina Baff, John Henry Cox, Steven Crossley, Rob Gomes, David Hall. *The Art of War* by George F. Walker. April 23, 1987. Directed by Stephen Katz; with June Gable, John Perkins, Michael Kemmerling, K.C. Wilson, Rudy Goldschmidt, Amy Griscom Epstein.

NEW YORK ART THEATER. *False Dawn*, adapted from Edith Wharton's *Old New York*. April 11, 1987. Directed by Donald T. Sanders.

NEW YORK GILBERT AND SULLIVAN PLAYERS. *Trial by Jury* and *The Sorcerer*. April 4, 1987. With Stephen M. Quint, Keith Jurosko, Jayne Lynch, Michael Collins, William Ledbetter, Alan Hill, Colby Thomas, Erin Langston, Judy Schubert, William Reynolds, Stephen O'Brien.

NEW YORK THEATER WORKSHOP. New Directors Project: *The Dispute* by Marivaux, translated by Daniel Gerould, directed by David Warren; *Farmyard* by Franz Xaver Kroetz, directed by David Esbjornson; *Burrhead* by Deborah Pryor, directed by Valerie Knight; *Seventy Scenes of Halloween* by Jeffrey Jones, directed by Michael Greif. October 28–December 13, 1986. *As It Is in Heaven* by Joe Sutton. April 1, 1987. *A Narrow Bed* by Ellen McLaughlin. May 19, 1987. Directed by Sarah Ream; with Christopher McCann, Debra Monk, Beth Dixon, Greg Germann, Kate McKillip.

92ND STREET Y. *Passionate Leave: Morris Traveller Takes a Vacation*. November 8, 1986. With The Moving Picture Mime Show.

NO SMOKING PLAYHOUSE. *On Extended Wings*, adapted by Sara Brooks from Diane Ackerman's memoirs. April 15, 1987. Directed by John Camera; with Norma Jean Giffin, Neil Lyons, Richard Willis, Jeff Vaughn.

NORTHERN LIGHT PRODUCTIONS. *Hitler's Childhood* by Niklas Raadstrom, based on Alice Miller's book *For Your Own Good*, translated by Irene Berman. September 4, 1986. Directed by Oeyvind Froeyland; with Brad Warner, Larry Attile, Priscilla Corbin, Dana Patton.

OHIO THEATER. *Bliss* by Mikhail Bulgakov, translated by Mirra Ginsburg. March 15, 1987. Directed by Charles Otte; with Jonathan Baker, Franca Barchiesi, Will Kepper, Elizabeth Gee, Carissa Channing.

ONTOLOGICAL-HYSTERIC THEATER. *Film is Evil: Radio Is Good* written and directed by Richard Foreman. April 29, 1987. With Kate Manheim, David Patrick Kelly, Lola Pashalinski.

OPEN SPACE THEATER. *Whispers* by Crispin Larangeira. January 1987. Directed by Nancy Gabor; with Stephen Rowe, Joan MacIntosh.

OUR STUDIOS. *Pinoc, the Barbarian* (musical) book by Dennis Soens and Mike Roberts, music and lyrics by Herb Martin and others. May 21, 1987. Directed by Dennis Soens; with Karla Bos, Rick Castillo, Nance McQuigg, Dennis Soens.

PARK ROYAL. *Johnny on the Pony* by Richard Vetere. April 10, 1987. Directed by Peter Miner; with Elizabeth Dennehy, Al D'Andrea, Albert Passeullo, Stephen Prutting.

PEARL THEATER. *Beautiful Dreamer* by Greg Zittel. October 7, 1986. Directed by Lori Lowe; with Carolyn Finney, David Newer, Valerie Brown Bickford, Mark Weil.

PERFORMANCE SPACE 122. *Pipedreams* (annual benefit). February 6, 1987. With performances by John Kelly, David Cale, Paul Zaloom, Kestutis Nakas.

PERFORMING GARAGE. *Epstein on the Beach* by Sarah Schulman and Robin Epstein. September 4, 1986. *Junk Love* written and directed by Robin Epstein and Dorothy Cantwell. September 12, 1986. With Stephanie Doba, Paul Walker, Jerry Turner, Robin Epstein, Dorothy Cantwell.

PRACTICAL CATS THEATER COMPANY. *Lady Moonsong, Mr. Monsoon* written and composed by Alice Eve Cohen. March 9, 1987. Directed by David Saint; with Mia Dillon, Reed Birney, Rick Lawless, Ennis Dexter Locke, George Ashiotis, Steve Silverstein.

PRIMARY STAGES COMPANY. *Free Fall* by Laura Harrington. February 18, 1987. Directed by Alma Becker; with Daniel Ahearn, Annette Helde, Marvin Einhorn, Anne O'Sullivan.

RIVERSIDE SHAKESPEARE COMPANY. *As You Like It* by William Shakespeare. July 18, 1986. Directed by Robert Mooney. (touring production)

RIVERWEST THEATER. *The Fox* adapted by Allan Miller from D.H. Lawrence's novella. November 28, 1986. Directed by Connie Grappo; with Pamela Moller, Brooke Palance, Stephen Caffrey.

ROGER FURMAN THEATER. *Like Them That Dream* by Edgar White. November 1986. Directed by Andre Robinson Jr.; with Kirtan Coan, Lorey Hayes, George Holmes, Lanyard Williams.

ROYAL COURT REPERTORY. *The Actors* by Ward Morehouse III. November 20, 1986. Directed by Phyllis Craig; with Jack Aranson, Ralph Douglas, Richard Waring, Lon Freeman, John Blaylock, Phyllis Craig.

ST. PETER'S CHURCH. *Living a Ragtime Life* (one-man show). November 26, 1986. With Max Morath.

SAMUEL BECKETT THEATER. *Cicero* by Sam Segal. October 17, 1986. Directed by Vince Tauro; with Hal Robinson, Charles Matheny, Neil Carpenter. *Miss Julie* by August Strindberg, translated by Michael Meyer. May 14, 1987. Directed by Maria Mazer; with Caroline Arnold, Shan Sullivan, Diane Tarleton, Douglas James Hamilton.

SANFORD MEISNER THEATER. *Jerker* by Robert Chesley. January 8, 1987. Directed by Nicholas Deutsch; with Jay Corcoran, John Finch.

SOUTH STREET THEATER. *Loveplay* by Arthur Schnitzler, translated by Lawrence Leibowitz. May 18, 1987. Directed by Susan Einhorn; with Sarah Hornby, John Hickok, Victor Raider-Wexler, Cynthia Crumlish.

STAGE ARTS THEATER COMPANY. *Better Living* by James van Maanen. January 16, 1987. With Richard Bowne, Tom Gerard, Gordon MacDonald, Charles Major. *Cowboy* (musical) book by Jess Gregg, based on an idea by Ronnie Claire Edwards; music and lyrics by Richard Riddle. May 1, 1987. Directed by Robert Bridges; with George Ball, Carolyn DeLany.

THEATER GUINEVERE. *Not Showing* by James Ryan. September 1986. Directed by Joe Gilford; with Ashley Gardner, W.T. Martin, Christina Moore, Jordan Roberts. *We Shall* by Karmyn Lott. January 22, 1987. Directed by Anderson Johnson; with Nicole Powell, Pa Sean Wilson, Timothy F. Murray, Consuelo Hill.

THEATER IN ACTION. *The House That Swift Built* by Grigori Gorin. September 20, 1986. Directed by L. Shekhtman.

THEATER IN VERSION. *Deus Duel Deux Duet* by Lee Ellickson (part 6 of 9-part *Back and Forth and Come and Go Again*). January 22, 1987.

TIME AND SPACE LIMITED. *Cross Way Cross* written and directed by Linda Mussman with Claudia Bruce. February 1987. With Claudia Bruce, Victoria Kelly.

TOMI THEATER. *Wicked Philanthropy* by Denis Diderot, translated by Gabriel John Brogyanyi. January 1987. Directed by Pamela Caren Billig; with Richard Pruitt, Gabriel Barre, Betsy Mohler.

TRIPLEX THEATER. *Le Cirque Imaginaire* developed and performed by Victoria Chaplin and Jean Baptiste Thierree. November 18, 1986.

UBU REPERTORY THEATER. *Trumpets of Death* by Tilly, translated by Timothy Johns. October 17, 1986. Directed by Pierre Epstein. *Vater Land, the Country of Our Fathers* by Jean-Paul Wenzel, translated by Timothy Johns; music by Hugh Levick. October 18, 1986. *A Man with Women* by Reine Barteve, translated by Richard Miller; music by Genji Ito. October 19, 1986. Directed by Francoise Kourilsky. (See also entry for *The Sleepless City* under LaMama ETC.)

THE UNOFFICIAL STAGE. *Never the Sinner* by John Logan. May 14, 1987. Directed by John Swanbeck; with Chet Carlin, Angel David, Janet Giangrasse, Neale Harper, John Petrella.

VIETNAM VETERANS ENSEMBLE THEATER. *The Grunt Childe* (staged reading) by Lawrence O'Sullivan. March 31, 1987. Directed by Thomas Bird.

VINEYARD THEATER. *How to Say Goodbye* by Mary Gallagher. November 29, 1986. Directed by Liz Diamond; with Cheryl McFadden, Kathryn Rossetter, Christine Jansen, D.W. Moffett, Jason Ruggiero.

VORTEX THEATER COMPANY. *Wretched Excess* by James Kantor. August 28, 1986. Directed by Robert Coles; with Kathryn Danielle, Katherine Kamhi, Bill Maul, Louie Mustillo, Alan Pratt. *A Show Boat in Deep Water* by Gary Weiz. September 1, 1986.

WESTBETH THEATER CENTER. *Annie Wobbler* by Arnold Wesker. October 22, 1986. Directed by Gerald Chapman; with Sloane Bosniak.

WINGS THEATER COMPANY. *The Casting of Kevin Christian* by Stephen Holt. May 7, 1987. Directed by Michael Hillyer; with Pete Benson, Stephen Holt, Ellaxis Smith.

THE WOOSTER GROUP. *The Road to Immortality—Part One* (Route 1 & 9). November, 1986. Directed by Elizabeth LeCompte. *The Road to Immortality—Part Two (. . . Just the High Points).* February, 1987. *Frank Dell's St. Antony* conceived by Elizabeth LeCompte and Peter Sellars. April, 1987. With Ron Vawter, Kate Valk. (Part 3 of trilogy)

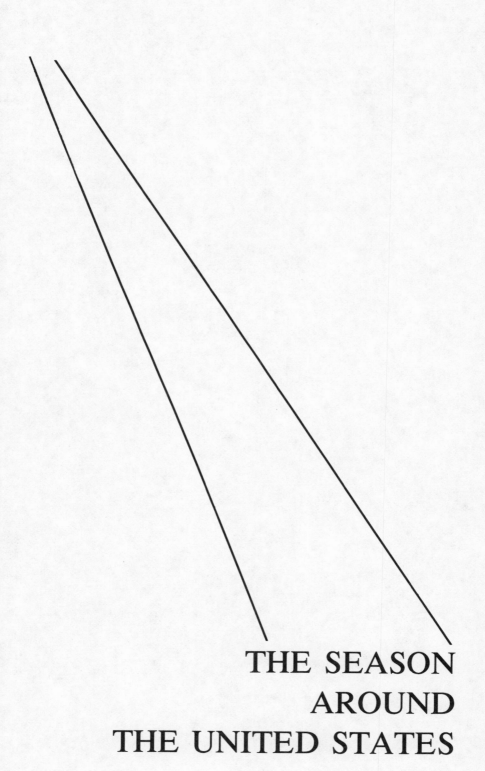

THE SEASON
AROUND
THE UNITED STATES

OUTSTANDING NEW PLAYS CITED BY AMERICAN THEATER CRITICS ASSOCIATION

and

A DIRECTORY OF NEW-PLAY PRODUCTIONS

THE American Theater Critics Association (ATCA) is the organization of 250 leading drama critics in all media in all sections of the United States. One of this group's stated purposes is "To increase public awareness of the theater as a *national* resource" (italics ours). To this end, ATCA has cited four outstanding new plays produced this season around the country, to be represented in our coverage of The Season Around the United States by excerpts from each of their scripts demonstrating literary style and quality. And one of these—Lee Blessing's *A Walk in the Woods*—was designated the first-place play and received the second annual ATCA New Play Award of $1,000.

The process for the selection of these outstanding plays is as follows: any ATCA member critic may nominate a play if it has been given a production in a professional house. It must be a finished play given a full production (not a reading or an airing as a play-in-progress). Nominated scripts were studied and discussed by an ATCA play-reading committee chaired by Dan Sullivan of the Los Angeles *Times* and comprising Ann Holmes of the Houston *Chronicle*, Damien Jaques of the Milwaukee *Journal*, Tom McCulloh of *Drama-Logue*, Julius Novick of the *Village Voice* and Bernard Weiner of the San Francisco

Chronicle. The committee members made their choices on the basis of script rather than production, thus placing very much the same emphasis as the editors of this volume in making the New York Best Play selections. There were no eligibility requirements except that a nominee be the first full professional production of a new work outside New York City within this volume's time frame of June 1, 1986 to May 31, 1987. If the timing of nominations and openings prevented some works from being considered this year, they will be eligible for consideration next year if they haven't since moved on to New York production. We offer our sincerest thanks and admiration to the ATCA members and their committee for the valuable insight into the 1986–87 theater season around the United States which their selections provide for this *Best Plays* record.

A WALK IN THE WOODS

A Play in Two Acts

BY LEE BLESSING

Cast and credits appear on page 444.

A WALK IN THE WOODS: Lee Blessing didn't take the easy way out when he decided to write a play about nuclear arms control and write it for only two characters: a Soviet arms negotiator and his American counterpart. But this inspired him as well as gave him something worth talking about. The outcome is a play that could be said to be profoundly pessimistic if it weren't for the fact that it's shot through with lashings of humanity and roaring good humor.

The Soviet negotiator, a long-time inhabitant of Geneva, has grown to believe that the arms and peace negotiations between the U.S.S.R. and the United States are window dressing. Both countries are determined to hang on to their ability to annihilate the entire world at the push of a button, because without it they wouldn't be superpowers. To him, the negotiators are in Geneva for one reason: to delay anything ever happening. They are, he believes, totally ineffectual nonentities.

The American negotiator, a newcomer to the arms-control table, arrives with all the optimism and fervor of any new broom. But as the days, weeks and months pass, he's forced to come to terms with the Russian's viewpoint and if not to agree with it, at least to see its validity. A prickly friendship develops as the two walk in the woods on the outskirts of Geneva between arms-control talks.

Their discussions seesaw between the profoundly disturbing and the purposely trivial. The Russian, after too many years of seriousness at the table and diplomatic receptions, yearns for frivolous chit-chat, which discombobulates the sober American. Along the way the play gives strong evidence of the personal price such negotiators pay, particularly when they are men of conscience.

The Russian is more outgoing, more at ease and more sophisticated. He's a charming rogue with a penchant for changing the subject. The American is almost priggish by comparison, a younger man who still believes he can contribute something to world peace. Both men care deeply about the fate of the world.

The entire two-act play takes place in "a pleasant woods . . . The path is

YALE REPERTORY THEATER—Kenneth Welsh as John Honeyman and Josef Sommer as Andrey Botvinnik in *A Walk in the Woods* by Lee Blessing, ATCA New Play Award winner

well-kept, but rustic. It leads to a wooden bench in a little clearing. The overall effect is light, airy, idyllic."

HONEYMAN: Your government rejected our proposal, didn't they?

BOTVINNIK: Not exactly.

HONEYMAN: What do you mean?

BOTVINNIK: They didn't reject your proposal itself. They rejected what your President has turned the proposal into.

HONEYMAN: Which is?

BOTVINNIK: Which is—in their words—a cynical public-relations scheme.

HONEYMAN: It is not a cynical . . .

BOTVINNIK: It is. From the moment he announced it to the world.

HONEYMAN: He had to announce it.

BOTVINNIK: Why? When we had not agreed to it yet.

HONEYMAN: You never agreed to anything! You accepted one small point, before our election, and since then—nothing, zero, no movement all winter. He couldn't wait any longer.

BOTVINNIK: You should have stopped him.

HONEYMAN: I tried. I argued him out of going public on this three times in the past five months. You know that.

BOTVINNIK: You should have argued again.

HONEYMAN: I did. But I was running out of ammunition.

BOTVINNIK: So. In one speech he destroys all the work we have done. Good. Fine. Why not?

HONEYMAN: You were the ones who destroyed it. By delay.

BOTVINNIK: Delay does not destroy agreements. One can always renew efforts. But to announce the proposal . . .

HONEYMAN: He had the right.

BOTVINNIK: He bears the responsibility!

HONEYMAN: For what? For telling the world? Why's that so terrible?

BOTVINNIK: Don't be ridiculous.

HONEYMAN: No, tell me. Why is it so bad if the world knows what we're discussing?

BOTVINNIK: Because it makes us look like fools. If we accept your proposal now, what will the rest of the world say? "Ah, the Americans have finally thought of a clever plan. Thank God the unimaginative Russians have agreed."

HONEYMAN: The rest of the world, if they said anything, would say, "At last—two maniacs have had a moment of sanity."

BOTVINNIK: Yes, they would say that too, but first they would say it is an American peace, an American security.

HONEYMAN: Who cares whose peace it is?

BOTVINNIK: You do. You do not want a Russian peace. Two years ago we announced to the world a plan of our own—just as good as yours. And you rejected it.

HONEYMAN: There were significant problems with that plan.

BOTVINNIK: Yes, it was ours. Now please, John—stop pretending. You know neither of our countries can afford to be second in the quest for peace.

HONEYMAN: What quest for peace? At this rate there is no quest for peace.

BOTVINNIK: But there's the quest for the appearance of the quest for peace. These are negotiations, John. There are rules. There are forms. You know them as well as I do. Your President knows them, too. When he announced the proposal, he knew we would have to reject it.

A beat. Honeyman expels a long sigh.

HONEYMAN: Why did your government delay so long? What was it about the proposal you objected to?

BOTVINNIK: Why go into it?

HONEYMAN: *It's our job. (A beat.)* Was it the total number of warheads?

BOTVINNIK: John . . .

HONEYMAN: Was it?

BOTVINNIK: No.

HONEYMAN: The percentage of land-based missiles?

BOTVINNIK: No.

HONEYMAN: The ratios? On-site inspections?

BOTVINNIK: It's useless to . . .

HONEYMAN: I want to know. Cruise-missile reductions? INF in general?

BOTVINNIK: Not really.

HONEYMAN: The testing moratorium? The research moratorium?

BOTVINNIK: No.

HONEYMAN: SDI? The ASAT provision?

BOTVINNIK: It wasn't any . . .

HONEYMAN: C3I questions? SLBMs? MX?

BOTVINNIK: No—not MX or SLBMs or SLCMs or SDI or FBS or CEP or SALT or START or any of it. We had no objections to anything in your proposal. You understand? Nothing.

A beat.

HONEYMAN: Nothing?

BOTVINNIK: Nothing. We liked the whole proposal.

HONEYMAN: I don't understand. You liked it?

BOTVINNIK: Very much.

HONEYMAN: Then why did you delay so long?

BOTVINNIK: Because your proposal was . . . too good.

HONEYMAN: Too good?

BOTVINNIK: It could have led to real arms reductions. Serious ones.

HONEYMAN: Don't you want that?

BOTVINNIK: Of course. But . . . also we are afraid of it.

HONEYMAN: Why? It's a treaty. We've made treaties before.

BOTVINNIK: Look at those treaties, John. They weren't treaties. They were blueprints. We determined what weapons we would build in the next few years, then agreed to let each other build them. Then we turned to the rest of the world and said, "See? We are capable of restraint." This proposal, on the other hand, could mean massive reductions. This we have never done before. We are afraid of it.

HONEYMAN: Andrey, each year, each month, each day someone is proposing a new weapons system. Someone is securing a grant for more research. Someone is dreaming up a new technology that will do God-knows-what destruction—to our economies, if nothing else. How, knowing that, can we let any opportunity slip through our fingers?

BOTVINNIK: I know, I know. But there is a problem for us with reductions such as these.

HONEYMAN: What is it?

BOTVINNIK: We don't trust you.

HONEYMAN: You don't trust us?

BOTVINNIK: Do you trust *us?*

HONEYMAN: Yes. Well—we try to. But whether we trust each other or not, the proposal has provisions. It has safeguards.

BOTVINNIK: We don't trust the safeguards.

HONEYMAN: There are checks on the safeguards. Verifications.

BOTVINNIK: We don't trust them.

HONEYMAN: Andrey . . .

BOTVINNIK: Even if there were checks on the checks on the checks, we wouldn't trust them.

HONEYMAN: Why not?

BOTVINNIK: Because we don't trust *you.* Who knows what you are making right now that lies outside this proposal?

HONEYMAN: We're not making any . . .

BOTVINNIK: Multiple warheads, SDI—these things came *after* treaties were signed, not before.

HONEYMAN: We can control new technologies. Together.

BOTVINNIK: Can we? How can you be sure of what's going on in your own country right now? Do you think they tell you everything? Face it, John—you can't even completely trust *your* side. And you want to trust ours?

HONEYMAN: We *can* work . . .

BOTVINNIK: Suppose we sign an agreement, and the next day you—or we— suddenly unveil a new weapon. What happens? Immediately, a new arms race.

HONEYMAN: Even if you're right—you're not, but even if you were . . .

BOTVINNIK: I am right. I am always right. And how do we appear to the rest of the world? As two warmongers who can't keep a treaty. If, however, we have never agreed to a treaty, then when a new technology comes along, we are simply two nations who are trying to make a treaty, but who must remain prepared for war. It creates a much better image.

HONEYMAN: Looking for peace, and purposely never finding it?

BOTVINNIK (*taking out his eyedrops, applying them*): It is better for everyone. Broken treaties make people too nervous, yes?

HONEYMAN: So this makes your job and my job—what? Sort of a nuclear nightlight? Providing no real hope, just . . .

BOTVINNIK: The appearance. Yes.

HONEYMAN: This is what you truly think is preferable?

BOTVINNIK: Not I. My leaders. Your leaders.

HONEYMAN: How long do you—do they—think this is supposed to go on?
BOTVINNIK *(shrugging, putting away his eyedrops):* Until the world ends.

A WALK IN THE WOODS *was produced by Yale Repertory Theater, New Haven, Conn. under the direction of Des McAnuff February 18, 1987.*

BACK IN THE WORLD

A Full-Length Play in One Act

BY STEPHEN MACK JONES

Cast and credits appear on pages 434-435.

BACK IN THE WORLD: Black veterans of the Vietnam War recall, reflect on and relive some of their searing experiences. One of them remembers that he promised God to spend his life helping others if God would spare him. Another remembers the anger, another the jungle smell, another the wounds and the suffering. Another proudly reviews the historical accomplishments of black soldiers from the Revolutionary War onwards and declares to the audience that blacks had a duty to fight in Vietnam and quotes General Westmoreland: "I have an intuitive feeling that the Negro servicemen have a better understanding than whites of what the war is all about," because it was about *freedom* (the veteran explains), freedom from Communism. He castigates the liberals for injecting moral issues when the only concern should have been victory.

Anthony "Jam" Brazil introduces himself. He is from Indianapolis, a rifleman of the Fourth Infantry Division: "Duc Pho, May '69. Saigon October 71, December 71." He saw a lot of action, and the memory of it hurts—he thinks about it every day, and it always hurts. He killed about as many people as are listening to him now, some Viet Cong, some Chinese, some innocent.

BRAZIL: I killed a seven-year-old boy once. Seven or eight. easiest thing I've ever done. Killin' that boy. Didn't look back, don't regret it. I mean, that's what bein' a soldier's all about, right? No frets, no regrets. They don't train you to be a—a philosopher or social worker. They train you to kill, to survive, and that's that. Find the enemy and kill 'um. And, I mean—when you're seventeen, eighteen years old and—

Pause.

We were taking fire outside of Duc Pho. The Fourth. My company was under some heavy fire and—in the first few seconds a couple of our guys bought it. *(Snaps his fingers.)* Just like that. One minute, they were there, next minute gone. One guy—a brotha—got it through the eye. Right next to me. Took the back of his head off. I didn't really think about it till later—and, man—all I could think was—"That coulda been me." This guy, we used to drink together, have some laughs, maybe, you know, do a little smoke. All that stuff. Got to be pretty friendly, I guess. After he's killed, I can't remember his name or what he looked like. I mean it was *like* that over there. Adrenaline. That's what you lived on for

ATTIC THEATER, DETROIT—Lou Beatty Jr. as Brazil in *Back in the World* by Stephen Mack Jones

six, eight, ten months at a time. Pure adrenaline. Pumped. Wired. Every sense is amplified. Anything that doesn't mean survival, forget it. Kick it out. You're hyped on what keeps you alive.

> *Pause.*

Insulation. When that blood was picked off next to me, I felt like a part of my insulation—part of my life-support system was gone. I mean—war strips you of compassion, of humanity. Makes you an animal. Shit, I was trained to be one—and baby let me tell you somethin'—I was king of the jungle.

> *Pause.*

When the fighting outside Duc Pho stops, the slicks fly in and we, you know, establish a purple-out zone. Get the wounded out. Scoop up the dead. Charlie's either dead or shakin' ass through a tunnel, right? Outta nowhere, this eight-year-old boy comes flyin' out of a hooch, runnin' as fast as he can for one of the Hueys. I see him and bring him down. Just like that. Funny thing, though. Before he even hits the ground—he blows up. Freaks the shit outta me. This kid—just—he just—All I could figure was—he was in a no-win situation from the get-go. Dead anyway you cut it. And, I mean, he probably didn't know what *any* of this shit was about.

> *Pause.*

I thought about that kid for maybe three, four days. *(Slight pause.)* You know, that was one of the worst things that could happen to you over there? Time to think. You start thinking, "What in the fuck am I *doin'* here?" *(Small laugh.)* That couple days I smoked enough Thai-stick, man, put a plow ox under! But—I couldn't get that kid outta my head.

> *The sound of weapon fire and explosion. The sound is more distant as if fading in a corner of memory.*

Started having these weird trips where I'd hold court in my head. Who was guilty? Charlie or me? I had to pull back like, whoa!, *right* damn now! I mean, you don't go in-country with a lot of questions. I passed judgment real fast, jack. It was the V.C. that killed that boy. Not me. The sentence? Death by *my* hand.

> *Pause.*

I mean—kids are supposed to be—sacred, right? Not—not somebody's goddamn cannon fodder. Somebody's weapon.

> *Pause.*

At least, that's the picture they paint here. But, shit—I been *out* there. Humpin' them damn boonies. Barely nineteen, runnin' through a damn jungle with live, flesh-eatin' ammo. All in the name of *"Democracy."* And hell, I don't even know what the shit it is!

Brazil remembers a particularly gruesome incident in which a white soldier—they called whites "rabbits"—shot a pregnant woman. He remembers that the war "got me all upside down" until he began collecting enemy ears. Finally, in 1970, they sent him home to Indianapolis with a bunch of medals on his chest.

BRAZIL: . . . . . Back in the world, if you call Indianapolis "the world." And all I'm trained to do is kill. Twenty years old now and that's all I know how to do. Not exactly the kind of thing you put on a résumé. *(Thoughtfully.)* 'Course,

Indianapolis ain't exactly the kind of town where you *need* a résumé. *(Brightening.)* Remember that TV show *Hawaii Five-O?* Remember that? Yeah. Steve McGarrett. "Book his ass, Dan-O." I caught some afternoon re-runs of that shit and got the shock of my life, man. I'm home, O.K.? Watchin' Steve McGarrett make Hawaii safe for rich white folk—and like in a *month,* man, I see *at least* three episodes about Viet vets off the nut. Shootin' and hackin' the shit outta Hawaii. Drugged out and shit. And I'm thinkin' to myself—what *is* this shit? Is this the way people see *me?* Hey, so like, I'm gettin' a little concerned, O.K.? Two months later, I reup. Four months later, I back in the 'Nam. Don't need no résumé. No references. Pay was steady. Plus, I get to ply my trade. I figured, yeah—if America can't deal with me at home—if I can't get a job and have to live some damn *niggah* in Indianapolis—*Indianapolis,* man!—I *will* go crazy! Bugs, man! Start shootin' up the town. *(Slight pause.)* Maybe even blow up Hawaii.

MAN: Book his ass, Dan-O!
> *Pause.*

BRAZIL: So listen. Where do they put me when I get back to the 'Nam? Where does the Army assign me? The "Pleasure Dome." Saigon. Guys walkin' 'round in civilian shirts, .45s slung real low like John Wayne. I mean, we was the *law* in Saigon! Shit! Cases of Johnnie Walker Black. Fresh meat and fish and fruit. And here I am—itchin'. *Need* my quota of blood. *Gotta* have it!
> *Pause.*

(Shrugs.) No action, so I start whorin' around.

In the midst of his headlong pursuit of liquor, drugs, women and black market activities, Brazil met a 16- or 17-year-old Vietnamese madam's daughter, Tai Lin, and established a relationship with her. He perceived that she really *liked* him, and he had special feelings for her—at 20, he didn't presume to judge whether or not this was love, but he set up housekeeping with Tai Lin and tried to learn a little about her language and customs. One day he brought home a fistful of wildflowers and couldn't resist telling her he loved her. She responded by stroking his face and calling him "Pretty man. pretty man;" and, Brazil remembers, "That afternoon was the first time in four, five months that we made love and I felt like—like I was makin' *love.* Not just gettin' off, but—you know—" It wasn't long before Tai Lin became pregnant.

BRAZIL: . . . . . By this time I'm just—she's my woman, O.K.? I love this lady, man. And—she's got my baby, *our* baby, inside her. And it's—it's incredible, you know? Just incredible. I mean, I feel like—like I've got a purpose now. Somethin' other than bein' this—this machine. A *real* purpose. I'm *makin'* life now. Creating it. Closest a man can get to being God.
> *Pause.*

That feeling is just so—it's—oh, man—
> *Pause.*

So what's the Army do? One day I'm carryin' flowers, next day they slap a sixteen in my hands and sayin' "Okay, son, go do your job." Shit! What fuckin' "job" you talkin' 'bout, man? Jesus, don't do this to me! Just don't—just don't *do* this to me! Please!

> *Pause. Helicopter sound.*

First day in-country, humpin' the boonies, I'm wounded. Rusty, you know? Bullet in the gut, shrapnel in the knee. Damn bullet severs my intestine, so I'm bleedin' and shittin' at the same time. Before I know it, I'm on a slick headin' out. The pilot, he's playin' music. Real loud. Over the chopper blades, man. Weird shit. Not your Rolling Stones kinda shit. But classical stuff. And I'm freakin' 'cause it sounds like, maybe, music dead people hear when they're goin' over.

> *Bring up the undercurrent sound of helicopter blades. Beneath the sound of the whirling blades we hear the instrumental beginnings of the opera "Rinaldo," Act I, the song "Cara Sposa."*

And this one rabbit motherfucker's hunched over me, sayin'—

MAN: You got a medal comin', son! You looked pretty good out there today! Shit! You're goin' *home,* boy! Back to the world—

BRAZIL: Fuck the world, man! I'm think' 'bout Tai! About my baby! I'm *beggin'* him to get ahold of her! Fly her to Japan with me! We're married! Shit, I got a kid on the way! I give him the address—everything, man! Everything!

MAN: Don't sweat it, soldier! Just another casualty! Hey, come on! You're goin' *home!* Get some of that sweet brown sugar! *(Addressing an unseen medic.)* I *am* holding him down, goddammit!

BRAZIL: Fuckin' rabbit.

> *Pause.*

Well, hey, I'm sorry, man. I can't forget her. I've looked at every picture of Saigon I can get my hands on. Fifteen goddamn *years!* Tryin' to see her face. See if she got on a Huey. Pictures of boat people. Lookin' for her. Fifteen goddamn years, you fuckin' bastards!

> *Pause.*

Jesus, I can't forget about her. I wish I could, but I can't! She's—it comes at night. When I'm alone. I see her. Holdin' those flowers. And I—I wonder about her and—my kid. If it's alive. A boy or girl. If it's livin' in the streets with all the other—casualties. And—and I—I think about that kid I shot and wonder if—I— oh, man—*(Brazil breaks down in tears.)*

BACK IN THE WORLD *was produced by the Attic Theater, Detroit under the direction of David L. Regal April 17, 1987.*

THE FILM SOCIETY

A Play in Two Acts

BY JON ROBIN BAITZ

Cast and credits appear on page 438.

THE FILM SOCIETY: At the beginning of his script, the playwright quotes Evelyn Waugh's *A Tourist in Africa:* "The consciences of the English are unnaturally agitated by Africa." This is Baitz's subject. His play has no blacks in it and there is precious little talk about the social problems swirling about Durban's Blenheim School for Boys. He makes his statement simply and powerfully by showing the disintegration of the elite South African white society in its insular decay.

Teacher Jonathon Balton has formed a "film society" as an alternative activity for his charges, somewhat oblivious to the radical posturings of his sodden colleague Terry Sinclair and the financial turmoils of Sinclair's wife, Nan, another teacher. Balton is also unaware that his mother's endowment of the school is about to change his position in Blenheim's hierarchy and his attitudes toward his own existence. Headmaster and owner of the school Neville Sutter, now in his 70s, begins to prepare Balton for the inevitable.

SUTTER: Well, moods change, you know. Parents been fairly passive till bloody Terry had to turn Centenary Day into a Commie-fest. Now they all think this is some sort of terribly, you know, Bohemian institution.

BALTON: Blenheim? Bohemian?

SUTTER: Well, have been a bit loose, haven't we? Been a bit soft, no?

BALTON: It's relative.

SUTTER: That's hardly the point. They want us to be more rigorous. You know, actually, it's quite amazing. These parents went here, right? Boys just like you. They're supposed to be well-informed, youthful, instead they're much worse than my generation, much more suspicious. They want discipline. They wanted Terry's blood.

BALTON: Tell them all to take their boys! Send off to bloody Ferrus or Durban Boys' High! We don't care.

SUTTER: Well, actually, we do care, is the thing. Can't have classrooms without boys.

BALTON: Marvelous idea.

SUTTER: You don't understand. They're complaining about everything. Length of the boys' hair, poor sporting performance, Nan Sinclair—

BALTON: Nan Sinclair? What about Nan? Nan is wonderful! You know that!

SUTTER: Yes, but her husband's gone Commie on us.

BALTON: He has not! And you make it sound like he's a rabid dog, must be put down. He's play-acting! He's out for a thrill. He's got new friends. Needn't take it out on Nan, Neville.

SUTTER: Appearances. You know nothing about it.

BALTON: And none of it has anything to do with film society. *Barefoot Contessa? Moon is Blue? Pillow Talk? Girl Can't Help It? The Killers?* Please, Neville. Great stories.

LOS ANGELES THEATER CENTER—Alan Mandell as Hamish Fox, William Glover as Neville Sutter and Daniel Davis as Jonathon Balton in a scene from *The Film Society* by Jon Robin Baitz

SUTTER: I'm sure.

BALTON: Besides. There has to be something besides cricket and rugger, hasn't there?

SUTTER: Yes. No. Look. Crucial match coming up against Durban Boys' High. And I drove by there yesterday and realized something. That they are quite on the ball. Quite rigorous. I mean, stupid, yes, poor, yes, certainly, but they've got something going on. Those boys are marching about the fields in their short-back-and-sides and it's all amazingly regimented and Lumpen Proletariat, working class, salt of the earth good value, South African hurrah-hurrah, earnestness, but you do see exactly what the parents and Hamish Fox have been complaining about. We should be more in the way of a trial.

BALTON: No we shouldn't.

SUTTER: A trial. It should be like—the commandos.

BALTON: Well, fine. Go backwards, why don't you? I agree one hundred percent. Drag 'em all off to the rugger field for twenty-four-hour-a-day practice. You know, my boys were led out of here looking like they'd been conscripted into the bloody navy. Right out of Captain Bligh, Neville. And these boys aren't rugby material. It's not for everyone being crunched in a scrum. And it's all very well to compare yourself to Durban Boys' High. Perhaps they do come out of there knowing how to tie knots and all that navigate-by-the-stars self-sufficiency business, but they are lacking a certain *imagination*—which to my mind Blenheim has always encouraged. And is exactly what separates Blenheim from all the rest.

SUTTER: That's all true. However, you have to know when to be politic.

BALTON: Baah! Travel films? Smashing. But look. *Charge of the Light Brigade?* Rigor and battle and honor galore and you can't have that in your travelogue of Bali, can you? *Moments,* Neville. Unforgettable moments. Glory—for boys who can't get it on the damn sporting fields! That's film society.

SUTTER: I really wish you wouldn't argue with me. I mean, I am the headmaster. I do know what I'm doing. I do own the school, remember. Sometimes it seems that everyone forgets.

BALTON: But let's be fair.

SUTTER: Well, fine, all very well. But let me try and clarify this. You and Terry decided, after teacher's college and radio theater, that instead of coming here right away, you'd go teach at Durban Boys' High, and I said, "Well, yes. But let's be realistic. You'll hate it." And you both said, "Oh, no, we need to expand and all."

BALTON: That's not fair!

SUTTER: Yes, but let me finish. You lasted a term, if I recall. So much for wanting a "less blue-nosed crowd."

BALTON: Well, it was a mistake. Different stock, more of the yoke of the trek-Boer. Only school I'd ever seen with compulsory marksmanship class. Quite a sight, those stocky little buggers with rifles.

SUTTER: Yes. And what happened?

BALTON: We started teaching here in the spring.

SUTTER: Exactly. *Back* at Blenheim. Do you get it? You're damn lucky that there was a Blenheim to come back to. You mustn't take survival for granted, Jonathon. In order to have a film society, there must first be a Blenheim. No Blenheim, no film society. They've added bloody Doric columns to the library at

Durban High, and I doubt that a single boy has set foot in the thing in twenty years. But they're subsidized. We're not. Terry Sinclair led you down the garden path and back home you came. Well, home is threatened. It's not just going on blithely. This is one of those gruesome periods of readjustment. Happens every fifteen years or so. All we needed was Terry Sinclair to push us over the edge.

BALTON: Is it that bad?

SUTTER: The board is most anxious. *(Beat.)* Interesting, the situations one finds oneself in, eh?

BALTON *(long pause):* How'd it be if once a week I showed a travel short?

SUTTER: I do hate to do this to you.

BALTON: Really, the film society should be a sacred cow, Neville. I don't ask for a lot, do I?

SUTTER: I shouldn't worry, Jonathon. A gesture, a genuflection in a certain direction. That's all that's needed. Interesting. I am fascinated by having to do all this—machinating. Doesn't go on very often.

BALTON: I mean, all they are is nice films.

SUTTER: Bit off-putting, to some. *(Beat.)* I do like this particular classroom, though. It is quite the best here.

BALTON: The Hannibal map? It's very old.

SUTTER: Was it here when you were a boy?

BALTON: Oh, no. No. I believe we had the Roman Empire's progression poster.

SUTTER: 'Course! Yes. Bloody good illustrations of Gauls and Visigoths. Looked like big apes, didn't they? Without genitalia. And the Romans had huge bulges. Fascinating artwork, eh?

BALTON: I showed *Julius Caesar* last month. Class went mad.

SUTTER: Keep the shades open, the lights on, that sort of thing. God knows what they're thinking, you know?

BALTON: But keep McNally away from my boys, will you?

SUTTER: Of course. Good. Right. You'll show travel films and tractor pictures?

BALTON: Once a week.

SUTTER: Right. That's settled then. *(Produces a flask from his jacket.)* Have you glasses?

BALTON: Teacups. Keep a bottle myself.

SUTTER: Only thing to do. One's spirits tend to flag at about half-past three.

BALTON: Blood sugar dropping, I expect.

SUTTER: A bit more than that, really. How'd you like to be assistant head?

BALTON: Pardon?

SUTTER: Hamish Fox has cancer.

BALTON: Cancer? Fox?

SUTTER: It's too ghastly. And my eyes are continuing to go out on me. Sting all the time.

BALTON: That's eyes for you.

SUTTER: Well? You are the most senior.

BALTON: It's a bit of a shock.

SUTTER: Yes. Well. Hamish can hardly walk. The spine, and the viscera, it seems. You needn't decide now but, you know, if you were to pass it up, well, I'm afraid I'd have to offer it to McNally, I suppose.

BALTON: Good Christ!

SUTTER: That's my point! Assistant head receives another four thousand.

BALTON: I'd be quite wealthy, wouldn't I?

SUTTER: Means a lot more on your plate.

BALTON: Won't mother be pleased.

SUTTER: Hamish saw to all the discipline.

BALTON: Yes. I know. I'm not much good at caning.

SUTTER: Well. Have McNally do it then, I don't care. Never enjoyed it. Except with bullies. Bullies I enjoy beating. Bullies I like to hit. Bullies are quite my favorite. McNally's a bully.

BALTON: Lots of bullies at Blenheim, Nev.

SUTTER: Yes. I wonder why.

BALTON: Always been. Your—

SUTTER: Well, never mind that. Also, you have to look after the African staff. They are all terrified of Hamish and it's best to make 'em terrified of you. 'Course, they all know you. Don't bully 'em, mind you, but still.

BALTON: Pool cleared of algae?

SUTTER: Shrubs kept trimmed. Written it all down for you. I do hope you understand, Jonathon. You have had a rather quiet time of it all, and it has, I'll admit, lurched forward unremarkably, but aside from the need to change things around here, you must be aware that you lose a certain mobility when you move from staff to suddenly being assistant headmaster. You find yourself becoming the representative and you have to acknowledge what it is you are representing, follow me? And it's all very well for you to be, you know, indignant and self-righteous about film society and McNally and all, but the fact is that parents have been ringing up in a panic—they see these indications of slack spirit outside the school, outside in the world—you have your hippies and your music and they get scared. "Don't let it happen here, please, Neville—not to our children." And then they come to celebrate the school and give us their money and boys and they get a mad black radical—the thing they fear the most—and really, if you listened to him, he wasn't all that frightening, but all they saw was this warrior—Shaka coming to get 'em. And the implication is, that there is something terribly wrong here, terribly incorrect and not the education which they, as parents in Durban, have assumed that their lads will get. So McNally and Fox, for all their—earnestness, are useful and devoted and friends. Do you understand all this?

BALTON (after a pause): I believe you're saying, "It's time for a change?"

SUTTER: My point exactly.

BALTON: No. I agree with you one hundred and ten percent. We can tighten up ship a bit. But really, if I may, the point seems to be, as I see it, that this is Blenheim. And Blenheim is Blenheim, isn't it? And what else is there in Durban, really?

SUTTER (quite exhausted): Ultimately, that's my point. Also, if you will, take the pellet gun and some dry ice and plug up the holes in the retaining wall.

BALTON: Lizards again?

SUTTER: A plague of 'em. I can't see the little buggers when they rush out any more. One of my small pleasures, and I'm giving it up. Quite a sight to see a gecko dashing about madly through your sights.

BALTON: Dare say it is.

SUTTER: Well. That's that, then. How 'bout a toast?

BALTON: Smashing!

SUTTER *(pause):* Er. Let's see—a toast—

> *They stand still for a moment, and then Sutter just shrugs, and Balton follows suit.*

THE FILM SOCIETY *was produced by Los Angeles Theater Center under the direction of Robert Egan January 22, 1987.*

THE STICK WIFE

A Play in Two Acts

BY DARRAH CLOUD

Cast and credits appear on page 438.

THE STICK WIFE: In a cluttered backyard setting "completely rendered in black and white and tones of gray," a husband and wife—Ed and Jessie Bliss—converse edgily about breakfast. They quarrel, and Ed departs despite Jessie's pleas to him to stay home.

That afternoon Jessie is hanging laundry on the line and indulging, as she does from time to time, in a fantasy about being a famous movie star in an interview with the press. A neighbor, Marguerite Pullet, comes over to tell Jessie the news (though Jessie refuses to hear it): somebody has bombed the church where black people go to worship.

When Ed returns, it's clear that he's not too happy to see Marguerite, and vice versa.

> *He stands there glaring a minute at them, then goes upstage, picks a blade of grass and brings it to Jessie, holding it up to her face.*

ED: See this?

JESSIE: Uh-huh.

ED: Grew.

JESSIE: Uh-huh.

ED: You said it wouldn't.

JESSIE: Did I say that?

ED: Uh-huh.

JESSIE: I thought it'd need some tendin' to, is all.

ED: Didn't.

JESSIE: No.

ED: Grew.
JESSIE (confused): Did I say it wouldn't?
ED: Well, I didn't.
JESSIE: Uh-huh.
ED: Don't ever bet against grass.
    He keeps holding it up in front of her face.
MARGUERITE: Well, I better get back before the phone rings and I'm not there.
JESSIE: I guess you better.
MARGUERITE: I am.

LOS ANGELES THEATER CENTER—Anne Gee Byrd as Jessie and Gene Ross as Ed in a scene from *The Stick Wife* by Darrah Cloud

Marguerite exits out back; Ed drops the grass blade, exits into house; Jessie pulls the wash down, re-hangs it.

JESSIE: I was born in a small town in the South . . . Decatur . . . you never heard of it . . . but I didn't get my start till I left home and moved to the city . . . where I was discovered, bein' a female at a cash register . . . I married the man who discovered me . . .

Red and yellow lights appear, skulking about the periphery; when Jessie turns to them directly, they disappear; Ed enters with a beer.

ED: Who you talkin' to?

JESSIE: Nobody. *He searches around for someone hiding. The phone rings once.*

ED: What's that?

JESSIE *(nervously):* People been callin' here all mornin'.

ED: Who?

JESSIE: I don't know. I didn't answer.

ED: How come?

JESSIE: Just didn't feel like talkin' today.

ED: That's all you been doin'!

JESSIE: But I didn't want to! Just happened!

ED: I was expectin' a call.

JESSIE: Now you're home you can answer.

ED: You hear the news?

JESSIE: You know I get distressed when I hear news. I get a buzz in my ears and have to sit down. Can't think. Can't do anythin'. Makes me sit at the winda, lookin' out. Watchin' for the mailman if it's not a Sunday, comin' closer and closer, stoppin' at every house like he was feedin' it till he gets to ours and slams the boxlid down on the bills and then just fades away like music . . . or that streetcleaner comin' around, you know, with that screamin' machine that eats whatever gets in its way, kittens and gym shoes, and all the little children run out of their houses screamin' and cryin' to save the lives of their toys, rushin' in fronta the streetmachine and grabbin' what they can before it runs 'em over, roarin' by as slow, as slow as a useless life . . .

ED: Somebody bombed a colored church.

Pause.

Blew the bottom out of it . . . Wish I'd a seen it.

He stands watching her work.

JESSIE *(in pain):* Who would do such a terrible, terrible thing as that?

ED: Somebody knew somethin' we didn't, I guess.

Pause; Jessie continues working.

JESSIE: Was anybody hurt?

ED: Only way some people learn.

JESSIE: Wouldn't it be awful if anybody was hurt?

ED: Have you ever wanted for a thing?

Ed exits into house; Jessie turns from laundry at a loss.

JESSIE: You . . . you want lunch? You want lunch? Ed? Dinner won't be till seven . . . Ed? . . . Ed?

He reappears with pants changed, hands the other ones to her.

ED: I gotta have these for work tomorrow.

JESSIE: Where you goin' now?

ED: One little bomb goes off, and the whole town explodes. I gotta see that.
He goes inside.

JESSIE: What did you get on these? . . . Ed? . . . Ed? . . . I don't think this is gonna come out! . . . What did you get on these? . . .
He re-enters, watching her silently.
This isn't gonna come out! This isn't gonna come out!

ED: Just dirt.

JESSIE *(jumps):* Not just dirt.

ED: Alabama dirt. *(He starts to leave.)*

JESSIE: Dinner's at seven.

ED: Too bad.

JESSIE: Why?

ED: Won't be here.

JESSIE: You won't be home for Sunday dinner?

ED: Don't feel like it.

JESSIE: We always have Sunday dinner!

ED: Look at you.

JESSIE: What's wrong?

ED: You fall for it every time.

JESSIE: I don't feel well.

ED: Look O.K.

JESSIE: Got a funny feelin' in my chest.

ED: Don't call the doctor.

JESSIE: Lord, no, I'd never call a doctor on a Sunday.

ED: Can't afford no doctor.

JESSIE: It's just a little thing. Too much Coca-Cola. Coke always makes me nervous. I been nervous all day.

ED: Don't drink my beer.

JESSIE: I won't.

ED: Don't be nervous, either. Don't want my wife nervous.

JESSIE: I don't mind bein' nervous once in a while.

ED: You tryin' to kill me?

JESSIE: No!

ED: Looks like it!

JESSIE: I worry!

ED: See there? See there?

JESSIE: I'm afraid!

ED: She's after me! She's after me!

JESSIE: What'd I do? What I do?

ED: You think I don't know what I'm doin'!

JESSIE: No I don't!

ED: How'm I sposed to do anythin' knowin' they's people in the world thinkin' I can't?

JESSIE: They just don't know you.

ED: That's right. People don't even know me are thinkin' I'm nothin' right now. Thinkin' less than that. Not thinkin' about me at all. Puttin' their thoughts up all over the country so's I can't get around them. I'm trapped in their brains. I'm trapped. I ain't ever gonna get out. And you just like them!

JESSIE: I didn't mean to hurt your feelin's.

ED: I accept what I am. You see me marchin' up Iron Mountain through the rich people's neighborhood, just to prove I'm equal as them? No you don't. I admit myself. I accept what I am. Don't I? Don't I?

JESSIE: Yes you do. *She goes to him; touches his back.*

ED: It's them that don't accept. They up there on that hill in they livin' rooms. Talkin' 'bout rights at cocktail parties. Holdin' they fingers out from the glass. No colored movin' into their neighborhood. Movin' into ours. We white as them, white as them. How come we don't get nothin' for it?

JESSIE *(sincerely):* Maybe we done somethin' wrong.

ED: I didn't do nothin'.

JESSIE *(desperate):* You sure?

ED: You don't know who you're livin' with. You don't know who I am.

JESSIE *(turns away from him):* I don't wanta know.

ED: That's my girl. *He sidles out quietly while her back is turned.*

JESSIE: Don't go . . . Please don't go . . . Ed? *(Turns.)* Ed? . . . Where'd you go? . . . Ed? . . .

> *Jessie turns back to line, pulls down laundry and re-hangs it; the lights appear again; Jessie whirls to look at them and they disappear immediately; she goes back to work.*

I have children . . . two children . . . Oh! I told you that! . . . Well . . . I have their pictures inside. You want me to get them? . . . Yes, I know Marlon Brando . . .

BIG ALBERT *(from inside house):* Ed? . . . Ed?

> *Jessie looks wildly around, steps in a few directions to escape, stops.* Ed?

> *Big Albert and Betty appear out of house.*

JESSIE: No!

BIG ALBERT: Jessie!

JESSIE: Yes.

BIG ALBERT: Ed around?

JESSIE: No.

BIG ALBERT: You know where he went?

JESSIE: Downtown. Just left.

> *Betty hangs back, staring at Jessie.*

BIG ALBERT: Shouldn't leave the house open like that when he's not around.

JESSIE: I never lock my door.

BIG ALBERT: Well, now, you better.

JESSIE: They need to be locked, Ed does it.

BIG ALBERT: Didn't you hear the news this mornin'?

JESSIE: News?

BIG ALBERT: Somebody bombed the colored church.

JESSIE *(shocked):* What?

BIG ALBERT: You heard me.

JESSIE: A church?

BIG ALBERT: That's where they gather.

JESSIE *(painfully):* Good Lord, who in the world would do such a terrible thing as that?

BIG ALBERT: Well, we got a war goin' on here now.

JESSIE: Not me. I don't!

BIG ALBERT: You a part of the country.

JESSIE: Not a part of no war.

BIG ALBERT: Well you are whether you like it or not. You a American.

JESSIE: Was anybody hurt, Albert? Nobody was hurt, where they?

BIG ALBERT: It's a war, Jessie.

> *Betty, behind Albert, nods; holds her hands out and indicates four little girls. Jessie, shocked, turns away from them.*

THE STICK WIFE *was produced by Los Angeles Theater Center under the direction of Roberta Livitow January 15, 1987.*

A DIRECTORY OF NEW-PLAY PRODUCTIONS

Compiled by Sheridan Sweet

Professional 1986–87 productions of new plays by leading companies around the United States that supplied information on casts and credits of first productions at Sheridan Sweet's request, plus a few reported by other reliable sources, are listed below in alphabetical order of the locations of the producing organizations. Date given is opening date, included whenever a record was obtainable from the producing management. All League of Regional Theaters (LORT) and other Equity groups were queried for this comprehensive Directory. Those not listed here either did not produce new or newly-revised scripts in 1986–87 or had not responded by press time. Most of the productions listed—but not all—are American or world premieres. Some are new revisions, second looks or scripts produced previously but not previously reported in *Best Plays*.

Albany: Capital Repertory Company

(Producing directors, Bruce Bouchard, Peter H. Clough)

DUSKY SALLY. By Granville Burgess. October 18, 1986. Director, Jack Chandler; scenery, Jack Chandler; lighting, Jane Reisman; costumes, Randy Barcelo; sound, Andrew G. Luft, Crispin Catricala.

James Hemings	L. Peter Callender
Thomas Jefferson	Pirie MacDonald
Marquis de Lafayette	Richard Maynard
Patsy Jefferson	Katherine Leask
Sally Hemings	Erica Gimpel
James Madison	Richard Maynard

Time: 1787–1826. Place: Paris and Monticello. One intermission.

COMMUNITY PROPERTY. By Darlene Young. November 22, 1986. Director, Peter H. Clough; scenery, Leslie Taylor; lighting, Jackie Manassee; costumes, Heidi Hollmann.

Jesse Tyler	Anne Newhall

Rose Sattorelli	Anna Berger
Paul Sattorelli	John Shepard
Danielo Sattorelli	Frank Biancamano

Time: 1967–1986. Place: The Sattorelli house, Queens. One intermission.

JUPITER AND ELSEWHERE. By Gram Slaton. March, 1987. Director, Tom Bloom; scenery, Robert Thayer; lighting, Lay Opitz; costumes, Lynda L. Salsbury.

Phil	Russ Jolly
Ginger	Nesba Crenshaw
Duncan	Michael Heintzman
Linus	Arch Johnson
Christy	Stephanie Saft
Danny	Doug Wert
Roach	Vincent Lamberti

Time: 1964–65. Place: Fendal, Ohio. Two intermissions.

Albany: Empire State Institute for the Performing Arts

(Producing director, Patricia B. Snyder)

POSSESSION—THE MURDER AT CHERRY HILL. By Sidney Michaels. October 18, 1986. Director, John Going; scenery, Stuart Wurtzel; lighting, John McLain; costumes, William Schroder; sound, Dan Toma; original score, Dennis Buck.

Maria Sanders Van Rensselaer	Sylvia O'Brien
Abraham Whipple	Ean Egas
Dinah Jackson	Louise Stubbs
George Wilson	John Romeo
Abraham Van Rensselaer	David Bunce

Catharine Lansing
  Van Rensselaer......... Tanny McDonald
Little Else............... Shannon Tierney
Arriete .... Kimberly Sajan
Maria P.................. Rosanne Raneri
Henrietta Patrick........... Laurel Murphy
Calvin Pepper ...... Joseph Larrabee-Quandt
Margaret Sandford .... Jeanne Vigliante
Jesse Strange .... Kevin O'Rourke
Elsie Lansing Whipple ..... Catherine Cooper
John Whipple............... David Combs
Stable Boys; Deputies;   Christopher Foster,
Hangmen.............. Christopher Howe
Sheriff Ten Eyck .... Thomas Carson
Jailer; Clown .... Gary O. Aldrich
Deck Officer...... John Thomas McGuire III
  Time and place: Act I: Autumn, September
1926. Scene 1: The house on Cherry Hill. Scene
2: On the hill behind the house, immediately
after. Scene 3: In the woods, a month later. Act
II: Winter. Scene 1: In the house, New Year's
Eve. Scene 2: February 1827. On the Schenec-
tady Turnpike in a buggy. Act III: The spring
murder, May 1827. Scene 1: In the house and
outside it. Scene 2: On the hill behind the house,
two days later. Scene 3: In the house, immediately after. Scene 4: In the Albany jail, a few days
later. Act IV: The summer trials and another
autumn. Scene 1: In the kitchen, July. Scene 2:
Aboard ship, on the pier, at the hanging. August.
Scene 3: The house, three years later. Autumn
1831. Scene 4. On the hill behind the house, a
week later. One intermission.

ALADDIN (musical). Book, Elisabeth Ruth-
man; lyrics, Dennis Buck and Elisabeth Ruth-
man; music, Dennis Buck. May 16, 1987. Director, Peter Webb; choreography, Patrice Soriero;
scenery and costumes, Alexander Okun; lighting,
Victor En Yu Tan; sound, Abe Jacob; musical
director, Maida Libkin.

Aladdin...................... Ron Bohmer
Khadijah .... Jeanne Vigliante
Magician..................... Alan Weeks
Sultan Mustafa the Magnificent.. Joel Aroeste
Zubaydah.................. Betsy Normile
Grand Vizir .... Gary O. Aldrich
Zoubir....................... John Romeo
Badralboudour............. Anny De Gange
Mariem.................... Dyann Arduini
Fatouma............... Jacqueline Serebrani
Slave of the Ring;
  Handmaiden .... Carole Edie Smith
Slave of the Lamp........... John Thomas
                              McGuire III
Rashid .... Christopher Foster
Iskander................. Christopher Howe
Fruit Seller; Abdallah the Jeweler;
  Executioner................. David Bunce
Captain
  of the Guard...... Joseph Larrabee-Quandt
Astrologer; Abd-El-Aziz the Jeweler;
  Tea Seller; Old Man........ Paul J. Villani
Lady of the Feast;
  Handmaiden .... Lea Charisse Woods
Handmaiden; Bat .... Kim Darwin,
                              Stacey Heinz
Guard; Merchant.......... John A. Hamelin
Guard; Sultan's Slave;
  Merchant................... Brent Griffin
  Technical Department Guards: Mark A.
Baird, Peter A. Davis, Jeffrey Helm, Olof Jan-
sson.
  Place: Drawn from the *Tales of the Arabian
Nights*. One intermission.

Staged Readings:
WINE OF SPECIAL VINTAGE. By W.A.
Frankonis. Director, W.A. Frankonis.
JUDGMENT IN JERUSALEM. By Thomas
Babbes. Director, W.A. Frankonis.

Allentown: Pennsylvania Stage Company

(Artistic director, Gregory S. Hurst)

THE HOUSEKEEPER. By James Prideaux.
January 9, 1987.

MORE FUN THAN BOWLING by Steven
Dietz. March 20, 1987. Director, Gregory S.
Hurst.

Staged Readings:
IVAN AND JANE. By Donald Drake.
AT LONG LAST LEO. By Mark Stein.

A QUIET COUNTRY PEOPLE. By Harry
Zimbler.
WHEN THE STARS BEGIN TO FALL. By
Lloyd Gold.
THE LOVE TALKER. By Deborah Pryor.
FAULT LINE. By Jon Klein.

Atlanta: Academy Theater

(Artistic director, Frank Wittow)

HEADLINES. By Frank Wittow. February 18, 1987. Director, Frank Wittow; lighting, Robert Corin; choreography, Terri Kayser; music and musical director, Phillip DePoy.

Gen. Sherman; Others .... Chris Kayser
Mr. Pitts; Others......... Kevin C.J. Crysler
Ivan Allen; Others .... Bill Johns
Rev. Finch; Others .... Kenny Leon
Estelle; Others .... Elizabeth Mercer
Rita; Others .... Carol R. Mitchell
Polly; Others .... Brenda Porter
Booker T. Washington;
    Others .... Tony Vaughn
    Time: 1864 to 1987. Place: In and around Atlanta. One intermission.

CYPARIS. By Barbara Lebow. May 13, 1987. Director, Barbara Lebow; scenery, Michael Halpern; lighting, Robert Corin; sound, Michael Keck; choreography, Terri Kayser.

Auguste Cyparis .... Kenny Leon
Loulouze................. Carol R. Mitchell
Therese..................... Cindy Martin
Papa .... Tony Vaughn
Marcellin .... Chris Kayser
Edouard .... Kimario Nanji
    Time: 1902. Place: The dungeon of the prison in St. Pierre, Martinique. One intermission.

Baltimore: Center Stage

(Artistic director, Stan Wojewodski Jr.; managing director, Peter W. Culman)

IN A PIG'S VALISE (musical). By Eric Overmyer. June 3, 1986. Director, Mark Harrison; musical staging, Marcia Milgrom Dodge; musical direction, Mike Huffman; scenery, Hugh Landwehr; lighting, Pat Collins; costumes, Jess Goldstein; sound, Janet Kalas.

James Taxi.................... Jack Kenny
Dolores Con Leche .... Yamil Borges
Shrimp Bucket......... Michael McCormick
Piles .... Rico T. Tavi
The Bop Op................. Keith Curran
Zoot Alors.................. Steve Pudenz
Root Choyce .... Stanford Egi
Blind Sax .... Arnold K. Sterling
Mustang Sally .... Sheila Peace
Dizzy Miss Lizzy .... Pamela Jame
Gut Bucket .... Alan Brasington
    Place: The Heartbreak Hotel at the corner of Neon and Lonely. One intermission.

DEADFALL. By Grace McKeaney. June 3, 1986. Director, Stan Wojewodski Jr.; scenery, Hugh Landwehr; lighting, Pat Collins; costumes, Jess Goldstein; sound, Janet Kalas.

Bay Brewer .... Jacqueline Knapp
Boo O'Banyon................. John Getz
Wash McComb .... Paul McCrane
Queenanne Fells .... Sally Sockwell
Price Fells .... William Foeller
Gosh Gowen .... Stuart Voytilla
    Time: 1938. Place: Waycross, Ga. One intermission.

REUNION. By Sybille Pearson. June 3, 1986. Director, Irene Lewis; scenery, Hugh Landwehr; lighting, Pat Collins; costumes, Jess Goldstein; sound, Janet Kalas.

D...................... Caitlin O'Connell
Lorraine .... Jennifer Harmon
Michael................... Carlos Carrasco
Leah .... Florence Stanley
Valerie;
    Fantasy Mother .... Anne Gerety
Desk Clerk;
    Man at Meeting; Danny;
    Doctor; Drunk; Pop;
    Mr. Welsh.................. Bob Horen
Maid; Mrs. Johnson;
    Woman at Meeting;
    Dr. Croyers; Nurse; Neighbor;
    Mom................. Rosemary Knower
    Voices of Rachel and Friends: Jennifer Kunzelman, Hillary Keyser, Katherine Williams.
    Time and place: Act I: The present, a hotel lobby; past, various locations in D's life. Act II: Valerie's living room, past and present. One intermission.

ROZA (musical). Book and lyrics by Julian More, music by Gilbert Becaud, based on La Vie Devant Soi by Romain Gary. December 12, 1986. Director, Harold Prince; choreography, Patricia Birch; musical direction and vocal and dance arrangements, Louis St. Louis; scenery, Alexander Okun; lighting, Ken Billington; cos-

CENTER STAGE, BALTIMORE—Caitlin O'Connell and Anne Gerety in a scene from *Reunion* by Sybille Pearson

tumes; Florence Klotz; sound, Lawrence R. Smith.

Hamil	Neal Ben-Ari
Madame Bouaffa	Michelle Mais
Jasmine	Yamil Borges
Doctor Katz	Jerry Matz
Madame Katz	Mary Lou Rosato
N'Da Amadee	Ira Hawkins
Salima	Monique Cintron
Michel	Max Barabas
Banania	Mandla Msomi
Young Momo	Brian Noodt
Max	Al DeCristo
Madame Roza	Georgia Brown
Lola	Bob Gunton
Young Moise	Stephen Rosenberg
Momo	Alex Paez
Moise	Manny Jacobs
Yussef Kadir	Neal Ben-Ari

Time: Not so long ago. Place: A house in Belleville, an immigrant quarter of Paris, inhabited by many different ethnic groups. One intermission.

Buffalo: Studio Arena Theater

(Artistic director, David Frank; managing director, Raymond Bonnard)

T BONE N WEASEL. By Jon Klein. April 2, 1987. Director, Kathryn Long.

PlayWorks (Staged Readings):
AMORPHOUS GEORGE. By Glen Merzer. October 13, 1986. Director, Kathryn Long. With Bess Brown, William Gonta, Carl Kowalkowski, Candace Lee, John Thyret.
IMMIGRANT VOICES. By John Urquhart.

February 9, 1987. Director, Heather T. Spicuzza. With Patricia Carreras, Brian Coatsworth, Eileen Dugan, Colin K. Jones, Moira A. Keenan, William Rauch.
THE MONKEYS COME OUT AT NIGHT. By Tom Williams. May 4, 1987. Director, Kathryn Long. With Peter Palmisano, Susan Toomey, Colin K. Jones, Mary McMahon, Tom Zindle.

Cambridge, Mass.: American Repertory Theater

(Artistic director, Robert Brustein; managing director, Robert J. Orchard)

ARCHANGELS DON'T PLAY PINBALL. By Dario Fo, translated by Ron Jenkins. June 1, 1986. Directors, Dario Fo, Franca Rame; scenery and costumes, Dario Fo; lighting, Robert M. Wierzel; music, Fiorenzo Carpi; sound, Stephen Santomenna.
   Cast: Tiny, Sunny Weather—Geoff Hoyle; 1st Friend, Clerk, Dog Pound Director, Mayor—Peter Gerety; 2d Friend, Clerk, Dogcatcher—Remo Airaldi; 3d Friend, Clerk, Stationmaster—Benjamin Evett; 4th Friend, Jules, Sergeant, Illusionist, Bum—John Bottoms; 5th Friend, Doctor, Clerk, Conductor—Dean Norris; Pastry Cook, Coptic Priest, Inspector, General—Richard Grusin; Blondie—Harriet Harris; 1st Girlfriend, Clerk, Woman at Dog Pound—Sally Schwager; 2d Girlfriend, Clerk, Dogcatcher—Alison Taylor; 3d Girlfriend, Woman at Window—Bonnie Zimering; 4th Girlfriend; 2d Woman at Window—Rima Miller.

TONIGHT WE IMPROVISE. By Luigi Pirandello, new adaptation by Robert Brustein. November 28, 1986. Director, Robert Brustein. With Diane d'Aquila, John Bottoms, Elizabeth Franz.

SWEET TABLE AT THE RICHELIEU. By Ronald Ribman. February 6, 1987. Director, Andrei Serban; scenery and costumes, John Conklin; lighting, Howell Binkley; sound, Stephen Santomenna.
Jeanine Cendrars . . . . Lucinda Childs

Frau Von Kessel . . . . Elizabeth Franz
Driver . . . . Ken Howard
Cathy; Lieder Singer . . . . Lynn Torgove
Henri Dusseau . . . . Nestor Serrano
Estelle Dusseau . . . . Sandra Shipley
Mrs. Karras . . . . Isabell Monk
Anthony . . . . Harry S. Murphy
Lester . . . . James Andreassi
Dr. Atmos . . . . Jeremy Geidt
Mimos Klein . . . . Harriet Harris
Franco Boupacha . . . . Thomas Derrah
Gabriella Bottivicci . . . . Pamela Gien
Cesare Bottivicci . . . . Ken Howard
   Place: Dessert at an elegant spa. No intermission.

Staged Readings:
POOR FOLK'S PLEASURE. By Len Jenkin. April 20, 1987. Director, Len Jenkin. With Steve Coats, Harriet Harris, Laura Innes, Will Patton, Rocco Sisto.
MARTIN NIGHT. By Joshua Goldstein. April 27, 1987. Director, Randy Testa. With Kevin Miller, Celia Wren, Jacqueline Brooks, Alexander Wierzbicki, Jeremy Geidt, Raymond Pape.
BILL. By Glenn Blumstein. May 4, 1987. Director, Randy Testa. With Michael Balcanof, Jacqueline Brooks, Donna Dinovelli, Sam Sifton, James McCarthy.
MOON CITY. By Paul Selig. May 4, 1987. Director, R.J. Cutler. With Sam Sifton, Christina Bynoe, Tamara Jenkins, Linus Gelber, Danielle Howe.

Chicago: Goodman Theater

(Artistic director, Robert Falls; producing director, Roche Schulfer)

GHOST ON FIRE. By Michael Weller. January 19, 1987. Director, Les Waters. With Joe Guzaldo, J.T. Walsh.

SHE ALWAYS SAID, PABLO. Conceived by Frank Galati; words, Gertrude Stein; music, Virgil Thompson and Igor Stravinsky; images,

Pablo Picasso. March 9, 1987. Director, Frank Galati; scenery, John Paoletti, Mary Griswold; lighting, Geoffrey Bushor; musical director, Edward Zelnis; choreographor, Steven Ivcich, Peter Amster; sound, Robert Neuhaus.

Gertrude................. Sussan Nussbaum
Alice........................ Marji Bank
Pablo...................... Larry Russo
Minotaur............... Steven Ivcich
Woman in White........... Carmen Pelton
    Ensemble: Peter Amster, Tom Aulino, Anita Berry, Mark S. Doss, Linda Marie Emond,

Robert Heitzinger, Kurt Johns, Janis Knox, Carmen Pelton, Barbara E. Robertson, Paula Scrofano.

Studio Theater:

ZOO THOUSAND ONE (musical). By and with Friends of the Zoo, music by Mark Nutter. November 12, 1986. Director, Rob Riley.

MY WEREWOLF. By John Schneider. January 22, 1987. Director, David Schweizer, a Theater X, Milwaukee production.

Chicago: Steppenwolf Theater Company

(Artistic director, Gary Sinise; managing director, Stephen B. Eich)

BANG. By Laura Cunningham. September 28, 1986. Director, Randall Arney; scenery and lighting, Kevin Rigdon; costumes, Erin Quigley; sound, Jeff Webb.
Sheila Calendar .... Rondi Reed

Len Calendar................. Rick Snyder
Bev LeFevre................. Moira Harris
Roy LeFevre .... Gary Cole
    Place: An underground condominium in Utah. One intermission.

Chicago: Victory Gardens Theater

(Artistic director, Dennis Zacek)

SHOOT ME WHILE I'M HAPPY. By Steve Carter. November 14, 1986. Director, Sydney Daniels; scenery, Nan Zabriskie; lighting, Barbara Reeder; costumes, Kerry Fleming; choreographer, Ronald Stevens.
Abel .... Ronald Stevens
Damselle; Nurse .... Kucha Brownlee
Louie; Orderly............... Robert Curry
Maman..................... Rita Warford
Belle .... Adjora Faith Stevens
Vanille Du St. Jacques .... Tom Towles

KIDS IN THE DARK. By Rick Cleveland and David Breskin. April 2, 1987. Director, Dennis Zacek; scenery, Patrick Kerwin; lighting, Michael Rourke; costumes, Maureen Kennedy; sound, Galen G. Ramsey.
Albert..................... Robert Bundy
Andrew.................... Philip Euling
Tracy .... Mary MacDonald Kerr
Randy....................... Dan Moser
Eddy..................... Patrick O'Neill
Rachel .... Karen Schiff
Mark....................... Jeremy Sklar
Ronny.................... Andrew White
    Time: Spring and summer 1984. Place: A quiet middle-class suburb anywhere in the United States.

Victory Gardens Theater and Body Politic Theater: The Great Chicago Playwrights Exposition, June 10–July 19, 1987, full-length productions:

GARDINIA'S 'N BLUM. By Nicholas A. Patricca. Director, Dennis Zacek; scenery, James Dardenne; lighting, Robert Shook; costumes, John Hancock Brooks Jr.; sound, Galen G. Ramsey.
Tony...................... Bernie Landis
Roberta.................. Petrea Burchard
Harry .... William J. Norris
Frazier .... Kenn E. Head
Ange..................... Joan Spatafora
Peppinu .... Phil Locker
    Time: The present. The action takes place over a two-week period. Place: The barbershop of Tony Gardinia.

IN THE SERVICE OF OTHERS. By Valerie Quinney. Director, James O'Reilly; scenery, Jeff Bauer; lighting, Michael Rourke; costumes, Kerry Fleming; sound, Mark Grinnel.
Hampton Wright............. Joe D. Lauck
Carey Wright............... Virginia Smith
Bert............... Johnny Lee Davenport
George Wright................ Charles Noel
Virginia Perkins............... Lee Guthrie
Epsie Perkins............ Virginia Harding
Vernon Perkins .... Jeffrey Steele
Preacher Dudley .... Gerry Becker
Dempsey.................. James McCance
    Time: The beginning of September 1918. Place: A mill village in Alamance County, North Carolina. One intermission.

Shorts Program:

CENTIPEDE. By Rick Cleveland. Director, Sandy Shinner; scenery, Jeff Bauer; lighting, Michael Rourke; costumes, Kerry Fleming; sound, Mark Grinnel. With Ed Blatchford.

JOHN WAYNE MOVIES. By John Logan. Director, Sandy Shinner; scenery, Jeff Bauer; lighting, Michael Rourke; costumes, Kerry Fleming; sound, Mark Grinnel.
Donna...................... Mary Seibel
Jerry...................... Charles Noel
    Time: The present. Place: Living room of Jerry and Donna's apartment in Queens.

MOTHERS AND SONS. By Lonnie Carter. Director, Sandy Shinner; scenery, Jeff Bauer; lighting, Michael Rourke; costumes, Kerry Fleming; sound, Mark Grinnel.
Evangeline Poole............... Pat Bowie
Deborah Libby............. Virginia Smith

TAKUNDA. By Charles Smith. Director, Nick Faust; scenery, Jeff Bauer; lighting, Michael Rourke; costumes, Kerry Fleming; sound, Mark Grinnel.
Takunda.................... Sydney Hardy
Woman....................... Pat Bowie
Man One........... Johnny Lee Davenport
Man Two.............. Michael E. Myers
    Time: 1973. Place: Salisbury, Rhodesia.

ROOF TOP PIPER. By David Hernandez. Director, Chuck Smith; scenery, Jeff Bauer; lighting, Michael Rourke; costumes, Maureen Kennedy.
Woman....................... Pat Bowie
Man .... Johnny Lee Davenport
Man .... Henry Godinez

THE NEWS FROM ST. PETERSBURG. By Rich Orloff. Director, Chuck Smith; scenery, Jeff Bauer; lighting, Michael Rourke; costumes, Maureen Kennedy.
Fyodor .... Charles Noel
Anya .... Mary Seibel
Sasha...................... Gerry Becker
Nikolai .... Jeffrey Steele
Cow of Noble Birth .... Bessie

Time: Afternoon. Place: Pre-Revolutionary Russia.

THEY EVEN GOT THE RIENZI. By Claudia Allen. Director, Chuck Smith; scenery, Jeff Bauer; lighting, Michael Rourke; costumes, Maureen Kennedy.
Ponzecki.................... Edgar Meyer
Man .... Henry Godinez
Woman....................... Pat Bowie
    Time: The present. Place: Various locales around Clark and Diversey.

FLOOR ABOVE THE ROOF. By Daniel Theriault. Director, Joseph Sadowski; scenery, Jeff Bauer; lighting, Michael Rourke; costumes, Maureen Kennedy.
Elroy..................... Henry Godinez
Cantor .... Johnny Lee Davenport
Jay .... Michael E. Myers
Swifty .... Ed Blatchford
    Time: The present, one August working day. Place: A loading dock of a warehouse on 20th Street and Broadway in New York.

BEFORE I WAKE. By William J. Norris. Director, Susan Osborne-Mott; scenery, James Dardenne; lighting, Robert Shook; costumes, Glenn Billings.
Daniel..................... Edgar Meyer
Molly .... Joan Spatafora

THE FIGURE. By Clifton Campbell. Director, Terry McCabe. scenery, James Dardenne; lighting, Robert Shook; costumes, Glenn Billings.
Keegan .... Phil Locker
Andecker .... Jerry Bloom
Bess............... Mary MacDonald Kerr
Kerry .... Ramsey Midwood
    Time: The present. Place: A small investigation room in central Florida.

Workshops:

MOONLIGHT DARING US TO GO INSANE. By E. Eugene Baldwin. Director, Pauline Brailsford.
THE TETHER DISORDER. By Clifton Campbell. Director, Sandy Shinner.

Cleveland: Cleveland Play House

(Acting artistic director, William Rhys)

THE PRAYING MANTIS. By Alejandro Sieveking, translated from *La Mantis Religiosa* by Charles Philip Thomas. September 16, 1986. Director, Evie McElroy; scenery, Keith Henry; lighting, D. Glen Vanderbilt; costumes, Estelle Painter.
Llalla .... Dawn Gray
Lina .... Catherine Albers

BODY POLITIC THEATER/VICTORY GARDENS THEATER, CHI-
CAGO—Joan Spatafora and Bernie Landis in *Gardenia's 'n' Blum* by Nicholas
A. Patricca, an offering of the Play Expo

Adela . . . . Sharon Bicknell
Juan . . . . Andrew May
Aparicio . . . . Robert Grey
Teresa . . . . Rebecca Manning
    Time: The present. Place: Talcahuano, Chile.
One intermission.

TO DIE FOR GRENADA. By Derek Walcott.
October 21, 1986. Director, Kay Matschullat;
scenery, Charles Berliner; lighting, Richard
Gould; costumes, Estelle Painter; sound, Steve
Shapiro; music, David Gooding.

Christine Field . . . . Jill Larson
Noel Birch . . . . Alan Coates
Captain Whitehead;
  Restaurant Sommelier;
  Man in Hat . . . . Roger Robinson
Rafiq "Max" Mohammed . . . . Erick Avari
Harlan Cade . . . . Morgan Lund
American Ambassador . . . . Bill Lewis
Mervyn Hospedales . . . . James P. Kisicki
Margot Hospedales . . . . Pamela Tucker-White
Nabo; Prisoner . . . . Terry Alexander
    Time: October 1983. Place: Monos, a small

island off the coast of Trinidad. One intermission.

MENSCH MEIER. By Franz Xaver Kroetz, translated by Roger Downey. January 27, 1987. Director, George Ferencz; scenery, Bill Stabile; lighting, Blu; costumes, Estelle Painter; music and sound, Steve Shapiro.

Otto .... Thomas Kopache
Martha .... Catherine Albers
Ludwig.................. Joseph Pecchio
    Two intermissions.

THE ARABIAN KNIGHT. Conceived and adapted by Joseph J. Garry Jr. and David O.

Frazier, based on the music, lyrics and poetry of Ann Mortifee. May 12, 1987. Director, Joseph J. Garry; musical direction, Jack Lee; scenery, Richard Gould; lighting, Kirk Bookman; costumes, Estelle Painter; sound, Greg Pauker.

Richard Burton .... David O. Frazier
Isabel Burton .... Debby Duffy Young
Scheherazade .... Ann Mortifee
    People of the Desert: Molly McGrath Cornwell, Jeffrey Guyton, Mary Michenfelder, Rex Nockengust, Robert C. Rhys, Jean Zarzour.
    Act I: Sir Richard Burton's last 1001 nights, Trieste, 1887. Act II: Trieste, 1890. One intermission.

Costa Mesa, Calif.: South Coast Repertory

(Producing artistic director, David Emmes; artistic director, Martin Benson)

HIGHEST STANDARD OF LIVING. By Keith Reddin. September 1986. Director, David Emmes; scenery, Ralph Funicello; lighting, Peter Maradudin; costumes, Susan Denison.

Bob .... Jeffrey Combs
Ludmilla............... Patricia Lodholm
Tatiana; Adele................ Anni Long
Lonnie; Jean................. Irene Roseen
Mother; Helen.......... Ann Siena-Schwartz
Yri; Gary .... Michael Tulin
Dmitri; Doug............... Ron Boussom
Vlad; Jack .... Art Koustik
Tom; Larry .... Richard Doyle
Sergei; Don .... Hal Landon Jr.
Rodger; Rick .... John Ellington
    Ensemble: Martin Henke, Brennan Howard, Steve Ingrassia, Ken Jensen, T. Bradshaw Yates.
    Children: Corbett Bufton, Steve Gribben, Kathleen Corey Staiger, Nicole Parker, Paul Root, Jason Cast, Laurie Cast, John Schnitzer, Zachary Okun, Todd Williamson.

BIRDS. By Lisa Loomer. November 7, 1986. Director, Ron Lagomarsino; scenery, Kent Dorsey; lighting, Cameron Harvey; costumes, Charles Tomlinson.

Gloria Vasquez .... Olivia Negron
Jasmine Vasquez .... Socorro Santiago
Lilly Vasquez............... Myriam Tubert
Manuel Vasquez .... Rick D. Telles
Chrystal Perkins;
    Christina Dart .... Heather Lee
Manny Vasquez.......... Manuel Santiago

THREE POSTCARDS (musical). Book, Craig Lucas; music and lyrics, Craig Carnelia. January 6, 1987. Director, Norman René; scenery, Loy

Arcenas; lighting, Debra J. Kletter; costumes, Walter Hicklin; sound, Bruce Cameron; choreographer, Linda Kostalik.

Bill .... Craig Carnelia
Big Jane .... Jane Galloway
Walter...................... Brad O'Hare
Little Jane .... Maureen Silliman
K.C. .... Karen Trott

COLD SWEAT. By Neal Bell. February 1987. Director, David Emmes; scenery, Michael Devine; lighting, Peter Maradudin; costumes, Nicole Morin; sound, Jim Rohrig.

Alice....................... Karen Hensel
Jamie .... Michael Canavan
Gordon............... Hubert B. Kelly Jr.
Hanson; Ray .... Tom Ligon
Emma............... Mary Anne McGarry
Bess............... Ann Siena-Schwartz
Court .... Jack Axelrod
Leon .... Richard Doyle

Staged Readings:

PLAY YOURSELF. By Harry Kondoleon.
HAUT GOUT. By Allan Havis.
THE VIRGIN MOLLY. By John Quincy Long.
BIG TIME: SCENES FROM A SERVICE ECONOMY. By Keith Reddin.
SWEET POWDER. By Eduardo Machado.

1987 Hispanic Playwrights Project:

THE PROMISE. By Jose Rivera.
PASSION. By Ana Maria Simo.
BLACKLIGHT. By Estela Portillo Trambley.
THE DEATH AND LIFE OF LUIS RODRIGUEZ. By Bernardo Solano.
MIDDLE GRAY. By Sam Garcia.
THE JUDAS GOAT. By Alfred Lopez.

Dallas: Theater Three

(Founding-artistic director, Norma Young; executive producer-director, Jac Alder)

ANIMAL FARM (musical). By George Orwell, adapted by Peter Hall; lyrics, Adrian Mitchell; music, Richard Peaslee. January 24, 1987. Director, Laurence O'Dwyer; musical director, Gary C. Mead; scenery, Cheryl Denson; lighting, Shari Melde; costumes, Bruce R. Coleman; sound, Tristan Wilson.

Boy . . . . Craig Ames
Snowball . . . . Sa'mi Chester
Squealer . . . . Dwain Fail

Boxer . . . . Lynn Mathis
Napoleon . . . . Kyle McClaran
Mollie . . . . Beverly Nachimson
Minimus . . . . Keith Oncale
Muriel . . . . Kati Porter
Old Major . . . . Stephanie Rascoe
Benjamin . . . . Kurt Rhoads
Mr. Jones . . . . Jeff Ricketts
Clover . . . . Karen Seal
One intermission.

Denver: The Changing Scene

(Artistic directors, Maxine Hunt, Alfred Brooks)

LEAVING THE PLANET SALE. By Lisa Williams. July 6, 1986. Director, Kirby Henderson; costumes, Nancy Bassett.
Sasha . . . . Sally Gunter
Amy . . . . Karen Casteel
Punk . . . . Ted Monte
Housewife . . . . Lizabeth Anne Roehrs
Moslem Man;
    Street Person . . . . Raymond Carreker
Moslem Wife; Woman . . . . . Jan Hetherington
Harry Skelter; Muscle Man . . . . . . Tim Elliott
Mr. Fix-it;
    Gay Caballero . . . . David T. Kottenstette
One intermission.

DEAL WITH A DEAD MAN. By Tom DeMers. September 4, 1986. Director, Kirby Henderson; scenery and lighting, Hugh Graham; costumes, Nancy Bassett.
Stone Wahl . . . . Rich Beall
Bonzo; Elroy Baggett . . . . Tim Sexton
Digger Fernandez; Doctor . . . . . Tom DeMers
Fruitfry . . . . John Fortin
Elinor Baggett; Judy Jerome . . . Leigh Armor
Hamlet; Kenny Bulova . . . . Bill Stewart
    Time: Twenty-four hours in 1933. Place: Los Angeles. One intermission.

FOIL. By Jay Derrah. October 9, 1986. Director and designer, Dennis Bontems.
Beatrice Buckler . . . . Kathryn Meistrell

Jake O'Drake . . . . Kevin Smith
Hank; Gov. Strongarm
    Armstrong . . . . Kenneth Dean
Drummer; Logger; Doctor . . . . . Ken Niemeier
Customer; Hedger; Bebe's Manager;
    Old Man . . . . Christopher Leo
Nurse . . . . Colleen Kirby
One intermission.

AMERICAN GOTHIC. By Joseph McDonough. February 17, 1987. Director and set designer, Edward Osborn; lighting, Eric Lassi; costumes, Rex Fuller.
Alma . . . . Lynn Johnstone Osborne
Ed . . . . James Aerni
Booney . . . . John Doyle
    Time: The Present. Place: An isolated farm in mid-America.

DESCENDING. By David Shawn Klein. March 17, 1987. Director, Stephen Kramer; scenery, Paul Sehnert. With Leigh Armor, F. Douglas Brown, Gary Carnes, David Andrew Dalton, John Fortin, Todd Fruth, Geoffrey Lasko, Margaret Sharp.

FAVORITE SPORTS OF THE MARTYRS. By Norman Lock. April 14, 1987. Director and set designer, Dennis Bontems; costumes, Nancy Bassett. With Heather Bean, John Fortin, Rebecca Harper, Brian Robertson, Peggy Russell.

Denver: Denver Center Theater Company

(Artistic director, Donovan Marley)

GOODNIGHT, TEXAS. By Terry Dodd. September 29, 1986. Director, Bruce K. Sevy; scenery, Pavel M. Dobrusky; lighting, Wendy Heffner; sound, Lora Mihelic.

Kristin .... Leslie Hendrix
Coleen................... Caitlin O'Connell
Alec .... Peter Lohnes
Guy........................... Kevin Gray
Brad .... Roderick Aird
     Time: Saturday, late August. Place: The Oaklawn section of Dallas, a borderline well-to-do neighborhood right off Turtle Creek Drive near downtown Dallas. One intermission.

THE WORLD OF MIRTH. By Murphy Guyer. September 30, 1986. Director, Peter Hackett; scenery, Pavel M. Dobrusky; lighting, Wendy Heffner; sound, Lora Mihelic.
Sweeney .... Jamie Horton
Buffy.................... Caitlin O'Connell
Emmett..................... Archie Smith
Augie .... Dougald Park
Patch .... Jim Baker
Ken Harley .... Jack Casperson
Kaspar .... Frank Georgianna
Accomplice .... John Stewart
Marcey...................... Anna Miller
     Time: Late evening and the following day. Place: A carnival. One intermission.

RACHEL'S FATE. By Larry Ketron. January 6, 1987. Director, Murphy Guyer; scenery and costumes, John Dexter; lighting, Michael W. Vennerstrom.
Cliffort .... Richard Elmore
Owen .... Mick Regan
Andrea .... Lynnda Ferguson
Fugut .... Stephen Lee Anderson
     Time and Place: Act I: Summer. A highway rest stop in South Carolina. Act II: The next morning. One intermission.

SHOOTING STARS. By Molly Newman. March 16, 1987. Director, Randal Myler; scenery, Richard L. Hay; lighting, Wendy Heffner; costumes, Janet S. Morris; sound, Benton Delinger.
Gay....................... Nancy Houfek
Butch .... Anna Miller

Tammy................... Wendy Lawless
Wilma................... Lynnda Ferguson
Birdie .... Sandra Ellis Lafferty
Shelby..................... Leslie Hendrix
Charlene................. Caitlin O'Connell
Cassius .... Archie Smith
     Time: Christmas Week, 1962. Place: A boys' high school locker room in a small Midwestern town. One intermission.

LOST HIGHWAY: THE MUSIC AND LEGEND OF HANK WILLIAMS. By Randal Myler and Mark Harelik. April 19, 1987. Director, Randal Myler; scenery, Richard L. Hay; lighting, Charles MacLeod; costumes, Andrew V. Yelusich; sound, John Pryor, Steve Stevens.
Tee-Tot...................... Ron Taylor
Hank Williams.............. Mark Harelik
Hoss .... Mick Regan
Jimmy...................... Jamie Horton
Audrey; Young Woman .... Fredi Olster
Leon .... Danny Wheetman
Mama; Cajun Woman...... Kay Doubleday
Pap .... Michael Winters
Voice of the Announcer .... Jim Baker
     Time: The Life of Hank Williams, 1923–1953. Place: From the hills of rural Alabama to the stage of the Grand Ol' Opry in Nashville. One intermission.

Prima Facie III: A Presentation of New American Plays, March 16, 17 and April 1, 2
WASPS. By Roger Cornish. Director, Bruce K. Sevy.
KOOSY'S PIECE. By Frank X. Hogan. Director, Donovan Marley.
VETS. By Donald Freed. Director, Laird Williamson.
GUS AND AL. By Albert Innaurato. Director, Peter Hackett.
TROPHY HUNTERS. By Kendrew Lascelles. Director, Donovan Marley.
TRIPLETS. By Constance Ray. Director, Bruce K. Sevy.

Detroit: Attic Theater

(Artistic director, Lavinia Moyer; managing director, Bruce Makous)

VAUDEVILLE. By Laurence Carr. November 21, 1986. Director, Laurence Carr; scenery and costumes, Philipp Jung; lighting, Gary Decker; sound, Bill Swayze, Dan Spahn.

BACK IN THE WORLD. By Stephen Mack Jones. April 17, 1987. Director, David L. Regal;

scenery, Eric M. Johnson; lighting, Timothy Alvaro; costumes, Anne Saunders; sound, Tony Vaillancourt.
The Man .... Clifford A. Reed
Sgt. Maj. Hannibal
Bellsen............... Von H. Washington
Pfc. Maurice T. Morton......... Tim Rhoze

Spec. 4 Anthony "Jam"
Brazil................... Lou Beatty Jr.
Cpl. James Norman
Stephens .... Reuben Yabuku
Time: The present. One intermission. (An ATCA selection; see introduction to this section.)

THE BALLAD OF CONRAD AND LORETTA (musical). Book, Christopher Reed, Ronald Martell; music and lyrics, Christopher Reed. Director, Ronald Martell; musical staging and choreography, Bick Goss; musical director, Richard Berent; scenery, Gary Decker; lighting,

Paul Brohan; costumes, Kristine Flones-Czeski; sound, Bill Swayze and Dan Spahn.
Conrad Stumblecram ...... Christopher Reed
Loretta Butts .... Cynthia Carle
Sammy California .... Robert Grossman
Johnny Worst .... Paul Hopper
Honey; Wanda May Billy Jean;
Beverly Hills................ Beth Taylor
Merle; Bus Driver;
Announcer.................. Joseph Reed
Time: The present, six days. Place: The action travels from Cactus Flats, Okla. to Albuquerque to Hollywood to Tijuana and back again. One intermission.

Detroit: Detroit Repertory Theater

(Artistic director, Bruce Millan; executive director, Robert Williams)

TIME CAPSULE. By Paul Simpson. April 30, 1987. Director, Bruce Miller; scenery, Bruce Millan; lighting, Kenneth R. Hewitt Jr.; costumes, B.J. Essen; sound, Reuben Yabuku, Karl

Yabuku.
Lisa.................. Fran L. Washington
Larry .... Council Cargle
Place: The bedroom. One intermission.

Dorset, Vt.: Dorset Theater Festival

(Artistic director, Jill Charles; producing director, John Nassivera)

THE ORCHARD. By John Nassivera. July 24, 1986. Director, Jill Charles; scenery, William John Aupperlee; lighting, Vincent DonVito; costumes, Deanna Majewski.

DOWN AN ALLEY FILLED WITH CATS. By Warwick Moss. August 21, 1986. Director, John Wood; scenery, William John Aupperlee; lighting, Timothy Foley; costumes, Deanna Majewski. With Alan Coates, Frank Anderson.

Evanston, Ill.: Northlight Theater

(Artistic director, Michael Maggio; managing director, Susan Medak)

DEALING. By June Shellene and Richard Fire. December 9, 1986. Director, Michael Maggio; scenery, Linda Buchanan; lighting, Robert Shook; costumes, Kaye Nottbusch.
Ronnie .... Tim Halligan
Sid........................... Ron Dean
Val .... Holly Fulger
John .... Kevin Dunn
Bob....................... B.J. Jones
Gary...................... Don Franklin
George .... Gary Houston
Brenda .... Barbara E. Robertson
Dealers: Terrance Auch, Brian Bakke, Stuart Greenman, Carlton Miller, Cristy Munden, Arthur Pearson, Rick Russo, Michael Sadowski.
Time: 1986. Place: A commodities exchange in Chicago. One intermission.

FREE ADVICE FROM PRAGUE—AN EVENING OF PLAYS: AUDIENCE and UNVEILING. By Vaclav Havel, translated by Jan Novak. October 22, 1986. Director, Kyle Donnelly; scenery, Eve Cauley; lighting, Rita Pietraszek; costumes, Jessica Hahn.
Audience
Ferdinand Vanek............. John Cothran
Brewmaster .... Gary Houston
Place: A brewmaster's office.
Unveiling
Ferdinand Vanek............. John Cothran
Vera .... Kathy Taylor
Michal .... Tom Amandes
Place: An apartment in Prague.

NORTHLIGHT THEATER, EVANSTON, ILL.—Tom Amandes, John Cothran and Kathy Taylor in the world premiere of *Free Advice From Prague,* a program of two one-acts, *Audience* and *Unveiling,* by Vaclav Havel, translated by Jan Novak

Hartford, Conn.: Hartford Stage

(Artistic director, Mark Lamos)

THE GILDED AGE. By Mark Twain and Charles Dudley Warner, adapted by Constance Congdon. October 4, 1986. Director, Mark Lamos; scenery, Marjorie Bradley Kellog; lighting, Pat Collins; costumes, Jess Goldstein; sound, David Budries.

Cast: Mrs. Nancy Hawkins—Wendy Brennan; George Washington Hawkins, Congressman Ames, Doctor, Reporter—Craig Bryant; Philip Sterling, Steamboat Pilot, Prosecuting Attorney, Senator, Policeman—Terrence Caza; Polly Sellers, Mrs. Grant, Steamboat Passenger—Constance Crawford; "Little Eva", Belle, Steamboat Passenger, Pearl Fairchild, Mrs. Newell, Mrs. Gilette, Lady Author—Melissa Gallagher; Col. Beriah Sellers, Congressman, Steamboat Pilot, "Topsy"—Philip Goodwin; Carpetbagger, "Mt. St. Clare", Steamboat Cub, Thurlo, Bixby, Senator, Arthur, Policeman, Usher—Joseph Houghton; Jeff Thompson, Bill O'Riley, Steamboat Passenger, Hardin, Gus, Senator, Lawyer, Uncle Jack—Douglas Krizner; President of the Columbus River Slack Water Navigation Project, Restaurant Manager, "Uncle Tom", Steamboat Steward, Hiram Grenville, Senator, Alienist,

Noble, Jury Foreman—Kevin McGuire; Harry Brierly, Steamboat Leadsman, Senator, Reporter, Actor—Michael McKenzie; Senator Abner Dilworthy, Ira, Steamboat Captain, J.C., Judge, Auctioneer—Joel Miller; Laura Hawkins, "Mrs. St. Clare"—Alison Stair Neet; Maj. Charles Langhorne Gillette, Pinchly, Clyde, Sen. Buckstone, Andrews—M. Bradford Sullivan; Edward Braham, Restaurant Waiter, Steamboat Passenger, Dale, Tailor, Senate Chairman, Hotel Clerk, Defense Attorney—Ralph Zito.

A DOLL'S HOUSE. By Henrik Ibsen, translated by Irene B. Berman, English text by Gerry Bamman. November 15, 1986. Director, Emily Mann; scenery, Andrew Jackness; lighting, Pat Collins; costumes, Dunya Ramicova; sound, David Budries; music, Mel Marvin.

Norma Helmer	Mary McDonnell
Messenger	Justin Pyrke-Fairchild
Torvald Helmer	Gerry Bamman
Helene	Diane Dreux
Mrs. Kristine Linde	Janet Zarish
Nils Krogstad	David Strathairn
Dr. Rank	Mark Lamos

Anne Marie . . . . Margot Stevenson
  The Helmer Children: William A. Friedle,
Jumper Lark, Meagan E. Seitz Smith.

CHILDREN. By A.R. Gurney Jr., based on a
John Cheever story. January 3, 1987. Director,
Jackson Phippin. With Scotty Bloch, Cara Duff-
MacCormick, Cynthia Mace, Jake Turner.

MOROCCO. By Allan Havis. May 9, 1987. Director, Mark Lamos.

Houston: Stages Repertory Theater

(Artistic director, Ted Swindley)

Plays-in-Progress:
IN LEBANON. By Tom White.
LITTLE LULU IN A TIGHT ORANGE
DRESS. By John G. Moynihan.

A MARRIAGE OF SORTS. By Jo Vander
Voort.
JANUARY. By Rosellen Brown.

Lansing, Mich.: BoarsHead Public Theater

(John Peakes, artistic director)

Winterfare '87, Jan. 28–March 22, 1987:
THE ONLY SONG I KNOW. By John C. Cam-
eron. Director, Jim Burton; lighting, James E.
Peters; costumes, Charlotte Deardoff; sound,
D.J. Krogol.
Anita. . . . . Laural Merlington
Margaret. . . . . Carmen Decker
Rachel Hern. . . . . Julie Lentz
John . . . . Kyle Euckert
Rachel Turner . . . . Wendy Keeley
Karl . . . . David Edward Jones
Tommy. Frederick Hill
  Time: The present and the memory of Marga-
ret Campbell. Flashbacks in the late 1920s and
early 1930s in Kentucky near the Tennessee bor-
der. Place: Margaret Campbell's room. One in-
termission.

BULLETS TO THE GUN. By Justin Peacock.
Director, Alan Benson; lighting, James E. Peters;
costumes, Charlotte Deardoff; sound, D.J. Krogol.
He. . . . . Jeff Gruszewski

She . . . . Terri Kent Gruszewski
  Time: The present. Place: An office building.

A PICTURE OF OSCAR WILDE. By Peter D.
Sieruta. Director, John Peakes; lighting, James
E. Peters; costumes, Charlotte Deardoff; sound,
D.J. Krogol.
Oscar Wilde. . . . . Mark Colson
  Time: September 1881. Place: The study of
Oscar's mother's home in London. One intermis-
sion.

PHOTOGRAPHIC MEMORY. By Kim Car-
ney. Director, John Peakes; lighting, James E.
Peters; costumes, Charlotte Deardoff; sound,
D.J. Krogol.
Goldina. . . . . Laural Merlington
Dennis . . . . Ian Peakes
Ernie. . . . . David Edward Jones
Barbara. . . . . Terri Kent Gruszewski
Jim . . . . Jim Burton
  Time: 1978. Place: A kitchen in Ionia, Michi-
gan.

Los Angeles: Los Angeles Theater Center

(Artistic producing director, Bill Bushnell)

SPAIN '36. By The San Francisco Mime
Troupe; book, Joan Holden; music and lyrics,
Bruce Barthol, Edward Barnes. June 5, 1986.
Director, Daniel Chumley; musical director, Ed-
ward Barnes; choreographer, Kimi Okada; sce-
nery, lighting and costumes, Timian Alsaker;
sound, Jon Gottlieb.
  Cast: Wilma Bonet, Charles Degelman, Ar-
thur Holden, Gustave Johnson, Jerry Kerrigan,
Ed Levey, Kate Lindsey, Sharon Lockwood,
Barrett A. Nelson, Muziki Duane Roberson,
Eduardo Robledo, Phillip Ray Rolfe, Joe
Romano, Maura Sandoval, Audrey Ann Smith,
Leonard L. Thomas, Deanar Ali Young.
  Time: 1936–39. Place: Spain and other locales.

ALFRED & VICTORIA: A LIFE. By Donald
Freed. November 19, 1986. Director, Gerald
Hiken; scenery, Clifton R. Welch; lighting,
Douglas D. Smith; costumes, Jill Brousard;
sound, Jon Gottlieb.
Victoria.................... Dinah Manoff
Alfred...................... Gerald Hiken
    Time and Place: Act I, Scene 1: Los Angeles,
August 1968. Scene 2: Los Angeles, December
23, 1970. Scene 3: Athens, August 14, 1974. Act
II, Scene 1: Bel Air, Calif., December 23, 1976;
Scene 2: Chapel, St. John's Hospital, Santa
Monica, Calif., August 1981. Scene 3: Los An-
geles, August 1981. Scene 4: St. John's Hospital,
Santa Monica, Calif., August 1981.

8th Los Angeles Theater Center Festival:
THE STICK WIFE. By Darrah Cloud. January
15, 1987. Director, Roberta Livitow; scenery,
lighting and costumes, Pavel M. Dobrusky;
sound, Jon Gottlieb.
Ed Bliss .... Gene Ross
Jessie Bliss .... Anne Gee Byrd
Marguerite Pullet .... Chris Weatherhead
Big Albert Connor .... Larry Drake
Betty Connor................ Camilla Carr
Tom Pullet.................. Richard Dean
    Time: Act I: September 1963. Act II: Novem-
ber 1963. Place: Birmingham, Ala. One intermission. (An ATCA selection; see introduction to
this section.)

THE FILM SOCIETY. By Jon Robin Baitz.
January 22, 1987. Director, Robert Egan; sce-
nery, D. Martyn Bookwalter; lighting, Martin
Aronstein; costumes, Robert Blackman; sound,
Jon Gottlieb; original music, Daniel Birnbaum.
Jonathon Balton .... Daniel Davis
Nan Sinclair................ Kate Mulgrew
Mrs. Balton .... Marrian Walters
Neville Sutter.............. William Glover
Terry Sinclair.............. Henry Woronicz
Hamish Fox................. Alan Mandell
    Time: 1970. Place: Durban, South Africa. One
intermission. (An ATCA selection; see introduc-
tion to this section.)

FOOLIN' AROUND WITH INFINITY. By
Steven Dietz. March 27, 1987. Director, Bill
Bushnell; scenery and lighting, Russell Pyle; costumes, Christine Lewis Hover; sound, Jon Gottlieb.

Sound .... Nick Scarmack
YOU..................... Karen Kondazian
Luke .... Suzann Calvert
John "Jesse" Randall .... Gregory Wagrowski
Arthur "Mac" McCormick ... Robert Darnell
Mr. Anderson .... Budge Threlkeid
    Time: The present. Place: A fallout shelter, a
missile silo command post and this theater.

New Works Project:
DAKOTA'S BELLY, WYOMING. By Erin
Cressida Wilson. February 18, 1987. Director,
Jody McAuliffe.
Dakota .... Jessie Nelson
Vern .... James Morrison
Trixie .... Theresa Karanik
    Time: The present. Place: Wyoming.

DEMON WINE. By Thomas Babe. February
18, 1987. Director, John Henry Davis.
Curly .... Vyto Ruginis
Jimmie .... Alan Rosenberg
Vinnie.................... Howard Witt
Fast Mail; Woman .... Grace Zabriskie
Mary...................... Cristine Rose
Billy .... Fredrick Lehne
Wanda .... Dana Hill
Smith .... Brent Jennings

VETS. By Donald Freed. February 19, 1987. Director, Gerald Hiken.
Leslie R. Holloway .... John McLiam
John MacCormick Butts........ Tom Rosqui
Walter Kercelik.............. Bill Pullman
    Time: Veteran's Day, the present. Place: A
small day-room in a large Veteran's Administration hospital.

ETTA JENKS. By Marlane Meyer. February 19,
1987. Director, Chris Silva.
Etta Jenks .... Roxanne Rogers
Clyde; Max .... Carl Lumbly
Burt; Sherman.............. Darrell Larson
Ben .... John Nesci
Dolly..................... Karmin Murcelo
Voice; Dwight; Alec .... Carmine Iannoccone
Sheri .... Vonetta McGee
James .... Tommy Swerdlow
Spencer..................... John Achorn
Kitty; Shelly.............. Laura Harrington
    Time: The present. Place: Los Angeles.

Los Angeles: Mark Taper Forum

(Artistic director/producer, Gordon Davidson; executive managing director, William P. Wingate)

Main Stage:

GREEN CARD. By JoAnne Akalaitis. May 29, 1986. Director, JoAnne Akalaitis; scenery, Douglas Stein; lighting, Frances Aronson; costumes, Marianna Elliott; choreographer, Carolyn Dyer; sound, Jon Gottlieb.

Cast: Raye Birk, Jesse Borrego, Rosalind Chao, George Galvan, Castulo Guerra, Jim Ishida, Josie Kim, Dana Lee, Alma Martinez, Jessica Nelson, Mimi Seton.

One intermission.

GHETTO. By Joshua Sobol, adapted by Jack Viertel from a literal translation by Kathleen Komar. October 30, 1986. Director, Gordon Davidson; choreography, Larry Human; scenery, Douglas Stein; lighting, Paulie Jenkins; costumes, Julie Weiss; original music, Gary William Friedman.

Gens .... Alan Feinstein
Kittel .... Harry Groener
Chaja .... Andrea Marcovicci
Srulik .... Peter Elbling
Dummy .... Barry Dennen
Weisskopf .... Ron Rifkin, Harvey Gold
Krup..................... David Spielberg
Heikin..................... Giora Feidman

Acting Company: Usha—David Wohl; Kuni—Jeremy Lawrence; Chaim—Joel Polis; Moishe—Harvey Gold, Ron Marasco; Gila—Jill C. Klein; Yusel—Ron Marasco; Leib—Ron Campbell; Yankel—Paul Haber; Itzak—Saul Phillip Stein; Elia—Seth Kurland; Lazer—Lee Arenberg; Duvid—David Kagen; Reizele—Naomi Goldberg; Lina—Lisa Harrison; Hannah—Dinah Lenney; Abba—Timothy Smith; Mordecai—Daniel Gerard Albert; Lionek—Ezra Kliger; Shmuel—Stuart Brotman; Umar—Jimmy Bruno; Feivel—Louis Fanucchi; Ephram—Zinovy Goro; Jewish Police—Scott Segall, Gary Dean Sweeney; Gestapo—Robert Fredrickson, D. Paul Yeuell.

Time: 1941–43. Place: In the mind of Srulik as he recollects the Vilna Ghetto. One intermission.

BURN THIS. By Lanford Wilson. January 22, 1987. Director, Marshall W. Mason; scenery, John Lee Beatty; lighting, Dennis Parichy; costumes, Laura Crow.

Anna..................... Joan Allen
Burton .... Jonathan Hogan
Larry .... Lou Liberatore

Pale..................... John Malkovich
Time: Act I: October-December. Act II: January-March. Place: A loft in a converted cast iron building, lower Manhattan. One intermission.

THE TRAVELER. By Jean-Claude van Itallie. March 5, 1987. Director, Steven Kent; choreography, Nancy Spanier; scenery, Douglas W. Schmidt, Jerome Sirlin; lighting, Beverly Emmons; costumes, Carol Brolaski; music and sound, Nathan Wang.

Traveler .... John Glover
Eva .... Gretchen Corbett
Orderly.................... Lance Roberts
Jed .... W. Dennis Hunt
Dr. Steiff.................. Michael Ennis
Lauri.................... Diane Diefendorf
Moira .... Ellen Gerstein
Intern .... Tony Maggio
EKG Lady.................. Ruth Hawes

Operating Room Doctors: Tony Maggio, Todd Jefferson Moore, Rose Portillo, Tina Preston. Souls, Doctors, Nurses, Orderlies, Patients: Glenn Berenbeim, Diane Diefendorf, Michael Ennis, Ellen Gerstein, Ruth Hawes, Tony Maggio, John Cameron Mitchell, Todd Jefferson Moore, Paul Oertel, Rose Portillo, Tina Preston, Lance Roberts.

Linda .... Paddi Edwards
Paul .... John Cameron Mitchell
Patient .... Todd Jefferson Moore
Dr. Sullivan .... Rose Portillo

Time and place: The mind and inner life of its main character. One intermission.

THE WOMAN WARRIOR. By Tom Cole and Joyce Chopra. April 30, 1987.

Taper Too:

THE DREAM COAST. By John Steppling. November 7, 1986. Time and place: A moody, dreamlike atmosphere populated by Los Angeles' underside—the homeless, the unrequited and the desperate.

Improvisational Theater Project (ITP):

ONE THOUSAND CRANES. By Colin Thomas. April 10, 1987. Director, Peter C. Brosius; choreography, Gary Mascaro; scenery, Richard Hoover; costumes, Nicole Morin. With John Allee, Rosie Lee Hooks, Karen Maruyama, Miho.

Los Angeles: Pasadena Playhouse

(Producing directors, Susan Dietz and Stephen Rothman)

MAIL (musical). Book and lyrics, Jerry Colker; music, Michael Rupert. May, 1987. Director, Andrew Cadiff; choreography, Grover Dale; scenery and lighting, Gerry Hariton, Vicki Baral; costumes, George T. Mitchell; musical director, Henry Aronson; sound, Jon Gottlieb.
Alex .... Michael Rupert

Dana .... Mara Getz
Max .... Robert Mandan
Franklin .... Brian Mitchell
Sandi .... Jonelle Allen
    Featured Ensemble: Mary Bond Davis, Robert Loftin, Michele Pawk, Rick Stockwell, Bradd Wong, Kathryn Ann Wright.

Louisville, Ky.: Actors Theater of Louisville

(Producing director, Jon Jory)

Humana Festival of New American Plays, Feb. 18–March 28, 1987:
GLIMMERGLASS. By Jonathan Bolt. Director, Jonathan Bolt.
    Cast: Robert Salas, Ben Siegler, Jordan Roberts, Anne Wessels, Frederic Major, Lanny Flaherty, Steve Rankin, David Garcia, Phillip Hinch, Christine Iaderosa, Ross Martineau, Patrick Husted, William McNulty, Bob Burrus, Vaughn McBride, Ray Fry, Mark Sawyer-Dailey, Adale O'Brien, David Garcia.
    Time and Place: Act I: The American wilderness, 1759. Act II: The American wilderness, 1779. Act III: An American settlement, 1809. Two intermissions.

ELAINE'S DAUGHTER. By Mayo Simon. Director, Jules Aaron.
Beth .... Jill Holden
Elaine .... Marilyn Rockafellow
Eliot .... Nick Bakay
Tom .... David Bottrell
Gus .... Andy Backer
    Time: The present. Place: Elaine's house in Los Angeles. One intermission.

Shorts (Three One-Act Plays):
CHEMICAL REACTIONS. By Andy Foster.

Director, Ray Fry.
Bern .... Peter Zapp
Ike .... Fred Sanders
    Time: Before dawn. Place: In a dumpsite.
FUN. By Howard Korder. Director, Jon Jory.
Casper .... Doug Hutchison
Denny .... Tim Ransom
Security Guard .... Nick Bakay
Workman .... Andy Backer
Waitress .... Lili Taylor
Matthew .... David Bottrell
Larry .... Dana Mills
THE LOVE TALKER. By Deborah Pryor. Director, Jon Jory.
The Red Head .... Janet Zarish
Gowdie Blackmun .... Lili Taylor
Bun Blackmun .... Suzanna Hay
The Love Talker .... Steve Hofvendahl
    Time: The present. Place: The Clinch Mountains of Virginia during the longest day of the year.

Staged Readings:
DIGGIN IN: THE FARM CRISIS IN KENTUCKY. Arranged by Julie Crutcher and Vaughn McBride from interviews. March 21, 1987. Director, Larry Deckel.

Malvern, Pa.: People's Light and Theater Company

(Producing director, Danny S. Fruchter)

THE STONE HOUSE. By Louis Lippa. June 17, 1986. Director, Jackson Phippin; scenery, James F. Pyne Jr.; lighting, Joe Ragey; costumes, P. Chelsea Harriman.
Tom Bianchi .... Tom Teti
Mary Bianchi .... Marcia Saunders

Flora Bianchi .... Edith Meeks
Sam Morelli .... Stephen Novelli
    Time: Late summer, 1937. Place: A South Philadelphia rowhouse. Act I, Scene 1: Early morning. Scene 2: A few hours later. Act II, Scene 1: A week later, early evening. Scene 2:

GEORGE STREET PLAYHOUSE, NEW BRUNSWICK, N.J.—Charlotte Booker, Steve Pudenz and Tom Celli in a scene from the new Langdon Brown translation of *Every Trick in the Book* by Georges Feydeau with Maurice Hennequin

Some hours later, about 2 in the morning. Scene 3: The next day, mid-morning. One intermission.

KABUKI OTHELLO. Conceived by Shozo Sato, script by Karen Sunde. September 17, 1986. Director, Shozo Sato; scenery, Joe Ragey and Shozo Sato; costumes, Shozo Sato; sound, Rob Milburn.

Othello . . . . Daniel Oreskes
(Desdemona) . . . . Susan Wilder, Kathy Santen
Emilia . . . . Alda Cortese
Iago . . . . Jarlath Conroy
Cassio . . . . Richard Roeder
(Parentheses indicate role in which the actors alternated)

Chorus, Puppetteers: Henry Godinez, Richard Wharton, Tim White, Susan Wilder, Kathy Santen.

Time and place: Feudal Japan.

Millburn, N.J.: Paper Mill Playhouse

(Executive producer, Angelo Del Rossi; artistic director, Robert Johanson)

Staged Readings:

KINGFISH (musical). Book and lyrics, Jeff Eric Frankel; music, John Franceschina. November 17, 1986. Director, Thomas Gruenewald; musical director, Donald W. Chan.

SAYONARA (musical). Book, William Luce; lyrics, Hy Gilbert; music, George Fischoff. December 8, 1986. Director, Robert Johanson; musical director, Jim Coleman.

JUBA (musical). Book and lyrics, Wendy Lamb; music, Russell Walden. January 19, 1987. Director, Sheldon Epps; choreographer, Mercedes Ellington; musical director, Donald W. Chan.

ONE MORE SONG (musical). Book, Anne Edwards, Mike Evans; music and lyrics, Stephen Citron. April 20, 1987. Director and musical staging, Philip Wm. McKinley; arrangements and musical supervision, Luther Henderson; musical director, Leonard Oxley; additional choreography, Norman Wendall Kauahi.

Milwaukee: Milwaukee Repertory Theater

(Artistic director, John Dillon; managing director, Sara O'Connor)

THE BLACK ROSE. By Mikhail Bulgakov, adapted by Barbara Field. October 3, 1986. With Kenneth Albers.

AN AMERICAN JOURNEY. By Kermit Frazier and John Leicht. January 16, 1987. Director, John Dillon; scenery, Laura Maurer and Tim Thomas; lighting, Victor En Yu Tan; costumes, Carol Oditz.

Sylvia Bell White.............. Tamu Gray
Dock Bell; Prospective Juror .... Lex Monson
Daniel Bell; Douglas White;
    Jimmy Bell .... Larry G. Malvern
Patrick Bell; Preacher........ Emil Herrera
Ernest Bell;
    Eugene Bradshaw..... Peter Jay Fernandez
Emma Clark; Prospective Juror.. Sylvia Carter
Patrolman Thomas
    Grady .... Matthew A. Loney
Patrolman Louise Krause...... Peter Silbert
District Attorney
    William McCauley......... Richard Riehle
Medical Examiner Joseph Lamonte; Chief of
    Police Johnson; Defense Lawyer;
    Inspector Glaser......... Kenneth Albers

Detective Russell Vorpagel.... Daniel Mooney
William Hochstaetter; Mayor Zeidler;
    Prospective Juror;
    Captain Woelfel .... James Pickering
Attorney Hamilton .... Julian E. Brown
Charles Wilson; Tucker;
    Defense Lawyer .... Steven J. Gefroh
Social Worker;
    Prospective Juror .... Johanna Melamed
Plaintiff Lawyers .... J. Michael Brennan,
                                        Rose Pickering
Police Sergeant .... Robert Bennett Jr.
Morgue Attendant.............. Ted Tyson
Judge .... J. Michael Brennan
    Crowd People, Wiretappers, Photographers,
Reporters, Voices: J. Michael Brennan, Julian E.
Brown, Robert Bennett Jr., Sylvia Carter, Sara
Chazen, Peter Jay Fernandez, Larry G. Malvern,
Johanna Melamed, Lex Monson, Ted Tyson.
    Time: Various times between 1936 and the
present. Place: America. One intermission.

Minneapolis: Cricket Theater

(Artistic director, William Partian; general manager, Sean Michael Dowse)

KILLERS. By John Olive. April 3, 1987. Director, Howard Dallin; scenery and lighting, Chris Johnson; costumes, Janet Daverne.

Charles Blackwell .... James D. Wallace
Lou........................ Bruce Bohne
Earl...................... David Lenthall
Husband.......... David Anthony Brinkley
Landlady .... Carolyn Ward
    Time: Early 1950s. Place: A boarding house in
a run-down section of a large American city.

THE ANGELS OF WARSAW. By Marisha Chamberlain. May 13, 1987. Director, George Sand; scenery, George Sand; lighting, Chris Johnson; composer, Tommy Wiggins.
Howie............. Michael Gilbert Tierney
Teresa.................... Jessica Zuehike

Jerzy.................... James R. Stowell
Miecz .... Ben Kreilkamp
Michael................. Dawn Renee Jones
Milo .... Chuck McQuary
Jophiel .... Karen Esbjornson
Raphael .... Allan Hickle-Edwards
    Time: 1984. Place: Act I: On a train from Paris
to Warsaw. Act II: Warsaw. One intermission.

"OH, MR. FAULKNER, DO YOU WRITE?" By John Maxwell and Tom Dupree. June 3, 1987. Director, Wiliam Partlan; scenery, Jimmy Robertson; costumes, Martha Wood. With John Maxwell.
    Place: William Faulkner's office at Rowan Oak, Oxford, Miss.

Minneapolis: Guthrie Theater

(Artistic director, Garland Wright; executive director, Edward A. Martenson)

INFIDELITIES. Translated and adapted from Pierre Marivaux by William Gaskill. January 16, 1987. Director, William Gaskill; scenery, John

Conklin; lighting, James F. Ingalls; costumes, John Conklin; sound, Tom Bolstad.
Silvia..................... Faye M. Price

Trivelin.................... Peter Thoemke
Prince................. Peter Francis-James
Flaminia.................. Lisbeth Bartlett
Lisette..................... Sandra Bogan
Harlequin.................... Tom Villard
Lord .... Richard Ooms
Singer .... Jevetta Andra Steele

Piano Player................. David Bishop
Ladies in Waiting, Courtiers, Servants: Ethan Adams, Megan Bacigalupo, Stephen Gee, John Hegge, Daniel Hershey, Kathleen Horner, Pamela Morrisey, Gena Petrella.
Time and place: In the 1700's at the Prince's palace. One intermission.

Minneapolis: Illusion Theater

(Executive producing director, Michael Robins)

FAMILY. By Cordelia Anderson, Bonnie Morris and Michael Robins. May 15, 1987. Director, Michael Robins; scenery, Dean Holzman; lighting, David Vogel; costumes, Linda Cameron. With Alfred Harrison, Marysue Moses, Pam Nice, Jose Alfredo Panelli, Lester Purry, Leslie Rapp, Ira Rosenberg, Walton Stanley, James A. Williams, Kimberly Wilson.

NO PLACE TO PARK. By Eric Anderson. May 29, 1987. Director, David Ira Goldstein; scenery, Linda Cassone; lighting, Jeff Bartlett; costumes, Sonya Berlovitz; choreographer, Randy Winkler.
Linda Porter .... Bonnie Morris
Mike O'Reilly .... Walton Stanley
Henry Thornhill III .... Ira Rosenberg
Connie Templeton.......... Mary McDevitt
Musician...................... Gary Rue
One intermission.

Montclair, N.J.: Whole Theater

(Artistic director, Olympia Dukakis; managing director, Laurence N. Feldman)

POPS. By Romulus Linney. September 30, 1986. Director, Romulus Linney; scenery, Michael Miller; lighting, Rachel Budin; costumes, Karen Gerson. With Jane Cronin, William Hardy, Robin Moseley, Adrienne Thompson, Peter Toran, Sam Tsoutsouvas.

STEAL AWAY. By Ramona King. January 16, 1987. Director, Billie Allen. With Louise Stubbs, Lizann Mitchell.

New Brunswick, N.J.: George Street Playhouse

(Producing director, Eric Krebs; associate artistic director, Maureen Heffernan)

THE LAST GOOD MOMENT OF LILLY BAKER. By Russell Davis. November 20, 1986. Director, Mark Lutwak; scenery, Rachel Buhner, Sarah Lenza; lighting, Greg Dohanic, Bill Van Billiard; costumes, Diane Salmonsen.
Bob Baker .... Michael Albert Mantel
Lilly Baker................ Susan Greenhill
Sam Kass.................. Stephen Singer
Molly Kass................ Katherine Udall
Time: June, 1980. Place: A country inn. One intermission.

EVERY TRICK IN THE BOOK. By Georges Feydeau with Maurice Hennequin, translated by Langdon Brown. December 12, 1986. Director, Peter Bennett; scenery, Gary English; lighting, Karl Haas; costumes, Patricia Adshead; sound, Vik Vaituzis.
Gusman .... Doug Tompos
Sophie................. Mabel McCormick

Angele .... Charlotte Booker
Ribadier .... Tom Celli
Thommereux .... Steve Pudenz
Savinet .... John Ranier
Time: The 1890s. Place: Paris, a salon on the ground floor of the Ribadier home. Two intermissions.

LITTLE HAM (musical). Book, Daniel Owens; lyrics, Richard Engquist, Judd Woldin; music, Judd Woldin. February 20, 1987. Director, Billie Allen; choreographer, John Parks; musical director, J. Leonard Oxley; scenery, Daniel Ettinger; lighting, Shirley Prendergast; costumes, Nancy Konrardy.
Mme. Lucille Bell .... Cheryl Alexander
Louie the Nail Mahoney .... David Brummel
Hot Stuff; Clarence .... Marion J. Caffey
Amanda .... Cleo
Tiny Lee.................... Ellia English

Shingle . . . . Luther Fontaine
Sugar Lou Bird . . . . Cheryl Howard
Mrs. Dobson; Divinity . . . . Adriane Lenox
Larchmont . . . . Gerry McIntyre
LeRoy Henson Smythe. . . . . . . Leon Morenzie
Bradford; Cop . . . . Steve Myers

Hamlet Hitchcock Jones. . . . . . Roumel Reaux
Rushmore. . . . . Dick Sabol
Opal . . . . Melodie Savage
Jimmy. . . . . Jeffrey V. Thompson
Time: 1936. Place. Harlem. One intermission.

New Haven, Conn.: Long Wharf Theater

(Artistic director, Arvin Brown; executive director, M. Edgar Rosenblum)

CAMILLE. By Pam Gems. November 28, 1986. Director, Ron Daniels; scenery, Ming Cho Lee; lighting, Ronald Wallace; costumes, Jess Goldstein.
    Cast: Jono Gero, Gina Gershon, Jane Hubert, David Jaffe, Kit LeFever, Christie McGinn, Bill Moor, David Pierce, Sasha von Scherler, William Swetland, Kathleen Turner, Ramy Zada.
    Time: Mid-1880s.

SELF DEFENSE. By Joe Cacaci. With Michael Wikes.

DALLIANCE. Adapted from Arthur Schnitzler's *Liebelei* by Tom Stoppard. March 13, 1987. Director, Kenneth Frankel.

THE TENDER LAND (opera). Libretto by Howard Everett, music by Aaron Copeland, new chamber version by Murray Sidlin. May 1, 1987. Director, Arvin Brown.

Stage II:
PROGRESS. By Doug Loucie. October 31, 1986. Director, John Tillinger; scenery, David Jenkins; lighting, Ronald Wallace; costumes, Jess Goldstein.

Cast: Lisa Banes, Stephen Bogardus, Jack Gilpin, Don Harvey, David Hunt, David Purdham, Tony Shalhoub, Brita Youngblood.
    Time: The Present.

NEAPOLITAN GHOSTS. By Eduardo DeFilipo. October 21, 1986.

WHEN IT'S OVER. By Geraldine Sherman and Eduardo Machado. February 24, 1987.

BALLEGANGAIRE. By Thomas Murphy. March 27, 1987.

Workshops:
DUSE DIED IN PITTSBURGH. By Paul Vincent. December 22, 1986. Director, Josephine Abady.
MEN IN THE KITCHEN. By Lorin-Paul Caplin. January 13, 1987. Director, Kenneth Frankel.
THE TRAVELLING SQUIRREL. By Robert Lord. February, 1987. Director, John Tillinger.
WHEN IT'S OVER. By Geraldine Sherman and Eduardo Machado. February 24, 1987. Director, Margaret Van Sant.

New Haven, Conn.: Yale Repertory Theater

(Artistic director, Lloyd Richards)

A WALK IN THE WOODS. By Lee Blessing. February 18, 1987. Director, Des McAnuff; scenery, Bill Clarke; lighting, Jennifer Tipton; costumes, Ellen V. McCartney; sound, Michael S. Roth, G. Thomas Clark; music, Michael S. Roth.
Andrey Botvinnik . . . . Josef Sommer
John Honeyman . . . . Kenneth Welsh
    Place: A pleasant woods on the outskirts of Geneva. One intermission. (ATCA Award winner; see introduction to this section.)

A PLACE WITH THE PIGS. By Athol Fugard. March 24, 1987. Director, Athol Fugard; scenery, Ann Sheffield; lighting, Michael R. Chy-

bowski; costumes, Susan Hilferty; sound, David Budries.
Pavel. . . . . Athol Fugard
Praskovya. . . . . Suzanne Shepherd
    Place: A pigsty in a small village, somewhere in the author's imagination.

ALMOST BY CHANCE A WOMAN: ELIZABETH. By Dario Fo. April 28, 1987. Director, Anthony Taccone; scenery, Tim Saternow; lighting, Michael Giannitti; costumes, Marina Draghici.
Elizabeth . . . . Joan MacIntosh
Martha . . . . Mary Lou Rosato

Egerton.................. Tom Mardirosian
Guards......... Tim MacLaren, Erik Onate
Mama Zaza .... Joe Morton
Boy....................... Daniel Chace
Assassin .... Peter Lewis
   Time: Final years of Queen Elizabeth I's reign.
Place: England. One intermission.

Winterfest 7, Jan. 13–Feb. 7, 1987:

APOCALYPTIC BUTTERFLIES. By Wendy
MacLeod. Director, Richard Hamburger; sce-
nery, E. David Cosier Jr.; lighting, Tim Sater-
now; costumes, Phillip R. Baldwin.
Hank Tater .... Steven Skybell
Muriel..................... Tessie Hogan
Francine................... DeAnn Mears
Dick .... Frank Hamilton
Trudi..................... Susan Gibney
   Time: Christmas, December 23, 24 and 25.
Place: Fryeburg, Me. A kitchen, a motel room,
a trailer home, and a field in front of a totem pole.
One intermission.

THE CEMETERY CLUB. By Ivan Menchell.
Director, William Glenn; scenery, Tamara Tur-
chetta; lighting, Michael R. Chybowski; costumes, Dunya Ramicova.
Ida .... Patricia Englund

Lucille...................... Sylvia Miles
Doris.................... Vera Lockwood
Sam......................... Rod Colbin
   Place: Ida's home in Forestville, Queens, and
at a nearby cemetery. One intermission.

EXACT CHANGE. By David Epstein. Direc-
tor, Jacques Levy; scenery, Marina Draghici;
lighting, Christopher Akerlind; costumes,
Dunya Ramicova.
Mary...................... Caris Corfman
Botts..................... Geoff Pierson
Bompkee.................. Kenneth Ryan
Merola .... Jon Korkes
   Time: The present. Place: New Jersey and
New York.

THE MEMENTO. By Wakako Yamauchi. Di-
rector, Dennis Scott; scenery and costumes,
George Denes Suhayda; lighting, Michael R.
Chybowski; sound, Ross S. Richards.
Marie .... Natsuko Ohama
Doug....................... Philip Moon
Ruth .... Ginny Yang
Judy .... Roxanne Chang
Junnichi .... Stanford Egi
   Time: Early 1970s. Place: California. One in-
termission.

New Rochelle, N.Y.: East Coast Arts

(Artistic director, Joe Cacaci)

THE EMPTY ROOM AND OTHER SHORT
PLAYS. Ten one-acts by Shel Silverstein. October 15, 1986. With Rose Gregorio, Val Bisoglio.

OLD BUSINESS. By Joe Cacaci. November 20,
1986 and March 12, 1987. With Michael Wikes.

THROUGH ROSES (music-theater). By Mark
Niekrug. April 21, 1987. Director, Brian Smiar.
With Harold Gould.

FLASHPOINT. By Julia Newton. May 28,
1987. Director, Joe Cacaci.

Omaha: Omaha Magic Theater

(Artistic director, Jo Ann Schmidman)

SLEAZING TOWARD ATHENS (musical).
Book and lyrics, Megan Terry; music, John J.
Sheehan, Joe Budenholzer. Director, Michelle
Hensley; scenery, Colin C. Smith; lighting,
Frank Xavier Kosmicki.
Mick...................... Gerry Ostdiek
Judy .... Hollie McClay
Henrik Ibsen .... Peggy Aufenkamp
   Time: The present. Place: University of Ne-
braska at Omaha.

FAMILY TALK (musical). Book and lyrics,
Megan Terry; music, John J. Sheehan, Joe
Budenholzer. Director, Jo Ann Schmidman.

Kevin .... Joe Budenholzer
Diane .... Diane Ostdiek
Davey .... David Fiedler
Jennifer................... Tammy Brown
Gregg .... Brian N. Beng
Debby.................. Jo Ann Schmidman
Phillip............... Frank Xavier Kosmicki
   One intermission.

SEA OF FORMS (musical). Book and lyrics,
Megan Terry, Jo Ann Schmidman; music, Joe
Budenholzer, John J. Sheehan, Mark Nelson, Ivy
Dow. Director, Jo Ann Schmidman.

Philadelphia: American Music Theater Festival

(Artistic director, Eric Salzman)

THE APPRENTICESHIP OF DUDDY KRA-VITZ (musical). September 22, 1986. By Morde-cai Richler, adapted by Austin Pendleton and Mordecai Richler; music, Alan Menken; lyrics, David Spencer. Director, Austin Pendleton.

Philadelphia: Philadelphia Drama Guild

(Producing director, Gregory Poggi)

Playwrights of Philadelphia Play Festival, March 3–15, 1987:

MOTHER. By Claude Koch. Director, Charles Conwell.
Thatcher..................... Doug Wing
Mother.................. Miriam Phillips
Father.................. Charles Walnut
Hilary................. Lydia Underwood
Geoffrey................ William Whelan
Wallace................. Allen Fitzpatrick
    Time: The early 1970's. Place: Wallingford, Pa., near Philadelphia. One intermission.

MEAN HARVEST. By John Erlanger. Direc-tor, Lon Winston.
Barbara.................... Karen Hurley
Ken..................... Tom McCarthy
Joe................... Peter De Laurier
Truly................... Margie Hanssens
    Time: The summer. Place: A well-appointed penthouse apartment in Manhattan. One inter-mission.

THE VIGIL. By Charles Jenkins. Director, Clay Goss.
Andy............ Vaughn Dwight Morrison
Wes......................... Mets Suber
Sonny....................... John Allen
    Time: A miserable, rainy night in the fall. Place: A basement room in an abandoned apart-ment building.

Playwrights Project May 12–13, 1987:

HEART AND SOUL. By Dick Goldberg. Di-rector, Charles Conwell.
Peter..................... Joey Lawrence
Sharon .... Janis Dardaris
Alan .... Tom Teti
Emily .... Susan Wilder

Philadelphia: Philadelphia Festival Theater for New Plays

(Artistic and producing director, Carol Rocamora; managing director, Stephen Goff)

EARLY ONE EVENING AT THE RAIN-BOW BAR & GRILLE. By Bruce Graham. De-cember 2, 1986. Director, Gloria Muzio; scenery, Eric Schaeffer; lighting, Curt Senie; costumes, Vickie Esposito; sound, Jeff Chestek.
Shep .... Anthony Fusco
Roy....................... Dave Florek
Willy...................... David Snizek
Bullard .... Jay Devlin
Shirley .... Phyllis Somerville
Virginia..................... Julie Boyd
Joe....................... William Wise
    Time: Beginning of summer. Place: A bar in a small Pennsylvania town. One intermission.

BETTER DAYS. By Richard Dresser. April 7, 1987. Director, Gloria Muzio; scenery, Eric Schaeffer; lighting, Curt Senie; costumes, Vickie Esposito; sound, Jeff Chestek.
Ray.................... Frank Girardeau
Arnie .... Stephen Bradbury
Faye .... Jayne Haynes
Phil...................... James Gleason
Crystal .... Jennifer Houlton
Bill .... Jude Ciccolella
    Place: A dying mill town near Lowell, Mass. Time: Act I: A Saturday in the dead of winter. Act I, Scene 1: Morning. Three days later. Scene 2: Later that day. Scene 3: A few hours later. One intermission.

THE DEAL. By William Witten. April 21, 1987. Director, William Partlan; scenery, Eric Scha-effer; lighting, Curt Senie; costumes, Vickie Es-posito; sound, Jeff Chestek.
Peter..................... William Carden
Jimmy...................... Paul Austin
Alex .... Gregg Daniel
Tommy.................... William Wise

PHILADELPHIA FESTIVAL THEATER—Phyllis Somerville, William Wise and Jay Devlin in a scene from *Early One Evening at the Rainbow Bar & Grille* by Bruce Graham

Time: Spring and summer, 1986. Place: Burnie, Pa., a small working-class city.

HEATHEN VALLEY. Written by Romulus Linney. May 5, 1987. Director, Romulus Linney; scenery, Eric Schaeffer; lighting, Curt Senie; costumes, Vickie Esposito; sound, Jeff Chestek.

Billy Cobb . . . . John David Cullum
Bishop. . . . . James Maxwell
Starns . . . . Thomas Kopache
Harlan . . . . Dan Patrick Brady
Cora . . . . Kate Levy
Juba . . . . Kathleen Chalfant

Time: 1840s. Place: The Appalachian Mountains of North Carolina. One intermission.

PENGUIN BLUES. By Ethan Phillips. May 19, 1987. Director, Gloria Muzio; scenery, Eric Schaeffer; lighting, Curt Senie; costumes, Vickie Esposito; sound, Jeff Chestek.

Angelita . . . . Helen-Jean Arthur
Gordon. . . . . Peter Zapp

Time: Summer, early evening. Place: A room somewhere in the Midwest. One intermission.

ABANDONED IN QUEENS. By Laura Maria Censabella. May 19, 1987. Director, Gloria Muzio; scenery, Eric Schaeffer; lighting, Curt Senie; costumes, Vickie Esposito; sound, Jeff Chestek.

Nick Gabriola . . . . Roger Serbagi
Frankie Gabriola. . . . . Doug Hutchison

Time: An unusually warm day in spring. Place: An apartment along the highway in Queens.

Philadelphia: Walnut Street Theater

(Executive director, Bernard Havard; literary manager, Deborah Baer Quinn)

ESCOFFIER, KING OF CHEFS. By and with Owen S. Rackleff. January 18, 1987.

EB & FLO. By Blake Walton and Amy Whitman. February 1, 1987. Director, Jimmy Bohr;

scenery, Robert Odorisio; lighting, Nina Chwast; costumes, Lynn A. Fox.

Jesse	Ann Morrison
Michael	Peter Samuel
Raymond	Allen Kennedy
Maggie	Jona Harvey

Time: Late spring. Place: A loft apartment in Lower Manhattan. One intermission.

DUMAS. By John MacNichols. February 7, 1987. Director, Larry Carpenter; scenery, John Falabella; lighting, Marcia Madeira; costumes, Lowell Detweiler.

Albert	Bob Hungerford
Alphonse; Honore de Balzac	Thomas Carson
Gustave Bocage;	
Baron de Stackelberg	Louis Lippa
Alexander Dumas père	Roger Robinson
Alexander Dumas fils	Geoffrey Owens
Nicolette	Lynn Chausow
Auguste Maquet	Don Auspitz
Soulougque	Ronal Stepney
Susanne	Katherine Buffaloe
Eugene Dejazet	Alex Corcoran

Marie Duplessis	Judith Hansen
Eugene DeMirecourt	Robin Chadwick
Lady Celeste Uppingham;	
Lola Montez	Cynthia Darlow
Lord John Uppingham	Bob Hungerford
Duc de la Tour Loungueville	Mark Capri

Time: The 1840's. Place: Paris and surroundings. One intermission.

NASTY LITTLE SECRETS. By Lanie Robertson. April 28, 1987. Director, Stuart Ross; scenery, Robert Odorisio; lighting, George McMahon; costumes, Robert Bevenger; sound, Cathy Ellen Slisky.

Joe Orton	Simon Brooking
Mr. Willoughby	Robin Chadwick
Kenneth Halliwell	Craig Fols
Carnes	Douglas Wing

Time: From fall 1952 through late summer 1967. Place: The bed-sitting room of Halliwell/Orton on the Islington section of London. A London courtroom. H.M. Prison Eastchurch at Sheerness and H.M. Prison Ford at Arundel. One intermission.

Pittsburgh: Pittsburgh Public Theater

(Producing director, William T. Gardner)

PRINCESS GRACE AND THE FAZZARIS. By Marc Alan Zagoren. May 26, 1987. Director, Peter Bennett; scenery, Gary English; lighting, Phil Monat; costumes, Laura Crow.

Lucille Fazzari	Rosemary DeAngelis
Rosemary Fazzari	Colleen Quinn
Cabrina Saviola	Vera Lockwood

Veronica Fazzari	Sally Prager
Vincent Fazzari	Victor Arnold
Joanne Saviola	Lorraine Serabian
Sal	A.J. Vincent

Time: The morning of April 19, 1956. One intermission.

Princeton, N.J.: McCarter Theater

(Artistic director, Nagle Jackson; managing director, Alison Harris)

DON'T TRIFLE WITH LOVE. By Alfred de Musset, translated by Nagle Jackson. March 11, 1987. Director, Nagle Jackson; scenery, Pavel M. Dobrusky; lighting, F. Mitchell Dana; costumes, Elizabeth Covey.

Chorus; Village Elder	Barry Boys
Baron	Jay Doyle
Perdican	Eric Conger
Master Blazius	Henson Keys
Master Bridaine	Richard Leighton
Camille	Michele Farr
Dame Pluche	Kimberly King
Rosette	Ann Tsuji
Messenger; Peasant	Randy Lilly
Peasants	Martin Hilson, Zoran Kovcic

Time: The early 1800s. Place: A country estate and its surroundings. One intermission.

NAPOLEON NIGHTDREAMS. By James McLure. March 25, 1987. Director, Nagle Jackson; scenery, Pavel M. Dobrusky; lighting, F. Mitchell Dana; costumes, Elizabeth Covey.

Josephine	Wanda Bimson
Laywer	Barry Boys
Architect	Jay Doyle
Sleeping Man	Henson Keys
Spider Woman	Kimberly King
Francois	Rob Lanchester
Napoleon	Richard Leighton
Gascon	Randy Lilly

Duroc...................... Gary Roberts
Boy.......................... Ann Tsuji
   Place: Partly in the mind of the "first modern man" and partly in the world which he created, the French Empire before 1812. No intermission.

Stage Two:
DEBUT. By Bruce E. Rodger. January 21, 1987. Director, Robert Lanchester; scenery and lighting, Don Ehman; costumes, Barb Taylor; sound, Stephen Smith.

Jimmy Gray................ Scott G. Miller
Grunt .... Basil Wallace
Evelyn Gray.............. Sally Chamberlin
Buck Gray............... Richard Leighton
Rachel .... Mary Martello

Staged Readings:
BREADALBANE. By Lawrence Crane.
THE DARK SONNETS OF THE LADY. By Don Nigro.
THREE WAYS HOME. By Casey Kurtti.

Rochester, N.Y.: GeVa Theater

(Producing director, Howard J. Millman; managing director, Thomas Pechar)

NATIONAL ANTHEMS. By Dennis McIntyre. January 13, 1987. Director, Allen R. Belknap; scenery, David Potts; lighting, Richard Winkler; costumes, Dana Harnish Tinsley.
Arthur Reed .... Tony Campisi
Leslie Reed .... Jacqueline Knapp
Ben Cook................... William Wise
   Time: The present, one night, early autumn.
Place: The Reeds' living room in Birmingham, Mich., a suburb of Detroit.

Plays in Progress:
CAPITAL CRIMES. By Tom Dulack. Director, Robert Furhmann.
ISOLATE. By Jule Selbo. Director, Allan Carlsen.
FORTUNE FOOLS. By Brian Reich. Director, Ann Patrice Carrigan.

St. Louis: Repertory Theater of St. Louis

(Artistic director, Steven Woolf; managing director, Mark D. Bernstein)

BEYOND HERE ARE MONSTERS. By James Nicholson. February 27, 1987. Director, Susan Gregg; scenery and lighting, Dale F. Jordan; costumes, Dorothy L. Marshall; sound, Brian Poissant.
Robin .... Boyd Heidenreich
Sophie.................... Susan Pellegrino
Uncas .... Naseer El-Kadi
Denzil..................... Arthur Hanket
Francis .... Jay E. Raphael
Eleazar de Carvalho .... Rohn Thomas
   Time: The recent present. Place: The Amazon. One intermission.

THE PHANTOM OF THE OPERA. By Gaston Leroux, adapted by Ken Hill. March, 1987. Director, Peter Farago; scenery, Joe Vanek; lighting, Max de Volder; costumes, Jim Buff; musical director, Diane Ceccarini.

James .... Crista Moore
Richard..................... Stan Rubin
Remy .... Bob Amaral
Debienne; Hauclair; Priest .... Stephen Berger
Raoul .... Merwin Foard
Mephistopheles; Persian .... Bob Morrisey
Faust.............. Richard Warren Pugh
Madame Giry .... Naz Edwards
Christine................. Victoria Brasser
Carlotta; Dominique; Rat Catcher;
   Chorus Girl.... Kathleen Mahoney-Bennett
The Phantom................ Sal Mistretta
Groom; Gravedigger; Old Man
   on the Roof.............. Stephen Berger
   Time: 1890's. Place: In and around the Paris Opera House. One intermission.

St. Paul: Actors Theater

(Artistic director, Michael Andrew Miner)

One-Act Festival Jan. 23–25, 1987:
MINNESOTA. By George Sand.
AN EDUCATED LADY. By Ken Jenkins.

BURNING DESIRE. By Steven Dietz.
THE BLUE MERCEDES. By Elan Garonzik.
BLUEGRASS. By Jon Klein.

San Diego: Old Globe Theater

(Executive producer, Craig Noel; artistic director, Jack O'Brien; managing director, Thomas Hall)

INTO THE WOODS (musical). Book, James Lapine; music and lyrics, Stephen Sondheim. Director, James Lapine; musical directors, Paul Gemignani, Eric Stern; scenery, Tony Straiges; lighting, Richard Nelson; costumes, Ann Hould-Ward, Patricia Zipprodt; sound, Michael Holten; orchestrator, Jonathan Tunick.

Narrator; Wolf; Steward... John Cunningham
Cinderella.................... Kim Crosby
Jack.......................... Ben Wright
Baker .... Chip Zien
Baker's Wife .... Joanna Gleason
Cinderella's Stepmother; Wolf..... Joy Franz
Florinda; Rapunzel .... Kay McClelland
Lucinda .... Lauren Mitchel
Jack's Mother .... Barbara Bryne
Little Red Riding Hood ...... LuAnne Ponce
Witch .... Ellen Foley
Mysterious Man;
    Cinderella's Father............ George Coe
Cinderella's Mother; Grandmother;
    Wolf; Giant................ Merle Louise
Rapunzel's Prince .... Chuck Wagner
Cinderella's Prince .... Kenneth Marshall
Footman..................... Ric Oquita
Snow White .... Pamela Tomassetti
Sleeping Beauty............ Terri Cannicott

ANOTHER ANTIGONE. By A.R. Gurney Jr. Director, John Tillinger; scenery and costumes, Steven Rubin; lighting, Kent Dorsey; sound, Corey L. Fayman.

Henry Harper .... George Grizzard
Judy Miller .... Marissa Chibas
Diana Eberhart .... Debra Mooney
David Appleton.............. Steven Flynn
    Time: Latter half of the spring term. Place: A university in Boston.

Play Discovery Program:

MESMER. By Joel Gross. October 14, 1986. Director, Robert Berlinger.
Dr. Anton Mesmer .... Bruce Davison
Maria-Theresa
    Von Paradis .... Madeleine Potter
Franzl...................... Lisa Pelikan
Dr. Otto Von Stoerk........ William Anton

THE BOILER ROOM. By Reuben Gonzalez. October 31, 1986. Director, Craig Noel.
Olga .... Karmin Murcelo

Anthony................... Victor Garron
Olivia .... Marsha Mercant
Doug..................... Frank A. Ross

THE GENTLEMEN OF FIFTH AVENUE. By James Penzi. November 7, 1986. Director, James Penzi.
Langley Collyer............... John Eames
Homer Collyer............ Ian Abercrombie
Alexander Campbell .... William Anton

UNCOMMON GROUND. By Jeremy Lawrence. January 26, 1987. Director, Gwen Arner. With Jonathan McMurtry, William Anton, Darla Cash, June Claman, Pippa Pearthree, Donald Moffat, Dann Florek, Eric Grischkat, Mark Hofflund, Mary Jackson.

RAINBOW'S RETURN. By Stephen Hanan. February 16, 1987. Director, Robert Berlinger.
Enid Peck................. Barbara Bosson
Shamey Peck .... Pamela Tomassetti
Donald Nussbaum............. David Wohl
Rainbow.................. Sam Woodhouse
Leota Miles .... Ellen Blake

CHINA WARS. By Robert Lord. March 2, 1987. Director, Robert Berlinger.
Dolly....................... Lois Foraker
Ken.................. Jonathan McMurtry
Holly.................... Lillian Garrett
Hal .... Wortham Krimmer

THE LADIES OF THE CAMELLIAS. By Lillian Garrett. March 30, 1987. Director, Raul Moncada. With Yareli Arizmendi, Jonathan McMurtry, Mitchell Edmonds, Katerine McGrath, Natalia Nogulich, B.J. Turner, Chuck Gregory, Ray Chambers, Ken Danziger.

VICTIMS (BLOOD FROM A STONE). By Anne Meara. April 20, 1987. Director, Robert Berlinger.
Joel......................... Joel Brooks
Dr. Probst .... Jonathan McMurtry
Maggie .... Kandis Chappell
Sid.......................... David Byrd
Stella....................... Erica Yohn
Little Boy.................... Kevin Six
Tante Rivka................. Irene Tedrow
Sharon .... Natalia Nogulich
Bubba..................... William Anton

OLD GLOBE THEATER, SAN DIEGO—Karmin Murcelo and Marsha Mercant in a scene from *The Boiler Room* by Reuben Gonzalez

San Francisco: Eureka Theater Company

(Artistic director, Anthony Taccone; managing director, Timothy Stevenson)

EVERY MOMENT. By OyamO. July 23, 1986. Director, Richard Seyd.

UBU UNCHAINED. By Amlin Gray. October 8, 1986. Director, Anthony Taccone; scenery, Peggy Snider; lighting, Jack Carpenter; costumes, Lydia Tanji; music and sound; Gina Leishman.

Cast: Mrs. Victorine Ubu—Joe Bellan; Court Clerk, Jeremy Bennett, Osip, Bippy, Cameraman, American-on-the-Street—Larry Holt; Hon. Frank Ubu—Geoff Hoyle; Sergeant-at-

Arms, Tommie the Technician, Warden Weems, Luther, AOK Newscaster—Esther Scott; Doyle Dermiss, Reggie, CLS Newscaster Reporter, American-on-the-Street—Richard Seyd; Defendants in Ubu's Court, Jackson Philpott, Guard Gantz, American-on-the-Street—Sigrid Wurschmidt; Orchestra—Gina Leishman.

One intermission.

THE WASH. By Philip Kan Gotanda. March 4, 1987. Director, Richard Seyd; scenery, Barbara Mesney; lighting, Ellen Shireman; costumes,

Roberta Yuen; music and sound, Steve Wein-stock.

Masi . . . . Nobu McCarthy
Nobu. . . . . Hiroshi Kashiwagi
Sado . . . . Wood Moy
Judy . . . . Judy Hoy
Chiyo . . . . Amy Hill
Blackie . . . . A.M. Lai
Kiyoko . . . . Diane Takei
Marsha . . . . Sharom Omi
One intermission.

ROOSTERS. By Milcha Sanchez-Scott. October 20, 1986. Director, Susan Marsden.
DAKOTA'S BELLY, WYOMING. By Erin Wilson. December 8, 1986. Director, Anthony Taccone.
PENGUIN BLUES. By Ethan Phillips. December 8, 1986. Director, Anthony Taccone.
YANKEE DAWG, YOU DIE. By Philip Kan Gotanda. February 9, 1987. Director, Oskar Eustis.

San Francisco: Magic Theater

(General manager, Marcia O'Dea)

Visions of Beckett: Nov. 4, 1986–Dec. 14, 1986:
THE OLD TUNE. By Robert Pinget, translated by Samuel Beckett. Director, Stan Gontarski; scenery, Andy Stacklin; lighting, Joe Dignan; costumes, Bill Brewer.
Gorman . . . . Dave Peichert
Cream. . . . . Morgan Uptown

WHAT WHERE. By Samuel Beckett. Director, Stan Gontarski; scenery, Andy Stacklin; lighting, Joe Dignan; costumes, Bill Brewer.
Bam . . . . Tom Luce
Bom . . . . Dave Peichert
Bim. . . . . Richard Wagner
Bem . . . . Morgan Uptown

TRUE BEAUTIES. By Julie Hebert. February 17, 1987. Director, Julie Hebert; scenery, John Mayne; lighting, Novella Smith; costumes, Lydia Tanji; sound, J.A. Deane.
Jolene . . . . Susan Brecht
Cordelia . . . . Kathleen Cramer
Nita. . . . . Christianne Hauber

Lou Ann. O-Lan Jones
Claude . . . . Gregory Pace
Aleda . . . . Carol Shoup-Sanders
Time: 1975 and memories of years gone by. Place: The outskirts of a small town in South Louisiana. One intermission.

ROSHI. By Lynne Kaufman. April, 1987. Director, Simon L. Levy; lighting, Margaret Anne Dunn; costumes, Lydia Tanji.
Tark . . . . Dennis Barnett
Lazar . . . . Don Bilotti
Zen Student . . . . James Fisk
Cora . . . . Karen Hott
Katatami . . . . Randall Nakano
Sam. . . . . Martin Pistone
Zen Student . . . . Katja Rivera
Heather. . . . . Rosemary Smith
Peter . . . . Anthony St. Martin
Place: A Zen Community in Southern California. Act I: 1976–1981. Acts II and III: The present. Two intermissions.

San Francisco: San Francisco Mime Troupe

(General manager, Patrick L. Osbon)

THE MOZAMGOLA CAPER: AN AFRICAN SPY/THRILLER (musical). Book, Joan Holden, John O'Neal, Robert Alexander. Director, Daniel Chumley; music, Bruce Barthol, Muziki Roberson; lyrics, Bruce Barthol; musical director, Bruce Barthol and Muziki Roberson; costumes, Jennifer Telford.

Cast: Ed Holmes, Barry Henley, Eloise Chitmon, Sigrid Wurschmidt, Jesse Moore, Eloise Chitmon, Edris Cooper, Muziki Roberson, Stacie Powers, Otobaji Stewart, Dan Hart.
Time: The near-distant future. Place: A not-entirely-fictitious nation in southern Africa.

Seattle: Empty Space Theater

(Artistic director, M. Burke Walker; managing director, Melissa Hines)

GLORIA DUPLEX (musical). By Rebecca Wells. April 15, 1987. Director, M. Burke Walker; musical director, Jim Ragland; choreog-rapher, Reggie Bardach; scenery, Bill Forester; lighting, Michael Davidson; costumes, Nina Moser.

Lu Gremillion . . . . Marjorie Nelson
Bud Joseph. . . . . Coby Scheldt
Reverend Mother Willie;
  Mae Felix . . . . Patrinell Wright

(Gloria Duplex). . Rebecca Wells, Susan Ronn
(Parenthese indicate role in which the actors alternated)

Seattle: Seattle Repertory Theater

(Artistic director, Daniel Sullivan; Benjamin Moore, managing director)

RED SQUARE. By Theodore Faro Gross. Director, Daniel Sullivan; scenery, Richard Seger; lighting, Pat Collins; costumes, Robert Wojewodski; sound, Michael Holten.
Bando; Nikolai Smirkov . . . . . John Procaccino
Julia; Yana Mihailovna. . . . . . Marianne Owen
Hal Jones;
  Alexandre Tarzi . . . . Mark Chamberlin
Oma; Major Gavrilov . . . . Pierre Epstein
Cornelia Whitehead. . . . . Eve Roberts
Roosevelt Wineglass . . . . Alexander Zale
Countess Marcella Tripoli . . . . Margo Skinner
Van Der Vane . . . . Brian Thompson
  Ensemble: William Keeler, Peter Lohnes, Cristine McMurdo-Wallis, Tom T. Skore.
  Time: The present. Place: New York City and Moscow. One intermission.

Stage Two:

THE UNDERSTANDING. By William Mastrosimone. April 15, 1987. Director Douglas Hughes; scenery, Thomas Fichter; lighting, Robert R. Scales; costumes, Rose Pederson; sound, Steven M. Klein.
Agostino Malatesta . . . . John Aylward
Raff Malatesta . . . . Scott MacDonald
Janice . . . . Sarah Brooke
  Time: The present. Place: The kitchen of a row house in Trenton, N. J.

Workshop Presentations:

PLAY YOURSELF. By Harry Kondoleon. Director, Douglas Hughes.
THE PRICE. By William Biff McGuire. Director, Robert Loper.

Stamford, Conn.: Hartman Theater

(Artistic director, Margaret Booker)

NEVER IN MY LIFETIME. By Shirley Gee. February 12, 1987. Director, Michael Bloom; scenery, Kate Edmunds; lighting, James F. Ingalls; costumes, Deborah Shaw; sound, David A. Schnirman.
Wife . . . . Anne Marie Bobby
Mother . . . . Aideen O'Kelly

Charlie . . . . Michael Wincott
Tom . . . . William O'Leary
Maire . . . . Elizabeth Berridge
Tessie . . . . Roma Downey
Soldier . . . . K. David O'Neil
  Time: The very recent past. Place: Scene 1: London. Subsequent scenes: Belfast.

Teaneck, N.J.: The American Stage Company

(Artistic director, Paul Sorvino)

VILLA SERENA. By Rick Johnston. November 18, 1986. Director, Paul Shyre. With Jack Betts, Anthony Call, Lisa Emery, Mary Orr, Marge Redmond, Lyn Greene, Frank B. McGowen.

OTHER PEOPLE'S MONEY. By Jerry Sterner. May 8, 1987. Director, John Ferraro. With Henderson Forsythe, Katherine Cortez, David Schramm.

Tucson: Arizona Theater Company

(Founding director, Sandy Rosenthan; artistic director, Gary Gisselman; managing director, Susan Goldberg)

A CIRCULAR FUNCTION. By Michael Grady. June, 1986. Director, Walter L. Schoen; scenery and lighting, Mitch Oomens; costumes,

Maryann Trombino; sound, Jeff Ladman.
Ray Daley . . . . Tony DeBruno
Marian Penwerth Daley . . . Kathleen Erickson

Doris Penwerth . . . . Darrie Lawrence
Martin Penwerth . . . . Kevin Bartlett
Michael Penwerth . . . . Stephen Stout
    Time: The present. Place: In and around the Penwerth home in a small city in central Illinois. One intermission.

Staged Readings:

IN PERPETUITY THROUGHOUT THE UNIVERSE. By Eric Overmyer. June, 1986. Director, Walter L. Schoen.

KATSINA. By Carol DuVal. March 13 and 15, 1987. Director, John Clark Donahue.
LUCK OF THE DRAW. By Michael Grady. March 20 and 22, 1987. Director, Michael Maggio.
ONLY YOU. By Timothy Mason. March 27 and 29, 1987. Director, Walter L. Schoen.
A SPANISH STORY. By Edit Villarreal. April 3 and 5, 1987. Director, Walter L. Schoen.

Venice, Calif.: L.A. Theater Works

(Producing director, Susan Albert Loewenberg)

BOUNCERS. By John Godber. Director, Ron Link; scenery, Cliff Faulkner; lighting, Peter Maradudin; sound, Nathan Wang; musical arrangement and choreography, Jeff Calhoun; original music, Bruce Goldstein.
Ralph . . . . Jack Coleman
Judd . . . . Dan Gerrity
Lucky Eric . . . . Gerrit Graham
Les . . . . Andrew Stevens
    Time: 1980s. Place: Outside a very popular nightclub in England.

New Play Reading Series:

ONLY THE DEAD KNOW BURBANK. By Peter Lefcourt. October 21, 1986. Director, Karen Austin.
OUR FATHER. By Michael Stephens. November 18, 1986. Director, Michael Haney.

CONTACT HIGH. By Mary Charles. November 25, 1986. Director, Sheila Hannigan.
PHANTOM LIMBS. By Charles Borkhuis. December 2, 1986. Director, Michael Arabian.
OTHER PEOPLE'S MONEY. By Jerry Sterner. December 9, 1986. Director, Clyde Ventura.
FALLS A GIANT SHADOW. By Ari Roth. January 14, 1987. Director, John-Frederick Jones.
SOLO FLIGHT. By John Reaves. March 3, 1987. Director, Mark Bringelson.
THE QUESTION OF ANTONIN ARTAUD. By Doug Kaback. March 24, 1987. Director, Chris Nixon.
AMORPHOUS GEORGE. By Glen Merzer. May 26, 1987. Director, Jeffrey Zimmerman.

Washington, D.C.: Arena Stage

(Producing director, Zelda Fichandler; managing director, William Stewart)

THE PIGGY BANK. By Eugene Labiche and A. Delacour, translated by Albert Bermel. December 5, 1986. Director, Garland Wright; scenery, John Arnone; lighting, Frances Aronson; costumes, Martin Pakledinaz; sound, Susan R. White; music, John McKinney.
Boursey . . . . Mark Hammer
Leonida . . . . Veronica Castang
Corden . . . . Marissa Chibas
Danne . . . . Stanley Anderson
Sylvain . . . . Henry Strozier
Felix . . . . Greg Pake
Penuri . . . . Robert Westenberg
Penuri; Benjamin . . . . Ralph Cosham
Poche . . . . Tana Hicken
Chute . . . . Terrence Currier
Joseph . . . . Morgan Duncan
Policeman . . . . Walt MacPherson

Tricot . . . . Terry Hinz
Madame Caramel . . . . Kim Staunton
Waiter . . . . Jason Adams
    Time: 1860s. Place: France. Act I: The Village of Endives-Under-Glass. Acts II, III, IV: Paris. One intermission.

CRIME AND PUNISHMENT. By Fyodor Dostoevsky, adapted by Yuri Lyubimov and Yuri Karyakin, translated by Michael Henry Heim. January 2, 1987. Director, Yuri Lyubimov; scenery, David Borovsky; costumes, Marjorie Slaiman; music, Adison Denisov.
Porfiry Petrovich . . . . Richard Bauer
Man With Ax . . . . Steven Dawn
Townsman; Priest . . . . Paul Walker
Rodion Raskolnikov . . . . Randle Mell
Pyotr Luzhin . . . . Mart Hulswit

ARENA STAGE, WASHINGTON, D.C.—Yuri Lyubimov, co-adapter and director of an American production of Dostoevsky's *Crime and Punishment,* translated by Michael Henry Heim

Nastasya................ Cary Anne Spear
Sonya .... Kate Fuglei
Svidrigailov; Marmeladov....... Kevin Tighe
Mikolka .... John Leonard
Zamyotov.......... Thomas Anthony Quinn
Lebezyatnikov .... John Gegenhuber
Katerina Ivanovna............. Helen Carey
(Polya) .... Leah Lipsky, April Lynn Lutz
(Kolya).... Adam Freedman, Ralph Pripstein
(Lyonya)...... W. Blair Larsen, Jason Minor
Raskolnikov's mother .... Halo Wines
Razumikhin .... Tom Hewit

German Landlady.......... Vivienne Shub
Dunya.................... Heather Ehlers
Pawnbroker ...... Beverly Brigham Bowman
Lizaveta; Prostitute...... Maggie Winn-Jones
(Parenthese indicate roles in which the actors alternated)

OURSELVES ALONE. By Anne Devlin. March 20, 1987. Director, Les Waters; scenery and costumes, Annie Smart; lighting, Nancy Schertler; sound, Susan R. White.
Danny.................... John Leonard

Frieda.................... Heather Ehlers
Gabriel; Liam;
  2d Soldier .... Christopher McHale
1st Man; 1st Policeman .... Marty Lodge
Josie .... Randy Danson
Donna.................. Christina Moore
Malachy .... Terrence Currier
Joe Conran............. Robert Westenberg
John McDermot .... Thomas Anthony Quinn

1st Soldier; 2d Policeman...... Jason Adams
Cathal O'Donnell .... John Finn

Staged Readings:

THE DEVIL AND ALL HIS WORKS. By Ernest Joselovitz. November 16, 1986. Director, James C. Nicola.
CHECKMATES. By Ronald Milner. January 25, 1987. Director, James C. Nicola.

Washington, D.C.: Studio Theater

(Artistic and managing director, Joy Zinoman)

CUTTIN' A RUG. By John Byrne. September 17, 1986. Director, Joy Zinoman; scenery, Russell Metheny; lighting, Daniel MacLean Wagner; costumes, Ric Thomas Rice; sound, David Crandall.
Phil McCann .... Michael Wells
George "Spanky" Farrell .... Simon Brooking
Hector McKenzie .... Tomas Kearney
Lucille Bentley............. Isabel Keating
Alan Downie .... Michael Russotto
Willie Curry.............. Harry A. Winter
Sadie....................... June Hansen
Miss Walkinshaw .... Eileen Russell
Bernadette Rooney ..... Jennifer Mendenhall
Terry Skinnedar............. Robert Carroll
  Time: A Friday evening in 1957. Act I takes place in the Ladies' and Gents' cloakrooms, Act II on the terrace overlooking the town. A starry night. One intermission.

STILL LIFE. By John Byrne. September 17, 1986. Director, Joy Zinoman; scenery, Russell Metheny; lighting, Daniel MacLean Wagner; costumes, Ric Thomas Rice; sound, David Crandall.
Phil McCann .... Michael Wells
George "Spanky" Farrell .... Simon Brooking
Lucille..................... Isabel Keating
Jack Hogg .... Chuck Lippman
Workman................... Joseph Scolaro
  Time: Act I takes place on a morning in the winter of 1967. Act II, a winter's afternoon five years later. Place: A corner of a municipal cemetary in Paisley known as the "The Garden of Remembrance." One intermission.

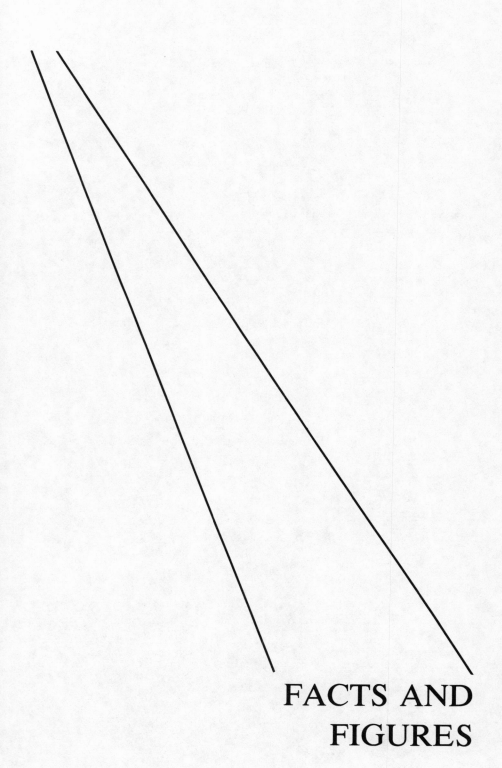

FACTS AND
FIGURES

LONG RUNS ON BROADWAY

The following shows have run 500 or more continuous performances in a single production, usually the first, not including previews or extra non-profit performances, allowing for vacation layoffs and special one-booking engagements, but not including return engagements after a show has gone on tour. In all cases the numbers were obtained directly from the shows' production offices. Where there are title similarities, the production is identified as follows: (p) straight play version, (m) musical version, (r) revival.

THROUGH MAY 31, 1987

(PLAYS MARKED WITH ASTERISK WERE STILL PLAYING JUNE 1, 1987)

Plays	Number Performances	Plays	Number Performances
*A Chorus Line	4,920	Dreamgirls	1,522
*Oh! Calcutta! (r)	4,786	Mame (m)	1,508
Grease	3,388	Same Time, Next Year	1,453
Fiddler on the Roof	3,242	Arsenic and Old Lace	1,444
Life With Father	3,224	The Sound of Music	1,443
Tobacco Road	3,182	How To Succeed in Business	
Hello, Dolly!	2,844	Without Really Trying	1,417
*42nd Street	2,816	Hellzapoppin	1,404
My Fair Lady	2,717	The Music Man	1,375
Annie	2,377	Funny Girl	1,348
Man of La Mancha	2,328	Mummenschanz	1,326
Abie's Irish Rose	2,327	Angel Street	1,295
Oklahoma!	2,212	Lightnin'	1,291
Pippin	1,944	Promises, Promises	1,281
*Cats	1,940	The King and I	1,246
South Pacific	1,925	Cactus Flower	1,234
The Magic Show	1,920	Sleuth	1,222
Deathtrap	1,793	Torch Song Trilogy	1,222
Gemini	1,788	1776	1,217
Harvey	1,775	Equus	1,209
Dancin'	1,774	Sugar Babies	1,208
Hair	1,750	Guys and Dolls	1,200
The Wiz	1,672	Amadeus	1,181
Born Yesterday	1,642	Cabaret	1,165
The Best Little Whorehouse in		Mister Roberts	1,157
Texas	1,639	Annie Get Your Gun	1,147
Ain't Misbehavin'	1,604	The Seven Year Itch	1,141
*La Cage aux Folles	1,577	Butterflies Are Free	1,128
Mary, Mary	1,572	Pins and Needles	1,108
Evita	1,567	Plaza Suite	1,097
The Voice of the Turtle	1,557	They're Playing Our Song	1,082
Barefoot in the Park	1,530	Kiss Me, Kate	1,070
Brighton Beach Memoirs	1,530	Don't Bother Me, I Can't Cope	1,065

Plays	*Number Performances*	Plays	*Number Performances*
The Pajama Game............	1,063	The Prisoner of Second Avenue.	780
Shenandoah	1,050	Oliver!.....................	774
The Teahouse of the August		The Pirates of Penzance (1980 r)	772
Moon....................	1,027	Woman of the Year..........	770
Damn Yankees...............	1,019	Sophisticated Ladies	767
Never Too Late	1,007	My One and Only	767
Any Wednesday.............	982	Bubbling Brown Sugar	766
A Funny Thing Happened on		State of the Union............	765
the Way to the Forum......	964	The First Year...............	760
The Odd Couple	964	You Know I Can't Hear You	
Anna Lucasta................	957	When the Water's Running..	755
Kiss and Tell	956	Two for the Seesaw...........	750
Dracula (r)..................	925	Joseph and the Amazing	
Bells Are Ringing	924	Technicolor Dreamcoat (r) ..	747
The Moon Is Blue............	924	Death of a Salesman	742
Beatlemania	920	For Colored Girls, etc........	742
The Elephant Man............	916	Sons o' Fun	742
Luv	901	Candide (mr)	740
Chicago (m).................	898	Gentlemen Prefer Blondes	740
Applause....................	896	The Man Who Came to Dinner.	739
Can-Can	892	Nine	739
Carousel	890	Call Me Mister..............	734
*Big River	889	West Side Story	732
Hats Off to Ice..............	889	High Button Shoes	727
Fanny	888	Finian's Rainbow............	725
Children of a Lesser God	887	Claudia	722
Follow the Girls	882	The Gold Diggers	720
Camelot	873	Jesus Christ Superstar........	720
I Love My Wife..............	872	Carnival	719
The Bat....................	867	The Diary of Anne Frank	717
My Sister Eileen	864	I Remember Mama...........	714
No, No, Nanette (r)	861	Tea and Sympathy...........	712
Song of Norway..............	860	Junior Miss.................	710
Chapter Two	857	Last of the Red Hot Lovers....	706
A Streetcar Named Desire	855	Company	705
Barnum....................	854	Seventh Heaven	704
Comedy in Music	849	Gypsy (m)	702
Raisin	847	The Miracle Worker	700
You Can't Take It With You...	837	That Championship Season	700
La Plume de Ma Tante........	835	Da........................	697
Three Men on a Horse	835	The King and I (r)	696
The Subject Was Roses........	832	Cat on a Hot Tin Roof........	694
Inherit the Wind	806	Li'l Abner..................	693
No Time for Sergeants	796	The Children's Hour.........	691
Fiorello!....................	795	Purlie	688
Where's Charley?.............	792	Dead End...................	687
The Ladder.................	789	The Lion and the Mouse	686
Forty Carats................	780	White Cargo................	686

Plays	Number Performances	Plays	Number Performances
Dear Ruth	683	A Little Night Music	600
East Is West	680	Agnes of God	599
Come Blow Your Horn	677	Don't Drink the Water	598
The Most Happy Fella	676	Wish You Were Here	598
The Doughgirls	671	A Society Circus	596
The Impossible Years	670	Absurd Person Singular	592
Irene	670	A Day in Hollywood/A Night in the Ukraine	588
Boy Meets Girl	669	The Me Nobody Knows	586
The Tap Dance Kid	669	The Two Mrs. Carrolls	585
Beyond the Fringe	667	Kismet (m)	583
Who's Afraid of Virginia Woolf?	664	Detective Story	581
Blithe Spirit	657	Brigadoon	581
A Trip to Chinatown	657	No Strings	580
The Women	657	Brother Rat	577
Bloomer Girl	654	Blossom Time	576
The Fifth Season	654	Pump Boys and Dinettes	573
Rain	648	Show Boat	572
Witness for the Prosecution	645	The Show-Off	571
Call Me Madam	644	Sally	570
Janie	642	Golden Boy (m)	568
The Green Pastures	640	One Touch of Venus	567
Auntie Mame (p)	639	The Real Thing	566
*I'm Not Rappaport	639	Happy Birthday	564
A Man for All Seasons	637	Look Homeward, Angel	564
The Fourposter	632	Morning's at Seven (r)	564
The Music Master	627	The Glass Menagerie	561
Two Gentlemen of Verona (m)	627	I Do! I Do!	560
The Tenth Man	623	Wonderful Town	559
Is Zat So?	618	Rose Marie	557
Anniversary Waltz	615	Strictly Dishonorable	557
The Happy Time (p)	614	Sweeney Todd, the Demon Barber of Fleet Street	557
Separate Rooms	613	A Majority of One	556
Affairs of State	610	The Great White Hope	556
Oh! Calcutta!	610	Toys in the Attic	556
Star and Garter	609	Sunrise at Campobello	556
The Mystery of Edwin Drood	608	Jamaica	555
The Student Prince	608	Stop the World—I Want to Get Off	555
Sweet Charity	608	Florodora	553
Bye Bye Birdie	607	Noises Off	553
Irene (r)	604	Ziegfeld Follies (1943)	553
Sunday in the Park With George	604	Dial "M" for Murder	552
Adonis	603	Good News	551
Broadway	603	Peter Pan (r)	551
Peg o' My Heart	603	Let's Face It	547
Street Scene (p)	601	Milk and Honey	543
Kiki	600		
Flower Drum Song	600		

Plays	Number Performances	Plays	Number Performances
Within the Law	541	Sunny	517
Pal Joey (r)	540	Victoria Regina	517
What Makes Sammy Run?	540	Fifth of July	511
The Sunshine Boys	538	Half a Sixpence	511
What a Life	538	The Vagabond King	511
Crimes of the Heart	535	The New Moon	509
The Unsinkable Molly Brown	532	The World of Suzie Wong	508
The Red Mill (r)	531	The Rothschilds	507
A Raisin in the Sun	530	On Your Toes (r)	505
Godspell	527	Sugar	505
The Solid Gold Cadillac	526	Shuffle Along	504
Biloxi Blues	524	Up in Central Park	504
Irma La Douce	524	Carmen Jones	503
The Boomerang	522	The Member of the Wedding	501
Follies	521	Panama Hattie	501
Rosalinda	521	Personal Appearance	501
The Best Man	520	Bird in Hand	500
Chauve-Souris	520	Room Service	500
Blackbirds of 1928	518	Sailor, Beware!	500
The Gin Game	517	Tomorrow the World	500

LONG RUNS OFF BROADWAY

Plays	Number Performances	Plays	Number Performances
*The Fantasticks	11,272	Sister Mary Ignatius Explains It All for You & The Actor's Nightmare	947
The Threepenny Opera	2,611		
*Forbidden Broadway	2,229		
Godspell	2,124	Your Own Thing	933
*Little Shop of Horrors	2,033	Curley McDimple	931
Jacques Brel	1,847	Leave It to Jane (r)	928
Vanities	1,785	The Mad Show	871
You're a Good Man Charlie Brown	1,597	Scrambled Feet	831
The Blacks	1,408	The Effect of Gamma Rays on Man-in-the-Moon Marigolds	819
One Mo' Time	1,372	A View From the Bridge (r)	780
Let My People Come	1,327	*Vampire Lesbians of Sodom	779
The Hot 1 Baltimore	1,166	The Boy Friend (r)	763
I'm Getting My Act Together and Taking It on the Road	1,165	True West	762
Little Mary Sunshine	1,143	Dime a Dozen	728
El Grande de Coca-Cola	1,114	Isn't It Romantic	733
One Flew Over the Cuckoo's Nest (r)	1,025	The Pocket Watch	725
		The Connection	722
The Boys in the Band	1,000	The Passion of Dracula	714
Fool for Love	1,000	Adaptation & Next	707
		Oh! Calcutta!	704
Cloud 9	971	Scuba Duba	692

Plays	Number Performances	Plays	Number Performances
The Foreigner	686	Dames at Sea	575
The Knack	685	The Crucible (r)	571
The Club	674	The Iceman Cometh (r)	565
The Balcony	672	The Hostage (r)	545
Penn & Teller	666	What's a Nice Country, etc.	543
America Hurrah	634	Six Characters in Search of an	
Hogan's Goat	607	Author (r)	529
The Trojan Women (r)	600	The Dirtiest Show in Town	509
*Nunsense	591	*Beehive	506
The Dining Room	583	Happy Ending & Day of	
Krapp's Last Tape & The Zoo		Absence	504
Story	582	Greater Tuna	501
The Dumbwaiter & The		The Boys From Syracuse (r)	500
Collection	578		

NEW YORK CRITICS AWARDS, 1935–36 to 1986–87

Listed below are the New York Drama Critics Circle Awards from 1935–36 through 1986–87 classified as follows: (1) Best American Play, (2) Best Foreign Play, (3) Best Musical, (4) Best, regardless of category (this category was established by new voting rules in 1962–63 and did not exist prior to that year).

1935–36—(1) Winterset
1936–37—(1) High Tor
1937–38—(1) Of Mice and Men, (2) Shadow and Substance
1938–39—(1) No award, (2) The White Steed
1939–40—(1) The Time of Your Life
1940–41—(1) Watch on the Rhine, (2) The Corn Is Green
1941–42—(1) No award, (2) Blithe Spirit
1942–43—(1) The Patriots
1943–44—(2) Jacobowsky and the Colonel
1944–45—(1) The Glass Menagerie
1945–46—(3) Carousel
1946–47—(1) All My Sons, (2) No Exit, (3) Brigadoon
1947–48—(1) A Streetcar Named Desire, (2) The Winslow Boy
1948–49—(1) Death of a Salesman, (2) The Madwoman of Chaillot, (3) South Pacific
1949–50—(1) The Member of the Wedding (2) The Cocktail Party, (3) The Consul
1950–51—(1) Darkness at Noon, (2) The Lady's Not for Burning, (3) Guys and Dolls
1951–52—(1) I Am a Camera, (2) Venus Observed, (3) Pal Joey (Special citation to Don Juan in Hell)

1952–53—(1) Picnic, (2) The Love of Four Colonels, (3) Wonderful Town
1953–54—(1) Teahouse of the August Moon, (2) Ondine, (3) The Golden Apple
1954–55—(1) Cat on a Hot Tin Roof, (2) Witness for the Prosecution, (3) The Saint of Bleecker Street
1955–56—(1) The Diary of Anne Frank, (2) Tiger at the Gates, (3) My Fair Lady
1956–57—(1) Long Day's Journey Into Night, (2) The Waltz of the Toreadors, (3) The Most Happy Fella
1957–58—(1) Look Homeward, Angel, (2) Look Back in Anger, (3) The Music Man
1958–59—(1) A Raisin in the Sun, (2) The Visit, (3) La Plume de Ma Tante
1959–60—(1) Toys in the Attic, (2) Five Finger Exercise, (3) Fiorello!
1960–61—(1) All the Way Home, (2) A Taste of Honey, (3) Carnival
1961–62—(1) The Night of the Iguana, (2) A Man for All Seasons, (3) How to Succeed in Business Without Really Trying

1962–63—(4) Who's Afraid of Virginia Woolf? (Special citation to Beyond the Fringe)
1963–64—(4) Luther, (3) Hello, Dolly! (Special citation to The Trojan Women)
1964–65—(4) The Subject Was Roses, (3) Fiddler on the Roof
1965–66—(4) The Persecution and Assassination of Marat as Performed by the Inmates of the Asylum of Charenton Under the Direction of the Marquis de Sade, (3) Man of La Mancha
1966–67—(4) The Homecoming, (3) Cabaret
1967–68—(4) Rosencrantz and Guildenstern Are Dead, (3) Your Own Thing
1968–69—(4) The Great White Hope, (3) 1776
1969–70—(4) Borstal Boy, (1) The Effect of Gamma Rays on Man-in-the-Moon Marigolds, (3) Company
1970–71—(4) Home, (1) The House of Blue Leaves, (3) Follies
1971–72—(4) That Championship Season, (2) The Screens, (3) Two Gentlemen of Verona (Special citations to Sticks and Bones and Old Times)
1972–73—(4) The Changing Room, (1) The Hot l Baltimore, (3) A Little Night Music
1973–74—(4) The Contractor, (1) Short Eyes, (3) Candide
1974–75—(4) Equus, (1) The Taking of Miss Janie, (3) A Chorus Line
1975–76—(4) Travesties, (1) Streamers, (3) Pacific Overtures

1976–77—(4) Otherwise Engaged, (1) American Buffalo, (3) Annie
1977–78—(4) Da, (3) Ain't Misbehavin'
1978–79—(4) The Elephant Man, (3) Sweeney Todd, the Demon Barber of Fleet Street
1979–80—(4) Talley's Folly, (2) Betrayal, (3) Evita (Special citation to Peter Brook's Le Centre International de Créations Théâtrales for its repertory)
1980–81—(4) A Lesson From Aloes, (1) Crimes of the Heart (Special citations to Lena Horne: The Lady and Her Music and the New York Shakespeare Festival production of The Pirates of Penzance)
1981–82—(4) The Life & Adventures of Nicholas Nickleby, (1) A Soldier's Play
1982–83—(4) Brighton Beach Memoirs, (2) Plenty, (3) Little Shop of Horrors (Special citation to Young Playwrights Festival)
1983–84—(4) The Real Thing, (1), Glengarry Glen Ross, (3) Sunday in the Park With George (Special citation to Samuel Beckett for the body of his work)
1984–85—(4) Ma Rainey's Black Bottom
1985–86—(4) A Lie of the Mind, (2) Benefactors (Special citation to Lily Tomlin and Jane Wagner for The Search for Signs of Intelligent Life in the Universe)
1986–87—(4) Fences, (2) Les Liaisons Dangereuses, (3) Les Misérables

NEW YORK DRAMA CRITICS CIRCLE VOTING 1986–87

The New York Drama Critics Circle voted August Wilson's *Fences* the best play of the season on the first ballot by a majority of 14 of the 21 members present or voting by proxy, against 4 votes for *Les Liaisons Dangereuses* and 1 each for *Broadway Bound*, *Coastal Disturbances* and *The Colored Museum*.

The critics then named Christopher Hampton's *Les Liaisons Dangereuses* the best foreign play of the season, also on the first ballot, by a majority of 11 votes against 6 votes for *The Common Pursuit*, 3 for *Asinamali!* and 1 for *Wild Honey*.

The critics also needed only one ballot to declare *Les Misérables* (the creation of a consortium of authors including Alain Boublil, Claude-Michel Schönberg and Herbert Kretzmer) the season's best musical by a majority of 11 votes against 8 for *Me and My Girl* and 1 each for *Rags* and *Three Postcards*.

FIRST BALLOTS IN CRITICS VOTING

Critic	Best Play	Best Foreign Play	Best Musical
Clive Barnes Post	Fences	Les Liaisons	Me and My Girl

John Beaufort *Monitor*	Fences	Les Liaisons	Les Misérables
Michael Feingold *Village Voice*	Fences	Asinamali	Three Postcards
Sylviane Gold *Wall St. Journal*	Fences	The Common Pursuit	Les Misérables
Mel Gussow *Times*	Fences	Les Liaisons	Les Misérables
William A. Henry III *Time*	Broadway Bound	The Common Pursuit	Les Misérables
Richard Hummler *Variety*	Fences	Asinamali!	Les Misérables
Howard Kissel *Daily News*	Fences	Les Liaisons	Me and My Girl
Jack Kroll *Newsweek*	Les Liaisons	Les Liaisons	Les Misérables
Jacques Le Sourd *Gannett Papers*	Fences	The Common Pursuit	Les Misérables
Michael Kuchwara *AP*	Fences	Wild Honey	Me and My Girl
Don Nelsen *Daily News*	The Colored Museum	The Common Pursuit	Les Misérables
Julius Novick *Village Voice*	Les Liaisons	Les Liaisons	Rags
Edith Oliver *New Yorker*	Coastal Disturbances	Asinamali!	Me and My Girl
William Raidy *Newhouse Papers*	Fences	Les Liaisons	Les Misérables
Frank Rich *Times*	Fences	Les Liaisons	Les Misérables
John Simon *New York*	Fences	The Common Pursuit	Me and My Girl
Marilyn Stasio *Post*	Les Liaisons	Les Liaisons	Les Misérables
Allan Wallach *Newsday*	Les Liaisons	Les Liaisons	Me and My Girl
Douglas Watt *Daily News*	Fences	Les Liaisons	Me and My Girl
Edwin Wilson *Wall St. Journal*	Fences	The Common Pursuit	Me and My Girl

CHOICES OF SOME OTHER CRITICS

Critic	*Best Play*	*Best Musical*
Judith Crist WOR-TV, TV Guide	Fences	Les Misérables
Susan Granger WMCA Radio, WICC, Conn.	Fences	Les Misérables
Stewart Klein WNYW	Fences	Les Misérables
Joel Siegel WABC	Fences	Les Misérables
Richard Scholem Radio Long Island	Fences, Broadway Bound	Les Misérables
Leida Snow WNYW-TV	Les Liaisons Dangereuses	Les Misérables

PULITZER PRIZE WINNERS, 1916–17 to 1986–87

1916–17—No award

1917–18—Why Marry?, by Jesse Lynch Williams

1918–19—No award

1919–20—Beyond the Horizon, by Eugene O'Neill

1920–21—Miss Lulu Bett, by Zona Gale

1921–22—Anna Christie, by Eugene O'Neill

1922–23—Icebound, by Owen Davis

1923–24—Hell-Bent fer Heaven, by Hatcher Hughes

1924–25—They Knew What They Wanted, by Sidney Howard

1925–26—Craig's Wife, by George Kelly

1926–27—In Abraham's Bosom, by Paul Green

1927–28—Strange Interlude, by Eugene O'Neill

1928–29—Street Scene, by Elmer Rice

1929–30—The Green Pastures, by Marc Connelly

1930–31—Alison's House, by Susan Glaspell

1931–32—Of Thee I Sing, by George S. Kaufman, Morrie Ryskind, Ira and George Gershwin

1932–33—Both Your Houses, by Maxwell Anderson

1933–34—Men in White, by Sidney Kingsley

1934–35—The Old Maid, by Zoë Akins

1935–36—Idiot's Delight, by Robert E. Sherwood

1936–37—You Can't Take It With You, by Moss Hart and George S. Kaufman

1937–38—Our Town, by Thornton Wilder

1938–39—Abe Lincoln in Illinois, by Robert E. Sherwood

1939–40—The Time of Your Life, by William Saroyan

1940–41—There Shall Be No Night, by Robert E. Sherwood

1941–42—No award

1942–43—The Skin of Our Teeth, by Thornton Wilder

1943–44—No award

1944–45—Harvey, by Mary Chase

1945–46—State of the Union, by Howard Lindsay and Russel Crouse

1946–47—No award

1947–48—A Streetcar Named Desire, by Tennessee Williams

1948–49—Death of a Salesman, by Arthur Miller

1949–50—South Pacific, by Richard Rodgers, Oscar Hammerstein II and Joshua Logan

1950–51—No award

1951–52—The Shrike, by Joseph Kramm

1952–53—Picnic, by William Inge

1953–54—The Teahouse of the August Moon, by John Patrick

1954–55—Cat on a Hot Tin Roof, by Tennessee Williams

1955–56—The Diary of Anne Frank, by Frances Goodrich and Albert Hackett

1956–57—Long Day's Journey Into Night, by Eugene O'Neill

1957–58—Look Homeward, Angel, by Ketti Frings

1958–59—J.B., by Archibald MacLeish

1959–60—Fiorello!, by Jerome Weidman, George Abbott, Sheldon Harnick and Jerry Bock

1960–61—All the Way Home, by Tad Mosel

1961–62—How to Succeed in Business Without Really Trying, by Abe Burrows, Willie Gilbert, Jack Weinstock and Frank Loesser

1962–63—No award

1963–64—No award

1964–65—The Subject Was Roses, by Frank D. Gilroy

1965–66—No award

1966–67—A Delicate Balance, by Edward Albee

1967–68—No award

1968–69—The Great White Hope, by Howard Sackler

1969–70—No Place To Be Somebody, by Charles Gordone

1970–71—The Effect of Gamma Rays on Man-in-the-Moon Marigolds, by Paul Zindel

1971–72—No award

1972–73—That Championship Season, by Jason Miller

1973–74—No award

1974–75—Seascape, by Edward Albee

1975–76—A Chorus Line, by Michael Bennett, James Kirkwood, Nicholas Dante, Marvin Hamlisch and Edward Kleban

1976–77—The Shadow Box, by Michael Cristofer

1977–78—The Gin Game, by D.L. Coburn

1978–79—Buried Child, by Sam Shepard

1979–80—Talley's Folly, by Lanford Wilson

1980–81—Crimes of the Heart, by Beth Henley

1981–82—A Soldier's Play, by Charles Fuller

1982–83—'night, Mother, by Marsha Norman

1983–84—Glengarry Glen Ross, by David Mamet

1984–85—Sunday in the Park With George, by James Lapine and Stephen Sondheim

1985–86—No award

1986–87—Fences, by August Wilson

THE TONY AWARDS 1986–87

The American Theater Wing's Antoinette Perry (Tony) Awards are presented annually in recognition of distinguished artistic achievement in the Broadway theater. The League of American Theaters and Producers and the American Theater Wing present the Tony Awards, founded by the Wing in 1947. Legitimate theater productions opening in eligible Broadway theaters during the eligibility season of the current year—May 1, 1986 to May 6, 1987—are considered for Tony nominations.

The Tony Awards Administration Committee appoints the Tony Awards Nominating Committee which makes the actual nominations. The 1986–87 Nominating Committee consisted of Joan Alleman, editor of *Playbill*; Schuyler Chapin, former Dean of the Columbia University School of the Arts; producer Jean Dalrymple; actor-director Alfred Drake; actor-director Jose Ferrer; writer-critic Leonard Harris; Dr. Mary Henderson, theater historian and author; caricaturist Al Hirschfeld; playwright-novelist-director Garson Kanin; David Oppenheim, dean of the Tisch School of the Arts; composer Mary Rodgers; and playwright-critic Jeffrey Sweet, associate editor of *Best Plays*.

The Tony Awards are voted by the members of the governing boards of the four theater artists organizations: Actors' Equity Association, the Dramatists Guild, the Society of Stage Directors and Choreographers and the United Scenic Artists, plus the members of the first and second-night theater press, the board of directors of the American Theater Wing and the membership of the League of American Theaters and Producers. Because of fluctuation within these boards, the size of the Tony electorate varies from year to year. In the 1986–87 season there were 615 qualified Tony voters.

The list of 1986–87 nominees follows, with winners in each category listed in **bold face type**.

BEST PLAY (award goes to both author and producer). *Broadway Bound* by Neil Simon, produced by Emanuel Azenberg; *Coastal Disturbances* by Tina Howe, produced by Circle in the Square (Theodore Mann and Paul Libin) in association with the Second Stage; **Fences** by **August Wilson**, produced by **Carole Shorenstein Hays** and the **Yale Repertory Theater**; *Les Liaisons Dangereuses* by Christopher Hampton, produced by James M. Nederlander, The Shubert Organization, Jerome Minskoff, Elizabeth I. McCann, Stephen Graham and Jonathan Farkas.

BEST MUSICAL (award goes to producer). **Les Misérables** produced by **Cameron Mackintosh**; *Me and My Girl* produced by Richard Armitage, Terry Allen Kramer, James M. Nederlander and Stage Promotions Limited & Co.; *Rags* produced by Lee Guber, Martin Heinfling and Marvin A. Krauss; *Starlight Express* produced by Martin Starger and Lord Grade.

BEST BOOK OF A MUSICAL. **Les Misérables** by **Alain Boublil** and **Claude-Michel Schönberg**; *Me and My Girl* by L. Arthur Rose, Douglas Furber, Stephen Fry and and Mike Ockrent; *Rags* by Joseph Stein; *Smile* by Howard Ashman.

BEST ORIGINAL SCORE (MUSIC & LYRICS) WRITTEN FOR THE THEATER. **Les Misérables**, music by **Claude-Michel Schönberg**, lyrics by **Herbert Kretzmer** and **Alain Boublil**; *Me and My Girl*, music by Noel Gay, lyrics by L. Arthur Rose, Douglas Furber, Stephen Fry and Mike Ockrent; *Rags*, music by Charles Strouse, lyrics by Stephen Schwartz; *Starlight Express*, music by Andrew Lloyd Webber, lyrics by Richard Stilgoe.

BEST LEADING ACTOR IN A PLAY. Philip Bosco in *You Never Can Tell*, **James Earl Jones** in *Fences*, Richard Kiley in *All My Sons*, Alan Rickman in *Les Liaisons Dangereuses*.

ALL MY SONS—Joyce Ebert and Richard Kiley in Arthur Miller's play, winner of the 1987 Tony for best revival

BEST LEADING ACTRESS IN A PLAY. Lindsay Duncan in *Les Liaisons Dangereuses*, **Linda Lavin** in *Broadway Bound*, Geraldine Page in *Blithe Spirit*, Amanda Plummer in *Pygmalion*.

BEST LEADING ACTOR IN A MUSICAL. Roderick Cook in *Oh Coward!*, **Robert Lindsay** in *Me and My Girl*, Terrence Mann in *Les Misérables*, Colm Wilkinson in *Les Misérables*.

BEST LEADING ACTRESS IN A MUSICAL (there were only three nominations in this category). Catherine Cox in *Oh Coward!*, **Maryann Plunkett** in *Me and My Girl*, Teresa Stratas in *Rags*.

BEST FEATURED ACTOR IN A PLAY. Frankie R. Faison in *Fences*, **John Randolph** in *Broadway Bound*, Jamey Sheridan in *All My Sons*, Courtney B. Vance in *Fences*.

BEST FEATURED ACTRESS IN A PLAY. **Mary Alice** in *Fences*, Annette Bening in *Coastal Disturbances*, Phyllis Newman in *Broadway Bound*, Carole Shelley in *Stepping Out*.

BEST FEATURED ACTOR IN A MUSICAL. George S. Irving in *Me and My Girl*, Timothy Jerome in *Me and My Girl*, **Michael Maguire** in *Les Misérables*, Robert Torti in *Starlight Express*.

BEST FEATURED ACTRESS IN A MUSICAL. Jane Connell in *Me and My Girl*, Judy Kuhn in *Les Misérables*, **Frances Ruffelle** in *Les Misérables*, Jane Summerhays in *Me and My Girl*.

BEST SCENIC DESIGN. Bob Crowley for *Les Liaisons Dangereuses*, Martin Johns for *Me and My Girl*, **John Napier** for *Les Misérables*, Tony Walton for *The Front Page*.

BEST COSTUME DESIGN. Bob Crowley for *Les Liaisons Dangereuses*, Ann Curtis for *Me and My Girl*, **John Napier** for *Starlight Express*, Andreane Neofitou for *Les Misérables*.

BEST LIGHTING DESIGN. Martin Aronstein for *Wild Honey*, **David Hersey** for *Les Misérables*, David Hersey for *Starlight Express*, Chris Parry and Beverly Emmons for *Les Liaisons Dangereuses*.

BEST DIRECTION OF A PLAY. Howard Davies for *Les Liaisons Dangereuses*, Mbongeni Ngema for *Asinamali!*, **Lloyd Richards** for *Fences*, Carole Rothman for *Coastal Disturbances*.

BEST DIRECTION OF A MUSICAL. Brian Macdonald for *The Mikado*, **Trevor Nunn** and **John Caird** for *Les Misérables*, Trevor Nunn for *Starlight Express*, Mike Ockrent for *Me and My Girl*.

BEST CHOREOGRAPHY. Ron Field for *Rags*, **Gillian Gregory** for *Me and My Girl*, Brian Macdonald for *The Mikado*, Arlene Phillips for *Starlight Express*.

BEST REVIVAL OF A PLAY OR MUSICAL. *All My Sons* produced by **Jay H. Fuchs, Steven Warnick** and **Charles Patsos**; *The Front Page* produced by Lincoln Center Theater, Gregory Mosher and Bernard Gersten; *The Life & Adventures of Nicholas Nickleby*, produced by The Shubert Organization, Three Knights, Ltd. and Robert Fox. Ltd.; *Pygmalion* produced by The Shubert Organization, Jerome Minskoff and Duncan C. Weldon.

SPECIAL TONY AWARDS. **Jackie Mason; The San Francisco Mime Troupe; George Abbott**; Lawrence Langner Award posthumously to **Robert Preston**.

TONY AWARD WINNERS, 1947–1987

Listed below are the Antoinette Perry (Tony) Award winners in the categories of Best Play and Best Musical from the time these awards were established (1947) until the present.

1947—No play or musical award
1948—Mister Roberts; no musical award
1949—Death of a Salesman; Kiss Me, Kate
1950—The Cocktail Party; South Pacific
1951—The Rose Tattoo; Guys and Dolls
1952—The Fourposter; The King and I
1953—The Crucible; Wonderful Town
1954—The Teahouse of the August Moon; Kismet
1955—The Desperate Hours; The Pajama Game
1956—The Diary of Anne Frank; Damn Yankees
1957—Long Day's Journey Into Night; My Fair Lady
1958—Sunrise at Campobello; The Music Man
1959—J.B.; Redhead
1960—The Miracle Worker; Fiorello! and The Sound of Music (tie)

1961—Becket; Bye Bye Birdie
1962—A Man for All Seasons; How to Succeed in Business Without Really Trying
1963—Who's Afraid of Virginia Woolf?; A Funny Thing Happened on the Way to the Forum
1964—Luther; Hello, Dolly!
1965—The Subject Was Roses; Fiddler on the Roof
1966—The Persecution and Assassination of Marat as Performed by the Inmates of the Asylum of Charenton Under the Direction of the Marquis de Sade; Man of La Mancha
1967—The Homecoming; Cabaret
1968—Rosencrantz and Guildenstern Are Dead; Hallelujah, Baby!
1969—The Great White Hope; 1776

1970—Borstal Boy; Applause
1971—Sleuth; Company
1972—Sticks and Bones; Two Gentlemen of Verona
1973—That Championship Season; A Little Night Music
1974—The River Niger; Raisin
1975—Equus; The Wiz
1976—Travesties; A Chorus Line
1977—The Shadow Box; Annie
1978—Da; Ain't Misbehavin'
1979—The Elephant Man; Sweeney Todd, the Demon Barber of Fleet Street

1980—Children of a Lesser God; Evita
1981—Amadeus; 42nd Street
1982—The Life & Adventures of Nicholas Nickleby; Nine
1983—Torch Song Trilogy; Cats
1984—The Real Thing; La Cage aux Folles
1985—Biloxi Blues; Big River
1986—I'm Not Rappaport; The Mystery of Edwin Drood
1987—Fences; Les Misérables

THE OBIE AWARDS, 1986–87

The *Village Voice* Off-Broadway (Obie) Awards are given each year for excellence in various categories of off-Broadway (and frequently off-off-Broadway) shows, with close distinctions between these two areas ignored. The 32d annual 1986–87 Obies were voted by a panel of *Village Voice* critics (Eileen Blumenthal, Michael Feingold, Robert Massa, Erika Munk, Julius Novick and Gordon Rogoff with Ross Wetzsteon as chairman) plus Billie Allen and Norris Houghton as guest judges.

BEST NEW PLAY. *The Cure* and *Film Is Evil, Radio Is Good* by Richard Foreman.

SUSTAINED ACHIEVEMENT. Charles Ludlam and The Ridiculous Theatrical Company.

PERFORMANCE. Philip Bosco and Black-Eyed Susan for sustained excellence. Robin Bartlett in *The Early Girl*, Rob Besserer and Anthony Holland in *The Hunger Artist*, Morgan Freeman and Dana Ivey in *Driving Miss Daisy*, Laura Hicks in *On the Verge*, John Kelly in *Pass the Blutwurst, Bitte (The Egon Schiele Story)*, Christine Lahti in *Little Murders*, Geina Mhlophe in *Born in the R.S.A.*, Bill Raymond in *Cold Harbor*, Clarice Taylor in *Moms*.

DIRECTION: Carole Rothman for sustained excellence. Garland Wright for *On the Verge*.

DESIGN. James Ingalls for sustained excellence in lighting. Andrew Jackness for sustained excellence in set design. Robert Israel for the sets and costumes of *On the Verge*, Paul Gallo for lighting *The Hunger Artist*.

SPECIAL CITATIONS. Dario Fo and Franca Rame; Non-Traditional Casting Project; Woza Afrika Foundation; Great Jones Repertory Company for its revival of *Fragments of a Greek Trilogy*; Judith Malina for *The Living Theater Retrospectacle*.

ADDITIONAL PRIZES AND AWARDS, 1986–87

The following is a list of major prizes and awards for achievement in the theater this season. In all cases the names and/or titles of the winners appear in **bold face type**.

2d ANNUAL ATCA NEW-PLAY AWARD. For an outstanding new play in cross-country theater, voted by a committee of the American Theater Critics Association. *A Walk in the Woods* by Lee Blessing.

1986 ELIZABETH HULL–KATE WAR-RINER AWARD. To the playwright whose work dealt with controversial subjects involving the fields of political, religious or social mores of the time, selected by the Dramatists Guild Council. **George C. Wolfe** for *The Colored Museum*.

9th ANNUAL KENNEDY CENTER HONORS. For distinguished achievement by individuals who have made significant contributions to American culture through the arts. **Jessica Tandy, Hume Cronyn, Lucille Ball, Ray Charles, Anthony Tudor, Yehudi Menuhin.**

1st AND 2d ANNUAL LUCILLE LORTEL AWARDS. For outstanding achievement off Broadway, voted by a committee comprising Clive Barnes, Andre Bishop, Paul Libin, Lucille Lortel, Lynne Meadow, Edith Oliver, Joseph Papp, Albert Poland and Willard Swire. 1986 award to **Lincoln Center Theater**, Gregory Mosher director, Bernard Gersten executive producer, for *Woza Afrika!* 1987 awards to *The Common Pursuit* by Simon Gray and to the **Manhattan Theater Club**, Lynne Meadow artistic director, Barry Grove managing director, for the body of work produced this season.

OUTER CRITICS CIRCLE AWARDS. For distinguished achievement in the 1986–87 New York theater season, voted by critics of foreign and out-of-town periodicals. Broadway play: *Fences*. Broadway musical: *Les Misérables*. Off-Broadway play: *The Common Pursuit*. Off-Broadway musical: *Stardust*. Performance by an actor: **James Earl Jones** in *Fences*. Performance by an actress: **Linda Lavin** in *Broadway Bound*. Director: **Trevor Nunn** and **John Caird** for *Les Misérables*. Scenery: **John Napier** for *Les Misérables*. Book of an off-Broadway musical: **Lanie Robertson** for *Lady Day at Emerson's Bar and Grill*. Music for an off-Broadway musical: **Allen Toussaint** for *Staggerlee*. Lyrics for an off-Broadway musical: **Barry Harman** for *Olympus on My Mind*. Debut of an actor: **Colm Wilkinson** in *Les Misérables*. Debut of an actress: **Frances Ruffelle** in *Les Misérables*. Revival of a play or musical: *All My Sons*.

Special award: *Jackie Mason's "The World According to Me!"* John Gassner Award for the author of a new American play: **August Wilson** for *Fences*.

43d ANNUAL THEATER WORLD AWARDS. For outstanding new talent in Broadway and off-Broadway productions during the 1986–87 season, selected by a committee comprising Clive Barnes, Mel Gussow, Douglas Watt and John Willis. **Annette Bening** and **Timothy Daly** of *Coastal Disturbances*, **Lindsay Duncan** of *Les Liaisons Dangereuses*, **Amy Madigan** of *The Lucky Spot*, **Demi Moore** of *The Early Girl*, **Molly Ringwald** of *Lily Dale*, **Frances Ruffele, Michael Maguire** and **Colm Wilkinson** of *Les Misérables*, **Frank Ferrante** of *Groucho: A Life in Revue*, **Robert Lindsay** of *Me and My Girl*, **Courtney B. Vance** of *Fences*.

32d ANNUAL DRAMA DESK AWARDS. For outstanding achievement, voted by an association of New York drama reporters, editors and critics. New play; *Fences*. Director, play: **Howard Davies** for *Les Liaisons Dangereuses*. Actor, play: **James Earl Jones** in *Fences*. Actress, play: **Linda Lavin** in *Broadway Bound*. Musical: *Les Misérables*. Director, musical: **Mike Ockrent** for *Me and My Girl*. Actor, musical: **Robert Lindsay** in *Me and My Girl*. Actress, musical: **Teresa Stratas** in *Rags*. Featured actor, play: **John Randolph** in *Broadway Bound*. Featured actress, play: **Mary Alice** in *Fences*. Featured actor, musical: **Michael Maguire** in *Les Misérables*. Featured actress, musical: **Jane Summerhays** in *Me and My Girl*. Book of a musical: **L. Arthur Rose, Douglas Furber, Stephen Fry** and **Mike Ockrent** for *Me and My Girl*. Music (tie): **Noel Gay** for *Me and My Girl* and **Claude-Michel Schönberg** for *Les Misérables*. Orchestration: **John Cameron** for *Les Misérables*. Scenery: **John Napier** for *Les Misérables* and *Starlight Express*. Lighting, **Chris Parry** for *Les Liaisons Dangereuses*. Costumes, **John Napier** for *Starlight Express*. One-person show: *Barbara Cook: A Concert for the Theater*.

Special awards: **Paul Davis** and **Frank Verlizzo** for "constantly inspired art work for theatrical productions; **Stanley Lebowsky** "in recognition of consistently outstanding musical direction and commitment to the theater"; **Henry Cohen, Donald Rose** and **Robert Kimball** for "their key roles in unearthing previously unpublished work" in a Secaucus, N.J. warehouse. Rosamond Gilder Award for outstanding creative achievement: **Fran Soeder**.

1985–86 GEORGE JEAN NATHAN AWARD. For dramatic criticism, selected by the heads of the Yale, Princeton and Cornell English departments. **Gordon Rogoff** of the *Village Voice* for the alert, imaginative quality of his writing about directors, performers, designers and (not incidentally) reviewers.

1986 GEORGE OPPENHEIMER/NEWSDAY PLAYWRITING AWARD. To the best new American playwright whose work is produced in New York City or on Long Island. **Reinaldo Povod** for *Cuba and His Teddy Bear*.

1986 JUJAMCYN THEATERS AWARD. Honoring a regional theater organization that has made an outstanding contribution to the development of creative talent in the theater. **Long Wharf Theater**, Arvin Brown artistic director, M. Edgar Rosenblum executive director.

51st ANNUAL DRAMA LEAGUE AWARDS. James Earl Jones for the most distinguished performance by an actor, in *Fences*. **Robert Lindsay** for outstanding achievement in a musical, in *Me and My Girl*. **Jose Quintero** for unique contribution to the theater in bringing to renewed life the plays of Eugene O'Neill.

EUGENE O'NEILL BIRTHDAY MEDAL. For furthering the playwright's works. **George C. White**, president of the Eugene O'Neill Theater Center, Waterford, Conn.

SUSAN SMITH BLACKBURN PRIZE. For playwriting by women. **Mary Gallagher** for *How to Say Goodbye* and **Ellen McLaughlin** for *A Narrow Bed* (co-winners).

3d ANNUAL GEORGE AND ELISABETH MARTON AWARD FOR PLAYWRITING. To recognize and encourage a new American playwright selected by a committee of the Foundation of the Dramatists Guild. **Wallace Shawn** for *Aunt Dan and Lemon*.

WILLIAM INGE AWARD. For lifetime achievement in playwriting, given by Independence, Kan., Community College. **Garson Kanin**.

GEORGE FREEDLEY MEMORIAL AWARD. For excellence in writing about the theater, given by the Library Association. **Mary C. Henderson** for *Theater in America*.

CLARENCE DERWENT AWARDS. For the most promising male and female actors on the metropolitan scene during the 1986–87 season. **Annette Bening** in *Coastal Disturbances* and **Courtney B. Vance** in *Fences*.

GEORGE LONDON AWARDS. Given by the National Institute for Music Theater. For musical theater: **Suzanne Douglas** (Mary Martin Award), **Brenda Pressley**, **Abra Bigham**. For opera: **Mark Doss** (George London Prize), **Ruth Golden**, **Michael Sylvester**.

MARGO JONES AWARD. To the producer and producing organization whose continuing policy of producing new theater works has made an outstanding contribution to the encouragement of new playwrights. **Lloyd Richards**, artistic director of **Yale Repertory Theater**.

THEATER HALL OF FAME. Annual election by members of the profession of nominees selected by vote of the members of the American Theater Critics Association. **George Balanchine, Ruby Dee, Dorothy Fields, Herbert Fields, Max Gordon, Danny Kaye, Siobhan McKenna, Mike Nichols, Elliot Norton, Paul Osborn**.

AMERICAN THEATER WING DESIGN AWARDS. For designs originating in the U.S., voted by a committee comprising Trish Dace, Henry Hewes, Edward F. Kook, Julius Novick and Patricia MacKay. Scenic design: **Robert Israel** for *The Hunger Artist* and **James D. Sandefur** for *Fences*. Costume design: **John Napier** for *Starlight Express* (redesigned for the American production). Lighting: **Paul Gallo** for *The Hunger Artist* and **Jennifer Tipton** for *Worstward Ho!* Noteworthy unusual effect: **Tom Kamm** and **Robert Wilson** for the tree in *The Civil Wars*.

COMMON WEALTH AWARD. For exceptional contributions to dramatic literature. **Samuel Beckett**.

1st ANNUAL ALAN SCHNEIDER AWARD. To assist mid-career directors who have exhibited unusual talent, have achieved local or regional reputations and who merit national attention, voted by a committee comprising Michael Kahn, Tony Giordano, Lloyd Richards and Peter Zeisler. **Mary B. Robinson**.

3d ANNUAL HELEN HAYES AWARDS. In recognition of excellence in the Washington, D.C. professional theater. Resident shows—Production of a play: **Shakespeare Theater at the Folger** for *The Miser*. Production of a musical: **Castle Arts Center** for *Quilters*. New play: *New York Mets* by **T.J. Edwards**. Leading actress: **Tana Hicken** in *The Wild Duck*. Leading actor: **Howie Seago** in *Ajax*. Supporting actress: **Pat Carroll** in *Romeo and Juliet*. Supporting actor: **Stanley Anderson** in *The Piggy Bank*. Performer in a musical: **Frank Kopyc** in *Hot Mikado*. Director: **John Going** for *The Miser*. Lighting design, **James Ingalls** for *Ajax*. Costume design: **Martin Pakledinaz** for *The Piggy Bank*. Set design: **Radu Boruzescu** for *The Wild Duck*.

Nonresident shows—Production: *Les Misérables*. Leading actor: **Colm Wilkinson** in *Les Misérables*. Leading actress: **Linda Lavin** in *Broad-*

way Bound. Supporting performer: **Frances Ruffelle** in *Les Misérables*.

American Express Tribute to a theatrical figure who received his start or whose career took a major turn in Washington: **James Earl Jones**.

14th ANNUAL JOSEPH JEFFERSON AWARDS. For excellence in Chicago area resident professional theaters during the 1985–86 season. Production of a play: **Remains Theater** for *Puntilla and His Hired Hand*. Production of a musical: **Candlelight Dinner Playhouse** for *Little Shop of Horrors*. Director, play: **Frank Galati** for *You Can't Take It With You*. Director, musical: **William Pullinsi** *for Little Shop of Horrors*. Director, revue: **Bill Castellino** for *Rap Master Ronnie*. Principal actor, play: **Denis Arndt** in *Puntilla and His Hired Hand*. Principal actor, musical: **Gene Weygandt** in *Little Shop of Horrors*. Actor, revue: **William M. Bush** in *Rap Master Ronnie*. Principal actress, play: **Joan Allen** in *A Lesson From Aloes*. Principal actress, musical: **Hollis Resnik** in *Little Shop of Horrors*. Actress, revue: **Hollis Resnik** in *The Middle of Nowhere in the Middle of the Night*. Supporting actor, play: **Robert Curry** in *Boesman and Lena* and **Danny Glover** in *A Lesson from Aloes*. Supporting actor, musical: **David Bedella** in *A Chorus Line* Supporting actress, play: **Amy Morton** in *You Can't Take It With You*. Ensemble: Steppenwolf in *You Can't Take It With You*. Cameo performance: **Laurie Metcalf** in *You Can't Take It With You*. Scene design: *The Government Inspector* (Goodman Theater). Lighting: *Boesman and Lena* (Northlight Theater). Costumes: *The Government Inspector* (Goodman Theater). Sound: *Little Shop of Horrors* (Candlelight Dinner Playhouse). Choreography: *Hello, Dolly!* (Marriott Lincolnshire). Musical direction: *Baby* (Marriott Lincolnshire). Original incidental music: *Puntilla and His Hired Hand* (Remains Theater).

Special awards: **Northlight Theater; Illinois Quilters** for *Quilters*; **Jane** and **Bernard Sahlins** as directors of the 1986 Chicago International Theater Festival.

18th ANNUAL LOS ANGELES DRAMA CRITICS CIRCLE AWARDS. For distinguished achievement in Los Angeles Theater during 1986. Production: *Bouncers* produced by Susan Albert Lowenberg for L.A. Theater Works in association with Joanne Jacobson, Sara Maultsby associate producer, Rich/Edrick Productions co-producers; *The Iceman Cometh* presented by UCLA Center for the Arts/The Theater Group, Inc., Lewis Allen, James Nederlander, Stephen Graham, Ben Edwards, American National Theater; *The Search for Signs of Intelligent Life in the Universe* presented by Tomlin and Wagner Theatricals, Lily Tomlin producer. Writing: **John Godber** for *Bouncers*, **Simon Gray** for *The Common Pursuit*, **Jane Wagner** for *The Search for Signs of Intelligent Life in the Universe*. Musical score: **Stephen Sondheim** for *Sunday in the Park With George*. Lead performance: **Charles Hallahan** in *Rat in the Skull*, **Brian Kerwin** in *Strange Snow*, **Esai Morales** in *Tamer of Horses*, **Jason Robards** in *The Iceman Cometh*, **Lily Tomlin** in *The Search for Signs of Intelligent Life in the Universe*. Featured performance: **Dana Hill** in *Picnic*, **Marie Windsor** in *The Bar off Melrose*. Ensemble performance: **Solomzi Bisholo, Thami Cele, Bongani Hlophe, Bheki Mqadi, Bhoyi Ngema** in *Asinamali!*; **Jack Coleman, Dan Gerrity, Gerrit Graham, Andrew Stevens** in *Bouncers*. Scene design: **John Lee Beatty** for *Picnic*, **Ben Edwards** for *The Iceman Cometh*. Lighting design: **Neil Peter Jampolis** for *The Search for Signs of Intelligent Life in the Universe*, **Peter Maradudin** for *Bouncers*, **Thomas R. Skelton** for *The Iceman Cometh*. Costume design: **Nicole Morin** for *Spain '36* (masks) and *Tartuffe*. Sound: **Bruce D. Cameron** for *The Search for Signs of Intelligent Life in the Universe*, **Nathan Wang** for *Bouncers*. Musical direction: **Corey Allen** for *Nite Club Confidential*. Choreography: **Jeff Calhoun** for *Bouncers*.

Margaret Harford Award: **Scott Kelman/Pipeline** "for unwavering commitment to innovative theater for Los Angeles that is unapologetically experimental and unashamedly political." Special awards: **Gordon Davidson** "for 20 years at the forefront of Los Angeles theater, helping to create the audiences and the atmosphere for its growth"; **Royal Shakespeare Company** "for translating Dickens's literary classic *The Life and Adventures of Nicholas Nickleby* into a stunning, once-in-a-lifetime experience."

SAN DIEGO THEATER CRITICS CIRCLE AWARDS. For outstanding achievement during the 1985–86 season, voted by 13 local critics. Best new play produced locally: *Emily* by **Stephen Metcalfe**. Best production: *Holy Ghosts* at San Diego Repertory Theater. Best actor: **Douglas Roberts** in *Billy Bishop Goes to War*. Best Actress: **Madolyn Smith** in *Emily*. Best supporting actor: **Michael Genovese** in *Gillette*. Best supporting actress: **Rebecca Nachison** in *In the Sweet Bye and Bye*. Best direction: **Douglas Jacob** for *Holy Ghosts*. Best scenic design: **Douglas Stein** for *Figaro Gets a Divorce*: Best costumes: **Robert Morgan** for *Pygmalion*. Best lighting: **David Thayer** for *The Diviners*. Best choreography: **Kenneth Green** for *Blues for a Gospel Queen*. Best new score: **Nat** and **Julian Adderley** for *Shout Up a Morning*. Best touring show: *Ajax*.

Special awards: **San Diego Theater League** for setting up the first discount theater ticket booth; **Sushi**, a performance art gallery.

1986–87 PUBLICATION OF RECENTLY-PRODUCED PLAYS

A . . . My Name Is Alice. Joan Micklin Silver and Julianne Boyd. Avon (paperback).
Biloxi Blues. Neil Simon. Random House.
Circe & Bravo. Donald Freed. Amber Lane (paperback).
Coming in to Land. Stephen Poliakoff. Methuen (paperback).
Courtship/Valentine's Day. Horton Foote. Grove Press. (also in paperback).
Danger: Memory! Arthur Miller. Grove Press. (also in paperback).
Death and the King's Horseman. Wole Soyinka. Hill & Wang. (also in paperback).
Educating Rita, Stags & Hens and *Blood Brothers*. Willy Russell. Methuen. (also in paperback).
Emerald City. David Williamson. Currency Press.
Flight. David Lan. Methuen (paperback).
Goose and Tomtom. David Rabe. Grove Press (paperback).
Highest Standard of Living. Keith Reddin. Broadway Play Publishing (paperback).
Lie of the Mind, A. Sam Shepard. New American Library.
Making Noise Quietly. Robert Holman. Methuen (paperback).
Month of Sundays, A. Bob Larbey. Amber Lane Press (paperback).
Mouthful of Birds, A. Caryl Churchill and David Lan. Methuen (paperback).
On the Verge. Eric Overmyer. Broadway Play Publishing (paperback).
Petition, The. Brian Clark. Amber Lane (paperback).
Prayer for Wings, A. Sean Mathias. Amber Lane (paperback).
Principia Scriptoriae. Richard Nelson. Broadway Play Publishing (paperback).
Rap Master Ronnie. Garry Trudeau and Elizabeth Swados. Broadway Play Publishing (paperback).
Rum & Coke. Keith Reddin. Broadway Publishing (paperback).
Search for Signs of Intelligent Life in the Universe, The. Jane Wagner. Harper & Row.
Sex and Death to the Age of 14. Spalding Gray. Vintage/Random House (paperback).
Talley & Son. Lanford Wilson. Hill & Wang. (also in paperback).
Unnatural Acts. Roger Karshner. Dramaline (paperback).
Wild Honey. Michael Frayn. New American Library (paperback).
Woza Afrika! Duma Ndlovu, editor. Braziller (also in paperback).

A SELECTED LIST OF OTHER PLAYS PUBLISHED IN 1986–87

Asian Plays, The. David Hare. Faber (paperback).
Best Short Plays 1987, The. Ramon Delgado, editor. Applause (also in paperback).
Classic American Monologues. Michael and Keil Earley. Applause (paperback).
Classical Comedy Greek and Roman. Robert W. Corrigan. Applause (paperback).
Collected Plays of David Williamson: Volume 1. David Williamson. Currency Press (paperback).
Collected Plays of Graham Greene, The. Graham Greene. Penguin (paperback).
Collected Plays of Neil Simon: Volume One and *Volume Two., The*. Neil Simon. New American Library (paperback).

Coming to Terms: American Plays & the Vietnam War. James Reston Jr., introducer. Theater Communications Group (paperback).
Complete Works and Letters of Georg Buchner. Georg Buchner. Continuum (paperback).
Dalliance/Undiscovered Country. Tom Stoppard. Faber & Faber (also in paperback).
Drama Contemporary France. Phillippa Wehle, editor. PAJ Publisher (paperback).
Edwin and Other Plays. John Mortimer. Penguin (paperback).
Ensemble Studio Theater: Marathon #84. David Mamet et al. Broadway Play Publishing (paperback).
Five of the Best Soviet Plays of the 1970s. Maya Cordeyeva and Mike Davidow, translators. Imported Publishers.
For Services Rendered/The Letter/Home and Beauty. W. Womerset Maugham. Pan (paperback).
Forty Years On and Other Plays. Alan Bennett. Faber & Faber (paperback).
Georges Feydeau: Three Farces. Georges Feydeau. University Press of America (paperback).
Guernica and Other Plays. Fernando Arrabal. Grove Press (paperback).
History Plays by David Hare, The. David Hare. Faber & Faber (paperback).
House of Blue Leaves, The and Two Other Plays. John Guare. New American Library (paperback).
In the Boom Boom Room. David Rabe. Grove Press and Samuel French (paperbacks).
Meeting the Winter Bike Rider. Wendy Lamb, editor. Dell (paperback).
More Racine. Racine. Oracle Press (paperback).
Nichols: Plays—One. Peter Nichols. Methuen (paperback)
Nine Plays by Black Women. Margaret B. Wilkerson, editor and introducer. New American Library (paperback).
One for the Road. Harold Pinter. Grove Press (also in paperback).
Plays by Steve Carter. Steve Carter. Broadway Play Publishing (paperback).
Plays From the New York Shakespeare Festival. Joseph Papp, introducer. Broadway Play Publishing (paperback).
Plays: One—by Simon Gray. Simon Gray. Methuen (paperback).
Selected Plays by Brian Friel. Brian Friel. Catholic University of America Press. (also in paperback).
Softcops & Fen. Caryl Churchill. Methuen (paperback).
Soliloquy! The Elizabethan and Jacobean Monologues. Carl Keil. Applause (paperback).
Strictly Dishonorable and Other Lost American Plays. Richard Nelson, introducer (paperback).
Three Children's Plays. David Mamet. Grove Press (also in paperback).
Three Plays by Derek Walcott. Derek Walcott. Farrar, Straus and Giroux (paperback).
Three Plays by Peter Shaffer. Peter Shaffer. Penguin (paperback).
Victory Celebrations/Prisoners/The Love-Girl and the Innocent: Three Plays. Alexander Solzhenitsyn. Farrar Straus and Giroux (also in paperback).

NECROLOGY

MAY 1986–MAY 1987

PERFORMERS

Abel, Walter (88)—March 26, 1987

Ackles, Kenneth Vincent (70)—November 5, 1986

Adams, Peter (69)—January 8, 1987

Alderman, John (53)—January 12, 1987

Aldre, Mart (46)—April 14, 1987

Allen, Wally (82)—June 19, 1986

Angel, Heather (77)—December 13, 1986

Anthony, Bob (71)—November 19, 1986

Argevitch, Simon (71)—October 12, 1986

Arren, Charlotte (75)—September 30, 1986

Ashby, Clem (62)—August 11, 1986

Baddeley, Hermione (79)—August 19, 1986

Baird, Bil (William Britton) (82)—March 18, 1987

Baker, Freddie (Alfred G. Casterioto) (79)—February 15, 1987

Baseleon, Michael (61)—October 9, 1986

Beachner, Louis (63)—September 19, 1986

Becher, John C. (71)—September 20, 1986

Benda, Helena (83)—December 24, 1986

Benline, Peggy Cornell (82)—August 30, 1986

Bernardi, Louis J. (77)—April 10, 1987

Black, Rosalie C. (59)—Winter 1986

Blake, Ted (82)—August 27, 1986

Blakely, Colin (56)—May 7, 1987

Bolger, Ray (83)—January 15, 1987

Bonelle, Dick (52)—July 5, 1986

Booker, Bernice Ingalls (91)—February 25, 1987

Brach, Robert (63)—August 2, 1986

Bressler, Morris (85)—July 22, 1986

Brewer, Jacqueline—June 14, 1986

Brooke, Walter (71)—August 20, 1986

Brumondi, Leone (76)—December 9, 1986

Burnell, Peter (44)—January 5, 1987

Burrows, Rachel (75)—April 15, 1987

Busch, Bobby (69)—September 29, 1986

Butterfield, Paul (44)—May 4, 1987

Cabot, Susan (59)—December 10, 1986

Cahn, David (29)—January 16, 1987

Caldwell, Don (51)—August 16, 1986

Campbell, Muriel (75)—July 1, 1986

Candelaria, Sanson (45)—October 30, 1986

Cannon, Lilo Alexander (76)—January 7, 1987

Canty, Marietta (80)—July 9, 1986

Carmel, Roger C. (54)—November 11, 1986

Carr, Larry (James Lawrence) (72)—January 7, 1987

Caruso, Enrico Jr. (82)—April 9, 1987

Case, Allen (51)—August 25, 1986

Chapin, Alene Olsen Dalton (71)—June 3, 1986

Chapman, Ted (63)—August 19, 1986

Clark, Mamo (72)—December 18, 1986

Clark, Norma A. (78)—September 2, 1986

Coco, James (56)—February 25, 1987

Coffin, Winnie (75)—December 18, 1986

Collier, William Jr. (86)—February 6, 1987

Colonna, Jerry (82)—November 21, 1986

Coluche (Michel Colucci) (41)—June 19, 1986

Como, Rossella (47)—December 20, 1986

Cook, Mark (86)—February 8, 1987

Cooper, Diana (93)—June 16, 1986

Cooper, Edna Mae (85)—June 27, 1986

Costello, Carole (48)—March 29, 1987

Council, Elizabeth (79)—February 3, 1987

Counsell, John (81)—February 23, 1987

Courtot, Marguerite (88)—May 28, 1986

Craig, Helen (74)—July 20, 1986

Crothers, Scatman (76)—November 26, 1986

Curran, Donald Francis (55)—May 30, 1986

Curran, Paul (73)—December 1, 1986

Currier, Thomas C. (79)—July 2, 1986

Dae, Sonny (Paschal S. Vennitti) (58)—February 23, 1987

Dainty, Bill (59)—November 19, 1986

Damon, Cathryn (56)—May 4, 1987

Dansby, William (44)—June 1, 1986

Dawson, Hal K. (90)—February 17, 1987

DeAngelis, Robert (40)—October 12, 1986

DeMarco, Joe (72)—October 23, 1986

Denton, Jack (61)—November 18, 1986

DeRue, Carmen (78)—September 28, 1986

Detroy, Gene (76)—July 11, 1986

Devlin, William (75)—January 25, 1987

Diaz Gimeno, Rosita (75)—Summer 1986

Donaldson, Gregory (31)—July 5, 1986

Donovan, Don (85)—December 6, 1986

Drake, Ken (65)—January 30, 1987

Draper, Freda (80)—July 6, 1986

Drew, Max (40)—January 8, 1987

Drivas, Robert (50)—June 29, 1986

Duncan, Vivian (84)—September 19, 1986

Dunlap, Romola Remus—February 17, 1987

Dunn, Clara Whips (90)—Winter 1986

Dwyer, Leslie (80)—December 29, 1986
Eaton, Vicki (32)—August 22, 1986
Edwards, Ken (42)—July 30, 1986
Elber, Samuel (71)—January 18, 1987
Elledge, Charles Cowles (78)—August 30, 1986
Ellin, David (61)—May 27, 1986
Elliott, Lou (61)—March 5, 1987
Engle, Eleanor (77)—September 3, 1986
Epping, Florence Lucilla (96)—Summer 1986
Fagon, Alfred (49)—Summer 1986
Fay, James Jr. (33)—April 20, 1987
Fisher, Al (69)—July 16, 1986
Flanagan, Neil (52)—June 4, 1986
Fonseca, Peter (28)—November 29, 1986
Forbes, Murray (80)—January 27, 1987
Fotopoulos, Mimis (73)—October 29, 1986
Francis, Ivor (68)—October 22, 1986
Franklin, Hugh (70)—September 26, 1986
Frees, Paul (66)—November 1, 1986
Gardner, Clark LaFollette (late 40s)—April 24, 1986
Gary, Sam (67)—July 21, 1986
Gaye, Freda (78)—Fall 1986
Géniat, Gilberte (70)—June 28, 1986
Gibney, Louise (90)—September 22, 1986
Gibson, Wynne (81)—May 14, 1987
Gigliotti, Yolande (58)—May 3, 1987
Gillmore, Margalo (89)—June 30, 1986
Gingold, Hermione (89)—May 24, 1987
Gladwin, Joe (82)—March 11, 1987
Gould-Porter, Arthur E. (81)—January 2, 1987
Grant, Cary (82)—November 29, 1986
Grantham, Tom (28)—July 26, 1986
Greenwood, Joan (65)—February 28, 1987
Gregg, Virginia (69)—September 15, 1986
Guardia, Albert H. (65)—November 15, 1986
Hagan, Billy (97)—June 10, 1986
Halop, Florence (63)—July 15, 1986
Hamlin, George (65)—July 5, 1986
Hamilton, Murray (63)—September 1, 1986
Hargrave, William (86)—December 6, 1986
Hart, Derek O. (61)—November 23, 1986
Hart, Maureen (36)—July 23, 1986
Haskin, Harold (80)—March 29, 1987
Hawkins, Dolores (58)—January 15, 1987
Hawthorne, Irene (69)—October 24, 1986
Haydock, Vincent S. (71)—August 17, 1986
Haynes, Lloyd (52)—December 31, 1986
Hayworth, Rita (68)—May 14, 1987
Helpmann, Robert (77)—September 28, 1986
Herbert, Tim (71)—June 20, 1986
Herron, Randolph Parks (44)—July 12, 1986
Hewitt, Alan (71)—November 7, 1986
Hiestand, John (80)—February 5, 1987
Hobby, Charles M. (62)—May 3, 1986

Hoffman, Beth Webb (89)—July 25, 1986
Hoffman, Jack (92)—March 8, 1987
Holden, Hal (47)—June 11, 1986
Howell, Edward (84)—August 20, 1986
Huberman, Edward I. (73)—December 4, 1986
Huet, Jacqueline (57)—October 8, 1986
Hutton, Marion (67)—January 9, 1987
Jackson, Clifford (72)—March 30, 1987
Jacob, Ruby (86)—February 27, 1987
Jameson, Joyce (55)—January 16, 1987
Jarboro, Caterina (90)—August 13, 1986
Jeffries, Lang (55)—February 12, 1987
Jerome, Suzie (26)—December 4, 1986
Johnson, Raymond (40)—March 26, 1987
Jones, Darby (76)—November 30, 1986
Jones, Paul R. (77)—February 24, 1987
Jordan, Charles (71)—June 27, 1986
Jordan, Sidney (66)—November 5, 1986
Kaapana, Regina (65)—November 19, 1986
Kay, Beatrice (79)—November 8, 1986
Kaye, Danny (74)—March 3, 1987
Kaye, Nora (67)—February 28, 1987
Kean, Betty (69)—September 29, 1986
Keenan, Paul (30)—December 11, 1986
Kendrick, Richard (early 80s)—February 10, 1987
King, Dennis Jr.—August 24, 1986
King, Mary Delores (88)—December 5, 1986
Klein, Howard (85)—February 24, 1987
Klein, Irving (97)—October 27, 1986
Knight, Esmond (80)—February 23, 1987
Knight, Ted (62)—August 26, 1986
Knuth, Gustav (85)—February 1, 1987
Kraber, Tony (81)—September 9, 1986
Kunii, Toshiaki (50)—February 28, 1987
Lake, Arthur (81)—January 9, 1987
Lambert, Douglas (50)—December 17, 1986
Lanchester, Elsa (84)—December 26, 1986
Lane, Lauri Lupino (64)—June 4, 1986
Langley, Ken (57)—February 4, 1987
Lawrence, Gary (35)—November 1, 1986
Lawrence, Philip (66)—February 19, 1987
Learn, Betsy (98)—February 5, 1987
Leland, David (65)—April 17, 1987
Lenard, Grace (mid-60s)—April 7, 1987
Liff, Arlene Friedrich—December 10, 1986
Long, Ronald (75)—October 23, 1986
Loos, Anne (70)—May 3, 1986
Louison, Robert C. (34)—September 17, 1986
Lys, Lya (78)—June 2, 1986
MacDonough, William A. (82)—January 18, 1987
MacGibbon, Harriet (81)—February 8, 1987
Mack, Helen (72)—August 13, 1986
MacLaughlin, Don (79)—May 28, 1986
Mandas, Catherine (56)—June 29, 1986

Marshall, Ray (66)—September 20, 1986
Martin, Dean Paul (35)—March 23, 1987
Martin, Vivian (95)—March 16, 1987
Marzano, Yvonne DuBarry (94)—September 30, 1986
Maskinas, Patricia (40)—June 12, 1986
Masyk, Robin David (29)—January 10, 1987
Maureen, Mollie (70s)—January 26, 1987
McCarthy, Bridget (39)—November 9, 1986
McDuffie, W. Alvin (37)—January 22, 1987
McKay, Scott (71)—Winter 1987
McKechnie, Hazel (81)—December 28, 1986
McKenna, Siobhan (63–64)—November 16, 1986
McKenzie, Ella—April 25, 1987
McKenzie, Ida Mae—June 29, 1986
McNamara, Ed (65)—October 11, 1986
Meer, Virginia Hewitt (58)—July 21, 1986
Mendez, Francisco (35)—July 7, 1986
Messinger, Marie (81)—April 4, 1987
Meyer, Emile G. (76)—March 19, 1987
Miles, Sally (53)—December 2, 1986
Milne, Maggie (Margaret) (79)—Fall 1986
Mirkin, Abraham (68)—July 28, 1986
Mollison, Clifford (89)—June 5, 1986
Montgomery, Earl (65)—March 4, 1987
Morgan, Doris (50s)—May 27, 1986
Morgana, Nina (94)—July 8, 1986
Moult, Edward (60)—September 3, 1986
Murphy, William H. (87)—September 26, 1986
Nanni, Daniel (38)—October 6, 1986
Neagle, Anna (81)—June 3, 1986
Nelson, Frank (75)—September 12, 1986
Nichols, Norman (87)—April 5, 1987
O'Brien, Virginia (90)—May 2, 1987
Ondra, Andy (83)—February 28, 1987
Onoe, Tatsunosuke (40)—March 28, 1987
Otero, Vincent (32)—October 20, 1986
Pagnano, Ernest (41)—April 18, 1987
Painchaud, Brian Roger (20)—July 27, 1986
Palmer, Norman (65)—November 25, 1986
Parker, Louise (60)—September 16, 1986
Partlow, Vern (76)—March 1, 1987
Paynter, Corona (88)—July 29, 1986
Phoenix, Pat (62)—September 17, 1986
Phillips, Owen—October 27, 1986
Pincus, Bobby (Peter J. Accardy) (78)—September 16, 1986
Pinheiro, Victor (58)—March 5, 1987
Pleshette, Geraldine—March 19, 1987
Poole, Roy (62)—July 1, 1986
Poplaski, William H. (31)—May 2, 1986
Preston, Robert (68)—March 21, 1987
Proach, Henry (66)—June 22, 1986
Reddick, Cecil (56)—December 10, 1986
Redding, Robert (38)—July 11, 1986

Reed, Dean (47)—June 17, 1986
Reid, Agnes Nan (67)—January 26, 1987
Repp, Guy (84)—November 24, 1986
Rey, Alejandro (57)—May 21, 1987
Robinson, Roosevelt (47)—July 7, 1986
Rocha, Victoria Joan (33)—March 12, 1987
Rollins, Bobby (79)—January 26, 1987
Romm, Harry A. (90)—August 27, 1986
Rubin, Benny (87)—July 15, 1986
Ruskin, Coby (75)—March 3, 1987
Russak, Gilbert P. (55)—July 14, 1986
Rutherford, Angelo (33)—January 30, 1987
Sanchez, Marcelino (28)—November 21, 1986
Schwartz, Arthur (39)—July 7, 1986
Scott, Haziel Money (85)—September 10, 1986
Scott, Ken (58)—December 2, 1986
Scott, Randolph (89)—March 2, 1987
Seidl, Lea (91)—January 4, 1987
Seymour, John D. (88)—July 10, 1986
Shawlee, Joan (61)—March 22, 1987
Shawn, Dick (63)—April 17, 1987
Shearing, Renee C. (86)—March 9, 1987
Shipp, Craig (32)—December 26, 1986
Shirley, Forest (30)—September 2, 1986
Sigmon, Patricia Lynn (60s)—November 17, 1986
Simpson, Bill (54)—December 21, 1986
Simpson, Joy (40)—March 25, 1987
Skulnick, Brucha (85)—November 17, 1986
Smith, Kate (79)—June 17, 1986
Soloviova, Vera (95)—November 9, 1986
Stephens, Harvey (85)—December 22, 1986
Stevens, Paul (65)—June 4, 1986
Stevens, Roy K. (40)—April 12, 1987
Stock, Nigel (66)—June 23, 1986
Stoltz, Arnold Theodore (83)—May 11, 1986
Styles, Herkie (65)—June 28, 1986
Sullivan, Maxine (Marietta Williams) (75)—April 7, 1987
Summers, David (34)—November 8, 1986
Sweet, Blanche (90)—September 6, 1986
Tamburo, Fred (74)—April 4, 1987
Tatum, Ellyna (60)—September 22, 1986
Taylor, Kent (80)—April 11, 1987
Teasdale, Verree (80)—February 17, 1987
Teitel, Carol (62)—July 27, 1986
Teruzzi, Lilliana W. (91)—January 15, 1987
Thatcher, Heather (early 90s)—Winter 1987
Thirkield, Robert (49)—July 9, 1986
Tilton, S. Webb (70)—June 22, 1986
Tracy, Steve (34)—November 27, 1986
Troughton, Patrick (67)—March 28, 1987
Tubbs, Helen (77)—December 23, 1986
Tucker, Forrest (71)—October 25, 1986
Tucker, Lorenzo (79)—August 19, 1986
Tuohy, Dermot (65)—December 14, 1986
Tuttle, Lurene (79)—May 28, 1986

Tyner, Penny (34)—February 26, 1987
Valenty, Lili (86)—March 11, 1987
Vallee, Rudy (84)—July 3, 1986
Valliere, Geraldine (96)—December 27, 1986
Vanagelis, Helene (69)—November 30, 1986
Vedrenne, Eddy (49)—June 23, 1986
Vern, Mildred—July 6, 1986
Victor, Paula (71)—March 17, 1987
Vigran, Herburt (76)—November 28, 1986
Volkie, Ralph (76)—March 6, 1987
von Trapp, Maria Augusta (82)—March 28, 1987
Wall, Lucille (87)—July 11, 1986
Wallace, Sippie (88)—November 1, 1986
Wallerstein, Pearl Avnet (91)—March 2, 1987
Ward, Charles (33)—July 11, 1986
Ward, Dorothy (96)—Spring 1987
Warner, Hazel (94)—April 11, 1987
Watkins, Toney Davis (39)—June 28, 1986
Watson, Claire (62)—July 16, 1986
Watson, Gladys Beck (71)—July 23, 1986
Webster, Hugh (58)—May 31, 1986
Welles, Paola Mori (57)—August 12, 1986
Wells, Sarajane (73)—January 11, 1987
Welting, Patricia Hollahan (40s)—June 23, 1986
Werris, Snag (75)—February 27, 1987
West, Rita Ann (64)—June 3, 1986
Wheel, Patricia (61)—June 3, 1986
White, Larry (33)—January 10, 1987
Wickman, Caryl Jean (47)—May 5, 1987
Wilson, Alfred (35)—August 25, 1986
Windy Blow (Charles Cole) (75)—Summer 1986
Withers, Tex (53)—Winter 1986
Wright, Tony (60)—Spring 1986
Wynn, Earl R. (74)—September 17, 1986
Wynn, Keenan (70)—October 14, 1986
Young, Vernon (73)—August 22, 1986
Zaremba, Jack C. (78)—December 15, 1986
Zega, Alfred Francis—July 13, 1986
Zins, Sidney Maurice (78)—November 26, 1986

PRODUCERS, DIRECTORS, CHOREOGRAPHERS

Abbot, Tom (52)—April 8, 1987
Allégret, Yves (79)—January 31, 1987
Allen, Seth (45)—August 14, 1986
Armitage, Richard (late 50s)—November 16, 1986
Bari, Liliane (55)—November 24, 1986
Bentley, Ronald (48)—September 11, 1986
Berger, Robert Allen (37)—September 19, 1986
Carey, Denis (77)—September 28, 1986

Carter, Frances Louise (78)—November 24, 1986
Casey, Eileen—March 30, 1987
Coe, Peter (58)—May 25, 1987
Cole, Harold (65)—December 30, 1987
Conklin, Jim (55)—March 25, 1987
Connelly, George (60)—October 12, 1986
Conrad, Arthur (51)—November 25, 1986
Crawford, Cheryl (84)—October 7, 1986
Crawley, F.R. (75)—May 13, 1987
Croft, Michael (64)—November 15, 1986
DeFore, Jimmy (63)—January 14, 1987
Dehn, Mura (84)—February 11, 1987
de Liagre, Alfred Jr. (82)—March 5, 1987
Dorn, Harding (63)—February 18, 1987
Elmore, Probien Lee (82)—December 2, 1986
Fregonese, Hugo (78)—Winter 1987
Garrett, Frederick P. (43)—August 29, 1986
Gay, Edward (72)—September 23, 1986
Gottlieb, Lester (73)—September 6, 1986
Gray, Harriette Ann (73)—April 20, 1987
Grose, Robert P. (56)—August 5, 1986
Grzimek, Bernhard (77)—March 13, 1987
Guercio, Corinne (59)—May 19, 1986
Hallenbeck, E. Darrell (64)—January 31, 1987
Harlan, Gregg (40)—February 15, 1987
Henriot, Rex Edward (55)—December 1, 1986
Huntington, Catharine (100)—February 27, 1987
John, Anthony (79)—April 24, 1987
Johnson, Carlton (52)—December 22, 1986
Keller, Harry (73)—January 19, 1987
Lewis, David (83)—March 13, 1987
Lifar, Serge (81)—December 15, 1986
Lister, Laurier (79)—September 30, 1986
Livitz, Barbara (44)—August 9, 1986
Lloyd-Lewis, Howard—Winter 1987
Loesser, Lynn (70)—November 19, 1986
Ludlam, Charles (44)—May 28, 1987
Maysles, David (54)—January 3, 1987
Merrill, Celeste Rush—February 15, 1987
Miller, John J. (49)—March 23, 1987
Minnelli, Vincente (83)—July 25, 1986
Minor, Michael (46)—May 4, 1987
Oestricher, Gerard L. (70)—May 25, 1987
Philbrick, Norman D. (73)—January 25, 1987
Roddy, James D. (38)—August 25, 1986
Ross, Duncan (68)—January 4, 1987
Sand, Jonathan (35)—August 12, 1986
Scism, Mack (61)—November 2, 1986
Sokol, Martin (56)—December 18, 1986
Tarkovsky, Andrei (54)—December 29, 1986
Tudor, Antony (78)—April 19, 1987
Tynes, Bill (30)—January 9, 1987
Wallis, Hal (88)—October 5, 1986
Watt, Harry (80)—April 2, 1987
Yarnell, Gwen (61)—January 27, 1987

DESIGNERS

Bates, Ronald (54)—August 25, 1986
Bay, Howard (74)—November 21, 1986
Boyt, John Thomas (65)—November 5, 1986
Emmons, David (34)—December 6, 1986
George, Herman (45)—May 20, 1986
Hearn, Eddie (72)—April 22, 1987
Hill, Roland E. (91)—November 10, 1986
Lancaster, Osbert (77)—July 27, 1986
Lavino, Steven (43)—July 31, 1986
Lusk, Gordon J. (39)—June 29, 1986
Piacentini, Vincent Jr. (64)—December 30, 1986
Reehling, Lawrence C. (45)—September 5, 1986
Westlund, R. Chris (37)—January 28, 1987
Whitmore, John (52)—March 17, 1987

CRITICS

Adams, Marjory Livingston (90)—September 2, 1986
Bilowit, Debbi Wasserman (40)—October 23, 1986
Bourke, George (82)—October 14, 1986
Bowman, Pierre (42)—September 22, 1986
Butler, Henry F. (82)—December 29, 1986
Clarens, Carlos (56)—February 8, 1987
Cone, Theresa Loeb (73)—August 18, 1986
Downie, Alison (70)—Summer 1986
Edwards, William J. (57)—March 5, 1987
Evans, Cecilia—November 18, 1986
Fergusson, Francis (82)—December 19, 1986
Gelatt, Roland Bernard (66)—December 3, 1986
Gilder, Rosamond (95)—September 5, 1986
Haggin, B.H. (86)—May 29, 1987
Harris, Sidney J. (69)—December 7, 1986
Jacobson, Robert M. (46)—May 9, 1987
Lambert, J.W. (69)—August 3, 1986
Levinson, Evelyn (76)—August 17, 1986
Morton, Lawrence (82)—May 8, 1987
Neville, Harry C. (56)—February 15, 1987
Reed, Edward A. (59)—August 27, 1986
Reid, Charles (86)—January 1, 1987
Sargeant, Winthrop (82)—August 1986
Sullivan, Lucile (82)—February 3, 1987

PLAYWRIGHTS

Anand, Inder Raj (68)—March 6, 1987
Arrighi, Mel (52)—September 16, 1986
Braine, John (64)—October 28, 1986

Burton, Russ J. (70)—April 22, 1987
De Cecco, Sergio—November 26, 1986
Dougherty, Richard (65)—December 30, 1986
Essex, Jon (62)—July 21, 1986
Galas, Philip-Dimitri (32)—August 12, 1986
Grael, Barry Alan (56)—March 14, 1987
Harshbarger, Clay (86)—April 26, 1987
Hemphill, A. Marcus (56)—August 11, 1986
Hill, Abram (76)—October 6, 1986
Hochwalder, Fritz (75)—October 20, 1986
Kohner, Frederick (81)—July 6, 1986
Langner, Ilse (87)—January 19, 1987
Marzban, Adi (73)—February 26, 1987
Mousseos, Platon (74)—November 24, 1986
Oboler, Arch (78)—March 19, 1987
O'Donnell, John (63)—July 21, 1986
Okie, William Raybon (71)—August 19, 1986
Reed, Henry (72)—Winter 1986
Ringkamp, Jonathan (57)—September 19, 1986
Salt, Waldo (72)—March 7, 1987
Speicher, John (52)—June 23, 1986
Taylor, Dwight (84)—December 31, 1986
Tibbles, George (73)—February 14, 1987

COMPOSERS, LYRICISTS

Albertine, Charles (57)—May 18, 1986
Aquaviva, Tony (61)—September 27, 1986
Avshalomov, Zevulon (77)—April 4, 1987
Bacon, W. Garwood Jr. (66)—July 5, 1986
Barthelson, Joyce (86)—December 1, 1986
Campbell, Alex—Winter 1987
Carroll, Joseph (59)—August 17, 1986
Colby, Robert (64)—March 10, 1987
Dick, Dorothy (85)—October 18, 1986
Dougherty, Celius (84)—December 22, 1986
Fassett, James (82)—December 17, 1986
Franklin, Mark (39)—October 9, 1986
Gallardo, Adrian (60)—July 27, 1986
Goodman, Simon Robert (31)—September 12, 1986
Greene, Joe (71)—June 16, 1986
Harris, Norman Ray (39)—March 21, 1987
Holmes, Leroy (72)—July 27, 1986
Lerner, Alan Jay (67)—June 14, 1986
Meeropol, Abel (83)—October 30, 1986
Montgomery, Merle (82)—August 26, 1986
Moore, Phil (70)—May 13, 1987
Petersen, Robert (50)—January 12, 1987
Poston, Elizabeth (81)—March 18, 1987
Pukui, Mary (91)—May 21, 1986
Reece, Florence (86)—August 3, 1986
Trimble, Lester (63)—December 31, 1986
Vidalin, Maurice (62)—October 10, 1986
Warren, Robert A. (71)—January 19, 1987

MUSICIANS

Adams, Park (55)—September 10, 1986
Aleinkoff, Harry (92)—July 26, 1986
Anderson, Donald H. (74)—September 18, 1986
Bass, Kenny (64)—January 13, 1987
Beau, Henry (76)—April 18, 1987
Bernhardt, Clyde, E.B. (80)—May 20, 1986
Bove, John J. (71)—June 15, 1986
Brenner, Engelbert F.J. (82)—September 16, 1986
Brown, Romaine (63)—June 2, 1986
Caulfield, Thomas (83)—March 11, 1987
Coe, Donald (71)—August 8, 1986
Cordaro, John (78)—September 11, 1986
Crosby, Billy (William Kroner) (80)—October 28, 1986
Darr, Jerome (75)—October 29, 1986
David, John Russell (47)—January 24, 1987
Davis, Eddie (65)—November 3, 1986
Dineen, Danny (83)—February 11, 1987
Doolittle, Jimmy (69)—April 12, 1987
Durham, Eddie (80)—March 6, 1987
Effron, Sigmund (74)—June 17, 1986
Escovedo, Thomas (45)—July 13, 1986
Evans, Pat (76)—April 9, 1987
Ferris, Tommy (80)—June 4, 1986
Fleet, Don (48)—December 31, 1986
Gaines, Charlie H. (86)—November 23, 1986
Galepides, François-Alexandre (58)—March 25, 1987
Goodman, Benny (77)—June 13, 1986
Gordon, David (34)—September 4, 1986
Gordon, Edith Wright (77)—October 14, 1986
Gordon, Herbert (83)—September 7, 1986
Green, Freddie (75)—March 1, 1987
Heim, Frederick William (72)—November 25, 1986
Higgins, Monk (50)—July 3, 1986
Howard, Marvin (60)—February 16, 1987
Hughes, Spike (78)—February 2, 1987
Huttenback, Dorothy (90)—April 10, 1987
Jackson, Clarence H. (67)—August 29, 1986
Jaffe, Allan (51)—March 9, 1987
Jefferson, Thomas (65)—December 3, 1986
Jenkins, Carroll L. (59)—November 28, 1986
Jenssen, Melvin P. (82)—November 11, 1986
Johnson, William (58)—April 29, 1987
Jones, Thad (63)—August 20, 1986
Kahgan, Philip (93)—June 6, 1986
Kiener, Barry (30)—May 25, 1986
Kleisinger, John Anton (67)—September 25, 1986
Lantz, J. Roscoe (82)—June 8, 1986
Liberace, Wladziu Valentino (Walter) (67)—February 4, 1987

Maddock, George E. (70)—January 12, 1987
Maresh, Ferdinand (68)—December 1, 1986
McCue, Claude (79)—April 25, 1987
McNelis, Declan (34)—April 13, 1987
McNelley, Bobby Gene (36)—January 7, 1987
Mobley, Henry (55)—May 30, 1986
Moore, Gerald (87)—March 13, 1987
Murphy, Turk (71)—May 30, 1987
Myers, Ray R. (75)—May 16, 1986
Namekelua, Alice (94)—April 27, 1987
Nyiregyhazi, Erwin (84)—April 13, 1987
O'Connor, Farrell B. (83)—April 8, 1987
Parker, John (68)—September 3, 1986
Ponce, Tommy (52)—November 2, 1986
Purnell, Alton (75)—January 16, 1987
Ragland, Thomas W. (74)—October 19, 1986
Rasul, Dawud Abdul (David Cruse) (38)—November 11, 1986
Rettenberg, Milton (87)—December 24, 1986
Reynolds, Tommy (69)—September 30, 1986
Rich, Buddy (69)—April 2, 1987
Rich, Jimmy—October 19, 1986
Roberts, Josephine (81)—January 1, 1987
Rosenbach, Melville (77)—December 17, 1986
Rubinoff, David (89)—October 6, 1986
Russell, Curly (69)—July 3, 1986
Salisbury, George Franklin (68)—May 16, 1986
Sayles, Emanuel (79)—October 5, 1986
Schipani, Alphonse (61)—September 29, 1986
Schlein, Irving (80)—July 11, 1986
Seaman, Eugene (66)—March 21, 1987
Sete, Bola (63)—February 14, 1987
Shu, Eddie (68)—July 4, 1986
Sino, Lou (55)—July 30, 1986
Skillman, Vince—January 18, 1987
Skrobacs, Lawrence (38)—March 10, 1987
Sleet, Don (48)—December 31, 1986
Spicer, Dempsey (74)—March 21, 1987
Stagliano, James (78)—April 11, 1987
Stanley, Roba (78)—June 9, 1986
Stein, Maurice (76)—January 9, 1987
Stricklin, Al (78)—October 15, 1986
Stroak, Dick (52)—Summer 1986
Sutherland, Esther (54)—December 31, 1986
Tapley, Rolland S. (85)—May 20, 1986
Tarto, Joe (84)—August 24, 1986
Thalben-Ball, George (90)—January 18, 1987
Thomas, Joseph (77)—August 3, 1986
Vandersall, David (66)—January 14, 1987
Wanderley, Walter (55)—September 4, 1986
Weis, Theodore M. (66)—February 14, 1987
Wilson, Teddy (73)—July 31, 1986
Wood, Henrietta (86)—December 18, 1986
Zimmerman, Oscar (76)—April 2, 1987

CONDUCTORS

Arnaz, Desi (69)—December 2, 1986
Baskerville, David (69)—December 27, 1986
Benack, Benny (64)—July 23, 1986
Block, Bert (74)—July 9, 1986
Brandon, Henry (71)—February 7, 1987
Caples, William T. (58)—July 9, 1986
Cicone, Victor (81)—September 19, 1986
Curtis, Duke (61)—December 9, 1986
Damiani, Leo (74)—November 4, 1986
DeSimone, Anthony (66)—June 12, 1986
Dowds, Bobby (83)—Spring 1987
Eidemiller, Herb (64)—January 29, 1987
Hackett, Ray (75)—March 29, 1987
Heidt, Horace (85)—December 1, 1986
Houston, James K. (60)—January 3, 1987
Lane, Marty (55)—June 27, 1986
Katz, David (62)—May 21, 1987
Kutin, Alexander Emelianoff (87)—May 31, 1986
Lebowsky, Stanley (59)—October 19, 1986
Louapre, Rene A. Jr. (71)—April 6, 1987
McArthur, Edwin (79)—February 24, 1987
Michalak, Thomas (45)—July 10, 1986
Owens, Harry (85)—December 12, 1986
Samuels, Eddy (52)—September 16, 1986
Sandiford, Preston (77)—June 6, 1986
Shaner, Bernie (85)—November 23, 1986
Spitalny, Maurice (93)—October 28, 1986
Stelt, Milo (71)—July 16, 1986
Twitchell, Jerome (95)—February 23, 1987
Williams, Earl Harris (75)—October 10, 1986

OTHERS

Abrams, Amos (44)—September 1, 1986
Agent
Agron, Oscar (75)—April 25, 1987
Las Vegas casino owner
Albanese, Carmen A. Jr. (29)—February 1, 1987
Stage manager
Alexander, Dorothy (82)—November 17, 1986
Founder, Atlanta Ballet
Amiel, Jack Joseph (77)—June 18, 1986
Jack Dempsey's Restaurant
Armhaus, Della—March 23, 1987
Receptionist
Atkin, Charles (83)—February 28, 1987
Production stage manager
Auerbach, Cynthia (44)—May 14, 1987
Opera director
Azar, Ted Jr. (early 50s)—October 17, 1986
Broadway hair, makeup designer

Bandy, Way (45)—August 13, 1986
Makeup artist
Bank, Gustave (74)—October 15, 1986
Maker of dance shoes
Barry, Francis J. (79)—June 7, 1986
Circle Line boat tours
Becker, Henry O. (73)—February 17, 1987
Stagehand
Bennewitz, John (64)—June 11, 1986
Broadway photographer
Bohm, William (74)—March 7, 1987
Theater manager
Bolker, Joseph (62)—November 28, 1986
Los Angeles Music Center
Bond, Henry (59)—January 3, 1987
"Preview Harry"
Borges, Jorge Luis (86)—June 14, 1986
Argentinian author
Brennan, James F. (late 40s)—October 7, 1986
AFTRA
Bromley, Paul (77)—July 22, 1986
Booking agent
Bundt, Ronald M. (34)—May 15, 1986
Alvin Alley American Dance Theater
Burke, Michael (70)—February 5, 1987
Madison Square Garden, Yankees
Caldwell, Erskine (83)—April 11, 1987
Novelist
Campbell, John B.T. Jr. (71)—September 6, 1986
President, Publicists Guild
Campbell, Margaret (87)—March 15, 1987
Washington Sq. Music Festival
Campbell, Tristram J. (58)—August 3, 1986
ASCAP
Canfield, F. Curtis (82)—June 8, 1986
Yale School of Drama
Chestnut, Sue G. (54)—June 5, 1986
Manager, agent
Cortez, Virginia (58)—Winter 1987
Civic Theater of Central Florida
Crangle, Nini Finkelstein (49)—August 14, 1986
Publicist
Crans, Thomas (50)—December 20, 1986
Technical director
Crosby, Mary—June 5, 1986
Writer, *Herald Tribune*
Davis, Eddie (93)—April 20, 1987
Leon & Eddie's
Diether, Jack (68)—January 23, 1987
Musicologist
DiStefano, Henry J. (72)—August 18, 1986
Victor's Cafe, Philadelphia
Doyle, Joe (68)—July 9, 1986
Theater manager

Duncan, Kenn (56)—July 26, 1986
Dance photographer
Dushkin, David (88)—September 2, 1986
Music teacher
Efros, Anatoly V. (61)—January 12, 1987
Taganka Theater, Moscow
Ellin, Stanley (69)—July 31, 1986
President, Mystery Writers of America
Esty, Harold M. (72)—September 16, 1986
Broadway show backer
Faulkner, Ralph B. (95)—January 28, 1987
Fencing instructor
Fitzgerald, Scottie (64)—June 18, 1986
Author
Geist, Harry (85)—August 24, 1986
Treasurer, Friars Club
Gelman, Harold S. (74)—October 16, 1986
Musicologist
Glankoff, Mort (85)—August 23, 1986
Cue magazine
Godwin, Harry (79)—May 27, 1986
Jazz historian
Gottlieb, Martha (36)—March 7, 1987
Capital Repertory
Grant, Alvin R. (65)—August 1, 1986
Madison Square Garden
Graves, Helen Louise (81)—November 27, 1986
St. Louis Symphony
Grogan, Frank (90)—August 29, 1986
Technician
Guterman, Mortie—March 18, 1987
Agent
Hamilton, Jake (59)—November 7, 1986
Stage manager
Harris, Lula (96)—January 6, 1987
Actors Fund of America
Heller, Sim E. (84)—May 21, 1987
Variety Club
Hepner, Lee Alfred (65)—July 25, 1986
Professor of music
Hoffman, Harold (79)—May 28, 1987
Union executive
Huie, William Bradford (76)—November 11, 1986
Author
Isaac, Al (50)—August 7, 1986
Company manager
Israel, William (90)—April 17, 1987
Theater manager
Jaffe, Mildred (79)—March 9, 1987
Arts patron
Kelley, Bruce M. (56)—September 4, 1986
Lighting director
Kephart, Daniel M. (34)—June 7, 1986
Publicist
Klein, Irv (67)—July 6, 1986
Agent

Lang, Robert Edward (70)—June 3, 1986
Radio Free Europe
Lartigue, Jacques-Henri (92)—September 12, 1986
Photographer
Lawrence, Justus Baldwin (83)—April 21, 1987
Publicist
Lebowitz, Ed (49)—September 24, 1986
Attorney
Le Bret, Robert Favre (92)—April 28, 1987
Cannes Film Festival
Lerner, Sol (77)—October 15, 1986
Attorney
Levine, Steve (37)—November 9, 1986
William Morris Agency
Lieberman, Abraham (86)—February 19, 1987
Friars Club
Loew, Mildred Zukor (86)—July 5, 1986
Little theater companies
London, Jack (66)—May 8, 1987
Attorney
Lorillard, Louis Livingston (67)—November 5, 1986
Newport Jazz Festival
Lowenthal, Jeffrey (37)—July 23, 1986
Wm. Morris Agency
Lundblad, Bertrum J. (77)—January 15, 1987
Ice Follies
Lyttle, Joseph—July 28, 1986
Agent
MacDonald, John D. (70)—December 28, 1986
Mystery writer
Maksik, Ben (78)—December 25, 1986
Town & Country nightclub
Mann, Frederic R. (83)—February 26, 1987
Director, N.Y. Philharmonic
Marek, George R. (84)—January 7, 1987
Music biographer
Mariano, Gene A. (77)—August 18, 1986
Resort niteries
Martini, Freddy—October 14, 1986
Freddy's nightclub
Matthews, Nat (75)—November 29, 1986
British theater manager
Maude, John C. (85)—August 16, 1986
British Drama League
McCarthy, Charles (62)—September 9, 1986
Abbey Theater
McCrae, John R. (69)—Winter 1986
Converse Opera Workshop
Meister, Eddie (79)—June 7, 1986
Boston's Showbar
Millay, Norma (92)—May 14, 1986
Millay Colony for the Arts
Millen, Norma J. (76)—August 1, 1986
Publicist

Minsky, Morton (85)—March 23, 1987
  Burlesque houses
Moll, James W. (70)—December 22, 1986
  Drama professor
Moss, Marvin (59)—June 19, 1986
  Agent
Nuddle, Seymour (60)—December 31, 1986
  Philadelphia Civic Center
O'Halloran, John F. (82)—April 22, 1987
  Waltham, Mass. Theater
Orhelein, William (58)—February 26, 1987
  Royal Palm Dinner Theater
Ossenfort, Robert (41)—July 8, 1986
  Company manager
Pagano, Carl (81)—May 31, 1986
  Arranger
Pagilaro, Sam (70)—December 31, 1986
  Company manager
Payne, David (49)—March 27, 1987
  Company manager
Peterson, William B. (75)—September 24,
  1986
  Agent
Poons, Marvin H. (57)—May 9, 1987
  American Dinner Theater Institute
Praeger, Soloman Leonard (74)—January 1,
  1987
  Agent
Primus, Sylvia (71)—July 11, 1986
  Backer
Randall, Paul E. (84)—June 27, 1986
  Drama professor
Rapp, Philip (75)—January 12, 1987
  Theater manager
Redstone, Michael (85)—April 4, 1987
  Theater owner
Riggs, L.A. "Speed" (79)—February 1, 1987
  Auctioneer
Roediger, Rolf (57)—December 24, 1986
  Puppetmaker
Rosenthal, Harold (69)—March 19, 1987
  Editor, *Opera* magazine
Rosenthal, Sandy (63)—December 27, 1986
  Arizona Theater Company
Salzer, Felix (82)—August 9, 1986
  Musicologist
Sanjek, Russell (70)—June 11, 1986
  Broadcast Music Inc.

Sanjurjo, Luis (45)—March 12, 1987
  Agent
Scholz, Jackson (89)—October 26, 1986
  Olympic sprinter
Schwartz, Jerome J. (62)—January 13, 1987
  Attorney
Shribman, Joe (70s)—December 24, 1986
  Personal manager
Simone, Peter (34)—September 18, 1986
  Publicist
Strauss, Helen M. (83)—May 4, 1987
  William Morris Agency
Streibert, Theodore (87)—January 18, 1987
  U.S. Information Agency
Townsend, Edward (73)—July 19, 1986
  Metropolitan Opera Club
Tussey, Clyde V. (62)—April 13, 1987
  Publicist
Valentino, Thomas J. (79)—August 4, 1986
  Special sound effects
Walker, Tommy (64)—October 20, 1986
  Director of entertainment, Disneyland
Wall, S. Leonard (71)—January 27, 1987
  Attorney
Walsh, Rose (85)—May 31, 1986
  Columnist
Weiss, Miriam (91)—February 19, 1987
  Variety staffer
Williams, Wade (53)—November 9, 1986
  Dance administrator
Williams, William B. (62)—August 3, 1986
  Radio personality
Wilson, Earl (79)—January 16, 1987
  Columnist
Wood, Billy (62)—April 28, 1987
  Agent
Wood, H. Thomas (80)—November 27, 1986
  Publicist
Workman, David (70)—May 6, 1986
  Still photographer
Yergin, Irving (79)—August 24, 1986
  Publicist
Yetman, Robert A. (27)—October 4, 1986
  Agent
Young, Stuart (52)—August 29, 1986
  Chairman, BBC

THE BEST PLAYS, 1894–1986

Listed in alphabetical order below are all those works selected as Best Plays in previous volumes in the *Best Plays* series. Opposite each title is given the volume in which the play appears, its opening date and its total number of performances. Two separate opening-date and performance-number entries signify two separate engagements off Broadway and on Broadway when the original production was transferred from one area to the other, usually in an off-to-on direction. Those plays marked with an asterisk (*) were still playing on June 1, 1987 and their number of performances was figured through May 31, 1987. Adaptors and translators are indicated by (ad) and (tr), the symbols (b), (m) and (l) stand for the author of the book, music and lyrics in the cast of musicals and (c) signifies the credit for the show's conception.

NOTE: A season-by-season listing, rather than an alphabetical one, of the 500 Best Plays in the first 50 volumes, starting with the yearbook for the season of 1919–1920, appears in *The Best Plays of 1968–69*.

PLAY	VOLUME	OPENED	PERFS
ABE LINCOLN IN ILLINOIS—Robert E. Sherwood	38–39.	.Oct. 15, 1938. .	472
ABRAHAM LINCOLN—John Drinkwater	19–20.	.Dec. 15, 1919. .	193
ACCENT ON YOUTH—Samson Raphaelson	34–35.	.Dec. 25, 1934. .	229
ADAM AND EVA—Guy Bolton, George Middleton	19–20.	.Sept. 13, 1919. .	312
ADAPTATION—Elaine May; and NEXT—Terrence McNally	68–69.	.Feb. 10, 1969. .	707
AFFAIRS OF STATE—Louis Verneuil	50–51.	.Sept. 25, 1950. .	610
AFTER THE FALL—Arthur Miller	63–64.	.Jan. 23, 1964. .	208
AFTER THE RAIN—John Bowen	67–68.	.Oct. 9, 1967. .	64
AGNES OF GOD—John Pielmeier	81–82.	.Mar. 30, 1982. .	486
AH, WILDERNESS!—Eugene O'Neill	33–34.	.Oct. 2, 1933. .	289
AIN'T SUPPOSED TO DIE A NATURAL DEATH—(b, m, l) Melvin Van Peebles	71–72.	.Oct. 7, 1971. .	325
ALIEN CORN—Sidney Howard	32–33.	.Feb. 20, 1933. .	98
ALISON'S HOUSE—Susan Glaspell	30–31.	.Dec. 1, 1930. .	41
ALL MY SONS—Arthur Miller	46–47.	.Jan. 29, 1947. .	328
ALL OVER TOWN—Murray Schisgal	74–75.	.Dec. 12, 1974. .	233
ALL THE WAY HOME—Tad Mosel, based on James Agee's novel *A Death in the Family*	60–61.	.Nov. 30, 1960. .	333
ALLEGRO—(b,l) Oscar Hammerstein II, (m) Richard Rodgers	47–48.	.Oct. 10, 1947. .	315
AMADEUS—Peter Shaffer	80–81.	.Dec. 17, 1980. .	1,181
AMBUSH—Arthur Richman	21–22.	.Oct. 10, 1921. .	98
AMERICA HURRAH—Jean-Claude van Itallie	66–67.	.Nov. 6, 1966. .	634
AMERICAN BUFFALO—David Mamet	76–77.	.Feb. 16, 1977. .	135
AMERICAN WAY, THE—George S. Kaufman, Moss Hart	38–39.	.Jan. 21, 1939. .	164
AMPHITRYON 38—Jean Giraudoux, (ad) S. N. Behrman	37–38.	.Nov. 1, 1937. .	153
AND A NIGHTINGALE SANG—C.P. Taylor	83–84.	.Nov. 27, 1983. .	177
ANDERSONVILLE TRIAL, THE—Saul Levitt	59–60.	.Dec. 29, 1959. .	179
ANDORRA—Max Frisch, (ad) George Tabori	62–63.	.Feb. 9, 1963. .	9
ANGEL STREET—Patrick Hamilton	41–42.	.Dec. 5, 1941. .	1,295
ANGELS FALL—Lanford Wilson	82–83.	.Oct. 17, 1982. .	65
ANIMAL KINGDOM, THE—Philip Barry	31–32.	.Jan. 12, 1932. .	183
ANNA CHRISTIE—Eugene O'Neill	21–22.	.Nov. 2, 1921. .	177
ANNA LUCASTA—Philip Yordan	44–45.	.Aug. 30, 1944. .	957
ANNE OF THE THOUSAND DAYS—Maxwell Anderson	48–49.	.Dec. 8, 1948. .	286

485

PLAY	VOLUME	OPENED	PERFS
ANNIE—(b) Thomas Meehan, (m) Charles Strouse, (l) Martin Charnin, based on Harold Gray's comic strip "Little Orphan Annie"	76–77.	.Apr. 21, 1977.	. 2,377
ANOTHER LANGUAGE—Rose Franken	31–32.	.Apr. 25, 1932.	. 344
ANOTHER PART OF THE FOREST—Lillian Hellman	46–47.	.Nov. 20, 1946.	. 182
ANTIGONE—Jean Anouilh, (ad) Lewis Galantiere	45–46.	.Feb. 18, 1946.	. 64
APPLAUSE—(b) Betty Comden and Adolph Green, (m) Charles Strouse, (l) Lee Adams, based on the film *All About Eve* and the original story by Mary Orr	69–70.	.Mar. 30, 1970.	. 896
APPLE TREE, THE—(b,l) Sheldon Harnick, (b, m) Jerry Bock, add'l (b) Jerome Coopersmith, based on stories by Mark Twain, Frank R. Stockton and Jules Feiffer	66–67.	.Oct. 18, 1966.	. 463
ARSENIC AND OLD LACE—Joseph Kesselring	40–41.	.Jan. 10, 1941.	. 1,444
AS HUSBANDS GO—Rachel Crothers	30–31.	.Mar. 5, 1931.	. 148
AS IS—William M. Hoffman	84–85.	.Mar. 10, 1985.	. 49
	84–85.	.May 1, 1985.	. 285
ASHES—David Rudkin	76–77.	.Jan. 25, 1977.	. 167
AUNT DAN AND LEMON—Wallace Shawn	85–86.	.Oct. 1, 1985.	. 191
AUTUMN GARDEN, THE—Lillian Hellman	50–51.	.Mar. 7, 1951.	. 101
AWAKE AND SING—Clifford Odets	34–35.	.Feb. 19, 1935.	. 209
BAD MAN, THE—Porter Emerson Browne	20–21.	.Aug. 30, 1920.	. 350
BAD HABITS—Terrence McNally	73–74.	.Feb. 4, 1974.	. 273
BAD SEED—Maxwell Anderson, based on William March's novel	54–55.	.Dec. 8, 1954.	. 332
BARBARA FRIETCHIE—Clyde Fitch	99–09.	.Oct. 23, 1899.	. 83
BAREFOOT IN ATHENS—Maxwell Anderson	51–52.	.Oct. 31, 1951.	. 30
BAREFOOT IN THE PARK—Neil Simon	63–64.	.Oct. 23, 1963.	. 1,530
BARRETTS OF WIMPOLE STREET, THE—Rudolf Besier	30–31.	.Feb. 9, 1931.	. 370
BECKET—Jean Anouilh, (tr) Lucienne Hill	60–61.	.Oct. 5, 1960.	. 193
BEDROOM FARCE—Alan Ayckbourn	78–79.	.Mar. 29, 1979.	. 278
BEGGAR ON HORSEBACK—George S. Kaufman, Marc Connelly	23–24.	.Feb. 12, 1924.	. 224
BEHOLD THE BRIDEGROOM—George Kelly	27–28.	.Dec. 26, 1927.	. 88
BELL, BOOK AND CANDLE—John van Druten	50–51.	.Nov. 14, 1950.	. 233
BELL FOR ADANO, A—Paul Osborn, based on John Hersey's novel	44–45.	.Dec. 6, 1944.	. 304
BENEFACTORS—Michael Frayn	85–86.	.Dec. 22, 1985.	. 217
BENT—Martin Sherman	79–80.	.Dec. 2, 1979.	. 240
BERKELEY SQUARE—John L. Balderston	29–30.	.Nov. 4, 1929.	. 229
BERNARDINE—Mary Chase	52–53.	.Oct. 16, 1952.	. 157
BEST LITTLE WHOREHOUSE IN TEXAS, THE—(b) Larry L. King, Peter Masterson, (m,l) Carol Hall	77–78.	.Apr. 17, 1978.	. 64
	78–79.	.June 19, 1978.	. 1,639
BEST MAN, THE—Gore Vidal	59–60.	.Mar. 31, 1960.	. 520
BETRAYAL—Harold Pinter	79–80.	.Jan. 5, 1980.	. 170
BEYOND THE HORIZON—Eugene O'Neill	19–20.	.Feb. 2, 1920.	. 160
BIG FISH, LITTLE FISH—Hugh Wheeler	60–61.	.Mar. 15, 1961.	. 101
BILL OF DIVORCEMENT, A—Clemence Dane	21–22.	.Oct. 10, 1921.	. 173
BILLY BUDD—Louis O. Coxe, Robert Chapman, based on Herman Melville's novel	50–51.	.Feb. 10, 1951.	. 105
BILOXI BLUES—Neil Simon	84–85.	.Mar. 28, 1985.	. 524
BIOGRAPHY—S. N. Behrman	32–33.	.Dec. 12, 1932.	. 267
BLACK COMEDY—Peter Shaffer	66–67.	.Feb. 12, 1967.	. 337
BLITHE SPIRIT—Noel Coward	41–42.	.Nov. 5, 1941.	. 657
BOESMAN AND LENA—Athol Fugard	70–71.	.June 22, 1970.	. 205

PLAY	VOLUME	OPENED	PERFS
ESCAPE—John Galsworthy	27–28.	.Oct. 26, 1927.	. 173
ETHAN FROME—Owen and Donald Davis, based on Edith Wharton's novel	35–36.	.Jan. 21, 1936.	. 120
EVE OF ST. MARK, THE—Maxwell Anderson	42–43.	.Oct. 7, 1942.	. 307
EXCURSION—Victor Wolfson	36–37.	.Apr. 9, 1937.	. 116
EXECUTION OF JUSTICE—Emily Mann	85–86.	.Mar. 13, 1986.	. 12
EXTREMITIES—William Mastrosimone	82–83.	.Dec. 22, 1982.	. 325
FALL GUY, THE—James Gleason, George Abbott	24–25.	.Mar. 10, 1925.	. 176
FAMILY BUSINESS—Dick Goldberg	77–78.	.Apr. 12, 1978.	. 438
FAMILY PORTRAIT—Lenore Coffee, William Joyce Cowen	38–39.	.May 8, 1939.	. 111
FAMOUS MRS. FAIR, THE—James Forbes	19–20.	.Dec. 22, 1919.	. 344
FAR COUNTRY, A—Henry Denker	60–61.	.Apr. 4, 1961.	. 271
FARMER TAKES A WIFE, THE—Frank B. Elser, Marc Connelly, based on Walter D. Edmonds's novel *Rome Haul*	34–35.	.Oct. 30, 1934.	. 104
FATAL WEAKNESS, THE—George Kelly	46–47.	.Nov. 19, 1946.	. 119
FIDDLER ON THE ROOF—(b) Joseph Stein, (l) Sheldon Harnick, (m) Jerry Bock, based on Sholom Aleichem's stories	64–65.	.Sept. 22, 1964.	.3,242
5TH OF JULY, THE—Lanford Wilson (also called *Fifth of July*).	77–78.	.Apr. 27, 1978.	. 159
FIND YOUR WAY HOME—John Hopkins	73–74.	.Jan. 2, 1974.	. 135
FINISHING TOUCHES—Jean Kerr	72–73.	.Feb. 8, 1973.	. 164
FIORELLO!—(b) Jerome Weidman, George Abbott, (l) Sheldon Harnick, (m) Jerry Bock	59–60.	.Nov. 23, 1959.	. 795
FIREBRAND, THE—Edwin Justus Mayer	24–25.	.Oct. 15, 1924.	. 269
FIRST LADY—Katharine Dayton, George S. Kaufman	35–36.	.Nov. 26, 1935.	. 246
FIRST MONDAY IN OCTOBER—Jerome Lawrence, Robert E. Lee	78–79.	.Oct. 3, 1978.	. 79
FIRST MRS. FRASER, THE—St. John Ervine	29–30.	.Dec. 28, 1929.	. 352
FIRST YEAR, THE—Frank Craven	20–21.	.Oct. 20, 1920.	. 760
FIVE FINGER EXERCISE—Peter Shaffer	59–60.	.Dec. 2, 1959.	. 337
FIVE-STAR FINAL—Louis Weitzenkorn	30–31.	.Dec. 30, 1930.	. 175
FLIGHT TO THE WEST—Elmer Rice	40–41.	.Dec. 30, 1940.	. 136
FLOATING LIGHT BULB, THE—Woody Allen	80–81.	.Apr. 27, 1981.	. 65
FLOWERING PEACH, THE—Clifford Odets	54–55.	.Dec. 28, 1954.	. 135
FOLLIES—(b) James Goldman, (m, l) Stephen Sondheim	70–71.	.Apr. 4, 1971.	. 521
FOOL, THE—Channing Pollock	22–23.	.Oct. 23, 1922.	. 373
FOOL FOR LOVE—Sam Shepard	83–84.	.May 26, 1983.	.1,000
FOOLISH NOTION—Philip Barry	44–45.	.Mar. 3, 1945.	. 104
FOREIGNER, THE—Larry Shue	84–85.	.Nov. 1, 1984.	. 686
FORTY CARATS—Pierre Barillet and Jean-Pierre Gredy, (ad) Jay Allen	68–69.	.Dec. 26, 1968.	. 780
FOXFIRE—Susan Cooper, Hume Cronyn, (m) Jonathan Holtzman; based on materials from the *Foxfire* books	82–83.	.Nov. 11, 1982.	. 213
*42ND STREET—(b) Michael Stewart, Mark Bramble, (m,l) Harry Warren, Al Dubin, (add'l l) Johnny Mercer, Mort Dixon, based on the novel by Bradford Ropes	80–81.	.Aug. 25, 1980.	.2,816
FOURPOSTER, THE—Jan de Hartog	51–52.	.Oct. 24, 1951.	. 632
FRONT PAGE, THE—Ben Hecht, Charles MacArthur	28–29.	.Aug. 14, 1928.	. 276
GENERATION—William Goodhart	65–66.	.Oct. 6, 1965.	. 299
GEORGE WASHINGTON SLEPT HERE—George S. Kaufman, Moss Hart	40–41.	.Oct. 18, 1940.	. 173
GETTING OUT—Marsha Norman	78–79.	.Oct. 19, 1978.	. 259
GIDEON—Paddy Chayefsky	61–62.	.Nov. 9, 1961.	. 236
GIGI—Anita Loos, based on Colette's novel	51–52.	.Nov. 24, 1951.	. 219
GIMME SHELTER—Barrie Keefe (*Gem, Gotcha* and *Getaway*)	78–79.	.Dec. 10, 1978.	. 17

PLAY	VOLUME	OPENED	PERFS
'NIGHT, MOTHER—Marsha Norman	82–83.	.Mar. 31, 1983. .	380
	83–84.	.Apr. 18, 1984. .	54
NINE—(b) Arthur L. Kopit, (m, l) Maury Yeston, (ad) Mario Fratti, from the Italian.	81–82.	.May 9, 1982. .	739
NO MORE LADIES—A. E. Thomas	33–34.	.Jan. 23, 1934. .	162
NO PLACE TO BE SOMEBODY—Charles Gordone	68–69.	.May 4, 1969. .	250
NO TIME FOR COMEDY—S. N. Berhman	38–39.	.Apr. 17, 1939. .	185
NO TIME FOR SERGEANTS—Ira Levin, based on Mac Hyman's novel.	55–56.	.Oct. 20, 1955. .	796
NOEL COWARD IN TWO KEYS—Noel Coward (Come Into the Garden Maud and A Song at Twilight)	73–74.	.Feb. 28, 1974. .	140
NOISES OFF—Michael Frayn	83–84.	.Dec. 11, 1983. .	553
NORMAN CONQUESTS, THE—(see Living Together, Round and Round the Garden and Table Manners)			
NUTS—Tom Topor.	79–80.	.Apr. 28, 1980. .	96
O MISTRESS MINE—Terence Rattigan.	45–46.	.Jan. 23, 1946. .	452
ODD COUPLE, THE—Neil Simon	64–65.	.Mar. 10, 1965. .	964
OF MICE AND MEN—John Steinbeck	37–38.	.Nov. 23, 1937. .	207
OF THEE I SING—(b) George S. Kaufman, Morrie Ryskind, (l) Ira Gershwin, (m) George Gershwin	31–32.	.Dec. 26, 1931. .	441
OH DAD, POOR DAD, MAMA'S HUNG YOU IN THE CLOSET AND I'M FEELIN' SO SAD—Arthur L. Kopit	61–62.	.Feb. 26, 1962. .	454
OHIO IMPROMPTU, CATASTROPHE and WHAT WHERE—Samuel Beckett.	83–84.	.June 15, 1983. .	350
OKLAHOMA!—(b, l) Oscar Hammerstein, II, based on Lynn Riggs's play Green Grow the Lilacs, (m) Richard Rodgers	42–43.	.Mar. 31, 1943. .	2,212
OLD MAID, THE—Zoë Akins, based on Edith Wharton's novel.	34–35.	.Jan. 7, 1935. .	305
OLD SOAK, THE—Don Marquis.	22–23.	.Aug. 22, 1922. .	423
OLD TIMES—Harold Pinter.	71–72.	.Nov. 16, 1971. .	119
OLDEST LIVING GRADUATE, THE—Preston Jones	76–77.	.Sept. 23, 1976. .	20
ON BORROWED TIME—Paul Osborn, based on Lawrence Edward Watkin's novel	37–38.	.Feb. 3, 1938. .	321
ON GOLDEN POND—Ernest Thompson.	78–79.	.Sept. 13, 1978. .	30
	78–79.	.Feb. 28, 1979. .	126
ON TRIAL—Elmer Rice.	09–19.	.Aug. 19, 1914. .	365
ONCE IN A LIFETIME—Moss Hart, George S. Kaufman	30–31.	.Sept. 24, 1930. .	406
ONE SUNDAY AFTERNOON—James Hagan	32–33.	.Feb. 15, 1933. .	322
ORPHEUS DESCENDING—Tennessee Williams.	56–57.	.Mar. 1, 1957. .	68
OTHERWISE ENGAGED—Simon Gray	76–77.	.Feb. 2, 1977. .	309
OUTRAGEOUS FORTUNE—Rose Franken.	43–44.	.Nov. 3, 1943. .	77
OUR TOWN—Thornton Wilder.	37–38.	.Feb. 4, 1938. .	336
OUTWARD BOUND—Sutton Vane.	23–24.	.Jan. 7, 1924. .	144
OVER 21—Ruth Gordon	43–44.	.Jan. 3, 1944. .	221
OVERTURE—William Bolitho	30–31.	.Dec. 5, 1930. .	41
P.S. 193—David Rayfiel.	62–63.	.Oct. 30, 1962. .	48
PACIFIC OVERTURES—(b) John Weidman, (m, l) Stephen Sondheim, additional material by Hugh Wheeler	75–76.	.Jan. 11, 1976. .	193
PACK OF LIES—Hugh Whitemore	84–85.	.Feb. 11, 1985. .	120
PAINTING CHURCHES—Tina Howe	83–84.	.Nov. 22, 1983. .	206
PARIS BOUND—Philip Barry.	27–28.	.Dec. 27, 1927. .	234
PASSION OF JOSEPH D., THE—Paddy Chayefsky	63–64.	.Feb. 11, 1964. .	15
PATRIOTS, THE—Sidney Kingsley	42–43.	.Jan. 29, 1943. .	173
PERFECT PARTY, THE—A. R. Gurney Jr.	85–86.	.Apr. 2, 1986. .	238
PERIOD OF ADJUSTMENT—Tennessee Williams	60–61.	.Nov. 10, 1960. .	132

PLAY	VOLUME	OPENED	PERFS
STAR-WAGON, THE—Maxwell Anderson	37–38.	.Sept. 29, 1937.	. 223
STATE OF THE UNION—Howard Lindsay, Russel Crouse	45–46.	.Nov. 14, 1945.	. 765
STEAMBATH—Bruce Jay Friedman	70–71.	.June 30, 1970.	. 128
STICKS AND BONES—David Rabe	71–72.	.Nov. 7, 1971.	. 121
	71–72.	.Mar. 1, 1972.	. 245
STONE AND STAR—Robert Ardrey (also called *Shadow of Heroes*).	61–62.	.Dec. 5, 1961.	. 20
STOP THE WORLD—I WANT TO GET OFF—(b, l, m) Leslie Bricusse, Anthony Newley.	62–63.	.Oct. 3, 1962.	. 555
STORM OPERATION—Maxwell Anderson.	43–44.	.Jan. 11, 1944.	. 23
STORY OF MARY SURRATT, THE—John Patrick	46–47.	.Feb. 8, 1947.	. 11
STRANGE INTERLUDE—Eugene O'Neill.	27–28.	.Jan. 30, 1928.	. 426
STREAMERS—David Rabe	75–76.	.Apr. 21, 1976.	. 478
STREET SCENE—Elmer Rice.	28–29.	.Jan. 10, 1929.	. 601
STREETCAR NAMED DESIRE, A—Tennessee Williams	47–48.	.Dec. 3, 1947.	. 855
STRICTLY DISHONORABLE—Preston Sturges.	29–30.	.Sept. 18, 1929.	. 557
SUBJECT WAS ROSES, THE—Frank D. Gilroy	64–65.	.May 25, 1964.	. 832
SUGAR BABIES—(ad) Ralph G. Allen from traditional material (special citation)	79–80.	.Oct. 8, 1979.	. 1,208
SUMMER OF THE 17TH DOLL—Ray Lawler	57–58.	.Jan. 22, 1958.	. 29
SUNDAY IN THE PARK WITH GEORGE—(b) James Lapine, (m, l) Stephen Sondheim.	83–84.	.May 2, 1984.	. 604
SUNRISE AT CAMPOBELLO—Dore Schary	57–58.	.Jan. 30, 1958.	. 556
SUNSHINE BOYS, THE—Neil Simon	72–73.	.Dec. 20, 1972.	. 538
SUN-UP—Lula Vollmer	22–23.	.May 25, 1923.	. 356
SUSAN AND GOD—Rachel Crothers.	37–38.	.Oct. 7, 1937.	. 288
SWAN, THE—Ferenc Molnar, (tr) Melville Baker	23–24.	.Oct. 23, 1923.	. 255
SWEENEY TODD, THE DEMON BARBER OF FLEET STREET—(b) Hugh Wheeler, (m,l) Stephen Sondheim, based on a version of *Sweeney Todd* by Christopher Bond	78–79.	.Mar. 1, 1979.	. 557
SWEET BIRD OF YOUTH—Tennessee Williams	58–59.	.Mar. 10, 1959.	. 375
TABLE MANNERS—Alan Ayckbourn	75–76.	.Dec. 7, 1976.	. 76
TABLE SETTINGS—James Lapine	79–80.	.Jan. 14, 1980.	. 264
TAKE A GIANT STEP—Louis Peterson	53–54.	.Sept. 24, 1953.	. 76
TAKING OF MISS JANIE, THE—Ed Bullins	74–75.	.May 4, 1975.	. 42
TALLEY'S FOLLY—Lanford Wilson	78–79.	.May 1, 1979.	. 44
	79–80.	.Feb. 20, 1980.	. 277
TARNISH—Gilbert Emery	23–24.	.Oct. 1, 1923.	. 248
TASTE OF HONEY, A—Shelagh Delaney	60–61.	.Oct. 4, 1960.	. 376
TCHIN-TCHIN—Sidney Michaels, based on François Billetdoux's play	62–63.	.Oct. 25, 1962.	. 222
TEA AND SYMPATHY—Robert Anderson	53–54.	.Sept. 30, 1953.	. 712
TEAHOUSE OF THE AUGUST MOON, THE—John Patrick, based on Vern Sneider's novel	53–54.	.Oct. 15, 1953.	. 1,027
TENTH MAN, THE—Paddy Chayefsky.	59–60.	.Nov. 5, 1959.	. 623
THAT CHAMPIONSHIP SEASON—Jason Miller	71–72.	.May 2, 1972.	. 144
	72–73.	.Sept. 14, 1972.	. 700
THERE SHALL BE NO NIGHT—Robert E. Sherwood	39–40.	.Apr. 29, 1940.	. 181
THEY KNEW WHAT THEY WANTED—Sidney Howard	24–25.	.Nov. 24, 1924.	. 414
THEY SHALL NOT DIE—John Wexley	33–34.	.Feb. 21, 1934.	. 62
THOUSAND CLOWNS, A—Herb Gardner	61–62.	.Apr. 5, 1962.	. 428
THREEPENNY OPERA—(b, l) Bertolt Brecht, (m) Kurt Weill, (tr) Ralph Manheim, John Willett	75–76.	.Mar. 1, 1976.	. 307
THURBER CARNIVAL, A—James Thurber	59–60.	.Feb. 26, 1960.	. 127

PLAY	VOLUME	OPENED	PERFS
WHITE STEED, THE—Paul Vincent Carroll	38–39.	.Jan. 10, 1939. .	136
WHO'S AFRAID OF VIRGINIA WOOLF?—Edward Albee	62–63.	.Oct. 13, 1962. .	664
WHOSE LIFE IS IT ANYWAY?—Brian Clark	78–79.	.Apr. 17, 1979. .	223
WHY MARRY?—Jesse Lynch Williams	09–19.	.Dec. 25, 1917. .	120
WHY NOT?—Jesse Lynch Williams	22–23.	.Dec. 25, 1922. .	120
WITCHING HOUR, THE—Augustus Thomas	99–09.	.Nov. 18, 1907. .	212
WILD BIRDS—Dan Totheroh	24–25.	.Apr. 9, 1925. .	44
WINGED VICTORY—Moss Hart, (m) David Rose	43–44.	.Nov. 20, 1943. .	212
WINGS—Arthur L. Kopit	78–79.	.June 21, 1978. .	15
	78–79.	.Jan. 28, 1979. .	113
WINGS OVER EUROPE—Robert Nichols, Maurice Browne	28–29.	.Dec. 10, 1928. .	90
WINSLOW BOY, THE—Terence Rattigan	47–48.	.Oct. 29, 1947. .	215
WINTERSET—Maxwell Anderson	35–36.	.Sept. 25, 1935. .	195
WINTER SOLDIERS—Daniel Lewis James	42–43.	.Nov. 29, 1942. .	25
WISDOM TOOTH, THE—Marc Connelly	25–26.	.Feb. 15, 1926. .	160
WISTERIA TREES, THE—Joshua Logan, based on Anton Chekhov's *The Cherry Orchard*	49–50.	.Mar. 29, 1950. .	165
WITNESS FOR THE PROSECUTION—Agatha Christie	54–55.	.Dec. 16, 1954. .	645
WOMEN, THE—Clare Boothe	36–37.	.Dec. 26, 1936. .	657
WONDERFUL TOWN—(b) Joseph Fields, Jerome Chodorov, based on their play *My Sister Eileen* and Ruth McKenney's stories, (l) Betty Comden, Adolph Green, (m) Leonard Bernstein	52–53.	.Feb. 25, 1953. .	559
WORLD WE MAKE, THE—Sidney Kingsley, based on Millen Brand's novel *The Outward Room*	39–40.	.Nov. 20, 1939. .	80
YEARS AGO—Ruth Gordon	46–47.	.Dec. 3, 1946. .	206
YES, MY DARLING DAUGHTER—Mark Reed	36–37.	.Feb. 9, 1937. .	405
YOU AND I—Philip Barry	22–23.	.Feb. 19, 1923. .	178
YOU CAN'T TAKE IT WITH YOU—Moss Hart, George S. Kaufman	36–37.	.Dec. 14, 1936. .	837
YOU KNOW I CAN'T HEAR YOU WHEN THE WATER'S RUNNING—Robert Anderson	66–67.	.Mar. 13, 1967. .	755
YOUNG WOODLEY—John van Druten	25–26.	.Nov. 2, 1925. .	260
YOUNGEST, THE—Philip Barry	24–25.	.Dec. 22, 1924. .	104
YOUR OWN THING—(b) Donald Driver, (m, l) Hal Hester and Danny Apolinar, suggested by William Shakespeare's *Twelfth Night*	67–68.	.Jan. 13, 1968. .	933
YOU'RE A GOOD MAN CHARLIE BROWN—(b, m, l) Clark Gesner, based on the comic strip "Peanuts" by Charles M. Schulz	66–67.	.Mar. 7, 1967. .	1,597
ZOOMAN AND THE SIGN—Charles Fuller	80–81.	.Dec. 7, 1980. .	33

INDEX

Play titles appear in **bold face**. *Bold face italic* page numbers refer to those pages where complete cast and credit listings for New York productions may be found.

503